THE
BOOK OF
RESOLUTIONS
OF THE UNITED METHODIST CHURCH
1992

THE
BOOK OF
RESOLUTIONS
OF THE UNITED METHODIST CHURCH
1992

The United Methodist Publishing House
Nashville, Tennessee

MANUFACTURED IN THE UNITED STATES OF AMERICA

PREFACE

The Book of Resolutions has been published after each General Conference since 1968. This edition includes all valid resolutions since that time. Resolutions which are no longer timely or have been rescinded or superceded have been omitted.

When approved by the General Conference, the resolutions state the policy of The United Methodist Church on many of the current social issues and concerns. Only the General Conference speaks for The United Methodist Church in its entirety.

This edition presents the resolutions in six sections: (1) The Natural World, (2) The Nurturing Community, (3) The Social Community, (4) The Economic Community, (5) The Political Community, and (6) The World Community. These section titles match the sections of the Social Principles, United Methodism's foundational statement on social issues (which appears at the front of this book). The date of General Conference adoption appears at the end of each resolution.

To further assist in study and use of the resolutions, this edition also includes:

—User's Guide.
—Cross referencing of related resolutions.
—Comprehensive indexes.

The Book of Resolutions is published by The United Methodist Publishing House, Robert K. Feaster, Publisher. Neil M. Alexander, Book Editor of The United Methodist Church, is responsible for editing the resolutions. Ronald P. Patterson, Senior Editor, along with Lee Ranck and Robert McClean, staff members of the General Board of Church and Society, served as the editorial team. Carolyn D. Minus, former General Board of Church and Society staff member, wrote the "User's Guide."

CONTENTS

User's Guide..17
Social Principles...31

THE NATURAL WORLD

Black-Owned Farm Land.. 53
Common Heritage...54
Energy Policy Statement... 57
Environmental Justice for a Sustainable Future..................... 62
Environmental Racism...67
Environmental Stewardship...70
Indian Lands Used by The United Methodist Church..............76
Indoor Air Pollution..77
Law of the Sea, The..79
Nuclear Safety in the United States.................................... 80
Protecting the Native American Land Base...........................86
Reduction of Water Usage by United Methodists................... 87
U.S. Agriculture and Rural Communities in Crisis................. 87
Use of Reclaimed Paper.. 112

THE NURTURING COMMUNITY

Adoption..113
Against Sterilization Abuse...113
AIDS and the Healing Ministry of the Church...................... 115
Care-Giving Teams for Persons with AIDS.......................... 120
Circumcision...121
Condemning Legal Prostitution.. 121
May as Christian Home Month... 122

Organ and Tissue Donation... 123
Pastoral Care and the AIDS Epidemic
  in Native American Communities................................. 123
Resources for AIDS Education..124
Responsible Parenthood.. 125
Sexual Violence and Pornography...................................128
Supportive Policies for Families with Children..................... 135
Understanding Living and Dying as Faithful Christians...........140

THE SOCIAL COMMUNITY

Accessibility of Meeting Places Beyond the Local Church........ 151
Access of Hispanics to Higher Education............................151
Act of Covenanting Between Other Christian Churches
  and The United Methodist Church................................. 153
Affirmation of Basic Rural Worth, An.............................. 157
Affirmation of Zoar United Methodist Church of
  Philadelphia...158
Affirmative Action... 159
Affirmative Action Plans and People with Disabilities............. 161
Affirming a Diversity of Language Usage in the
  United States and Opposing a Constitutional
  Amendment Making English
  the Official Language..162
African-American Family Life...164
Aging in the United States of America.............................. 165
American Indian Religious Freedom Act.............................176
America's Native People,
  The United Methodist Church and................................ 178
Anna Howard Shaw Day... 182
Annual Accessibility Audit.. 184
Appointment of Clergy to Rural Ministry........................... 185
Available and Affordable Housing.................................... 185
Ban on Alcohol Beverage Advertisements...........................189
Barrier-Free Construction for the Handicapped.....................189
Black Church Growth... 190
Black Leadership.. 191
Call to the Bishops to Undergird Cooperative Parish
  Ministry... 191

CONTENTS

Celebrate and Support the Ongoing Work of the General
Commission on the Status and Role of Women................192
Celebrate and Affirm the Work of General Commission
on Religion and Race..193
Celebrating 100 Years of Lay Education
in the Tradition of Scarritt-Bennett Center.....................194
Charter for Racial Justice Policies in an
Interdependent Global Community, A.........................196
Church and Community Workers, 1988.......................199
Church and Community Workers, 1992.......................200
Church and Persons with Mentally, Physically, and/or
Psychologically Handicapping Conditions, The................200
Church's Response to Changing Rural Issues, The..............204
COCU Consensus: In Quest of A Church of Christ Uniting.....205
Comity Agreements Affecting Development of Native
American Ministries by The United Methodist Church.........206
Communications Access for Persons Who Have Hearing
and Sight Impairments..207
Compliance with the Americans with Disabilities Act
for Employers..208
Comprehensive Approach to Native American Ministries.......209
Confession to Native Americans...............................210
Confronting the Drug Crisis...................................211
Considering Community Contexts in the
Appointment-Making Process.................................215
Continuance of Funding to the Evangelical Seminary
of Puerto Rico...216
Continuing Membership in the Consultation on
Church Union..217
Continuing Membership in the National Council of Churches..217
Continuing Membership in the World Council of Churches.....218
Declare Zoar United Methodist Church a Primary
Historical Emphasis..219
Dependent Care..219
Domestic Violence and Sexual Abuse..........................223
Driving Under the Influence...................................228
Drug and Alcohol Concerns...................................229
Ecumenical Decade: Churches in Solidarity with Women........242
Ecumenical Interpretations of Doctrinal Standards..............245

Education on Alcohol and Substance Abuse............................246
Education Responsibilities Concerning
   Native American Cultural Traditions..............................247
Elimination of Racism in The United Methodist Church.......... 248
Enlist and Involve the Youth in the Life of the Church........... 249
Equal Rights of Women.. 251
Eradication of Racism...254
Ethnic Membership on Boards and Agencies.......................254
Federal Funds for Indian Health Services........................... 254
Full Personhood... 255
Global Racism.. 256
Goals and Recommendations on Participation of Women.........261
Guidelines for Interreligious Relationships "Called to Be
   Neighbors and Witnesses"...263
Health and Wholeness.. 273
Health for All by the Year 2000..278
Health in Mind and Body...280
Higher Education Training and Scholarships........................ 284
History of Blacks in The United Methodist Church................ 285
History of Racial/Ethnic United Methodists......................... 285
Homelessness in the United States.................................... 286
Housing.. 293
In Support of Women, Infants, and Children's Supplemental
   Food and Nutrition Education Program (WIC Program)........302
Inclusive History... 303
Inclusiveness of the Physically Challenged at All Conferences..304
Increased Support for Programs Impacting the Higher
   Education of Native Americans.................................... 304
Ku Klux Klan and Other Hate Groups in the United States..... 306
Medical Rights for Children and Youth............................... 308
Membership in Clubs or Organizations that Practice
   Exclusivity.. 311
Ministries in Social Conflict... 312
Ministries on Mental Illness... 313
Ministry to Runaway Children.. 317
Mutual Recognition of Members..318
National Convocation on the Ordained Ministry
   for Native Americans.. 320

CONTENTS

Native American History and Contemporary Culture as
Related to Effective Church Participation........................ 321
Native American Representation in
The United Methodist Church.................................322
Native American Social Witness Program........................ 324
Native American Young Adults in Mission...................... 324
New Developments in Genetic Science...........................325
Observance of Dr. Martin Luther King, Jr., Day.................338
Oxford House Model for Treatment of Drug and
Alcohol Abuse, The.. 338
Pacific Islanders Included as Racial and Ethnic Minority
Group...339
Pan Methodist Unity...340
Population..342
Prejudice Against Muslims and Arabs in the U.S.A............. 345
Program to Emphasize Inclusiveness in All Dimensions
of the Church... 346
Project Equality..349
Promote the Observance of Native American
Awareness Sunday... 349
Protecting and Sustaining Children............................350
Racial Harassment.. 360
Recruitment and Development Plan for Local Pastors............361
Relationship between The United Methodist Church and
the New Affiliated Autonomous Methodist Church
of Puerto Rico..362
Resourcing Black Churches in Urban Communities..............364
Rights of Native People of the Americas...................... 366
Rural Chaplaincy as a Ministry of Laity and Clergy.............366
Sale and Use of Alcohol and Tobacco on Church Property...... 367
School Busing...368
Shared Financial Support for the Native American Center....... 368
Spanish Language Hymnal.....................................370
Special Emphasis on Reclaiming the Cities.....................370
Status of Women, The.. 371
Strengthening the Black Church for the 21st Century.............376
Suicide: A Challenge to Ministry.............................. 377
Support the Consultation on Church Union Proposal.............382
Support to Strengthen Ethnic Minority Local Church.............383

Tent-Building Ministries..384
To Love the Sojourner..384
Toward an Ecumenical Future...385
Toward a New Beginning Beyond 1992............................386
Treatment of Women in the United States Under
  Social Security, The...392
Universal Access to Health Care in the United States
  and Related Territories...395
Use of Alcohol and Drugs on Campuses, The....................398
Use of Church Facilities by Community Groups...................399
Vision Interfaith Satellite Network..................................399

THE ECONOMIC COMMUNITY

Appalachian Challenge..401
Appalachian Mission, The...401
Economic Justice...403
Extension of the Right to Organize and Bargain Collectively....411
Gambling..412
Gambling, the United Methodist Church's Position on............413
Global Debt Crisis...414
Guidelines for Initiating or Joining an Economic Boycott.........423
Investment Ethics...427
National Incomes Policy..431
Nuclear Weapons Production at the General Electric
  Company..433
Pay Equity in the U.S.A..434
Rights of Workers...438
Safety and Health in Workplace and Community..................443
Self-Help Efforts of Poor People......................................446
Sexual Harassment in Church and Society in the U.S.A..........447
Sexual Harassment and The United Methodist Church............449
Special Needs of Farm Workers.......................................452
Unemployment..453

THE POLITICAL COMMUNITY

A Call for Increased Commitment to End
  World Hunger and Poverty...457
Assistance and Sanctuary for Central American Refugees........463

CONTENTS

Bilingual Education..464
Capital Punishment..465
Certification of Conscientious Objectors............................467
Church/Government Relations............................468
Church-Government Relations, The United Methodist
  Church and..480
Church in a Mass Media Culture, The............................484
Community Life..488
Concerning the Draft in the United States............................490
Criminal Justice..492
Domestic Surveillance..496
Enabling Financial Support for Domestic Programs............................498
Equal Justice..499
Grand Jury Abuse..503
Gun Control..504
Human Rights..506
Immigration..507
Juvenile Justice..511
Literacy, The Right to Learn: A Basic Human Right............................512
Local Church and the Local Jail, The............................516
New Issues in Human Rights..517
Opposition to a Call for a Constitutional Convention............................520
Penal Reform..524
Police Firearms Policies..526
Prevention and Reduction of Juvenile Delinquency............................526
Public Education in the United States............................527
Ratification for District of Columbia Representation............................528
Religious Liberty..529
Repression and the Right to Privacy..532
Support of Conscientious Objectors to Registration............................535
Support Legislation Prohibiting Malicious Harassments............................536
U.S. Gun Violence..536
Use of Church Facilities for Operating Private Schools............................540
Victims of Crime..540

THE WORLD COMMUNITY

Arab-Israeli Conflict, The..542
Bishops' Call for Peace and the Self-Development of Peoples...547
Black Hills Alliance, The..554

Boycott of Royal Dutch/Shell...555
Central America: Peace and Justice with Freedom...................557
Christian Faith and Disarmament.......................................561
Church and the Global HIV/AIDS Epidemic, The..................564
Comprehensive Test Ban Treaty...568
Concern for El Salvador...570
Consequences of Conflict...570
Current Arab-Israeli Crisis, The...571
End U.S. Military Presence in Bolivia..................................573
Fort Laramie Treaty, The...574
Free Flow of Information Among All Peoples of the Earth.......575
Global Nature of The United Methodist Church, The.............579
Holy Land Tours...580
In Support of Self-Determination and Non-Intervention..........581
Infant Formula Abuse...584
Justice for Reverend Alex Awad..589
Justice, Peace, and the Integrity of Creation........................591
Mission and Aging of Global Population..............................593
"New House" of Europe...597
Nuclear Disarmament: The Zero Option..............................600
Nuclear-Free Pacific...605
Oppose Food and Medicine Blockade or Embargoes..............605
Our Muslim Neighbors..606
Peace Colleges...612
Peace, Justice, and Reunification of Korea...........................613
Peace, The United Methodist Church and............................617
Peace with Justice as a Special Program..............................623
Persons Missing in Action..629
Philippines, The..629
Puerto Rico and Vieques...632
Ratification of Human Rights Covenants and Conventions.......633
Recognition of Cuba..634
Southern Africa..636
Support Amnesty International...640
Support and Concern to Mozambique.................................641
Terrorism...643
United States-Mexico Border..644
Understanding The United Methodist Church
    as a Global Church...647

CONTENTS

United Nations, In Support of the.................................. 648
United Nations, On the... 650
United States–China Political Relations.............................. 651
United States Church–China Church Relations..................... 653
Web of *Apartheid*, South Africa and the Destabilization
   of Its Neighbors.. 658

OTHER RESOLUTIONS

Biblical Language... 663
Evangelism the Number 1 Priority for the Next
   Quadrennium, Make... 663
Proper Use of Name: The United Methodist Church............. 663
Spiritual Directors' Program.. 664
Tithing Church, A.. 665
New Beginning, A.. 666

Topic and Category Index.. 667

Subject Index... 675

USER'S GUIDE

What's the purpose of the *Book of Resolutions?*

The *Book of Resolutions 1992,* published by The United Methodist Publishing House, collects in one volume all current and official social policies and other resolutions adopted by the General Conference of The United Methodist Church since 1968. These resolutions are:

• *Official policy statements* for guiding all the work and ministry of The United Methodist Church on about 200 subjects.
• *Educational resources* for The United Methodist Church on many of the important issues affecting the lives of people and all God's creation.
• *Guides and models* for helping United Methodist members and groups relate a lively biblical faith to action in daily life.
• *Resource materials* for persons preparing public statements about United Methodist concerns on current social issues.

The *Book of Resolutions 1992* is primarily a reference tool for church members and leaders. It is not a book that you will sit down to read from cover to cover.

You may not get acquainted with these resolutions until you are in the midst of some controversy in your congregation, or something happens in your community (state, the nation) on a particular subject. You may find that your denomination's policies give you more "food for thought." Maybe you will agree with the denomination's position. On the other hand, you may disagree. Either is all right. At the least you know your church cares and wants you to be a knowledgeable and caring Christian about the issues of the day.

Furthermore, you may look to some of the statements in this book for spiritual guidance as you make an important decision in your life about work, home, family life, or use of money and other resources.

Can you answer some of my questions?

Why do we have all these social policies and resolutions?

The resolutions say, "We care!" Delegates to the General Conference of The United Methodist Church believe that we each need and deserve the guidance of the whole denomination as we face daily hopes, struggles, joy, or pain. The resolutions and Social Principles express our church community's beliefs and give us evidence that the church means for God's love to reach into situations faced each day, not just on Sunday mornings. Not all of us are intimately involved with each issue, but someone, somewhere is.

Isn't *The Book of Discipline* enough?

Most of *The Book of Discipline* is legislation and legally sets up the framework for each part of United Methodism. The General Conference decided in 1968 that for reasons of length these resolutions should be published in a volume separate from the *Discipline*. While the *Book of Resolutions* is not legally binding, it is an official guide from our denomination to be used responsibly for reference, encouragement, study and support.

Why do the Social Principles appear in both the *Discipline* and in the *Book of Resolutions?*

The United Methodist Church puts the Social Principles in the *Discipline* (¶¶ 70-76) as one of our denominational foundation statements suggesting how faith is translated into action. Its broad principles (guides, not rules) are declarations to help us be in dialogue with one another about how faith motivates us to "get off the fence" and act.

The United Methodist Church puts the Social Principles in the front of the *Book of Resolutions* to help us relate the broad strokes of the Social Principles to more specific exploration and applications in resolutions.

Where do these policies and resolutions come from?
How do they get adopted by General Conference?

They are sent in as petitions to General Conference every four years by general agencies, annual conferences, local churches, individual members, and groups. Once submitted as petitions, most of them are worked on by delegates in the Church and

Society Legislative Committee. The legislative committee accepts, rejects, or amends the petitions, then reports its recommendations to the General Conference plenary; all delegates then vote on their recommendations.

Can I trust the statistics and data in these resolutions?

General source references are usually given when statistics are used in a resolution. Because such data may change during the years the resolution is valid, sometimes the resolution will provide more general descriptions of social conditions which make it urgent for the church to speak on a particular topic. Resolutions will take on more meaning when you secure local statistics and data on relevant topics.

Why do church social policies and U.S. government policies or positions seem so far apart on some of these issues?

The United Methodist Church membership extends beyond the U.S. boundaries; it is global. So, in many cases we are speaking to, from, or with more than one national government. Further, the Christian Church must never be a mirror image of any government, whether Democrat or Republican, totalitarian or democratic. We know that Christians are obligated to be responsible and participating citizens under any governmental system, but that response and participation is to be interpreted in light of our faith.

As the Social Principles states, "Our allegiance to God takes precedence over our allegiance to any state." And our church's public witness is first and foremost to be judged by God by whether it supports justice, love and mercy, particularly for the poor and powerless.

Why can't the church just let us make up our own minds on these matters after it presents us neutral information on both sides of an issue?

Most importantly, The United Methodist Church believes God's love for the world is an active and engaged love, a love seeking justice and liberty. We cannot just be observers. So we care enough about people's lives to risk interpreting God's love, to take a stand, to call each of us into a response, no matter how controversial or complex. The church helps us think and act out a faith perspective, not just responding to all the other "mind-makers-up" that exist in our society.

No information is truly neutral. This is true even of the most "hard scientific" data secured from the most advanced technology. These resolutions do strive for objectivity, not neutrality. There are usually more than "two sides" in important social controversies. Dialogue between different sides is critical in taking a stand. Faithfulness requires favoring what best demonstrates God's love *and* being willing to change when new perspectives or data emerge.

Is this something new in United Methodism?

Taking an active stance in society is nothing new for followers of John Wesley. He set the example for us to combine personal and social piety. Ever since predecessor churches to United Methodism flourished in the United States, we have been known as a denomination involved with people's lives, with political and social struggles, having local to international mission implications. It is an expression of the personal change we experience in our baptism and conversion.

Is there a difference between a "social policy" and a "resolution"?

The terms are used almost interchangeably in The United Methodist Church. Most social issue resolutions refer to public policy matters, such as local, state, and federal government programs and legislation. Other statements focus on conditions affecting the church and the church's programs or funding.

How do people use this *Book of Resolutions?*

• An ordained minister went to console neighbor parents after their son committed suicide. At home later that evening the pastor and his own family struggled in their grief to apply their faith to this troubling situation. What did the church say about suicide? How should a Christian act? The pastor found the 1980 *Book of Resolutions* absolutely silent on this topic. During the six years after that first personal encounter with ministry after a suicide, the pastor wrote letters and articles and talked with seminary faculty and national church staff. As a result the 1988 General Conference adopted its first resolution on suicide. Instead of wishing for guidance from our church on this most difficult subject, this pastor gave constructive leadership to the church and we now can find helpful perspectives in the 1992 *Book of Resolutions.*

• A bishop and an annual conference Board of Church and Society wanted to share a United Methodist position against the death penalty with their governor, who had to consider clemency for a death row inmate. They visited the governor and delivered a letter stating their own views of this particular situation and described why The United Methodist Church opposes the death penalty. They used the resolution on capital punishment in the *Book of Resolutions* as the official policy of The United Methodist Church to support their plea for clemency.

• An adult church school group studied the foreign policy discussion topics called "Great Decisions," issued annually by the Foreign Policy Association. They compared its resources with positions in the relevant United Methodist policies from the *Book of Resolutions* for several evenings of lively study.

• Another adult class meeting on Sunday morning always studied faith and contemporary issues. For nearly six months the members used the *Book of Resolutions* to guide their study and discussion. Different members made presentations on some aspect of the resolutions; then they used the study questions provided to stimulate some challenging discussion. Occasionally they had guest speakers or used an audiovisual from their conference media center to amplify the subject.

• A nurse who is an active church member found the resolutions on "Universal Access to Health Care in the United States and Related Territories" and "Ministries on Mental Illness" helpful as she reflected on the strains in her job. She found it more possible to connect her faith to her discussions with co-workers about some of the major issues facing her profession in a big city hospital.

• A local church's Outreach Work Area asked its Administrative Council to approve a congregational statement to the county zoning board favoring the construction of several low-income housing units. As part of their homework, the work area members reviewed the "Housing" resolution in the *Book of Resolutions.* That resolution then served as a basis for their initiative; they even quoted from it when they testified at the zoning board.

How do I use the *Book of Resolutions?*

Read the preface   ⟶ It provides an orientation to the whole book

Skim through the Table of ⟶ Note: resolutions are list-
Contents.   ed alphabetically according to the section of the
Social Principles to which
they most closely relate.

Look at the index in the ⟶ The index helps you find
back of the book.   subject references which
may be more specific than
titles.

Example: If you want to know whether our denomination has
spoken about "teenage pregnancy," you find that entry
in the index. This subject is referred to in two different
resolutions.

Example: What is there on "schools"? The index tells you to look
under "public education," which includes a number of
references.

Find the text of the   • Note that the Social Principles include
Social Principles   broad, fundamental statements grouped in
six sections between a preamble and a
creedal summary, "Our Social Creed."
• Review the "How can I understand the
Social Principles?" section in this User's
Guide. Use the diagrams in this section to
help interpret and look for meaning in the
Social Principles

How can I understand the Social Principles?

The Book of Resolutions organizes almost all resolutions into the six areas of concern which form the major sections of the Social Principles. You may find it helpful to consider these six areas of concern as you explore specific resolutions.

One way of understanding the Social Principles is to consider the six sections as areas of concern: (1) the natural world, (2) the nurturing community, (3) the social community, (4) the economic community, (5) the political community, and (6) the world community.

The Natural World, the starting point for the areas of concern, provides the essential resources of life for all humankind.

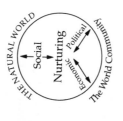

All of us also become a part of **The Nurturing Community.** Through the people with whom we interact most often—family, friends, local church, etc.—we shape our lives and the way we relate to other communities.

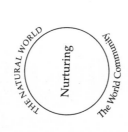

Then add to the natural world the people of the world—of **The World Community.** All of us live in community, oftentimes becoming part of several communities. Together we make up the world community.

Three other communities impact both the nurturing community and the world community.

The Social Community (or cultural community) provides the arena where we live out our responsibilities and rights in our treatment of others.

The Economic Community, in which each of us functions, establishes production, distribution and employment systems; it creates both wealth and poverty.

The Political Community determines whether our rights are guaranteed and our basic freedoms are upheld. Directions and goals of our social and economic communities are debated and decided in this arena.

Decisions in all these communities have an impact on the natural world and vice versa.

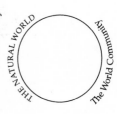

Our Social Creed

"Our Social Creed" (Section VII of the Social Principles) is a summarization of the foregoing sections of the Social Principles in the form of a creed. While it is recommended by the general church for separate use in worship services, "Our Social Creed" is an integral part of the Social Principles.

Another way of considering the six sections of the Social Principles (the six areas of concern) is to look at: (1) the role of each section, (2) the predominant faith statement in each section, (3) our responsibility defined in each section, and (4) the issues discussed in each section. The chart on the next two pages summarizes the Social Principles in this way.

The Social Principles

CATEGORY	I The Natural World	II The Nurturing Community	III The Social Community	IV The Economic Community	V The Political Community	VI The World Community
ROLE	Provides for sustenance of all creation to be used with integrity.	Provides the potential to nurture human beings into the fullness of their humanity.	Provides for means for determining the rights and responsibilities of the members toward one another.	Provides directions for influencing economic policies.	Provides for the ordering of society.	Provides the setting for the interaction of nations.
FAITH STATE-MENT	All creation is God's.	All persons are important and loved by God.	All persons are equally valuable in the sight of God.	All economic systems are under God's judgment.	All political systems are under God's judgment.	All of God's world is one world.

OUR RESPONSIBILITY	To value and conserve all natural resources.	To innovate, sponsor, and evaluate new forms of community.	To work toward societies in which social groups and individual values are recognized, maintained and strengthened.	To insure that sound policies are developed that provide for full employment adequate income, etc.	To take active responsibility for our government.	To work to develop the moral and spiritual capacity to achieve a stable world of love.
ISSUES	Water, air, soil, plants, energy utilization, animal life space.	Family, Christian community, marriage, human sexuality, abortion, death.	Rights of minorities children, youth and young adults, the aging, women, persons with handicapping conditions; alcohol/drugs, rural life.	Property, collective bargaining work/leisure, consumption, poverty, migrant workers, gambling.	Basic liberties, political responsibility, freedom of information, civil obedience and civil disobedience, crime and rehabilitation military service.	Nations and cultures, national power and responsibility, war and peace, justice and law.

How can I better understand the resolutions?

The following model or method for studying any of the resolutions shows:

• The Social Principles paragraph to which that resolution relates (found in the cross-reference at the conclusion of any resolution).
• The biblical references and/or theological concerns identified in this resolution.
• The major actions called for in that resolution for churches, individuals, church agencies, local, state, or national governments.
• Hymns found in the *United Methodist Hymnal* which may be especially appropriate to sing in relation to this resolution. (For page number see index of first lines and common titles in the hymnal.)

For some subjects you may need to consult the Topic and Category Index.

Natural World

Resolution	Social Principles Paragraph	Biblical References Theological Concerns	Actions called for	Hymns to use
Indoor Air Pollution	¶ 70A	Jesus' abundant life embraced physical well-being as well as emotional and spiritual health. Wesley and his followers have a long record of health/welfare ministries.	• Urge local churches, all church agencies and institutions to learn of suffering due to indoor air pollution; prohibit smoking indoors; provide adequate fresh air ventilation; audit for sources of pollution. • Urge general United Methodist agencies, with consultation with those most seriously affected, to prepare guidelines addressing indoor air pollution; advocate legislation to adopt standards and regulatory laws. • Ask all United Methodists to inventory indoor pollution levels and to take steps to reduce environmental pollution.	"Open my eyes, that I may see." "God who shaped creation."

Natural World

Resolution	Social Principles Paragraph	Biblical References Theological Concerns	Actions called for	Hymns to use
Nuclear Safety in the United States	¶ 70B	The God-given charge to humans to "guard and keep the earth" (Gen. 2:15). To ensure that God's creation is protected for present and future generations.	• Urge general United Methodist agencies to assist annual conferences on all aspects of information and action strategies on this issue. • Advocate for public policy, particularly regarding nuclear power, reviewing safety of operating plants, researching designs for plant safety, phasing out nuclear weapons production, establishing uniform safety standards for civilian and military nuclear operations, re-evaluating U.S. nuclear waste policy, and conserving energy and enhancing alternative energy sources.	"A charge to keep I have" "Creating God, your finger trace."

God's gift of the land is a common gift to all humanity, requiring just patterns of land use (Lev. 25).

Jesus commands us to love neighbor as self.

Gospel challenges an ethic based on "bigness is better."

Issues over 72 comprehensive calls for change by the church at all levels, by local communities, state and federal governments. For example:

• Churches to develop intentionally ministry to meet major needs in today's rural USA; to become public policy advocates; to model and support team and cooperative ministries; to emphasize ecology as part of Christian stewardship.

• Federal legislation and programs to enable farm families to receive just return for their labor and investments; to develop just water and energy policies; to recognize and protect rights of farm workers.

• State and governments, private lending agencies, local governments and community groups to be involved, together and separately. Overall, to develop a vision for agricultural life where programs and relations are just, participatory and sustainable.

"Great is Thy faithfulness."

"Faith, while trees are still in blossom."

What do I do next?

Consider these questions for study and response to any of the resolutions:

• How familiar am I with the situation(s) described in this resolution?

• What are my reactions to this call for action by our church?

• How might reactions be different if we lived in another part of this country? Came from another country to the U.S.? Lived in another country? If we were of a different economic class? Attended a different church? If members of my family were present? Or not present?

• How could our local congregation creatively respond to the calls for action in the resolution?

• Are there groups in my area or state at work on this issue where I could join in action or learn more?

• What models for action or conditions do we know about on this subject in our community or region?

• What have I communicated to our congressional members or state legislators about our church's position on an issue of great importance?

• Who could we contact for more information or resources? Write to or call: Communications, General Board of Church and Society, 100 Maryland Ave., N.E., Washington, D.C. 20002; (202) 488-5632.

SOCIAL PRINCIPLES

Preface

The United Methodist Church has a long history of concern for social justice. Its members have often taken forthright positions on controversial issues involving Christian principles. Early Methodists expressed their opposition to the slave trade, to smuggling, and to the cruel treatment of prisoners.

A social creed was adopted by the Methodist Episcopal Church (North) in 1908. Within the next decade similar statements were adopted by the Methodist Episcopal Church, South, and by the Methodist Protestant Church. The Evangelical United Brethren Church adopted a statement of social principles in 1946 at the time of the uniting of the United Brethren and The Evangelical Church. In 1972, four years after the uniting in 1968 of The Methodist Church and The Evangelical United Brethren Church, the General Conference of The United Methodist Church adopted a new statement of Social Principles, which was revised in 1976.

The Social Principles are a prayerful and thoughtful effort on the part of the General Conference to speak to the human issues in the contemporary world from a sound biblical and theological foundation as historically demonstrated in United Methodist traditions. They are intended to be instructive and persuasive in the best of the prophetic spirit. The Social Principles are a call to all members of The United Methodist Church to a prayerful, studied dialogue of faith and practice. (*See* ¶ 610.)

Preamble

We, the people called United Methodists, affirm our faith in God our Creator and Father, in Jesus Christ our Savior, and in the Holy Spirit, our Guide and Guard.

31

We acknowledge our complete dependence upon God in birth, in life, in death, and in life eternal. Secure in God's love, we affirm the goodness of life and confess our many sins against God's will for us as we find it in Jesus Christ. We have not always been faithful stewards of all that has been committed to us by God the Creator. We have been reluctant followers of Jesus Christ in his mission to bring all persons into a community of love. Though called by the Holy Spirit to become new creatures in Christ, we have resisted the further call to become the people of God in our dealings with each other and the earth on which we live.

Grateful for God's forgiving love, in which we live and by which we are judged, and affirming our belief in the inestimable worth of each individual, we renew our commitment to become faithful witnesses to the gospel, not alone to the ends of earth, but also to the depths of our common life and work.

¶ 70. I. The Natural World

All creation is the Lord's and we are responsible for the ways in which we use and abuse it. Water, air, soil, minerals, energy resources, plants, animal life, and space are to be valued and conserved because they are God's creation and not solely because they are useful to human beings. Therefore, we repent of our devastation of the physical and nonhuman world. Further, we recognize the responsibility of the Church toward life-style and systemic changes in society that will promote a more ecologically just world and a better quality of life for all creation.

A) Water, Air, Soil, Minerals, Plants.—We support and encourage social policies that serve to reduce and control the creation of industrial by-products and waste; facilitate the safe processing and disposal of toxic and nuclear waste; provide for appropriate disposal of municipal waste; and enhance the rejuvenation of polluted air, water, and soil. We support measures which will halt the spread of deserts into formerly productive lands. We support regulations designed to protect plant life, including those that provide for reforestation and for conservation of grasslands. We support policies that retard the *indiscriminate* use of chemicals, including those used for growing, processing, and preserving food, and encourage adequate research into their effects upon God's creation prior to utilization. We urge development of international agreements concerning equitable utilization of the ocean's resources for human benefit so long as the integrity of the seas is maintained. Moreover, we support policies on the part of governments and industries that conserve fossil and other fuels, and that eliminate methods of securing minerals that destroy plants, animals, and soil. We encourage creation of new sources for food and power, while maintaining the goodness of the earth.

B) *Energy Resources Utilization.*—We support and encourage social policies that are directed toward rational and restrained transformation of parts of the nonhuman world into energy for human usage, and which de-emphasize or eliminate energy-producing technologies that endanger the health, safety, and even existence of the present and future human and nonhuman creation. Further, we urge wholehearted support of the conservation of energy and responsible development of all energy resources, with special concern for the development of renewable energy sources, that the goodness of the earth may be affirmed.

C) *Animal Life.*—We support regulations that protect the life and health of animals, including those ensuring the humane treatment of pets and other domestic animals, animals used in research, and the painless slaughtering of meat animals, fish, and fowl. Furthermore, we encourage the preservation of animal species now threatened with extinction. We also recognize the necessity of the use of animals in medical and cosmetic research; however, we reject the abuse of the same.

D) *Space.*—The moon, planets, stars, and the space between and among them are the creation of God and are due the respect we are called to give the earth. We support the extension of knowledge through space exploration, but only when that knowledge is used for the welfare of humanity.

E) *Science and Technology.*—Concerning that which science has offered the world, facts alone can be empty and confusing without an integrating interpretation best accomplished through dialogue with the scientific community. Given the emptiness of scientific facts alone, the Church could "bless" the scientific community with depths of interpretation drawn from things of the Spirit. The Church has affirmed from the beginning that God is the Creator of all and that God has given us the command to participate in taking care of and enhancing that creation. This age-old belief could take on new life, given the fresh awareness and knowledge of the discoveries of science and the resulting technology which provides new and powerful tools to complete the Church's divinely appointed task of saving and transforming the world.

We therefore encourage dialogue between the scientific and theological communities, and seek the kind of participation which will enable humanity to sustain life on earth and, by God's grace, increase the quality of our common lives together.

¶ 71. II. The Nurturing Community

The community provides the potential for nurturing human beings into the fullness of their humanity. We believe we have a responsibility to innovate, sponsor, and evaluate new forms of community that will encourage development of the fullest potential in individuals. Primary for us is the gospel understanding that all persons are important—because they are human beings created by God and loved through and by Jesus Christ and not because they have merited significance. We therefore support social climates in which human communities are maintained and strengthened for the sake of all persons and their growth.

A) The Family.—We believe the family to be the basic human community through which persons are nurtured and sustained in mutual love, responsibility, respect, and fidelity. We understand the family as encompassing a wider range of options than that of the two-generational unit of parents and children (the nuclear family), including the extended family, families with adopted children, single parents, stepfamilies, couples without children. We affirm shared responsibility for parenting by men and women and encourage social, economic, and religious efforts to maintain and strengthen relationships within families in order that every member may be assisted toward complete personhood.

B) Other Christian Communities.—We further recognize the movement to find new patterns of Christian nurturing communities such as Koinonia Farms, certain monastic and other religious orders, and some types of corporate church life. We urge the Church to seek ways of understanding the needs and concerns of such Christian groups and to find ways of ministering to them and through them.

C) Marriage.—We affirm the sanctity of the marriage covenant which is expressed in love, mutual support, personal commitment, and shared fidelity between a man and a woman. We believe that God's blessing rests upon such marriage, whether or not there are children of the union. We reject social norms that assume different standards for women than for men in marriage.

D) *Divorce.*—Where marriage partners, even after thoughtful consideration and counsel, are estranged beyond reconciliation, we recognize divorce as regrettable but recognize the right of divorced persons to remarry. We express our deep concern for the care and nurture of the children of divorced and/or remarried persons. We encourage that either or both of the divorced parents be considered for custody of the minor children of the marriage. We encourage an active, accepting, and enabling commitment of the church and our society to minister to the members of divorced and remarried families.

E) *Single Persons.*—We affirm the integrity of single persons, and we reject all social practices that discriminate or social attitudes that are prejudicial against persons because they are single.

F) *Human Sexuality.*—We recognize that sexuality is God's good gift to all persons. We believe persons may be fully human only when that gift is acknowledged and affirmed by themselves, the Church, and society. We call all persons to the disciplined, responsible fulfillment of themselves, others, and society in the stewardship of this gift. We also recognize our limited understanding of this complex gift and encourage the medical, theological, and social science disciplines to combine in a determined effort to understand human sexuality more completely. We call the Church to take the leadership role in bringing together these disciplines to address this most complex issue. Further, within the context of our understanding of this gift of God, we recognize that God challenges us to find responsible, committed, and loving forms of expression.

Although all persons are sexual beings whether or not they are married, sexual relations are only clearly affirmed in the marriage bond. Sex may become exploitative within as well as outside marriage. We reject all sexual expressions which damage or destroy the humanity God has given us as birthright, and we affirm only that sexual expression which enhances that same humanity, in the midst of diverse opinion as to what constitutes that enhancement.

We deplore all forms of the commercialization and exploitation of sex with their consequent cheapening and degradation of human personality. We call for strict enforcement of laws prohibiting the sexual exploitation or use of children by adults. We call for the establishment of adequate protective services, guidance, and counseling opportunities for children thus abused. We insist that all persons, regardless of age, gender, marital status, or sexual orientation, are entitled to have their human and civil rights ensured.

We recognize the continuing need for full, positive, and factual sex education opportunities for children, youth, and adults. The Church offers a unique opportunity to give quality guidance/education in this area.

Homosexual persons no less than heterosexual persons are individuals of sacred worth. All persons need the ministry and guidance of the Church in their struggles for human fulfillment, as well as the spiritual and emotional care of a fellowship which enables reconciling relationships with God, with others, and with self. Although we do not condone the practice of homosexuality and consider this practice incompatible with Christian teaching, we affirm that God's grace is available to all. We commit ourselves to be in ministry for and with all persons.

G) Rights of Homosexual Persons.—Certain basic human rights and civil liberties are due all persons. We are committed to support those rights and liberties for homosexual persons. We see a clear issue of simple justice in protecting their rightful claims where they have: shared material resources, pensions, guardian relationships, mutual powers of attorney, and other such lawful claims typically attendant to contractual relationships which involve shared contributions, responsibilities, and liabilities, and equal protection before the law. Moreover, we support efforts to stop violence and other forms of coercion against gays and lesbians.

H) Abortion.—The beginning of life and the ending of life are the God-given boundaries of human existence. While individuals have always had some degree of control over when they would die, they now have the awesome power to determine when and even whether new individuals will be born. Our belief in the sanctity of unborn human life makes us reluctant to approve abortion. But we are equally bound to respect the sacredness of the life and well-being of the mother, for whom devastating damage may result from an unacceptable pregnancy. In continuity with past Christian teaching, we recognize tragic conflicts of life with life that may justify abortion, and in such cases support the legal option of abortion under proper medical procedures. We cannot affirm abortion as an acceptable means of birth control, and we unconditionally reject it as a means of gender selection. We call all Christians to a searching and prayerful inquiry into the sorts of conditions that may warrant abortion. We call for the Church to provide nurturing ministries to those persons who terminate a pregnancy. We encourage the Church to provide nurturing ministries to those who give birth. Governmental laws and regulations do not provide all the guidance required by the informed Christian conscience. Therefore, a decision concerning abortion should be made only after thoughtful and prayerful consideration by the parties involved, with medical, pastoral, and other appropriate counsel.

I) Adoption.—Children are a gift from God to be welcomed and received. We recognize that some circumstances of birth make the rearing of a child difficult. We affirm and support the birth parent(s) whose choice it is to allow the child to be adopted. We recognize the agony, strength, and courage of the birth parent(s) who choose(s) in hope, love, and prayer to offer the child for adoption. In addition, we affirm the receiving parent(s) desiring an adopted child. When circumstances warrant adoption, we support the use of proper legal procedures. We commend the birth parent(s), the receiving parent(s), the child to the care of the Church, that grief might be shared, joy might be celebrated, and the child might be nurtured in a community of Christian love.

J) Death with Dignity.—We applaud medical science for efforts to prevent disease and illness and for advances in treatment that extend the meaningful life of human beings. At the same time, in the varying stages of death and life that advances in medical science have occasioned, we recognize the agonizing personal and moral decisions faced by the dying, their physicians, their families, and their friends. Therefore, we assert the right of every person to die in dignity, with loving personal care and without efforts to prolong terminal illnesses merely because the technology is available to do so.

¶ 72. III. The Social Community

The rights and privileges a society bestows upon or withholds from those who comprise it indicate the relative esteem in which that society holds particular persons and groups of persons. We affirm all persons as equally valuable in the sight of God. We therefore work toward societies in which each person's value is recognized, maintained, and strengthened.

A) *Rights of Racial and Ethnic Persons.*—Racism is the combination of the power to dominate by one race over other races and a value system which assumes that the dominant race is innately superior to the others. Racism includes both personal and institutional racism. Personal racism is manifested through the individual expressions, attitudes, and/or behaviors which accept the assumptions of a racist value system and which maintain the benefits of this system. Institutional racism is the established social pattern which supports implicitly or explicitly the racist value system. Racism plagues and cripples our growth in Christ, inasmuch as it is antithetical to the gospel itself. Therefore, we recognize racism as sin and affirm the ultimate and temporal worth of all persons. We rejoice in the gifts which particular ethnic histories and cultures bring to our total life. We commend and encourage the self-awareness of all racial and ethnic groups and oppressed people which leads them to demand their just and equal rights as members of society. We assert the obligation of society, and groups within the society, to implement compensatory programs that redress long-standing systemic social deprivation of racial and ethnic people. We further assert the right of members of racial and ethnic groups to equal opportunities in employment and promotion; to education and training of the highest quality; to nondiscrimination in voting, in access to public accommodations, and in housing purchase or rental; and positions of leadership and power in all elements of our life together. We support affirmative action as one method of addressing the inequalities and discriminatory practices within our Church and society.

B) *Rights of Religious Minorities.*—Religious persecution has been common in the history of civilization. We urge policies and practices that ensure the right of every religious group to exercise its faith free from legal, political, or economic restrictions. In particular, we condemn anti-Semite, anti-Muslim, and anti-Christian attitudes and practices in both their overt and covert forms, being especially sensitive to their expression in media stereotyping. We assert the right of all religions and their adherents to freedom from legal, economic, and social discrimination.

C) *Rights of Children.*—Once considered the property of their parents, children are now acknowledged to be full human beings in their own right, but beings to whom adults and society in general have special obligations. Thus, we support the development of school systems and innovative methods of education designed to assist every child toward complete fulfillment as an individual person of worth. All children have the right to quality education, including a full sexual education appropriate to their stage of development that utilizes the best educational techniques and insights. Christian parents and guardians and the Church have the responsibility to ensure that children receive sexual education consistent with Christian morality, including faithfulness in marriage and abstinence in singleness. Moreover, children have the rights to food, shelter, clothing, health care, and emotional well-being as do adults, and these rights we affirm as theirs regardless of actions or inactions of their parents or guardians. In particular, children must be protected from economic, physical, and sexual exploitation and abuse.

D) *Rights of Youth and Young Adults.*—Our society is characterized by a large population of youth and young adults who frequently find full participation in society difficult. Therefore, we urge development of policies that encourage inclusion of youth and young adults in decision-making processes and that eliminate discrimination and exploitation. Creative and appropriate employment opportunities should be legally and socially available for youth and young adults.

E) *Rights of the Aging.*—In a society that places primary emphasis upon youth, those growing old in years are frequently isolated from the mainstream of social existence. We support social policies that integrate the aging into the life of the total community, including sufficient incomes, increased and non-discriminatory employment opportunities, educational and service opportunities, and adequate medical care and housing within existing communities. We urge social policies and programs, with emphasis on the unique concerns of older women and ethnic persons, that ensure to the aging the respect and dignity that is their right as senior members of the human community. Further, we urge increased consideration for adequate pension systems by employers with provisions for the surviving spouse.

F) Rights of Women.—We affirm women and men to be equal in every aspect of their common life. We therefore urge that every effort be made to eliminate sex role stereotypes in activity and portrayal of family life and in all aspects of voluntary and compensatory participation in the Church and society. We affirm the right of women to equal treatment in employment, responsibility, promotion, and compensation. We affirm the importance of women in decision-making positions at all levels of church life and urge such bodies to guarantee their presence through policies of employment and recruitment. We support affirmative action as one method of addressing the inequalities and discriminatory practices within our Church and society. We urge employers of persons in dual career families, both in the Church and society, to apply proper consideration of both parties when relocation is considered.

G) Rights of Persons with Handicapping Conditions.—We recognize and affirm the full humanity and personhood of all individuals as members of the family of God. We affirm the responsibility of the Church and society to be in ministry with all persons, including those persons with mentally, physically, and/or psychologically handicapping conditions whose disabilities or differences in appearance or behavior create a problem in mobility, communication, intellectual comprehension, or personal relationships, which interfere with their participation or that of their families in the life of the Church and the community. We urge the Church and society to receive the gifts of persons with handicapping conditions to enable them to be full participants in the community of faith. We call the Church and society to be sensitive to and advocate programs of rehabilitation, services, employment, education, appropriate housing, and transportation.

H) Population.—Since the growing worldwide population is increasingly straining the world's supply of food, minerals, and water, and sharpening international tensions, the reduction of the rate of consumption of resources by the affluent and the reduction of current world population growth rates have become imperative. People have the duty to consider the impact on the total world community of their decisions regarding childbearing, and should have access to information and appropriate means to limit their fertility, including voluntary sterilization. We affirm that programs to achieve a stabilized population should be placed in a context of total economic and social development, including an equitable use and control of resources; improvement in the status of women in all cultures; a human level of economic security, health care, and literacy for all.

I) Alcohol and Other Drugs.—We affirm our long-standing support of abstinence from alcohol as a faithful witness to God's liberating and redeeming love for persons. We support abstinence from the use of any illegal drugs. Since the use of alcohol and illegal drugs is a major factor in crime, disease, death, and family dysfunction, we support educational programs encouraging abstinence from such use.

Millions of living human beings are testimony to the beneficial consequences of therapeutic drug use, and millions of others are testimony to the detrimental consequences of drug misuse. We encourage wise policies relating to the availability of potentially beneficial or potentially damaging prescription and over-the-counter drugs; we urge that complete information about their use and misuse be readily available to both doctor and patient. We support the strict administration of laws regulating the sale and distribution of all opiates. We support regulations that protect society from users of drugs of any kind where it can be shown that a clear and present social danger exists. Drug-dependent persons and their family members are individuals of infinite human worth deserving of treatment, rehabilitation, and ongoing life-changing recovery. Misuse should be viewed as a symptom of underlying disorders for which remedies should be sought.

J) Tobacco.—We affirm our historic tradition of high standards of personal discipline and social responsibility. In light of the overwhelming evidence that tobacco smoking and the use of smokeless tobacco are hazardous to the health of persons of all ages, we recommend total abstinence from the use of tobacco. We urge that our educational and communication resources be utilized to support and encourage such abstinence. Further, we recognize the harmful effects of passive smoke and support the restriction of smoking in public areas and workplaces.

K) Medical Experimentation.—Physical and mental health has been greatly enhanced through discoveries by medical science. It is imperative, however, that governments and the medical profession carefully enforce the requirements of the prevailing medical research standard, maintaining rigid controls in testing new technologies and drugs utilizing human beings. The standard requires that those

41

engaged in research shall use human beings as research subjects only after obtaining full, rational, and uncoerced consent.

L) *Genetic Technology.*—The responsibility of humankind to God's creation challenges us to deal carefully with the possibilities of genetic research and technology. We welcome the use of genetic technology for meeting fundamental human needs for health, a safe environment, and an adequate food supply.

Because of the effects of genetic technologies on all life, we call for effective guidelines and public accountability to safeguard against any action which might lead to abuse of these technologies, including political or military ends. We recognize that cautious, well-intended use of genetic technologies may sometimes lead to unanticipated harmful consequences.

Human gene therapies that produce changes that cannot be passed to offspring (somatic therapy) should be limited to the alleviation of suffering caused by disease. Genetic therapies for eugenic choices or that produce waste embryos are deplored. Genetic data of individuals and their families should be kept secret and held in strict confidence unless confidentiality is waived by the individual, or by his or her family, or unless the collection and use of genetic identification data is supported by an appropriate court order. Because its long-term effects are uncertain, we oppose genetic therapy that results in changes that can be passed to offspring (germ-line therapy).

M) *Rural Life.*—We support the right of persons and families to live and prosper as farmers, farm workers, merchants, professionals, and others outside of the cities and metropolitan centers. We believe our culture is impoverished and our people deprived of a meaningful way of life when rural and small-town living becomes difficult or impossible. We recognize that the improvement of this way of life may sometimes necessitate the use of some lands for nonagricultural purposes. We oppose the indiscriminate diversion of agricultural land for nonagricultural uses when nonagricultural land is available. Further, we encourage the preservation of appropriate lands for agriculture and open space uses through thoughtful land use programs. We support governmental and private programs designed to benefit the resident farmer rather than the factory farm, and programs that encourage industry to locate in nonurban areas.

N) *Urban-Suburban Life.*—Urban-suburban living has become a dominant style of life for more and more persons. For many it furnishes economic, educational, social, and cultural opportunities. For others, it has brought alienation, poverty, and depersonalization. We in the Church have an opportunity and responsibility to help shape the future of urban-suburban life. Massive programs of renewal and social planning are needed to bring a greater degree of humanization into urban-suburban life-styles. Christians must judge all programs, including economic and community development, new towns, and urban renewal, by the extent to which they protect and enhance human values, permit personal and political involvement, and make possible neighborhoods open to persons of all races, ages, and income levels. We affirm the efforts of all developers who place human values at the heart of their planning. We must help shape urban-suburban development so it provides for the human need to identify with and find meaning in smaller social communities. At the same time such smaller communities must be encouraged to assume responsibilities for the total urban-suburban community instead of isolating themselves from it.

O) Media Violence and Christian Values.—The unprecedented impact which the media (principally television and movies) are having on Christian and human values within our society becomes more apparent each day. We express disdain at current media preoccupation with dehumanizing portrayals, sensationalized through mass media "entertainment" and "news." These practices degrade humankind and violate the teachings of Christ and the Bible.

United Methodists, along with those of other faith groups, must be made aware that the mass media often undermine the truths of Christianity by promoting permissive lifestyles and detailing acts of graphic violence. Instead of encouraging, motivating, and inspiring its audiences to adopt lifestyles based on the sanctity of life, the entertainment industry often advocates the opposite: painting a cynical picture of violence, abuse, greed, profanity, and a constant denigration of the family. The media must be held accountable for the part they play in the decline of values we observe in society today. Yet the media remain aloof to the issue, claiming to reflect society rather than to influence it. For the sake of our human family, Christians must work together to halt this erosion of moral and ethical values in the world community.

¶ 73. V. The Economic Community

We claim all economic systems to be under the judgment of God no less than other facets of the created order. Therefore, we recognize the responsibility of governments to develop and implement sound fiscal and monetary policies that provide for the economic life of individuals and corporate entities, and that ensure full employment and adequate incomes with a minimum of inflation. We believe private and public economic enterprises are responsible for the social costs of doing business, such as employment and environmental pollution, and that they should be held accountable for these costs. We support measures that would reduce the concentration of wealth in the hands of a few. We further support efforts to revise tax structures and eliminate governmental support programs that now benefit the wealthy at the expense of other persons.

A) Property.—We believe private ownership of property is a trusteeship under God, both in those societies where it is encouraged and where it is discouraged, but is limited by the overriding needs of society. We believe that Christian faith denies to any person or group of persons exclusive and arbitrary control of any other part of the created universe. Socially and culturally conditioned ownership of property is, therefore, to be considered a responsibility to God. We believe, therefore, governments have the responsibility, in the pursuit of justice and order under law, to provide procedures that protect the rights of the whole society, as well as those of private ownership.

B) Collective Bargaining.—We support the right of public and private (including farm, government, institutional, and domestic) employees and employers to organize for collective bargaining into unions and other groups of their own choosing. Further, we support the right of both parties to protection in so doing and their responsibility to bargain in good faith within the framework of the public interest. In order that the rights of all members of the society may be maintained and promoted, we support innovative bargaining procedures that include representatives of the public interest in negotiation and settlement of labor/management contracts including some that may lead to forms of judicial resolution of issues. We reject the use of violence by either party during collective bargaining or any labor/

44

management disagreement. We likewise reject the permanent replacement of a worker who engages in a lawful strike.

C) *Work and Leisure.*—Every person has the right and responsibility to work for the benefit of himself or herself and the enhancement of human life and community and to receive adequate remuneration. We support social measures that ensure the physical and mental safety of workers, that provide for the equitable division of products and services and that encourage an increasing freedom in the way individuals may use their leisure time. We recognize the opportunity leisure provides for creative contributions to society and encourage methods that allow workers additional blocks of discretionary time. We support educational, cultural, and recreational outlets that enhance the use of such time. We believe that persons come before profits. We deplore the selfish spirit which often pervades our economic life. We support policies which encourage the sharing of ideas in the workplace, cooperative and collective work arrangements. We support rights of workers to refuse to work in situations that endanger health and/or life, without jeopardy to their jobs. We support policies which would reverse the increasing concentration of business and industry into monopolies.

D) *Consumption.*—We support efforts to ensure truth in pricing, packaging, lending, and advertising. We assert that the consumers' primary responsibility is to provide themselves with needed goods and services of high quality at the lowest cost consistent with economic practices. They should exercise their economic power to encourage the manufacture of goods that are necessary and beneficial to humanity while avoiding the desecration of the environment in either production or consumption. Those who manufacture goods and offer services serve society best when they aid consumers in fulfilling these responsibilities. Consumers should evaluate their consumption of goods and services in the light of the need for enhanced quality of life rather than unlimited production of material goods. We call upon consumers to organize to achieve these goals and to express dissatisfaction with harmful economic practices through such appropriate methods as boycott, letter writing, corporate resolution, and advertisement. For example, these methods can be used to influence better television and radio programming.

E) *Poverty.*—In spite of general affluence in the industrialized nations, the majority of persons in the world live in poverty. In order to provide basic needs such as food, clothing, shelter, education, health care, and other necessities, ways must be found to share more equitably the resources of the world. Increasing technology and exploitative economic practices impoverish many persons and make poverty self-perpetuating. Therefore, we do not hold poor people morally responsible for their economic state. To begin to alleviate poverty, we support such policies as: adequate income maintenance, quality education, decent housing, job training, meaningful employment opportunities, adequate medical and hospital care, and humanization and radical revisions of welfare programs.

F) Migrant Workers.—Migratory and other farm workers, who have long been a special concern of the Church's ministry, are by the nature of their way of life excluded from many of the economic and social benefits enjoyed by other workers. Many of the migrant laborers' situations are aggravated because they are racial and ethnic minority persons who have been oppressed with numerous other inequities within the society. We advocate for the rights of all migrants and applaud their efforts toward responsible self-organization and self-determination. We call upon governments and all employers to ensure for migratory workers the same economic, educational, and social benefits enjoyed by other citizens. We call upon our churches to seek to develop programs of service to such migrant people who come within their parish.

G) Gambling.—Gambling is a menace to society, deadly to the best interests of moral, social, economic, and spiritual life, and destructive of good government. As an act of faith and love, Christians should abstain from gambling, and should strive to minister to those victimized by the practice. Where gambling has become addictive, the Church will encourage such individuals to receive therapeutic assistance so that the individual's energies may be redirected into positive and constructive ends. Community standards and personal life styles should be such as would make unnecessary and undesirable the resort to commercial gambling, including public lotteries, as a recreation, as an escape, or as a means of producing public revenue or funds for support of charities or government.

¶ 74. V. The Political Community

While our allegiance to God takes precedence over our allegiance to any state, we acknowledge the vital function of government as a principal vehicle for the ordering of society. Because we know ourselves to be responsible to God for social and political life, we declare the following relative to governments:

A) *Basic Freedoms.*—We hold governments responsible for the protection of the rights of the people to free and fair elections and to the freedoms of speech, religion, assembly, and communications media, and petition for redress of grievances without fear of reprisal; to the right to privacy; and to the guarantee of the rights to adequate food, clothing, shelter, education, and health care. The form and the leaders of all governments should be determined by exercise of the right to vote guaranteed to all adult citizens. We also strongly reject domestic surveillance and intimidation of political opponents by governments in power, and all other misuses of elective or appointive offices. The use of detention and imprisonment for the harassment and elimination of political opponents or other dissidents violates fundamental human rights. Furthermore, the mistreatment or torture of persons by governments for any purpose violates Christian teaching and must be condemned and/or opposed by Christians and churches wherever and whenever it occurs.

The Church regards the institution of slavery as an infamous evil. All forms of enslavement are totally prohibited and shall in no way be tolerated by the Church.

B) *Political Responsibility.*—The strength of a political system depends upon the full and willing participation of its citizens. We believe that the state should not attempt to control the Church, nor should the Church seek to dominate the state. "Separation of church and state" means no organic union of the two, but does permit interaction. The Church should continually exert a strong ethical influence upon the state, supporting policies and programs deemed to be just and compassionate and opposing policies and programs which are not.

C) *Freedom of Information.*—Citizens of all countries should have access to all essential information regarding their government and its policies. Illegal and unconscionable activities directed against persons or groups by their own governments must not be justified or kept secret even under the guise of national security.

D) *Education.*—We believe responsibility for education of the young rests with the family, the Church, and the government. In our society this function can best be fulfilled through public policies which ensure access for all persons to free public elementary and secondary schools and to post-secondary schools of their choice. Persons in our society should not be precluded by financial barriers from access to church-related and other independent institutions of higher education. We affirm the right of public and independent colleges and universities to exist, and we endorse public policies which ensure access and choice and which do not create unconstitutional entanglements between Church and state. The state should not use its authority to inculcate particular religious beliefs (including atheism) nor should it require prayer or worship in the public schools, but should leave students free to practice their own religious convictions.

E) *Civil Obedience and Civil Disobedience.*—Governments and laws should be servants of God and of human beings. Citizens have a duty to abide by laws duly adopted by orderly and just process of government. But governments, no less than individuals, are subject to the judgment of God. Therefore, we recognize the right of individuals to dissent when acting under the constraint of conscience and, after having exhausted all legal recourse, to disobey laws which they deem to be unjust or laws which are discriminately enforced. Even then, respect for law should be shown by refraining from violence and by accepting the costs of disobedience. We offer our prayers for those in rightful authority who serve the public and we support their efforts to afford justice and equal opportunity for all people. We assert the duty of churches to support everyone who suffers for the cause of conscience, and urge governments seriously to consider restoration of rights to such persons while also maintaining respect for those who obey.

F) *Criminal Justice.*—To protect all citizens from those who would encroach upon personal and property rights, it is the duty of governments to establish police forces, courts, and facilities for the confinement, punishment, and rehabilitation of offenders. We support governmental measures designed to reduce and eliminate crime, consistent with respect for the basic freedom of persons. We reject all misuse of these necessary mechanisms, including their use for the purpose of persecuting or intimidating those whose race, appearance, life-style, economic condition, or beliefs differ from those in authority, and we reject all careless, callous, or discriminatory enforcement of law. We further support measures designed to remove the social conditions that lead to crime, and we encourage continued positive interaction between law enforcement officials and members of the community at large. In the love of Christ who came to save those who are lost and vulnerable, we urge the creation of genuinely new systems for the care and support of the victims of crime, and for rehabilitation that will restore, preserve, and nurture the humanity of the imprisoned. For the same reason, we oppose capital punishment and urge its elimination from all criminal codes.

G) Military Service.—Though coercion, violence, and war are presently the ultimate sanctions in international relations, we reject them as incompatible with the gospel and spirit of Christ. We therefore urge the establishment of the rule of law in international affairs as a means of elimination of war, violence, and coercion in these affairs.

We reject national policies of enforced military service as incompatible with the gospel. We acknowledge the agonizing tension created by the demand for military service by national governments. We urge all young adults to seek the counsel of the Church as they reach a conscientious decision concerning the nature of their responsibility as citizens. Pastors are called upon to be available for counseling with all young adults who face conscription, including those who conscientiously refuse to cooperate with a system of conscription.

We support and extend the ministry of the Church to those persons who conscientiously oppose all war, or any particular war, and who therefore refuse to serve in the armed forces or to cooperate with systems of military conscription. We also support and extend the Church's ministry to those persons who conscientiously choose to serve in the armed forces or to accept alternative service.

¶ 75. VI. The World Community

God's world is one world. The unity now being thrust upon us by technological revolution has far outrun our moral and spiritual capacity to achieve a stable world. The enforced unity of humanity, increasingly evident on all levels of life, presents the Church as well as all people with problems that will not wait for answer: injustice, war, exploitation, privilege, population, international ecological crisis, proliferation of arsenals of nuclear weapons, development of transnational business organizations that operate beyond the effective control of any governmental structure, and the increase of tyranny in all its forms. This generation must find viable answers to these and related questions if humanity is to continue on this earth. We commit ourselves, as a Church, to the achievement of a world community that is a fellowship of persons who honestly love one another. We pledge ourselves to seek the meaning of the gospel in all issues that divide people and threaten the growth of world community.

A) *Nations and Cultures.*—As individuals are affirmed by God in their diversity, so are nations and cultures. We recognize that no nation or culture is absolutely just and right in its treatment of its own people, nor is any nation totally without regard for the welfare of its citizens. The Church must regard nations as accountable for unjust treatment of their citizens and others living within their borders. While recognizing valid differences in culture and political philosophy, we stand for justice and peace in every nation.

B) *National Power and Responsibility.*—Some nations possess more military and economic power than do others. Upon the powerful rests responsibility to exercise their wealth and influence with restraint. We affirm the right and duty of people of all nations to determine their own destiny. We urge the major political powers to use their nonviolent power to maximize the political, social, and economic self-determination of other nations, rather than to further their own special interests. We applaud international efforts to develop a more just international economic order, in which the limited resources of the earth will be used to the maximum benefit of all nations and peoples. We urge Christians, in every society, to encourage the governments under which they live, and the economic entities within their societies, to aid and to work for the development of more just economic orders.

C) *War and Peace.*—We believe war is incompatible with the teachings and example of Christ. We therefore reject war as an instrument of national foreign policy and insist that the first moral duty of all nations is to resolve by peaceful means every dispute that arises between or among them; that human values must outweigh military claims as governments determine their priorities; that the militarization of society must be challenged and stopped; that the manufacture, sale, and deployment of armaments must be reduced and controlled; and that the production, possession, or use of nuclear weapons be condemned.

D) *Justice and Law.*—Persons and groups must feel secure in their life and right to live within a society if order is to be achieved and maintained by law. We denounce as immoral an ordering of life that perpetuates injustice. Nations, too, must feel secure in the world if world community is to become a fact.

Believing that international justice requires the participation of all peoples, we endorse the United Nations and its related bodies and the International Court of Justice as the best instruments now in existence to achieve a world of justice and law. We commend the efforts of all people in all countries who pursue world peace through law. We endorse international aid and cooperation on all matters of need and conflict. We urge acceptance for membership in the United Nations of all nations who wish such membership and who accept United Nations responsibility. We urge the United Nations to take a more aggressive role in the development of international arbitration of disputes and actual conflicts among nations by developing binding third-party arbitration. Bilateral or multilateral efforts outside of the United Nations should work in concert with, and not contrary to, its purposes. We reaffirm our historic concern for the world as our parish and seek for all persons and peoples full and equal membership in a truly world community.

¶ 76. VII. Our Social Creed

We believe in God, Creator of the world; and in Jesus Christ the Redeemer of creation. We believe in the Holy Spirit, through whom we acknowledge God's gifts, and we repent of our sin in misusing these gifts to idolatrous ends.

We affirm the natural world as God's handiwork and dedicate ourselves to its preservation, enhancement, and faithful use by humankind.

We joyfully receive, for ourselves and others, the blessings of community, sexuality, marriage, and the family.

We commit ourselves to the rights of men, women, children, youth, young adults, the aging, and those with handicapping conditions; to improvement of the quality of life; and to the rights and dignity of racial, ethnic, and religious minorities.

We believe in the right and duty of persons to work for the glory of God and the good of themselves and others, and in the protection of their welfare in so doing; in the rights to property as a trust from God, collective bargaining, and responsible consumption; and in the elimination of economic and social distress.

We dedicate ourselves to peace throughout the world, to the rule of justice and law among nations, and to individual freedom for all people of the world.

We believe in the present and final triumph of God's Word in human affairs, and gladly accept our commission to manifest the life of the gospel in the world. Amen.

(It is recommended that this statement of Social Principles be continually available to United Methodist Christians and that it be emphasized regularly in every congregation. It is further recommended that "Our Social Creed" be frequently used in Sunday worship.)

THE NATURAL WORLD

Black-Owned Farm Land

Whereas, according to the agricultural census of 1978, black farmland loss was two-and-a-half times greater than the loss rate for white farmers; black farmers as a group, compared to other farmers, depend more heavily on farming for an income and have less off-farm income; the continuing loss of ownership and control of agricultural land by black American farmers has reduced their ability to achieve economic viability and financial independence; this loss has been accelerated by the black land owners' lack of access to capital, technical information, and legal resources needed to retain and develop agricultural land holdings into stable income-producing, self-sustaining operations;

Whereas, the 1982 Civil Rights Commission study entitled "The Decline of Black Farming in America" reported many actions and inactions on the part of the US Department of Agriculture and, in particular, the Farmers Home Administration, that have contributed to black land loss; a follow-up study in 1983 showed the Farmers Home Administration's record to be worse than the year before; there were many specific recommendations in the two reports that are yet to be followed through on;

Whereas, the U.S. Civil Rights Commission's study predicted that, if present trends continue, there will be no black-owned farms by the year 2000;

Whereas, the dislocation of blacks in agriculture and the disruption of rural black family life contributes to unemployment, drug and alcohol abuse, child and spouse abuse, loss of identity, loss of community leadership, increasing absentee land ownership and a decline in attendance and participation in rural black churches across the countryside;

W<small>HEREAS</small>, we as United Methodists take seriously Paul's advice: "If one member suffers, all suffer together;"

Therefore be it resolved, that The United Methodist Church go on record supporting the crucial need for the church and the government to provide financial, technical and management assistance to help stop the decline of black-owned farmland in America.

Be it further resolved, that the General Conference of The United Methodist Church call upon the Secretary of Agriculture to provide additional grants to predominantly black colleges to research the plight of black farmers in their state and to identify and document the extent of black land ownership and land loss.

Be it further resolved, that the General Conference of The United Methodist Church call upon the Secretary of Agriculture to provide grants to agricultural colleges to help develop new marketing strategies for limited-resource farmers and to help disseminate information on existing viable marketing strategies; preference to be given to historically black agriculture (1890 land grant) colleges where available.

Be it further resolved, that the General Conference of The United Methodist Church ask the Secretary of Agriculture to seek initiatives linking government, private, church and other community resources to offer support and aid black farm owners.

Finally be it further resolved, that the General Conference of The United Methodist Church ask the President of the United State and the Secretary of Agriculture to press for a just and enlightened public farm policy that will preserve the diverse ownership of land as well as the continuation of black-owned family-operated farms.

ADOPTED 1988

See Social Principles, ¶ 70, "U.S. Agriculture and Rural Communities in Crisis," "Environmental Racism."

Common Heritage

Common Heritage Concept

The common heritage is a pioneering concept in actual international cooperation and sharing of the benefits of the world's resources. This concept stems from the underlying premise that resources outside the control of different nations should be under a just and equitable system of management. Several principles are a general guide to what a common heritage area may be. These include the need for full participation in decision-making for all nations; the use of the resource area only for peaceful purposes; no nation allowed an exclusive claim; the transfer of technology; and development of the resources for the benefit of all humanity while insuring future generations the use of the area and resources as well.

Past, Present, and Future Implementation

The international community has been developing the concept of common heritage through the United Nations Law of the Sea Treaty and the Agreement Governing the Activities of States on the Moon and Other Celestial Bodies. The system that has evolved in the Law of the Sea is one to which most countries have agreed, although no one nation has been totally satisfied. Nations are continuing in the process to complete the implementation of the concept through the ongoing Law of the Sea process. The concept of the common heritage is being expanded to include, but is not limited to, the air we breathe; water which sustains all life; the genetic variability of plants and animals upon which future agriculture and medicine may depend; Antarctica; the moon and other planets; and outer space.

Biblical and Theological Base

The common heritage concept has its roots for people of faith in the biblical understanding that all creation is under the authority of God and that all creation is interdependent. Our covenant with God requires us to be stewards, protectors, and defenders of all creation. The use of natural resources is a universal concern and responsibility of all as reflected in Psalm 24:1, "The earth is the Lord's and the fullness thereof."

The New Testament confronts us with the implication of the Old Testament understanding when it asks us how we use our resources in relation to our brothers and sisters. John the Baptist prepared us for Jesus' ministry by stating, "Those who have two coats let them share with those who have none; and those who have food let them do likewise" (Luke 3:11). This philosophy was carried forth into the early church by incorporating the belief that the way in which one shares one's goods is a reflection of how one loves God. This is stated in I John 3:17; "But if anyone has the world's goods and sees his brother in need, yet closes his heart against him, how does God's love abide in him?"

Our Denominational Witness

The Social Principles of The United Methodist Church applies these basic biblical perceptions to how we use the resources of creation when it says: "We believe that Christian faith denies to any person or group of persons exclusive and arbitrary control of any other part of the created universe. Socially and culturally conditioned ownership of property is, therefore, to be considered a responsibility to God."

The Social Principles also reminds us that "upon the powerful rests responsibility to exercise their wealth and influence with restraint." Furthermore, the statement says that as United Methodists "we applaud international efforts to develop a more just international economic order, in which the limited resources of the earth will be used to the maximum benefit of all nations and peoples."

United Methodists have affirmed the common heritage since 1976 and have worked to see the common heritage become codified into international agreements for Law of the Sea, the moon, and Antarctica.

Statements of Understanding

In light of the uneven patterns of utilization of the world's resources and in light of our own understanding of the gospel and United Methodist tradition, we affirm these principles:

1. Specific natural resources belong to all humanity, and therefore must be developed and preserved for the benefit of all, not just for the few, both today and for generations to come.

2. All people have the right to enough of the resources of the universe to provide for their health and well-being.

3. God's creation is intended to be used for the good of all as a precious gift, not for warfare or economic oppression of others.

Recommended Actions

Therefore as United Methodists we are called to:

1. Work for and support the process of legal implementation of the common heritage concept as understood in the Law of the Sea Treaty and the Agreement Governing the Activities of States on the Moon and Other Celestial Bodies, as vehicles to address a more just and responsible use of God's creation.

2. Request that the appropriate general agencies of The United Methodist Church study and develop a broad biblical and theological understanding of the common heritage concept, which should include but not be limited to Antarctica, outer space, plant and animal genetics, air and water.

3. Request that the appropriate general agencies of The United Methodist Church develop and distribute resources for education about, and become advocates for, the common heritage concept.

4. Study these materials on the common heritage as individuals, local congregations, general program agencies, and other groups.

ADOPTED 1984

See Social Principles, ¶ 70, "Environmental Justice for a Sustainable Future," "Environmental Stewardship."

Energy Policy Statement

Preamble

In 1979 our nation experienced two shocks which are compelling us to reassess our energy future: the revolution in Iran and the accident at Three Mile Island. It is already clear that by the turn of this century our sources of power will be radically altered. Just as the first half of this century was marked by a rapid shift from wood, water, and coal to the fossil fuels that currently supply 90 percent of the U.S. energy needs, so we today are at the beginning of a rapid transition from these fuels, which are running out, to the renewable sources which must supply our energy future. Because society runs on its energy and is shaped by the fuels it uses and the way it uses them, we will, in effect, be shaping a new world by the energy policies we adopt in the next few decades. The stakes are high: the decisions which human societies are now making will either enhance or degrade the quality of life on our planet; they will either more closely approximate the vision of the reign of God which fires the Christian imagination or they will make that vision more remote from actual human existence. Furthermore, as our world comes up against limits and undergoes the stress of rapid change, fears will be raised and conflicts will become inevitable. Our responses to these stresses can either produce more repressive societies or ones in which liberty is enhanced.

Stewards of the Spaceship Earth

The recognition that a new world is emerging and that the Church of Jesus Christ may have a role to play in shaping that world calls us to re-examine the biblical sources out of which we as Christians live our lives.

Humankind enjoys a unique place in God's universe. On the one hand we are simply one of God's many finite creatures, made from the "dust of the earth," bounded in time and space, fallible in judgment, limited in control, dependent upon our Creator, and interdependent with all other creatures. On the other hand we are created in the very image of God, with the divine spirit breathed into us, and entrusted with "dominion" over God's creation (Gen. 1:26, 28; 2:7, Ps. 8:6). We are simultaneously co-creatures with all creation, and, because of the divine summons, co-creators with God of the world in which we live. This hybrid human condition produces both the opportunity and the twin dangers for humans on this planet.

The first danger is arrogance: that we may overestimate the extent of human control over our environment and the soundness of human judgments concerning it (after all, we still know very little about the ecosystem in which we live); that we may underestimate the limits of the planet where we live; and that we may misunderstand "dominion" to mean exploitation instead of stewardship.

The second danger is irresponsibility: that we may fail to be the responsible stewards of the earth that God has called us to be, choosing instead to bury our "talents" while awaiting the Master's return (Mt. 25:24-28). As stewards entrusted with dominion, then, we will demonstrate our faith in God by becoming God's avante garde in shaping the new human society which will emerge in the twenty-first century. We cannot, therefore, eschew the task of seeking to embody in the new-world-aborning the values which we hold in covenant

58

with God. At the same time, however, we dare not overlook the limits of our control; nor can we forget the forgiving grace in Jesus Christ which alone makes us bold enough or the hope in Christ which alone keeps us from despair.

The Values Involved in Energy Policy

The scripture which provides the motive for our action in the present energy crisis also lays the foundation for the values which we seek to realize. These values underlying the policies we advocate are justice and sustainability.

1. *Justice.* Ever since the first covenant between God and Israel, and especially since the eighth century prophets, the people of God have understood that they bear a special concern for justice. "Let justice roll down like waters, and righteousness like an everflowing stream" (Amos 5:24) is a cry echoed in hundreds of contexts throughout the Old and New Testaments. Biblical righteousness includes a special concern for the least and the last: the poor, the captive, the oppressed (Lk. 4:18; cf. Isa. 61:1-2). Energy policies which Christians can support, then, will seek to actualize the multifaceted biblical vision of justice. They will be policies which close rather than widen the gap dividing wealth and poverty, rich nations and poor. They will be measures which liberate rather than oppress. They will be programs which distribute fairly the benefits, burdens, and hazards of energy production and consumption, taking into consideration those not yet born as well as the living. They will thus be strategies which give priority to meeting basic human needs, such as air, water, food, clothing, and shelter.

2. *Sustainability.* Only recently have we humans come to recognize that creation (finitude) entails limits to the resources entrusted to us as stewards of the earth. In particular we have come up against limits to the non-renewable fuels available for our consumption and limits to our environment's capacity to absorb poisonous wastes. These double limits mean that humans can betray their stewardship either by using up resources faster than they can be replaced or by releasing wastes in excess of the planet's capacity to absorb them. We now know that humans have the capacity to destroy human life and perhaps even life itself on this planet, and to do so in a very short period of time. Energy policy decisions, therefore, must be measured by sustainability as a criterion in addition to justice. In terms of energy policy, sustainability

means energy use which will not (a) deplete the earth's resources in such a way that our descendants will not be able to continue human society at the level which is adequate for a good quality of life, and (b) pollute the environment to such an extent that human life cannot be sustained in the future. These guidelines for sustainability must include considerations of quality of life as well as mere biological continuance.

Until such time as a truly inexhaustible source of power is developed, we must create and expand all of the energy resources available to us with special emphasis on renewable energy resources. We enjoy a highly sophisticated, industrialized world. It is not a realistic option for us to retrogress to a world where people read by candlelight and heat with wood. Also we should be aware of the tragic effects that steadily increasing energy costs will have, especially upon the aged and poor members of our society. All options available in the United States are not open to peoples in other parts of the world; hence we should endeavor to develop all available energy sources. We must creatively explore all of the energy options available to us.

There are environmental problems connected with these energy options that cause people to raise objections to their development and use. We believe that the objections to each energy source should be calmly assessed and then the risks and benefits of its use compared with the use of the other energy options. For example, the large-scale use of our coal resources poses many problems. Underground mining, in addition to operational accidents, causes disabling illness or death from black lung. Strip mining can despoil an area and ruin it for further use if restoration measures are not practiced. The actual burning of coal causes large-scale pollution and could seriously alter the environment by increasing the CO_2 content of the atmospheric envelope.

Hydroelectric power also has its problems. In addition to deaths from industrial accidents, many dam sites are (or were) attractive scenic areas. Destroying (or diminishing) such natural beauty areas as the Grand Canyon would be objectionable to most of us. Possible dam failure with the resultant flood damage must also be considered in evaluation of this source of power.

The use of petroleum products creates environmental problems which are on the increase. Tankers and off-shore wells have created spills which have devastated sea coast areas; the damage is long-lasting or permanent. Atmospheric pollution, far from being under control, is a most serious health problem in centers of dense population.

Our nuclear energy option also has many problems to be faced. The hazards in storing radioactive wastes for thousands of years and the destructive potential of a catastrophic accident involve a great risk of irreversible damage to the environment or to the human genetic pool.

1. We support a strenuous national effort to conserve energy. Economists have concluded that in the next decade a greater increase in end-use energy can be gained through conservation than through any single new source of fuel. Furthermore, conservation is non-polluting and job-producing. We include under conservation: insulation, cogeneration, recycling, public transportation, more efficient motors in appliances and automobiles, as well as the elimination of waste and more simplified lifestyle. The technology for such steps is already known and commercially available; it requires only dissemination of information and stronger public support, including larger tax incentives than are presently available.

2. All United Methodist churches are encouraged to be models for energy conservation by doing such things as: installing dampers in furnaces, insulating adequately all church properties, heating and lighting only rooms that are in use, using air circulation, and exploring alternative energy sources such as solar energy.

3. We also urge all our members and agencies to assess their own energy consumption, finding ways to conserve, to eliminate waste, to revise transportation patterns, and to simplify lifestyles as a model for sound stewardship of the limited resources entrusted to us.

4. We support increased government funding for research and development of renewable energy sources, especially solar energy, and government incentives to speed the application of the resulting technologies to our energy needs, wherever appropriate. The greatest national effort should be made in the areas of conservation and renewable energy sources.

5. We oppose any national energy policy which will result in continuing exploitation of Native American lands without the consent of the persons who control those lands. The despoiling of Native American lands and the increased health problems which have resulted among Native Americans because of the mining of coal and the milling of uranium must cease.

6. We support a national energy program which will not increase the financial burden on the poor, the elderly, and those with fixed incomes. If a rapid rise in the price of fuel is necessary to smooth out

distortions in the energy economy, as many economists believe, then legislative means should be found to cushion the impact of such price increases on the poor.

7. We support full U.S. cooperation in international efforts to ensure equitable distribution of necessary energy supplies and rapid development and deployment of appropriate technologies based on renewable energy resources such as solar, wind, and water energy generation.

8. We strongly encourage The United Methodist Church at all levels to engage in a serious study of these energy issues in the context of Christian faith and the values of justice and sustainability.

ADOPTED 1980

See Social Principles, ¶ 70.B, "Nuclear Safety in the United States," "Environmental Stewardship."

Environmental Justice for a Sustainable Future

Humankind is destroying the global ecological balance which provides the life-support systems for the planet. Signs of the crisis are evident all around us. The global ecological imbalance produces environmental destruction.

Polluted air pervades the atmosphere. Garbage abounds with little space for disposal. Polluting gases destroy the ozone layer and cause global warming. Deforestation leads to soil erosion, a lack of carbon storage, inadequate water quantity and poor quality and the loss of species, thus a reduction in biological diversity. The misuse of pesticides and fertilizers contributes to the poisoning of our soils and creates products harmful to all life.

Present social, political, and economic development structures fail to provide the basic necessities of food, clothing, and shelter for an estimated 5.4 billion people. Additionally, at least one billion people live in absolute poverty. The environmental crisis results in social unrest and mounting violence.

Historical and Theological Concerns

Through the ages a theological base for the domination of creation was found in Genesis 1:28. "Be fruitful and multiply, and fill the earth and subdue it; and have dominion over . . . every living thing that moves upon the earth." Misinterpretation of "subdue" and "dominion" has been used to justify much of the nature-destroying aspects of modern civilization.

The scale of human activity has grown so large it now threatens the planet itself. Global environmental problems have become so vast that they are hard to comprehend. Between 1955 and 1990 the human population has doubled to 5.4 billion. During the same time, the consumption of fossil fuels has quadrupled. Increasing evidence suggests that the carbon dioxide from fossil fuels has already caused a noticeable warming of the globe. Destruction of habitat, especially tropical rain forests, is causing the loss of species at an ever-increasing rate. Valuable topsoil is being depleted. There is a recurring hole in the ozone layer. More ultraviolet radiation now reaches the earth which may cause more cancers, poorer crop growth, and damage to the immune systems of humans and other animals.

Confronted with the massive crisis of the deterioration of God's creation and faced with the question of the ultimate survival of life, we ask God's forgiveness for our participation in this destruction of God's creation. We have misused God's good creation. We have confused God's call for us to be faithful stewards of creation with a license to use all of creation as we see fit. The first humans had to leave the Garden of Eden when they decided they had permission to use all of creation despite warnings to the contrary. We have denied that God's covenant is with all living creatures (Gen. 9:9). We have even denied that all of the human family should enjoy the covenant. We forget that the good news that we are called to proclaim includes the promise that Jesus Christ came to redeem all creation (Col. 1:15-20).

We believe that at the center of the vision of *shalom* is the integration of environmental, economic, and social justice.

We are called to eliminate over-consumption as a life-style, thus using lower levels of finite natural resources.

We are called to seek a new life-style rooted in justice and peace.

We are called to establish new priorities in a world where 40,000 children die of hunger each day.

Therefore, we are called to a global sense of community, solidarity leading to a new world system of international relationships and economic/environmental order. In this way the misery of one billion poor now living in absolute poverty can be alleviated and the living ecosystem be saved.

Principles for a Sustainable Future

The Social Principles of The United Methodist Church reminds us that "all creation is the Lord's and we are responsible for the ways in which we use and abuse it" (¶ 70). Development must be centered in the concept of sustainability as defined by the World Commission of Environment and Development: "to meet the needs of the present without compromising the ability of future generations to meet their own needs." The Christian understanding of sustainability encompasses this concept. Fundamental to our call as faithful witnesses is the meeting of human needs within the capacity of ecosystems. This insures the security of creation and a just relationship between all people. Sustainable development, therefore, looks toward a healthy future in three vital areas: the social community, the economy, and the environment.

Conclusion

The United Methodist Church will strive for a global sense of community to help achieve social, economic, and ecological justice for all of creation.

We will focus on the conversion to sustainable practices in the following areas:

Atmosphere

• Support measures calling for the reduction of carbon dioxide, chlorofluorocarbons (CFCs), methane, nitrogen oxides, and sulfur dioxide, believed to cause the greenhouse effect and acid rain.
• Support measures calling for the elimination of CFCs to stop the depletion of the ozone layer.
• Support the cleanup of environmental problems through economic incentive, appropriate enforcement measures, and sanctions against those causing pollution.

Earth

• Support integrated and sustainable natural resource management.
• Commit to the "Greening of the World" through the limiting of all emissions of pollutants that damage forests and reforestation.
• Work for ecologically sound agricultural practices that produce healthy food and a clean environment.
• Protect biodiversity among both animals and plants.

Water

• Support integrated sustainable management to reduce or eliminate factors contributing to limited water quantity and poorer quality.

Energy

• Support improved energy conservation and greater reliance on new and renewable sources of energy.
• Support the development of efficient mass transportation.
• Support a call for a sustainable National Energy policy.

Actions/Recommendations

We call upon the agencies and local congregations of The United Methodist Church to take the following actions:

Council of Bishops

• Communicate to the Church the urgency of responding to the ecological crisis.
• Model for the Church a "ministry of presence" by going to places where humans and ecosystems are endangered by environmental destruction.

General Council on Ministries

• Initiate basic research on the changing attitudes on environmental issues among United Methodist members.
• Request each United Methodist agency to include an evaluation of their corporate action taken towards sustainable environmental practices as a part of their 1993–1996 Quadrennial Report.

General Board of Church and Society (GBCS)

• Develop programs which help annual conferences and local churches become more involved in sustainable practices in public policy and personal aspects of the ecological crisis. These programs would emphasize conversion to a sustainable society.

General Board of Discipleship

• Develop curricula and programs (for all ages), in consultation with GBCS, that emphasize ecological responsibility as a key element of discipleship.

General Board of Global Ministries (GBGM)

- Join with the GBCS in working with mission partners through the National, World, and Women's Divisions to prepare for and participate in the environmental recommendations which will flow from the United Nations Conference on the Environment and Development (UNCED).
- Conduct a survey, with the assistance of all mission partners, to identify environmental concerns and develop projects geared to the solution of common concerns.
- Initiate an audit of all National, World, and Women's Division- and UMCOR-sponsored projects as to their environmental effect on the global ecological balance.
- Establish an eco-mission intern group to work on ecology issues under the sponsorship of the National and World Divisions.
- Include global environmental issues in the training of all GBGM missionaries.
- Facilitate dialogue between religious groups, other non-government organizations, and government agencies on the formation and methods of popular participation.

General Board of Higher Education and Ministry

- Include a greater awareness in clergy education and training of the global ecological crises.

United Methodist Communications

- Produce programs which stress Christian responsibility for the future of creation and include models of The United Methodist Church's involvement in environmental justice.

General Council on Finance and Administration

- Assist the church in its effort to be ecologically responsible in its own use of resources by collecting statistics on local churches' and general agencies' use of energy, water, paper, and recycling to monitor the progress of the church in these aspects of stewardship.

General Board of Pensions

- Develop investment guidelines, in consultation with agencies, to evaluate its securities in light of whether those corporations have a positive history of care for creation.

Local Congregations

• Develop programs to incorporate the concerns of ecological justice into their work in evangelism, social concerns, mission activities, stewardship, trustees, and worship.

ADOPTED 1992

See Social Principles, ¶ 70, "Environmental Stewardship," "Energy Policy Statement."

Environmental Racism

The United Methodist Church is committed to understanding and eliminating racism. One generally ignored aspect is environmental racism. People of color are disproportionately affected by toxic contamination due to the production, storage, treatment, and disposal process of hazardous materials and wastes. African-American, Hispanic North American, Asian-American, Native American, and Third-World communities are usually the least able, politically and economically, to oppose the sitings of these facilities.

Research has documented that:

a) Race is consistently the most statistically significant variable in the location of commercial hazardous waste facilities. Three of the five largest commercial hazardous waste landfills in the United States are located in communities of color; communities with commercial hazardous waste facilities have two to three times the average minority population of communities without such facilities; and three out of every five African Americans and Hispanic North Americans live in communities with toxic waste sites.[1] The predominantly African-American and Hispanic south side of Chicago has the greatest concentration of hazardous waste sites in the United States.

b) Communities where hazardous waste incinerators are sited tend to have large minority populations, low incomes, and low property values. The minority portion of the population in communities with existing incinerators is 89 percent higher than the national average. In Houston, Texas, six of eight municipal incinerators are located in predominantly African-American neighborhoods.[2]

---

[1]"Toxic Wastes and Race," Commission for Racial Justice, United Church of Christ, 1987.
[2]*Playing with Fire: Hazardous Waste Incineration,* Greenpeace, 1991.

c) Communities of color have greater cancer rates than white communities.[3] Many environmental groups are calling for a study of the linkage between environmental contamination and increased cancer rates.

d) Fifty percent of the children in the United States suffering from lead poisoning are African-American.

e) Farm workers' children (mainly Hispanics) in the United States suffer a higher rate of birth defects due to their mothers' exposure to pesticides during the early stages of pregnancy. In farm worker communities children with cancer are common. Pesticide exposure among farm workers causes more than 300,000 pesticide-related illnesses each year.[4]

f) Navajo teenagers have cancer rates 17 times the national average, due to countless uranium spills on Navajo lands that contaminated their water, air, and soil.[5]

g) The growing trend during the 1980s and 1990s has been to dump toxic wastes in developing countries.[6] Countries such as Liberia have been offered much-needed foreign capital if they accepted several shipments of toxic wastes in the past few years. Unfortunately, these countries often lack the appropriate infrastructure to handle adequately the environmental and health problems that accompany these wastes.

Other evidence suggests that the problem is worsening. The findings of the Inter-Denominational Hearings on Toxics and Minorities, held in September, 1990, in Albuquerque, N.M., and the General Board of Church and Society-sponsored consultation on "Responding to Communities Facing Toxic Hazards," held in Baton Rouge, La., in October, 1990, poignantly demonstrated that communities are still having problems related to toxic contamination more than 10 years after the media exposed the problems.

Our society's attitude toward the production and disposal of hazardous products is one of "out of sight, out of mind." But "out of sight, out of mind" is most often where the poor and powerless live and work. These communities have thus become toxic "sacrifice zones." This pattern of racism represents a serious challenge to the

---

[3]*Health and Status of Minorities and Low-Income Groups*, Third Edition. U.S. Department of Health and Human Services, 1991.
[4]Dr. Marion Moses, M.D., Pesticide Education Network.
[5]Center for Third World Organizing.
[6]Greenpeace Waste Trade Campaign.

conscience of all Christians. We ask our local churches, conferences, and general agencies to join with other religious bodies and groups in actions to end this form of racism.

1. We request the Council of Bishops to address environmental racism in any formal communication to the denomination concerning racism or the environment.

2. We urge annual conferences, districts, local churches, and general agencies to become more involved with community groups working to alleviate environmental racism.

3. We urge all general program agencies and the Commission on Religion and Race to:

a. disseminate the "stories" of people and communities affected by environmental racism;

b. find expertise, build leadership, and develop networks that can help empower people within communities in crisis; and

c. provide financial support to grassroots groups and programs working to alleviate environmental racism.

4. We call upon the General Board of Church and Society to:

a. advocate a moratorium on the siting of hazardous waste treatment, storage, and disposal facilities in low-income/people-of-color communities;

b. advocate comprehensive legislation that remedies these injustices and adequately protects all citizens and the environment; and

c. develop programs that help annual conferences, districts, and local churches respond to these concerns.

5. We request the General Council on Ministries to assist the General Board of Church and Society in conducting research in this area.

6. We call upon the General Board of Pensions and other church investors to sponsor shareholder resolutions on environmental racism issues and to urge corporations to sign guidelines for corporate conduct on the environment (such as the Valdez Principles developed in cooperation with the Interfaith Center on Corporate Responsibility).

7. We urge individual United Methodists to:

a. become aware of how and where their community's wastes are disposed and who in their community is adversely affected by the production and disposal of industrial chemicals; and

b. make a personal commitment to reduce their use of hazardous chemicals by one each day.

8. We call upon the U.S. federal government to:

a. institute comprehensive risk assessment studies of communities at risk and their affected populations;

b. enable these communities to participate in clean-up decisions that affect them directly;

c. institute a budget and staff in the Environmental Protection Agency to monitor toxic waste siting in low-income/people-of-color communities;

d. give these communities priority in receiving Superfund funding to clean up existing sites; and

e. prohibit hazardous waste exports and imports.

9. We urge industry to:

a. assess the adverse impacts of their production and disposal processes on workers and surrounding communities;

b. implement comprehensive Toxics Use Reduction (TUR) programs;

c. develop non-toxic alternatives to commonly used hazardous materials;

d. comply with local, state, and federal environmental and safety laws;

e. respond to community concerns and grievances;

f. sign comprehensive environmental guidelines developed with public input, such as the Valdez Principles; and

g. develop industrywide standards for environmental accounting and auditing procedures similar to those required for financial accounting.

ADOPTED 1992

See Social Principles, ¶ 70, "Environmental Justice for a Sustainable Future," "A Charter of Racial Justice Policies in an Interdependent Global Community."

Environmental Stewardship

I. *A Theology of Stewardship and the Environment*

Many of today's "environmental problems" have their roots in humanity's short-sighted use of God's creation. While focusing on the stewardship of monetary resources, we forget that the source of all wealth is God's gracious creation.

In the Bible, a steward is one given responsibility for what belongs to another. The Greek word we translate as steward is *oikonomos*, one who cares for the household or acts as its trustee. The world *oikos*, meaning household, is used to describe the world as God's household. Christians, then, are to be stewards of the whole household (creation) of God. *Oikonomia*, "stewardship," is also the root of our word "economics." *Oikos*, moreover, is the root of our modern word, "ecology." Thus in a broad sense, stewardship, economics, and ecology are, and should be, related. Indeed, a "faithful and wise steward" (Luke 12:42) must relate them.

The Old Testament relates these concepts in the vision of *shalom*. Often translated "peace," the broader meaning of *shalom* is wholeness. In the Old Testament, *shalom* is used to characterize the wholeness of a faithful life lived in relationship to God. *Shalom* is best understood when we experience wholeness and harmony as human beings with God, with others, and with creation itself. The task of the steward is to seek *shalom*.

Stewards of God's Creation. The concept of stewardship is first introduced in the creation story. In Genesis 1:26, the Bible affirms that every person is created in God's image. But this gift brings with it a unique responsibility. Being created in God's image brings with it the responsibility to care for God's creation. God chose to give human beings a divine image not so we would exploit creation to our own ends, but so we would be recognized as stewards of God. To have dominion over the earth is a trusteeship, a sign that God cares for creation and has entrusted it to our stewardship. Our stewardship of all the world's resources is always accountable to God who loves the whole of creation and who desires that it exist in *shalom*. The intention of creation was that all should experience *shalom*, to know the goodness of creation. In the Old Testament, "fullness of life" means having enough, sufficient, to experience the goodness of creation. By contrast, our age has come to define "fullness of life" as more than enough. The desire of many for excess begins to deny enough for others, and *shalom* is broken. That all should participate in creation's goodness is a fundamental of stewardship.

Another theme of *shalom* is that in creation we are all related. Humans are not self-sufficient. We need God, others, nature. The story of the garden (Genesis 2) attempts to picture the complete and harmonious interrelatedness of all creation. There is *shalom* only when we recognize that interrelatedness and care for the whole. When we violate the rules of the garden, we are dismissed. In ecological terms, when we violate the principles of ecology, we suffer environmental damage.

As the story of the garden shows, God's intention of *shalom* was not carried out. Sin intervened, and the *shalom* was broken. But God offered a way to restore *shalom*—redemption. And as God's stewards we have a role in that redemption. Stewardship, then, is to become involved wherever wholeness is lacking and to work in harmony with God's saving activity to reconcile, to reunite, to heal, to make whole. Stewardship has to do with how we bring all of the resources at our disposal into efficient use in our participation in the saving activity of God. Environmental stewardship is one part of our work as God's stewards. As stewards of the natural environment we are called to preserve and restore the very air, water, and land on which life depends. Moreover, we are called to see that all persons have a sufficient share of the resources of nature. The environmental crises that face us need not exist. With new hope rooted in Christ and with more obedient living as stewards of the earth, the creation can be healed.

II. *United Methodist Historical Concerns*

Since the beginnings of the Methodist movement, there has been a concern with what we today call "environmental concerns." Wesley's emphasis on "cleanliness" came as he observed a land of open sewers, impure water, unplanned cities, and smoke-filled air. In the mines and mills, squalor and filth were everywhere, as was disease. The substantial decline in the death rate in England from 1700 to 1801 can be traced to improvements in environment, sanitation, and a wider knowledge of concepts of basic health such as those advocated by Wesley.

The first Social Creed, adopted by the 1908 General Conference of The Methodist Episcopal Church (North) focused on the environmental and health hazards facing workers.

As the problems of soil erosion and dwindling reserves of natural resources became more obvious, General Conferences in the 40s, 50s, and 60s called for the development of programs stressing careful stewardship of the soil and conservation of natural resources. In 1968, a United Methodist Church concerned with continuing pollution of the environment insisted that community rights take precedence over property rights and that "no individual should be permitted to degrade the environment . . . for the sake . . . of profit."

In the mid-1980s, the environmental problems of the world are no less acute than they were in the 1960s and 1970s. While some parts of the industrialized world have less pollution of some sorts, polluting factories have been relocated to the industrializing nations. Hazardous chemicals have been banned in one nation, while their use increases in another. In the United States, children have been poisoned by toxic wastes under their schools; in Central America children have been poisoned when the fields they have worked in have been sprayed with pesticides banned in other countries.

Sometimes our solutions create new problems. Some thought higher smokestacks would help disperse air pollutants; instead we have more acid rain. Herbicides, used in "no till" agriculture, while helping to control soil erosion, have begun to pollute aquifers. The environmental problems of the next few decades will require more effort and more initiative to solve than the problems of the past.

The Christian church should actively support programs to implement principles which will safeguard the environment. Some of the areas we now recognize as key are: responsible use of resources, toxic and hazardous substances, air quality, pesticide use, use of wild and agricultural lands, water quality, the military and the environment, and the impact of new technologies on the environment.

III. *Principles for Christian Stewardship of the Environment*

A. *Responsible Use of Natural Resources.* We support measures which will lead to a more careful and efficient use of the resources of the natural world. We encourage programs which will recycle solid materials of all sorts—paper, glass, metals, plastics, etc. We urge United Methodists to participate actively in community recycling programs and urge the establishment of such programs in communities without these programs.

B. *Toxic and Hazardous Substances.* We advocate that governments devote sufficient monetary and human resources to assessing the extent of possible toxic and hazardous waste disposal problems within their jurisdictions. We believe that the entity or entities responsible for the problem should pay the costs related to the site's cleanup and for any health damages caused by the improper or inadequate disposal of such substances. We call upon those agencies responsible for enforcing existing laws to adopt a more aggressive strategy in responding to violators. We support strong penalties for those convicted of illegal disposal of hazardous and toxic materials. We oppose the practice of exporting materials banned in one nation for use in another nation. We advocate that all parties with information on the health effects of a potentially toxic or hazardous substance make these data available to users of the substance. We support the right of those groups that would be affected by a nuclear, toxic, or hazardous material waste repository to be involved actively in all decisions to locate such repositories in their neighborhoods or jurisdictions.

Finally, in order to preclude serious environmental threats to the world population, we urge a discontinuation of the dumping of nuclear waste at sea and support the monitoring of waste disposal of a toxic nature in the soil.

C. *Clean Air.* We believe all persons have the right to breathe clean air. Where the air quality is now poor, steps should be taken to improve its quality including the elimination of toxic pollutants, the limiting of pollutants from cars, trucks and buses, the clean-up of smokestack emissions. Where the air is now good, every effort should be made to maintain such good air quality. We advocate the adoption and strict enforcement of adequate standards to control indoor air pollutants, including toxic substances and tobacco smoke. Special attention should be given to such long-range air quality problems as the depletion of the ozone layer, the heating of the atmosphere, and acid rain. We support international and bilateral efforts to eliminate the cause of such long-term problems.

D. *Chemical Use.* Many chemicals are used for agricultural purposes. These include pesticides, herbicides, and fertilizers. These are required to maximize yields in feeding a hungry world, but their use may be detrimental to the crops or to the environment if improperly selected and/or applied.

We recommend the concept of integrated pest management (IPM), natural control systems, and crop rotation. We urge that greater restrictions be placed on the export of restricted agricultural chemicals from the United States and that the U.S. development agencies encourage the use of agricultural techniques which rely less heavily on agricultural chemical use.

A wide variety of chemicals is used for the processing and preservation of food products. There is growing suspicion, and some scientifically confirmed knowledge, that some of these chemicals are harmful to animals and humans. We recommend that continual aggressive investigation and study be made on the long-range effect of these chemicals by industry, consumer groups, and governmental agencies. We urge policies that retard the indiscriminate use of chemicals, including those used for growing, processing, and preserving food.

E. *Land Use.* All agricultural productivity relies on our careful stewardship of a few inches of topsoil. We encourage economic and farming practices which conserve and promote the improvement of topsoil. We urge that governments provide farmers with incentives for more careful management of this precious resource.

Just as the best farm land is lost through erosion, so too is it lost when it is used for purposes other than farming (e.g., highways, reservoirs, housing, industrial uses and surface mining). Likewise, land that has become poisoned with salt through poor irrigation practices or with pesticides may become less productive as an agricultural resource. We urge that the careful maintenance of the productivity of the land be the central goal of all management of agricultural lands. We urge governments to preserve the most productive soils for agricultural purposes. Careful management of agricultural lands can help discourage the so-called "reclamation" of forests, wetlands, and wild areas. These areas are valuable in their own right and should be preserved for the contribution they make to ecological balance, wildlife production, water, and air quality, and the human spirit.

F. *The Diversity of Life.* We believe that the wondrous diversity of nature is a key part of God's plan for creation. Therefore, we oppose measures which would eliminate diversity in plant and animal varieties, eliminate species, or destroy habitats critical to the survival of endangered species or varieties.

G. *Water.* We live on what has aptly been called the "Water Planet." More than 70 percent of the surface of the earth is covered with water; yet only a small part of that water can be used for drinking, industrial, and agricultural purposes. Our careless use of water in the past means that it will cost more in the future. Decisions over how to allocate increasingly costly supplies of pure water for drinking, industry and agriculture will be among the most contentious resource policy questions of the next decades. We urge that steps be taken by all concerned parties to ensure more careful management and preservation of existing groundwater sources. We support the right of native peoples to the first use of waters on their lands. We urge that industrial, municipal, agricultural and individual consumers of water find ways to use more efficiently the water we now have. We believe that conservation of an area's existing water supplies, not costly transfers of water from basin to basin, or other large-scale projects, usually offers the most efficient and environmentally sound source of new water. Finally, we believe that all persons have a right to a sufficient supply of high quality water free from toxic chemical or pathogenic impurities.

H. *Impact of Technology.* We urge that the ethical and environmental effects of new technologies be fully examined before these technologies are used on a widespread basis. We acknowledge the constantly imperfect state of our knowledge of the effects of our creations and urge the development of those technologies most in accord with God's plan of wholeness for all creation.

I. *The Military and the Environment.* We oppose the military's imperious claim to our planet's resources and its willingness to risk massive environmental contamination through accidental or intentional release of nerve gas, preparation for biological warfare, or continued testing and possible use of nuclear weapons for the sake of claimed offensive and defensive needs.

We also oppose the production of nuclear weapons and the resultant production of tremendous amounts of nuclear waste that endangers the environment.

IV. *Involvement*

We urge all United Methodists to examine their roles as stewards of God's earth and to study, discuss and work to implement this resolution.

ADOPTED 1984

See Social Principles, ¶ 70, "Environmental Justice for a Sustainable Future."

Indian Lands Used by The United Methodist Church

The General Conference directed:

that the General Board of Global Ministries develop a comprehensive study and report on the use by The United Methodist Church of American Indian Lands for mission purposes since 1784, in consultation with the Native American International Caucus and the Oklahoma Indian Missionary Conference;

that the board report include the intended disposition of any unused land.

ADOPTED 1988

See Social Principles, ¶¶ 70 and 72.A, "The United Methodist Church and America's Native People," "Toward a New Beginning Beyond 1992," "Confession to Native Americans."

Indoor Air Pollution

The United Methodist Church stands in a long tradition of profound concern for the health and physical well-being of the human family.

For Jesus, the abundant life embraced the physical well-being as well as emotional and spiritual health; he performed acts of healing as signs of the reign of God.

John Wesley was in his day at the forefront of the advocates of physical health, and the churches which formed The United Methodist Church have a long record of health and welfare ministries.

Our church has addressed in various ways the issues of environmental contamination, especially outdoor pollution and workplace hazards. Indoor air pollution has also emerged as an important dimension of overall air contamination, and extensive research has demonstrated the acuteness of this problem. Indoor air pollution affects in a very serious way persons with respiratory problems, allergies, chemical sensitivities and ecological illnesses. This is an emerging problem for churches, for air pollutants in church buildings can be serious deterrents against attendance at worship and other church activities for some persons.

Churches are generally unaware of the extent to which persons are either prevented from being in church facilities by pollutants or endure them only at considerable personal discomfort or illness.

Sources of indoor pollution in church buildings include chemical fumes from gas stoves and furnaces, pesticides, cleaning materials, formaldehyde, candles, paint, photocopy machines, rest room deodorizers, and radon, as well as particulates such as dust, mold, and asbestos fibers.

Additional pollutants are brought into church buildings in the form of perfume, cologne, and other scents, dry cleaning odors, and cigarette smoke (which itself releases over 1000 chemicals into the air).

The problem in church buildings is compounded by a) the general absence of effective air circulation systems which can mechanically circulate fresh air, and b) the improved insulating of buildings in recent decades, which while conserving heat, also reduces the rate of air exchange and allows the build-up of concentration of the indoor pollution. U. S. government studies have shown indoor air pollution levels to be as much as eight times higher than outdoor air pollution.

Indoor air pollution is not only a problem for those most seriously affected. The long-term effects of such pollution could potentially be detrimental to everyone. In our century the human body is forced to cope with an incredible level of chemical exposure, for which the long-term effects are only partially known. Lung cancer and other sickness resulting from exposure to smoke, whether to smokers themselves or to involuntary smokers exposed to sidestream smoke are the most widely publicized of the potential long-term effects on everyone.

There is much that churches and church institutions can do to minimize the effect of indoor air pollution. Some churches have already taken steps to reduce indoor air pollution and to address the needs of those seriously affected.

We urge local churches and church agencies and institutions at all levels to: a) invite those with special sensitivities to share the handicaps and suffering which they bear due to indoor air pollution, b) prohibit smoking in all indoor facilities, c) provide adequate fresh air ventilation, or high quality air cleaning equipment, if necessary d) take an audit of sources of indoor air pollution and take remedial steps.

We ask the Health and Welfare Division of the General Board of Global Ministries, with consultation with those most seriously affected, a) to draw up and promote guidelines for addressing indoor air pollution, and b) to investigate and develop a vigorous program to eliminate the use of tobacco in churches and church institutions.

Further, we ask the General Board of Church and Society and conference Church and Society agencies to advocate strong legislation in all nations at all levels of government for the adoption and attainment of indoor air pollution standards and for laws which regulate chemical contamination of public areas, workplaces and the overall environment.

Finally, we ask all United Methodists to make an inventory of the pollution levels in their homes, schools, workplaces, and public areas and to take steps to reduce environmental pollution for the sake of ourselves, our loved ones, our communities, and future generations.

ADOPTED 1988

See Social Principles, ¶ 70.A, "Environmental Stewardship."

The Law of the Sea

We recognize that "All creation is the Lord's and we are responsible for the ways in which we use and abuse it." (1980 Statement of Social Principles.)

We are called to repent of our devastation of the physical and non-human world, because this world is God's creation and is therefore to be valued and conserved.

Nowhere is this need greater than in relation to the sea. In 1970 the United Nations agreed that those areas of the seabed beyond national boundaries were the "common heritage" of humankind. This means that the resources belong to everyone.

But this ideal is not yet expressed in international treaty. So the race is one to see who will be able to exploit and control the resources of the seas. The question facing the peoples of the world is whether global cooperation or global anarchy will prevail.

The best hope for global cooperation is through the United Nations, where representatives of the nations of the world are at work in the conference on the Law of the Sea.

The conference hopes to produce a fair and just law for the ocean, in which all nations will benefit. No one nation will have all of its interests satisfied, but mechanisms will be set up to maintain order and peace, and both developed and developing countries will have worked on the regulations.

The United Nations, concerned with protecting this "common heritage" of humankind, is negotiating international agreements to:
—guarantee unimpeded access to over 100 straits, facilitating commercial transportation;
—prevent conflicts or "cod wars" like the one between Iceland and England over fishing waters;
—enforce environmental regulations forbidding countries to dump harmful wastes which spoil the ocean waters;
—share equitably the ocean resources, oil, fish, minerals, and prohibit unjust exploitation of these resources by the powerful;

—regulate access to the waters of coastal countries to permit research of the marine environment;

—limit the continuing extension of national sovereignty over international waters and settle legal disputes arising therefrom;

—prevent the division of the world into competing camps depending on powerful navies;

—create an international agency to manage cooperatively the international seabed resources.

We also affirm our support for the evolution of effective "commons" law, such as treaties now under development for the Antarctic and outer space, which supports our obligations of stewardship, justice, and peace.

Therefore, we urge all United Methodists to become informed about all of the aspects of "Law of the Sea," one of the most critical and least understood issues of our day.

Further, we urge all United Methodists to call upon their governments to commit themselves to the development of a just and equitable treaty through the United Nations Conference on Law of the Sea, and to ratification of the treaty by our respective governments.

ADOPTED 1980

See Social Principles, ¶ 70.A, "Common Heritage," "Environmental Justice for a Sustainable Future."

Nuclear Safety in the United States

Theology

God has given humans a special charge to "guard and keep" the earth (Genesis 2:15). Nuclear technology presents a special challenge to our call to be stewards of God's creation because of the risks involved in the production, handling, and disposal of long-lived nuclear by-products (such as plutonium) in the energy and weapons-production cycles. As long as society continues to use nuclear power to produce energy and weapons, we have a special responsibility to ensure that God's creation be protected for present and future generations by insisting that the entire production cycle be as safe as possible.

The problem of nuclear safety is of worldwide concern. It is the responsibility of the church to use its influence internationally to prevent the devastation that could result from nuclear disasters.

NUCLEAR SAFETY IN THE UNITED STATES

United Methodist Policy

The United Methodist General Conference affirmed the use of nuclear power for energy production, but noted that the "nuclear energy option also has many problems to be faced" (1984 Book of Resolutions, p. 160). Among these many problems it particularly identified the health hazards from "ionizing radiation (which) threatens the exposed individual to additional hazards such as cancer and sterility and also threaten future generations with birth defects and gene mutations" (p. 238).

The General Conference urged society to examine the ethical and environmental effects of technological developments, and ensure that these technologies be in accord with God's plan of wholeness for all creation. It also "opposed the production of nuclear weapons and the resultant production of tremendous amounts of nuclear waste that endangers the environment" (1984 Book of Resolutions, p. 339).

Background

Nuclear Power

The accident at Chernobyl on April 26, 1986, demonstrated the dangers involved in the production of nuclear energy. This accident was much larger than the one at Three Mile Island. However, the Nuclear Regulatory Commission's Reactor Safety Study points out that accidents even larger than Chernobyl are possible for U.S. reactors. Despite the difference between the design of the Chernobyl plants and the designs of most U.S. plants, there are, according to the Reactor Safety Study, many accident scenarios possible in U.S. plants that could lead to substantial releases of radiation. These safety analyses indicate that even after the improvements instituted after the Three Mile Island accident, there is a substantial chance of a core meltdown among the 107 currently licensed U.S. commercial nuclear power plants over the next 20 years.

In the past few years, while other nations with a sizable commitment to nuclear power have increased their efforts to improve nuclear power plant safety, the U.S. efforts have been inadequate. Countries such as Japan, West Germany, and Sweden have demonstrated that there are practical and reasonable options available to improve reactor safety. These nations' records show outstanding quality in plant construction, plant materials and equipment, extensive preventive maintenance programs, outstanding levels of human performance, plant reliability, and few unplanned shutdowns, equipment failures, or personnel errors. In the U.S. the nuclear power industry is plagued by human error (operators falling asleep on the job), poor maintenance practices, poor management, poor design, and a serious gap in contractor accountability. In 1985 alone, there were almost 3000 plant mishaps and 764 emergency shutdowns, up 28% from 1984.*

Department of Energy Reactors

The Department of Energy (DOE) operates over 200 nuclear facilities. Among its main responsibilities are the production and testing of this country's nuclear weapons program. The DOE facilities are generally more antiquated than civilian plants and are not subject to review by outside agencies. Five of these facilities are the main nuclear weapons production reactors. Four are located on the Savannah River in South Carolina, the fifth is the "N-Reactor" at Hanford, Washington (a complex where poor disposal of wastes in the past has created a radioactive landfill known as "one of our largest contaminated areas"). The containment systems in these plants have been criticized as being inadequate and not capable of meeting minimum civilian standards. In 1986, the DOE agreed to submit its five weapons reactors to state and federal waste disposal rules and shut-down the Hanford "N-Reactor" for safety improvements. The cleanup of the Hanford site alone could cost over $100 billion. Yet most DOE plants continue to be exempt from the far more rigorous examination of commercial reactors by the Nuclear Regulatory Commission.

Emergency Planning and State Rights

After the Three Mile Island accident, rules were instituted to improve public safety in case of a nuclear accident. The new rules required the participation, in emergency planning exercises, of local and state officials. In 1986, the Nuclear Regulatory Commission, in response to two state governors' challenge to the viability of utility-produced emergency plans, requested that it be allowed to approve utility emergency evacuation plans in the event that state and

*Source: Joshua Gordon as cited by Christopher Flavin, Worldwatch Paper 75: Reassessing Nuclear Power: The Fallout from Chernobyl, March 1987.

local officials refuse to participate in the emergency planning process. This rule change would ease the licensing of future nuclear reactors and seriously diminish public participation and review of safety measures, as well as increase the dangers of a serious accident.

Nuclear Wastes

One of the most controversial and costly components of the nuclear fission process is the creation of radioactive by-products. The Nuclear Regulatory Commission divides wastes into two different categories according to the level and duration of radioactivity: high-level and low-level wastes. Since the 1950's the Department of Energy has been searching for a viable way to dispose of the wastes created by commercial nuclear reactors (irradiated fuels) and high-level wastes from weapons production. These wastes are highly radioactive and will remain radioactive for long periods of time. Presently, these wastes are stored within nuclear facility sites, creating what one member of Congress called hundreds of "de facto nuclear waste dumps."

The Nuclear Waste Policy Act of 1982 set a schedule for the location, construction, and operation of two high-level waste geologic repositories, one in the East, and one in the West. Unfortunately, the U.S. nuclear waste policy remains in disarray. Political considerations have taken precedence over safety and scientific considerations, and there has been improper and inadequate consultation and cooperation with state governments and Native American tribes. Clear examples of the fragmented and problem-ridden condition of the U.S. nuclear waste policy include: an April 1985 proposal to build a Monitored Retrievable Storage (MRS) facility within the state of Tennessee (an interim facility to make up for expected delays in the permanent repository schedule); and a May 1986, DOE recommendation for a permanent waste storage site in Texas, Nevada, or Washington, and postponement of further siting activities for an Eastern site (in order to avoid placing a nuclear waste site in states where the Department of Energy expects strong political opposition). The MRS facility is intended to receive 15,000 metric tons of nuclear waste (20% of the capacity of the permanent repository) and package it for delivery to a permanent repository for final disposal. Critics feel that the MRS proposal is being offered by DOE solely as an expedient way of relieving utilities of the burden of on-site, spent fuel storage. Little research has been done as to the increased hazards of such a plan. Building the MRS would increase the likelihood of a transportation accident due to the need to ship waste twice. Moreover, there will likely be political pressure to convert the MRS into a "semi-permanent" repository without careful environmental review.

Recommendations

The United Methodist Church expresses its deep concern over the use of a technology with severe environmental and health impacts, without appropriate and extensive safety measures in the production, handling, and disposal processes. We also reiterate our opposition to the use of nuclear technology for the production of weapons.

We recommend

A) Reviewing safety of operating plants.

Each of the 107 operating commercial plants in the U.S. should be reviewed by the Nuclear Regulatory Commission and the Office of Technology Assessment of the U.S. Congress, to identify design deficiencies and weaknesses that could contribute to or cause an accident.

B) Instituting improvement programs.

Improvement programs should be instituted in areas of demonstrated weak performance such as management, personnel performance, equipment reliability, and contractor accountability.

C) Researching new designs for plant safety.

New designs for existing and future nuclear plants should be researched and developed so as to eliminate the potential of a core meltdown accident.

D) Phasing out nuclear weapons production.

We urge the closing down of the five weapons-producing reactors and the Rocky Flats Plutonium Processing Plant, a thorough cleanup of any remaining nuclear wastes at these sites, and no more nuclear arms testing.

E) Establishing uniform safety standards for civilian and military nuclear operations.

We support having all nuclear operations in the U.S. subject to uniform basic safety provisions. All Department of Energy nuclear operations should be licensed and reviewed by an independent agency such as the Nuclear Regulatory Commission or the

Environmental Protection Agency. Department of Energy contractors should be held accountable to the same standards as civilian facility contractors and operators.

F) Protecting neighboring populations.

We urge that due attention be given to the protection of population living near nuclear power plants or along routes used to transport nuclear materials by ensuring the communities participation in emergency evacuation plans. We support maintaining evacuation planning zones for all areas within 10 miles from a nuclear facility, and engaging the full participation of state and local officials in the planning process. We believe that the safety of all potentially exposed populations should be the guide in safety improvements to nuclear power plants, not narrow cost-benefit analysis.

G) Instituting full liability and compensation.

We hold that those corporations and governments responsible for nuclear accidents should be liable for cleanup and restitution to all victims of an accident.

H) Re-evaluating the U.S. nuclear waste policy.

1) We urge a moratorium on DOE's proposed nuclear waste repository program.

2) We urge Congress to establish an independent commission to review DOE's nuclear waste repository and Monitored Retrievable Storage Programs, and provide increased funding for the development of waste management technologies which will allow prolonged storage at the reactor site.

3) We urge that full public participation and consultation in any future nuclear waste repository siting and transportation routing be guaranteed through provision of grants to affected localities, states, and Native American tribes.

4) We urge a moratorium of the building of nuclear power facilities until an adequate national plan is developed and implemented for the permanent disposal of nuclear waste products.

I) Decommissioning.

We urge that the full cost of decommissioning (the dismantling and disposing of obsolete or closed power plants) be paid by the entities responsible for the construction and operation of nuclear facilities, not ratepayers or taxpayers.

J) Conserving energy and finding alternative energy sources.

The greatest national effort should be made in the areas of

conservation and renewable energy sources. We support increased government funding for research and development of technologies that would decrease dependence upon nuclear energy as an electricity source and urge the development of incentives, including tax and appliance standards, to speed the adoption of these technologies.

K) Cooperating with annual conferences.

We urge the general church agencies of The United Methodist Church to assist central and annual conferences in their efforts to learn more about nuclear safety. Specifically, we urge general agencies of The United Methodist Church to assist annual conferences who have identified nuclear safety problems related to nuclear facilities, waste sites, and transportation routes within the bounds of those annual conferences.

We particularly urge the General Board of Church and Society to identify qualified nuclear safety experts who could assist annual conferences to understand and respond to nuclear waste and nuclear safety concerns in their areas.

ADOPTED 1988, REVISED 1992

See Social Principles, ¶ 70, "Environmental Stewardship," "Energy Policy Statement."

Protecting the Native American Land Base

W<small>HEREAS</small>, protection of the Native American land base is an issue of prime importance today as it has been historically, and

W<small>HEREAS</small>, Native American tribal organizations are seeking to consolidate and increase their land base for economic and cultural purposes, and

W<small>HEREAS</small>, intrusion on tribal lands and subsequent attempts to seize Indian lands by non-Indian parties continues to be a source of tension and insecurity among Native American people, and

W<small>HEREAS</small>, The United Methodist Church has historically held tribal lands for mission purposes and contemporarily holds Indian lands originally secured for purposes of missionary work of the church among Native Americans, and

W<small>HEREAS</small>, some of their land is no longer used for purpose of mission among Native Americans,

Be it resolved, that all such lands held by the church, where there is no intention of continuing or developing ministries among the respective Native Americans, be transferred without compensation to the ownership of the Indian Nation within whose bounds it exists, or to the Indian Nation which was the original owner.

ADOPTED 1988

See Social Principles, ¶¶ 70.A and 72.A, "Indian Lands Used by The United Methodist Church," "The United Methodist Church and America's Native People."

Reduction of Water Usage by United Methodists

Be it resolved, that members of all churches of The United Methodist Church be called upon to analyze their usage of water as a matter of conscientious Christian stewardship; and

Be it further resolved, that The United Methodist Church calls on industry, makers of government policies and regulations, manufacturers, developers, and consumers to reflect on the importance of water conservation and difficulties being faced by society because of water problems, and to develop and utilize water-conserving technology and practices.

ADOPTED 1992

See Social Principles, ¶ 70, "Environmental Stewardship," "Environmental Justice for a Sustainable Future."

U.S. Agriculture and Rural Communities in Crisis

I. Preface

The United Methodist Church has long witnessed to rural peoples and their concerns. Each General Conference since 1940 has suggested responses for improving community life, and the economic and environmental well-being of rural peoples.

The 1984 General Conference directed that a writing team composed of five farmers, one from each jurisdiction, and board and staff representatives from the General Boards of Church and Society and Global Ministries, carry out dialogues with grass-roots persons throughout the Church. Six regional meetings were conducted in Missouri, California, West Virginia, Georgia, Texas, and South Dakota during 1986 and 1987. Approximately 200 persons presented written and/or verbal testimonies at these hearings which then were processed by the writing team and incorporated into the content of this document. Additional reviews of the team's work were conducted by the National United Methodist Town and Country Network, the United Methodist Rural Fellowship, and other individuals and groups.

This resolution calls The United Methodist Church to reaffirm its historic commitment to rural ministry and agricultural concerns, examines the nature of three intertwined crises—the farm crisis, the crisis of rural community, and the global ecological crisis affecting rural areas—and proposes steps the Church and society must take in order to address more effectively the urgent needs of life in rural society today.

II. Theological Statement: Land, People & Justice

The Books of the Law in the Old Testament make clear that God did not intend for human destiny to be separate from that of creation. Several basic themes repeat themselves regarding nature and the land: God is the owner of the land (Lev. 25), thus it is a gift in covenant which involves the stewardship of keeping and tending the land for present and future generations; as God's creation, land has rights and needs—the need to be regenerated that it may sustain life and be a place of joy. It is a common gift to all of humanity requiring just patterns of land use.

Social, economic, and ecological justice with regard to the use of land was central to the Law. The care of the land and the rights of the poor and those in need were at the center of the Law. Adequate food was regarded as an inherent right of all. The poor could eat grapes in a neighbor's vineyard or pluck grain when passing by a field (Deut. 23:24-25). Owners were urged not to be too efficient in their harvest (Lev. 19:9-10). The land itself was to receive a rest every seven years. (Lev. 25:4). Voluntary charity or occasional care of the land was not enough. Israel's failure to follow the laws related to the land was considered a cause of the exile to Babylon (2 Chron. 36:21).

Indeed, the concept of equal access to community resources according to need formed the basis of the covenant the community was expected to embody. The caring for one's neighbor, especially one in need, becomes a religious obligation. Jesus both inherits and fulfills this tradition when he lists the commandment to love your neighbor as yourself as second only to love God (Matt. 22:38-40).

It is no accident that prophetic voices in the history of the Church seemed to emerge as the society around them diverged from the Shalom ideal of caring for God's creation and one's neighbors.

The prophets saw the patterns of economic exploitation, social class consciousness, judicial corruption, political oppression, failing to care for the land, and exclusiveness as opposed to God's desire for full life and wholeness for all (Amos 2-8; Isa. 5:1-1, 58:3-7, Jer. 2:7-8; Hos. 4:1-3). Some would suggest that both the contemporary world and Israel under the monarchy came to worship "bigness" more than God. Under Solomon, the temple itself became the symbol of both the bigness-is-better ethic and the separation of the people from God. The temple became bigger, and God smaller. God was no longer among the fields and villages, but living in the temple (Ps. 132:13-14).

Today, rural parts of the globe suffer from many of the same maladies as did ancient Israel. Land holdings have become more concentrated. Bigness is worshipped as the solution to both spiritual and economic problems. Creation itself groans under a burden of eroding topsoil, toxic wastes, and polluted waters. Neither the land nor most of the people who work it can celebrate the wholeness God intended.

III. The Farm Crisis

Across the American countryside, the 1980s will be remembered as a time of painful crisis and fundamental changes. Like many land-based peoples in the Third World, Americans now face the displacement of farm families and the disruption of rural communities. Entire regions of the country that have depended on natural resources see their economic and social systems in jeopardy.

As the adverse economic conditions affecting rural America become chronic, the patterns of diverse land ownership and control are disappearing. The structure of agriculture is changing. The Office of Technology Assessment of the U.S. Congress estimates that by the year 2000, half of the existing 2.2 million farms in the United States will disappear. Most of the farms expected to be lost are family sized units. About 72,000 farms may be lost each year. Some 50,000 very large farms will produce three-quarters of the nation's food. These "super" farms will make extensive use of new biotechnologies. Ethnic-minority-owned and small-scale farms may become less innovative and will decline further if present trends continue.

The Family Farm—A definition

In this resolution, a family farm is defined not by the number of acres in operation, but as an agricultural production unit and business in which the management, economic risk, and most of the labor (except in peak seasons) are provided by the family, and from which the family receives a significant part, though not necessarily the majority, of its income.

Losing the Family Farm

Land Values

Rural land values and the value of farmland in particular declined sharply in the early 1980s. The erosion of farm equity continued through the middle '80s. While total farm debt declined by $16 billion in 1986 (mostly due to forced liquidation of farm assets), total farm asset values fell by $59.4 billion in the same year according to the US Department of Agriculture's (USDA) Economic Research Service. The Federal Reserve Bank of Kansas reported in February of 1987 that farmland values declined 14% in 1986 and 55% from their peak in 1981 in Kansas, Missouri, Nebraska, Oklahoma, Colorado, New Mexico, and Wyoming.

Most farmers rely on their asset values to secure their operating loans. When land values decline, so does the farmer's ability to borrow in order to produce this year's crop.

Farm Product Prices and Income

Even if land prices were to stabilize, farm income would not necessarily rise.

Short-range farm policies and frequent adjustments to programs have made it very difficult for farmers to make the long-range plans needed for a stable family farm system of agriculture. The rationale of recent farm bills has been that farmers must accept a lower commodity price in order to increase U.S. exports abroad. Yet, while most farm commodity prices declined by about half between 1981-86, U.S. exports have declined from 44 billion to 26 billion between the same period. The few successes in the programs have disproportionately benefited larger corporate farms.

In 1986, the U.S. Department of Agriculture reported that the prices farmers received for raw material products fell nearly 6 percent. For that year, the average production cost to farmers for wheat, corn, rice, soybeans, and cotton was in every case substantially higher than the market value, even counting government subsidies. In each case, the market price in early 1987 was less or about the same as 1932 depression levels when adjusted for inflation. Prices are expected to fall still further. Several independent research facilities expect further declines in net farm income if present farm policies continue.

Farm Bankruptcies

By 1987 farm bankruptcies had risen for six years in a row. Since the new Chapter 12 farm bankruptcy law took effect on November 26, 1986, farm bankruptcy filings have been easier to track. A twelve-state survey of the filings between November 1986 and March 1987 found that some 400 farmers in those North Central states had filed for bankruptcy. Interestingly, another survey showed a markedly lower bankruptcy rate in those states that require lenders to enter into mandatory mediation with their farm borrowers.

Forced Land Transfers and Foreclosures

Much of the reduction in total farm debt during 1986 and 1987 was due to the forced liquidation of farm assets. In the Dakotas and Minnesota, studies show that for the first time in recent history more than half of the land sales in 1986 were caused by foreclosure or "other financial stress." Farmland purchased by farmers when interest rates were 18%, and later lost in foreclosure, was advertised in Midwest papers during 1987 for sale at 4.9% interest. Many of the farmers might have been able to save their farms had they been offered the lower interest rate.

The Structure of Agriculture and Farm Size

Land ownership is being concentrated in fewer and fewer hands because of the ongoing farm crisis. As far back as 1978, the USDA reported that 75 percent of the land in private ownership at the time was owned by 5 percent of the nation's landowners. The Office of Technology Assessment predicts that along with an increase in the number of "super" farms will come increased concentration of agricultural resources—including land—into fewer and larger farms.

By the mid 1980s the best determiner of the degree of poverty in agricultural areas of the United States was the size of the land holdings. Counties with larger-sized land holdings had greater poverty than those with smaller-sized land holdings (350 acres or less per land owner).

Tax Policy

The general effect of the U.S. income tax policy on the structure of U.S. agriculture has been to encourage non-farm investment, concentration of production, and separation of ownership from operation. Many large farming corporations are still eligible to use cash accounting and tax procedures more appropriate to family farm operations.

While the occupation of farming requires large investments of capital in livestock, land, equipment and supplies, the farmers are not protected by a tax system appropriate to the anticipated income. In many counties the tax base has reached an unbalanced condition so that adequate funds are not provided for needed services.

Farm Debt Concentrated Among Family Farmers

Despite the fact that farm debt is being reduced through bankruptcies, foreclosures, and improved prices for some commodities, significant problems remain. While land prices have declined to a point that land might be worth purchasing again, those farmers with even modest debt are unable to purchase land. Some 925,000 of roughly 1.5 million farmers surveyed by the USDA in January 1987 were in no position to purchase land due to cash losses, insolvency, or both. Only one-fifth of the 1.5 million farmers were in a position to expand their operations. These farmers were mostly older farmers with little debt or farmers with significant off-farm income.

The younger the farmer, the more likely his or her operation will be highly in debt. Some 45% of those 34 years of age or younger, and 43% percent of those between 35-44 had debt/asset ratios higher than the 40 percent level considered "highly leveraged." But only 21% of those between 45 and 54 years of age had debt/asset ratios in this category. Only 11 percent of 55 to 64 year olds, and 3% of those 65 years and older were highly leveraged. Moreover, most of the debt (82%) was held by farmers listing their primary occupation as farming. In short, much of the farm debt falls on younger full-time farmers who began farming when land costs were at their highest. Rebuilding for these farmers will be difficult even after bankruptcy. As older farmers retire, fewer and fewer farmers will be full-time family farmers. Presently, only 16 percent of farmers are less than 30 years old.

Racial and Ethnic Minorities in Farming

Black and other minority farmers are even less likely to be in a position to benefit from any changes in the rural/farm economy than young farmers in general. In May 1987, the Federation of Southern Cooperatives/Emergency Land Fund reported that land owned by black Americans was being lost at a rate of half of a million acres a year, worth an estimated $250 million. At this rate, black Americans will be landless by 1994. Virtually no new farms are being established by black farmers. The Farmers Home Administration made only 34 farm ownership loans to black farmers in 1986. While racism plays a clear part in the failure to grant more funds to black borrowers, unequal access to markets, information and technical assistance hinder black entry or reentry into farming.

Farming is the leading occupation among Native Americans living on reservation lands. Surveys of Native American farmers suggest that their situation may be nearly as bleak as that of black farmers. A U.S. Government Accounting Office study of Farmers Home Administration borrowers on fourteen reservations in Montana and the Dakotas found that 40% of the Native American farmers were expected to lose their land through forced or voluntary foreclosures in 1987. On some reservations the total was as high as 75%.

Native American lands are also adversely affected by a number of other factors. Water rights of many tribes are being violated by water diversion and control by state, federal, and corporate entities. Hunting and fishing rights of the tribes are being similarly challenged. Most of the proposed locations for high-level nuclear waste facilities are on or near tribal lands.

Asian Americans were historically excluded from significant farm ownership through a series of exclusionary immigration acts between 1882 and 1924. Nonetheless, many Asians became farmers settling often in the most marginal lands. Many of these farmers brought into production land that otherwise would have gone unused. Unfortunately, many of these same farmers were denied access to credit and formed their own cooperatives to survive. Japanese farmers lost their farms during their internment in World War II relocation camps. Many were unable to reenter farming after they were released, despite the fact that most worked as agricultural laborers for the camps.

Migrant Workers

Despite technical advances in harvest equipment, much of America's food is still harvested by seasonal and migrant workers, the majority of whom are Hispanic (mostly Mexican or Mexican-American). The work is difficult and often dangerous; too many are injured or poisoned by toxic substances each year. At the same time, inadequate wages, benefits and living facilities keep most in poverty. The H-2 provisions of the new immigration law are believed by church advocates possibly to further perpetuate poverty and expand unemployment among these workers.

Migrant workers are at the mercy of crew bosses, agribusiness managers, and others who may exploit them. State and federal legislation is often adequate, but poorly enforced. Workers themselves are either not organized, or poorly organized, to deal with labor and health issues confronting workers in agriculture.

Human Costs of the Farm Crisis

Many farmers have internalized the responsibility for their losses and this has caused their deep sense of guilt, frustration and anger. The results have included deep depression, spouse and family abuse, alcoholism, mental breakdown, divorce, suicide, participation in extremist groups, and at times, murder.

The Farm Crisis Expands to a Rural Crisis

Many experts expect the farm crisis to continue for at least several more years, and predict that more farmers and rural businesses will be lost. The farm crisis will accelerate the loss of rural community.

For every five to seven farms that go out of business, one business in town will fold. When even one business in a small community closes, it creates a ripple effect that is felt throughout the town. Each job lost means there is that much less money being spent at the grocery store, the hardware store, and the barber shop. As the tax base erodes, schools must consolidate, eliminating more jobs. The closing of schools can be the deathblow for many small towns where the school is the major employer.

IV. Rural Community in Crisis

The rural United States today is a paradox of beauty and desecration, isolation and industrialization, wealth and poverty, power and oppression, freedom and exploitation, abundance and hunger, and individualism and dependence. The nation's poorest housing and health facilities occur disproportionately in rural communities, as do the worst education, the worst roads and transportation systems, the least progressive justice systems, and the greatest poverty and malnutrition. Towns which not long ago were vibrant communities of economic, social and spiritual life now have become ghost towns with empty businesses, abandoned homes, closed churches, and broken spirits. Broken homes, broken lives, suicides, bankruptcies, spouse and child abuse, employment, drug and alcohol abuse, and other social catastrophes often make up the local news for many rural communities.

In some sections of the country, these problems are intensified. Such areas are plagued by historic isolation, marked by plantation attitudes and colonial economic relationships, and characterized by external (absentee) ownership of land and resources and the use of natural and human resources as expendable commodities.

Small Town Services and Businesses

In 1985 and 1986, small towns in the Midwest lost businesses at the rate of 5% a year, according to the Federal Reserve Bank of Kansas City. Twenty-five percent of these non-farm businesses were in severe financial difficulty. Farm related businesses in rural areas have been especially hard hit. Nationwide, sales of all major farm equipment items declined during 1985, 1986 and 1987.

Community Banks

In 1986, 138 banks failed in the United States—a new post-Depression record topping the 130 failures in 1985. Most of these banks were rural lenders that made agriculture-or-energy-related loans. The loss of rural lenders will mean that decisions on the investment funds available to a community increasingly will be made in distant urban areas.

Unemployment/Underemployment

Replacing income lost from a farm or other natural resource-based business is difficult in rural areas because of a lack of other jobs. Also, women and men whose livelihood has been derived from farming often find themselves without the skills needed for employment off the farm. Even young persons with job skills often find themselves unemployed or underemployed. About 80% of the well-educated and well-prepared youth migrate out of rural areas. Those persons who do stay in rural areas may take away jobs traditionally filled by the poorer segments of the community.

Poverty

Images of poverty in the United States are largely urban images—crowded tenements, inner city missions, and street gangs. But this picture leaves out over half of the nation's poor. Rural poverty is characterized by these statistics:

—Ninety-one of the nation's 100 poorest counties are located in rural areas. In some Appalachian counties one out of every three households is below the poverty level.

—The numbers of rural persons in poverty has grown from 9.4 million in 1978, to 13.4 million in 1983.

—The rural poverty rate is almost 40% higher than in urban centers. The rates of low birth weights, stunted growth and infant mortality have increased in rural areas while dropping in the rest of the nation.

—Within the rural black population, over 70% of the children living in households headed by women are poor.

Rural Aging, Children and Women

More than one-third of U.S. residents over 65 years old live in rural areas. For these persons, the problems of poverty, housing, isolation, and transportation are interrelated. Transportation to medical and social service centers cannot be found or cost too much.

Historically, women played key roles in developing the rural community and economy. Rural women are now involved in every aspect of their community and economic life, but like their urban sisters continue to suffer from inequalities in the job market, in social service delivery, and in legal matters. Poverty is a stark reality.

Among older women who live alone, 82% are poor. Many other women who live alone find that there are no persons available to hire to do home maintenance or health care tasks that they can no longer do for themselves.

Other concerns of rural women include a lack of accessibility to adequate health care services, lack of public transportation, and a lack of emergency services. In addition, a study by Dr. Lee Morical of the University of Wisconsin for the National Division of the General Board of Global Ministries indicates that three major psychological issues rural women face today are loneliness, guilt, and a feeling of powerlessness. Also reported are startlingly high rates of stress, mental health problems, and abuse by spouses.

While many rural women are single heads of households, subsidized child care is virtually nonexistent. The disruption of family life, brought about by the dislocation of farmers and rural business people, contributes to unemployment, drug and alcohol abuse, spouse and child abuse, loss of identity and loss of community leadership, all of which are affecting rural children. Rural youth now suffer the highest suicide rate in the nation.

Rural Governments and Social Services

In order for rural communities to remain viable in the United States today, they must be able to maintain a desired quality and quantity of social services for their members, including health care, housing, transportation, education, fire and police protection, jobs, and recreation. Persons who live in rural areas have a right to sufficient resources to meet their need. Healthy communities must have adequate leadership as well as a skilled population of sufficient size from which to draw that leadership.

Rural governments often provide these services in the face of declining tax bases, increased demand for services, and sharp reductions in federal revenue sharing funds. School and county services budgets are being severely strained in many rural areas. Some local and county governments have had to stop providing services, hoping that volunteers or state programs or rural churches will pick up what is dropped.

V. The Ecological Crisis in Rural Areas

Access to pure water is the common heritage and right of all persons. An abundant supply of pure water in rural areas is essential for domestic use, livestock and irrigation, recreation, and urban water systems.

Half of the rural population of the United States depends on ground water from shallow wells. Half of these sources are already polluted.

Contaminated surface waters threaten the quality of water for both urban and rural use. Our next crisis is already upon us. The lack of sufficient quantities of high quality water will strain both rural and urban areas.

Mining

Great hope was placed in laws concerning land restoration, but recent studies by the Commission on Religion in Appalachia reveal that mining interests often pay little heed to such laws, and have the political clout to get away with ignoring them. Absentee land ownership and all its shortcomings are endemic to mining. A study on land ownership done for the Appalachian Regional Commission in 1981 found that ownership of land and minerals was concentrated in the hands of a few persons. Only 1 percent of the local population, along with absentee holders, corporations and government agencies, control at least 53 percent of the total land surface in the 80 counties studied. Both land and minerals rights were largely absentee owned. Nearly three-fourths of the surface acreage, and four-fifths of the mineral acres in Appalachia were owned by out-of-stage entities.

Land and Soil Conservation

Responding to changes in agriculture policies, during the 1970s and 1980s, many farmers abandoned soil conservation practices in order to produce more crops on larger fields. Practices such as contour plowing, crop rotation, windbreaks, and cover-cropping conflicted with the push to farm more and more acres with bigger and bigger equipment. Fertilizer inputs went up rapidly. Wetlands and other marginal lands such as those with steep slopes were put into production.

The resulting increases in production enabled some farmers to keep ahead of their creditors for a few years, but the cost to the soil itself was devastating. In the past 200 years, the United States has lost one-third of its cropland, and another third is seriously threatened at this time. When the land was first plowed it had an average of twelve inches of topsoil; it has since lost half of that. In 1975 the annual soil loss by erosion was about three billion tons; by 1987, over four billion tons. In much of the corn belt, two bushels of topsoil are lost for every bushel of corn harvested.

In addition to erosion losses, the soils of North America suffer massive losses to salinity and alkalinity, and to non-agricultural land conversion. Every day about twelve square miles of U.S. cropland are converted for urban, industrial and highway use. Other land uses such as hydroelectric development, power-lines, recreational lakes, and strip-mining whittle away at prime farmland.

Pesticides/Herbicides

The decline of conservation practices was paralleled by an increase in pesticide and herbicide use. A number of factors combined to move farmers rapidly into the chemical age—changing cropping patterns that relied less on crop rotations, a desire to reduce labor inputs, and the need to have a form of chemical "insurance" for already high input costs. Farm magazines blossomed with multi-page advertisements for agricultural chemicals.

While pesticides and herbicides have brought many desired benefits, there are still unanswered questions that need to be carefully examined. Chemicals should be used with great care and as prescribed. Testing should be continued to determine any harmful effects including residue buildup.

Some environmentally dangerous chemicals have been replaced with substances that have a less profound environment effect, but we still have much to learn. Our incomplete understanding of the nature of chemicals has led to many problems. We now know that compounds, excellent for killing insects, build up in the tissues of animals and fish and will not break down. Farmers and their families, and migrant workers may become victims of the pesticides and herbicides they use. Harmful levels of toxic chemical residues are increasingly found in vegetables, fruits, meats, and cereals, and process foods. The U.S. food processing industry uses well over one billion pounds of food additives per year, involving some 25,000 different chemicals.

The Loss of Genetic Diversity

The created order contains hundreds of thousands of species of plants. Of these about 200 to 300 are widely eaten in their present form. We depend upon only about a dozen plant species for 95% of our food calories. Even within these species we rely primarily on a few varieties of each plant. An additional factor has entered into this source of food plants—genetic manipulation. Plant breeders have manipulated the genetic design of plants to make them highly responsive to chemical fertilizers and an abundance of water. Older seed varieties, developed through centuries of the "survival of the fittest" in resisting disease, insects, and weather, have been driven from the field by "improved varieties." The consequences of the loss of native seed varieties are staggering; in one short generation, human beings could throw away key evolutionary links in the food system.

Adding to this concern is the patenting of plants and animals. As natural seed varieties disappear and are replaced by those controlled by commercial interests, low income farmers around the world are placed in a very dangerous situation. Fifty years ago, most US farmers saved and used their own seed corn. Today they pay as much as $75.00 a bushel for hybrid seed corn, which must be purchased each year. If the patenting of animals is permitted, a farmer might be prohibited from breeding a patented animal, further raising costs and concentrating livestock production.

VI. The Church Responding to Crisis

The people of God are called to become the salt and the leaven in working to create communities of "Shalom." The United Methodist Church is spread across rural USA. Since our Church works as a connection, and our rural churches are strategically located to both suffer from and minister in the rural crises, the whole Church has a responsibility and a special opportunity to help our rural churches rebuild broken lives and communities. Combining our strength with that of the ecumenical community will allow a comprehensive ministry of presence and advocacy.

We have a proud history of service to the rural community. The predecessors of The United Methodist Church moved with the frontier to minister to the community; established churches, schools, hospitals, homes for persons in need; and welcomed immigrants. The dynamic spirit, the circuit pattern and lay preacher, and the travelling elder furnished the flexibility necessary for ministering to people on the move. Rural churches became centers of community life. Vital rural churches still serve this function. Today United Methodism's rural churches face grave stresses as they minister in the face of radical change with diminishing resources.

Today, approximately 88 percent of our members are located in population areas of 50,000 or less; 78 percent of our churches and 51 percent of our members are located in population areas of 10,000 or less. About 59 percent of our churches and 24 percent of our members are located in population areas of 1,000 or less. Ours is a denomination of small membership churches; 65 percent of our churches have fewer than 200 members, and 40 percent have fewer than 100 members. The multiple church charge is the primary pattern of pastoral assignments. Our 37,880 churches are lodged deep in the fabric of rural America.

The United Methodist Church is widely represented across the rural United States, with at least one church in all but around 100 counties. One would assume that such a Church, with the sources of a major denomination only a phone call away, would have been a major help in ministering to the needs of the rural population during the recent farm crisis. In 1986, Judith and Bill Heffernan of the University of Missouri interviewed 46 families that had lost their farms in one Missouri county. The farmers reported that of all agencies or persons, including the agencies that foreclosed on them, the church in their county was of the least help in their time of need. Reports from across the nation echoed this situation.

A number of reasons have been cited for the Church's shortcoming in this time of rural crisis:

—Many church members are still accepting a theology that "goodness" means "success," and that failure means that God has punished the person for his/her "sins." Many have not heard or heeded the theology of grace and the concept of human worth aside from human accomplishments. As a result many farm families found walls instead of bridges between them and their "successful" neighbors.

—Many clergy have been incapable of adequately ministering to the needs of the hurting families in their communities. Most ministers are from urban areas, and seminaries are not equipping them for ministering in rural areas. Many rural ministers are students, with little time for their congregations. Others are part-time ministers with limited time and training. Most appointments are far too brief for the minister to build relationships through which pastoring is possible.

—Congregational needs are generally taken into consideration, but the needs of the larger community generally are not.

—In the vast majority of rural areas, churches are still operating under a competitive rather than a cooperative model. Real cooperative parishes, where the skills of laity and clergy alike are shared in a total ministry to a total region, are scarce, though fully proven. The usual model of congregational independence (instead of interdependence) simply accentuates the lack of working together for the common good in these communities. When cooperation does happen it is after a last ditch effort, rather than a move born out of creativity and strength.

There are notable exceptions where local churches have given strong support to persons and families who are hurting, and also ministers have been able to be pastors to an entire community, but for the most part the ministry of the rural church to farm and town families in this time of crisis has been "too little and too late."

VII. A Call for Change: What Needs To Be Done?

Complex problems that have developed over long periods of time have no quick and simplistic solutions. We call upon the Church, local communities, state and federal governments to make the following changes:

A. *We call upon the United Methodist churches, charges, and cooperative parishes to:*

Intentionally develop ministries to meet four major needs that exist today in rural U.S.A.

1. Mend the brokenness of community life in rural U.S.A.

2. Strengthen its ministry in rural U.S.A. In order to do this we suggest that the churches:

a) Encourage seminaries to develop much stronger and more specific programs for equipping ministers to be pastors in rural settings.

b) Encourage bishops and cabinets to lengthen greatly the tenure of ministers in rural areas, and to discover ways in which the local church can cooperate in such a process.

c) Become adept at analyzing the needs of their own community, and in responding to them. (See *Book of Discipline* ¶ 261.)

d) Urge every local United Methodist church to study the plight of the racial/ethnic farmer.

e) Encourage local churches and their pastors to offer counsel, support and emergency aid to all farm families in trouble in their community.

f) Support and become involved in cooperative and ecumenical ministry, sharing in specific geographic areas. (See *Discipline* ¶¶ 257.8, 524.3.)

3. Call our nation to a stewardship of its natural resources.

We support maintaining the quality of air, water, soil, land, vegetation and wildlife so that they might be preserved for future generations. We oppose the use of rural areas as waste dumps or the use of the soil as a nonrenewable resource. We support the development of alternative disposal methods including technology to render the substances harmless.

4. Build bridges of understanding and partnership between rural and urban congregations and communities.

Some proven models for doing this are:

a) A Sunday visit/exchange where several carloads of people from an urban church go to a rural church or parish and worship, study, visit farms, and dialogue together.

b) Ministerial exchanges of a month or more allowing the leadership of both rural and urban churches to understand each other better.

B. *We call upon districts to:*

1. Develop and or strengthen their missional stance in rural areas.

2. Create cluster groups and other supportive networks within the district to facilitate spiritual formation.

3. Encourage cooperative leadership through more creative use of available personnel and appropriate technology.

C. *We call upon the annual conferences to:*

1. Analyze their rural crisis response and provide funding for an effective and ongoing response. (See *Discipline* ¶ 726.10*d*.)

2. Place personnel strategically in order to respond to rural needs. Insist that pastoral appointments be made with the needs of entire communities in mind, and not just the needs of the congregation. (See *Discipline* ¶ 532.1*c*.)

3. Become public policy advocates, speaking out as a church, creating awareness and understanding, and in bringing about positive change.

4. Cooperate with other Church and secular agencies in a rural response. (See *Discipline* ¶ 726.10*f*.)

5. Be in partnership with seminaries to develop programs, including "teaching" parishes and internships, to equip ministers to serve in rural areas.

6. Develop programs to invest conference foundation funds in rural economic development needs.

7. Discover ways to enable the ethnic ownership of farmland.

8. Model and support the team ministry concept at every level.

9. Develop programs for volunteers in mission in rural areas.

D. *We call upon the general church to:*

1. Use its seminaries to prepare clergy to be more effective *pastors* in rural areas, using the "missionary training" model, knowing that many ministers not accustomed to rural life enter into an area where there is a new "language," a new lifestyle, and a new culture.

2. Cooperate ecumenically with groups such as Interfaith Action for Economic Justice, the National Council of Churches' Rural Crisis Issue Team, and the National Save the Family Farm Coalition to develop responses to the problems of rural areas in the U.S. and abroad.

3. Better learn the skills of personnel placement, so that appointed ministers in rural areas will have a tenure that is long enough for them to build trust/understanding relationships necessary for becoming *pastors* to the *community*. Place more mission (and similar) personnel in rural ministries.

4. Recognize Rural Life Sunday as a special day in the Church year, combining in this one day the emphasis of Rural Life Sunday, Soil Stewardship Day, World Environment Day, and Rogation Sunday.

5. Provide opportunities for U.S. and Third World farmers to share innovations and knowledge to assist each other's lands.

6. Carefully analyze and monitor all Church agencies' programs to insure sensitivity to the present rural crisis.

7. Emphasize, in all appropriate literature and training programs, the importance of soil stewardship and ecology as a part of total Christian stewardship. Examine Church-owned land holdings for their use and stewardship, and report findings yearly to annual conferences and general agencies.

8. Consider using a significant portion of the investment funds of all Church agencies for investment in local church based community economic development in rural areas.

9. Urge all Church agencies to continue to promote the cooperative style of ministry as a model of God's desire for life in community. (See *Discipline* ¶ 206.2.)

10. Aggressively research corporate ownership of agriculture and its effects upon life in rural areas, and advocate necessary responses based upon the findings of this research.

11. Request all general board staff and directors to study this document and to use the resources of their offices to respond.

12. Develop and distribute an educational curriculum on global education with emphasis on rural development in the Third World and in the United States.

13. Request that the General Board of Discipleship Curriculum Resources Committee develop curriculum resources on the issues raised in this resolution in coordination with the General Board of Church and Society and the General Board of Global Ministries and make such materials available to all churches.

14. Call upon the General Board of Church and Society and the General Board of Global Ministries to develop other materials to interpret this resolution, including, but not limited to, materials generated from the hearings used to develop this resolution.

E. *We call upon the Council of Bishops to:*

1. Develop and promote a pastoral letter document, similar to "In Defense of Creation," on the crisis in rural life, both present and long term.

2. Encourage Cabinets to work toward longer term rural appointments (with a goal of a minimum of 4 years) of clergy leadership to provide more stability in rural areas.

3. Foster a cooperative style of leadership by more creative use of available personnel and appropriate technology.

F. *We call upon the annual conference episcopal leaders to:*

1. Consider adjusting the work load of district superintendents to provide more time to be a pastor to pastors.

G. *We call upon federal legislators and administrators as they develop farm and rural policies to:*

1. Develop policies that will enable farm families to receive a just return for their labor and investments. These new policies would:

a. Reverse the loss of family farms.

b. Provide for credit to family farmers at affordable interest rates.

c. Develop a marketing and government support system which will guarantee the cost of production to farm families.

d. Initiate participatory democratic processes with farmers to determine if mandatory production goals, which would halt current over-production of some commodities, are needed to move toward a balance between supply and demand.

e. Greatly reduce government payments to large corporate farming interests.

f. Create programs that would enable new families to enter farming as a vocation.

g. Create incentives for family farmers to shift from current production-oriented modes to a sustainable and regenerative agriculture.

2. Discourage concentration in ownership and control of land and money and move toward land reforms that broaden ownership of land by all persons.

3. Require soil and water conservation practices for farm operations which participate in federal programs; include farmers in the planning of such requirements.

4. Reduce the federal deficit, which will serve to reduce the international valuation of the dollar, thereby enhancing export sales.

5. Reform federal tax laws to remove unfair competition and discourage tax-shelter motivated capital in agriculture.

6. Maintain the Farmers Home Administration (FmHA) traditional emphasis on direct loan activity, resist attempts to reduce the

level of direct loans in favor of guarantees, and increase the Limited Resources Loan program for qualified farmers.

7. Provide for commodity reserves, isolated from the market, to be established at a level adequate to protect consumers from supply disruption and meet domestic agricultural disaster and global humanitarian food aid requirements.

8. Ensure that most federally-supported programs of research and education in agriculture focus on small and medium-sized family farm operations, and that such programs be especially targeted to minority farmers.

9. Fund major new research initiatives and programs through the federal land grant institutions, including black land grant colleges, to ensure the development of long-term, sustainable and regenerative agriculture.

10. Develop farm policies that will encourage farm owned and controlled businesses and cooperatives for processing, distributing and marketing farm products.

11. Develop policies that will respect the guaranteed land and water rights of all minority peoples.

12. Develop and support programs to upgrade the quality of life in depressed rural areas, with attention given to health care, transportation, education, employment, law enforcement, housing, and job training.

13. Develop national and regional water and energy policies which assure that those who benefit from energy and water projects pay a substantial portion of those costs.

a) The institution by the United States Congress of the 960-acre limitation on subsidized irrigation water is a step forward. We call on the bureau of Reclamation to institute strict enforcement of this 960-acre limitation and compel farming operations larger than 960 acres to pay full cost of reclamation irrigation water.

14. Recognize and protect the right of farm workers to organize into unions of their own choosing, be covered by minimum wage laws, and receive adquate benefits, including social security, health care, and unemployment.

15. Discourage export policies that would hurt small farm agriculture in developing countries and hinder efforts toward food self-sufficiency in those countries.

16. Prohibit the importation of produce containing residues of pesticides or other chemicals that are banned for U.S. producers and revise permitted pesticide residue levels when the pesticide is banned.

17. Urge the federal government to declare moratoriums on foreclosures in states where lenders are participating in debt restructure or mediation programs.

18. Seek out international cooperation in developing an international food policy.

H. We call upon state governments to:

1. Develop systems of mediation to resolve conflicts between borrower and lender.

2. Develop and enforce fair and just tax systems that ensure that those with great wealth and political power pay their fair share of taxes.

3. Ensure that state subsidies for water benefit small and medium-sized operations.

4. Protect security of farm products stored by farmers in elevators.

5. Continue to develop and support farmers markets and marketing cooperatives.

6. Pay special attention to the education and relocation of jobless persons, commit state resources to the establishment of industries or agencies that will increase the job/tax base, and the maintenance of an acceptable quality of social services for all.

7. Allocate funds to monitor all state programs and economic development projects for their impact upon the socioeconomic and natural environment.

8. Urge the development and maintenance of conservation programs that supplement federal programs and environmental standards that exceed federal minimums.

9. Sell bonds to help farmers secure low-interest loans, with special attention given to minority farmers and others with similar needs. Assist such families in identifying and securing loans from such sources.

10. Assure that state marketing regulations benefit small-and-medium-sized operators.

11. Ensure that most state-supported programs of research and education in agriculture focus on small-and-medium-sized family

farm operations, and that such programs be especially targeted to minority farmers.

12. Fund major new research initiatives and programs through state and/or corporate grants to ensure the development of long-term, sustainable, and regenerative agriculture.

I. We call upon government and private lending agencies to:

1. Continue to restructure existing loans to allow for lower payments over a longer period of time, and with lower interest rates, as agreed to by lender and borrower through a mediation process.

2. Require FmHA and other lending agencies to have more balanced and consistent lending policies and practices, and to assess fairly the spending of authorized funds on farm operations.

3. Urge government to change accounting procedures to allow banks that participate in debt restructure agreements to write off any potential losses over a ten-year period.

4. When foreclosed land is offered for sale by government, farm credit system, private banks, and insurance, priority for purchase should be given to minority foreclosed, beginning and re-entering farmers.

J. We call upon local government and community groups to:

1. Develop land use and land reclamation policies, supported by adequate funding, to preserve productive farmlands.

2. Organize and support local groups to provide legal aid, financial advice, counseling and other support services for rural persons.

3. Monitor programs to assure that all community planning is ecologically sound and socially responsible.

4. Intentionally foster a positive community spirit with a variety of local programs that enhance the community members' well-being and self-worth.

5. Develop and support measures that ensure a fair tax treatment of all in the community.

6. Support the development of local programs to meet such special needs as better housing, health care, transportation, and recreation.

7. Develop local representative, long range planning committees to monitor and advise elected or appointed officials, and community groups.

8. Cooperate with state agencies to develop policies so that farmers markets in their communities may be able to accept food stamps and WIC certificates for purchases.

K. We call upon multinational, national, and local business groups to:

1. Consciously examine their corporate policy in relationship to an understanding of and responsiveness to the values of rural lifestyles represented by smaller farm size units.

2. Specifically analyze and implement policies in relationship to (but not necessarily limited to) research; short-term and long-term residual effects; conservation of resources; water and energy utilization; local, national, and export marketing; labor use; and the availability and access to financing and credit.

The More Difficult Task

This document, up to this point, has dealt largely with immediate solutions to immediate problems within the agricultural communities of the United States. The larger and more difficult task is to look toward the centuries ahead, and to look at agriculture in a global context. Also, this paper has focused on a pastoral role for the Church and society—to ease the hurt being felt across our rural areas, and short-term "fixes."

The next task for the Church is to take clearly and intentionally the prophetic role. The Church has a clear record of helping the world address such issues as clean water and air, civil rights, nuclear warfare, arms expenditures, and world hunger. The Church must likewise take responsibility for addressing the problem of agriculture. The outcome of human history will be determined by our resolve to achieve a favorable future for agriculture.

Unless we change some basic directions, we are not just in a period of transition; we are headed for disaster for all the nations. Some basic directions that must be changed include:

—The movement toward investor-owned land in increasingly larger corporate units; the separation of ownership, management, and labor.

—The increased reliance upon high inputs of non-renewable resources such as fossil fuels and chemicals.

—The continued decline in rural populations from rural areas, especially of those who have been directly involved in food production.

—The increasing chemical toxicity of our water systems, air, rain, waste dumps and vegetable and animal products.

110

—The continuing loss of cropland through erosion, salinization, urbanization, conversion, and other processes.

—The disappearance of world forest resources, and changing weather patterns resulting from that.

—The loss of atmospheric ozone.

—The continuing and growing use of the world's basic resources for armaments.

—The loss of our centuries-old genetic seed bank.

Three Ethical Guidelines

The above trends are not irreversible. We can change, but we need guidelines. Some visionaries suggest that a preferred agriculture must have three attributes:

(1) It must be *just*. A just society and a just agriculture provide the means whereby people can share in the inheritance of the earth so that all can fully be maintained in freedom and community. To seek justice is an act of love. The purpose of a just agriculture should be for the maintenance and renewal of the necessary resources for food, clothing and shelter, for now and for the future.

(2) It must be *participatory*. For an agriculture to be just everyone has the right to be consulted. Participation in society and in the ongoing process of creation is the necessary condition for justice. Participation requires a recognition of everyone's right to be consulted and understood, regardless of that person's economic, political, or social status. Participation is not possible without power. In such decision-making everyone has the right to be consulted about such issues as expenditures for armaments, nuclear power, forms of employment, social services, etc.

(3) It must be *sustainable*. Peruvian farmers have been farming their steep slopes for 3,500 years, and in any of our U.S., heavily cropped areas, half our topsoil has disappeared in 100 years. We may have far more to learn from Peruvian farmers than we have to teach them.

A sustainable society and a sustainable agriculture is one where the idea of permanent carrying capacity is maintained, where yields (agriculture, energy production, forestry, water use, industrial activity) are measured by whether or not they are sustainable, rather than by the criteria of yields per acre or profits. In a sustainable agriculture waste products can be absorbed back into the ecosystem without damage.

The Church—Visionary and Model

"Where there is no vision, the people perish" (Proverbs 29:18a). The Church must envision and create models for a preferred agriculture and a preferred future. We must be the salt and the leaven to bring about the vision of the Lord's Prayer, that God's will might indeed be done "on earth as it is in heaven."

The Church as congregation can deal with personal and community concerns. The Church as connection can deal with the systemic issues that cause hurt. Our immediate task is twofold. We are to bring a priestly ministry of healing to a rural society that is broken. At the same time we must proclaim with words and action a prophetic word about the Shalom with God of which we dream.

ADOPTED 1988

See Social Principles, ¶¶ 70.A, 72.M, "An Affirmation of Basic Rural Worth," "Special Needs of Farmworkers."

Use of Reclaimed Paper

Be It Resolved, that the General Conference request the publisher, boards, agencies, and all local churches to seek diligently suppliers of recycled or reclaimed paper for all possible uses whenever practicable and possible.

Be It Further Resolved, that the General Conference request that all said agencies use only recycled or reclaimed paper whenever possible for all printing, mimeographing, correspondence, and other uses of paper.

ADOPTED 1972

See Social Principles, ¶ 70, "Environmental Stewardship."

THE NURTURING COMMUNITY

Adoption

W<small>HEREAS</small>, all privately arranged placement of a child for adoption without a license to place children for adoption is frequently in violation of state laws; and

W<small>HEREAS</small>, all those concerned with the placement of a child for an (non-relative) adoption, shall abide by the laws of their state in using only licensed child placing agencies; and

W<small>HEREAS</small>, by so doing, the needs of the birth parents can be met by appropriate counseling as they make decisions regarding their life and the life of their child; and

W<small>HEREAS</small>, licensed-child placing agencies have a more diverse group of approved prospective parents which enables them to serve the best interest of the child;

Therefore, be it resolved that United Methodists planning to enter the adoption process be encouraged to work only with licensed adoption agencies.

ADOPTED 1988

See Social Principles, ¶ 71.I.

Against Sterilization Abuse

We recognize, especially in this country, that the choice of sterilization as a method of limiting family size is winning more acceptance. When voluntary, this practice is a matter of personal choice; however, when someone else makes the decision, the chances of abuse are great.

Sterilization abuse is recognized as a problem of low-income women, particularly Third World women. According to *Family Digest,*

May 1972, 35 percent of married Puerto Rican women of child-bearing age were sterilized. In November 1977 the U.S. General Accounting Office issued a report indicating that Health Service had sterilized approximately 5.5 percent of all Indian women of child-bearing age in the Aberdeen, Phoenix, Albuquerque, and Oklahoma City areas. In 1979, a study conducted by the Women's Division in New York City found, in face-to-face interviews with 600 women ages 18-45, that of the first 50 interviews, 26 women had had tubal ligations and 8 had had hysterectomies. Of those who had tubal ligations, 13 were black, 9 were Puerto Rican, and 4 were white. Ten of the 26 were receiving public assistance. In 13 cases a doctor suggested the operation and 12 of these women indicated that the doctor was the single most influential person in the decision. Only 8 of the 26 brought up the subject themselves; 3 women did not remember how the subject came up; and in one case the woman's mother influenced her. Fifty per cent of the women showed regret over having been sterilized.

WHEREAS the decision to be sterilized is unique in the area of reproductive freedom because it is irreversible, the dangers of coercion, deception, and misinformation and the desire of some for population control, particularly among the poor, Third World (in the U.S. and overseas) people, require safeguards against an uninformed and involuntary decision with such inexorable consequences;

WHEREAS the importance of the sterilization decision for most people cannot be overestimated, since reproductive ability is key to the identity of many people, both male and female, the decision to become sterilized can have tremendous psychological as well as physical repercussions;

WHEREAS sterilization abuse—the sterilizing of people against their will or without their knowledge—is still occurring;

It Is Therefore Recommended That:
1. The United Methodist Church support the following principles:
   a. The patient, not her physician or any other party, should make the ultimate decision in accordance with law, as to whether she will be sterilized. Involuntary sterilizations (for minors or persons adjudged to be mentally incompetent) are justifiable only if ordered by a competent court after a hearing according to due process of law.

b. Adequate and accurate information should be given to women concerning sterilization and its alternatives.

c. The decision to be sterilized should not be made during a time of stress, particularly during hospitalization for abortion or childbirth.

2. In order that the sterilization decision be both informed and voluntary, there is a need that:

a. women considering sterilization be given specific information in their own language using understandable terms about the nature and consequences of the sterilization procedure to be performed, as well as the risks and benefits of that procedure;

b. they have adequate time in which to make this irreversible decision in a non-coercive atmosphere—thus a thirty-day waiting period which would enable them to leave the hospital and consult with family, friends, or other physicians.

3. Local churches monitor the implementation of the guidelines in local hospitals.

4. Local churches be encouraged to ascertain women's attitudes toward and experience with sterilization in their communities.

5. Education and information about sterilization and other forms of contraception be included in family life programs with special note taken of the guidelines for voluntary consent.

6. The United Methodist Church oppose racist population control policies and practices aimed at Third World peoples (in the U.S. and overseas).

7. The United Methodist Church oppose all forms of sterilization abuse, including lack of informed consent, arbitrary measures for handicapped and institutionalized women and industrial exposure to radiation.

ADOPTED 1980

See Social Principles, ¶¶ 71 and 72.A, "Eradication of Racism," "Equal Rights of Women."

AIDS and the Healing Ministry of the Church

I. AIDS and the Gospel of Wholeness

As United Methodists we confess that the God known in Jesus Christ is the One who "makes all things new," who promises to redeem past failures and sends an empowering Spirit to support us when we seek to enact the divine will.

According to the Gospel of Luke (4:16-21), Jesus identified himself and his ministry with that of the servant Lord: the one who Isaiah tells us was sent to bring good tidings to the afflicted; to bring hope to the brokenhearted; to proclaim liberty to the captives; to comfort all who mourn; to give them the oil of gladness, and the mantle of praise instead of a faint spirit (Isaiah 61:1-3).

There is no doubt that the Gospel entrusted to the church as the body of Christ is a Gospel of wholeness that calls us to a ministry of healing: a ministry which understands healing not only in physiological terms but as wholeness of mental, physical, spiritual, relational and social being.

Diseases spring from complex conditions, factors, and choices. It is not helpful to speak of diseases in inflammatory terms like "punishment for sin." The Gospel challenges us to respond with compassion that seeks to enable the physical and spiritual wholeness God intends in the lives of all persons affected by Acquired Immune Deficiency Syndrome (AIDS).

With the Apostle Paul, we assert that "neither death, nor life, nor angels, nor principalities, nor things present, nor things to come, nor powers, nor height, nor depth, nor anything else in all creation will be able to separate us from the love of God in Jesus our Lord" (Romans 8:38-39).

In the spirit of the One who makes all things new, who empowers the people of God for ministries of healing and hope even in the midst of a frightening epidemic, The United Methodist Church and its members are called to respond to the epidemic of Acquired Immune Deficiency Syndrome by engaging in ministry, healing, and social responsibility consistent with the Church's understanding of the Gospel imperatives.

II. AIDS and the Church as a Healing Community

The Church as a healing community, empowered by the Holy Spirit, is called to confession, celebration and action.

A. As a Church we confess: that until now our response to AIDS has been tardy and inadequate; that we have failed to call political leaders to account for their slowness and lack of compassion; and that when

116

challenged by the assertion that AIDS is God's punishment, we have failed to offer a grace-filled alternative, consistent with an understanding of the whole Gospel of Jesus Christ.

B. As a Church we celebrate and offer thanksgiving: for the pioneering and self-sacrificial work of persons who have developed volunteer ministries of service to persons with AIDS (PWA's), and for the disease prevention education work which has reduced both the sexual transmission and blood transfusion associated transmission of AIDS.

We celebrate the leadership of local churches and annual conferences which have begun ministries in response to AIDS; the guidance provided during the 1984-88 quadrennium by the General Boards of Global Ministries, Church and Society, and Discipleship.

C. As a Church we resolve that:

1. Churches should be places of openness and caring for persons with AIDS and their loved ones. The church should work to overcome attitudinal and behavioral barriers in church and community that prohibit the acceptance of persons who have AIDS and their loved ones.

2. Ministries in response to AIDS will be developed, whenever possible, in consultation and collaboration with local departments of public health and community based groups that have already identified priorities for action, and will be supportive of ecumenical and interfaith efforts.

3. Educational efforts must include reliable medical and scientific information and theological and biblical components that enable participants to address issues related to death and dying, human sexuality, and recognition of people's lack of knowledge and fear. Such educational efforts can prepare congregations to respond appropriately when they learn that a member has been infected by the HIV (Human Immunodeficiency Virus) or diagnosed with AIDS, and can lead to the development of compassionate rational policies, educational materials and procedures related to the church school, nurseries, and other issues of institutional participation.

4. Pastors, paid workers and other volunteer Church workers should prepare themselves to provide appropriate pastoral care and counseling to persons living with AIDS or AIDS Related Complex (ARC) and the loved ones of these persons.

5. Liturgical and worship life should provide opportunities for education as well as an expression of pastoral care. Worship provides a time for celebration and the lifting up of special concerns.

6. Congregations should organize to provide emotional, physical and/or financial support to those in their community who are caring at home or elsewhere for a person who has AIDS.

7. Local churches should use their resources to respond to the AIDS crisis. These may include support groups, counseling, grants, providing a location for recreational activities for persons with AIDS, and recruiting volunteers or offering office or meeting space for community based organizations.

D. As a Church we call upon our general agencies, annual conferences, local churches, and members to:

1. Work for public policies and the allocation of resources to ensure the availability of appropriate medical, psychological and support services for all persons infected by the HIV. These programs should afford the greatest amount of independence and self-determination possible for persons with AIDS within the framework of their individual circumstances.

2. Advocate that children infected by the HIV be permitted to attend regular school so long as they are able and wish to do so and while their presence does not constitute a threat to their own health or the health of others.

3. Advocate for the development of accurate testing procedures which are voluntary and which guarantee confidentiality including counseling services. The ability to test for antibodies to the AIDS virus is a useful AIDS prevention strategy in some instances. However, even voluntary use of antibody testing as a preventive effort will require the assurance of levels of confidentiality and anonymity.

4. Support AIDS prevention education in church and society that provides both the information and motivation required for persons to change their behavior so as to reduce or eliminate the risk of infection. Because sexual and intravenous drug using activities can begin at a very young age, we encourage school boards to initiate AIDS education activities at the elementary school level. We afirm the necessity for comprehensive health education including human sexuality and drug abuse prevention designed for children and youth. We call for the development of adequate numbers of drug treatment programs to care for persons who are dependent on the use of illicit

drugs. We support the provision of detailed information and other resources that will prevent intravenous drug users from sharing needles as a part of the larger effort to prevent the further spread of AIDS.

5. Urge implementation and enforcement of policies and, if necessary, legislation to protect the human and civil rights of persons infected by the HIV, persons perceived to be at risk for such infection, and persons with AIDS or AIDS Related conditions. We urge efforts to investigate thoroughly, document, and prevent prejudice and violence against all persons who have AIDS or are perceived as being at risk for AIDS.

6. Support the development of workplace policies that permit all persons with AIDS/ARC to work as long as they are able and wish to do so, with medical assurance that their presence in the workplace does not constitute a threat to co-workers or others.

7. Encourage health care providers to regard persons with AIDS as the appropriate decision makers about their care, to respect their wishes to seek or refuse specific treatments, and to honor their determination about persons who will make decisions on their behalf should they become unable to decide themselves.

8. Request the health-related and health-care institutions of The United Methodist Church to provide leadership in the creation of service including hospices and home health-care facilities for patients with AIDS and HIV patients, and to publicize their services to these patients in beneficial ways; and to further request that wherever possible these institutions join with other agencies in research activities.

9. Work for public policies and the allocation of public resources for research and prevention, treatment, and elimination of AIDS-related diseases. Monitor private insurance company policies related to coverage and benefits for persons with AIDS- and HIV-related diseases.

10. Encourage worldwide cooperation by all countries in sharing research facilities and findings in battling this disease, mindful that governments, churches, families, and persons in every region of the world are affected by the AIDS epidemic.

E. We commend the interagency efforts by the General Boards of Discipleship, Church and Society, and Global Ministries to address the AIDS crisis and urge the continuation and growth of this work to envision, create, and help facilitate a plan for AIDS ministry and education within The United Methodist Church. We urge these boards immediately to inform and enlist the annual conferences in the work of this ministry and to continue to report their action to the General Conference.

The global AIDS pandemic provides a nearly unparalleled opportunity for witness to the Gospel and service to human need among persons, many of whom would otherwise be alone and alienated from themselves, other people and from God. The Christian gospel of wholeness calls us to a complete and full dedication of our bodies as temples of the Holy Spirit. We are called, also, to a ministry with and among all persons, including those whose lives are touched by AIDS. As members of The United Methodist Church we covenant together to assure ministries and other services to persons with AIDS, based on the reality of meaning and hope in and for their lives, whatever duration they may have. We acknowledge the spiritual and personal growth that can be experienced by persons facing AIDS in their own life or the life of a loved one, and we give thanks for the witness to God's empowering love contained in that growth. We ask for God's guidance that we might respond in ways that bear witness always to Jesus' own compassionate ministry of healing and reconciliation; and that to this end we might love one another and care for one another with the same unmeasured and unconditional love that Jesus embodied.

ADOPTED 1988

See Social Principles, ¶ 71, "Care-Giving Teams for Persons with Aids," "Pastoral Care and the AIDS Epidemic in Native American Communities," "Resources for AIDS Education."

Care-Giving Teams for Persons with AIDS

WHEREAS, AIDS has emerged in epidemic proportions in the United States and in the world; and

WHEREAS, AIDS is being transmitted more and more through contaminated needles used to inject drugs; and

WHEREAS, recent statistics indicate that Black Americans are being disproportionately infected and that cultural needs are not being adequately addressed; and

WHEREAS, current information often does not reach black communities;

Therefore, be it resolved, that each local church be encouraged to establish care-giving teams which will be trained to minister specifically to persons with AIDS and their families, giving particular attention to those communities where needs are not being addressed; and

Be it further resolved, that using materials from general Church agencies, these teams would be trained to provide AIDS education in churches and communities.

ADOPTED 1992

See Social Principles, ¶ 71, "AIDS and the Healing Ministry of the Church," "Pastoral Care and the AIDS Epidemic in Native American Communities," "Resources for AIDS Education."

Circumcision

The United Methodist Church encourages all involved doctors and medical institutions to inform fully the parents of every newborn male concerning all the risks and benefits of circumcision prior to the giving of their consent for the procedure.

ADOPTED 1992

See Social Principles, ¶ 71, "Health and Wholeness."

Condemning Legal Prostitution

WHEREAS, the Social Principles of The United Methodist Church states that "sexuality is a good gift of God, and "we reject all sexual expressions which damage or destroy the humanity God has given us as birthright, and we affirm only that sexual expression which enhances that same humanity . . . ;" and

WHEREAS, one such damaging and destroying practice is prostitution, which treats sex as a market commodity rather than a shared gift from God, and which treats persons as things to be used rather than as human beings with the potential to grow in grace; and

WHEREAS, many public officials and law enforcement officers are reported to disregard statutes against prostitution; and

WHEREAS, the State of Nevada by statute permits cities and counties to license and regulate brothels;

Therefore, Be It Resolved, that The United Methodist Church strongly condemns the practice of prostitution, legal or illegal, while supporting programs of care, counseling, and rehabilitation for those who have been victimized by the practice; and

Be It Resolved, that United Methodist congregations are urged to develop strategies for influencing state and local officials in their communities to enforce laws on prostitution, and to minister to the victims of the practice of prostitution who are in their midst; and

Be It Further Resolved, that the General Conference strongly urges United Methodists in the state of Nevada, and anywhere legalized prostitution exists, to implement strategies leading to the repeal of such laws; and

Be It Finally Resolved, that the General Conference calls upon all United Methodists including the leadership of general agencies, district superintendents, and bishops in areas where prostitution is legal to be persistent in:

1. Communicating The United Methodist Church's understanding of the degrading, sinful nature of prostitution, and

2. Contacting government executives and legislators to influence them to give leadership to the enactment of legislation repealing laws which authorize the practice of prostitution.

ADOPTED 1988

See Social Principles, ¶ 72.F, "Sexual Violence and Pornography."

May as Christian Home Month

WHEREAS, we believe that families in our nation, at this hour, stand at a critical juncture, in the midst of destructive pressures that are daily taking their toll; and that The United Methodist Church has the opportunity, potential, and responsibility to respond to the urgent needs of families;

Be it resolved, that General Conference declare the month of May as Christian Home Month, with emphasis upon family worship in the home, a Day of Prayer for the Family set aside in May, and emphasis on the family by local churches in worship and program planning. We call upon the Family Life Committee and Curriculum Resources Committee to gather existing family curriculum materials and, where necessary, create a core of curriculum materials across age levels.

ADOPTED 1992

See Social Principles, ¶ 71.A, "Responsible Parenthood," "Supportive Policies for Families with Children."

Organ and Tissue Donation

W<small>HEREAS</small>, selfless consideration for the health and welfare of others is at the heart of the Christian ethic; and

W<small>HEREAS</small>, organ and tissue donation is a life-giving act, since transplantation of organs and tissues is scientifically proven to save the lives of persons with terminal diseases and improve the quality of life for the blind, the deaf and others with life-threatening diseases; and

W<small>HEREAS</small>, organ donation may be perceived as a positive outcome of a seemingly senseless death and is thereby comforting to the family of the deceased and is conducted with respect, and with the highest consideration for maintaining the dignity of the deceased and his/her family; and

W<small>HEREAS</small>, moral leaders the world over recognize organ and tissue donation as an expression of humanitarian ideals in giving life to another; and

W<small>HEREAS</small>, thousands of persons who could benefit from organ and tissue donation continue to suffer and die due to lack of consent for donation, due primarily to poor awareness and lack of an official direction from the Church;

Be It Resolved, that The United Methodist Church recognizes the life-giving benefits of organ and tissue donation, and thereby encourages all Christians to become organ and tissue donors by signing and carrying cards or driver's licenses, attesting to their commitment of such organs upon their death, to those in need, as a part of their ministry to others in the name of Christ, who gave his life that we might have life in its fullness.

ADOPTED 1984

See Social Principles, ¶ 71.J, "Understanding Living and Dying as a Faithful Christian."

Pastoral Care and the AIDS Epidemic in Native American Communities

W<small>HEREAS</small>, the AIDS disease is of epidemic proportions; and

W<small>HEREAS</small>, pastoral care training does not take into consideration the unique cultural and spiritual healing methods of the Native American community; and

WHEREAS, a national consultation on pastoral care and AIDS for Native Americans would provide sound cultural insights for The United Methodist Church in the area of pastoral care for Native American pastors; and

WHEREAS, a program of this nature would provide nurture for Native American pastors and their continuing education;

Therefore, be it resolved, that the General Board of Higher Education and Ministry and the National United Methodist Native American Center continue to develop culturally relevant curriculum materials regarding pastoral care and AIDS in the Native American community; and

Be it further resolved, that General Conference encourage the National United Methodist Native American Center and the Board of Higher Education and Ministry to hold as soon as possible, a National Consultation on Pastoral Care and AIDS in the Native American Community using this curriculum, consistent with the availability of independent funding.

ADOPTED 1992

See Social Principles, ¶ 71, "AIDS and the Healing Ministry of the Church," "Resources for AIDS Education," "Care-Giving Teams for Persons with AIDS."

Resources for AIDS Education

WHEREAS, the virus which causes Acquired Immune Deficiency Syndrome (AIDS) has proven itself to be a deadly killer of children, women and men; and

WHEREAS, the AIDS virus is being carried and may be transmitted by millions of persons world-wide; and

WHEREAS, the AIDS virus is known to be transmissible through exchange of blood, semen or vaginal fluids or other suspected bodily fluids of the carrier; through sexual intercouse (anal, oral or vaginal); by injection of a contaminated hypodermic needle; or transfusion/ contamination with infected blood; or organ transplant; and

WHEREAS, massive efforts will be required to change the behaviors that result in continued transmission of the virus, and to care for the victims who develop AIDS or AIDS-related Complex (ARC);

Therefore be it resolved, that the 1988 General Conference directs the General Boards of Church and Society, Discipleship and Global

Ministries to provide or continue providing the Annual Conferences and local churches with equipping resources to carry out a multi-faceted effort of education and awareness for all, including school-age children; legislative lobbying at federal, state and local levels; and direct ministry to persons who have been or may be exposed to or infected with the AIDS virus; and

Further be it resolved, that the delegates to the 1988 General Conference encourage their respective Annual Conferences:

1. to utilize the resources developed by the General Boards or other organizations such as the National Council of Churches or the United States Public Health Service; or
2. to develop their own resources; and
3. to make these resources available to their own churhces as quickly as possible.

Further be it resolved, that these efforts and resources

1. be explicit and clear in describing AIDS virus and the process of its transmission;
2. promote the prevention and treatment of AIDS and ARC;
3. educate the public about the needs of the victims of AIDS and ARC;
4. encourage United Methodist clergy and laity to participate in direct ministries with human imuno virus victims and their families.

ADOPTED 1988

See Social Principles, ¶ 71, "AIDS and the Healing Ministry of the Church."

Responsible Parenthood

We affirm the principle of responsible parenthood. The family in its varying forms constitutes the primary focus of love, acceptance, and nurture, bringing fulfillment to parents and child. Healthful and whole personhood develops as one is loved, responds to love, and in that relationship comes to wholeness as a child of God.

Each couple has the right and the duty prayerfully and responsibly to control conception according to their circumstances. They are in our view free to use those means of birth control considered medically safe. As developing technologies have moved conception and reproduction more and more out of the category of a chance happening and more closely to the realm of responsible choice, the decision whether or not to give birth to children must include acceptance of the responsibility to provide for their mental, physical, and spiritual growth, as well as consideration of the possible effect on quality of life for family and society.

To support the sacred dimensions of personhood, all possible efforts should be made by parents and the community to ensure that each child enters the world with a healthy body, and is born into an environment conducive to realization of his or her full potential.

When, through contraceptive or human failure, an unacceptable pregnancy occurs, we believe that a profound regard for unborn human life must be weighed alongside an equally profound regard for fully developed personhood, particularly when the physical, mental, and emotional health of the pregnant woman and her family show reason to be seriously threatened by the new life just forming. We reject the simplistic answers to the problem of abortion which, on the one hand, regard all abortions as murders, or, on the other hand, regard abortions as medical procedures without moral significance.

When an unacceptable pregnancy occurs, a family, and most of all the pregnant woman, is confronted with the need to make a difficult decision. We believe that continuance of a pregnancy which endangers the life or health of the mother, or poses other serious problems concerning the life, health, or mental capability of the child to be, is not a moral necessity. In such cases, we believe the path of mature Christian judgment may indicate the advisability of abortion. We support the legal right to abortion as established by the 1973 Supreme Court decision. We encourage women in counsel with husbands, doctors, and pastors to make their own responsible decisions concerning the personal and moral questions surrounding the issue of abortion.

We therefore encourage our churches and common society to:

1. Provide to all education on human sexuality and family life in its varying forms, including means of marriage enrichment, rights of children, responsible and joyful expression of sexuality, and changing attitudes toward male and female roles in home and marketplace.

2. Provide counseling opportunities for married couples and those approaching marriage on the principles of responsible parenthood.

3. Build understanding of the problems posed to society by the rapidly growing population of the world, and of the need to place

personal decisions concerning childbearing in a context of the well-being of the community.

4. Provide to each pregnant woman accessibility to comprehensive health care and nutrition adequate to assure healthy children.

5. Make information and materials available so all can exercise responsible choice in the area of conception controls. We support the free flow of information on reputable, efficient and safe nonprescription contraceptive techniques through educational programs and through periodicals, radio, television, and other advertising media. We support adequate public funding and increased participation in family planning services by public and private agencies, including church-related institutions, with the goal of making such services accessible to all, regardless of economic status or geographic location.

6. Make provision in law and practice for voluntary sterilization as an appropriate means for some for conception control and family planning.

7. Safeguard the legal option of abortion under standards of sound medical practice, and make abortions available to women without regard to economic status.

8. Monitor carefully the growing genetic and biomedical research, and be prepared to offer sound ethical counsel to those facing birth-planning decisions affected by such research.

9. Assist the states to make provisions in law and practice for treating as adults minors who have, or think they have, venereal diseases, or female minors who are, or think they are, pregnant, thereby eliminating the legal necessity for notifying parents or guardians prior to care and treatment. Parental support is crucially important and most desirable on such occasions, but needed treatment ought not be contingent on such support.

10. Understand the family as encompassing a wider range of options than that of the two-generational unit of parents and children (the nuclear family); promote the development of all socially responsible and life-enhancing expressions of the extended family, including families with adopted children, single parents, those with no children, and those who choose to be single.

11. View parenthood in the widest possible framework, recognizing that many children of the world today desperately need functioning parental figures, and also understanding that adults can realize the choice and fulfillment of parenthood through adoption or foster care.

12. Encourage men and women to demonstrate actively their responsibility by creating a family context of nurture and growth in which the children will have the opportunity to share in the mutual love and concern of their parents.

13. Be aware of the fears of many in poor and minority groups and in developing nations about imposed birth planning, oppose any coercive use of such policies and services, and strive to see that family-planning programs respect the dignity of each individual person as well as the cultural diversities of groups.

ADOPTED 1976

See Social Principles, ¶¶ 71.A, F, and H, "Supportive Policies for Families with Children."

Sexual Violence and Pornography

"So God created humankind in God's own image, in the image of God was the human created; male and female God created them. . . . And God saw everything that was made, and behold, it was very good. . . ." (Genesis 1:27; 31, RSV-AILL). Human sexuality is a sacred gift of God. It "is crucial to God's design that creatures not dwell in isolation and loneliness, but in communion and community . . . sexual sins lie not in being too sexual, but in not being sexual enough in the way God has intended us to be." ("Reuniting Sexuality and Spirituality" by James B. Nelson, The Christian Century, Feb. 25, 1987.)

God created human beings with an ability to make a choice for good or evil. This divinely created freedom is one to be cherished as are all gifts from God.

We face a massive public health problem based on people's choosing violence. In 1977, the Centers for Disease Control initiated a program to study the nature of violence in our society. In 1985, violence was declared a major health problem.

Violence takes many forms and many different weapons are being used. Many people use their bodies as weapons to abuse children, their spouses and the elderly or to commit rape and other forms of violent battery. Deprivation of many kinds are forms of violence. Discrimination and poverty are forms of social violence. Indeed, Ghandi once said that poverty is the worst form of violence.

And the threat of nuclear war constitutes a violent cloud over all of us.

The causes of violence and the escalation of violence in the U.S. are varied. However, public attitudes toward violence play a major factor in the cause and acceptance of violence in our society. In the United States is a large-scale tolerance of interpersonal violence. This society is permeated with images and myths about violence from the old cowboy movies where justice and violence became synonymous, to the new type of stalk and slash movies which combine sexual exploitation with violence.

New technology has made sexually violent and pornographic films more available to more people regardless of age, location, or level of moral understanding. Now persons of all ages can go to their own video stores and secure a wide variety of tapes for play on their videotape recorders or telephone-dial-a-porn from the privacy of their own homes.

These new phenomena are especially dangerous for several reasons:

1. A wide variety of videos are easily available at low cost.

2. Violent or sexually explicit scenes can be played over and over again, teaching through powerful visual images and repetition.

3. The highly erotic stimulation of dial-a-porn is particularly damaging to children and youth.

4. Videos and dial-a-porn are used without parental knowledge, consent or interaction.

As a result, the sex education of our children is shifting dramatically from parents and the responsible institutions of our society to the powerful mass media of film, television, cable TV and video cassettes.

Carefully documented research has found false messages that predominate in many media images of sexuality:
• Violence is a normal part of sexual relationships;
• Women "enjoy" being forced into sex;
• Women "invite" men to violate them;
• Sex is something you "do to" rather than share with someone else.
The repeated viewing of sexually violent material by men:
• Desensitizes men to violence on the screen;
• Decreases their empathy with victims of sexual violence;
• Increases their belief in the "rape myths" that women ultimately enjoy being raped, that "no" doesn't mean no, that women are responsible for their own rape.

As Christians and as citizens, we recognize the need to differentiate between sex education materials, erotica, sexually explicit material and obscenity. The lines are neither self-evident nor clear and will differ among persons and groups. The Supreme Court has not defined pornography while finding "obscenity" not protected under the free speech provisions of the First Amendment.

We affirm the need for sex education in our schools, community youth organizations and churches. Our young people need to know the biological facts, the health risks, the emotional impact and consequences of their choices, and the moral basis of their faith. We recognize the appropriateness and need for explicit sexual information both verbally and visually. In all instances, information should be used with restraint and a clear attempt should be made to minimize erotic qualities.

Child pornography uses children alone, in sexual relationships with other children, or in sexual relationships with adults. Children are psychologically or physically coerced into participation by older children, or adults. Child pornography victimizes children and harms them physically, emotionally and spiritually. Child pornographers and distributors should be prosecuted to the full extent of the law.

The Supreme Court declared that obscenity is not protected by the free speech provisions of the First Amendment. Material to be judged illegal must be offensive to community standards and appeal to prurient interests, lack serious scientific, educational, literary, political or artistic value. We believe that sexually violent material should be judged "obscene" within the context of the Supreme Court decision.

In order to discuss issues related to sexually explicit material more clearly and precisely, we propose the following definitions:

Erotic material is sexually explicit and arousing but does not use coercion, inflict pain, use violence in any way, and rarely depicts sexual intercourse. Some of the world's greatest masterpieces are erotic.

Soft pornography may show persons in sexual intercourse, but does not use coercion, inflict pain or use violence. However, we believe that soft-core pornography usually is harmful and erotica may be harmful to disturbed or immature persons.

Hard core pornography may show persons in intercourse using coercion, or using violence and inflicting pain. It generally presents women in subordinate situations and degrades both men and women.

Sexual exploitation is a form of social violence that, when communicated to a large number of people, can create both tolerance of sexual violence and increase the incidence of such violence. The National Council of Churches conducted a study of "Violence and Sexual Violence in Film, Television, Cable and Home Video." Some key points that are relevant to this issue include: violence in all of its forms—whether social as in the cases of discrimination and sexual exploitation or physical as in the cases of battery or sexual abuse—is a major public health problem in this nation. Therefore, a combined Christian and public health approach to resolving the problem needs to be applied.

As Christians, we need to examine those materials with which we interact to determine their social or physical violence characteristics. We must insure that we do not communicate myths that perpetrate violence or allow images of violence, victimization, or exploitation to become a part of institutional communications.

A public health approach instructs our secular institutions to imitate educational and communication strategies that enable people to learn alternatives to violence, as well as other violence prevention measures. People must be encouraged to seek help when victimized.

Institutions such as family counseling centers, drop-in crisis nurseries, battered women shelters, runaway shelters need to be provided by both church and community.

In examining our own and secular media the following points adopted by the National Council of Churches are helpful:

1. Our media environment is more complex than ever before. As entertainment forms increasingly include excessive portrayals of violence, parents and other concerned citizens often feel helpless before a media system that is seemingly out of control.

2. Christians are called to a ministry of concern and constructive response so that moral values which have emanated from families of faith can be preserved, perpetuated and shared with others in our society. Christians also are called upon to bring prophetic judgement to bear on threats to public welfare through what is seen as a moral pollution of our media environment.

3. Only a genuinely open marketplace of ideas can guarantee the search for truth. For this reason we are determined to defend the First

Amendment guarantees of freedom of religion, of speech and of the press. Society should seek to maximize the diversity of sources and ideas, and to minimize the power of government or individuals to block or constrict this diversity of sources.

4. However, prior control of the content of media does exist in our society exercised by the government, by business, by education, by the power of money and monopoly. With respect to any program, someone must decide what shall be included or what is left out. The issue is not whether there should be prior control, but who should exercise it, and how it should be exercised.

5. As Christians we affirm our adherence to the principles of freedom of expression as a right of every person, both individually and corporately. We oppose any law which attempts to abridge the freedom of expression guaranteed by the First Amendment. At the same time, as Christians we affirm that the exercise of this freedom must take place within a framework of social responsibility.

6. Children are especially threatened by the pervasiveness of violence and sexual violence in media. Both ethically and constitutionally it is the responsibility of the entire society to protect the interests of children and to provide for their education and welfare. We support the 1968 Supreme Court ruling that children may legally be barred from theatre showings of films deemed unsuitable for them. Parents should be helped to avoid the showing of that same material in their homes via television, cable and videocassette.

7. The airwaves are held in trust for the public by radio and television broadcasters with licenses regulated by the government. The broadcaster is therefore responsible for the content of programming. However, this right does not abridge the public's "right to know" and to be fairly represented.

8. Federal regulation should require broadcast licensees and cable operators to make available regularly scheduled constructive programming to enlighten and entertain children.

9. We support criminal obscenity laws which do not embody prior restraint but which punish after the fact certain kinds of speech which the Supreme Court has determined are not protected by the First Amendment.

10. In any competitive business environment, some rules are necessary to bring about positive change. Laws and governmental regulation are essential in dealing with reform in the communication

industry, because they can place all competitors on an equal basis and thus not disturb the working of the economic marketplace.

11. All mass media are educational. Whether they deal with information, opinion, entertainment, escape, explicit behavior models or subtle suggestion, the mass media always, directly or indirectly, shape values.

12. In all broadcast and film media, advance information about the products offered should be made available by the industry to parents so they can guide their children's viewing.

13. It is important for research into the effect of media to continue, under a variety of auspices, so society will have increasingly accurate information as the basis for remedial action to the problems presented by violence and sexual violence in the media. The Church has a special role for congregational education and public policy relative to pornography, violence and sex exploitation. The NCCC developed action strategies for churches on local, annual conference and national levels:

a) Communication agencies within the denominations and through the National Council of Churches' Communication Commission should monitor programs in order to assess danger levels of violence and sexual violence. Findings should be published for the guidance of parents, educators and others.

b) Theologians should examine the moral and spiritual implications of the violence phenomenon in media.

c) Clergy, parents and teachers within Christian communions should be trained and equipped to prepare children and youth to survive with integrity in a complex media environment.

d) Churches and their agencies should join forces with other groups in society who share the same concern over the extent of violence in media, in order to plan concerted counteraction.

e) Religious communities should establish dialogue with creative media professionals. Their objective should be to support and encourage those producers, directors, writers, and actors who are willing to seek ways within the industry to provide viable alternatives to programming that exploits violence and sexual violence.

f) Churches and church agencies should assist in funding and promoting general distribution programming which presents positive messages and does not contain exploitative sex and gratuitious violence.

g) Opinions, both positive and negative, should be solicited from members of Christian churches and their leaders, to be presented to those responsible for media productions. Affirmation and encouragement should be sent to those responsible for quality presentations that lift the human spirit while complaints and protests should go to those responsible for programs that exploit, demean or desensitize audiences through excessive applications of violence and sexual violence.

Since United Methodists represent a broad spectrum of American society, and since pornography is no respecter of age, social, economic or even religious condition, there are undoubtedly those among our constituency who are afflicted and dependent on the habit of sexually violent material. There are persons within our congregations who need help. There are young people who need guidance. There are children who are being sexually abused, and women who are being physically abused.

Therefore, we encourage our congregations to:

a. Use United Methodist sex education curriculum.

b. Study the issues surrounding pornography.

c. Undertake training programs to learn to hear the "cries of help" from abused children and women and develop a plan of referral of these persons to appropriate community service organizations.

d. Support shelters for battered women and children.

e. Join with other community groups in taking appropriate steps to curb distribution of sexually violent material and child pornography in our communities.

Further, we request that The United Methodist Church should, through all its agencies which manage investments, monitor such investments to assure that no church funds are invested in companies which are involved in the production, distribution or sale of pornographic material, and further, if such investments are found, should move to divest holdings in such companies.

The misuse of our human sexuality through violence and coercion separates us from one another by making women and children fearful of men and separates us from our creator God.

ADOPTED 1988

See Social Principles, ¶ 72.F, "Sexual Harassment in Church and Society in the U.S.A."

Supportive Policies for Families with Children

The United Methodist Church in its Social Principles paragraph 72.C affirms: "Rights of children—Once considered the property of their parents, children are now acknowledged to be full human beings in their own right, but beings to whom adults and society in general have special obligations. . . . Moreover, children have the rights to food, shelter, clothing, health care, and emotional well-being as do adults, and these rights we affirm as theirs regardless of actions or inactions of their parents or guardians. In particular, children must be protected from economic and sexual exploitation."

The Problem

Children today face seriously weakened support systems when they are struggling with unprecedented stresses and being forced to make very important life related choices at a younger age than ever before. This is evidenced by the following information:

1. Today many marriages end in divorce, and more than a million children each year have their families broken up in this way. According to government statistics, one out of four of these children will slip into poverty because of the loss of a father's income.

2. Today a child can grow up in one of ten different types of family units ranging from those headed by never-married mothers to those headed by two parents to those headed by divorced fathers.

3. There were more than 270,000 out-of-wedlock births to women under the age of twenty in 1984, a threefold increase since 1960. These children are most likely to be born with low birth weight, not have adequate health care and nutrition, and live in poverty.

4. In the United States, 21.3 percent of all children, (one out of five children, including 46.5 percent of all Black children, 39 percent of all Hispanic children), grow up in families where there is not sufficient income. Children living below the poverty line are likely to be living in inadequate housing, not have adequate health care, and have an inadequate diet and inappropriate clothing.

5. In the United States, between 1983 and 1984 there was a 16 percent increase in reported cases of child abuse and neglect and a 57 percent increase in report cases of sexual abuse.

6. Over 90 percent of the cases of child abuse and neglect take place in the child's own home with the abuser being someone known to the child.

7. One out of every five handicapped children entitled to special education services is not receiving them.

8. Suicides among teenagers have been increasing rapidly and now are the second-ranking cause of death for them.

9. Infant mortality in the United States is higher than that in several developing nations, as one out of every sixty-five infants born dies.

Policy Recommendations

Because of the rapid increase in the number of children whose lives are affected by poverty, and the increased number of persons who within the U.S. society can work full time and still remain in poverty (the working poor), the problem described above becomes even more critical. Thus, as these problems are examined, various public and church related policy stances must be expressed. Some very important lines from the 1972 resolution on "Children, Their Welfare and Health Care" must be reiterated:

"The United States has dropped to thirteenth (1985—now seventeenth) place in infant mortality. Physical brutality, i.e. child abuse, is increasingly widespread. Children have little chance in courts where the child is the property of the parents. The practice of juvenile law has a position of low prestige in the profession.

"The result of such victimizing is a generation of youth and adults who struggle for identity, trust and the basic values of responsible citizenship. The Church can and must speak out on behalf of children. It can order an environment in which children's rights are protected. . . The rights of children for love, health, security and emotional well-being must be recognized in the home, in the Church and in the ordering of priorities in government planning.

"We therefore seek a creative partnership with national government agencies concerned with children, including utilization of federal funds and services."

Our public policy position should not change; we need to press for policies that:

1. Guarantee basic income for all families regardless of structure (the major U.S. welfare program in many states excludes two-parent

families and persons who work yet earn well below the poverty line) and provide basic support services, for families in economic crisis, including food and nutrition services (like food stamps, women, infants children's programs, child care food programs, etc.), crisis respite care and homemaker services.

2. Assure safe, sanitary and affordable housing for families without discrimination based on age of children, race or religious affiliation.

3. Mandate full and complete access to health and medical care including health maintenance, well-baby care, and prenatal services, mental health services (for all family members including the highly under-served group of young children and teens).

Churches must increase and formalize their commitment to ministry with families, realizing that it is almost impossible to care fully for the needs of children without addressing the family situation. For example, children of alcoholics cannot be fully ministered to without care and concern being shown for the entire family. The physical, emotional and mental health of each family member has a strong impact on the health and well-being of other family members.

A coordinated ministry that reaches out to join with the health services, mental health and professional community is needed in every local area.

Ministry to families must, of necessity, include the broadest definition of family structure so that the variety of configurations (grandparent as parent; blended families resulting from divorce(s) and extended family structures) can be considered. The basic definition of children, from infancy through age eighteen, should not eliminate the needs of children who, through injury or other handicapping conditions, may maintain a child/dependent relationship over a longer period of time.

The Church must recognize and reaffirm a commitment to its long-standing professional institutions in almost every annual conference that provide ministry to children and families in extreme crisis. These institutional ministries provide 24-hour care for children who have been abused or neglected, have run away, or are in emotional distress. Many provide care and counseling for families to allow re-unification where possible. United Methodist Community Centers provide many of these services and need the special support of local churches.

The funds from the public sector have been greatly reduced over the past few years; thus there is a need for local churches and annual conferences to advocate for increased funding from the Church and the government for these institutional ministries of the Church.

Every annual conference of The United Methodist Church should establish and support a child advocacy committee in the conference. The committee could: form a network of child advocate groups from local churches and communities; establish a child advocacy agenda for the annual conference; train for child and family advocacy; and make an annual report to the conference on the needs of children and their families as well as the initiatives, developments and needs of the Conference Child Advocacy Committee.

Each charge across the whole of The United Methodist Church should be encouraged to form a children's council or committee as prescribed by the *Discipline* (Para. 264.1 1984) and this council/committee should broaden its mandate and concern to include advocacy for children and families within and outside the charge.

There is a need for churches to realize that the problems described are not outside the congregation or charge. In 1980 a survey was conducted relative to family problems of active United Methodists; some of the results showed:

1. Substance abuse. One in every 50 respondents had abused some drug; one in five reported that a family member or close friend had abused drugs; one of every 33 respondents had abused alcohol; and one in three reported that a family member or close friend had abused alcohol.

2. Family violence—One in every 13 respondents had been abused by a spouse; one in every nineteen had experienced abuse as a child; one in nineteen had abused a child.

3. Teenage pregnancy—One in every 19 respondents had a teenage and/or unmarried pregnancy; one in four reported that a family member or close friend had experienced that situation.

Supportive services for families to enable them to survive is crucial in every local area. Local churches and annual conferences can aid in the development of services like: homemaker services, child day care, respite care or mothers day out, nutritional programs, and others.

One special family support service is child day care. There is a dramatic rise in the need for child day care services because of the increased economic need for single parents and for both parents in a two parent family to be in the paid work force. Local churches provide up to 70 percent of all child care centers.

A basic standard of health, safety and nutrition in the form of state licensing becomes crucial in the face of the high demand. Families surveyed want safe and secure places for their children. However, one-third of the states exempt church-based care from basic licensing standards.

It is important for the Church to reaffirm its 1984 commitment to child care as a valid part of the mission of the Church. Local churches that provide child care should work cooperatively and intentionally with those programs, valuing those services as a ministry to families and providing support to enhance the quality of the services offered to children and their families. Congregations in states that presently exempt child care programs from licensing regulations must meet state licensing requirements as one way of promoting quality and enhancing services.

The United Methodist Church advocates improved licensing standards in order to strengthen the quality of child care programs and adopts the 1985 Child Care Policy Statement of the National Council of Churches as its own policy position.

The United Methodist Church affirms its commitment to children as stated in the Social Principles and pledges to work to involve every adult in the church and society in general to fulfill their obligations to children and to ensure the rights of children.

We recommend that a task force be formed of persons from general church boards and agencies which have departments and/or programs related to children, youth and families, and the Children, Youth and Family Section of the United Methodist Association of Health and Welfare Ministries. That task force would:

1) set the national agenda of The United Methodist Church related to children;

2) establish guidelines for the creation of child advocacy networks within each annual conference across The United Methodist Church;

3) do research on the needs of children, youth and families;

4) share the research findings with the general Church;

5) participate in developing educational materials on the needs of children, issues facing children and responses to the needs and issues;

6) develop recruiting and training materials for conferences and churches to use as they form child advocacy groups;

7) survey the general Church to determine

    a) program services for children and youth taking place in local churches and annual conferences, and

    b) child advocacy efforts in churches and annual conferences and then share the findings with the church at-large;

8) establish networking with other church bodies, United Methodist related agencies, and national organizations presently involved in organized child advocacy programs.

Each member of The United Methodist Church should extend help to children, become an advocate for children because of our faith commitment and response to Jesus Christ who said, "Let the children come to me and do not stop them, because the Kingdom of God belongs to such as these" (Mark 10:14 Good News Bible).

In order to address appropriately the needs, issues, stresses and decisions confronting children in today's society, the General Conference of The United Methodist Church establishes a special program for the quadrennium 1989-92 "Focus on Children, Youth and Families." This special program is to be coordinated through General Council on Ministries.

ADOPTED 1988

See Social Principles, ¶ 71.A and 72.C, "Dependent Care," "In Support of Women, Infants, and Children's Supplemental Food and Nutrition Education Program (WIC Program)."

Understanding Living and Dying as Faithful Christians

I. Theological and Ethical Affirmation

A. Divine Creation of Human Life

All human life is the gift of God. Distinct from other creatures, we are created male and female in God's image with intellect and free will. Thus endowed with the capacities for knowledge, freedom, responsibility, and personal relationships, we are called in community to realize the divine purpose of living, which is to love God and one another. As Christians, we believe that God reaffirms the value of all human life through the incarnation of Jesus Christ and through the empowering presence of the Holy Spirit.

B. *The Human Condition*

Humanity is subject to disease and the inevitability of death. Death as well as life is a part of human existence. Given this relationship, we should be free from either denying or exalting death. Our propensity, however, to distrust God leads us to distort the ordered place and meaning of death. When we do, our fears and anxieties become exaggerated and we are led into despair, believing God has forsaken us.

Our human situation is further exacerbated by our sins of indifference, greed, exploitation, and violence, and by the moral failure engendered by stupidity and narrow-mindedness. As a result we have rendered our earthly environment unhealthy and produced unjust social structures perpetuating poverty and waste. This deprives much of the human family of health, robs persons of dignity, and hastens death.

C. *The Healing Christ*

Through Jesus Christ, God has entered human suffering even to the point of dying on the cross. In the healing ministry and sacrificial death of Jesus Christ, God transforms suffering and death into wholeness and life. These realities call us to witness to God's presence in the midst of suffering by sharing compassionately in the tasks of healing the sick and comforting the dying.

D. *Stewardship of Life*

Life is given to us in trust: not that we "might be as gods" in absolute autonomy, but that we might exercise stewardship over life while seeking the purposes for which God made us. In this life we are called by God to develop and use the arts, sciences, technologies, and other resources within ethical limits defined by respect for human dignity, the creation of community, and the realization of love.

The care of the dying must always be informed by the principle of the loving stewardship of life. The direct, intentional termination of human life either of oneself or another generally has been treated in the history of Christian thought as contradictory to such stewardship because it is a claim to absolute dominion over human life.

Such stewardship, however, allows for the offering of one's life when a greater measure of love shall be realized through such action than otherwise would be possible, as in the case of sacrificing one's life for others or choosing martyrdom in the face of evil. When a person's suffering is unbearable and irreversible or when the burdens of living outweigh the benefits for a person suffering from a terminal or fatal illness, the cessation of life may be considered a relative good.

Christian theological and ethical reflection shows that the obligations to use life-sustaining treatments cease when the physical, emotional, financial, or social burdens exceed the benefits for the dying patient and the care givers.

E. Christian Hope

In the face of the ultimate mystery of why humans suffer and die, our hope rests in the God who brought again Jesus from the dead. God offers us, in the midst of our struggle and pain, the promise of wholeness within the unending community of the Risen Christ. Nothing, neither life nor death, can separate us from the love of God in Jesus Christ.

II. Pastoral Care

A. Healing Ministry

Pastoral care should be an expression of the healing ministry of Christ, empowering persons in the experience of suffering and dying. Those who give pastoral care create a relationship wherein signs of God's presence are revealed. Pastoral care may come from the church and wider community of family, friends, neighbors, other patients, and the health-care team. Suffering and dying persons remain autonomous and have a right to choose their relationships with pastoral care givers.

Persons offering pastoral care empathize with suffering patients and share in the wounds of their lives. In providing comfort, they point beyond pain to sources of strength, hope, and wholeness. They may join in prayer with a person who is facing death. Such prayer should focus on healing that points to wholeness of personhood, even in death. Healing implies affirmation of the goodness of life, while recognizing death is not always an enemy.

B. Reconciliation

In both the healing ministry and the death of Jesus Christ, God enters into our suffering, sustains us, and provides the resources for reconciliation and wholeness. This means assisting a person in reactivating broken or idle relationships with God and with others, and being at peace with oneself.

C. Relationships and Care

Pastoral care provides families and friends an opportunity to share their emotions, including hurt and anger as well as grief, and provides help for complex questions that frequently require difficult decisions. Religious, cultural, and personal differences among family and friends must be considered with special sensitivity. Grieving persons need to be reminded that their feelings are normal human responses. Such feelings need not cause embarrassment or guilt. Families at the bedside usually act according to long-established patterns of relationships. Attention to the entire family as a unit must be incorporated into pastoral care.

Health-care workers also need pastoral care. Doctors and, especially, support staff have intimate contact with dying persons in ways experienced by few others. They live in the tension of giving compassionate care to patients while maintaining professional detachment. Pastoral care for health-care workers means helping them to take loving care of themselves as well as their patients.

D. Specific Pastoral Concerns

1. Communications with the dying person and family

Pastoral-care persons are trained to help patients understand their illness. While they usually do not communicate medical information to patients, they can assist in assimilating information provided by medical personnel. Pastoral-care persons are especially needed when illness is terminal and neither patients nor family members are able to discuss this reality freely.

The complexity of treatment options and requests by physicians for patient and family involvement in life-prolonging decisions require good communication. Pastoral-care persons can bring the insights of Christian values and Christian hope to the decision-making process. If advance directives for treatment, often called "living wills," are contemplated or are being interpreted, the pastoral-care persons can offer support and guidance to those involved in decision making. They can facilitate discussion of treatment options, including home and hospice care.

2. Suicide

Some persons, confronted with a terminal illness that promises prolonged suffering and anguish for themselves and for loved ones, may consider suicide as a means to hasten death. When the natural process of dying is extended by application of medical technology, the emotional, economic, and relational consequences for self and others may lead a responsible person seriously to question whether continued living is faithful stewardship of the gift of life. Some may ask care givers for assistance in taking their lives. Churches need to provide preparation in dealing with these complex issues.

Among the issues of stewardship to be considered in such a decision are: (a) God's sacred gift of life and the characteristics or boundaries of meaningful life; (b) the rights and responsibilities of the person in relationship to the community; (c) the exercise and limits of human freedom; (d) the burdens and benefits for both the person and the community. Engagement with these issues is necessary for persons considering suicide.

When possible, others who are related to and care about the dying person should be included in discussion. The loving presence of Christ as manifested in the church community should surround those contemplating suicide and the survivors of those who take their own lives. An important pastoral concern is the guilt and stigma often felt by survivors, particularly when they have not been included in prior considerations.

3. Donation of organs for transplantation, or of one's body, after death to medical research

The gift of life in organ donation allows patients and survivors to experience positive meaning in the midst of their grief. Donation is to be encouraged, assuming appropriate safeguards against hastening death and with determination of death by reliable criteria. Pastoral-care persons should be willing to explore these options as a normal part of conversation with patients and their families.

4. Holy Living

A major concern of pastors and chaplains is the sustaining ministry to and spiritual growth of patients, families, and health-care personnel.

Pastoral-care persons bear witness to God's grace, with words of comfort and salvation. In our United Methodist tradition, spiritual growth is nurtured by persons who offer prayers and read the Scriptures with patients and loved ones, by Holy Communion, the laying on of hands, and by prayers of repentance, reconciliation, and intercession. A ritual of prayer or anointing with oil after miscarriage, or after a death in a hospital, nursing home, or hospice are examples of means to bring comfort and grace to the participants. Rituals developed in connection with a diagnosis of terminal illness, of welcome to a hospice or nursing home, or of return to a local congregation by persons who have been absent for treatment or in the care of a loved one, may also enhance spiritual growth. Preparation of these rituals with and by the persons involved is strongly encouraged.

Pastoral care givers and the community of faith are called to be open to God's presence in the midst of pain and suffering, to engender hope, and to enable the people of God to live and die in faith and in holiness.

III. The Social Dimension

Ethical decisions about death and dying are always made in a social context that includes policies and practices of legislative bodies, public agencies and institutions, and the social consensus that supports them. Therefore, it is important for Christians to be attentive to the social situations and policies that affect the dying. The social context of dying decisively affects individual decisions to continue or forego treatment or to accept death. Social policies and practices must protect the fundamental values of respect for persons, self-determination, and patient benefit of treatment.

A. Respect for Persons: Holy Dying

Dying with dignity calls for care that puts emphasis on compassion, personal interaction between patient and care givers, respect for the patient as a whole person with social as well as medical needs.

To the extent that medical technology is used to sustain, support, and compensate for human functions, it supports the preservation of human dignity. Indeed, medical technology is a gift of our age, supported by the will and resources of a society that values life and is willing to apply the measures necessary for extending life when possible. When technology becomes an end in itself, however, unduly prolonging the dying process, it creates a paradox in which human dignity may be undermined and the goals of treatment distorted in the interest of technology.

When a person is dying and medical intervention can at best prolong a minimal level of life at great cost to human dignity, the objective of medical care should be to give comfort and maximize the individual's capacity for awareness, feeling, and relationships with others. In some cases of patients who are without any doubt in an irreversibly comatose state, where cognitive functions and conscious relationships are no longer possible, decisions to withhold or withdraw mechanical devices which continue respiration and circulation may justly be made by family members or guardians, physicians, hospital ethics committees, and chaplains.

B. Justice for All

All persons deserve to be able to die with dignity, regardless of age, race, social status, life-style, communicability of disease, or ability to pay for adequate care. The biblical witness of God's concern for justice, particularly for those most marginalized and powerless in society, demands such commitments. Equitable allocation of economic resources is necessary to assure the protection of individuals in their dying from neglect, social isolation, unnecessary pain, and unreasonable expense.

C. Self-Determination

The right of persons to accept or reject treatment is protected in a just society by norms and procedures that involve the patient as an active participant in medical decisions. In order to safeguard the right of self-determination at a time when one may lack decision-making capacity due to dementia or unconsciousness, individuals are encouraged to designate a proxy or execute a durable power of attorney and to stipulate, in written advance directives, guidelines for their treatment in terminal illness.

All persons are endowed with the gift of freedom and are accountable to God and their covenant community for their decisions. Congregations and other church groups can play a particularly important role helping their members provide written guidance for their treatment in terminal illness and find support for implementing their own directives or those of others.

D. Pain and Dying

In spite of the belief held by some that euthanasia and suicide may be the humane solution for the problem of excruciating pain experienced by the terminally ill, use of these options is minimized by effective medical management of pain. Presently, the proper application of medical science, as demonstrated by hospice care, can in most cases enable patients to live and die without extreme physical suffering. Such methods of controlling pain, even when they risk or shorten life, can be used for terminally ill patients, provided the intention is to relieve pain and not to kill. The law should facilitate the use of drugs to relieve pain in such cases.

If adequate support by community, family, and competent pastoral care givers is provided, the mental suffering of loneliness, fear, and anguish, which is often more painful than physical suffering, can be alleviated. This support is particularly important in those patients who are without any physical pain but who suffer emotional trauma in knowing that they are in the early stages of certain diseases currently considered incurable, such as Alzheimers disease, amyo-

147

trophic lateral sclerosis, Huntington's disease, and HIV-related diseases.

E. Social Constraints

Certain social constraints militate against the ideals of holy dying.

1. Attitudes toward dying

The attempt to deny death frequently results both in reluctance by individuals to plan ahead for their dying and unwillingness in professionals to "let go" even when a patient is beyond medical help or benefit. This denial is intensified by negative attitudes toward old age, poverty, and disability.

2. Ethos of the medical profession

The emphasis on curing, healing, and restoration can contribute to uneasiness among physicians in making the transition from cure to care when possibilities of cure are exhausted. Members of the medical profession are to be commended when they accept the legitimacy of medicine oriented toward relief of suffering rather than extension of the inevitable process of dying. This is not easily done; institutional pressure encourages the use of sophisticated technology even when it can only prolong a patient's dying. This is heightened by the fear of physicians concerning legal liability for failing to use all available technologies.

3. Failures in distributive justice

Budget allocations and reimbursement policies for medical care by both private and government health plans give priority to funding technologically sophisticated diagnosis and treatments. At the same time, they often deny or minimize payments for less costly services that are critical for humane dying.

In addition, medical professionals are often constrained in their efforts to implement health-care plans that have patient benefit as their goal by payment policies of government and insurance companies that dictate the length and modalities of treatment. A society committed to helping every person realize a humane death will reverse these policies and give highest priorities to such services as hospice and home care, social services, and pastoral resources. This will include an adequately funded national health plan that assures all persons access to these resources.

4. Use of the legal system

Persons increasingly have sought to redress perceived injustices in medical treatment or to resolve difficult cases in the adversarial setting of the courtroom. As a result, the courts have become the site of medical decisions. The failure of society to provide effective support systems in health-care facilities, including the use of ethics committees, leaves individuals and institutions vulnerable to outside interference. The resulting practice of defensive medicine has frequently increased the use of futile diagnostic and treatment procedures by physicians and added to the cost of patient care.

F. United Methodist Response

Churches need to work together to overcome these social constraints. It is recommended that United Methodists:

1. Acknowledge dying as part of human existence, without romanticizing it. In dying, as in living, mercy and justice must shape corporate response to human need and vulnerability.

2. Accept relief of suffering as a goal for care of dying persons rather than focusing primarily on prolongation of life. It is within human and financial means, if made a priority, to provide pain control and comfort-giving measures in a setting of communal affection and support, such as a hospice.

3. Advocate equitable access for all persons to resources, including a national health care plan, needed to relieve the dying and their loved ones from financial crises created by extended terminal illness.

4. Promote effective personal support systems, such as pastoral care teams, ethics committees in hospitals and nursing facilities and

church groups, for medical personnel who must implement difficult decisions on behalf of dying persons and their families.

5. Participate in congregational, ecumenical and community-wide dialogue to help shape consensus on treatment of dying persons.

6. Encourage persons to use advance directives for their treatment in terminal illness and dying. Congregations can be supportive by providing information, opportunities for considering alternatives and assistance in implementing the directives.

Holy dying, with loving pastoral care and without efforts to prolong terminal illness, will be enhanced to the extent that the church and the human community embody mercy and justice for all persons.

ADOPTED 1992

See Social Principles, ¶ 71.J, "Suicide: A Challenge to Ministry," "Organ and Tissue Donation,""Universal Access to Health Care in the United States and Related Territories."

THE SOCIAL COMMUNITY

Accessibility of Meeting Places beyond the Local Church

Be it resolved, that all meetings scheduled by general, jurisdictional, and annual conferences and their boards and committees shall be "accessible." This accessibility refers to architectural, communication, and attitudinal barriers.

Be it further resolved, that guidelines for what constitutes an accessible meeting shall be established in each annual conference by their Accessibility Advocates Association/Committee on Ministry with Persons with Handicapping Conditions, or, if such a committee has not been formed, by their Division on Health and Welfare Ministries.

ADOPTED 1992

See Social Principles, ¶ 72, "Barrier-Free Construction for the Handicapped," "The Church and Persons with Mentally, Physically, and/or Psychologically Handicapping Conditions."

Access of Hispanics to Higher Education

WHEREAS, the Hispanic population in the United States and Puerto Rico has increased dramatically over the last decade (up 39 percent, compared to the general population increase of 9.5 percent) to a total of 21 million in 1960s; and

WHEREAS, reliable reports indicate that Hispanics are the most undereducated segment of the U.S. population, with an average dropout rate of 49 percent, with 11.9 percent of Hispanics 25 years and older considered illiterate in 1987, compared with an estimated 1.8 percent failure of literacy tests in the non-Hispanic population; and

WHEREAS, a study funded by the Division of Higher Education, Board of Higher Education and Ministry, and conducted by a research team of the faculty of the Methodist Theological School in Ohio over a two-year period, concluded the following important factors in consideration of this issue:

- In 1987, the thirteen United Methodist theological schools graduated 1093 students, seven of whom were identified as "Hispanic."
- In 1987, 263 Hispanics were graduated as part of a class of 12,775 from 201 theological schools of more than 11 denominations.
- Many private colleges and more than forty public colleges, universities, and university systems were found to have created methods and programs to increase substantially the number of Hispanic graduates from their institutions.

These creative intervention programs (often involving thousands of potential Hispanic students) focused on the causes of non-enrollment of Hispanic students. These causes concerned financial need, cultural estrangement from large, impersonal institutions, the creation of inappropriate admission tests, the need for assistance with language and study skills, the need to provide mechanisms of nurture in which the culture of Hispanics is honored and cultivated, and the special need to create educational bridges between the unusually large community college population of Hispanics and neighboring four-year institutions.

- Few innovative programs for Hispanics were identified as initiated or shared in by universities, colleges, theological schools, or medical/nursing schools associated with the University Senate of The United Methodist Church. In fact it was found that "only a paucity of United Methodist schools are intentional in their efforts to recruit and support Hispanic students."

- The study revealed that in the fall enrollment of 1988, among those United Methodist-related schools with the largest enrollment of Hispanics, only one school was found to have an enrollment of at least 5 percent Hispanics. This amounted to a total of 280 students. This is in contrast with other systems not related to The United Methodist Church that enroll thousands of Hispanics, especially in certain geographical areas.

- On the positive side, the study learned—as a result of a national poll undertaken by the team—that there are a number of "successful recruitment and retention" programs for Hispanics. Typically, these have been developed by boards of regents, state-level boards of higher education, and a few state-wide community college systems. These programs have been undertaken as a consequence of "high institutional commitment," and typically feature the creation of a broad range of intervention strategies. In many well-documented cases these creative programs, motivated by the desire to significantly intervene in the dire educational situation of Hispanics, have turned negative statistics around in a single student generation. Unfortunately, the team was not able to discover any similar results in member schools of the United Methodist University Senate.

- This study also discovered that the motivation to change the composition of the student body to be far more inclusive of Hispanics is, in and of itself, the determinative factor in the formula for change. Further, the study concluded that since motivation to change the character of the campus to become more inclusive of Hispanics is the most critical issue, it follows that primary responsibility must be lodged at the highest levels of higher education leadership (boards, presidents, chancellors, deans, etc.). These leaders know well how to lead expert staff persons to create the changes necessary, inspire their associates to make necessary changes, and lead their institutions in a process of change.

Therefore, be it resolved, that the General Conference request that all University Senate-related institutions be informed of this research, the needs it identifies, and the intervention strategies it surveys by means of the most appropriate method identified by the Board of Higher Education and Ministry.

ADOPTED 1992

See Social Principles, ¶ 72.A, "Bilingual Education," "Public Education in the United States."

Act of Covenanting Between Other Christian Churches and The United Methodist Church

The United Methodist Church must always be open to the leading of God's Spirit. Today there is an expressed need for new relationship in the Body of Christ. We believe that an Act of Covenanting between consenting churches may be one response to the need and to the witness of the Holy Spirit. In such an act the participating churches will continue independence in their structures, traditions, styles of implementation of ministry, existing partnerships, agreements and explorations, forms of worship and programs. The United Methodist Church will continue to see itself as an international church.

The focus of an act of covenanting is the larger Body of Christ and thus it is open to potential covenanting churches of all Christian heritages. It is rooted both in the Apostolic Faith and in our contemporary experience of God's love and will.

The following sample elements of an act of covenanting with other Christian churches are adopted by the 1988 General Conference of The United Methodist church for implementation and negotiation as indicated in the text:

Elements of an Act of Covenanting

1. *Introduction.* Covenants have been integral in the history of God's relationships with the People of God. Indeed, as the General Conference of 1968 stated (*On the Ecumenical Road,* A Statement on the Cause of Christian Unity): ". . . the profoundest imperative to Christian unity springs from God's own design and providence for his covenant people." In the Preamble to the Constitution of The United Methodist Church we are alerted to the dangers of all dividedness: "The Church of Jesus Christ exists in and for the World, and its very dividedness is a hindrance to its mission in that world." In recent decades we have received clearer understanding of the relationship between Christian unity and our covenant with God. At the same time we have new insight into the nature of the Christian Church and new sense of common global mission. Geographical and political boundaries do not limit the Body of Christ.

The United Methodist Church has a stake in the faithful discipleship of other communions. Other communions have a stake in the faithful discipleship of The United Methodist Church. Thus, The United Methodist Church now seeks a new form of acceptance of God's gift of unity. We seek to engage in covenant with other Christian churches wherever more visible Christian unity can increase effective mission in the modern world. This covenant is a symbol of the search for deeper relationships with churches that are a part of the whole Covenant People of God.

2. *Possible Definition and Commitments.* In this Act of Covenanting, the emphasis is on our roots in the Apostolic Faith and in our contemporary experience of God's love and will. It is aimed at encouraging a new sense of global common cause, mutual support, mutual spiritual growth, common study of scripture and culture, creative interaction as ministers in the mission of God's Church, cross-fertilization of ideas about ways to be in that mission, sharing of resources, and exploring new forms of service directed at old and emerging needs.

In this covenant, the _____ Church and The United Methodist Church acknowledge the centrality of the sovereignty of Jesus Christ, as basic to all relationships. Our links with the Apostolic Faith through Scripture, Tradition, Experience and Reason lead us now solemnly to affirm to each other that "all who are baptized into Christ are members of Christ's ministry through the people of the one God, Father, Son and Holy Spirit." (COCU Digest, 1974, p. 335; *Official Record*, XII, 1974)

a. We therefore recognize our respective baptisms as different facets of the one baptism and mutually recognize the members of the _____ Church and of The United Methodist Church are members one of the other;

b. We, therefore, recognize each other as authentic expressions of the One, Holy, Catholic, and Apostolic Church of Jesus Christ.

c. We, therefore, recognize the ordained ministries of our churches and pledge our mutual efforts at effecting forms of reconciliation of those ministries, including the exchange or transfer of ordained ministers between properly constituted bodies where the approval and consent of the appropriate authorities involved is given. The assumption of pastoral care of members visiting or residing in each other's countries is another instance of this aspect of the Act of Covenanting.

d. We are committed to systematic participation in full Eucharistic fellowship as a symbol of transcendence over manifestations of human divisions.

e. We expect that the various agencies of our two churches will function in new ways of partnership in mission and evangelism, in education and implementation of the Gospel. Mutual sharing of principles and methods can improve our functioning in our separate contexts and especially in continuance or new development of joint projects in mission between the _____ Church and The United Methodist Church.

f. We expect that an expanded and focused international linkage of visitations and partnerships will take place. The bishops or presidents of the churches will arrange for mutually agreeable visitations and exchanges that will provide contact with and some knowledge of the social, political, economic, moral and religious context in which the people of the world struggle for existence, meaning and purpose. Mutual visitations may include occasional presence at each other's appropriate assemblies.

g. Extended partnerships might be possible between, for example a covenanting church or its parts and a particular congregation, Annual Conference or Episcopal Area of The United Methodist Church. Such participation in this covenant would be by special action subsequent to adoption of the covenant. Such an extended partnership, perhaps in consultation with specific United Methodist agencies as well, might be for a defined period to enable a mutual flow of persons, interest and commitment. The partnership can be extended or ended by mutual agreement. Such extended partnerships would make palpable the global stake we have in each other in various parts of the world. These focused partnerships would be integrated with visitations by leaders and the sharing by agencies of time, ability and funding resources.

h. Our covenant assumes the continuing independence and autonomy of the covenanting churches in their structures, traditions, styles of implementation of ministry, existing partnerships, agreements and explorations, forms of worship and program. But we look forward to knowing each other in love, to losing our fear of difference and our fear of differences for the same of more effective participation in the mission of God's Church. We make bold to anticipate that out of our experience we will be led by the Spirit to new forms of covenant and to new relationships for the global Christian community.

3. *Oversight of Covenant Projects and Participation.* For The United Methodist Church, oversight of the covenantal relationships is the responsibility of the Council of Bishops with the assistance of the General Commission on Christian Unity and Interreligious Concerns,

while participation in specific projects is the responsibility of the appropriate general agency or agencies.

4. *Authorization.* The Council of Bishops shall represent The United Methodist Church in developing an Act of Covenanting with a prospective partner church. The Council of Bishops shall make recommendations to General Conference on such specific covenanting agreements. The Act of Covenanting becomes effective immediately upon approval by the General Conference and by the chief legislative body of the partner church, signed by the president of the Council of Bishops and the secretary of the General Conference of The United Methodist Church and by the authorized persons in the covenanting church.

5. *Enabling Legislation.* Submitted separately for adoption and publishing in the *Book of Discipline* are several items of enabling legislation related to an Act of Covenanting.

6. *Liturgical Celebration.* A brief liturgical celebration of the Act of Covenanting shall be prepared by representative of our two churches and shall be celebrated at the chief legislative bodies of both covenanting churches.

ADOPTED 1992

See Social Principles ¶ 72, "Continuing Membership in the Consultation on Church Union," "Toward an Ecumenical Future," "COCU Consensus: In Quest of a Church of Christ Uniting."

An Affirmation of Basic Rural Worth

W{HEREAS}, rural life often is romanticized or devalued by the culture of the nation; and

W{HEREAS}, approximately 50 percent of United Methodist churches are located in rural areas that have populations of 2,500 or less; and

W{HEREAS}, more than 55 percent of all United Methodist churches are on circuits; and

W{HEREAS}, the rural church is an integral part of the United Methodist connection; and

W{HEREAS}, more elderly, homeless, sick, and poor increasingly live in rural areas; and

W{HEREAS}, rural peoples are employed in farming, ranching and other agricultural endeavors, trucking, migrant work, timbering, recreation, fishing and river work, rural factories, and small business of numerous kinds; and

WHEREAS, rural peoples now are a minority population in the United States;

Therefore, be it resolved, that The United Methodist Church affirm the following statements on the basic worth of rural peoples, rural life and rural places:

1. Like other peoples, persons who live in rural places are persons of sacred human worth to whom God's grace is available and operative.

2. God is present in all places, whether few, any, or many persons live there.

3. Each rural church, regardless of large or small size and location, is valuable to The United Methodist Church as a connectional church.

4. Rural residents deserve the option of living and prospering in the communities where they live, and the goals and policies of the governments that relate to rural places should be to provide this option.

5. Rural peoples deserve equitable and continuing spiritual care, recreational opportunities, security for the elderly and disabled, nurture and protection for children and youth, satisfying economic opportunity, and a sense of purpose and hope.

6. As stewards of the creation, rural people have a right to determination of how land, water, air, and other resources within their communities, especially in areas of limited population, are to be used, with particular attention to land use and control being exercised by all who live within an area rather than by only a few persons.

ADOPTED 1992

See Social Principles, ¶ 72, "Appointment of Clergy to Rural Ministry," "The Church's Response to Changing Rural Issues," "Rural Chaplaincy as a Ministry of Laity and Clergy."

Affirmation of Zoar United Methodist Church of Philadelphia

WHEREAS, Zoar United Methodist Church represents the historic continuity of the African American within the traditional stream of The United Methodist Church; and

WHEREAS, some of the African-American members left Old St. George's

Church in Philadelphia and formed a new denomination known as the African Methodist Episcopal Church; and

WHEREAS, the remaining African Americans stayed and endured racial discrimination until 1794; and

WHEREAS, the eighteen men and three women moved out of St. George's to form a new congregation, the Church of African Mother Zoar; and

WHEREAS, this congregation has received a number of citations;

Therefore, be it resolved, that the denomination focus prayerful support for Zoar Church, Philadelphia, as it celebrates 200 years of service and ministry to its constituency and its communities.

ADOPTED 1992

See Social Principles, ¶ 72.A, "Declare Zoar United Methodist Church a Primary Historical Emphasis."

Affirmative Action

The concept of "affirmative action" emerged and developed during the period of the 1960's along with many other programs designed to address the inequalities and discriminatory practices within our society. It was defined as measurable efforts by employers and educational institutions to hire and admit those who had traditionally been excluded. While it has been actively resisted in many ways, especially where it has meant change from long existing patterns, significant though small gains for women, ethnic and racial minorities, and persons with handicapping conditions have been achieved, but much more needs to be done.

Gunnar Myrdal reminded us in his book, *An American Dilemma* (published in 1944), that the race problem in America is basically a moral dilemma, not a legal problem. The premise upon which affirmative action is built is essentially moral and spiritual in nature. Concern for the disadvantaged, the disinherited, and the oppressed is a major feature of both the Old Testament prophets and the message and ministry of Jesus. According to biblical teaching, what is required is a redress of grievances and a sincere effort to make amends. Strong leadership from the religious community is demanded when efforts to correct the injustices and evils of the past and present are under attack.

The characterization of affirmative action as "unfair" often appears to rest on the dubious assumption that conditions for women, racial and ethnic minorities and persons with handicapping conditions have improved so radically that further special efforts on their behalf are unnecessary. Unemployment of racial and ethnic minority persons remains much higher than the national average, and women workers continue to earn less than male workers. Affirmative action has been proven to have a significant impact in opening opportunities and increasing the participation of racial and ethnic minority persons, women, and persons with handicapping conditions in employment and educational settings.

Affirmative action recognizes the need to broaden the definition of compensatory, protective and preferential programs that now exist in our society and the traditional preferential treatment given to non-minority groups and males. Affirmative action is a management plan to achieve a more inclusive work-force or enrollment. Effective plans usually include:

a) A clear and forthright policy statement calling for nondiscrimination and for the inclusion of ethnic minority persons, women, and persons with handicapping conditions;

b) An assignment of responsibility to achieve the policy by executive, managers, and supervisors;

c) An analysis of workforce patterns by race, sex, and job category compared to availability to determine the extent of inclusiveness;

d) Establishment of goals and objectives to achieve a representative inclusiveness;

e) Development of recruitment, selection, training, and other personnel of admissions practices to achieve the objectives and goals;

f) Procedures for monitoring personnel or admissions practices and to measure results of the plan.

The discrimination of the past, which automatically excluded certain groups of people—by color, by sex, by age, and because of handicapping conditions—is being corrected with due regard for the compensation necessary for the disadvantages of the past to be transformed into equality of opportunity in the future. Affirmative action plays an important role in "releasing captives" and "setting the oppressed at liberty." The Church has an important role to play in ministering which is designed to effect reconciliation and healing for those who suffer the pain caused by societal change, as well as in supporting the continuation of those changes.

We therefore call upon individuals and institutions, including United Methodists individually and as congregations, to:

1. Forthrightly and clearly affirm their support of affirmative action legislation and programs.

2. Reaffirm and increase their support of those efforts that seek to insure effective representation of ethnic minority persons and women.

3. Continue to provide a much-needed role model for others in society by affirming, strengthening, and practicing their own affirmative action policies.

4. Affirm and proclaim the Judeo-Christian heritage of restitution, inclusiveness, justice, and grace as the best possible support for affirmative action.

5. Affirm the equal consideration of lay people in church-related positions where not prohibited by the *Book of Discipline* of The United Methodist Church.

6. Seek to interpret the true purpose and meaning of affirmative action against claims of reverse discrimination.

7. Support actively church-related programs such as Project Equality which seek to support equal opportunity and to promote an inclusive society.

8. *Be it resolved*, that the 1988 General Conference mandate intentional implementation of affirmative action programs and procedures in general church boards and agencies, annual conferences, church-related institutions, districts, and local churches;

9. *Be it further resolved*, that the General Commissions on Religion and Race and Status and Role of Women and Project Equality continue to monitor and provide assistance to United Methodist agencies and institutions in affirmative action programs and processes in an effort to lead The United Methodist Church toward a more inclusive society.

ADOPTED 1988

See Social Principles, ¶ 72.A, "Affirmative Action Plans and People with Disabilities," "A Charter for Racial Justice Policies in an Interdependent Global Community," "Ethnic Membership of Boards and Agencies."

Affirmative Action Plans and People with Disabilities

Affirmative Action Plans (AAPs) have greatly increased the numbers of ethnic minorities and females in the workplace and have increased the hope and pride of racial/ethnic people and women.

People with disabilities have been underutilized by public and private employers as evidenced by surveys showing an unemployment rate of over 60 percent.

People with disabilities have also experienced discrimination in employment. They have been excluded from the workplace by physical barriers which have denied workplace accessibility.

People with disabilities are defined as individuals who meet the disability definitions found in Section 504 of the Rehabilitation Act and the Americans with Disabilities Act (ADA).

1. We urge that all United Methodist Church agencies, annual conferences, and the General Conference include persons with disabilities in their existing AAPs and set forth goals and timetables for persons with disabilities, comparing the percentages of people with disabilities on their staffs with either job availability studies or the percentage of persons with disabilities in the latest U.S. Census population figure within their respective service areas.

2. We urge all public and private employers to include people with disabilities in their existing, respective AAPs, using the same comparison criteria as listed in number one.

ADOPTED 1992

See Social Principles, ¶ 72, "Affirmative Action," "The Church and Persons with Mentally, Physically and/or Psychologically Handicapping Conditions."

Affirming a Diversity of Language Usage in the United States and Opposing a Constitutional Amendment Making English the Official Language

The United States is a land whose inhabitants are enriched by diverse traditions, languages, and cultures. While English is the commonly used or primary language of the country, there have always been other languages present throughout the history of the nation. Native American languages and Spanish were already spoken when the first English colonists arrived at Plymouth. Throughout that same history, there have been various efforts to prescribe the use of English and proscribe the use of other languages. These efforts sometimes resulted in legislation which had the effect of legalizing discrimination against various language minority groups. However, such legislation was eventually overcome by the constitutional principles of equal rights for all. The acknowledgement of English as the primary language of the United States, does not deny the right and contribution of other languages, or the inherent right of people to retain and speak their mother tongues.

In recent years there have been renewed efforts in different parts of the country to make English the official language of the nation. We are concerned that the movement to declare constitutionally English as the official language of the nation is not based upon any real need but, in fact, may be motivated by an effort to deny the pluralistic foundation of the country, and to deny the dignity and wholeness of persons from different racial and ethnic groups who rightly considered their languages an integral part of their cultures. We fear the real purpose of some may be not so much to make English the official language of the U.S. as to make English the exclusive language of the nation.

For example, there is an English-only "movement" which has, within the last year, gained more national recognition. Organizations, such as "U.S. English" and "English First" continue gaining support through active national activities and local English-only campaigns. In addition to promotion of their principles through the media, they are also involved in various legislative and lobbying activities. Those include: efforts to pass a constitutional amendment making English the official language of the United States; opposition to federal legislation for bilingual education, voting rights bills, and the FCC licensing applications for Spanish language broadcasts.

These efforts and their implications are another manifestation of the systemic racism which has infected this country for generations. The English-only movement blames the deterioration of the American fabric on immigration and the use of languages other than English. It contends that the nation's unity rests upon the use of an official language. It defines multi-culturalism and multi-lingualism as "anti-unity." Consequently, the movement, if successful, could further discriminate and segregate the racial/ethnic minority population of the U.S. Essential information such as the 911 emergency telephone number, hospital emergency rooms, police, fire fighters, language services, bilingual education, and interpreters in the judicial system might be denied.

As Christians, we believe that we are children of God, created in God's image, and members of the family of God;

We believe that diversity is a gift of the creative genius of God and that languages are an expression of the wisdom of God;

We believe that competence in the English language is important to participate fully in the life of the United States, but that we also live in a global context, the global Family of God, where people and nations experience interdependency at all levels;

We believe that our nation needs to take advantage of the rich contributions that the ethnic/language groups bring to this country by preserving those languages and encouraging North Americans to learn other languages;

We believe that it is the will of God that each human being is affirmed as a whole person and that it is in the acceptance and interchange of our uniqueness that we find Oneness—total wholeness—Shalom;

We oppose the attempt to rob a person of his/her language as dehumanizing and as a denial of that person's wholeness;

We oppose the English-only movement as a manifestation of the sin of racism; therefore,

The General Conference shall:

1) Express in writing, to the President of the United States its support for practices and policies which permit provision of information in languages appropriate to the residents of communities and its opposition to the movement which seeks to make English the only language of the United States, which movement is discriminatory and racist;

2) Forward this resolution to members of Congress, governors and the legislatures of the fifty states and territories;

3) Commend this resolution to all annual conferences for promotion and interpretation within the annual conferences; and

4) Ask the General Board of Church and Society to make this resolution an urgent item in their agenda for lobbying, constituency education and advocacy.

ADOPTED 1988

See Social Principles, ¶ 72.A, "A Charter for Racial Justice Policies in an Interdependent Global Community," "Bilingual Education," "Literacy, the Right to Learn: A Basic Human Right."

African-American Family Life

WHEREAS, our Social Principles state that "we believe the family to be the basic human community through which persons are nurtured and sustained in mutual love, responsibility, respect, and fidelity"; and

Whereas, families of all types in the United States are vulnerable to social and economic change; and

Whereas, research shows that strong African-American families are highly religious, but that the local church has limited resources to assist them in resolution of problems and crises; and

Whereas, African-American families today face problems of epidemic proportions from violence within the geographical community, new and virulent health problems, a high rate of cardiovascular illness, economic stress, etc.;

Be it resolved, that the General Board of Discipleship identify or create resources and materials to assist local churches in developing a program of mentoring, counseling, and referral which includes strategies to strengthen African-American family life.

ADOPTED 1992

See Social Principles, ¶ 71.A and 72.A, "Protecting and Sustaining Children," "Universal Access to Health Care in the United States and Related Territories," "Supportive Policies for Families with Children."

Aging in the United States of America

I. Preamble

The elderly in the United States of America occupy a new frontier in a rapidly changing industrial society. A frontier has two aspects: its hazards, uncharted ways, unknowns, anxieties; its promises, hopes, visions, and fulfillments. A frontier becomes a promised land when guides chart the way, pioneers settle and builders develop the land. But this new frontier is yet to be charted for the aged. Existing institutions have not been able to adapt fast enough nor have new institutions been created to meet the new conditions. Some research, however, has recently begun to topple some myths and stereotypes about the aging process and older persons.

This statement is for study, discussion, and implementation and action by The United Methodist Church in the United States. It contains brief sections on the current situation of the older population, on a theological response and on calls to the society and to the church. There has, however, been no attempt to set priorities for ministries in this new frontier described within this statement; it is hoped that appropriate church agencies and units will set their own priorities.

II. The Situation

During the past 100 years, life expectancy in the United States has increased about 27 years, a fact to be celebrated. The number of persons 65 years of age and older has grown from 3.1 million in 1900. (4.1% of the total population) to 28 million in 1984 (11.9% of the total population). This number is expected to increase from 34.9 million in the year 2000 (13.0%) to 65 million in 2030 (21.1%). The older population includes a disproportionate number of women (148 women to 100 men) and persons with a wide range of capacities, from active and employed to fragile, frail, to chronically disabled. The fastest growing age group in the population is 85 years of age and over, and the second most rapidly growing is the 75 to 84 age group.[1]

The trend in recent years has been for older persons to live alone rather than with family members or in a formal care setting, primarily in nursing homes. In 1984, only 2% of those persons 65-74 years old were in nursing homes, while 7% of the 75-84 year olds and 23% of those 85 years and over were living in long-term care facilities. Social security provides some benefits to about 92% of the older adult population.[2] However, about 12.4%,[1] or 3.3 million persons 65 and older had incomes below a subsistence poverty level in 1984.[1] The median annual income for older men in 1984 was $10,000, for women about $6,000, only $1,000 above the official poverty level[3] ($4,979 for individuals living alone and $6,282 for older couples' households in 1984).[1] It is not surprising that 72% of the elderly poor are women and 28.1%[4] of the total elderly minority population are considered marginally poor.[4]

Clearly, the elderly are not a homogenous group. These data point out that not all subgroups fit into the normative situation of the larger population of the elderly. In addition, middle class persons with much higher incomes often find themselves reduced to poverty by the cost of health treatment and long-term care. The increased probability of widowhood and divorce also may produce economic instability for older women. For example, in the case of pensions, about 28% of men and 10% of women receive pensions.[5] "Currently, only one woman in five receives any type of pension, public or private, to supplement her

Social Security payments. The median income for women from pensions in 1984 was $233 per month, about half of what men received. And only half as many women received pensions, whether as retired workers or as spouses of retired workers."[3]

The current health system is more adequate for persons who are younger and have excellent insurance plans. Even though aging itself is not a disease, older people have more illness for a longer period of time than younger people do. Adequate health insurance coverage for millions of uninsured women has been identified as the most pressing health issue faced by older women today. Older women under 65 who are neither married nor in the work force often find health insurance so expensive that it is unaffordable or impossible to buy because of the exclusions for "existing conditions." This problem is made worse because they have no claim on employer-based group policies in which their husbands participated if divorce or death occurs, as well as having fewer job options with good insurance plans if they choose to work outside the home.

Medicare is a health insurance program primarily for persons over the age of 65. Medicaid provides a supplement to Medicare as well as coverage for younger persons in poverty. Out-of-pocket health costs for older Americans rose to an average of $1,666 per person in 1985.[6] Medicare only covers about 40% of most older adults' individual medical expenses.[7]

In 1984, 78% of older men were married while 50% of older women were widowed. There are about five times as many widows as widowers. Women are likely to live six more years as widows,[8] and 68% of them will live alone. A number of factors signal problems. For instance: because of traditional sex-role socialization, older men are psychologically ill-prepared for living alone, and older women are often inadequately prepared for assertiveness in financial and other management decisions when they find themselves alone. Since most people have been socialized to live in families, they are not prepared to live alone in old age. We need to develop adequate responses to single persons in a society that is oriented toward family living.

Although most older persons live in urban places, they also comprise a large proportion of rural populations where facilities and resources for them are extremely limited. This condition is complicated further by a disproportionately low allocation of federal funds to meet the needs of the rural elderly.

Race and ethnicity are important determinants of the residential patterns of elderly people. While about one-third of all older persons live in central cities, one-half of all Blacks and Hispanics over 65 is heavily concentrated in urban areas. The popular shifts in housing patterns brought about by urban renewal and gentrification (higher-income persons buying property in formerly poor neighborhoods) and the resultant increase in homeowner taxes have a major impact on the elderly, especially minorities. Houses that have been paid for are lost because of the tax increases, or low rents rise astronomically.

We need to dispel the common misunderstanding that aging is senility and that older persons are unable or not motivated to learn, grow, and achieve. Opportunities for continuing education and growth have long been unmet by a system geared to the needs of the young. This demand for continuing education will become acute as better educated, younger generations grow older. We need to counteract the impact of racism and sexism on later life because of underemployment, no employment, inequitable access to education, and language or nationality barriers.

Some problems that beset older persons are the result of the social and physical process of aging. These include change in work, family and community roles; the reduction of energy; and the increase in chronic illness and impairments. These conditions can lead to increased dependence on others for life's necessities. Other problems faced by the elderly are the result of social and political institutions that sometimes victimize the elderly through various techniques of both subtle and overt discrimination. Being old today is not easy, either in the church or society. If the situation of older persons is to be improved, the church must act.

III. The Technological Response

Aging is a process involving the whole life span from birth to death. A theological understanding of aging, therefore, must be concerned with the whole life process, rather than with only its final stages. The meaning of life, rather than death, is the central point from which to theologize about aging. In our pluralistic church, there is a certain legitimacy for several traditional, biblical and theological understandings of the meaning of life in its progression from birth to death. The position presented here is one attempt to express this meaning.

A. All of creation is God's work (Gen. 1). Human beings are only a small part of the totality of life forms. The aging process is universal in all life forms. Birth, aging, and death are all part of divine providence, and are to be regarded and taught as positive values. This does not, in any way, mean that such things as birth defects, disease or deaths at an early stage in life are the will of God.

B. As Christians, the mystery of God's involvement in the person of Jesus Christ provides us with a unique source of divine help (grace) in our passage through life's successive stages. This is especially significant in the later stages, when spiritual maturation and well-being can be experienced even in times of physical decline. The power of the cross is a special revelation of how suffering can be reconciling and redemptive. Faith in the Resurrection provides us with an assurance of the abiding presence of the Risen Lord (Matthew 28:20) and the Holy Spirit (John 14:16-19; 2 Cor. 3:17-18; Rm. 8:9-11), and the permanence of our relationship with God beyond the mystery of death. In this spiritual presence we also find the source of the potential of all persons for self-transcendence. God's act in Christ was for life abundant (John 10:10) in all stages of life. Christ also gives us our traditional Wesleyan vision of the goal of ultimate perfection (Matt. 5:48). The grace of God in Christ is therefore important throughout life, including its last stages.

C. In response to this saving grace, we believe in the inevitable need to walk in the ways of obedience that God has enabled (Eph. 2:8-10). These ways are defined by love for God and neighbor (Mark 12:28-31; Rom. 13:8-9). It is therefore the privilege of Christians to serve all persons in love, including older persons with their special needs. Furthermore, since God's grace is not conditioned by any human standards of worthiness or usefulness (2 Cor. 5:19), we should regard all persons as valuable to God (Matt. 6:25-30). In the larger pattern of human needs and rights, those of elderly persons must be consciously and intentionally included.

D. Older persons are not simply to be served, but are also to serve; they are of special importance in the total mission of the church. Since the Christian vocation has no retirement age, the special contributions of elderly persons need conscious recognition and employment. The experience of all older persons, and the wisdom of many, are special resources for the whole church.

E. The church as the Body of Christ in the world today (1 Cor. 12:27) is God's method for realizing the reconciliation accomplished by Christ (Col. 1:16-20). As such, it intentionally sponsors institutional forms that help reconcile persons of all ages to one another and to God. This especially includes those institutions designed to meet the needs of elderly persons and to keep them fully incorporated into the Body of Christ. The church also is charged with an abiding concern for justice for all. It should work tirelessly for the freedom of all persons to meet their own fullest potential and to liberate those who are captive to discrimination, neglect, exploitation, abuse or poverty.

IV. The Call

A. To society at all levels

United Methodist people are called upon to engage in sustained advocacy for the elimination of age discrimination in personal attitudes and institutional structures. We should pursue this advocacy vigorously and in cooperation with appropriate private and public groups, including all levels of government. We recognize that there needs to be creativity in developing the proper cooperative mix of private and public programs to serve the elderly, but all our efforts should be based on the following assumptions:

1. Religious institutions can make a unique and significant contribution to the context of care provided for persons. Secular society involves ethical issues and value decisions; therefore, a religious presence in neighborhoods and institutions is important to the quality of total community life.

2. Government should play a critical role in assuring that all benefits are available to all elderly persons to improve their quality of life. Christians should support governmental policies that promote sharing with those who are less fortunate. This does not absolve either the institutional church or individual Christians from responsibility for persons in need.

3. A standard of basic and necessary survival support systems should be accepted and established in our society and made available to all persons. These should include at minimum: health care, transportation, housing, and income maintenance. Church people need to identify and promote those facilities and services that assure

opportunities for prolonged well-being. These services should be provided at a cost within the financial means of the elderly with appropriate public subsidy when necessary. They include the following:

a) Health resources systems special to the needs of the elderly which are comprehensive, accessible and feasible within available resources. (These include long-term care, hospice care, home health care and health maintenance organizations.)

b) Health education systems that emphasize proper nutrition, proper drug use, preventive health care, and immunization as well as information about the availability of health resources within the community.

c) Training for medical and social service personnel concerning the special cultural, physical, psycho-social, and spiritual aspects and needs of the elderly.

d) Adequate housing, that is both affordable and secure, with protections that massive tax and rental increases will not create displacement, and transportation systems that meet the special needs of the elderly.

e) Basic governmental income maintenance system adequate to sustain an adequate standard of living affording personal dignity. (This system should be supplemented when necessary by private pension programs. Both public and private pension systems must be financed in a manner that will assure their ability to meet all future obligations, as well as guarantee equitable consideration of the needs of women and minorities.)

f) When basic pension systems benefit levels are not adequate to meet economic needs at least equal to the defined poverty level, supplementation by benefits from public funds.

g) Continuing educational and counseling opportunities for the elderly in preretirement planning, in work-related training, in interpersonal retirement relationships, and in personal enrichment.

h) Formal and informal community associations such as public and private centers that foster social, recreational, artistic, intellectual, and spiritual activities to help persons overcome loneliness and social isolation.

i) Continuing employment opportunities for those who desire them in flexible, appropriate work settings related to varying life styles.

j) Opportunities for volunteer work and paid employment that best utilize the skills and experiences of the elderly.

Finally, our society is called upon to respond to a basic human right of the elderly: the right to die with dignity and to have personal wishes respected concerning the number and type of life-sustaining measures that should be used to prolong life. Living wills, requests that no heroic measures be used, and other such efforts to die with dignity should be supported.

B. *To the church at all levels*

1. Each local church is called upon:

a) To become aware of the needs and interests of older people in the congregation and in the community and to express Christian love through person-to-person understanding and caring.

b) To affirm the cultural and historical contributions and gifts of ethnic minority elderly.

c) To acknowledge that ministry to older persons is needed in both small and large churches.

d) To assure a barrier-free environment in which the elderly can function in spite of impairments.

e) To motivate, equip, and train lay volunteers with a dedication for this important ministry.

f) To develop an intentional ministry with older adults which:

i. Assures each person health service, mobility, personal security, and other personal services.

ii. Offers opportunities for life enrichment including intellectual stimulation, social involvement, spiritual cultivation, and artistic pursuits.

iii. Encourages life reconstruction when necessary, including motivation and guidance in making new friends, serving new roles in the community and enriching marriage.

iv. Affirms life transcendence including celebration of the meaning and purpose of life through worship, Bible study, personal reflection, and small-group life.

g) To recognize that older persons represent a creative resource bank available to the church and involve them in service to the community as persons of insight and wisdom. (This could include not only ministry to one another, but also to the larger mission of the church for redemption of the world, including reaching the unchurched.)

h) To foster intergenerational experiences in the congregation and community including educating all age groups about how to grow old with dignity and satisfaction.

i) To assure that the frail are not separated from the life of the congregation, but retain access to the sacraments and are given assistance as needed by the caring community.

j) To provide guidance for adults coping with aging parents.

k) To cooperate with other churches and community agencies for more comprehensive and effective ministries with older persons including radio and television ministries.

l) To accept responsibility for an advocacy role in behalf of the elderly.

m) To develop an older-adult ministry responsible to the Council on Ministries involving an adult coordinator or older-adult coordinator, volunteer or employed. (An older-adult council may be organized to facilitate the ministry with older adults.)

2. Each annual conference is called upon:

a) To provide leadership and support through its Council on Ministries for an intentional ministry to older persons in its local churches with special attention to the needs of women and minorities.

b) To develop a program of job counseling and retirement planning for clergy and lay employees.

c) To share creative models of ministry and a data bank of resources with the local churches and other agencies.

d) To define the relationship between the annual conference and United Methodist-related residential and nonresidential facilities for the elderly, so that the relationships can be clearly understood and mutually supportive.

e) To relate to secular retirement communities within its boundaries.

f) To recruit persons for professional and volunteer leadership in working with the elderly.

g) To serve as both a partner and critic to local church and public programs with the elderly, promoting ecumenical linkages where possible.

h) To support financially, if needed, retired clergy and lay church workers and their spouses who reside in United Methodist long-term care settings.

i) To promote Golden Cross Sunday and other special offerings for ministries by, for, and with the elderly.

j) To recognize that other persons within the conference, both lay and clergy, represent a significant and experienced resource that should be utilized in both the organization and mission of the conference.

3. General boards and agencies are called upon:

a) To examine the pension policies of the General Church and their impact related to the needs of those who are single (retired, divorced, or surviving dependents of pensioners).

b) To create specific guidance materials for ministry by, for, and with the elderly.

c) To prepare intergenerational and age-specific materials for church school and for other special studies in the local church.

d) To promote advocacy in behalf of all the elderly, but especially those who do not have access to needed services because of isolation, low income, or handicap. (This might include advocacy for health care, income maintenance and other social legislation.)

e) To assist institutions for the elderly to maintain quality care and to develop resource centers for ministry with and by the elderly.

f) To create a variety of nonresidential ministries for the elderly, such as Shepherd's Centers.

g) To coordinate general Church training in ministry with the elderly.

h) To provide for formal coordination on aging issues.

i) To advocate the special concerns and needs of older women and minorities.

j) To utilize older persons as a creative resource bank in the design and implementation of these objectives.

4. Retirement and long-term care facilities related to the church are called upon:

a) To develop a covenant relationship with the church to reinforce a sense of joint mission in services with the elderly.

b) To encourage the provision of charitable support and provide a channel for the assistance of the whole church.

c) To encourage both residential and nonresidential institutional settings that emphasize the spiritual, personal, physical, and social needs of the elderly.

5. Seminaries and colleges are called upon:

a) To provide seminarians instruction on aging and experiences with older persons in the curriculum.

b) To prepare persons for careers in the field of aging.

c) To develop special professorships to teach gerontology, and to provide continuing education for those who work with the elderly.

d) To stimulate research on the problems of aging, special concerns of minorities, the status of the elderly, and ministries with the elderly, the majority of whom are women.

e) To enable the elderly to enroll in courses and degree programs and to participate generally in the life of educational institutions.

6. Finally, all levels of the church are called upon:

a) To include ministries for, with, and by the elderly as an essential component of the church and its mission.

b) To promote flexible retirement and eliminate mandatory retirement based solely on age.

c) To develop theological statements on death and dying that recognize the basic human right to die with dignity.

d) To develop ethical guidelines for dealing with difficult medical decisions that involve the use of limited resources for health and life insurance.

e) To authorize appropriate research, including a demographic study of members of The United Methodist Church, to provide greatly-needed information on the socio-religious aspects of aging.

f) To establish a properly-funded pension system with an adequate minimum standard for all clergy and church-employed lay persons and their spouses, including the divorced spouse.

V. Summary

Life in the later years has caused older persons to ask two questions: How can my life be maintained? What gives meaning and purpose to my life in these years? Both questions have religious implications.

Concern for older persons in the church is theologically grounded in the doctrine of Creation, in the meaning of God's work in Christ, in the response to grace that leads us into service, in the continuing value of older persons in the larger mission, and in the nature of the church as an agent of redemption and defender of justice for all.

Older adults in the United States deserve respect, dignity, and equal opportunity. The United Methodist Church is called to be an advocate for the elderly, for their sense of personal identity and dignity, for utilization of experience, wisdom and skills, for health maintenance, adequate income, educatonal opportunities, and vocational and avocational experiences in cooperation with the public and private sectors of society.

The graying of America implies also the graying of The United Methodist Church. The church, however, is called to be concerned, not only for its own, but also for all older people in our society.

As the aging process is part of God's plan of creation, with the good news of Christ's redemption giving hope and purpose to life, United Methodist people are called upon to help translate this message through words and deeds in the church and in society.

[1] *A Profile of Older Americans,* 1985 (AARP brochure).
[2] *Social Security Administration,* 1986. (Figure includes recipients of Railroad Retirement and Social Security benefits; it does not include SSI, or other disability related payments that are based on need and/or condition.)
[3] *The O.W.L. Observer: National Newspaper of the Older Women's League,* Special Edition: Women and Pensions, November 1985, p. 1.
[4] Nineteen eighty five *Bureau of Census, Poverty Report.*
[5] *Tomorrow's Elderly: A Report Prepared by The Congressional Clearinghouse of the Future,* House of Representatives, Ninety-Eighth Congress, October, 1984, p. 8.
[6] *Cut the Cost: Keep the Care: New Action Steps for 1986* (AARP brocure), p. 5.
[7] *The Prudent Patient: How to Get the Most for Your Health Care Dollar* (AARP booklet), p. 3.
[8] *Mortality Report, Divison of Vital Statistics* (National Center for Health Statistics).
[9] Nineteen eighty four *Bureau of Census Housing Report.*

ADOPTED 1988

See Social Principles, ¶ 72.E.

American Indian Religious Freedom Act

WHEREAS, tribal people have gone into the high places, lakes, and isolated sanctuaries to pray, receive guidance from God, and train younger people in the ceremonies that constitute the spiritual life of Native American communities; and

WHEREAS, when tribes were forcibly removed from their homelands and forced to live on restricted reservations, many of the ceremonies were prohibited; and

WHEREAS, most Indians do not see any conflict between their old beliefs and the new religion of the Christian church; and

WHEREAS, during this century, the expanding national population and the introduction of corporate farming and more extensive mining and timber industry activities reduced the isolation of rural America, making it difficult for small parties of Native Americans to go into the mountains or to remote lakes and buttes to conduct ceremonies without interference from non-Indians; and

WHEREAS, federal agencies began to restrict Indian access to sacred sites by establishing increasingly narrow rules and regulations for managing public lands; and

WHEREAS, in 1978, in an effort to clarify the status of traditional Native American religious practices and practitioners, Congress passed a Joint Resolution, entitled "The American Indian Religious Freedom Act," which declared that it was the policy of Congress to protect and preserve the inherent right of American Indians to believe, express, and practice their traditional religions; and

WHEREAS, today a major crisis exists in that there is no real protection for the practice of traditional Indian religions within the framework of American constitutional or statutory law, and courts usually automatically dismiss Indian petitions without evidentiary hearings; and

WHEREAS, while Congress has passed many laws which are designed to protect certain kinds of lands and resources for environmental and historic preservation, none of these laws are designed to protect the practice of Indian religion on sacred sites; and

WHEREAS, the only existing law directly addressing this issue, the American Indian Religious Freedom Act, is simply a policy which provides limited legal relief to aggrieved American Indian religious practitioners;

Therefore, be it resolved, that the General Board of Global Ministries and the General Board of Church and Society make available to the church information on the American Indian Religious Freedom Act; and

Be it further resolved, that the General Board of Church and Society support legislation which will provide for a legal cause of action when sacred sites may be affected by governmental action; proposed legislation should also provide for more extensive notice to and consultation with tribes and affected parties; and

Be it further resolved, that the General Board of Church and Society may enter and support court cases relating to the American Indian Religious Freedom Act; and

Be it further resolved, that the General Board of Church and Society communicate with the Senate Select Committee on Indian Affairs, declaring that the position of The United Methodist Church, expressed through the 1992 General Conference, is to strengthen the American Indian Religious Freedom Act of 1978 and preserve the God-given and constitutional rights of religious freedom for American Indians.

ADOPTED 1992

See Social Principles, ¶ 72, "Confession to Native Americans," "Rights of Native People of the Americas," "The United Methodist Church and America's Native People."

The United Methodist Church and America's Native People

Most white Americans are isolated from the issues of justice for the United States' native people by the lapse of time, the remoteness of reservations or native territories and the comparative invisibility of natives in the urban setting, the distortions in historical accounts, and the accumulation of prejudices. Now is the time for a new beginning and The United Methodist Church calls its members to pray and work for that new day in relationship between native peoples, other minorities, and white Americans.

The United States has been forced to become more sharply aware and keenly conscious of the destructive impact of the unjust acts and injurious policies of the United States government upon the lives and culture of U.S. American Indians, Alaskan and Hawaiian natives. In the past the white majority population was allowed to forget or excuse the wrongs which were done to the indigenous peoples of this land. Today, U.S. American Indians, Alaskan and Hawaiian natives are speaking with a new and more unified voice, causing both the government and the American people to re-examine the actions of the past and to assume responsibility for the conditions of the present.

A clear appeal is being made for a fresh and reliable expression of justice. The call is being made for a new recognition of the unique rights which were guaranteed in perpetuity of U.S. American Indians by the treaties and legal agreements which were solemnly signed by official representatives of the United States government. A plea is being raised regarding the disruption of Alaskan and Hawaiian natives who were not granted the legal agreements protecting their culture and land base.

The time has come for the American people to be delivered from beliefs which gave support to the false promises and faulty policies which prevailed in the relations of the United States government with U.S. America's native peoples. These beliefs asserted that:

1. White Europeans who came to this continent were ordained by God to possess its land and utilize its resources.
2. Natives were not good stewards of the environment, permitting nature to lie in waste, as they roamed from place to place living off the land.
3. The growing white population tamed nature and subdued the natives and thus gave truth to the assumption that the white race is superior.
4. The forceful displacement of the natives was a necessary and justifiable step in the development of a free land and a new country.
5. The white explorers and pioneers brought civilization to the natives and generously bestowed upon them a higher and better way of life.

Rarely are these beliefs now so blatantly set forth, yet they are subtly assumed and furnish the continuing foundation upon which unjust and injurious policies of the government are based.

These beliefs, in former times, permitted the government, on the one hand, to seize lands, uproot families, break up tribal communities, and undermine the authority of traditional chiefs. On the other hand, the beliefs enabled the government to readily make and easily break treaties, give military protection to those who encroached on native lands, distribute as "free" land millions of acres of native holdings which the government designated as being "surplus," and systematically slay those natives who resisted such policies and practices.

In our own time these beliefs have encouraged the government to:

1. Generally asume the incompetence of natives in the management and investment of their own resources.
2. Give highly favorable leasing arrangements to white mining companies, grain farmers, and cattle ranchers for the use of native lands held in trust by the federal government or historically used as supportive land base.

3. Use job training and other government programs to encourage the relocation of natives from reservations or native territories to urban areas.

4. Utilize government funds in projects which are divisive to the tribal or native membership and through procedures which co-opt native leadership.

5. Extend the control of state government over native nations which are guaranteed federal protection.

6. Terminate federal services and protection to selected native nations and further deny federal recognition to others.

7. Engage in extensive and expensive litigation as a means of delaying and thus nullifying treaty rights and aboriginal land claims.

8. Pay minimal monetary claims for past illegal confiscation of land and other native resources.

9. Lump together United States natives with other racial minorities as a tactic for minimizing the unique rights of native peoples.

10. Punitively prosecute the native leaders who vigorously challenge the policies of the federal government.

The Church is called to repentance, for it bears a heavy responsibility for spreading false beliefs and for unjust governmental policies and practices. The preaching of the gospel to America's natives was often a preparation for assimilation into white culture. The evangelizing of the native nations often effected the policies of the government.

The Church has frequently benefitted from the distribution of native lands and other resources. The Church often saw the injustices inflicted upon native peoples but gave assent or remained silent, believing that its task was to "convert" the heathen.

The Church is called through the mercy of Almighty God to become a channel of the reconciling Spirit of Jesus Christ and an instrument of love and justice in the development of new relations between native nations, other minorities, and whites, in pursuit of the protection of their rights.

The United Methodist Church recognizes that a new national commitment is needed to respect and effect the rights of American Indians, Alaskan and Hawaiian natives to claim their own identities, maintain their cultures, live their lives, and use their resources.

The United Methodist Church expresses its desire and declares its intention to participate in the renewal of the national responsibility to U.S. America's native people.

The United Methodist Church calls its congregations to study the issues concerning American Indian, Alaskan and Hawaiian native relations with the government of the United States; to develop an understanding of the distinctive cultures and the unique rights of the native people of the United States; to establish close contacts wherever possible with native persons, tribes and nations; and to furnish support for:

1. The right of native people to live as native people in this country.
2. The right of native people to be self-determining and to make their own decisions related to the use of their lands and the natural resources found on and under them.
3. The right of native people to plan for a future in this nation and to expect a fulfillment of the commitments which have been made previously by the government, as well as equitable treatment of those who were not afforded legal protection for their culture and lands.
4. The right of American Indian nations to exercise the sovereignty of nationhood, consistent with treaty provisions.
5. The right of Alaskan natives to maintain a subsistence land base and aboriginal rights to its natural resources.
6. The right of native Hawaiians to a just and amicable settlement with the United States through federal legislation related to aboriginal title to Hawaiian lands and their natural resources.

The United Methodist Church especially calls its congregations to support the needs and aspirations of America's native peoples as they struggle for their survival and the maintenance of the integrity of their culture in a world intent upon their assimilation, westernization, and absorption of their lands and the termination of their traditional ways of life.

Moreover, we call upon our nation, in recognition of the significant cultural attainments of the native peoples in ecology, conservation, human relations, and other areas of human endeavor, to receive their cultural gifts as part of the emerging new life and culture of our nation.

In directing specific attention to the problems of native peoples in the United States, we do not wish to ignore the plight of native people in many other countries of the world.

*Note: This statement was reaffirmed by the 1984 General Conference.

ADOPTED 1980

See Social Principles, ¶ 72.A., "Confession to Native Americans," "Toward a New Beginning Beyond 1992," "American Indian Religious Freedom Act," "Native American Representation in The United Methodist Church," "Rights of Native People of the Americas."

Anna Howard Shaw Day

WHEREAS, The United Methodist Church, a union of several branches sharing a common historical and spiritual heritage, affirms "the importance of women in decision-making positions at all levels of church life"; and

WHEREAS, Barbara Heck and a slave girl named Betty helped form a Methodist society in New York in the fall of 1766; and

WHEREAS, although women class leaders and "exhorters" were part of Methodism from the beginning, it was not until 1847 that the United Brethren in Christ gave Charity Opheral a "vote of commendation" to engage in public speaking and then licensed Lydia Sexton to preach in 1851, and it was not until 1869 that Margaret (Maggie) Newton Van Cott became the first woman officially to be licensed to preach in the Methodist Protestant Church; and

WHEREAS, the Woman's Foreign Missionary Society of the Methodist Episcopal Church was formed in Boston in 1869 and, beginning with Isabella Thoburn and Dr. Clara Swain who went to India in 1870 as the first missionaries, a stream of women from all branches of United Methodism have ministered throughout the world; and

WHEREAS, Anna Snow Den Oliver and Anna Howard Shaw, first women graduates of Boston University School of Theology, were not able to be ordained under the provisions of the 1876 *Discipline* of the Methodist Episcopal Church but Anna Howard Shaw was ordained in the Methodist Protestant Church in 1880; and

WHEREAS, the 1880 General Conference of the Methodist Episcopal Church withdrew approval of the licensing of women as local preachers, not to be granted again until 1920; and

WHEREAS, Frances E. Willard and four other women were elected as delegates to the 1888 General Conference of the Methodist Episcopal Church but were denied seats; and

WHEREAS, in 1889 the General Conference approved the ordination of women and, at the 1890 Michigan Annual Conference, Mrs. L. J. Batdorf and Mrs. S. A. Lane were ordained and admitted to the itinerant ministry; and

WHEREAS, in 1895 a Mrs. Hartman from Oregon was acclaimed as "the first female member of an Evangelical Annual Conference"; and

WHEREAS, Bell Harris Bennett, educator and missionary advocate, worked diligently in the Methodist Episcopal Church, South, to gain full lay rights for women, approved in 1922; and

WHEREAS, Georgia Harkness, recognized in 1947 as "one of the 10 most outstanding Methodists in America" and the first woman to be a professor of theology at a Methodist seminary, was one of the major champions of equal clergy rights for women; and

WHEREAS, the 1956 General Conference of The Methodist Church did approve equal rights and privileges so that today "both men and women are included in all provisions of the Discipline which refer to the ordained ministry" (¶ 412.2), and Maud Keister Jensen of Northern New Jersey became the first woman to become a clergy member of an annual conference under the new provision; and

WHEREAS, it was not until 1967 that a woman was appointed a District Superintendent of the Maine Annual Conference; and

WHEREAS, The United Methodist Church did establish new professional standards for ordained ministry in 1968 which made it possible for the eventual 1980 election of the first woman bishop, Marjorie Swank Matthews, to be followed in 1984 by Leontine T. Kelly and Judith Craig, and in 1988 by Susan Murch Morrison and Sharon A. Brown Christopher; and

WHEREAS, in 1989 Anna Snowden Oliver and Anna Howard Shaw were elected posthumously as full members of the Southern New England Conference; and

WHEREAS, during her lifetime Anna Howard Shaw, S.T.B., M.D., ministered to the physical, emotional, and spiritual need of disadvantaged mothers and children, organized and lectured for the causes of temperance and women's suffrage, and sought for political solutions for the problems of women throughout the world; and

WHEREAS, Anna Howard Shaw was the best-known clergywoman in the world at the turn of the century so that, at the time of her death in 1919, *The New York Times* would say that she was "an American with the measureless patience, the deep and gentle humor, the whimsical and tolerant philosophy, and the dauntless courage, physical as well as moral, which we find most satisfyingly displayed in Lincoln, of all our heroes";

Therefore, because Methodism has been in the forefront against discrimination of any kind, and Anna Howard Shaw has become a role model for women in mission and ministry:

1) each local United Methodist church around the world may set aside an "Anna Howard Shaw Day" annually as a time to remember the continuing struggles of "women and men to be equal in every aspect of their common life";

2) this shall be communicated each year through United Methodist publications; and

3) appropriate agencies shall plan for the 150th anniversary of Anna Howard Shaw's birth on February 14, 1997.

ADOPTED 1992

See Social Principles, ¶ 72.F, "Equal Rights of Women," "Goals and Recommendations on Participation of Women," "The Status of Women."

Annual Accessibility Audit

WHEREAS, our Social Principles state, "We affirm the responsibility of the Church and society to be in ministry with all persons, including those persons with mentally, physically and/or psychologically handicapping conditions"; and

WHEREAS, the Americans with Disabilities Act calls for all public buildings to be made accessible to persons with handicapping conditions;

Therefore, be it resolved, that all United Methodist churches shall conduct an annual audit of their facilities to discover what barriers impede full participation of persons with handicapping conditions. Plans shall be made and priorities determined for the elimination of all barriers including architectural, communication, and attitudinal barriers. The Accessibility Audit for Churches, available from the Service Center, shall be used in filling out the annual church/charge conference reports.

ADOPTED 1992

See Social Principles, ¶ 72.G, "Barrier-Free Construction for the Handicapped," "The Church and Persons with Mentally, Physically, and/or Psychologically Handicapping Conditions."

Appointment of Clergy to Rural Ministry

WHEREAS, The United Methodist Church seeks to affirm individuals in the exercise of their God-given gifts and areas of expertise; and

WHEREAS, there are unique differences in the needs, struggles, and strengths or urban, suburban, and rural communities; and

WHEREAS, primary emphasis in the form of funding and the appointment of experienced and well-trained pastors tends to focus on urban and suburban settings; and

WHEREAS, the 1988 *Book of Discipline* (¶ 532) states that "appointments shall take into account the unique needs of a charge in a particular setting and also the gifts and evidences of God's grace of a particular pastor";

Therefore, be it resolved, that pastors who have the unique gifts, training, experience, and interests needed to serve rural churches and communities creatively and effectively shall be appointed to rural assignments; and

Be it further resolved, that pastors assigned to rural appointments shall be equitably and adequately compensated for their work of ministry.

ADOPTED 1992

See Social Principles, ¶ 72.M, "An Affirmation of Basic Rural Worth," "The Church's Response to Changing Rural Issues," "Rural Chaplaincy as a Ministry of Laity and Clergy."

Available and Affordable Housing

The lack of available and affordable housing leads not only to economic hardship and instability but also to a sense of hopelessness among families and individuals who must live without the security and well-being that comes with a home to call their own.

The church's interest in housing has been linked historically with its concern for alleviating poverty. One part of the United Methodists' efforts to eradicate poverty and to provide a decent standard of living for all persons has focused on better housing in both rural and urban settings.

All persons are equally valuable in God's sight. When persons are denied access to, or opportunity for, decent housing, their humanity is diminished. The Bible in the Old and New Testaments correlates the term *house* with identity, security, protection, power, and authority.

House becomes more than a dwelling place; it is a space where rootage can take hold and where personal history begins and ends.

Therefore, God's vision of the new creation for human beings includes the affirmations to the effect that [all persons] shall live in the houses they build (Isa. 65:21a), and even the birds and foxes have places that they call their own (Matt. 8:20).

A dwelling place becomes an inherent part of God's design for the creation in which human beings are an important part. Housing may be understood to be the means of preserving and protecting the human body which is characterized by the Apostle Paul as the Temple of God.

The need for adequate housing at affordable costs is critical. Millions of families around the world huddle together in densely overcrowded apartments, rural shacks, ancient house trailers, converted warehouses, and condemned or abandoned buildings. Because the remainder of us fail to recognize their plight or simply do not care enough, millions live in adequate housing that lacks such necessities as running water or plumbing, through no fault of their own. Still others, many of whom are children, have no shelter at all. While The United Methodist Church affirms the pervasive powers of families as "creators of persons, proclaimers of faith perspectives and shapers of both present and future society," it must continue its condemnation of policies that ignore the causal relationship between shortages of low-income housing and the lack of political will to ensure that safe and affordable housing is available to all.

Whatever the form of community organization, housing protection, management, or ownership of a housing project, every effort should be made at each developmental step to ensure that those who are being aided are afforded the opportunity, and indeed required, to take every action necessary to direct the undertaking. Recognizing housing conditions and needs over time has brought about trends which cannot be ignored. Only through concrete actions and a commitment to the goal of fit, livable, and affordable housing will we begin to see the demise of unfit conditions and increased rates of home ownership. The time has come to take steps to promote the more equitable distribution of wealth and resources so that a decent place for a family to live becomes the foundation for dignity and self-respect.

The religious community has a vital role to play in offering hope to those who see no reason for hope in their future. The United Methodist Church has been actively involved in social issues since its beginnings. As a significant presence in local communities, churches can make an impact in the area of affordable housing in the following ways:

1. Using volunteers who have technical expertise in the building and renovation of physical structures. Such volunteers must be committed to the hours of hard work and paperwork that housing ministries demand.

2. Funding projects and pooling resources to create, maintain, and improve affordable housing while improving the community. Members with experience in finance, construction, and advocacy work can be especially helpful in tackling the issue of affordable housing.

3. Providing the widest possible range of supportive assistance to individuals, congregations, districts, conferences, and all forms of interfaith and cooperative groups sharing similar goals and policies so that our fellow citizens may achieve as their right safe, sanitary, and affordable housing as soon as possible.

Within the United States, we urge:

1. *Community organizing.* Church members are urged to contact national religious and secular organizations dealing with affordable housing to become familiar with opportunities for specific ministries and to advocate adequate affordable housing. Newsletters, fact sheets, and other resources are available from religious and secular agencies and organizations, including every level of government, business, and housing producers.

2. *Advocacy.* On the basis of sound facts and ethical concerns, individual members or church groups in the United States should write to government leaders in support of programs that would guarantee fair housing practices, provide more low-cost housing units, include units for rural residents and farm workers, prevent activities that would eliminate low-cost housing, and urge adequate funding for provisions under the National Affordable Housing Act of 1990 to provide more low-cost housing units such as by modular construction techniques.

3. *Prophetic role/denouncing.* Of great importance for providing nongovernmental funding are provisions of the Community Reinvestment Act as they affect banks and savings and loan institutions in

the local community. Lending institutions that continue to discriminate against certain neighborhoods and communities in lending and financing should be challenged by churches and neighborhood organizations regarding practices that mirror past racial and geographical redlining procedures.

4. *Sensitizing*. Churches can take a lead in raising consciousness around the issues of affordable housing and homelessness. Many local agencies are in need of volunteers to conduct testing for fair housing. Opportunities are available for forming community trust funds and cooperative housing agreements that can provide financing and organizational opportunities for individuals or communities in need.

5. *Creating alternatives*. Congregations can even take on individual building or renovation projects. We offer praise to the Salkehatchie Summer Service sponsored by the South Carolina Conference Board of Missions. This program, which includes high school and college-age youth and adult community leaders, is engaged in upgrading housing and motivating people to help themselves. The Kentucky Mountain Housing Corporation of Morefield, Kentucky, and Camp Hope of First United Methodist Church, Frostburg, Maryland, are other innovative housing ministries congregations can emulate.

Hundreds of local church volunteers and millions of dollars in financial aid are needed annually to construct affordable housing in many countries around the world.

In response to the housing needs of our world community we urge that United Methodists use resources such as:

1. General Advance Specials which provide an appropriate way to channel financial resources.

2. The General Board of Global Ministries Volunteers in Mission Program which provides appropriate opportunities for volunteers to work side by side with people as they seek to achieve improved living conditions.

3. Habitat for Humanity and the Cooperative Housing Foundation which have proven records of success. Both provide many opportunities in more than 25 developing countries for sharing in similar self-help partnership efforts to develop quality affordable housing with those who need it desperately.

4. We also urge that government, labor, and economic resources which are too often directed toward involvement in efforts of war and other destructive endeavors be utilized instead to build communities, assist in development, and bring modern technologies to destitute situations around the world.

Adequate human shelter is a primary goal for ministry of all who accept John Wesley's challenge that the world is our parish.

ADOPTED 1992

See Social Principles, ¶ 72, and "Housing."

Ban on Alcohol Beverage Advertisements

WHEREAS, alcohol is the number one drug of abuse in the United States; costs associated with alcohol use/abuse are more than the costs associated with all illegal drugs combined; and

WHEREAS, the use/abuse of alcohol is closely associated with the two leading causes of death among adolescents (suicide and motor vehicle accidents); and

WHEREAS, chronic alcohol consumption causes damage to many body organs, including brain, liver, heart, stomach, intestines, mouth; and

WHEREAS, even in moderate amounts, alcohol can interfere with learning and impair physical coordination, including driving ability; and

WHEREAS, fetal alcohol syndrome is one of the most common causes of mental retardation, cardiac defects, pre- and postnatal growth retardation, and other abnormalities among infants;

Therefore, we petition that those responsible ban any alcoholic beverage advertisements from television or radio transmissions. We feel this is a logical step in the national "War on Drugs" commitment that is long overdue.

ADOPTED 1992

See Social Principles, ¶ 72.I, "Drug and Alcohol Concerns," "Education on Alcohol and Substance Abuse."

Barrier-Free Construction for the Handicapped

Be it resolved, that Church monies from agencies of The United Methodist Church beyond the local church be granted, loaned, or otherwise provided only for the construction of church sanctuaries, educational buildings, parsonages, camps, colleges, or other church-related agencies or facilities that meet minimum guidelines in their plans for barrier-free construction.

That local churches utilizing their own funds or funds secured through lending agencies and institutions beyond The United Methodist Church be urged to make adequate provision in their plans to insure that all new church buildings shall be of barrier-free construction.

That local churches be urged to adapt existing facilities, through such programs as widening doorways, installing ramps and elevators, eliminating stairs where possible, providing handrails, adequate parking facilities, and rest rooms so that handicapped persons may take their appropriate place in the fellowship of the church.

That the appropriate national agencies provide technical information for local churches to assist in providing barrier-free facilities.

ADOPTED 1980

See Social Principles, ¶ 72.G, "Accessibility of Meeting Places Beyond the Local Church," "The Church and Persons with Mentally, Physically and/or Psychologically Handicapping Conditions."

Black Church Growth

WHEREAS, Black Americans are becoming the new residents in transitional communities, and represent an excellent opportunity to plant new churches in established communities utilizing existing buildings;

Therefore, be it resolved, that The United Methodist Church address racial transition as a model for building Black churches by providing denominational resources and pastors to cultivate and promote Black church growth;

Be it further resolved, that each annual conference identify a test group of Black clergy/laity and empower the Boards of Discipleship and Higher Education and Ministry to train these selected persons for effective leadership in local churches, utilizing the most capable resource persons across denominational lines.

ADOPTED 1992

See Social Principles, ¶ 72, "Black Leadership," "Resourcing Black Churches in Urban Communities," "Strengthening the Black Church for the 21st Century," "Support to Strengthen Ethnic Minority Local Church."

Black Leadership

Be it resolved, that The United Methodist Church in all of its annual conferences will actively seek to identify Black clergy and laity for leadership positions at the local, district, annual conference, jurisdictional, and general church levels. Such active identification may be accomplished through:

- The conducting of district leadership training seminars to which at least three members of each predominantly Black church has been invited;
- The establishment of a "mentor system" in which an effective Black leader would become a mentor to a potential Black leader and would encourage and assist that person into the full development of his or her leadership skills;
- The frequent fellowshipping of racial/ethnic congregations leading to an understanding and knowledge of racial differences;
- Bishops and district superintendents actively choosing Black United Methodists to fill appointive positions in the district, annual conference, jurisdictional, and general church levels.

ADOPTED 1992

See Social Principles, ¶ 72.A, "Strengthening the Black Church for the 21st Century," "Resourcing Black Churches in Urban Communities."

Call to the Bishops to Undergird Cooperative Parish Ministry

WHEREAS, cooperative parish ministry is a style of ministry by which laity can participate in and take ownership of ministry and mission, and also is a way for pastors to give and receive support from colleagues in ministry; and

WHEREAS, cooperative parish ministry is a way through which groups of churches, with the guidance of the Holy Spirit, intentionally and intensively witness to the unity of the Church in Christ through more effective responses to both local and global issues and needs; and

WHEREAS, cooperative parish ministry is a way for churches, especially small membership churches, in rural and urban settings, to remain viable and to develop what can be done better together than alone; and

WHEREAS, the bishops, laity, and clergy present at the Third National Consultation on Cooperative Parish Ministries, which met in November of 1991, affirmed cooperative ministry as one of the primary forms of ministry for United Methodism at the present time and in the future; and

WHEREAS, those present at the consultation emphasized the need for all bishops to provide specific leadership for cooperative ministries within their episcopal areas; and

WHEREAS, those present at the consultation also stressed the need for the development of recommendations as to how connectional agencies of the Church can undergird cooperative ministries;

Therefore, be it resolved, that the Council of Bishops be called on to develop recommendations to enable the implementation of United Methodist and ecumenical cooperative ministries, and to urge the implementation of their recommendations by annual conference and general church boards and agencies; and

Further, be it resolved, that the Council of Bishops be called on to create a continuing process for the training and regular updating of bishops and district superintendents regarding the cooperative parish ministry paradigm; and

Also, be it further resolved, that all bishops be called on to give attention within their cabinets to developing organizational structures and processes that will facilitate more effective appointment making to cooperative ministries.

ADOPTED 1992

See Social Principles, ¶ 72, "Considering Community Contexts in the Appointment-Making Process."

Celebrate and Support the Ongoing Work of the General Commission on the Status and Role of Women

Progress has been made by the General Commission on the Status and Role of Women toward eliminating sexism in our church from 1975 to 1992.

The United Methodist Church is committed to inclusiveness in our church; but females and males are not yet equally represented in policy- and decision-making bodies, especially in administration and finance.[1]

The United Methodist Church stands in opposition to the sin of sexual harassment in our church and in society;[2] however, sexual harassment in our church continues to victimize both females and males, both clergy and laity.[3]

Be it resolved that The United Methodist Church:
- celebrate the twentieth anniversary of the General Commission's efforts to be advocate, catalyst, and monitor for a gender-inclusive church;
- affirm the work and the necessity for the continuance of the General Commission in its ministry;
- support the work being done by the General Commission throughout the entire church to educate United Methodists in understanding and responding to the issues of sexual harassment through training, resources, policies, and procedures; and
- support the work and funding of the General Commission to strengthen effective participation and insure equitable representation of female in policy- and decision-making positions at all levels in our church as encouraged by United Methodist disciplinary guidelines.

ADOPTED 1992

---

[1]"Survey on the Participation of Women in the Local Church." General Commission on the Status and Role of Women, 1991.
[2]"Sexual Harassment in Church and Society in the U.S.A." (See p. 446.)
[3]"Sexual Harassment in The United Methodist Church." Office of Research, General Council on Ministries, November 1990.

See Social Principles, ¶ 72, "Sexual Harassment and The United Methodist Church," "Sexual Harassment in Church and Society in the U.S.A."

Celebrate and Affirm the Work of General Commission on Religion and Race

WHEREAS, The United Methodist Church is committed to the elimination of racism and to incarnate the inclusive community of God; and

WHEREAS, the journey for racial inclusiveness has been long but also rewarding; barriers have come down and accomplishments have taken place since the establishment of the General Commission on Religion and Race; and

WHEREAS, the denomination has begun to express the diversity of God's people in general agencies, the Council of Bishops, theological seminaries, and annual conference leadership; and

WHEREAS, the task is far from being completed: racism is still very much alive in our midst—not only in society but in our own church's bosom; attitudes and ingrained racial beliefs are still at work in annual conferences, church schools and institutions, and most certainly in the local church; and

WHEREAS, the journey toward the elimination of racism and toward an inclusive church has taken us to a crucial and challenging point: to live and embody the true community of God where diversity is affirmed and shapes the Body who from many is one; and

WHEREAS, this is the moment when the presence of Asians and Pacific Islanders, Blacks, Hispanics, and Native Americans in our denomination needs to go beyond presence in order to make a difference in our life together—a difference that will make our denomination a vital, powerful, diverse, and inclusive church—a difference that will affect our worship style, management, appointment system, programs, budgets, and the entire church structure;

Therefore, let it be known, that the 1992 General Conference celebrates the ministry of the General Commission on Religion and Race, affirms its function and mission, and commits itself to continue struggling against racism and institutional racism.

ADOPTED 1992

See Social Principles, ¶ 72.A, "Affirmative Action," "Elimination of Racism in The United Methodist Church," "Eradication of Racism."

Celebrating 100 Years of Lay Education in the Tradition of Scarritt-Bennett Center

WHEREAS, the Woman's Board of (Foreign) Missions of the Methodist Episcopal Church, South, in 1888 resolved that the matter of a training school for missionaries should be investigated by naming Miss Belle Harris Bennett its agent and provided the necessary credentials to enlist the sympathy and aid of the workers and to collect funds and to report results to the board; and

WHEREAS, in 1890 the General Conference and Woman's Board of (Foreign) Missions both met in St. Louis and resolved the establishment of a Bible and Training School under the auspices, control, and management of the Woman's Board, for the education of missionaries and other Christian workers; and

WHEREAS, on September 14, 1892, the Scarritt Bible and Training School was opened in Kansas City, Mo., moving to Nashville in 1924 and becoming Scarritt College for Christian Workers, becoming Scarritt Graduate School in 1981; and

WHEREAS, the creation of the office of deaconess by the Methodist Episcopal Church, South, in 1902 expanded Scarritt's role in the preparation and training of lay workers in the church; and

Whereas, Scarritt carried forward the tradition and interests of the Methodist Training Institute founded by Bishop Walter Lambuth, Methodist Episcopal Church, South; and of the National College, founded by the Woman's Home Missionary Society of the Methodist Episcopal Church; and

Whereas, Scarritt has continually led the way in educational innovation, having the first departments of sociology, anthropology, and missions in the Nashville university system; and

Whereas, graduates of these various institutions in this tradition are now serving the church, educational institutions, social service agencies, and many other arenas of work in many states and countries; and

Whereas, buildings at the Scarritt-Bennett Center are named to honor women who have given major leadership in the church, such as: Maria Layng Gibson, Belle Harris Bennett, Maria Davis Wightman, Grace L. Bragg, Anna Ogburn, Virginia Davis Laskey and Susie Gray; and

Whereas, the Women's Division as successor to the Women's Board of (Foreign) Missions has been related to Scarritt since Belle Bennett first proposed her "vision" of a training school for women; and

Whereas, The Scarritt Foundation is successor to the Scarritt Graduate School; and

Whereas, a partnership between the Scarritt Foundation and the Women's Division of The United Methodist Church has resulted in a lay training program called the Scarritt-Bennett Center; and

Whereas, the Scarritt-Bennett Center Board of Directors held its organizational meeting on November 10-11, 1988, and is functioning with a Mission Statement which says:

> The Scarritt-Bennett Center shall be a place of education for Christian ministries of justice and equality, reconciliation and renewal, cooperation and interaction within the ecumenical and global context. Rooted in mission, the Center shall have a strong commitment to the eradication of racism, the empowerment of women, the education of the laity and spiritual formation.

Be it resolved, that the General Conference of The United Methodist Church in session in Louisville, Kentucky, May 5-15, 1992, commemorates this 100 years of lay training in the Scarritt tradition by:

1) Recognizing all present at this General Conference who are Scarritt

graduates, former students, and faculty, or members of the Board of Trustees.

2) Sending greeting to the International Celebration of 100 Years of Lay Training to be held at the Scarritt-Bennett Center in Nashville, November 14, 1992, and September 18, 1993.

3) Encouraging the use of the Scarritt-Bennett Center conference facilities by all boards and agencies requiring space for meetings and workshops.

ADOPTED 1992

See Social Principles, ¶ 72.

A Charter for Racial Justice Policies in an Interdependent Global Community

Racism is the belief that one race is innately superior to all other races. In the United States, this belief has justified the conquest, enslavement, and evangelizing of non-Europeans. During the early history of this country, Europeans assumed that their civilization and religion were innately superior to those of both the original inhabitants of the United States and the Africans who were forcibly brought to these shores to be slaves. The myth of European superiority persisted and persists. Other people who came and who are still coming to the United States by choice or force encountered and encounter racism. Some of these people are the Chinese who built the railroads as indentured workers; the Mexicans whose lands were annexed; the Puerto Ricans, the Cubans, the Hawaiians, and the Eskimos who were colonized; and the Filipinos, the Jamaicans, and the Haitians who lived on starvation wages as farm workers.

In principle, the United States has outlawed racial discrimination but, in practice, little has changed. Social, economic, and political institutions still discriminate, although some institutions have amended their behavior by eliminating obvious discriminatory practices and choosing their language carefully. The institutional church, despite sporadic attempts to the contrary, also still discriminates.

The damage of years of exploitation has not been erased. A system designed to meet the needs of one segment of the population cannot be the means to the development of a just society for all. The racist system in the United States today perpetuates the power and control of those of European ancestry. It is often called "White racism." The fruits of racism are prejudice, bigotry, discrimination, and dehumanization. Consistently, Blacks, Hispanics, Asians, Native Americans, and Pacific Islanders have been humiliated by being given inferior jobs, housing, education, medical services, transportation, and public accommodation. With hopes deferred and rights still denied, the deprived and oppressed fall prey to a colonial mentality which acquiesces to the inequities, occasionally with religious rationalization.

Racist presuppositions have been implicit in U.S. attitudes and policies toward Asia, Africa, the Middle East, and Latin America. While proclaiming democracy, freedom, and independence, the U.S. has been an ally and an accomplice to perpetuating inequality of the races and colonialism throughout the world. The history of The United Methodist Church and the history of the United States are intertwined. The "mission enterprise" of the churches in the United States and "westernization" went hand in hand, sustaining a belief in their superiority.

We are conscious that "we have sinned as our ancestors did: we have been wicked and evil" (Psalm 106:6, Today's English Version). We are called for a renewed commitment to the elimination of institutional racism. We affirm the 1976 General Conference Statement on The United Methodist Church and Race, which states unequivocally: "By biblical and theological precept, by the law of the Church, by General Conference pronouncement, and by episcopal expression, the matter is clear. With respect to race, the aim of The United Methodist Church is nothing less than an inclusive church in an inclusive society. The United Methodist Church, therefore, calls upon all its people to perform those faithful deeds of love and justice in both the church and community that will bring this aim into reality."

Because We Believe

1. that God is the Creator of all people and all are God's children in one family;
2. that racism is a rejection of the teachings of Jesus Christ;
3. that racism denies the redemption and reconciliation of Jesus Christ;
4. that racism robs all human beings of their wholeness and is used as a justification for social, economic, and political exploitation;

5. that we must declare before God and before each other that we have sinned against our sisters and brothers of other races in thought, in word, and in deed;

6. that in our common humanity in creation all women and men are made in God's image and all persons are equally valuable in the sight of God;

7. that our strength lies in our racial and cultural diversity and that we must work toward a world in which each person's value is respected and nurtured;

8. that our struggle for justice must be based on new attitudes, new understandings, and new relationships, and must be reflected in the laws, policies, structures, and practices of both church and state;

We commit ourselves as individuals and as a community to follow Jesus Christ in word and in deed and to struggle for the rights and the self-determination of every person and group of persons. Therefore, as United Methodists in every place across the land we will unite our efforts within The United Methodist Church:

1. to eliminate all forms of institutional racism in the total ministry of the Church, giving special attention to those institutions which we support, beginning with their employment policies, purchasing practices, and availability of services and facilities;

2. to create opportunities in local churches to deal honestly with the existing racist attitudes and social distance between members, deepening the Christian commitment to be the Church where all racial groups and economic classes come together;

3. to increase efforts to recruit people of all races into the membership of The United Methodist Church and provide leadership development opportunities without discrimination;

4. to create workshops and seminars in local churches to study, understand, and appreciate the historical and cultural contributions of each race to the Church and community;

5. to increase local churches' awareness of the continuing needs for equal education, housing, employment, and medical care for all members of the community and to create opportunities to work for these things across racial lines;

6. to work for the development and implementation of national and international policies to protect the civil, political, economic, social,

and cultural rights of all people such as through support for the ratification of United Nations covenants on human rights;

7. to support and participate in the world-wide struggle for liberation in church and community;

8. to support nomination and election processes which include all racial groups employing a quota system until the time that our voluntary performance makes such practice unnecessary.

ADOPTED 1980

See Social Principles, ¶ 72.A, "Global Racism," "Eradication of Racism," "Elimination of Racism in The United Methodist Church," "Racial Harassment," and a number of other resolutions in "The Social Community" dealing with aspects of racial justice.

Church and Community Workers, 1988

WHEREAS, during the past quadrennium the National Division of the General Board of Global Ministries has shown commendable progress in financially supporting and in deploying additional church and community workers to serve as national missionaries of the church; and

WHEREAS, for many years Church and Community Ministry has proven itself to be an effective response of national missionary outreach for The United Methodist Church in rural areas that have needed caring and creative leadership; and

WHEREAS, church and community workers as 'national' missionaries have numerous skills that have enriched Christian ministry in town and country communities where personal, family, and community crises have existed; and

WHEREAS, rural America continues to be in great transition due to crises being faced by family farmers, the loss of industrial employment opportunities, and the break up of rural communities;

Therefore, be it resolved that the General Conference direct the National Division through the General Board of Global Ministries to increase the number of church and community workers; and

Be it further resolved that special attention be given to assigning church and community workers to work closely with cooperative parish ministries and districts in order to provide leadership, ministering skills, and other supports to:

—local churches located in rural communities that are experiencing high levels of transition;

—the 'new' poor in rural communities;

—the initiation of economic development alternatives; and

Be it further resolved that the National Division make every effort to raise the salary of the church and community workers to a more commensurate level.

ADOPTED 1988

See Social Principles, ¶ 72.N, "Church and Community Workers 1992."

Church and Community Workers, 1992

Be it resolved, that the 1992 General Conference of The United Methodist Church commend the National Program Division of the General Board of Global Ministries for its continuing support of Church and Community Ministry, and offer grateful recognition to these church and community workers; and

Be it further resolved, that congregations be encouraged to enter covenant relationship agreements in support of these national mission workers as Mission Link partners; and

Be it further resolved, that the National Program Division be requested to enlarge the number and expand the deployment of church and community workers, giving special consideration to cooperative parishes of various types, community development opportunities, relief of human need, ministries seeking human justice, and economic development efforts; and

Be it further resolved, that the National Program Division be urged to increase support for church and community workers to a level more commensurate with their valuable contributions to the ministry of the church.

ADOPTED 1992

See Social Principles, ¶ 72.N, "Church and Community Workers, 1988."

The Church and Persons with Mentally, Physically, and/or Psychologically Handicapping Conditions

We call United Methodists to a new birth of awareness of the need to accept, include, receive the gifts of and respond to the concerns of those persons with mentally, physically, and/or psychologically handicapping conditions, including their families.

Because the experience of handicapping conditions is included in all racial, social, sexual, and age groupings, and this experience is common to every family and at some time in every life;

And because a large part of the ministry of our Lord focused on persons with mentally, physically, and/or psychologically handicapping conditions;

And because the Body of Christ is not complete without people of all areas of life;

And because we cannot afford to deny ourselves fellowship with these persons and must intentionally develop more healthy attitudes and behavioral responses to persons with handicapping conditions;

And because there exist inadequacies in the church and in society with regard to concerns for the rights of persons with handicapping conditions, utilization of talents, and their full participation within the life of the church and society;

And because of more suffering and exclusion from the fellowship of the church of persons with mentally, physically, and/or psychologically handicapping conditions;

And believing that the church is most faithful to the teachings and example of Jesus when it expresses love in concrete ways in a mutual ministry with those who are outcasts, neglected, avoided, or persecuted by society;

And believing in the legacy of John Wesley, Phillip Otterbein and Jacob Albright who held that vital piety flows into compassionate ministry;

And knowing that prevailing societal norms unduly glorify the conditions of youthful beauty, mental alertness, and material affluence to the exclusion and avoidance of those whose handicapping conditions put them outside these norms.

Therefore, we pledge ourselves to:

Accessibility

• Renew and increase our commitments as a church to the development of a barrier-free society, especially in the many facilities of the church and parsonages. To indicate the seriousness of our intent we must set time limits to assure the greatest physical accessibility in the shortest feasible periods and extend our policy of not providing funding through or approval by United Methodist agencies unless minimum guidelines are met which include but are not limited to:

A. Providing adequate access to sanctuary pews, altars, chancel areas and pulpit, classrooms, and restrooms.
B. Providing curb cuts, ramps with at least a 1:12 inclination or platform lifts.
C. Providing facilities with equipment and supplies to meet the needs of persons with seen and unseen handicapping conditions including persons with vision and/or hearing impairments.

• All meetings of The United Methodist Church, beyond the local church, be accessible to persons with handicapping conditions. As general church agencies, jurisdictions, annual conferences, and districts nominate persons with handicapping conditions to their boards and committees, it is necessary for these boards and committees to accommodate these persons.

• All United Methodist churches are asked to conduct an audit of their facilities to discover what barriers impede the full participation of persons with handicapping conditions. Steps should then be taken to remove those barriers. *The accessibility audit for churches* is a recommended resource available from the General Board of Global Ministries.

Awareness

• Sensitize and train local church pastors to the needs and opportunities for those who are handicapped and their families to better minister to and with them.

• Lead the local chuches in attitudinal change studies to the end that the people called United Methodists are sensitized to the gifts, needs, and interests of persons with handicapping conditions, including their families.

• Take advantage of the great opportunities for our church to work cooperatively with other denominations who also are addressing these issues and extend an active invitation to work jointly where possible.

• Suggest one Sunday a year as Access Sunday to sensitize people to our accessibility concerns.

Adequate Resources

• Provide resources through the church at all levels, including curricula, for persons with various handicapping conditions, such as those who are blind, deaf, para-or-quadriplegic, mentally retarded, psychologically or neurologically disabled, etc., so that each individual has full opportunity for growth and self-realization with the community of faith and the society at large.

• Strongly recommend that all curriculum material be so designed that it can be adapted to meet the needs of persons with handicapping conditions; that curriculum material portray persons with handicapping conditions in leadership roles within church and society; that curriculum material reflect the Guidelines for the Elimination of Handicappist Language as produced by the General Council on Ministries.

Affirmative Action

• Include in all our efforts of affirmative action the concerns and interests of persons with handicapping conditions, particularly in the active recruitment and encouragement of these persons for leadership roles, both clergy and lay, within the church and its agencies, in hiring practices, in job security, housing and transportation.

That the General Board of Higher Education and Ministry monitor Annual Conference Boards of Ordained Ministry so that persons with handicapping conditions are given equal treatment in the steps to ordained ministry.

• Strongly urge that our schools of higher education and theological training provide specialized courses for faculty and students in the awareness of and appreciation of gifts, needs, and interests of persons with handicapping conditions. This must include the emphasis of accessibility and equal employment in these institutions as well as in those in the larger society. Accreditation by the University Senate should be withdrawn where handicapped persons are excluded, either from attendance, services, or employment.

• Strongly urge local churches to conduct needs assessment surveys. Such a survey would suggest to a local church what particular actions must be taken to include fully persons with handicapping conditions within the life of the church.

Advocacy Within the Church

• Implement within each Annual Conference methods of recruiting, sensitizing, and training persons as advocates to work with and on behalf of persons with handicapping conditions on a one-to-one basis and to enable them to achieve their human and civil rights as well as to assume their rightful place in the life of the church and community. Each Annual Conference should also develop the larger concern of advocacy for persons with handicapping conditions to enable them to achieve appropriate housing, employment, transportation, education, and leisure time development.

Advocacy Within the Society

While there is much to be done within the church to make real the gospel of inclusiveness with regard to persons with handicapping conditions, yet there is a world society which also must be made aware of the concerns and needs of these persons. We admonish the church and its people to stand alongside persons with handicapping conditions and to speak out on their rights in society. These rights include access to jobs, public transportation, and other reliable forms of transportation, adequate housing, and education. We are people under orders to minister to and with all God's children. We are all a people in pilgrimage! We have too often overlooked those of God's children who experience life in different ways than ourselves. We pledge ourselves to an inclusive, compassionate, and creative response to the needs and gifts of persons with mentally, physically, and/or psychologically handicapping conditions.

ADOPTED 1984, REVISED 1992

See Social Principles, ¶ 72.G, "Accessibility of Meeting Places Beyond the Local Church," "Barrier-free Construction for the Handicapped," "Compliance with the Americans with Disabilities Act for Employers," "Communications Access for Persons Who Have Hearing and Sight Impairments."

The Church's Response to Changing Rural Issues

Be it resolved, that each board and agency of The United Methodist Church, and district and conference programming agencies, encourage and assist urban, suburban, and rural churches to address and respond to the following issues, which while present in rural society often are not recognized or acknowledged by the larger society:

* The poor self-esteem of many rural residents and communities.
* The abandonment of the elderly and breakdown of the extended family.
* Homelessness and poor housing.
* The changing role of the family.
* Deterioration of the family, including an increase of divorces and a high level of domestic violence.
* The incidence of alcohol and substance abuse.
* Poor basic government services such as good health care, rural public transportation, children's services, and legal assistance.
* Rural crime and an absence of good police protection.
* The effects of regional consolidations of local community agencies such as banks, businesses, and industries.
* Lack of consumer goods and feelings that consumers are at the mercy of businesses and industries.
* Poor stewardship of the environment, including the pollution of the soil, air, and water.
* Ownership and control of land and its use by nonresident persons and entities.
* Spiritual irrelevance.
* The changing role of the church within the rural community.

ADOPTED 1992

See Social Principles, ¶ 72, "Affirmation of Basic Rural Worth," "Appointment of Clergy to Rural Ministry," "Rural Chaplaincy as a Ministry of Laity and Clergy."

COCU Consensus: In Quest of A Church of Christ Uniting

1. WHEREAS, The United Methodist Church believes that Christ wills for the church to be visibly one; and
2. WHEREAS, the 1984 *Book of Discipline* (¶ 69) affirms that "along with all other Christians, [we] are a pilgrim people under the Lordship of Christ"; and
3. WHEREAS, throughout the Church of Jesus Christ significant ecumenical proposals continue to emerge which envision the achievement of visible unity through a series of covenants

which unite our memberships, ministries, observances of the sacraments and mission; rather than a single act of merger of structures; and

4. WHEREAS, The Evangelical United Brethren Church and The Methodist Church were founding members of the Consultation on Church Union and in successive General Conferences The United Methodist Church has affirmed its strong participation and has adopted specific aspects related to mutual recognition of memberships and theological agreements; and

5. WHEREAS, The United Methodist Church (Preamble to the Constitution) recognizes that "The Church of Jesus Christ exists in and for the world, and its very dividedness is a hindrance to its mission in that world;" and

6. WHEREAS, United Methodists diligently have participated in the development of the Consultation Consensus as a way of reducing dividedness among Christians: therefore,

Be it resolved: That the 1988 General Conference claims the 1984 Consultation Consensus on these three points:

a. The United Methodist Church recognizes in Consensus an expression in the matters with which it deals of the apostolic faith, order, worship, and witness of the church.

b. The United Methodist Church recognizes in Consensus an anticipation of the Church Uniting which the participating bodies, by the power of the Holy Spirit, wish to become.

c. The United Methodist Church recognizes in Consensus a sufficient theological basis for the covenanting acts to be proposed by the Consultation that we expect to be recommended to the General Conference of 1992.

d. Therefore, The United Methodist Church requests that the Council of Bishops transmit this action to the Consultation on Church Union.

ADOPTED 1988

See Social Principles, ¶ 72.B, "Continuing Membership in the Consultation on Church Union," "Act of Covenanting Between Other Christian Churches and The United Methodist Church."

Comity Agreements Affecting Development of Native American Ministries by The United Methodist Church

WHEREAS, certain annual conferences of The United Methodist Church have used the alleged Comity Agreement as the basis for their functional relationship among Native Americans, limiting their capability to develop Native Americans ministries in certain geographical areas, and

WHEREAS, the effects of practicing the concept of a Comity Agreement by The United Methodist Church have resulted in the failure of the Church to follow through with the biblical mandate of propagating the gospel to all nations and, further, caused the failure of the Church to create the climate for leadership development of Native Americans, and

WHEREAS, it is concluded, on the basis of data collected, that a Comity Agreement limiting The United Methodist Church to certain geographical areas of ministry to Native Americans, does not exist, and

WHEREAS, such a Comity Agreement would be discriminatory in that it would violate the right of Native Americans to associate with the denomination of their choice, now

Therefore Be It Resolved, that The United Methodist Church states, as a matter of policy, that it is not a party to any interdenominational agreement that limits the ability of any annual conference in any jurisdiction to develop and resource programs of ministry of any kind among Native Americans, including the organization of local churches where necessary.

ADOPTED 1980

See Social Principles, ¶ 72.A, "The United Methodist Church and America's Native People," "Confession to Native Americans."

Communications Access for Persons
Who Have Hearing and Sight Impairments

BECAUSE The United Methodist Church believes that all United Methodists are full members of the church and is committed to ministry by and with persons with handicapping conditions; and

BECAUSE the churches are excused from compliance with the Americans with Disabilities Act of 1990:

Public accommodations such as restaurants, hotels, theaters, doctors' offices, pharmacies, retail stores, museums, libraries, parks, private schools and day care centers, may not discriminate on the basis of disability, effective January 26, 1992. Private clubs and religious organizations are exempt.

Auxiliary aids and services must be provided to individuals with vision or hearing impairments or other individuals with disabilities so that they can have an equal opportunity to benefit, unless an undue burden would result.

*From a synopsis prepared by
the Civil Rights Division,
U.S. Department of Justice*

AND BECAUSE, despite sincere efforts on the part of the church, persons with handicapping conditions are still confronted by barriers to communications within and without the church.

We call upon the church to:

- Increase its awareness of and sensitivity to the special needs of persons who are deaf and hard of hearing and persons who are blind and partially sighted with respect to media and communications.
- Keep abreast of existing and developing technologies which could make the church's communications accessible to persons who are blind and partially sighted and persons who are deaf and hard of hearing.
- Use appropriate technologies to make essential communications accessible to persons who are hard of hearing and deaf, including:

Considering production of alternative versions of church-produced videos, films or other audiovisuals for persons who are hard of hearing and deaf and persons who are partially sighted and blind at meetings.

Considering the use of assistive technologies for persons who are hard of hearing and deaf for telephone communications.

ADOPTED 1992

See Social Principles, ¶ 72.G, "The Church and Persons with Mentally, Physically, and/or Psychologically Handicapping Conditions."

Compliance with the Americans with Disabilities Act for Employers

WHEREAS, the General Board of Global Ministries, on October 16, 1979, called "United Methodists to a new birth of awareness of the need to include, assimilate, receive the gifts, and respond to the needs, of those persons with mental, physical, and/or psychologically handicapping conditions, including their families"; and

Whereas, the General Conference resolved in 1980, to take major steps in adapting facilities, new and existing, such as "church sanctuaries, educational buildings, parsonages, camps, colleges, or other church-related agencies or facilities" so that they meet minimum guidelines for "barrier-free construction" (see "Barrier-Free Construction for the Handicapped"); and

Whereas, President Bush signed into law the Americans with Disabilities Act (ADA) which, however, would not pertain to most churches; and

Whereas, love without justice is empty and meaningless, and it is unjust to deny anyone employment based solely on human-created obstacles; and

Whereas, it is fitting that Christians be a "cloud of witnesses" for the secular world;

Therefore, be it resolved, that all United Methodist churches investigate and attempt to comply with Title I of the ADA, which states that employers "may not discriminate against qualified individuals with disabilities" and will "reasonably accommodate the disabilities of qualified applicants or employees unless undue hardship would result."

ADOPTED 1992

See Social Principles, ¶ 72.G, "The Church and Persons with Mentally, Physically, and/or Psychologically Handicapping Conditions," "Barrier-Free Construction for the Handicapped."

Comprehensive Approach to Native American Ministries

Whereas, there is a growing Native American population which is shifting from reservation and rural to urban centers in the United States; and

Whereas, 50% of Native Americans live in urban centers today with little being done by The United Methodist Church to address their physical and spiritual needs; and

Whereas, there is a serious shortage of Native American pastors and their leaders to address this growing need; and

Whereas, many annual conferences are trying to create new ministries and are hampered by the lack of trained Native American leaders; and

WHEREAS, there is now a National Native American Center created to recruit, train, and deploy Native American leadership; and

WHEREAS, it will take great amounts of time and finances to train new Native American leadership;

Therefore, be it resolved, that in 1988 General Conference request the General Board of Higher Education and Ministry (BHEM) to design a comprehensive plan that is sensitive to the culture of Native Americans and appropriate for recruitment, training, and deployment of Native American clergy and other Native American leadership during the 1989-92 quadrennium.

Be it further resolved, that the 1988 General Conference request BHEM to develop and implement, in cooperation with the National United Methodist Native American Center, an intentional program of recruitment, enlistment, and training and deployment, in consultation with the Oklahoma Indian Missionary Conference, Native American International Caucus, related general agencies, and other church leaders during the 1989-92 quadrennium.

Be it further resolved, the 1988 General Conference request BHEM to provide adequate financial assistance for the recruitment and training of native American persons for ministry with special attention being given to the Oklahoma Indian Missionary Conference and annual conferences with Native Americans.

Be it further resolved, that the 1988 General Conference request BHEM to develop and recruit Native ministers for Native American urban ministries.

ADOPTED 1988

See Social Principles, ¶ 72.A, "National Convocation on the Ordained Ministry for Native Americans," "Native American Social Witness Program," "Native American Young Adults in Mission," "Native American Representation in The United Methodist Church."

Confession to Native Americans

WHEREAS, the Gospel calls us to celebrate and protect the worth and dignity of all peoples; and

WHEREAS, the Christian churches, including The United Methodist Church and its predecessors, have participated in the destruction of Native American people, culture, and religious practices; and

WHEREAS, the churches of this country have not sufficiently confessed their complicity in this evil; and

WHEREAS, the churches have been blessed by having members who are Native Americans as well as by engaging in dialogue with Native Americans who practice their traditional religions; and

Whereas, confession of our guilt is a first step toward the wholeness which the churches seek through the ecumenical movement;

Therefore, be it resolved, that the United Methodist General Conference confesses that The United Methodist Church and its predecessor bodies has sinned and continues to sin against its Native American brothers and sisters and offers this formal apology for its participation, intended and unintended, in the violent colonization of their land, and

Be it further resolved, that The United Methodist Church pledges its support and assistance in upholding the American Indian Religious Freedom Act (P.L. 95-134, 1978) and within that legal precedent affirms the following:

1) The rights of the Native Peoples to practice and participate in traditional ceremonies and rituals with the same protection offered all religions under the Constitution of the United States of America.

2) Access to and protection of sacred sites and public lands for ceremonial purposes.

3) The use of religious symbols (feathers, tobacco, sweet grass, bones, etc.) for use in traditional ceremonies and rituals.

Therefore, be it further resolved, that the General Conference recommends that local churches develop similar statements of confession as a way of fostering a deep sense of community with Native Americans, and encourages the members of our church to stand in solidarity on these important religious issues and to provide mediation when appropriate for ongoing negotiations with state and federal agencies regarding these matters.

ADOPTED 1992

See Social Principles, ¶ 72, "Native American Religious Freedom Act of 1978," "Native American History and Contemporary Culture as Related to Effective Church Participation," "Comity Agreements Affecting Development of Native American Ministry by The United Methodist Church," "The United Methodist Church and America's Native People."

Confronting the Drug Crisis

Over the past decade, the alcohol and drug crisis has reached global proportions. More alcohol and drugs are produced and consumed in more places around the world than ever before. Illegal drug traffic and abuse is fed both by sustained political and economic turmoil in drug-producing nations and by the social, economic, and spiritual crisis in consuming countries, with their attendant problems of poverty, racism, domestic violence, hopelessness, and despair.

The church has a critical role to play in addressing the crisis. To date, government responses to the crisis have largely been inadequate or misplaced.

The United Methodist Church has waged a long-standing opposition to the abuse of alcohol and other drugs. As far back as 1916, the General Conference authorized the formation of a Board of Temperance, Prohibition and Public Morals, "to make more effectual the efforts of the church to create public sentiment and crystallize the same into successful opposition to the organized traffic in intoxicating liquors."

Over the past quadrennium the church has launched a comprehensive Bishops' Initiative on Drugs and Drug Violence which, through regional hearings across the United States, has deepened the church's awareness of alcohol and other drug problems. The report of these hearings concluded: "The United Methodist Church must play a key role in confronting drug and alcohol addition in [the United States]." Today, The United Methodist Church remains committed to the church's involvement in curbing drug traffic and the abuse of alcohol and other drugs.

As God's children and heirs to the gift of eternal life, we recognize the need to answer the cry of those for whom life holds only condemnation and death. The widespread abuse of legal and illegal drugs in our world points to a need for knowledge of God's saving grace—wholeness offered to each individual through Christ Jesus.

The solution to this problem requires that we, as representatives of Christ, dedicate ourselves to searching for and living out the truth. Jesus spoke often of truth and its crucial place in our lives on earth and in our relationship with God. He promised that those who hold to his teachings "will know the truth, and the truth will make you free" (John 8:32, NRSV). In recognizing the truth, we must commit ourselves to overcoming the denial that keeps individuals and nations from overcoming their struggle with drug traffic and abuse.

Abuse of legal drugs (alcohol, tobacco, and pharmaceuticals) remains a leading cause of disease and death around the world. While "casual" use of illegal drugs in the United States has declined, the use of drugs remains socially acceptable and levels of addiction and abuse continue to rise.

Growing numbers of U.S. cities, small towns, and rural areas are caught in a web of escalating drug-related violence. As the findings of the regional hearings stressed: "Drug addiction crosses all ethnic, cultural and economic backgrounds." U.S. social service systems are dangerously strained under the heavy weight of drug-related health and social problems. Meanwhile the supply of drugs from impoverished developing countries in Latin America and Asia continues to grow in response to high demand.

Tragically, the U.S. policy response to the drug crisis has focused almost exclusively on law enforcement and military solutions, often with dangerous and counterproductive consequences. Not only has the policy failed, but it has led to the erosion of precious civil liberties and human rights, especially for poor and minority communities.

Regardless of how many prisons are built and drug crops are eradicated, those engaged in drug abuse cannot "just say no" to drugs unless they have something to which they can say "yes," such as quality education, purposeful employment, and a spiritually fulfilled life. These people must be given an alternative to drugs to fill the void caused by the breakdown of community and family life and the alienation caused by an increasingly fragmented and impersonal society.

The drug crisis must therefore be redefined as a social, economic, spiritual, and health problem, rather than primarily a criminal problem requiring tough law enforcement and military strategies. Costly supply-reduction strategies that have proven ineffective and destructive at home and abroad should be reassessed and funds redirected toward curbing the demand for drugs.

International strategies should reflect the need for balanced, equitable economic growth and stable democratic governments in drug-producing developing nations. Most important, any alternative strategy must be rooted in local communities. The most creative and effective approaches to the present crisis begin at the local level.

The church has a fundamental role in reorienting the public debate on drugs by shifting the policy focus from punishment to prevention and treatment. To be effective, we must recognize that there remains widespread denial of the drug problem in many of our congregations. If this denial is faced squarely, members of the church have the ability and responsibility to reach out to those individuals, communities, and nations in most need.

Policy Statement/Actions

In response to the alcohol and other drug crisis, The United Methodist Church commits itself to a holistic community health approach, incorporating emphases on prevention, intervention, treatment, community organizing, public advocacy, abstinence and mission evangelism. Out of love for God and our neighbors, the church must have a positive role by offering a renewed spiritual perspective on this crisis.

The following actions are commended to general agencies and seminaries, annual conferences, and/or local congregations:

To General Agencies and Seminaries:

1. Develop alcohol and other drug education programs and materials (sensitive to different ethnic communities) for children, youth, and adults.

2. Urge professional schools of theology, medicine, education, and other graduate schools to develop alcohol and other drug education courses.

3. Encourage United Methodist publications to publish and circulate articles and church school curriculum that focus on the church's role in presenting alternatives to alcohol and other drugs, including abstinence.

4. Utilize the church's communication resources to increase awareness of the widespread misuse of legal drugs, such as alcohol, tobacco, and pharmaceuticals.

5. Develop a network of annual conferences and local churches to share and exchange information and workable models for intervention and healing, and about the changing needs of ministries responding to alcohol and other drugs.

To Annual Conferences:

1. Develop leadership training opportunities and resources for local church pastors and laity to help them with: counseling individuals and families who have alcohol- and other drug-related problems; counseling those bereaved by alcohol- and other drug-

related deaths and violence; and teaching stress management to church workers in communities with high alcohol and other drug activity.

To Local Churches:

1. Encourage integration of alcohol and other drug education programs and materials into the public school curriculum.

2. Join with others engaged in programs of education, prevention, and treatment; support community-based efforts to provide services and facilities to those in need.

To the People Called United Methodist:

1. Work with local, state, and federal government representatives on legislation to limit advertisement of alcohol and tobacco.

2. Advocate policy initiatives at the local, state, and federal levels that shift funding priorities toward alcohol and other drug prevention and treatment.

3. Advocate policy initiatives at the local, state, and federal levels that address the global dimensions of the drug crisis, including the often negative impact of our government's militarized foreign drug control strategy.

ADOPTED 1992

See Social Principles, ¶72.I, "Drug and Alcohol Concerns."

Considering Community Contexts in the Appointment-Making Process

W<small>HEREAS</small>, congregations of all sizes need to understand and respond to the dynamics of their contexts in order to become "a strategic base from which Christians move out to the structures of society"; and

W<small>HEREAS</small>, The United Methodist Church has responsibility for enabling every church to fulfill the holistic "expectations of an authentic church, through community outreach as a key for Christian witness; and

W<small>HEREAS</small>, church profiles developed by the pastor, the Pastor-Parish Relations Committee, and the district superintendent for use with appointment making are to include information on the church's size, finance, lay leadership, spiritual life, and the church's ministry for the sake of its community;

Therefore, be it resolved, that our episcopal and other United Methodist leaders challenge and guide the churches toward an increased understanding that the contextual communities where their congregations are located are as important to their ministries as are the needs of their members; and

Further, be it resolved, that the bishops of the church and their appointive cabinets be open to making intentional appointments to communities as well as to congregations so that Christian responses can be made through ministries of service, organizing, advocacy, and economic development relevant to specific and diverse community contexts.

ADOPTED 1992

See Social Principles, ¶ 72.

Continuance of Funding to the Evangelical Seminary of Puerto Rico

WHEREAS, the Methodist Episcopal Church, one of the predecessors of The United Methodist Church, was one of the founders of Evangelical Seminary of Puerto Rico through the Board of Home Missions and Church Extension in 1919; and

WHEREAS, close to 30 graduates of the Evangelical Seminary of Puerto Rico are serving The United Methodist Church in the United States, and it is expected that the flow of pastors coming from Puerto Rico to serve in The United Methodist Church will continue;

Therefore, be it resolved, that the General Conference of The United Methodist Church mandates the General Board of Global Ministries and the General Board of Higher Education and Ministry to: consult with the Evangelical Seminary of Puerto Rico, study the impact of any reduction of funds in the aforementioned institution, and continue the funding up to 1996. Both agencies should consider the continuation of the present financial support at the current level through the year 2000, and what financial assistance is possible beyond the beforementioned period in the light of our ecumenical and moral responsibilities as founders. Both agencies shall report their findings and recommendations to the 1996 General Conference.

ADOPTED 1992

See Social Principles, ¶ 72, "Puerto Rico and Vieques."

Continuing Membership in the Consultation on Church Union

WHEREAS, the Constitution of The United Methodist Church states that the dividedness of the Church is a "hindrance to its mission" in the world and has committed us to ecumenical involvement; and

WHEREAS, the predecessor churches of The United Methodist Church were founding members of the Consultation on Church Union, and The United Methodist Church has been an active supporter of COCU for almost 25 years; and

WHEREAS, the 1988 General Conference of The United Methodist Church affirmed *The COCU Consensus* as an authentic expression of the apostolic faith and a sufficient theological foundation for covenanting; and

WHEREAS, the 1988 General Conference of The United Methodist Church voted to move forward toward covenanting; and

WHEREAS, the United Methodist Council of Bishops stated in May, 1992, "we celebrate God's call to the concept of covenant relationships expressed in *Churches in Covenant Communion* . . . [and] long for the day when the covenant may be realized among us, and acknowledge with joy our eagerness to enter into covenant";

Therefore, be it resolved, that the General Conference directs:

1. The Council of Bishops and the General Commission on Christian Unity and Interreligious Concerns to continue in dialogue with covenanting partners, clarifying questions, and developing the covenanting process; and

2. The Council of Bishops and the General Commission on Christian Unity and Interreligious Concerns to lead The United Methodist Church in continuing prayer and study as we move toward a vote on *Churches in Covenant Communion* at the 1996 General Conference.

ADOPTED 1992

See Social Principles, ¶ 72, "Toward an Ecumenical Future."

Continuing Membership in the National Council of Churches

WHEREAS, the Constitution of The United Methodist Church states that the dividedness in the Church of Jesus Christ "is a hindrance to its mission" in the world and has committed us to ecumenical involvement; and

Whereas, The United Methodist Church and its predecessor churches have been charter members of the National Council of the Churches of Christ in the U.S.A.; and

Whereas, the NCCC/USA is a "community through which the churches are seeking to make visible their unity given in Christ"; and

Whereas, the NCCC/USA is "an instrument of the churches' ecumenical witness to live responsibly in mutual accountability and service"; and

Whereas, the NCCC/USA provides a unique opportunity for denominational representatives to share divergent traditions in matters of faith and practice; and

Whereas, the NCCC/USA provides a channel for denominational cooperation in Christian education, mission and justice issues, communications, interfaith matters, evangelism, and relationships with local ecumenical expressions; and

Whereas, the United Methodist delegates from each of the jurisdictions have offered distinguished leadership to the NCCC/USA, and successive general conferences have supported the continuing membership in the NCCC/USA since its founding in 1950;

Therefore, be it resolved, that the 1992 General Conference of The United Methodist Church reaffirms its membership in and support of the National Council of the Churches of Christ in the U.S.A., in accordance with the *1988 Book of Discipline* (¶ 2402.2).

ADOPTED 1992

See Social Principles, ¶ 72.B, "Toward an Ecumenical Future."

Continuing Membership in the World Council of Churches

Whereas, the Constitution of The United Methodist Church states that the dividedness in the Church of Jesus Christ "is a hindrance to its mission" in the world and has committed us to ecumenical involvement; and

Whereas, The United Methodist Church and its predecessor churches have been charter members of the World Council of Churches (WCC); and

Whereas, membership in the WCC is tested by the confession of each member church in "the Lord Jesus Christ as God and Saviour according to the Scriptures"; and

WHEREAS, the WCC provides a worldwide forum and a channel for cooperation in unity, mission, and service; and

WHEREAS, United Methodist delegates in leadership positions among the 317 member churches continue to make significant contributions to this worldwide body, and the 1984 Conciliar Review Committee of the United Methodist Council of Bishops strongly affirmed continuation of commitment to the WCC;

Therefore, be it resolved, that the 1992 General Conference of The United Methodist Church reaffirms its membership in and support of the World Council of Churches, in accordance with the *1988 Book of Discipline* (¶ 2402.3).

ADOPTED 1992

See Social Principles, ¶ 72.B.

Declare Zoar United Methodist Church a Primary Historical Emphasis

WHEREAS the Eastern Pennsylvania Annual Conference has declared Zoar United Methodist Church of Philadelphia, Pennsylvania to be an historic site;

AND WHEREAS the Annual Conference has declared Zoar United Methodist Church to be its primary historical emphasis for the 1980s and has committed itself to provide funds toward the refurbishing of the church;

AND WHEREAS the Annual Conference has undertaken appropriate research and development of the church as an historical center for United Methodism;

Therefore, Be It Resolved, that the General Conference of The United Methodist Church likewise declares Zoar United Methodist Church of Philadelphia to be one of its primary historical emphases for the 1980s.

ADOPTED 1980

See Social Principles, ¶ 72, "Affirmation of Zoar United Methodist Church of Philadelphia."

Dependent Care

The Problem

Almost all families at one time or another need assistance from persons outside the immediate family structure. Increasing numbers of families require some degree of help in the day-to-day care of family members who, because of age or disability, need constant supervision. With a growing number of women entering the paid labor force and with the increased mobility of families away from communities where elderly parents and relatives reside, more and more families need some kind of support care.

1. *Need for a Safe Environment for Children.* Children are often victims at an age when they should be developing trust and confidence in persons and in life itself. Children determine neither what food they will eat nor who will care for them in the absence of parents. Adults make these and other life-affecting decisions for them.

The church has a special responsibility to children and their families to demonstrate concern for and responsiveness to human need. The Christian faith proclaims that children are to be valued not as potential adults but as persons in their own right—persons deserving of dignity, joy, and a protected environment. Because of their vulnerability, children need defenders and guardians, both within the family circle and in the larger extended family of the community. They must be protected from prejudices that may victimize them because of their racial, ethnic, and socio-economic backgrounds.

In many communities are large numbers of latchkey children—children who are unsupervised during parts of the day or night because their parents are at work and no one is available to care for them. Unfortunately these children are often victimized by persons who prey on the unprotected. To avert potential problems, the U.S. Department of Agriculture and the 4-H community clubs have initiated a nationwide program to teach latchkey children various techniques for survival and self-protection. But these children also need to have someone reach out to them, sharing love, care, and security.

2. *Need for Long-term Dependent Care.* The ability of families to remain intact is severely strained when a child, a spouse, or an older relative is disabled and needs constant health-monitoring or supervised care. Families often need help with these situations in the form of in-home health care or custodial care. In many cases, a small amount of assistance could enable these families to function well and maintain healthy relationships with minimal stress. But without aid, stress related to these circumstances can result in divorce, separation,

or institutionalization of loved ones—eventualities neither wanted nor necessary.

The need for long-term dependent care frequently arises from several trends in modern society. Among them, the increased mobility of persons worldwide and the movement from rural to urban areas often result in the isolation of family units from their network of relatives. Older relatives then find themselves separated by long distances from other family members.

Too, the need of many families to rely on the cash economy has moved more women—traditionally the caregivers for family members with long-term needs—into the paid work force, rendering them no longer available to provide free care. Recent statistics show that in the United States:

- Eighty percent of home health care is provided by female relatives whose average age is 55. Forty-four percent of these care-givers are also in the paid work force.
- Two-thirds of the women in the paid work force are either sole providers or have husbands who earn less than $15,000.
- Forty-six percent of all preschool children and 46 percent of all school-age children have mothers in the paid workforce.

A myriad of problems—ranging from inadequate facilities to the high cost of securing persons who can provide care—is placing an unnecessary strain on many modern families who have limited resources and nowhere to turn for help.

The Call

The Christian faith mandates us to recognize and respond to the value of each human person. Our task as the church is to minister to the needs of all persons and to insure for them a caring community where all may be nurtured in a dignified and loving manner. This mandate is to be seen not as a burden, but rather as an opportunity. We are called to participate in the creative, redemptive work of God. Jesus, who provides our example, said: "The Spirit of the Lord is upon me, because he has anointed me to preach the good news to the poor. He has sent me to proclaim release to the captives and recovering of sight to the blind, to set at liberty those who are oppressed, to proclaim the acceptable year of the Lord" (Luke 4:18-19).

Christians who take their commission seriously will accept the challenge to become responsive to the needs of families for external support systems. God has given each person an element of sacredness by the very nature of having been born into the world. This blessing carries the need for a commitment by families, church, and community to help enable persons to live life in the fullness that Jesus proclaimed.

We have answered the call in the past by building hospitals, homes for the elderly, and institutional settings for children who need them. This has been done on a worldwide basis. Now we must take seriously the opportunity to create and support responsive systems of child care and long-term care for those persons who are elderly or who have handicapping conditions (in independent living situations or within family settings).

The Task

In matters of public concern, the church has a responsibility to make its voice heard. Since dependent care (such as child day care, senior day care, home health handicaps) is important to the present and future well-being of various segments of our society, the church's position on the system of dependent care delivery constitutes an appropriate public policy concern. The role of dependent care in its various forms should be seen as a support system for families. Such services enable rather than usurp the traditional role of families.

A national survey of church-based child care discovered that in the United States, churches are the major providers of out-of-home child care. These child care workers listed as a priority task the provision of care that benefits the emotional, social, and learning needs of children. Within this context, persons sponsoring or overseeing church-based programs and churches with special ministries to families have a responsibility to be involved in policy discussions on the form and function of dependent care.

It becomes the obligation of churches to urge and promote coherent, inclusive, and equitable policies that affect families. There is a temptation to separate dependent care from the various programs designed to support and aid families in their life in the church and community, but it must be recognized that most families, at some time or another, rely on formal or informal support systems relative to the care of children, the elderly, or persons with handicapping conditions.

As it approaches public advocacy for dependent care, the church must be guided by the variety of forms of its ministry. The church must acknowledge the importance and implement the provision of affordable and high-quality family support systems that are equitably distributed to those who need them.

Toward this end, the church on all levels is called to advocate the following policies:

1. Public policies that enhance the availability of dependent care in its varied forms to meet the needs of families by providing:

a. Adequate financial aid (such as private foundation grants, tax credits, tax reimbursement, sliding fees) to allow families to care for loved ones at home rather than having these persons institutionalized when that option is not desired, needed, or economically possible.

b. Sufficient information on the availability of dependent care services as well as on methods of evaluating the care provided.

2. Church policies and ministries that enhance the spiritual and psychological needs of families who care for dependent members.

3. Community services that help families/individuals who are under psychological and psycho-social pressures resulting from the responsibilities of caring for dependent family members.

ADOPTED 1984

See Social Principles, ¶ 72.C, "Supportive Policies for Families with Children."

Domestic Violence and Sexual Abuse

The deafening and disabling silence that has surrounded the abuse of women and children must be broken. Overwhelming numbers of women and children in our churches and communities are being battered, raped, emotionally and psychologically abused, physically and sexually assaulted. The abuse occurs in similar percentages in communities of every racial composition and every economic status, in rural areas as well as cities, in families adhering to every religion and to no religion. Silence shields us from our complicity in the violence as well as our failure to overcome it. The facts are grim:

One out of three girls and one out of seven boys in the United States will be sexually abused before the age of 18.[1] Fifteen million U.S.

[1]Sexual Assault Center, Harborview Medical Center, Seattle, Wash.

adults alive today were incest victims as children.[2] Forty-nine percent of reported rape cases in Malaysia involve children under 15 years of age, with the majority of abusers being fathers, stepfathers, or another relative.[3] In 80 percent of wife assault cases in Canada, children are present.[4] One out of every two U.S. women is battered by her spouse or intimate partner sometime during her lifetime.[5] Fourteen percent of married women report being raped by their husbands.[6] In Peru, 70 percent of all crimes reported to the police are of women beaten by their partners.[7] Dowry deaths in India (a wife killed by her husband for failing to produce requested monies from her family) increased by 100 percent in two years during the 1980s.[8] Two million children in the U.S. are victims of physical abuse and neglect, and between two and five thousand children die each year as the result of child abuse.[9] Fifty-four percent of all murders in Austria are committed within the family, with children and women constituting 90 percent of the victims.[10] One-third of all U.S. women are raped during their lifetimes; approximately 70 percent of those rapes are by persons known to the victims. Only one in ten rapes are ever reported; only 40 percent of reported rapes result in arrest; about 1 percent of rapists are convicted.[11] International attention to the prevalence of rape is increasing: the 1991 murder of 19 girls and rape of 71 others at a rural boarding school in Kenya was described in a statement by two leading Kenyan women's organizations as "a mirror of the kind of abuse and violence that women and girls are going through at home, in the workplace and in public places."[12] Children in one out of ten U.S. families hit, beat, stab, or shoot their parents. More than one million parents over 60 years of age will be abused by their own children this year.[13]

We must acknowledge the ways in which misinterpretation and misuse of Christian scriptures and traditions have contributed to

---

[2] ABC network documentary on incest.
[3] Women's International Network, Lexington, Mass.
[4] Ibid.
[5] Fund for the Feminist Majority, Washington, D.C.
[6] Ibid.
[7] Worldwatch Institute.
[8] *New York Times*, January 15, 1989.
[9] Clearinghouse on Child Abuse and Neglect Information.
[10] Worldwatch Institute.
[11] Winters, *Laws Against Sexual and Domestic Violence*.
[12] Fund for the Feminist Majority.
[13] *New York Times, August 4, 1991*.

violence against women and children, to the guilt, self-blame, and suffering which victims experience and to the rationalizations used by those who abuse. A reexamination of those misused passages can help us reclaim traditions in a way which supports victims and challenges abuse in the family.

Stories of violence against women and children are so common that we scarcely notice them, even in the Bible. Yet they are there. Women, only a few of them even named, are abused, rejected, and raped by brothers, husbands, and strangers. Daughters are traded and sacrificed. A concubine wife is sliced into pieces by the master who had traded her body for his own safety.[14] Yet even this last most violent story, in Judges 19, cannot be used to justify abuse, for it ends with this command: "Consider it, take counsel and speak" (vs. 30). It is the silence, the unwillingness to acknowledge the horror, which leaves victims isolated, protects perpetrators, and thwarts healing. We are commanded to break the silence, to give credence to the stories, to be agents of wholeness and justice.

Jesus' concern for the victim is seen in the story of the Good Samaritan (Luke 10:25-37). By concluding this parable with the words, "Go and do likewise," Jesus indicates that we are to receive all people who have been violated or abused, who are weak or vulnerable, with compassion and caring. It is significant that those who failed to come to the aid of the assault victim in the parable were religious leaders. Jesus made it clear that meeting a legalistic obligation is not enough; we must go beyond the letter of the law in reaching out to comfort and assist those who have been harmed.

The church must reexamine the theological messages it communicates in light of the experiences of victims of domestic violence and sexual abuse. We must treat with extreme care the concepts of suffering, forgiveness, and the nature of marriage and the family.

The Social Principles of The United Methodist Church affirms the family as "the basic human community through which persons are nurtured and sustained in mutual love, responsibility, respect, and fidelity." Clearly violence and abuse cannot be tolerated within such an understanding. The Social Principles "reject social norms that

---

[14]Phyllis Tribble, *Texts of Terror* (Fortress Press, 1984)

assume different standards for women than for men in marriage," thus eliminating most of the tacit rationalizations which undergird spouse battering. The Social Principles also call for the protection of children from all forms of exploitation and abuse.

Situations of violence and abuse exist in families in virtually every congregation; tragically, no church or community is exempt. Numerous pastors have been asked, after asserting their conviction that there were no families experiencing violence or abuse in their congregations, to mention the issues from the pulpit, using words like battering, rape, incest, child abuse. Virtually without exception, they have reported that members have subsequently come to them with current stories of abuse in their families. Clearly, church families are not immune, and many are waiting for a signal that these concerns are appropriate ones to share and struggle with within a Christian community.

The church is being challenged to listen to the stories of victims and survivors and to obtain information and guidance which will lead to wiser and more effective ways of ministry with persons who experience domestic violence and sexual abuse. The church must be a refuge for people who are hurting, and is an entirely appropriate place for these issues to be addressed. We must find ways to demonstrate that the church is a place where people can feel confident in turning first, not last, for comfort and healing.

People of faith should take the lead in calling for a just response by the community in the face of domestic violence and sexual abuse. A just response involves several steps: righteous anger; compassion for the victim; advocacy for the victim; holding the offender legally and spiritually accountable for his or her sin against the victim and the community; treatment for the offender; and prevention of further abuse by addressing the societal roots and not merely the symptons of violence and abuse.

Policy Statements and Actions

The United Methodist Church affirms the sacredness of all persons and their right to safety, nurture, and care. It names domestic violence and sexual abuse as sins and pledges to work for their eradication. The church commits itself to listen to the stories of battered spouses, rape victims, abused children, adult survivors of child sexual abuse, and all others who are violated and victimized. The church further commits itself to provide leadership in responding with justice and compassion to the presence of domestic violence and sexual abuse among its membership and within the community at large.

The following actions are commended to general agencies, seminaries and annual conferences:

1. Provide to clergy and laity education and training which address domestic violence and sexual abuse. Seminaries are urged to include mandatory courses in their curriculum, and annual conferences are urged to offer courses in their continuing education programs for clergy.

2. Support policies, programs, and services which protect victims, hold offenders accountable for the offense, provide appropriate incarceration and treatment for offenders, and provide support for other family members.

3. Provide training in abuse prevention, detection, and intervention to church school teachers, youth leaders, and pastors and encourage them to use abuse protection curriculum. Urge churches to sponsor marriage enrichment and parenting classes.

4. Develop and implement clear policies to deal with sexual abuse by clergy.

5. Encourage governments to ratify the United Nations Conventions on the Elimination of all Forms of Discrimination Against Women and on the Rights of the Child.

The following actions are commended to local congregations:

1. Create a church climate of openness, acceptance, and safety that encourages victims to speak their pain and seek relief.

2. Encourage all clergy and lay leaders to work with specialized community agencies on prevention strategies and to provide for the physical, emotional, and spiritual needs of victims, offenders, and other family members.

3. Assess currently available prevention and response resources in the community and, where indicated and appropriate, initiate new programs and services. Wherever possible, undertake new programs ecumenically or as part of a community coalition.

4. Set up peer support groups for battered spouses, for adults who were sexually abused as children, for rape victims. A trained resource person or professional counselor should be consulted for assistance in setting up peer support groups.

5. Encourage church members to volunteer their services to existing shelters, crisis centers, and other community services. Insist upon training for volunteers.

6. Reexamine and change scriptural and theological messages, cultures, and traditions that validate violence or abuse or support a view of women as subordinate to men or children as property of adults.

7. Maintain a library of printed and video resources on domestic violence, sexual abuse, and the role of the church. Develop a utilization plan.

8. Participate in Domestic Violence Awareness Month each October and Child Abuse Prevention Month each April in the United States, or similar emphases in other countries. Clergy are urged to preach on domestic violence and sexual abuse topics; congregations are urged to host or cooperate in community education events and to highlight opportunities for involvement in prevention and service activities.

ADOPTED 1992

See Social Principles, ¶ 72, "Protecting and Sustaining Children."

Driving Under the Influence

Summary: Christian values cause us as United Methodists to protest openly the high rate of injury and loss of life caused by drivers who are impaired by alcohol and other drugs. Many of these crashes are preventable, and we intend to do what we can to reduce the losses.

WHEREAS, in the United States:

We lose more than 60 persons per day by death in vehicle crashes involving drivers impaired by alcohol. This is nearly 50 percent of all highway deaths. Through legislation and education, the 50 percent rate represents a 19 percent reduction from 10 years ago, but is still 10 times the rate in Europe;

We injure 1,370 persons per day in alcohol-related crashes. About half are serious injuries. Many persons are paralyzed for life;

In addition to the great pain and suffering, we have a direct cost of over $12 billion per year which drives up auto and health insurance costs;

The National Highway Traffic Safety Administration provides research and recommendation regulations which reduce the incidence of driving impaired and the resulting losses; effective changes are possible!; and

WHEREAS, our Scripture and our tradition place high value on persons, their welfare, and their potential; however, we have complacently accepted deaths and losses of personal potential caused by impaired drivers;

Therefore, be it resolved, that we ask our congregations and members to:

1. Study and discuss the facts of driving impaired and the moral values related to it.

2. Decide that driving while seriously impaired by alcohol or other drugs—even prescription drugs—is not acceptable action.

3. Support legislation which has reduced impaired driving.

ADOPTED 1992

See Social Principles, ¶ 72.I, "Drug and Alcohol Concerns," "Education on Alcohol and Substance Abuse."

Drug and Alcohol Concerns

I. Drugs

We recognize the widespread use and misuse of drugs which alter mood, perception, consciousness, and behavior of persons among all ages, classes, and segments of our society. We express deep concern for those persons who must depend on the effects of chemical substances to medicate emotional problems or to meet personal, social, and/or recreational needs to an extent that debilitates the individual's health or functioning.

The church can offer a religious and moral heritage which views each individual as a person of infinite worth and significance, sees meaning and purpose in all of life, supports the individual and the society in the quest for wholeness and fulfillment, and seeks healing for the afflicted and liberty for the oppressed. The church should act to develop and support conditions in which responsible decision making by both individuals and corporate bodies can occur.

We are also deeply concerned about the widespread ignorance and fear of drugs and their effects on part of the general public. Such lack of knowledge and understanding makes for hysterical and irrational responses. Humane and rational approaches to solutions require an enlighted public capable of making discriminating judgments.

We understand the drug problem to be a "people problem" rather than merely a chemical, medical, or legal problem. As such, a human-problems approach is required, focusing on why people use drugs in their lives, and the social and cultural conditions which may contribute to or alleviate the destructive use of drugs. Such an approach sees drug use and misuse in the larger context of health care, inadquate education, and inadequate, substandard housing, poverty in the midst of plenty, affluence without meaning, rapid social change and technological development, changing moral values and growing alienation, hostility and war between peoples, environmental pollution, the waste of natural resources, the quest for purpose and meaning of life, and the lack of self-understanding, self-affirmation, and self-reliance.

The human-problems approach is interdisciplinary, i.e., it involves all relevant fields of human knowledge in the search for solutions. It requires community involvement from professionals, self-help groups, volunteer services, concerned individuals in the public and private sectors. Such active motilization of community resources makes possible the consideration of all relevant dimensions of the situation, personal and social.

With all the conflicting opinions and misinformation available, accurate definitions are essential to clear understanding and constructive action on human problems involving the use and misuse of drugs. Pharmacologically, a drug is "any substance which by its chemical nature alters the structure or function of the human organism." This broad definition encompasses a wide range of substances, including medicines, food additives, and household remedies such as aspirin, as well as psychoactive substances such as alcohol, tobacco, caffeine, heroin, barbiturates, amphetamines, *cannabis sativa* (marijuana), tranquilizers, LSD, and miscellaneous substances such as glue and paint thinner. Even the proper medical use of drugs under guidance of a competent physician carries risks to health and functioning, and nonmedical use increases those risks considerably. We understand drug misuse to mean taking a substance irresponsibly in an amount, frequency, strength, or manner that is likely to result in damage to the user's health or impair his or her ability to function psychologically, socially, or vocationally, or proves harmful to society. The meaning of drug abuse is covered in the definition of misuse and is thus omitted, since it has generally confused rather than clarified understanding. No drug may be considered harmless, but the effects of any given drug must be judged in the light of such variables as dosages, manner of ingestion, the user's personality and disposition, and the social setting in which the drug is taken.

The ministry of the church should be directed both to the prevention and the treatment of problems related to drug use and misuse. All members of society, including churchmen and church-women, should become thoroughly informed about drug issues so that they can make intelligent and responsible decisions about personal use and social policy controlling drug use.

Therefore:

1. We encourage and seek funding for the church and the larger community to develop various forms of drug education for children, youths, and adults that deal with drug issues in an honest, objective, and factual manner. Informed public discussion is essential to enlightened public action.

2. We urge churches and their members to join with others engaged in positive and constructive programs of prevention and treatment to form a comprehensive, ecumenical, interfaith, and multidisciplinary approach to the wide range of drug problems. Therefore, churches should become involved in prevention and rehabilitation efforts and should encourage and support community-wide efforts to provide services and facilities to the total population in need.

3. We call upon the helping professions in general to develop an increased awareness of drug problems and to utilize their various skills in the search for solutions to these problems. The pastor should serve as a member of this interprofessional community service team.

4. We encourage public schools to integrate drug education into the curriculum in such a way that children and youths of the total community may learn about drugs in an open and supportive atmosphere that facilitates personal growth and responsible decision making.

5. We urge professional schools in theology, medicine, education, and other graduate schools to develop drug education courses for the

training of their students. Opportunities for continuing education and in-service training should also be provided for professionals.

6. We encourage the efforts by city, state, and national government to find ways and means to deal with people who have drug-related problems within the framework of social, health, and rehabilitation services, rather than in the framework of law and punishment. The fundamental role of law enforcement agencies should be to reduce the traffic in drugs by apprehending the professional profiteers. We ask the legislative bodies to provide sufficient funding for an adequate drug education program.

7. We call upon members of the medical profession to join with the church, all community agencies, and government in finding ways and means of preventing the misuse of those drugs intended to be therapeutic.

8. We urge research into the effects, the extent, the causes, the prevention, and the treatment of all aspects of the use and misuse of drugs, and believe that such research is urgent and should be pursued in an atmosphere of flexibility and freedom.

9. We support the efforts of the President, the Congress, and state legislative bodies to develop social policy about drugs that is rational, humane, based on factual evidence, and commensurate with the known dangers of the drugs to the individual and to society.

II. Alcohol

Alcohol presents a special case of drug abuse because of its widespread social acceptance. We affirm our long-standing conviction and recommendation that abstention from the use of alcoholic beverages is a faithful witness to God's liberating and redeeming love.

This witness is especially relevant in a pluralistic society where drinking is so uncritically accepted and practiced; where excessive, harmful, and dangerous drinking patterns are so common; where destructive reasons for drinking are so glamorized that youthful immaturity can be exploited for personal gain; where alcohol contributes to a great proportion of fatal traffic and industrial accidents; where millions of individuals and their families suffer from alcoholism and countless others from various drinking problems; and where alcohol is a factor in many other social problems such as crime, poverty, and family disorder.

Thus the recommendation of abstinence to members of The United Methodist church is based on critical appraisal of the personal and socio-cultural factors in and surrounding alcohol use, the detrimental effects of irresponsible drinking on the individual and society, and a concrete judgment regarding what love demands. The church recognizes the freedom of the Christian to make responsible decisions and calls upon each member to consider seriously and prayerfully the witness of abstinence as a part of his or her equipment for Christian mission in the world. The understanding of the social forces that influence people either to drink or to abstain must be encouraged. Christian love in human relationships is primary, thereby making abstinence an instrument of love and always subject to the requirements of love. Persons who practice abstinence should avoid attitudes of self-righteousness which express moral superiority and condemnatory attitudes toward those who do not abstain.

We believe that concern for the problems of alcohol carries with it the inherent obligation to seek the healing and justice in society that will alleviate the social conditions which contribute to and issue from alcohol problems.

Therefore:

1. We urge every local congregation and each member to demonstrate an active concern for alcoholics and their families and for all persons with drinking problems.

2. We urge all legislative bodies and health-care systems to focus on and implement measures to meet the special needs of women, racial minorities, juveniles, and the elderly. Basic to this concern is an informed mind and compassionate heart which views the alcoholic without moralism and with empathy.

3. We urge churches to make education about alcohol problems and the value of abstinence an integral part of all drug education efforts.

4. We encourage churches to develop special action programs on alcohol problems which include prevention education in the family, church, and community; utilizing mass media to develop responsible attitudes toward alcohol-related problems; care, treatment and rehabilitation of problem drinkers; measures to prevent persons from driving while under the influence of alcohol; the achievement of appropriate and effective legal controls; and the stimulation of sound empirical research.

5. We favor laws to eliminate the advertising of alcoholic beverages. Working toward this end, we urge the Board of Church and Society and local churches to increase efforts to remove all advertising of alcoholic beverages from television (as was done with cigarette advertising). We urge special attention to curbing promotions on use of alcoholic beverages on college campuses.

6. We urge the health system, especially United Methodist-related hospitals, to accept alcoholism as a medical-social-behavioral problem and to treat the alcoholic person with the same attention and consideration as is given any other patient.

7. We urge the Federal Trade Commission to continue its efforts to develop better health hazard warning statements concerning the use of alcohol as a beverage, and that labels which are affixed to all alcoholic beverages offered for sale are enlarged to facilitate easier reading of the message by the consumer.

8. We urge the federal government to better coordinate its drug and alcohol abuse efforts in treatment and prevention.

9. We urge all United Methodist churches in the United States to work for a minimum legal drinking age of 21 years in their respective states.

III. Tobacco

Tobacco presents another special case of drug abuse. Constrained by the overwhelming evidence linking cigarette smoking with lung cancer, cardio-vascular diseases, emphysema, chronic bronchitis, and related illnesses, and moved to seek the health and well-being of all persons, we urge private and public health organizations to initiate intensive programs to demonstrate the link between smoking and disease. The United Methodist Church discourages persons, particularly youths and young adults, from taking up this generally habit-forming practice.

We are especially concerned about the portrayal of smoking in connection with commercial advertising. We commend the suspension of cigarette advertising on radio and television. Smoking in other advertisements is still depicted in ways which identify it with physical and social maturity, attractiveness, and success. We support the Federal Trade Commission's rules requiring health warning statements in cigarette packaging.

We are also concerned that the tobacco industry is implementing marketing strategies that focus on the sales of tobacco in developing countries.

Therefore:

1. We support expanded research to discover the specific agents in tobacco which damage health, to develop educational methods which effectively discourage smoking, to organize services to assist those who wish to stop smoking.

2. We urge the Department of Agriculture and other government agencies to plan for and assist the orderly economic transition of the tobacco industry—tobacco growers, processors, and distributors—into other, more benign, lines of production.

3. We recommend that tobacco smoking in our churches and in other public facilities be discouraged in support of the right of nonsmokers to clean air.

4. We recommend the prohibition of commercial advertising of tobacco products in order to reduce enticement toward use of a proven health hazard.

IV. Marijuana

Marijuana is one form of the common hemp plant, *cannabis sativa*, which consists of the dried and crushed leaves and flowering tops of the plants. High concentration of the plant resin alone is called hashish and is six to eight times as potent as the usual marijuana.

In 1990, the National Institute of Drug Abuse (NIDA) released its National Household Survey on Drug Abuse which showed: (1) that of the youth between the ages of 12 and 17, 14.8 percent have used marijuana, 11.3 percent used it during the past year and 5.2 percent used marijuana during the past month; (2) that as many as 66.5 million Americans have tried marijuana at least once and 10 million have used it during the past month. Despite decriminalization efforts on the part of some states, in 1990, 1,089,500 persons were arrested for possession of all illegal drugs. Of that number, the arrests for marijuana possession was 6.1 percent and 23.9 percent for sale and manufacturing of the drug.

Research conducted at the Institute of Behavioral Science at the University of Colorado concluded that "personal control variables—

whether religiosity, moral standards, or attitudes about transgression—were shown to be powerful in regulating whether marijuana use occurred at all, how early, and with what degree of involvement."

We recommend the following:

1. Abstinence from the use of marijuana.

2. Special attention be given to marijuana in drug education programs. It is necessary to deal with the fear and misinformation which surround attitudes about this drug in order that discussion can be conducted on a rational basis.

3. We continue to support strong law enforcement efforts against the illegal sale of all drugs.

4. We encourage continued medical and scientific research to determine the potential dangers of marijuana use to the individuals.

5. We urge development of a social policy regarding the use of marijuana based upon accurate knowledge and enlightened understanding.

V. Narcotics

Narcotics are a group of drugs whose analgesic action relieves pain and produces sleep or stupor. They include derivatives of the opium plant such as heroin, morphine, codeine, and percodan, synthetic substances such as methadone and meperidine. Medically, narcotics are employed primarily for the relief of pain, but the risk of physical and psychological dependence is well established. Dependence of both kinds refers to compulsive behavior characterized by a preoccupation with procuring and using the drug. The exact number of persons, commonly called "addicts," dependent on self-administered doses is unknown, but estimates place the number of persons who used illicit drugs in the past month at 6.4 percent of the population, or approximately 13 million persons.

The action of the narcotic reduces hunger, pain, and aggressive and sexual drives; it is the desire or need for the drug rather than its effects which motivates criminal activity associated with compulsive narcotic abuse. While the availability of heroin has long been prevalent in many inner-city ghetto communities, it is a growing problem in all segments of our society.

Therefore:

1. We urge members of the church to consider the compulsive users of narcotics as persons in need of treatment and rehabilitation, and to show compassion and supportive concern for them and their families.

2. We urge that public, private, and church funds be made available for prevention of drug abuse and for treatment and rehabilitation methods for compulsive narcotics users, including types of chemical therapy, which emphasize becoming productive and emotionally stable members of society.

3. We urge continual reform of the law to make it easier for the compulsive users to be treated not as criminals but as persons in need of medical treatment, pastoral care, and social rehabilitation.

4. We support strong enforcement measures aimed at reducing the illegitimate organized production, manufacture, distribution, and sale of narcotics for profit.

VI. Sedatives and Stimulants

Sedatives, which include barbiturates and the major and minor tranquilizers, are prescribed appropriately for treatment of psychiatric illnesses. However, habitual use of these drugs to relieve the everyday stresses of life constitutes misuse and may represent irresponsible prescribing.

Severe physical dependence on barbiturates can develop at doses higher than therapeutic doses, and withdrawal is severe and dangerous. Overdose of barbiturates is currently one of the major methods of committing suicide. Accidental overdoses sometimes occur with sleeping pills are left by the side of the bed and an already sedated, confused person ingests a lethal dose. Alcohol and barbiturates combined multiply their effects so that drinking after taking medication is especially hazardous. Enough barbiturate capsules are manufactured by pharmaceutical companies annually to supply thirty capsules for each person in the United States. A significant proportion of these legitimately produced pills are diverted into illegitimate channels.

Stimulants range from amphetamines to mild stimulants such as caffeine and nicotine. Therapeutically, some are used to treat obesity, narcolepsy, hyperkinesis, fatigue, and depression. Stimulants produce a temporary sense of vitality, alertness, and energy plus the ability to do without sleep for long periods.

Cocaine is one of the most powerfully addictive of the drugs of abuse—and it is a drug that can kill. Cocaine is a strong central nervous system stimulant that heightens the body's natural response to pleasure and creates a euphoric high. It is an extremely dangerous drug. When inhaled, its occasional use can easily lead to heavy use of the drug. It is not possible for individuals to predict or control the extent to which they will use the drug.

"Crack" is a crystallized form of cocaine which gets it name from the crackling sound made when the substance is smoked (heated). It is readily available because of its lower cost, and addiction often comes from one use of the substance.

Studies by the Department of Health and Human Services on amphetamines (uppers, speed, etc.) show their excessive use causing increased blood pressure, brain damage, kidney failure, severe weight loss and malnutrition, irritability, violence, and severe delusions of persecution.

The stimulant misuser cannot be stereotyped but ranges from diet pill abusers to the "speed freak." Few people die from the direct overuse of stimulants but long-term misuse may result in disorientation and paranoid psychosis. Stimulants are not a major source of energy but instead push the user to a greater expenditure of his or her own physical resources, often to a hazardous point of fatigue. The body builds a tolerance so that larger doses are required to maintain the same "high." Stimulants such as amphetamines are available legally on a written prescription of a physician. These prescriptions cannot be refilled but can be obtained from one or more physicians, and filled by one or more pharmacists.

Therefore:

1. We urge members of the medical profession to exercise special care in their prescription of sedatives and stimulants and to provide therapeutic nonchemical alternatives where available and possible, especially to those eligible for third-party payments.

2. We urge the federal government to take the necessary protective step to curtail excessive production and distribution of sedative and stimulant drugs by setting quotas, requiring precise record keeping of receipts, and positions to be filed with the government periodically,

and the insuring of adequate drug storage procedures by the manufacturer and wholesalers through licensing requirements.

3. We call upon both the governmental and private sectors of society to develop cooperatively a comprehensive regulatory system in which the drug industry, the drug distributors, advertisers, the medical profession, and the consumers will be required to assume collective responsibility for the proper production, distribution, promotion, and the use of prescription and nonprescription drugs.

4. We call upon the mass media, advertising agencies, and the drug companies to frame advertisements which promote appropriate drug use rather than to encourage their indiscriminate use to solve personal problems.

5. Because mood-altering drugs have often been promoted and prescribed for uses beyond those that are medically indicated, we recommend (1) the development of an independent drug information/evaluation system; (2) the upgrading of medical school training in regard to the prescribing of mood-altering drugs as well as postgraduate education for already practicing physicians; (3) the education of the public to the inherent dangers and inappropriate uses of such substances.

6. We encourage and support the efforts of the federal government to continue to monitor and reduce the manufacture and distribution of amphetamines.

VII. Psychedelics or Hallucinogens

Psychedelics or hallucinogens are a class of drugs which include LSD, psilocybin, mescaline, PCP, and DMT. These drugs produce radical changes in perception and altered states of consciousness. "Hallucinogenic" refers to the illusion-producing properties of these drugs, and psychedelic means, literally mind-opening. PCP (Phencyclidine, "Angel Dust") has been determined by the federal government to have no recommended human medical use. It is a depressant, although it is sold on the street as a hallucinogen. Depending on the dosage, PCP can cause increased heart rate, elevated blood pressure, flushing, sweating, impaired coordination, speech and vision, drooling, nausea, and vomiting. The simple manufacture and easy distribution of PCP enables its production by a vast number of persons, making it the drug of choice of the 15- to 25-year-old age group in the United States.

Scientific experimentation to determine therapeutic uses for LSD-type drugs includes treatment of alcoholism, narcotic addition, and terminal cancer patients. As far as is now known, these drugs do not produce physical dependence. The full dangers are still under investigation.

Some persons take LSD in the search for self-knowledge and self-awareness, others in quest of mystical or religious consciousness, still others because of disillusionment with reality and rebellion. Casual or promiscuous use is particularly hazardous since serious adverse reactions are common where warm and supportive settings are absent. These dangers include fear and panic, which can lead to bizarre and self-destructive behavior or temporary psychosis. Long-term risks include prolonged depression, paranoia, psychosis, and the "flashback"—the recurrence of some aspect of the drug experience after the influence of the drug has gone. Buying LSD-type drugs through illicit channels carries the additional larger danger of unknown dosage and impure forms.

Therefore:

1. We urge individuals to refrain from the use of psychedelics.

2. We urge modification of current legal controls of psychedelic drugs in order to make possible more controlled professional therapeutic research with these drugs.

VIII. Drug Trafficking and Operations

Although the current drug crisis has condemned many people to lives of violence and despair, destroyed families and communities nationwide, and become a national priority, nevertheless, present federal anti-drug programs overlook a critical component of the drug-crisis—specifically, that the influx of drugs into our country has been fueled by government agency and private contractor relationships with drug traffickers in the name of national security and under the cover of covert operations.

A report by the Senate Foreign Relations Subcommittee on Narcotics, Terrorism, and International Operations, the findings of the Christic Institute, and other independent investigations report the following to be true:

1) U.S. government officials have turned a blind eye to drug trafficking by allies in exchange for the rebels support of U.S. foreign policy goals.

2) Drug money has been an integral financial component of covert military operations for many years, funding covert activities from the Vietnam War in the 1960s to the Contra War in the 1980s.

3) Drug traffickers have been employed to carry out covert operations on behalf of our government.

4) Federal officials have protected drug smugglers and undermined drug investigations for foreign policy purposes.

5) The State Department paid U.S. tax money to companies owned by known drug kingpins in return for their support of covert operations.

These relationships with drug dealers have led to a significant increase in the flow of drugs into the United States, opening our borders to traffickers who come and go with little fear of detection or prosecution. Further, these relationships have made it difficult, if not impossible, for U.S. officials to rein in members of drug cartels and drug-corrupted foreign government officials with whom they have been involved in the past. Government collusion with drug dealers could indeed be continuing today, given the length and depth of these relationships and the consistent failure to prosecute known criminal activity.

Therefore:

1. We call on the President, the Congress of the United States, and all appropriate federal agencies to pledge publicly to end all support of and involvement with individuals engaged in drug trafficking, and to end support for drug-corrupted military allies.

2. We call upon the President and the Congress of the United States to remove from the National Security Act any wording that allows or enables the CIA to develop and carry on covert actions separate from and in addition to intelligence-gathering activities.

3. We call upon the House and Senate Judiciary Committee to investigate and support the prosecution of government officials who have worked unlawfully with drug traffickers or have obstructed the prosecution of drug traffickers.

ADOPTED 1992

See Social Principles, ¶¶ 72.I and J, "Ban on Alcohol Beverage Advertisements," "Confronting the Drug Crisis," "Driving Under the Influence," "Education on Alcohol and

Substance Abuse," "Oxford House Model for Drug and Alcohol Abuse," "The Use of Alcohol and Tobacco on Church Property," "The Use of Alcohol and Drugs on Campus."

Ecumenical Decade: Churches in Solidarity with Women

When we look at women across the world we discover millions who are still on the margin of their societies. Some are there largely because they were born female instead of male. Others are on the fringe because they are old in societies which want women to be eternally young. Young women who are single parents with families have few marketable skills and cannot support their children. Women may find themselves on the fringes of society because of age, caste, class, color, ethnic or national origin or marital status.

The margin of society is dangerous. Women are forced to live there by reason of poverty, famine, war, illiteracy, ageism, handicapping conditions, refugee or illegal alien status, homelessness, or incarceration. Women are not the only ones to suffer. When women suffer, there is a ripple effect. So central are the well-being and economic security of a woman to the lives of others that her marginalization adversely impacts not only the quality of her development but that of her family and her community as a whole. The well-being of women is central to the well-being of all.

Signs of hope are emerging across the world as women are making the journey away from the fringes of society, empowering one another through care and struggle for life.

The United Nations Decade for Women (1975-1985) has pointed the way to what can be done. Much is still before us. The United Nations "End of The Decade" Conference held in Nairobi, Kenya, in 1985 was a milestone. It was the starting point for the sustained hard work required for the decades to come.

The "Forward Looking Strategies for the Advancement of Women by the Year 2000" which emerged from the 1985 End of the Decade Conference should be implemented. But in the churches there is need for another decade. The World Council of Churches at Easter 1988 launched a new focus called "An Ecumenical Decade: Churches in Solidarity with Women." It builds on the momentum of the United Nations Decade for Women and gives the churches a new opportunity to respond to God's call for inclusiveness and solidarity and sharing of power. Some of the obstacles women face were cited in the World Council of Churches report to the national conference:

—In time of economic recession women are among the first to be thrown out of work;

—Women in rural areas receive least attention in development plans and are not consulted about their basic needs;

—The effects of famine are hardest on women, who bear the heaviest responsibility for the family;

—As socio-economic situations deteriorate, frustration of jobless men often leads to increased sexual abuse and violence against women;

—Growing poverty, the spread of military bases and promotion of sex-tourism have greatly increased the plague of prostitution, involving even younger women and children.

—Among the victims of nuclear testing are women, such as in the Pacific, who bear the burden of increased miscarriages and deformed children;

—Women industrial workers are often without protection and receive the lowest wages from local and multinational industries, exploiting women's vulnerable positions;

—Apartheid and other forms of racism oppress women in a specific way and make them suffer often double and triple oppression as women, as poor and as racial/ethnic people.

Men of the church and in society are joining women in acts of reformation and even re-creation working to transform old orders of relationships and systems to better serve the needs of women and men and whole communities.

When we strive together to end the physical and emotional abuse of women, their economic insecurity and political powerlessness, their exclusion from decision-making processes, we ensure that women will be able to make their full contribution to every aspect of society. We work out of a faith commitment which proclaims that through Christ a new humanity can be established for all persons in all places.

The World Council of Churches directs us to the biblical and theological roots for the ecumenical decade. Rooted in the biblical accounts of the genesis of the world and the human family is the declaration that all persons, female and male, are created in the image of God, the giver of life. Human relationships have failed to mirror this imagery of creation in God's image, but women's experiences, their struggles for life and for nurturing life are crucial perspectives for safeguarding and liberating the creation.

In calling for an ecumenical decade for women, the World Council of Churches reminds us that the prophetic tradition calls the people of God to take on the task of living and working in solidarity with the oppressed to bring oppression to an end. We are also reminded of the affirmation that through our Baptism, we are incorporated into the body of Christ, the new community in which old patterns of relationships among classes, races, and genders have been ended and new patterns are embodied which reflect the caring of the new age. The Call reminds us of the diversity of gifts which the Spirit imparts upon persons in the human family and the challenge to enable all persons to utilize those gifts for the building up of the community for justice and reconciliation in the world.

In the words of the 1981 World Council of Churches Consultation on the Community of Women and Men in the Church, "We receive a foretaste of a global community of women and men vulnerable to the pain of all forms of oppression and united in struggle against them."

We Call Upon the United Methodist Church to:

1. Participate fully in "The Ecumenical Decade—Churches in Solidarity with Women" (1988-1998) launched by the World Council of Churches (WCC) including support for:
   a. Women's full participation: includes the question of power, power sharing and empowerment; women's presence on decision-making bodies and in bodies where ideas (e.g. theology, public policy) and plans are developed.
   b. Women's visions and perspectives, concerns and commitments related to the ecumenical study, "Justice, Peace and the Integrity of Creation".
   c. Women doing theology and sharing spirituality: how can we enable an integrated process of study, sharing, acting and celebrating?
2. Produce educational resources and programs on the marginalization and oppression of women, their struggle for human dignity and a better life, and their creative contribution in theology, spirituality and ministry.

3. Encourage all levels of the church—general, jurisdictional annual conference, district, and local church—to participate in the Ecumenical Decade by studying the root causes of sexism, exploring ways to increase participation of women in all aspects of church life, and be open to ways of addressing injustices toward women through the church and society.

4. Urge all commissions and program agencies to study and implement as appropriate the priorities of the "Forward Looking Strategies";

5. Increase the involvement of racial, ethnic and national minority women as well as other oppressed women;

6. Improve relationships with women suffering under sexism, racism and casteism and support the World Council of Churches' Women Under Racism Programme;

7. Continue efforts which both the church and the society accomplished during the United Nations Decade for Women towards the goals of equality, development and peace;

8. Work for women to participate equally with men in the decisions of the church and the society concerning justice and peace;

9. Urge United Methodists to encourage governments to commit themselves to appropriate action for the implementation of the strategies within the framework of their national development plans and programs;

10. Monitor and be supportive of the continual emphasis on women by the United Nations and participate in all the United Nations arenas where Non-Governmental Organizations have potential for influence;

11. Support the "United Nations Convention on the Elimination of All Forms of Discrimination Against Women" and urge United Methodists to work through local and national organizations to encourage their governments not only to ratify but to implement the Convention.

ADOPTED 1988

See Social Principles, ¶ 72.F, "Equal Rights of Women," "The Status of Women," "Full Personhood."

Ecumenical Interpretations of Doctrinal Standards

WHEREAS, the 1970 General Conference passed a "Resolution of Intent" concerning the ecumenical interpretation of the Thirty-Nine

Articles, which was mistakenly deleted from the 1970 *United Methodist Book of Resolutions;* and

WHEREAS, it is common knowledge that the context of the original Thirty-Nine Articles (1563) and specifically Articles XIV, XIX, XXI, XXII, XXIV, XXV, XXVIII, XXX, XXXI, XXIV, were bitterly polemical, it is of prime importance that they should be reconsidered and reassessed in the contemporary context. They were aimed, deliberately, at the Roman Catholic Church in a time of strife and were a mix of the theological and nontheological convictions of embattled schismatics, fighting as they believed for national survival and evangelical truth. John Wesley's hasty abridgment (1784) of the original Thirty-Nine Articles (down to twenty-four) retained seven out of ten of these anti-Roman references-XIV, XV, XVI, XVII, XIX, XX, XXI—in his enumeration. This reflects his conviction as to their applicability to the Roman Catholic Church as he perceived it. This much must be recognized and acknowledged as belonging to our inheritance from our Anglican-Wesleyan past. It is, however, one of the virtues of historical insight that it enables those in a later age to recognize the circumstances of earlier events and documents without being bound to their historical evaluation, especially in a subsequent epoch when relationships have been radically altered; and

WHEREAS, we rejoice in the positive relationships developed between The United Methodist Church and the Roman Catholic Church, at levels both official and unofficial;

Therefore, be it hereby resolved, that we declare if our official intent to interpret these Articles in consolance with our best ecumenical insights and judgment.

And be it further resolved, that this resolution be printed in its entirety in the *1992 Book of Resolutions* and that appropriate reference be noted in the *Book of Discipline* to correct the inaccuracies found in page 30, footnote #3, and page 64, footnote #5.

ADOPTED 1992

See Social Principles, ¶ 72.B, "Toward an Ecumenical Future."

Education on Alcohol and Substance Abuse

WHEREAS, The United Methodist Church has recognized the widespread use and misuse of drugs which alter mood, perception, consciousness, and behavior of persons among all ages, classes, and segments of our society, and

WHEREAS, we as a church are concerned about the widespread ignorance and fear of drugs and their effect on the general public; and

WHEREAS, The United Methodist Church's recommendation of abstinence to its members is based on the detrimental effects of irresponsible drinking on the individual and society; and

WHEREAS, the church recognizes the freedom of Christians to make responsible decisions and encourage an understanding of the social forces that influence people to either drink or abstain; and

WHEREAS, the church urges the churches to include education about alcohol problems and prevention in the family, church, and community;

Now therefore, be it resolved, that the General Board of Discipleship be directed, through The United Methodist Publishing House, to incorporate education on alcohol and substance abuse materials in its graded literature and produce special materials that address the drug and alcohol problem that confronts our society.

ADOPTED 1992

See Social Principles, ¶ 72.I, "Drug and Alcohol Concerns," "Confronting the Drug Crisis."

Education Responsibilities Concerning Native American Cultural Traditions

WHEREAS, non-Native American pastors are being appointed to Native American churches with little or no awareness of the history, culture, and language of Native Americans in that particular community; and

WHEREAS, these non-Native American pastors may not realize that Native Americans are being hurt by their insensitivity and/or ignorance; and

WHEREAS, the non-Native American pastors need to obtain some form of training regarding the do's and don't's on Native American history, culture, and language; and

WHEREAS, the history of Christian missions among Native Americans invariably shows that well-intentioned missionaries were accomplices in the colonial conquest and ongoing oppression of Native Americans, usually confusing the proclamation of the gospel with the proclamation of European values; and

WHEREAS, the responsibility of The United Methodist Church is to make sure these non-Native American pastors are sensitized, educated, and made aware of Native American history, culture, and language.

Therefore, be it resolved, that the 1992 General Conference encourage the General Board of Higher Education and Ministry with the National United Methodist Native American Center to develop a curriculum that deals with The United Methodist Church and colonial conquest and that this curriculum be made available to all United Methodist seminaries. This curriculum shall include a process for the non-Native American pastor to become sensitive to Native American culture, history, and language.

ADOPTED 1992

See Social Principles, ¶ 72.A, "The United Methodist Church and America's Native People," "Native American History and Contemporary Culture as Related to Effective Church Participation," "Toward a New Beginning beyond 1992."

Elimination of Racism in The United Methodist Church

WHEREAS, The United Methodist Church continues to exhibit an indifference to the creative and the courageous leadership of ethnic minority persons in their local congregations and the communities where they serve;

WHEREAS, we continue to practice the exclusion of Asian, Black, Hispanic and Native American clergy persons from full and total participation in the appointment process of the itinerant ministry;

WHEREAS, the General Commission on Religion and Race has identified the persistent presence of racism within our lives and within local churches, annual conferences, general agencies, seminaries, and other institutions, as one of the underlying causes for the inability of the denomination to meet fully the goals and expectations of the Missional Priority, "Developing and Strengthening the Ethnic Minority Local Church: For Witness and Mission";

WHEREAS, we profess an understanding of the will of God and a willingness to surrender our lives to Jesus Christ; and

WHEREAS, we realize the necessity to engage regularly in events/activities which will enable us to grow toward Christ-like perfection;

Therefore, the General Commission on Religion and Race petitions:

1) That, the 1988 General Conference calls on all annual conferences, local churches, seminaries, general agencies, institutions, and Council of Bishops to make the elimination of racism a priority in all of their agendas; and,

2) That, General Conference calls on all annual conferences, local churches, seminaries, general agencies, institutions, and Council of Bishops to pursue more intentionally the attitudinal and systemic changes that need to take place in order to be, in word and in deed, a truly racially inclusive church; and

3) That, bishops, cabinets and the Boards of Ordained Ministries engage in workshops and personal growth training sessions to deepen their sensitivity to the positive contribution of Asian, Black, Hispanic and Native American clergy persons and lay persons to the development of local congregations and empowering of local communities; and

4) That, by August 1, 1991, each annual conference report to the General Commission on Religion and Race the number of sessions they have had and their results, as they strive to fulfill recommendation #3; and

5) That, during the next quadrennium, annual conference agencies, general agencies, seminaries, and other denomination-related institutions provide for their staff and members of their policy-making organizations racism workshops, which focus on the subtle and the overt racial, cultural, attitudinal and behavioral forces in the work place of The United Methodist Church-related institutions; these workshops should include an emphasis on strategies for inclusiveness in our multi-cultural church; and

6) That, a report of those workshops with their findings be forwarded to the General Commission on Religion and Race by August 1, 1991.

ADOPTED 1988

See Social Principles, ¶ 72.A, "Eradication of Racism," "Celebrate and Affirm the Work of the General Commission on Religion and Race," "Racial Harassment."

Enlist and Involve the Youth in the Life of the Church

Introduction

From August 2-4, 1991, a group of some 25 persons who had been active in the youth work of the Methodist denominations that merged to form The Methodist Church in 1939 met at Baker University, Baldwin City, Kansas. They came together with the cooperation of Archives and History leaders of the Kansas East Annual Conference to observe the fiftieth anniversary of the founding of the Methodist Youth Fellowship.

Nearly all of them had played a leading role as state student representatives or conference youth presidents in the programs of the predecessor denomination, in the deliberations of the Uniting Conference (1939), in the Youth Study Commission created by action of the 1940 General Conference of the new church, in the work of the general boards as full, voting youth members, and/or in the leadership of the National Conference of the Methodist Youth Fellowship, created to coordinate and represent the youth and student leadership of The Methodist Church.

After the presentation of papers reviewing the youth programs of those days, the group heard from two representatives of the current NYMO youth program: Jenny Devoe, a youth leader from Helena, Montana, and Lynn Strother Hinkle of the NYMO staff in Nashville, Tennessee. They spoke of the program and answered questions at length.

The group also had in their hands copies of a letter addressed by Harold W. Ewing, director of youth work in The Methodist Church during the 1950s, to Ezra Jones of the General Board of Discipleship. In his letter, Dr. Ewing wrote, "We are raising teen-agers in a 'pressure-cooker' of cultural problems we have created. The direction of the future may depend upon how the church can minister to them as they develop their values, life style and priorities." Such an EMPHASIS (sic) to involve every board, every conference and every local church in a creative program/ministry with the youth of the church and community."

The discussion of this question led the group of former leaders to contrast the substantial staff and funds devoted in the 1940s and 1950s to work with youth and students with the scanty resources now available on both national and annual conference levels. There was unanimity that United Methodism must place a higher priority on such work if its membership decline is to be reversed.

Resolved,

1) That the General Conference direct the General Council on Ministries, the General Council on Finance and Administration, the

General Board of Discipleship, the General Board of Higher Education and Ministry, and other general agencies to allocate sufficient funds and mobilize the necessary staff and resources for a major emphasis on youth and students commensurate with the risks and problems confronting young people in society today.

2) That the General Conference urge the annual conferences to increase their efforts and resources in youth and student work.

3) That the General Conference urge that at least one half-time staff position be provided within each conference to work in connection with the Conference Council on Youth Ministries and that adequate funding be provided within each annual conference budget for youth ministry as outlined in the *Book of Discipline*.

4) That the General Conference encourage local churches to enlist and involve youth in the life and work of their congregations.

5) That the General Council of Ministries plan to recommend youth ministry as a program emphasis for the 1997–2000 quadrennium.

ADOPTED 1992

See Social Principles, ¶ 72.

Equal Rights of Women

The gospel makes it clear that Jesus regarded women and men as being of equal worth. Nowhere is it recorded that Jesus treated women in a different manner than he did men. Although the gospel writers recorded little in the way of verbal statements of Jesus *about women*, they have preserved for us many incidents in the life of Jesus which indicated that he understood the equality of all people, male and female alike, to be a significant element of his message.

While Jesus called only males to be part of the 12, biblical evidence indicates that others, including women, were considered disciples or followers of Jesus. In open defiance of the customs of his society, Jesus taught women, spoke to them in public, and refused to confine women to the traditionally accepted roles. Moreover, women were the first witnesses to the resurrection and were directed to go and tell their brothers.

While both the Old and New Testaments came out of male-centered cultures and necessarily reflect that culture, interpretations of the Scriptures by the church have unduly emphasized male "superiority." For example, popular interpretations of the two creation stories often assume the women as "help mate" or "helper," which implies female inferiority or subordination. In the original Hebrew, however, the word translated "helper" described a person of at least equal status to the one helped. Indeed, the majority of times this word appears in the Old Testament it is speaking of God as "helper." Rather than defining women as secondary to man, each creation story points to the equality of the male and female, both of whom are made "in the image of God."

A number of statements attributed to Paul have frequently been cited to support the idea of feminine subordination and submission. However, when these statements are taken in context and balanced against the rest of the New Testament, especially against the message of Jesus, there can be no doubt that women are of equal value with men and should enjoy the same rights, privileges, and obligations as men.

The support of The United Methodist Church for equal rights of women derives from our traditional concern for justice, human dignity, and equality of all persons.

Examples of courageous action throughout our history inspire us as we move into our third century. Grounded in our biblical understanding, experience, and tradition, equal rights for women in church life, public institutions, and personal relationships have been, and will continue to be, fundamental in our call to be faithful as United Methodists.

Since 1972 this commitment was focused through our denomination's effort to support ratification of the Equal Rights Amendment to the United States Constitution. Three successive General Conferences, with practically unanimous votes, supported involvement in the ratification effort for the proposed 26th amendment which would have guaranteed equity in the formation and implementation of the legal statutes in the United States. Yet, the deadline for ratification occurred in 1982 with only three states lacking the necessary approval. Thus, in the United States citizens continue to live in a situation where the laws at the local, state, and federal levels discriminate against persons. Social policies which view women as dependents continue to the extent that many women reach mature adulthood and their senior years to find themselves in poverty. Trends indicate that women, children, and other dependents living in families headed by women will compose almost all the persons living in poverty in the United

States by the year 2000 if current social policies continue. These social conditions include social services cutbacks, unemployment, salary discrimination, inequality of opportunity, and the weakening of affirmative action and Equal Employment Opportunity regulations. For women of racial or language minority groups or women who are older, the burden of these conditions is the most extreme.

Be it therefore resolved, that we, as United Methodists will continue:

1. To lift up our historic concern for the equality of women and men, to confess those times when we have failed to confront discrimination, and to rejoice in efforts to support human dignity.

2. To work through local churches, councils of churches, conference committees, general agencies, and appropriate coalitions to research laws and policies that discriminate on the basis of gender and to advocate changes that enable equality of rights and opportunities. (This work will continue to require strategic focus and coordination on every level.)

3. To support the passage of the Equal Rights Amendment to the U.S. Constitution; to educate United Methodists and others to its history, meaning and purpose; and to work through all appropriate channels for its passage.

4. To monitor those public policies and practices which affect unemployment, pay inequity, inequality of opportunity, and in the United States the weakening of affirmative action (with special concern for the interlocking impact of discrimination on the basis of gender, race, age); to support those public policies and practices that create new jobs, that encourage women to move into non-traditional jobs and that alleviate competition between women and minorities for jobs.

5. To encourage United Methodist general program agencies and annual conferences to develop creative approaches for the development of governmental social policies that will eliminate the burden of poverty on women and children; to offer opportunities for service and action to United Methodists who want to be involved in eradicating those conditions; and to work for economic justice.

ADOPTED 1984

See Social Principles, ¶ 72.F, "The Status of women," "Ecumenical Decade: Churches in Solidarity with Women."

Eradication of Racism

WHEREAS, racism continues to be a pervasive and systematic force within our church; and

WHEREAS, racism deprives the church and society of the opportunity to utilize some of the best minds, skills, and talents which they have; and

WHEREAS, racist attitudes and practices in this country and in the church do not abate without intensive effort on the part of those who seek to ensure justice and equality;

Therefore, be it resolved, that the General Conference continue the General Commission on Religion and Race and its mandate that there be a Commission on Religion and Race in every annual conference; and

Be it resolved, that each annual conference be urged, through its commission to design programs specifically aimed at eradicating racism and achieving equality and inclusiveness; and

Be it resolved, that each annual conference be encouraged to urge its local churches to develop programs and activities which are directed at promoting inclusiveness within the local congregations.

ADOPTED 1992

See Social Principles, ¶ 72, "A Charter for Racial Justice Policies in an Interdependent Global Community," "Elimination of Racism in The United Methodist Church," "Racial Harassment," "Global Racism."

Ethnic Membership on Boards and Agencies

Be it resolved, that the delegates at the various jurisdictional conferences be urged to be intentional in their nominations to the various general boards and agencies to assure that ethnic minorities are elected to these boards and agencies in representative numbers; and

Be it further resolved, that the nominating committees of each annual conference include in its nomination and election process and equitable number of ethnic minorities on every board and agency.

ADOPTED 1992

See Social Principles, ¶ 72, "Affirmative Action."

Federal Funds for Indian Health Services

WHEREAS, Native Americans are the most socioeconomically deprived minority group in the United States; and

WHEREAS, the United States government is bound by treaty to

provide health care for all Native Americans and their descendants; and

WHEREAS, the United States government now provides these medical services through Indian Health Services, United States Public Health Service, Department of Health and Human Services; and

WHEREAS, medical services currently provided by the Indian Health Services for health education and prenatal care have contributed to an even more rapid decline in infant mortality among Native Americans than among more affluent whites; and

WHEREAS, similar success of these health programs are likely to have occurred for all Native Americans living in the United States; and

WHEREAS, despite these successes, the current administration proposes substantial funding cuts for the Indian Health Services; and

WHEREAS, any funding cuts could severely curtail or cancel health care for a large number of eligible Native Americans; and

WHEREAS, a small number of Native Americans have private health insurance, and an even larger number cannot afford to buy such insurance.

Be it resolved, that all Native Americans have access to adequate medical services to ensure a balance of physical, mental, and spiritual well-being for the "Journey Toward Wholeness;" and that the current appropriation committee allow no decrease in federal funds to operate Indian health facilities.

Be it further resolved, that the General Board of Church and Society submit this resolution, on behalf of the General Conference, to all United States senators and legislators that have Indian Health Services within their respective state.

ADOPTED 1988

See Social Principles, ¶ 72.F, "The United Methodist Church and America's Native People," "Rights of Native American People of the Americas."

Full Personhood

WHEREAS, We, as a General Conference, have taken steps to ensure the participation of women in the church, such as the establishing of a Commission on the Status and Role of Women; and

WHEREAS, The call to serve Christ with all our gifts, time and abilities is made to both men and women;

Therefore, be it resolved, That all persons, boards and agencies

255

responsible for programming at every level of the church be encouraged to evaluate their programs as to their explicit and implicit impact on women and take such steps necessary to affirm programs which encourage full personhood for everyone.

ADOPTED 1976

See Social Principles, ¶ 72.F, "Equal Rights of Women," "Celebrate and Support the Ongoing work of the General Commission on the Status and Role of Women."

Global Racism

God through creation has established a mode whereby, through a reconciling process, human beings can achieve the full potential of their existence.

The worth of every human being resides in the intrinsic value which God has given to each individual. This affirmation is echoed in Jesus' parables where each human being is valued according to God's special love for that person.

Any person who places another person, by thought or deed, outside of the possibility of human growth and development violates God's sacred mandate to humanity: "Love your neighbor as yourself."

This mandate sets the conditions for human existence through justice, mutual respect, and trust. Our failure to fulfill this mandate has resulted in oppression and racism.

Racism is a system of domination in which one racial group claims superiority and oppresses other groups for economic, political, cultural, psychological and/or religious reasons. Racism confers certain privileges on a small group of people who benefit from the resultant inequities. It is the creation and defense of these privileges that underlie and maintain the systems of racial domination. For this reason, racial domination is exceedingly complex. It is enforced and maintained both consciously and unconsciously by the legal cultural, educational, economic, political, and military institutions of a society. This oppression is a pervasive, worldwide phenomenon, not confined to certain countries or continents. No economic system— socialism, capitalism or any other—is immune to it.

Racism is encountered whenever:

1. Persons, even before they are born, are assigned to a group,

severely limited in freedom of movement, choice of work and places of residence because of their race.

2. Groups of people, because of their race, are denied effective participation in the political process and are compelled, often by physical force, to obey the edicts of governments which they were not allowed to have a part in choosing.

3. Racial groups within a nation are excluded from the normal channels available for gaining economic power, through denial of educational opportunities and entry into occupational/professional groups.

4. Policies of a nation ensure benefits for that nation from the labor or racial groups, migrant or otherwise, while at the same time denying to such people commensurate participation in the affairs of the nation.

5. The identity of persons is defamed through stereotyping of racial and ethnic groups in textbooks, cinema, mass media, interpersonal relations and other ways.

6. People are denied equal protection of the law, because of race, and when constituted authorities of the state use their power to protect the interests of the dominant group at the expense of the powerless.

7. Groups or nations continue to profit from regional and global structures that are historically related to racist presuppositions and actions.

The Social Principles states that:

Racism plagues and cripples our growth in Christ, inasmuch as it is antithetical to the gospel itself. Therefore, we reject racism in every form, and affirm the ultimate and temporal worth of all persons. We rejoice in the gifts which particular ethnic histories and cultures bring to our total life. We commend and encourage the self-awareness of all racial and ethnic minorities and oppressed people which leads them to demand their just and equal rights as members of society. We assert the obligation of society, and groups within the society, to implement compensatory programs that redress long-standing systemic social deprivation of racial and ethnic minorities. We further assert the right of members of racial and ethnic minorities to equal opportunities in employment and promotion; to education and training of the highest quality; to nondiscrimination in voting, in access to public accommodations, and in housing purchase or rental; and positions of leadership and power in all elements of our life together.

Confession of Racism in Today's Church

As a religious community, both as United Methodist congregations and individuls, we often have failed to proclaim and live out the gospel message of love toward our neighbors in terms of salvation and liberation for all of God's people. Too often we have not recognized the struggle against racism as central to our church's missions to the world.

Confession of Racism in Today's Society

Within the larger secular society, it is the economic and political manifestations of racism that are the most obvious. Usually, it is people of color, women and children, and those people in developing countries who suffer most from the priorities of racist policies and attitudes.

As United Methodists we recognize the need to:

1. Examine our direct and indirect roles in retarding the self-determination and development of racially oppressed people.

2. Critique immigration patterns and promote nonracially determined immigration policies.

3. Recognize the exploitation of the world's resources and people by many transnational corporations who place profit before people.

4. Demand greater corporate responsibility and accountability.

5. Demand greater responsibility from the communications/media industry in their role of attitude formation and perpetuation of racist stereotypes and mythology.

6. Assess the continued exploitation inherent in the dichotomies of north/south, rich/poor, industrialized nations/world of color.

7. Critique and reform legal and judicial systems which disproportionately jail, imprison, and execute people of color.

8. Support the restructuring of the educational systems to enable all children to learn to their fullest potential under conditions of maximum opportunity.

9. Support the enforcement of affirmative action in employment, housing, health care institutions, and governmental system, even in the face of laws which compel such behavior.

10. Support changes in laws and practices which doubly discriminate against women of color.

As United Methodists who have adopted a "Charter for Racial Justice Policies in an Interdependent Global Community," we recognize the need to:

1. Condemn the Ku Klux Klan, the Nazi Party, the Posse

Comitatus, Aryan Nations, Christian Identity Movement, and similar militantly racist movements.

2. Assess the increasing militarism of the United States, which is based on racist enlistment patterns growing out of economic forms of racism; the ultimate wrong of U.S. minorities fighting in the Third World on behalf of an elitist group of economic interests.

3. Understand the implications of bilingual and multicultural experiences in relationship to racism.

4. See our actions on racism in the light of histories and issues of Black Americans, Hispanic Americans, Native peoples, Asians, and Pacific Islanders.

5. Examine the domination by the United States of Puerto Rico's development, particularly the Island of Vieques.

6. Examine the racist actions in the United States involving refugees coming from Africa, Asia, the Caribbean, Latin America, and the Pacific Islands.

7. Halt racist actions directed at Native peoples, related to sacred lands, broken treaties, land rights and natural resources questions.

8. Challenge the inherent racism of United States immigration policy, its unfair application to people of color, and the treatment of the undocumented persons.

9. Examine the racism of the welfare system in the United States.

Therefore, as United Methodists, Committed to Understanding and Eliminating Racism

We affirm the use of nonviolent action and resistance as alternatives to human abuse, injustice, war, and exploitation, and that nonviolence become one of the strategies for a new international coalition to combat racism:

We recommend the following actions:

1. That the General Commission on Religion and Race make known, monitor, and address throughout the denomination the new manifestations of racism and strategies as revealed in the National and Jurisdictional Convocations held in the 1985-1988 Quadrennium.

2. That the general agencies, the Council of Bishops and local congregations affirm and encourage the use of theologies of ethnic peoples which will free all people from the domination of Anglo-European theologies and make ethnic faith relevant to their own communities.

3. That individuals and local congregations be encouraged to

explore how their invested money is being used and to question the racial practices of those companies in which they invest.

4. That the General Boards of Church and Society and Global Ministries work to:

a) Urge the U.S. government to cease all collaboration with the government of South Africa until it abandons its policy on *apartheid*.

b) Encourage the U.S. Senate to ratify and become an advocate for the International Convention on the Elimination of All Forms of Racial Discrimination.

c) Provide an opportunity for dialogue among United Methodists in the United States, Methodists in South Africa, representatives from the African National Congress (ANC), Southwest Africa People's Organization (SWAPO), and United Methodist persons living in the Front Line States of Southern Africa. The dialogue will focus on *apartheid* as the source of violence in Southern Africa, South Africa's use of "anti-communism" as a way to divert global attention away from the racism and brutality of *apartheid*, and the special circumstance of women and children under *apartheid*.

5. That the General Board of Global Ministries and the General Board of Discipleship promote study and use of interpretive materials for local churches on the World Council of Churches' Program to Combat Racism and encourage individuals and local churches to consider financial support for the "Special Fund to Combat Racism" of the World Council of Churches.

6. That the Commission on Religion and Race and the General Board of Global Ministries make a careful analysis of the perspective of indigenous and aboriginal people vis-a-vis racism, especially in those cases where genocide is being practiced.

7. That the appropriate United Methodist agencies sponsor a convocation in the United States for members of the mass media to:

a) Examine racism in reporting both in the United States and outside.

b) Examine racism in advertising.

ADOPTED 1984, REVISED, 1988

See Social Principles, ¶ 72.F, "A Charter for Racial Justice Policies in an Interdependent Global Community," "Eradication of Racism."

Goals and Recommendations on Participation of Women

Goals

The United Methodist Church, in serious consideration of the issue of the role of women in the Christian community and their participation in the life and work of The United Methodist Church, believes that it should direct its energies and resources:

1. To move toward the liberation of all persons so that all may achieve full humanity.

2. To bring about attitudinal changes in relation to (a) theological, philosophical, and biblical interpretations and understandings of the role of women and (b) expectations for achievement and contributions of women.

3. To make all United Methodists sensitive to the issues involved in the rights of women.

4. To overcome rigid sex-role distinctions which have traditionally characterized church structures and society.

5. To eliminate all discriminatory language, images, and practices in the life and work of The United Methodist Church.

6. To create an openness and receptivity for women in the professional ministry of The United Methodist Church.

7. To utilize the full potential of both men and women in elections and appointments at all levels in The United Methodist Church.

8. To establish a process for evaluation of the performance of The United Methodist Church regarding the role and participation of women in its life and work.

Recommendations for the Enhancement of the Participation of Women

1. That every programming agency in the denomination give serious attention to developing new avenues of participation for younger adult members of the denomination, particularly women in the 20-35 age range; and further that this attention be in the form of staff time and financial resources needed to explore varied styles of family life, that alternative life styles be considered, and that new styles (e.g., single women, employed women) be made more acceptable in the overall church population; and

2. That, inasmuch as the Study Commission has been pre-

occupied with the study of the problems of women's roles in general, to the exclusion of the particular problems of women in racial and ethnic groups, the study should be continued with special attention given to the roles of women of minority racial groups and ethnic groups within The United Methodist Church; and

3. That experimental ministries be developed to and by women, in order to increase awareness of roles and potential of women through consciousness-raising, counseling, education, and political action; and

4. That the media development agencies of the church produce and disseminate materials which would aid a sensitization process concerning the role of women with consideration being given to all forms of media presentation; and

5. That there be a development of curriculum which would help United Methodists avoid sustaining an inadequate image of male and female roles and understand how our rigidly held sexual roles deprive us of our full humanity, and which would assist in the exploration and development of new and alternative life styles; and

6. That careful consideration be given to the professional ministry, beginning with the traditional practices of entering the profession, continuing through recruitment and acceptance at the schools of theology, educational programs for women in the schools of theology, the processes and attitudes of annual conference boards of ministry and the attitudes of local congregations toward women clergy; and

7. That the Theological Study Commission on Doctrine and Doctrinal standards be requested to study and report on the role of women from a theological and doctrinal perspective; and

8. That all nominating committees in local churches, annual, jurisdictional, and general conferences give attention to the nomination of women for membership on committees, commissions, boards, councils, and other organizations, so that women are included in all of these units in significant numbers (bearing in mind that at least 50 percent of the membership of The United Methodist Church is made up of women); and

9. That the General Conference take whatever action is necessary to

a. assure an increased proportion of women in all levels of professional staff in general boards and agencies; and

b. create a more favorable setting for the recruitment, education, and appointment of women clergy; and

c. encourage local churches to be open to the acceptance of women as clergy (senior ministers, associate ministers, and ministers in special appointments) and as lay employees; and

10. That the General Conference establish a Commission on the Role of Women in The United Methodist Church to foster an ongoing awareness of the problems and issues relating to the status of women and to stimulate progress reports on these issues from the various borads and agencies. (The legislation for the organization and work of the commission is in the *Discipline*.)

ADOPTED 1972

See Social Principles, ¶ 72.F, "Full Personhood," "Celebrate and Support the Ongoing Work of the General Commission on the Status and Role of Women," "Equal Rights of Women."

Guidelines for Interreligious Relationships
"Called to Be Neighbors and Witnesses"

Nations of the world are growing increasingly interdependent politically and economically, and the various world religious communities are also encountering each other in new ways. Religions of Asia and Africa are showing new life and power within their homelands and are spreading to other continents, creating new multireligious societies, especially in western nations. New sects, cults, and ideologies merge and seek converts to their faith.

The emergence of these religiously diverse societies and the new dynamics in old religious communities have forced many faiths to reconsider how they relate to one another and to secular ideologies. There is danger that religious tensions will lead to oppression of religious minorities and curtailment of religious freedom with real potential for armed conflict. Worldwide problems of human suffering due to poverty, wars, and political oppression are so vast and pervasive that no one faith group can solve them, yet tensions between religious groups often prevent cooperation in solving these urgent human problems. As ancient religions demonstrate new life and power to speak to the deepest human concerns, questions are raised for Christians regarding their understanding of these faiths and regarding their claims to a global mission to all people.

What are the implications of this religiously diverse situation for Christian theology? What does it mean to be a faithful follower of and witness to Jesus Christ? Can we of different faiths live together as neighbors, or will diverse religious loyalties result in mutual antagonism and destruction? What are the resources of United Methodist Christians for building constructive relationships between persons of different faiths?

The United Methodist Church provides this statement as guidance to its members and congregations in facing these questions in their relations with persons of other faiths.

Called to Be Neighbors

For some Christians, it seems strange even to refer to "persons of other faiths." We are accustomed to calling them "non-Christians" or "non-believers." These attitudes have developed out of confidence in the ultimate truth of our own faith, and from ignorance of and insensitivity to other faiths, to the truth they contain, and to the profound meaning and purpose they give to the lives of people.

In conversation with a lawyer (cf. Luke 10:25), Jesus reminded him that his neighbor, the one to whom he should show love and compassion, included a stranger, a Samaritan. Today, our Lord's call to neighborliness (cf. Luke 10:27), includes the "strangers" of other faiths who have moved into our towns and cities. It is not just that historical events have forced us together. The Christian faith itself impels us to love our neighbors of other faiths and to seek to live in contact and mutually beneficial relationships, in community, with them.

What does it mean to be a neighbor? It means to meet other persons, to know them, to relate to them, to respect them, and to learn about their ways which may be quite different from our own. It means to create a sense of community in our neighborhoods, towns, and cities and to make them places in which the unique customs of each group of people can be expressed and their values protected. It means to create social structures in which there is justice for all and in which everyone can participate in shaping their life together "in community." Each race or group of people is not only allowed to be who they are, but their way of life is valued and given full expression.

Christians distinguish several meanings of "community." One

definition expresses their relationships as members of one another in the body of Christ, the Church, a people called together by Christ, a "communion of saints" who look to the reign of God. A broader definition points to the relationship that is shared with others in the wider human community, where Christians are concerned for peace, justice, and reconciliation for all people. Other faiths also have their understanding of "community." The vision of a "worldwide community of communities" commends itself to many Christians as a way of being together with persons of different faiths in a pluralistic world. That suggests that we United Methodist Christians, not just individually, but corporately, are called to be neighbors with communities of other faiths (Buddhist, Jewish, Muslim, Hindu, and others), and to work with them to create a human community, a set of relationships between people at once interdependent and free, in which there is love, mutual respect, and justice.

Within this religiously diverse community, Christians, trusting in Jesus Christ for their salvation, are called to witness to him as Lord to all people, (cf. Acts 1:8). We witness to our Lord through words which tell of his grace, through deeds of service and social change that demonstrate his love, and through our life together in the Christian community, exhibiting God's power to heal, reconcile, and unite.

As relationships with persons of other faiths deepen, Christians discover how often their witness has been unneighborly, how much we have talked and how little we have listened, and how often insensitive and unappreciative approaches have alienated sincere truth seekers and persons who already have strong faith commitments. We become aware that we frequently communicate attitudes of superiority regarding our own faith and inferiority toward that of others, and that in so doing, we perpetuate walls and hostilities between us as human beings which lessen chances that our witness will be received.

As we United Methodist Christians reflect anew on our faith and seek guidance in our witness to, and encounter with, our new neighbors, we rediscover that God who has acted in Jesus Christ for the salvation of the whole world, is also Creator of all humankind, the "one God and Father of all men, who is Lord of all, works through all, and is in all," (Ephesians 4:6 TEV). The God to whom we point in Jesus Christ is the God who is at work in every society in ways we do not fully understand and who has not left himself without witness in any human community. Here Christians confront a profound mystery, the awareness of God who is related to all creation and at work in the whole of it, and the experience of God who has acted redemptively for the whole creation in Jesus Christ. Christians witness to God in Jesus Christ in the confidence that here all people find salvation and in the trust that because of what we know of God in Jesus, God deals graciously and lovingly with all people everywhere.

Dialogue: A Way to Be Neighbors and Witnesses

"Dialogue" is the word which has come to signify a different approach to persons of other faiths, one which takes seriously both the call to witness and the command to love and be neighbors, and sees witnessing and neighborliness as interrelated activities. Rather than a onesided address, dialogue combines witnessing with listening. It is the intentional engagement with persons of other faiths for mutual understanding, cooperation, and learning.

"Dialogue" may be as informal as a conversation in the marketplace, or as formal as the leader of one religious group explaining to others its philosophy or worship life. Dialogue is more than an individual or academic enterprise. It also involves groups or communities of people holding different faiths, who reach out to one another. This community orientation gives a practical bent to interreligious dialogue.

In dialogue, one individual or group may seek a relationship with another in order to expose misunderstandings and stereotypes, and to break down barriers that separate and create hostility and conflict. Ethnic or religious communities may approach each other in dialogue in order to resolve particular problems or to foster cooperation in dealing with a local, national, or even global situation of human suffering. At its deepest level, dialogue is both learning about and sharing our respective faiths. Each partner learns from the rich store of wisdom of the other, and each expresses his or her own deepest conviction in the faith that it has a truth worth sharing with the other.

Through dialogue with persons of other faiths, new insights are received regarding God's activity in the world today and the divine purpose for humankind as a whole, and the place of the Christian community within these purposes. It is also a common experience for Christians to feel the need to express their own faith with greater clarity. We can expect the Holy Spirit to make known new and different insights through our encounter with persons of other faiths.

Because the Jewish community is the largest community of another faith in the United States, Jews will be a major partner in dialogue for the United Methodists. Christians need Judaism lest their faith in God be compromised and truncated in a rootless Christianity. For many United Methodists, especially in Asia, Buddhists, Hindus, or Muslims will be their natural partners in dialogue. Dialogue with persons in these faith groups is increasingly important for United States Christians as well, since their numbers there are increasing. Muslims and Christians also share a close but often unrecognized relationship, since both have roots that go back to Abraham. In many nations, long histories of separation between Buddhist, Hindu, and Christian communities have yet to be bridged, while in the United States many youth have been attracted to the deep spirituality of Buddhist and Hindu adherents. Dialogue offers the possibility of sharing mutually beneficial insights, as well as overcoming past hostilities.

Dialogue frequently has been misunderstood. Some see it as limited to the commonalities between persons and communities of different faiths. It is important to discern and explore those commonalities and to utilize them to strengthen relationships. But there is more! Dialogue offers to both partners the opportunity of enriching their own faith through the wisdom of the other. In the process it helps overcome the deep mistrust, hatred, hostility, and conflict that characterize so many intercultural and interreligious relations. Each religious community asserts that its faith offers a way to resolve conflict in positive ways and has resources for building community among diverse peoples. Dialogue seeks to provide an environment which allows space for differences and to build on the positive affirmations of each faith and to bring them into relationship with each other.

The only precondition for dialogue is a willingness to enter a relationship of mutual acceptance, openness, and respect. Effective dialogue requires that both partners have deep convictions about life, faith, and salvation. True dialogue requires that Christians *not* suspend their fundamental convictions concerning the truth of the Gospel but enter into dialogue with personal commitment to Jesus Christ and with the desire to witness to that faith. Effective dialogue also requires that Christians be open to persons of other faiths, to their convictions about life, truth, and salvation and to their witness, as others also feel called to witness to their faith and teachings about the meaning of life.

Dialogue: An Exchange of Witness

Is not this urge to witness an obstacle to interreligious dialogue? It often has been but it need not be. Where there is listening as well as speaking, openness and respect as well as concern to influence, there is dialogue *and* witness. Indeed, dialogue at its most profound level is an *exchange of witness*. Participants share with each other their perceptions of the meaning of life, of ultimate reality, salvation and hope, and the resources of their faith for enabling community. In genuine "dialogue," we "witness and are witnessed to." The most effective dialogue takes place when both sides really do care that the other hear, understand, and receive their wisdom. Part of our witness is our openness to hearing the witness of the other.

Dialogue at these depths holds great promise. Long cherished convictions may be modified by the encounter with others. Misunderstandings may be clarified, potential hostilities reconciled, and new insights regarding one's own faith may emerge in contrast to that of another. The depths of another's faith may be so disclosed that its power and attractiveness are experienced. Dialogue is a demanding process, requiring thorough understanding of one's own faith and clear articulation of it to the other person.

Dialogue is *not* a betrayal of witness. Dialogue and witness are wrongly placed in opposition to each other. They need each other. Dialogue creates relationships of mutual understanding, openness, and respect. Witness presses dialogue to the deepest convictions about life, death, and hope.

Many persons of other faiths are suspicious that dialogue is a new and more subtle tool for conversion. In some ways this is inevitable since Christians do want others to learn of and receive the truth and grace we know in Jesus Christ. The difference between dialogue and other forms of witness is that it is a context for learning from the other the truth and wisdom of the other faith as well as sharing with the other the truth and wisdom of our own. We leave to the Holy Spirit the outcome of our mutual openness. Our concern is to be obedient to our own call to witness and to the imperative to be loving and neighborly to persons of other faiths. In dialogue, these deeply held truths encounter each other in witness and love, so that larger wisdom and larger understanding of truth may emerge which benefit all parties in the dialogue. As we exhibit courtesy, reverence and respect, and become neighbors, our fears of each other are allayed, and the Holy Spirit works within these relationships.

Neighbors and Witnesses

The command to love one's neighbors and the call to witness to Jesus Christ to all people are inseparably linked. The profound challenge which this represents for United Methodist Christians can be seen most sharply in the new religious movements which have arisen in recent years. These movements have become a source of concern for many Christians. Some groups seem to utilize methods that are manipulative and coercive. However, many people have found new vision, meaning, and hope in some of these new faiths. These new religious movements are very diverse and they should not be lumped together indiscriminately, condemned and dismissed. Neither should they automatically be embraced as valid expressions of human dignity and freedom.

Careful study and contact will enable Christians to distinguish those which are manipulative and coercive and which are to be challenged for reasons of faith. Questions of basic human rights are raised both by tactics sometimes employed by some religious movements and by acts of opposition against them. In particular, enforced deprogramming represents a violation of the personality of individuals and their rights of free choice. The question of what means are justified in trying to win back persons who have joined cults is a difficult one, and one to which Christians will respond differently. Where children of church members are involved, the parents are in special need of pastoral counseling and support. The best preparation for meeting these groups is the development within families and through the educational program of the Church a deeper understanding of and commitment to Jesus Christ and his claims, especially the costliness of following our "suffering servant" Lord. This commitment is deepened through the experience of acceptance and personal relationship within the fellowship of the Christian community.

As we take seriously this calling to be witnesses and neighbors, to people of all faiths old and new, we become aware of the biblical caution not to bear false witness (cf. Matthew 19:18) and the admonition to live at peace with all people (cf. Hebrew 12:14). How are we to avoid bearing false witness unless we know our neighbors and understand their faith commitments? How can one truly love a neighbor and hold back what to Christians is the greatest of all gifts—God becoming present to people in Jesus Christ? How can we live peacefully together, unless we are willing to be neighborly? How can we say we love our neighbor if we are unwilling to be attentive to the message and the gifts which God has given him or her? Love of neighbor and witness to Christ are the two primary attitudes of United Methodist Christians in their relationship with persons of other faiths. And when we become this kind of neighbor, we discover that God has given us another gift—people of different faiths.

Guidelines for Interreligious Relationships

The following guidelines will assist United Methodists to be faithful to their call to witness and to the call to be neighbors with persons of other faiths.

1. *Discover and find out about the persons of other faiths in your town or city and educate your congregation about them.*

a. Plan experiences that bring Christians into contact with persons of other faiths. Whenever possible initiate these experiences ecumenically. In the absence of cooperative efforts to develop relationships and explore tensions and difficulties, United Methodist initiative is encouraged.

b. Visit the services and meeting places of other faiths, but respect their sacred times and places and do not treat them as "tourist" attractions.

c. Study the new religious movements carefully and develop attitudes of courtesy towards them.

Support efforts in the community to insure that their human rights are not violated. Seek assistance in cases where efforts are being made to insure the human rights of members of a group by testing their freedom to leave it, and in developing perspectives on Christian witness to these new religious movements.

2. *Initiate dialogues with other faith communities.*

a. Seek relationships with Jews, Muslims, Buddhists, and Hindus, and their respective organizations. Initiate conversations, programs, and dialogues leading to: understanding of each faith, appreciation of their particular gifts, discovery of commonalities and differences, and areas of mutual cooperation.

b. With the Jewish community seek an awareness of both our common roots and the tragic interlocking of our histories, sensitivity to anti-Semitism among Christians, and an understanding of the significance of the Holocaust and the importance of Israel for Jews.

c. With the Muslim community, explore the negative stereotypes which perpetuate misunderstanding and continue to hinder the establishment of positive relationships, and seek an understanding of the role of the Islamic faith in various Middle Eastern societies.

d. With the Buddist and Hindu communities, explore their spiritual practices and understandings which have attracted many people in the west.

Prepare for dialogue through reflection on the following:

(1) Clarity regarding your understanding of and commitment to your own faith is absolutely essential.

(2) Each partner must believe the other is speaking in good faith.

(3) Each partner must strive for a clear understanding of the faith of the other and be willing to interpret it in its best light rather than its worst.

(4) Each partner must forthrightly face the issues that cause separation as well as those that create unity.

3. *Share in common enterprises with persons of other faiths in practical ways.*

a. Work together to resolve economic, social, cultural, and political problems in the community. Together become sensitive to infringements of the human rights of groups within the community and threats to their cultural values and heritage and initiate steps to protect them.

b. Jointly plan community celebrations with an interreligious perspective.

c. Participate in interreligious associations.

d. Seek to generate interreligious educational efforts in the community. This could include enlisting the aid of school authorities in the examination of texts used in schools to see that the various religious groups are depicted fairly and accurately. Other educational ventures might include providing courses in adult schools and for people who are planning trips abroad; or developing special programs for media such as television and radio to reach a wider audience.

4. *Prepare carefully before sharing in celebrations, rituals, worship, and meditation with persons of other faiths.*

It will not be possible for Christians to participate fully in another faith's rituals and worship, nor should they expect it. However, it is appropriate, where invited, to share in such occasions. Some may wish to share in joint prayer services. On such occasions, care should be taken not to relativize all religious symbols and practices to make religious differences unimportant. It is unwise to juxtapose symbols of different religions. Each partner must approach such occasions out of the integrity of his or her own faith.

Intent

The intent in developing interreligious relationships is not to amalgamate all faiths into one religion. We Christians have no interest in such syncretism. To engage in interreligious dialogue is not to say that any religion is all right just so you have one. Far from requiring a lessening of commitment to Christ, effective dialogue is only possible when one's own faith is strong.

We Christians are seeking to be neighbors with persons of other faiths whose religious commitments are different from our own, and to engage each other about the deepest convictions of our lives. In our assurance of and trust in God's grace in Jesus Christ, we open ourselves to dialogue and engagement with persons of other faiths and to other Christians whose understandings may be different from our own.

This interreligious engagement challenges United Methodist Christians to think in new ways about our life in the broader human community, about our mission, evangelism, service, and our life together within the Christian church. We seek to promote peace and harmony with persons of other faiths in our various towns, cities, and neighborhoods.

Yet we do not hide our differences, nor avoid conflicts, but seek to make them constructive. In each place we share our lives with each other, we witness and are witnessed to, we invite others into the

Christian community and we are invited into theirs. Our prayer is that the lives of all in each place will be enriched by the differences of others, that a new sense of community may emerge, and that others may receive the gift of God in Christ, while we receive the gifts which have been given them.

ADOPTED 1980

See Social Principles, ¶ 72.B, "Our Muslim Neighbors," "The Global Nature of The United Methodist Church."

Health and Wholeness

Introduction

All human beings have been created in the image of God and are called to the abundant life. In the biblical story of the woman with the hemorrhage, Jesus provides an example of his healing ministry that includes the spiritual as well as the physical status of the person.

"And behold, a woman, who had suffered from a hemorrhage for twelve years came up behind and touched the fringe of his garment; For she said to herself, 'If I only touch his garment, I shall be made well.' Jesus turned and seeing her, he said, 'Take heart, daughter; your faith has made you well.' And instantly the woman was made well" (Matt. 9:20-22).

The United Methodist Church, as an entity, believes that its mission is to continue the redemptive ministry of Christ, including teaching, preaching and healing. Christ's healing was not peripheral but central in his ministry. The church, therefore, understands itself as called by the Lord to the wholistic ministry of healing: spiritual, mental and emotional, and physical.

Health in this sense is something beyond, but not exclusive of, biological well-being. In this view, health care is inadequate when it fixes its attention solely on the body and its physiological functions, as is any religion that focuses its interest entirely on the spirit. Taking the gospel mandates seriously, United Methodists are called to work toward a healthy society of whole persons. Part of our task is to enable people to care for themselves and to take responsiblity for their own health. Another part of our task is to ensure that people who are ill whether from illness of spirit, mind, or body are not turned aside or ignored but given care that allows them to live a full life. We see this task as demanding concern for spiritual, political, ethical, economic, social, and medical decisions that maintain the highest concern for the condition of society, the environment, and the total life of each person.

Human suffering is caused by a variety of factors, the environmental, social and personal factors mentioned as well as others which remain unknown to us.

Environmental Factors. Clean air, pure water, effective sanitary systems for the disposal of wastes, nutritious foods, adequate housing and hazard-free work places are essential to health. The best medical system cannot preserve or maintain health when the environment is disease-producing.

Social Factors. Inadequate education, poverty, unemployment, lack of access to food, stress-producing conditions, and social pressures reinforced by marketing and advertising strategies that encourage the use of tobacco, alcohol, and other drugs are detrimental to good health.

Personal Habits. Overeating or eating non-nutritious foods, substance abuse (including alcohol, tobacco, barbiturates, sedatives, etc.) are clearly destructive of health. Failure to exercise or to rest and relax adequately are also injurious to health.

Although medical care represents a very important part of health care it does not include the whole. More medical care does not always equal better health.

Medical care in much of the world has evolved too much as disease care rather than health care. Disease prevention, public health programs, and health education appropriate to every age level and social setting are needed globally. Services should be provided in a compassionate and skillful manner on the basis of need; without discrimination as to economic status, mental or physical handicap, race, color, religion, sex, age, national origin, or language.

A Just Health System

Within a just society every person has a right to:

1. Basic health services that are accessible and affordable in each geographic and cultural setting.

2. An environment that promotes health.

3. Active involvement in the formulation of health care activities that meet local needs and priorities.

4. Information about his or her illness and to be an active participant in treatment and rehabilitation.

5. Receive compassionate and skilled care.

6. A health care system sensitive to cultural needs.

7. Access to funding sources where necessary for basic health services. •

Health Insurance

For all persons to have adequate access to needed health care services, public financing must be a significant part of an overall health insurance plan. Public funding is necessary to pay for insuring those who cannot pay part or all of the necessary premiums required.

Health Maintenance

Many health problems and illnesses are preventable if we accept the fact that health maintenance requires understanding of the unity of the human body, mind and spirit. The whole person needs proper nutrition, exercise, the challenge to learn and grow, and an acknowledgement that this is a life-long process. We recognize that these needs are difficult to meet when environmental factors contribute to ill health. But we must acknowledge the fact that we have separated spiritual health from physical health. In Western Protestant interpretation of health and healing, the union of the body and spirit are often dismissed. Cultures that respect and revere that union are often disregarded or looked upon in a condescending manner. The early church did not make these distinctions, nor did Jesus in his healing ministry. We must, if we are to obtain good health, unite the body and spirit in our thinking and actions.

Therefore, as Christians we accept responsibility for modeling this wholistic, preventive style of health maintenance. We commit ourselves to examining the value systems at work in our society as they impact the health of our people and to working for programs and policies that enable people to breathe clean air, drink clean water, eat wholesome food, and have access to adequate education and freedom that enable mind and spirit to develop.

Medical Services

We support the following principles of access to health services:

1. In a just society all people are entitled to basic maintenance and health care services. We reject as contrary to our understanding of the gospel the notion of differing standards of health care for various segments of the population.

2. Health care should be comprehensive, including preventive, therapeutic, and rehabilitative services.

3. Religious and other appropriate forms of counseling should be available to all patients and families when they are called upon to make difficult medical choices, so that responsible decisions, within the context of the Christian faith, may be made concerning organ transplants, use of extreme measures to prolong life, abortion, sterilization, genetic counseling, institutionalization, and death with dignity.

4. We encourage development of community support systems that permit alternatives to institutional care for such groups as the aging, the terminally ill and mentally ill, and other persons with special needs.

5. Professional health care personnel should be recruited and appropriately educated to meet the health care needs of all persons. Especially urgent is the need for physicians trained in geriatric medicine. Special priorities should be established to secure among the professional group at least proportional representation of women and minorities who are now seriously underrepresented.

6. In areas where medical services are not available, or are in undersupply, we urge private or public funding to provide the full range of needed services. To meet these goals, we recommend the reallocation of funds from armaments to human services, both nationally, and internationally (Social Principles ¶ 75.C).

7. Regional planning processes should coordinate the services rendered by all health care institutions, including those funded by governments, to create a more effective system of health services in every area. Priorities should be established for the provision of health services, such as preventive care, mental health services, home care, and health education.

8. Corrective measures should be taken where there is maldistribution or unavailability of hospital beds, intermediate care and nursing

home care, home-delivered care, neighborhood health centers, community mental health centers, and emergency care networks.

9. We encourage medical education for laypersons that will enable them to evaluate effectively medical care they need and are receiving.

10. We support the medical community in its effort to uphold ethical standards and to promote quality assurance.

Health and Wholeness Ministry

As United Methodists we are called to a ministry of health and wholeness. Therefore, we challenge our membership to:

1. Make health concerns a priority in the church with special emphases that include but are not limited to women's health concerns; appropriate, unbiased, informed diagnosis and treatment of older adults; preventive care (including health education); special health concerns and needs of children and youth; and establishment of networks for information sharing and action suggestions.

2. Support the provision of direct health services where needed and to provide, as we are able, such services in hospitals and homes, clinics, and health centers.

3. Accept responsibility for educating and motivating members to follow a healthy lifestyle reflecting our affirmation of life as God's gift.

4. Become actively involved at all levels in the development of support systems for health care in the community including: dependent care (respite and 24-hour care, in-home and short-term out-of-home care), meals, programs for women in crisis, halfway houses, support systems for independent living, and family support systems.

5. Become advocates for: a healthful environment, accessible, affordable health care, continued public support for health care of persons unable to provide for themselves, continued support for health-related research and provision of church facilities to enable health related ministries.

6. Become involved in a search for Christian understanding of health, healing and wholeness and the dimensions of spiritual healing in our congregations and seminaries.

7. Encourage colleges, universities, hospitals and seminaries related to The United Methodist Church connectional units to gain an added awareness of health issues and the need for recruitment and

education of persons for health-related ministries who would approach such ministries out of a Christian understanding and commitment.

8. Support public policies and programs that will ensure comprehensive health care services of high quality to all persons on the principle of equal access.

In the United States, we affirm the findings of the President's Committee on Medical Ethics of 1983. While noting the importance of cost containment, the committee wrote: "Measures designed to contain health care costs that exacerbate existing inadequacies or impede the achievement of equity are unacceptable from a moral standpoint."

A positive response to these challenges within the Christian context will help assure to all persons an abundant mental, emotional, and spiritual life.

ADOPTED 1984

See Social Principles, ¶ 72, "Health for All by the Year 2000," "Health in Mind and Body," "Universal Access to Health Care in the U.S. and Related Territories."

Health for All by the Year 2000

WHEREAS, The United Methodist Church is global in its outreach and has a strong commitment to work with other churches and secular organizations which are concerned about the health of the world's people; and

WHEREAS, The United Methodist Church has had a long history of medical missions, training of health personnel, support of health facilities, involvement of local churches in health education and direct service programs; and

WHEREAS, The United Methodist Church affirms health as a condition of physical, mental, social, and spiritual well-being to be desired and worked for by all persons, and that all persons are entitled to basic health care, while at the same time having a responsibility to care for their own health and to protect the health of others; and

WHEREAS, it is recognized that more than anything else people's health is affected by the circumstances of their lives including living and environmental conditions, education and employment opportunities, resources and life style, political and socio-economic realities, spiritual nurture, and supportive relationships; and

WHEREAS, it has been a part of the prophetic, redemptive and healing ministry of The United Methodist Church to identify always with those persons whose needs are not being met; to focus clearly on those factors which impede individuals and communities in their search for health and wholeness; and to point to what must be done if people are to be freed from those powers and practices which stand in the way of healthy development, physically, mentally, socially and spiritually; and

WHEREAS, the member states of the World Health Organization, including the United States, affirmed in 1977 at the 30th World Health Assembly that one of the most important social goals of the world community in the coming decades should be the attainment by all people of the world by the year 2000 of a level of health that will permit them to lead a socially and economically productive life; and

WHEREAS, the Director General of the World Health Organization has affirmed that cooperation between sectors of society, with an emphasis on religious as well as secular bodies, is essential toward the goal of health for all by the year 2000; and

WHEREAS, The United Methodist Church through its seven central conferences, 73 annual conferences, 38,000 local churches, 9,500,000 members, and its involvement with health ministries around the world, has a unique opportunity to protect and promote health; minister with persons who have illnesses of body, mind and/or spirit; create opportunities for individuals and communities to participate in determining local health priorities and methods for delivery of needed services, identify unmet needs and advocate that those needs be met; and address those political, economic and social factors which contribute to ill health and the unequal distribution of those opportunities, goods, and services which are essential to attaining and maintaining health;

Therefore be it resolved, that The United Methodist Church:

Joins with the international community affirming health for all by the year 2000 as one of the most important social goals of the 20th century;

Asks its annual conferences, central conferences, their related institutions, local churches, and all church members to be informed about the goal of health for all by the year 2000, and to work with other groups to develop means of promoting and protecting health, giving particular attention wherever possible to the needs of mothers and infants; children, youth and families; older persons; persons with handicapping conditions; and immigrants and refugees; being aware of how ageism, sexism, racism, handicappism, poverty and other forms of discrimination impede persons and communities in their achievement of health and wholeness; and

Encourages each annual conference and central conference to focus on health for all by the year 2000 through its health and welfare unit, or other most appropriate unit; and

Assigns responsibility to the Health and Welfare Ministries Program Department of the General Board of Global Ministries to develop and make available interpretive material about health for all by the year 2000 and to suggest ways in which the various units of The United Methodist Church can be involved in this goal.

ADOPTED 1984

See Social Principles, ¶ 72, "Health in Mind and Body," "Universal Access to Health Care in the U.S. and Related Territories," "Ministries on Mental Illness," "Health and Wholeness."

Health in Mind and Body

Mental health is intimately linked with the fundamental purpose of the church—the love of God, others, and self. Mental, physical, social, emotional, and spiritual health are intricately interwoven. How persons think about themselves, about life, and about the future has an impact on other areas of health. A healthy mind is necessary to get the most out of living. Positive mental health results in constructive activities and enables persons to use both good and bad experiences as opportunities for personal growth.

This concepts are consistent with biblical themes in which God reassures the people of God to have faith and hope, and not to fear. Wisdom literature refers again and again to the grounding of integrity and character in wisdom, insight, and a heart of purity (Job 42:1-6; Ps. 51:6-12; Prov. 4:7; 28:6). In the New Testament, Jesus reshapes these traditions to the teaching that real obedience to God begins in the heart (Matt. 5:8, 21-32; 15:1-20). Paul, too, expresses his confident hope in the face of suffering: "We are troubled on every side yet not distressed; we are perplexed, but not in despair" (2 Cor. 4:8).

There are clear indications and opportunities for the church to harness and use its worship, preaching, church school, group life, and evangelism as strategic educative, preventive, and therapeutic resources to bring hope and healing. The 1990 World Summit on Children addressed the fact that the world's children are living in conditions without hope. The National Institute on Mental Health in its annual report shared that "in the last three decades mood disorders will afflict more than 20 million Americans at some point in their lifetime."

I. Reasons for Actions

Mental health and those factors that affect it can be seen in global, national, community, and individual contexts.

A. Children and youth across the world suffer from war, regional conflicts, and national resources spent on the military rather than on human services such as education, housing, clean air and water, and health care. Children are often exploited for economic gain. As a result, many see the world as hostile and violent. They respond out of fear, anxiety, anger, and aggression.

B. National daily news reports about killings, family violence, gang violence, suicide, racial attacks, child abuse and neglect, and random street shootings all contribute to individuals and communities feeling insecure, anxious, and afraid.

C. The changing forms of the family in the United States—from an extended, close-knit one, to a two-parent nuclear one, to an ever-increasingly younger, female-headed single-parent family—have left children and adults with fewer supportive, nurturing family members. Families are facing more stressful, episodic crises than previous generations. Some of these stresses are a result of inadequate wages to support families and the lack of health insurance, all of which affect the overall emotional well-being of families.

D. Substance abuse has become a national crisis, especially the use of crack cocaine and its related violence. Children born to parents who abuse drugs are increasing in number, and too many children no longer feel safe or secure at home, in school, or within the community. Families and communities are becoming dysfunctional units because of this crisis.

E. People of color face the ordinary demands of life in addition to the vicissitudes of racism, sexism, and classism. The constant emotional and psychic energies used to thwart daily social pressures of inequality prevent people of color from reaching their full potential. The increasing incidences of racial violence in neighborhoods add to the emotional toll of alienation, isolation, and lack of acceptance of people of color in God's global community.

f. Clergy are also under stress. Today's clergy are expected to meet their traditional duties of pastoral care, teaching, preaching, and worship while simultaneously addressing the daily adversities that affect members of their congregations and communities. Ministry is increasingly more complex. The personal and vocational expectations and demands of ministry may drain clergy, their families, and congregations of healthy coping skills.

G. Laity in the life of the church may find themselves alone and without emotional support as they cope with the loss of a loved one because of suicide, murder, or traumatic circumstances such as terrorism; as their lives are touched by AIDS; as they care for the chronically ill parent or child; as they are confronted with physical, sexual, and emotional abuse; and as they face unemployment and other life-shattering experiences.

II. Policy Statement

The church's concern for mental health lies at the center of its mission to enable persons to develop and maintain peace and strength of mind.

We affirm the need for the church to avoid policies that harm mental health, such as those emphasizing status and power rather than Christ-like service to God in daily vocation. We affirm the need for the church to receive all persons as children of God, so that none are considered more holy than others. Likewise, we affirm the need for the church to consider the effect of human dignity of every sermon that is preached, every lesson that is taught, and every program that is planned and developed. We affirm the development of mental health ministries at all levels of the church through seminars, model sharing, skill-building opportunities, and direct services that bring healing and wholeness.

III. Action

The Christian faith encourages people to become whole with sound minds. This faith enables persons to care for their physical bodies, to live in harmony with the environment, and to face adversities with balance. It urges one to care about one's mental outlook toward life, living in peace and acceptance of oneself, with respect, fair play, justice, and acceptance of others as children of God.

• We urge all United Methodists to use the resources of the church to affirm positive mental health as an essential part of the gospel of Jesus Christ and make this affirmation a reality by planning appropriate programs and events through the local church's health and welfare ministries representative.

• We urge local churches to be in mission within the congregation and community through support groups, advocacy, public policy education, information-sharing, and direct service ministries with individuals and families.

• We urge United Methodist-related institutions of higher education to make mental health a part of the educational process by shaping a vision of human community that is inclusive of all persons, hopeful about the future, and confident of God's sustaining presence, through holding convocations and special educational events and including in the curriculum the concept of cultural diversity, the responsibility of Christians to participate in public life, and ethical practices stemming from the Christian belief that material resources are to be used in service to alleviate human suffering.

• We urge United Methodist schools of theology to continue to develop practical theology that instills in students the need for the mental health aspects of preaching, pastoral care, administration, and church polity. Seminary education should provide opportunities for prospective clergy to become involved in multidisciplinary settings and with challenges from other professionals to help congregations develop and maintain good mental health.

We ask the General Board of Global Ministries to:

• Develop models for mental health that relate to the local church.

• Provide research on mental health to other general agencies for their work on policy development, curriculum development, and programs.

- Provide to annual conferences specific plans on how conferences can develop programs that develop and promote good mental health within congregations and communities.
- Develop resources for local churches and annual conferences health and welfare representatives of specific actions they can take that will affirm good mental health.

ADOPTED 1992

See Social Principles, ¶¶ 71 and 72, "Ministries on Mental Illness," "Universal Access to Health Care in the U.S. and Related Territories," "Drug and Alcohol Concerns."

Higher Education Training and Scholarships

WHEREAS, The United Methodist Church supports the public education system in America and realizes that in an ever-changing society "Excellence in Education" can be achieved with proper nourishing; and

WHEREAS, church, community, and federal government involvement is imperative if the current trend in public education is to be reversed; and

WHEREAS, The United Methodist Church believes that every person has a right to an education and it is society's responsibility to enable every person to obtain this right; and

WHEREAS, The United Methodist Church believes in universal public education and supports public educational institutions; and

WHEREAS, individuals have the right and freedom to inquire, discuss, and teach, regulated by self-discipline of scholarship and good judgment;

Be it therefore resolved, that the General Conference:

1. Encourages all local churches to establish learning enrichment centers with tutors who can provide supplementary instruction for students to ensure academic excellence according to each one's potential;

2. Supports the training and recruitment of qualified ethnic minority teachers who will serve as positive role models for ethnic minority students;

3. Directs the General Board of Higher Education and Ministry to seek additional funding for scholarships for ethnic minority persons.

ADOPTED 1992

See Social Principles, ¶ 72.A, "Public Education in the United States," "A Charter for Racial Justice in an Interdependent Global Community."

History of Blacks in the United Methodist Church

W<small>HEREAS</small>, an examination and assessment of the Methodist legacy in America reveal that Black persons and their contributions continue to receive inadequate credits; and

W<small>HEREAS</small>, at the present time there are more written resources available about Blacks in the history of Methodism; and

W<small>HEREAS</small>, literature about Black persons in the Methodist history and/or literature written from the perspective of the Black ethos is perceived as resources primarily for Black persons; and

W<small>HEREAS</small>, an important element in the interrelationship of the different groups within the church family is to respect thoroughly and understand the uniqueness and contributions of Black persons in the evolving history of Methodism and the U.S.A.;

Therefore, be it resolved, that The General Commission on Archives and History and The United Methodist Publishing House in joint consultation with The General Commission on Religion and Race determine the most effective means to identify additional Black literary and historical records which have not been acknowledged and/or published; promote the use of these and other such resources among whites and other racial/ethnic minorities; and encourage training sessions led by Blacks using these resources which acknowledge the contributions of Black persons to the legacy and heritage of Methodism in the United States of America and the world.

ADOPTED 1992

See Social Principles, ¶ 72.A, "History of Racial/Ethnic United Methodists."

History of Racial/Ethnic United Methodists

W<small>HEREAS</small>, persons of Pacific Island, Asia, African, Hispanic, and Native American descent have made significant contributions to the history of The United Methodist Church and its predecessors; and

W<small>HEREAS</small>, these contributions have received scant attention and acknowledgement by the church and its historians; and

W<small>HEREAS</small>, this lack has begun to be addressed with the publication in 1991 of four histories of Asian Americans, African Americans, Native Americans, and Hispanic Americans within the United Methodist tradition and with four accompanying bibliographies;

Be it resolved, that the General Commission on Archives and History commends these histories and bibliographies to the United Methodist denomination and urges that archivists and historians at all levels of the church continue to collect, document, research, and disseminate sources and publications of racial/ethnic persons within United Methodism.

ADOPTED 1992

See Social Principles, ¶ 72, "Elimination of Racism in The United Methodist Church."

Homelessness in the United States

Homelessness is a scourge upon the nation's conscience. In the most materially rich nation in the world, the homeless are people who sleep 300 to a room in an old tire factory in San Diego. They are the lonely who pass their time talking to themselves in every big city and small town in the nation. They are rural families without the economic means to travel long distances to shelters and other public services. The homeless are people who have been displaced and discarded. Their numbers alone make them a nation of strangers, highly mobile and rootless, surrounded by wealth, glamor, and excess of all of that which they so desperately lack. On any given night in the United States, it is estimated that at least 735,000 individuals are without shelter. As many as two to three million people are without shelter one or more nights during the course of the year.

They are people with past histories and future hopes. They are young and old. They are from rural areas and big cities. They are black, brown, and white. They are Native Americans and recent Asian immigrants. They are women and men, families and children. The homeless are people who shiver in doorways and cower in subway tunnels. They are migrants who live in the back seats of cars and mothers with children who wait daily in soup lines for something to eat. They are multiple families crammed together in small apartments and mothers with children living in dilapidated chicken coops. They are farmers evicted from the land. Homelessness is a crisis that strikes at the soul of the nation and at the heart of the church. As Christians and as the church we must come to know the homeless and know these facts:

• Between 25 percent and 33 percent of homeless people are families with children.

- In some rural areas of the nation, 65 percent of the homeless are families.
- Approximately one-fourth of homeless people suffer from chronic mental illness or personality disorders.
- Veterans (especially Vietnam-era veterans) make up 22 percent to 46 percent of the homeless population.
- Around 4 percent of homeless people are unaccompanied youths.
- Migrant workers and migrant worker families are increasingly among the homeless.
- The homeless are disproportionately African Americans and other peoples of color.
- A substantial percentage (22 percent) of the homeless is employed full or part time, albeit in low-paying jobs.
- Males make up the majority of homeless people (66 percent)
- The median age for homeless people is around 35 years.
- Only about one-third of the homeless receive public assistance.
- More than 50 percent have been homeless for less than one year.

But the homeless are most assuredly the people of God—the people of God who call the church to both repentance and action. They are the hungry we are asked to feed, the strangers we are to welcome, the naked whom we are to clothe. They are the sick and imprisoned we are commanded to visit (Matt. 25:31-36). The homeless are our neighbors, living in closer proximity to our church buildings than many of our members.

The 1990 annual report of the U.S. Conference of Mayors reports a hardening of attitudes and a growing callousness among the larger population to the plight of the homeless. Yet the church cannot turn its face from the poor. It must continue to respond to those who have been left out and shunted aside. Few biblical mandates are clearer than those charging us to care for the poor. In isaiah 58:6-7, God says, "Is not this the fast that I choose . . . to share your bread with the hungry, and bring the homeless poor into your house; and when you see the naked, to cover him?" Theologian Walter Brueggemann says, "The Bible itself is primarily concerned with the issue of being displaced and yearning for a place." What we must seek as a nation for all of our people is safe, sanitary, and affordable housing. But as Christians and as the church, we must seek more than just shelter. We must do more than house the homeless and feed the hungry. We must build community. We must strive to make the kingdom of God evident upon the earth. We must seek solutions that both ease the pain but ultimately heal the wound. We must seek justice—the kind of justice which calls evil to task and then redeems or destroys it. The church must be that voice which calls us all to account for what we have done and to covenant around what we must to do. The church must ever promise that the broken will be made whole and that which is rent will be sewn together again. Home as a promise to the homeless must be the ongoing commitment of the church.

Homelessness has many faces and many causes, but its root is in the failure of the nation to commit itself through public policies and programs to eradicate poverty. In the United States today more people are living in poverty than at any time since 1965. Homelessness has increased each year since 1980 and shows no sign of lessening or leveling off. In fact, indications are that, if something is not done, by the year 200 more than 15 million citizens will be homeless, and the majority of these will be women and children. A poor child born in the United States in 1990 has a better chance of being homeless sometime in his or her growing up than he or she has of being a high-school graduate. "Today families with children make up one-third of the nation's homeless population." In some parts of the country they make up the majority. Nationwide, one in every five homeless people is a child. Every night 100,000 children go to sleep without homes.

A comprehensive all-out attack on poverty must be waged. Poverty must be eliminated in order for homelessness to be eradicated. This nation proved during the 1960s that poverty can be drastically reduced by a combination of public response and private commitment. Investments by the government in its citizenry through job training, aid to education, community economic development, child care, family support services, low-income housing initiatives, income maintenance, and public-private partnership covering a broad spectrum of creative responses to the crisis of poverty can and will work. The cost of eliminating poverty in the United States is less than one might think. Outlays of $53.8 billion or the equivalent of one percent of our 1990 gross national product could do the job. This cost to eliminate poverty pales in comparison to what it will cost the nation to bail out the bankrupt savings and loan industry, estimates of which now exceed $200 billion. Homelessness and poverty cannot be separated. One is a child of the other, and the two must be confronted together.

Many factors contribute to the growing ranks of the homeless: lack of community support for deinstitutionalized people with chronic mental illness; discontinuance or reduction of public benefits to significant numbers of elderly and disabled people; a minimum wage structure that locks the working poor into poverty; loss of family farms; closure of plants and businesses; an economy increasingly built on low-paying temporary and seasonal jobs with few or no benefits; the increasing number of single-parent households with associated low incomes; lack of housing for people with AIDS; and displacement of inner-city residents by urban renewal.

But the biggest factor contributing to today's alarming homelessness crisis is the acute and growing shortage of affordable housing for low-income persons. Since 1980 the total number of low-income housing units has decreased by 2.5 million units nationally. In particular, this country has seen a dramatic loss of single-room units, the number of which fell from 126,000 units in 1974 to less than 50,00 units in 1988. All types of affordable housing continue to be lost to abandonment, foreclosure, gentrification, and destruction. The rate of replacement falls far short of the rate of loss.

Low incomes, economic shifts, and the growing numbers of people who live in poverty, coupled with the loss of affordable housing, mean that people must pay more and more of their income for shelter. A 1990 study shows that 63 percent of U.S. citizens are paying more than 50 percent of their incomes for housing. Forty-five percent of citizens pay 70 percent or more of their incomes for housing. Thirty-two million people live below the poverty line, and the numbers continue to increase.

Homelessness is both a rural and urban problem. In some areas of the northwestern United States the percentage of homeless people in rural areas exceeds those found in cities. The rural homeless tend to be young, white, and female. Rural shelters are scarce, so homeless people often double up with friends and relatives. The Housing Assistance Council has found that rural homeless people are migrant workers, displaced renters, bankrupt farmers, and laid-off workers. Native Americans and other residents on Indian reservations are increasingly found among the rural homeless. Extremely high unemployment, coupled with the increased numbers of Native American people returning to live on reservations, has placed undue burdens on an already overtaxed and inadequate social service system. Rural homeless people often migrate to cities, thus contributing to urban homelessness.

The tragedy of the homeless in the United States, however, cannot be told in statistics alone. Homelessness often has a hidden face. Homeless persons are hidden due to the fact that they might be living with friends or relatives, camping in public recreation areas, seeking cover in barns or in other inappropriate shelters. They are hidden because they are often too proud to ask for help. The homeless are people with no place to go and little to call their own.

The United Methodist Church and all people of faith must seize the moment and demand an end to homelessness in the United States. It must raise an outcry against the injustice of such suffering toward homeless persons as individuals while advocating with others for just societal responses that address the root causes of homelessness. Piecemeal solutions are not enough. The people of this nation must insist that a safe, affordable, and sanitary place to live is a basic human right to be enjoyed by all citizens.

Policy Statement and Actions

The United Methodist Church affirms the right of all persons to live without deprivation in safe, sanitary, and affordable housing. The United Methodist Church asserts that inequitable public policies and unfair and discriminatory private-sector practices have deprived many of that right. The church views homelessness as a violation of human dignity and an affront to the biblical mandate to do justice. It pledges to do all in its power to eliminate the causes of homelessness and to work along with others to eradicate it. The church commits itself to welcoming the stranger into its midst and to seeing all people as belonging to the family of God. The church recognizes homeless people as its neighbors, seeking to learn their names and speaking out on their behalf in the councils of government, in their own congregational settings, and in the larger community. The church further commits itself to stand with homeless people as they organize to speak out on their own behalf. The United Methodist Church through its prayers, policies, and actions will make its voice heard in the land, affirming that all human beings are bound by sacred trust to God and that God, in faithfulness to that trust, will never abandon God's people.

The following actions are commended to general agencies, annual conferences, and local churches:

1. General Agency Recommendations

1.1 Provide to clergy and laity educational and training resources and opportunities which address the root causes of homelessness and provide models for addressing the problem. Urge seminaries to include courses in their curricula that help prepare clergy for effective leadership around systemic contradictions in our society that create poverty and homelessness. Encourage annual conferences to include courses in their plans for continuing education for clergy at least once a quadrennium.

1.2 Continue to support and work with national, regional, and local housing advocacy groups to implement this resolution. Endorse a National Interfaith Conference on the Church and Homelessness, as soon as possible after the 1992 General Conference, to build a base for impacting Congress to pass comprehensive national housing legislation.

1.3 Join with other communions to promote affordable housing for low-income persons through the National Low-Income Housing Coalition and other appropriate networks.

1.4 Document and affirm the work of local churches and service providers who provide needed ministries of compassion to homeless persons through church-based soup kitchens, transitional housing programs, shelters, food pantries, clothes closets, and rent and utility assistance programs. Promote their efforts throughout the local church, by soliciting financial contributions and volunteer support, and by encouraging members to contribute specialized skills and technical assistance.

1.5 Identify effective existing models and provide new models for local congregations and clergy who wish to undertake Bible study/theological reflection around the root causes of homelessness. Provide outlines for both study and action on the local level.

2. Annual Conference Recommendations

2.1 Adopt the "One Church—One Home" campaign of the Churches' Conference on Shelter and Housing and push for implementation of the campaign through the districts and their local congregations. This program encourages each United Methodist church throughout the world to reach out in a people-to-people action to adopt at least one of the world's millions of homeless persons or families, to ensure that these people's basic needs for food, housing, health care, education, and employment are met and to enable them, warmed in body and soul, to face the future with hope.

2.2 Inform clergy and laity about avenues available to churches seeking to become involved in housing developing through creative ventures such as cooperating housing with other area congregations, development of unused or underutilized church land or building space for housing, development of affordable rental units, or renting apartments for subleasing at a subsidized rate.

2.3. Adopt a resolution on homelessness encouraging actions at the congregational level to address the homeless crisis in local communities.

2.4 Encourage local churches to conduct a survey on homelessness in their areas to determine what services are currently being provided and to discover gaps in services toward which the church should direct its efforts.

2.5 Undergird cooperative parishes as a major strategy for responding to the problem of homelessness.

3. Local Church Recommendations

3.1 Involve clergy and laity in local church volunteer networks, direct service programs, and ecumenical coalitions for the homeless. Provide directories of local service providers, speaking opportunity for groups such as Habitat for Humanity, and workshops led by local homeless advocates and the homeless themselves.

3.2 Promote local church-based community organizing efforts to empower neighborhoods and influence government at every level.

4. All Levels of Church

4.1 Call upon Congress to pass comprehensive National Housing Legislation, as outlined in the General Conference resolution on housing.

ADOPTED 1992

See Social Principles, ¶ 72, "Housing," "Available and Affordable Housing."

Housing

The Scriptures look ahead to that ideal day when all persons will enjoy pleasant, peaceful, and secure shelter under their own vines and fig trees and "none shall make them afraid" (Micah 4:4).

In many portions of the gospel, we find Jesus seeking out homes for retreat and renewal, for fellowship and hospitality. Similarly, all persons are entitled to dwelling places that provide for privacy and recreation.

The Social Principles statement of The United Methodist Church declares: "We hold governments to be responsible for . . . guarantee of the right to adequate . . . shelter." We reaffirm this right as well as the assertion of the 1972 General Conference that "housing for low income persons should be given top priority. . . ."

There are approximately eighty-eight million occupied housing units in the United States. Of these seven and one half million are seriously substandard; another 25 to 30 million are marginal for human habitation. Nationally, it has been estimated by the Low Income Housing Coalition that by 1985 there were twice as many low-income households as there were low-cost housing units. In California, the ratio of low-income households to low-cost housing units in 1985 was four to one. Between 1970 and 1980, available housing in Detroit decreased by 11%, more than any other U.S. city. Furthermore, six and one third million U.S. citizens, (almost half of all low income households), are paying more than 40% of their incomes for housing. The need for adequate housing at affordable costs is critical. (Congressional Research Service)

Love for neighbor demands that Christians care about how adequately their neighbors are sheltered. Christians should identify with those who suffer daily from a shortage of available, decent, safe, and sanitary housing. There are many levels and forms of deprivation. Nearly every American town and city has its "homeless" those who exist literally without any form of shelter, living under bridges, in cars and abandoned buses, carrying their entire possessions with them in a few shopping bags.

Millions of families huddle together in densely overcrowded apartments, rural shacks, ancient house trailers, converted warehouses, and condemned or abandoned buildings. At least seven million of our fellow citizens live in housing that lacks such necessities as running water or plumbing, and an additional estimate of one to three million have no permanent housing (the homeless) because the remainder of us fail to recognize their plight or simply do not care enough.

Since December of 1986, families with children have become the fastest growing homeless group and now comprise an estimated 38% of all homeless persons in the U.S. The National Housing Law Center estimates that 2.5 million people lose their homes each year to condominium conversion, redevelopment and building abandonment. Ninety-two percent of cities in the United States surveyed show an increase in the number of homeless families. While The United Methodist Church affirms the pervasive powers of families as "creators of persons, proclaimers of faith perspectives and shapers of both present and future society," it must continue its condemnation of policies that ignore the causal relationship between shortages of low-income housing and the lack of initiative or political will to insure that safe and affordable housing is available to all citizens.

The de-institutionalization of persons diagnosed as mentally ill or recovering, or who could live full lives with minimal supervision is a concept of worth. However, a lack of regional and community planning has allowed many people to be released from a variety of institutions with no place to go, no affordable housing on the budgets allotted to persons through federal or state funds, and no supervised environment for those who need it. Few services exist to maintain supervised, semi-independent, safe, affordable housing. The National Institute of Mental Health estimates that one third of the homeless has mental health problems. Some are persons who were de-institutionalized with no support, others became ill because of the environment of homelessness.

"Am I my brothers keeper?" (Genesis 4:8) becomes a challenging alternative when concerned United Methodists begin to address the phenomenon of increased homeless families in our country. We must grapple with ways to meet the needs of the homeless. We must be more open to using church buildings that are outmoded and excess land in urban and rural areas. We must examine needs and services in our communities and develop a better understanding of our role in local, state and federal policy development. We commend United Methodists who are engaged in the effort to change such intolerable housing conditions. We commend every such individual, local church, interfaith group, nonprofit, for-profit, and government effort. We endorse with gratitude and appreciation the thousands of dollars and untold hours of voluntary service that United Methodists dedicate to this battle to improve human shelter in our country. We urge local churches, districts, and annual conferences to strengthen every housing ministry taking place within their communities by providing additional financial, technical, counseling and spiritual resources.

Many specific activities deserve greater United Methodist support.

A. At the local level

Local churches, individually or in cooperation with other churches, can identify specific housing needs existing in their communities. Often, bringing to public consciousness the plight of people in need of shelter is the first step toward alleviating such need. Sometimes the use of existing church buildings can graphically demonstrate both the need and a solution which then can be developed more fully through the use of other facilities and financial resources.

Formation of nonprofit and limited-divided housing corporations or housing cooperatives is a viable approach in many situations. There are excellent opportunities for establishing housing construction, management, and advocacy programs. However, expert consultative and technical services generally are needed from the earliest conception. We urge the use of the services provided by the General Board of Global Ministries, National Division, Housing Consultant Services and Economic Development Programs. We urge landowners, apartment and housing managers, and policy boards to allow federally subsidized tenants to inhabit their dwellings. This is a serious problem at this time because U.S. government policy recommends selling up to 30% of public housing units for private development. The net result is displacement of the poor. Availability of housing for them is limited because of discrimination and a reluctance on the part of the government to maintain federally subsidized housing monies for privately owned housing.

B. At the regional level

The atmosphere of conflict infects the relationship between cities, towns, suburban areas, counties, and states throughout our nation.

Too often competition for use of land cloaks subtle racism. Economic profit, likewise, often is used to justify a lack of concern for the impact of taxation measures. Uncoordinated planning and development results in jobs being located beyond the reach of those most in need of work. The "trickle down theory" of housing occupancy masks a selfish motivation and results in the maintenance and expansion of existing ghettos, causes the formation of new ghettos, and enforces negative attitudes that support class and racial segregation. We urge United Methodists to challenge all such practices and to engage in every activity to eliminate such vestiges of discrimination from our nation.

Every urbanized area in our country is required to have some form of a regional planning agency. Most rural areas have some similar agency, such as an area development district. Generally these political structures have considerable influence upon housing patterns, planning, production, and usage. Most can have citizens' advisory groups which develop strategy proposals and monitor private and governmental housing activities. We urge United Methodists to become knowledgeable of, and involved in such planning agencies.

C. At the national level

Since the enactment of the National Housing Act of 1949 the United States has set a goal that every citizen be housed in "decent, safe and sanitary housing." Yet the reality is that we are farther from that goal today than ever before. In part this is due to growth of population and the ever-increasing gap between those who are economically well off and those who are not. But in large measure the disparity is due to an unwillingness of our elected representatives to use general tax revenues to achieve the goals more fully. Generally, legislators feel they represent the views of their electorate, and receive very little support for using tax dollars to build more housing for low- and moderate-income families. The moral commitment first stated in 1949, and restated in every subsequent Housing Act by Congress (1959, 1968, 1974, 1978) has gone greatly unheeded. If "decent, safe and sanitary housing" is to be a citizen right, a much greater moral outcry must be raised.

Therefore, we call upon United Methodists to undertake a concerted effort to impress upon their elected representatives a profound concern over the continuing housing deficiencies existing in our cities, towns, and rural areas. Much more effort needs to be made to influence the legislative processes which affect housing, improving existing law, developing more imaginative approaches where possible, and providing adequate funding for housing designated to meet the needs of the ill-sheltered.

1. Subsidized rental housing (Section 8) and Public Housing

Under the Section 8 Housing Assistance Payments Program, renters normally pay a percent of their income for rent and the federal government makes up the difference between that and the HUD-established Fair Market Rent. We support this program for subsidizing rents as one way of opening up more housing units to low-income families and yet expecting such families, when possible, to provide their fair share of costs. However the reality is that there are just not enough units of housing available at a cost that can be afforded by the poor, even with payment assistance. There is a great need for developing more housing units. In 1985 more than 8 million low income renters were in the market for the only 4.2 million units available at an affordable (minimum of 25% of income) price.

Aid to Families with Dependent Children (AFDC) is the primary source of income for many people who now find themselves homeless. The amount of money that many families with children receive is lower than the average cost of housing in many states.

We are greatly concerned over the rapidly increasing trend toward converting rental housing to condominiums for sale. Too often in practice this means pushing people out of housing they can afford to rent but can't afford to buy. We therefore recommend that the rate of condominium conversion of rental units be slowed, or that percentages of the units be set aside with affordable rental rates. Further, we urge local housing authorities to offset this trend by encouraging increased housing stock of subsidized rental units.

We support use of a wide variety of subsidized housing approaches in order to meet a greater demand to house needy people. However, the development of a "voucher" program with no ceiling on the actual rent that can be charged and no local community guarantee of housing set aside for the poor will not alleviate the present situation.

Public housing continues to be a vital necessity in both urban and rural areas. Every incorporated city, town, and county can and should provide public, well-constructed and well-managed rental housing for those who cannot obtain it on the open market. Nearly 50 percent of all housing now is occupied by the elderly. Since the church has traditionally expressed concern and provided care of the aging, it is especially crucial that this program is continued, expanded, and adequately funded.

We must at all times critically examine the setting at the local, state, and federal levels because governmental policies affect the funding improvement and provision of housing resources for any given community. The Federal Administration between 1981 and 1988 has tried to eliminate or reduce the main federal programs used by states and local governments to help the poor and the homeless. The Community Development Block Grant Program, General Revenue Sharing and the Temporary Emergency Food Assistance Program have all been affected. The Community Development Block Grant program budget has been cut almost yearly. General Revenue Sharing was eliminated. The Administration has targeted for elimination the Temporary Emergency Food Assistance Program. Congress has repeatedly come to the rescue of these programs and in 1986 passed a law allowing the homeless to receive Aid to Families with Dependent Children, Social Security and Medicaid.

2. Fair Housing

Fair housing in our nation has regressed in the past decade. Because housing remains segregated in most places in the United States, schools tend to be segregated and jobs tend to be located at inconvenient distances from ethnic minority neighborhoods.

We therefore call upon the U.S. Congress to provide the Department of Housing and Urban Development with "cease and desist" enforcement powers and we encourage HUD to apply these powers evenly and with relentless determination to assure equal access to affordable housing in all markets. We support state and local legislation that would strengthen fair housing enforcement across the country; we also support HUD and Farmers Home Administration funding for states with laws that are substantially equivalent to federal law. We also call for the expansion of coverage in the Fair Housing Act to provide protection for persons with handicapping conditions.

Equal access to housing not available represents an unrealizable right. Therefore, to fulfill equal opportunity objectives we urge that more housing be built and offered at prices most persons can afford to pay.

A. Redlining

We deplore the practice of "redlining" as it occurs in many urban areas. This generally means that financial institutions, insurance companies, and mortgage brokers collectively make it difficult for homeowners to secure adequate financing and insurance at reasonable rates in a certain neighborhood of a given urban community. We ask that all steps necessary be taken, through negotiation and legislation, to eliminate this immoral practice and that churches take the lead in encouraging financial support arrangements that rejuvenate instead of destroy our neighborhoods. Vigilant monitoring by the religious community can forestall such unhealthy practices.

We support existing laws such as the Home Mortgage Disclosure Act, which provides information to the public on where banks and savings and loans make their loans, and the enlarged Community Reinvestment Act, which mandates that banks and savings and loans have the responsibility to serve the credit needs of moderate and lower-income communities.

We urge compliance of the institutions in which the church deposits funds with the Home Mortgage Act; and we support such additional regulations and laws that will assure reinvestment in currently redlined communities, in a way that will not result in unjust displacement of elderly, poor, ethnic minority, and other persons.

B. Housing for Older Adults and Persons with Handicapping Conditions

The Section 202 federal program is a bright spot in an otherwise dismal picture of housing for older adults and persons with handicapping conditions of any age. Restricted to sponsorship by nonprofit groups (the majority of which are related to religious groups), the 202 continues to offer a direct ministry opportunity. Since it is a loan guarantee program with lower than market interest rates, it needs to be funded at much more realistic levels than in the past.

There is also a need for expanding the congregate housing services project for semi-independent older adults or persons with handicapping conditions. The steady increase in age of our population is evidence for the need to expand the 202 program until the need for this type of rental housing for the elderly has been met. This program provides support services for persons using 202 housing and is cost effective because it allows people who might have to be institutionalized to live in much lower cost housing.

3. Housing for Native Americans

Housing policy, as in other aspects of national policy and practices toward Native American tribes, is grossly inadequate. We call for a substantial increase in programs at the federal level and for the implementation of state and local housing programs in every possible way, so that the shocking condition of substandard reservation housing can be quickly improved. Special efforts through programs of United Methodist general agencies, in partnership with ethnic conferences and funds for ethnic minority ministry, should be supportive of actions to improve housing for Native Americans.

4. Financing of Housing

Traditionally, the vast majority of housing in our country has been financed through the private money-lending industry. There is little likelihood that this would need to change if the traditional principles against usury are followed. But more attention needs to be given to developing ways mortgage money can be made available to low income persons for home ownership, and to provide rental housing for low income people. Federal and state programs aid the moderate and upper income segments of our population quite well, but similarly helpful programs for the lower income sector of the population do not exist. The 1980's have seen the greatest benefit go not to the neediest families, but to those who are sufficiently well off to purchase homes. In 1985, tax relief to home owners totalled $30.4 billion (up from 8.2 billion in 1970) in the form of federal income tax deductions for mortgage interest rates. An additional $8.6 billion in relief came through state and local property tax deductions.

The higher the family income the more these tax breaks help.

Three-fourths of these tax breaks go to homeowners in the top 15% of the income bracket. Poor or lower middle class homeowners (with incomes of $15,000 or below) get only 3% of the tax breaks. Government subsidized mortgage programs need to be developed that can also aid the lower middle-class and poor individuals and families.

In contrast to the rapid growth in federal aid to more well-to-do homeowners through the tax code, use of federal budget authority for low-income housing programs declined from an annual average of 24.3 billion during the 1977-1981 years to 8.4 billion a year between 1982-86.

New methods of private financing need to be developed so that traditional money sources are not withdrawn from the housing industry in favor of other more profitable forms of investment.

Recommendations

A number of federal programs as well as some state programs exist today to make possible the meaningful participation of church groups in providing adequate housing in a wholesome environment. We encourage churches to join in such programs that require minimal capital investment but substantial commitment of time and energy. Churches should be aware that these programs are available in both urban and rural areas. More church groups ought to: 1) be concerned about the conditions of housing in their communities; 2) use the tools available (e.g. National Division, General Board of Global Ministries Housing Consultant Services) to provide better housing; 3) dedicate a special day or Sunday as a Day of Prayer and Action for Shelter, as has been developed by Habitat for Humanity (contact the General Board of Church and Society for special resources); and, 4) develop a sense of mission and assume responsibility as stewards to meet these needs without expectation of monetary reward.

In implementing any housing ministry, church people must maintain great sensitivity to community needs and work to achieve community participation and control. Tenants' need for adequate, reasonably-priced and energy-efficient housing should be recognized. Care always must be exercised to assure our Christian involvement as "enablers" rather than "controllers." Our goal must always be to enable those we help to be in control of their own lives, future, and destiny. Whatever the form of community organization, housing production, management, or ownership of a housing project, every effort should be made at each developmental step to insure that those who are being aided are afforded the opportunity, and indeed required, to take every action necessary to direct the undertaking. Wherever possible, we must train rather than service, transfer power rather than decide, empower rather than control. In this as in all other aspects of housing ministries, United Methodists should seek the best technical guidance, and ensure the greatest professional competence for such a ministry. Let us equip ourselves and provide the widest possible range of supportive assistance to individuals, congregations, districts, conferences, and all forms of cooperative groups sharing similar goals and policies, so that our fellow citizens may achieve as their right, "decent, safe and sanitary housing" as soon as possible.

ADOPTED 1988

See Social Principles, ¶ 72, "Available and Affordable Housing."

In Support of Women, Infants, and Children's Supplemental Food and Nutrition Education Program (WIC Program)

WHEREAS, the Women, Infants, and Children's Supplemental Food and Nutrition Education Program (WIC Program) provides nutrition education and food coupons for needy high-risk pregnant women, lactating women, and children under five years of age, and

WHEREAS, the WIC food coupons are available to high-risk needy pregnant women such as those who are anemic, overweight or underweight, teenage or over 35, or those who have had problems with a previous pregnancy, and

WHEREAS, the WIC coupons, costing an average of $27 per month per person on the program, can be used only for milk, cheese, eggs, juices high in Vitamin C, iron-fortified cereal, and iron-fortified formula and not for high caloric junk foods that are low in certain essential nutrients, and

WHEREAS, malnutrition is a primary cause of low birth weight babies, and

WHEREAS, low birth weight babies get off to a slow start in life at great emotional expense to the parents and financial hardship to families, insurance companies, and the taxpayers, and

WHEREAS, the cost of putting weight on a newborn baby in a "premie nursery" is about $600 per day and about $5,000 per pound of weight gain, and

WHEREAS, inadequate diet in the formative years is a major cause of some types of mental retardation, and

WHEREAS, 60 percent of the total number of brain cells are already developed at the time of birth, the other 40 percent are developed by the age of 3, and from 3 to age 5 the brain cells increase in size, but not in number, and

WHEREAS, the cost of institutional care of a mentally retarded child is $1,400 per month or more, and of a mentally retarded adult is $700 to $1,400 per month for life;

Now Therefore Be It Resolved, that The United Methodist General Conference go on record as supporting the Women, Infants, and Children's Supplemental Food and Nutrition Education Program, Public Law 95627 of the Child Nutrition Act, as a positive, cost-effective, malnutrition prevent measure.

ADOPTED 1980

See Social Principles, ¶¶ 71.F and 72.C, "A Call for Increased Commitment to End World Hunger and Poverty," "Protecting and Sustaining Children."

Inclusive History

WHEREAS, The United Methodist Church celebrates regularly the growth and development of the Methodist legacy in America; and

WHEREAS, the influence of the literary records has shaped the images, values, and perceptions of racial ethnic minority groups toward one another; and

WHEREAS, the most positive images and dominant contributions in the Methodist legacies are credited and related to Caucasian persons; and

WHEREAS, nominal historical recognition is given to Asian, Black, Hispanic, Native Americans, and Pacific Islanders and their contributions to the Methodist legacy in America; and

WHEREAS, The United Methodist Church proclaims a commitment to the goal of realizing racial ethnic minority inclusiveness,

Therefore, be it resolved, that The General Commission on Archives and History, The United Methodist Publishing house in joint consultation with The General Commission on Religion and Race determine the most effective means to identify all Asian, Black,

Hispanic, Native American, and Pacific Islanders literary and historical records which have not been acknowledged and/or published; promote the use of these resources among whites and racial ethnic minorities; and encourage training sessions led by Asians, Blacks, Hispanics, Native Americans, and Pacific Islanders using these resources which acknowledge the contributions of these racial ethnic minorities to the legacy and heritage of Methodism in the United States of America and the world.

ADOPTED 1992

See Social Principles, ¶ 72, "History of Racial/Ethnic United Methodists," "History of Blacks in The United Methodist Church," "Native American History and Contemporary Culture as Related to Effective Church Participation."

Inclusiveness of the Physically Challenged at All Conferences

WHEREAS, all minority groups should be represented at all conferences of The United Methodist Church; and

WHEREAS, those who are physically challenged are indeed a minority group; and

WHEREAS, those who have lived with a physical handicap are able to address issues which affect those with handicapping conditions; and

WHEREAS, a person with a physical handicap is just as capable of acting on important issues as that of an able-bodied person; and

WHEREAS, persons with a physical handicap wish to serve the Lord through The United Methodist Church with their prayers, presence, gifts, and, last but not least, their *service*;

Be it therefore resolved, that the physically challenged be considered for representation at all conferences within The United Methodist Church.

ADOPTED 1992

See Social Principles, ¶ 72.G, "The Church and Persons with Mentally, Physically, and/or Psychologically Handicapping Conditions," "Affirmative Action Plans and People with Disabilities."

Increased Support for Programs Impacting
the Higher Education of Native Americans

WHEREAS, the National United Methodist Native American Center, Inc., supports and endorses the goal of optimum educational achievement for all United Methodist Church members; and

WHEREAS, the concept of illiteracy is unacceptable in a time when society projects a formal demeanor of progress and opportunity for all members; and

WHEREAS, past support for The United Methodist Church for the participation of Native Americans in higher education has been minimal, productive, and appreciated; and

WHEREAS, a trend of decreasing Native American participation in higher education is beginning to appear at the national and regional levels; and

WHEREAS, the consistently rising costs of higher education contribute considerably to decrease of Native American participation in higher education; and

WHEREAS, recent statistics suggest an upward trend of academic success for Native Americans currently participating in higher education; and

WHEREAS, the National United Methodist Native American Center, Inc., supports the philosophy that every person has a right to an education and it is society's responsibility to enable every person to obtain this right; and

WHEREAS, the foundation to Native American growth and progress in society lies within the domain of formal education;

Be it therefore resolved, that the General Conference encourage the Board of Higher Education and Ministry, if monies are available, to sponsor a Native American Higher Education Forum in the Fall of 1993 to:

1. Collect data about the causes for higher dropout rates among Native American students.

2. To identify self-help trends among Native Americans who feel isolated from mainstream society on college and university campuses.

3. To develop practical strategies that will appropriately address these causes within the Native American community.

Be it further resolved, that the General Conference endorse and support the funding, development, implementation, and assessment of a higher education recruitment/retention forum, sponsored by The United Methodist Church for Native Americans throughout the denomination's regions, to be organized and managed by the National United Methodist Native American Center, Inc., in cooperation with local churches reflecting a significant population of Native Americans.

Be it further resolved, that the General Conference encourage The United Methodist Church to utilize the information and materials generated, as a result of the forum, for sensitizing and familiarizing non-Indian membership about Native Americans in their respective communities.

ADOPTED 1992

See Social Principles, ¶ 72, "Shared Financial Support for the Native American Center," "National Convocation on the Ordained Ministry for Native Americans," "The United Methodist Church and America's Native People."

Ku Klux Klan and Other Hate Groups in the U.S.A.

The Charter for Racial Justice Policies holds us accountable as United Methodists in the United States to be conscious that "we have sinned as our ancestors did; we have been wicked and evil" (Psalm 106:6, *Today's English Bible*). We are called to a renewed commitment to the elimination of institutional racism. We affirm the 1976 General Conference statement "The United Methodist Church and Race," which states unequivocally:

> By biblical and theological precept, by the law of the Church, by General Conference pronouncement, and by episcopal expression, the matter is clear. With respect to race, the aim of The United Methodist Church is nothing less than an inclusive church in an inclusive society. The United Methodist Church therefore calls upon all its people to perform those faithful deeds of love and justice in both the church and community that will bring this aim into full reality.

The United Methodist Church has expressed its opposition to all forms of racism and anti-semitism in the past. Racism replaces faith in the God who made all people with a belief in the superiority of one race over another.

Nevertheless racism still exists in the United States, congealed in its most violent, anti-democratic form—the white supremacist movement.

The white supremacist movement has developed into two distinct trends: a clandestine and semi-clandestine movement committed to terror and violence to popularize its aims and achieve its goals. The other trend has specialized in developing an elaborate facade, designed to win new supporters who would otherwise be repelled by an open appeal to violence and neo-nazism. Together these groups form a facist movement with a stable core and expanding spheres of influence, despite the temporary fortunes or misfortunes of its constituent groups.

An underground composed of members of different Klan factions, the Aryan Nations (which include "The Church of Jesus Christ-Christian," "The Mountain Kirk," and other nonchurch organizations) and other neo-nazi formations continue to exist. The underground was typified by "The Order," a basic philosophy of the

Ku Klux Klan. Activities carried out under this philosophy include murder, theft, vandalizing synagogues, counterfeiting, bombing churches and public buildings, and bank robbery.

The racist movement has already entered the twenty-first century with an increasingly sophisticated technical apparatus. The Aryan Nations organization operates five different "Liberty Net" computer bulletin boards that relay messages among white supremacists which allows them a wider public audience for their ideas.

Ku Klux Klan and neo-nazi groups engage in open paramilitary activity. Training bases of groups are located in all sections of the country. From the White Aryan Resistance in the West, to the Christian-Patriots Defense League in the Midwest, to the Ku Klux Klan in the South, hate groups are trained with highly sophisticated weaponry.

On the other hand Posse Comitatus-type groups have recruited farm and rural whites throughout the depressed agricultural sections of the country. They have used clever schemes based on providing fraudulent legal assistance and grassroots organizing to win new recruits. Although organizers of groups such as National Agricultural Press Association (NAPA), Farmer Liberation Army, and the Iowa Society of Educated Citizens don't openly identify themselves as neo-nazi—they do place the blame for the crisis in agriculture on a mythical international Jewish conspiracy. Some of the members of the Posse Comitatus-like groups have been involved in violent altercations with the law.

In addition to the paramilitary, economic, and political organizing of the fascist movement, a powerful religious movement called "Christian Identity" has developed. "Christian Identity" is derived from a century-old religious doctrine known as British Israelism. It provides theological unity to disparate sections of the white supremacist movement, and an attraction to the racist movement for those whose beginning interests are primarily religious. "Christian Identity" functions in the religious sphere much like fraudulent legal schemes do among economically distressed farmers. "Christian Identity" theology teaches that people of color are "pre-Adamic," lower forms of species than white people; that Jews are children of Satan and that the white people of northern Europe are the Lost Tribes of Israel.

Therefore, be it resolved, that the General Conference, in solidarity with victims of recent outbreaks of racial violence:

A. Calls upon the appropriate boards and agencies of The United Methodist Church to:

1. Educate clergy and laity to the insidiousness of the "Christian Identity" movement, the Ku Klux Klan and other hate groups which claim their values and practices are based in Christianity. Education should include courses in seminaries as well as education for children, youth and adults in church programs.

2. Develop special programs to support churches and persons harassed by hate groups, particularly in rural areas where the social institutions that mediate conflict are weak and hate group activity is prevalent.

3. Support coalitions that oppose bigotry and hate groups.

4. Oppose the involvement of minors in paramilitary training sponsored by the Ku Klux Klan and other racist groups.

B. Calls upon government and its agencies to:

1. Assure that law enforcement personnel take the necessary steps to maintain accurate records on racist violence and bring to justice the perpetrators of such violence and intimidation.

2. Hold hearings on racist violence, particularly in those states where statistics reveal an increase in the activity of the Ku Klux Klan and other hate groups. Congressional hearings should be held when there are allegations of government involvement or negligence exacerbating such violence.

ADOPTED 1988

See Social Principles, ¶ 72.A, "Support Legislation Prohibiting Malicious Harassment," "Racial Harassment," "Prejudice Against Muslims and Arabs in the USA."

Medical Rights for Children and Youth

Out of long tradition our society has valued the family as its fundamental social institution. The family is seen as the primary locus for the nurture and protection of children and youth. To preserve, protect, and defend the family as a social unit, the family's right to privacy has been protected in almost absolute fashion by law and custom. The rights of parents to determine the conditions and circumstances of their children have known little limitation.

When children are abused or maltreated, therefore, the tragic facts are often hidden or little known. We must awaken now to the reality that some of our children, at some times and places, have been battered and beaten within their own families. It has been estimated that "10,000 children are severely battered every year, at least 50,000 to 75,000 are sexually abused, 100,000 are emotionally neglected, and another 100,000 are physically, morally, and educationally neglected."

In light of these tragic facts, we as church people should particularly bear witness to our conviction that parental rights over children are limited, that all children are gifts of God and belong to God, and that parents do not own their children. Children have fundamental rights as persons—rights that are to be protected by the community at large when the family system fails any particular child.

Medical care represents a particularly crucial area of the rights of children. We therefore call particular attention to the following statement of the medical rights due children and youth, and commend its principles for adoption:

The Pediatric Bill of Rights Preamble

Every child, regardless of race, religion, ethnic background, or economic standing, has the right to be regarded as a person and shall have the right to receive appropriate medical care and treatment. The Pediatric Bill of Rights shall not be construed as a bypassing of the family's right to personal privacy, but shall become operative when parental rights and the child's rights are in direct conflict and it becomes necessary to act in the best interests of the child. Provision shall be made for adequate counseling of the child as to his right to receive and deny medical care. To the extent that a child cannot demand his rights as a person, those involved in his health care shall move to protect that child's medical interests to the best of their ability.

Canon I. Every person, regardless of age, shall have the right of timely access to continuing and competent health care.

Canon II. Every person, regardless of age, shall have the right to seek out and to receive information concerning medically accepted contraceptive devices and birth-control services in doctor-patient confidentiality. Every person, regardless of age, shall have the right to receive medically prescribed contraceptive devices in doctor-patient confidentiality.

Canon III. Every person, regardless of age, shall have the right to seek out and to receive information concerning venereal disease, and every person, regardless of age, shall have the right to consent to and to receive any medically accepted treatment necessary to combat venereal disease in doctor-patient confidentiality.

Canon IV. Every person, regardless of age, shall have the right to seek out and to accept in doctor-patient confidentiality the diagnosis and treatment of any medical condition related to pregnancy. Every person, regardless of age, shall have the right to adequate and objective counseling relating to pregnancy and abortion in doctor-patient confidentiality and every person, regardless of age, shall have the right to request and to receive medically accepted treatment which will result in abortion in doctor-patient confidentiality.

Canon V. Every person, regardless of age, shall have the right to seek out and to receive psychiatric care and counseling in doctor-patient confidentiality.

Canon VI. Every person, regardless of age, shall have the right to seek out and to receive medically accepted counseling and treatment for drug or alcohol dependency in doctor-patient confidentiality.

Canon VII. Every person, regardless of age, shall have the right of immediate medical care when the life of such person is in imminent danger. The decision of imminent danger to the life of such person is a decision to be made solely by the attending physician; and the attending physician shall decide what treatment is medically indicated under the circumstances.

Canon VIII. Any person, regardless of age, who is of sufficient intelligence to appreciate the nature and consequences of the proposed medical care and if such medical care is for his own benefit, may effectively consent to such medical care in doctor-patient confidentiality. The same shall not apply to Canons II through VIII which are deemed to be absolute rights.

Canon IX. In every case in which a child is being examined by, treated by, or is under the medical care of a qualfied medical practitioner, and where, in the opinion of that qualified medical practitioner, the child is in need of immediate medical care and where the parent or the legal guardian of said child refuses to consent to such needed, immediate medical treatment, said medical practitioner shall notify the juvenile court or the district court with juvenile jurisdiction immediately. The juvenile court or the district court with juvenile jurisdiction shall immediately appoint a guardian ad litem, who shall represent the child's interests in all subsequent legal proceedings. The juvenile court or the district court with juvenile jurisdiction shall immediately set a date for hearing, not to exceed 96 hours from the receipt of the initial report. The court shall determine at the hearing, based upon medical and other revelant testimony and the best interests of the child, whether or not said medical treatment should be so ordered by the court.

Canon X. Every person, regardless of age, shall have the right to considered and respectful care. During examinations, every attempt shall be made to insure the privacy of every patient, regardless of age; and every person, regardless of age, has the right to know, if observers are present, what role the observer may have in regard to the patient's treatment and shall have the right to request that observers remove themselves from the immediate examining area.

Canon XI. Every person, regardless of age, shall have the right to know which physician is responsible for his care. Every person, regardless of age, shall have the right to be informed concerning his diagnosis, his treatment and his prognosis in language that is readily understandable to him. Every person, regardless of age, shall have the right to ask pertinent questions concerning the diagnosis, the treatment, tests and surgery done, on a day-to-day basis in a hospital setting; and every person, regardless of age, shall have the right to immediate response to the best of the attending physician's knowledge and in language that the patient clearly understands.

ADOPTED 1976

See Social Principles, ¶ 72.C, "Health and Wholeness," "Universal Access to Health Care in the U.S. and Related Territories."

Membership in Clubs or Organizations which Practice Exclusivity

WHEREAS, membership held in any club or organization which practices exclusivity based on gender, race, or socioeconomic condition is clearly in violation of the stance of the United Methodist Social Principles,

Therefore, it is recommended, that United Methodists who hold memberships in clubs or organizations which practice exclusivity based on gender, race, or socioeconomic condition prayerfully consider whether they should work for change within these groups or resign their membership. If one decides to resign, we urge that the decision and reasons be made public. This reflects the intent and purpose of the Social Principles of The United Methodist Church.

ADOPTED 1992

See Social Principles, ¶ 72, "Eradication of Racism," "Charter for Racial Justice Policies in an Interdependent Global Community."

Ministries in Social Conflict

Conflict is an integral aspect of the human condition that creates both positive and negative changes. The presence of conflict inspires us to move toward the vision of peace with justice. As Christians, we are called to live out God's reconciling spirit in the activities of our daily lives, both corporately and individually. Christ summons us to show social, civic and personal righteousness to insure our integrity as a community of faith. Our response to the call must be informed by Paul's lesson to the Corinthians: "God chose what is foolish in the world to shame the wise, God chose what is weak in the world to shame the strong, God chose what is low and despised in the world, even things that are not, to bring to nothing things that are, so that no human being might boast in the presence of God."

Like Christ, the church must continue intercession and formal engagement in crisis intervention and conflict resolution. In these areas, United Methodism has a long history of involvement. The past involvements of the church in the continuing struggle for the affirmation of the dignity of women, people of color, and the poor, have all enriched the church and society. Social changes caused by technology, value systems, cross cultural influences, and poverty are creating conflicts within the global community, radically changing the lives of people and the nature of institutions. The church is neither exempt from these dynamics nor is it alone in experiencing these crises. However, the church is unique in its responsibility to respond to these conflicts with models which glorify God.

Many institutions and organizations have recognized the role of conflict and crisis in human relations. Blessed with materials, human resources, and a legacy of conflict resolution activities, The United

Methodist Church has the mandate to develop and sustain a comprehensive Ministry for Conflict Resolution. Consistent with our Social Principles and the resolutions concerning Human Rights, Peace, and Conciliation Ministries, we call The United Methodist Church to summon its resources to organize and develop a Ministry for Conflict Resolution.

To further the leadership role of The United Methodist Church in the area of crisis intervention and conflict resolution, the General Board of Church and Society is committed to promote a ministry of Conflict Resolution as a significant component of the Board's program. In addition we call upon the General Board of Global Ministries to provide leadership in the area of cross-cultural and international conflict; and call upon the General Board of Global Ministries to work with the General Board of Church and Society to provide training in conflict resolution to all missionaries, community developers, church and community workers and staff involved in the administration and deployment of such workers. We call upon the Board of Higher Education and Ministry to establish a system that will grant continuing education units as credit for clergy receiving training under this program, and urge all seminaries of The United Methodist Church to provide their students with opportunities to gain exposure to the field of conflict resolution and conciliation. Furthermore, we call upon the appropriate personnel within the general boards and agencies to prepare a proposal for the 1992 General Conference on the establishment of a formal Ministry of Conflict Resolution.

ADOPTED 1988

See Social Principles, ¶ 72, "Support Legislation Prohibiting Malicious Harassments," "Racial Harassment."

Ministries on Mental Illness

Mental illness is a group of brain disorders that cause severe disturbances of thinking, feeling, and acting. Treatment should recognize the importance of a nonstressful environment, good nutrition, and an accepting community as well as medical and psychiatric care in regaining and maintaining health. Churches in every community are called to participate actively in expanding care for the mentally ill and their families and communities.

John Wesley's ministry was grounded in the redemptive ministry of Christ with its focus on healing that involved spiritual, mental, emotional, and physical aspects. His concern for the health of those to whom he ministered led him to create medical services at no cost to those who were poor and in deep need, refusing no one for any reason. He saw health as going beyond a simple biological well-being to wellness of the whole person. His witness of love to those in need of healing is our model for ministry to those who are suffering from mental illness.

All aspects of health—physical, mental, and spiritual—were of equal concern to Jesus Christ, whose healing touch reached out to mend broken bodies, minds, and spirits with one common purpose: the restoration of well-being and renewed communion with God and neighbor. But those whose illness brought social stigma and isolation, such as the man of Gadara, whose troubled spirit caused fearsome and self-destructive behavior, were embraced and healed with special compassion (Mark 5:1-34). When the man of Gadara said his name was "Legion, for we are many," his comment was suggestive of the countless individuals, in our time as well as his, whose mental dysfunction, whether genetically, environmentally, chemically, socially, or psychologically induced, causes fear, rejection, or shame, and to which we tend to respond with the same few measures no more adequate for our time than his: stigmatization, isolation, incarceration, and restraint.

We confess that our Christian concepts of sin and forgiveness, at the root of our understanding of the human condition and of divine grace, are sometimes inappropriately applied in ways that heighten paranoia or clinical depression. Great care must be exercised in ministering to those whose brain disorders result in exaggerated self-negation, for, while all persons stand in need of forgiveness and reconciliation, God's love cannot be communicated through the medium of forgiveness for uncommitted or delusional sins.

We reaffirm our confidence that God's unqualified love for all persons beckons us to reach out with fully accepting love to all, but particularly to those with disabling inability to relate to themselves or others due to mental illness.

Research published since 1987 has underscored the physical and genetic basis for the more serious mental illnesses, such as schizophrenia, manic-depression, and other affective disorders.

Public discussion and education about mental illness are needed so that persons who suffer from brain disorders and their families can be free to ask for help. This includes freedom from the stigma attached to mental illness that derives from a false understanding that it is primarily an adjustment problem caused by psychologically dysfunctional families. Communities need to develop more adequate programs to meet the needs of their mentally ill members. This includes the need to implement state and local programs that monitor and prevent abuses of mentally ill persons as well as those programs that are intended to replace long-term hospitalization with community-based services.

The process followed in recent years of deinstitutionalizing mental patients has corrected a long-standing problem of "warehousing" mentally ill persons. However, without adequate community-based mental health programs to care for the de-hospitalized, the streets, for too many, have become a substitute for a hospital ward. Consequently, often the responsibility, including the costs of mental-health care, have simply been transferred to individuals and families or to shelters for the homeless, already overloaded and ill-equipped to provide more than the most basic care. Furthermore, the pressure to deinstitutionalize patients rapidly has caused some mental-health systems to rely unduly upon short-term chemical therapy to control patients rather than upon more complex programs that require longer-term hospitalization or other forms of treatments where research provides successful outcomes achieved. Such stopgap treatment leads to repeated short-term hospitalizations with little or no long-term improvement in a person's ability to function.

The Church, as the body of Christ, is called to the ministry of reconciliation, of healing and of salvation, which means to be made whole. We call upon the church to affirm ministries related to mental illness that embrace the role of community, family, and the healing professions in healing the physical, social, environmental, and spiritual impediments to wholeness for those afflicted with brain disorders and for their families.

1. We call upon all local churches, districts, and annual conferences to support the following community and congressional programs to support:

    a. adequate public funding to enable mental health systems to provide appropriate therapy;

b. expanded counseling and crisis intervention services;

c. workshops and public awareness campaigns to combat stigmas;

d. housing and employment for de-institutionalized persons;

e. improved training for judges, police, and other community officials in dealing with mentally ill persons;

f. community and congregational involvement with patients in psychiatric hospitals and other mental health care facilities;

g. community, pastoral, and congregational support for individuals and families caring for mentally ill family members;

h. more effective interaction among different systems involved in the care of mentally ill persons, including courts, police, employment, housing, welfare, religious, and family systems;

i. education of their members in a responsible and comprehensive manner about the nature of the problems of mental illness facing society today, the public-policy advocacy needed to change policies and keep funding levels high;

j. active participation in helping their communities meet both preventive and therapeutic needs related to mental illness;

k. the work of the National Alliance for the Mentally Ill (NAMI), Washington, D.C., a self-help organization of mentally ill persons, their families, and friends, providing mutual support, education, and advocacy for those persons with severe mental illness and urge the churches to connect with NAMI's religious outreach network. We also commend to the churches, Pathways to Promise: Interfaith Ministries and Prolonged Mental Illnesses, St. Louis, Missouri, as a necessary link in our ministry on this critical issue.

2. We call upon seminaries to provide:

a. technical training, including experience in mental-health units, as a regular part of the preparation for the ministry in order to help congregations become more knowledgeable about and involved in mental-health needs of their communities.

3. We call upon the general agencies to:

a. advocate systemic reform of the health-care system to provide more adequately for persons and families confronting the catastrophic expense and pain of caring for mentally ill family members;

b. support universal access to health care, insisting that public and private funding mechanisms be developed to assure the availability of services to all in need, including adequate coverage for mental-health services in all health programs;

c. advocate community mental-health systems, including public clinics, hospitals, and other tax-supported facilities, being especially sensitive to the mental-health needs of culturally or racially diverse groups in the population;

d. support adequate research by public and private institutions into the causes of mental illness, including, as high priority, further development of therapeutic applications of newly discovered information on the genetic causation for several types of severe brain disorders;

e. support adequate public funding to enable mental-health-care systems to provide appropriate therapy;

f. build a United Methodist Church mental-illness network at the General Board of Church and Society to coordinate mental-illness ministries in The United Methodist Church.

ADOPTED 1992

See Social Principles, ¶ 72, "Health in Mind and Body."

Ministry to Runaway Children

The United Methodist Church calls its members to follow Jesus Christ in his mission to bring all persons into a community of love. The Social Principles upholds the potential of the community for nurturing human beings into the fullness of their humanity through its basic unit, the family. We as United Methodists acknowledge children as beings to whom adults and society in general have obligations: the rights to food, shelter, clothing, health care, and emotional well-being. We also recognize youth and young adults as those who frequently find full participation in society difficult.

The United Methodist Church, having accepted its commission to manifest the life of the gospel in the world within the context of hope and expectation, deplores the fact that in this nation 1,000,000 children are reported missing every year, that countless thousands are forced out or "thrown-away," and that homicide is one of the five leading causes of death among children between the ages of one and seventeen. We recognize the prevalence of physical, sexual or emotional abuse as the underlying cause for almost half of the behaviors classified as running away.

317

Running away is not unique to any social class. The average age for runaways is dropping and the majority are girls. We are alarmed that a whole new category of children known as street children are living degrading and dangerous lives in the streets of our towns and cities.

We believe these runaways should neither be a police problem nor processed through the legal system where they are usually incarcerated rather than protected and adjudicated rather than enlightened. Most such youths require temporary shelter and supervision instead of secure detention.

We commend those congregations and annual conferences already engaged in outreach to runaway youth, providing food, shelter, and protection from personal exploitation as well as referral to sources of help. We feel that the runaway crisis offers a further opportunity to help families when they want and are receptive to such help. Therefore, we support immediate crisis intervention and counseling for youth and their families with the primary objective of returning the youth to his/her home. When there is no possibility of it becoming a healthy environment, we support the development of alternate living arrangements that provide a nurturing environment.

We further urge that United Methodist agencies join in efforts to develop innovative ministries of support and protection for street children who would not usually come to a runaway shelter.

We encourage local church efforts toward prevention by programming to strengthen and support families within their congregations. We call Christians everywhere into service wherever God and a loving heart may call them; into the schools where poor school performance is often the precipitating crisis to running; into their own neighborhoods and community where there are countless opportunities to help troubled youth; into supporting programs in the community which deal compassionately with abusing parents.

"And the King will answer them, 'Truly, I say to you, as you did it to one of the least of my brethren, you did it to me' " (Matt. 25:40).

ADOPTED 1984

See Social Principles, ¶ 72.C, "Protecting and Sustaining Children."

Mutual Recognition of Members

Introduction

The General Conferences of 1976 and 1980 adopted affirmations of the basic Consultation on Church Union principle of mutual recognition of memberships based on baptism. All other member churches have done the same. Now as the Consultation is moving forward on further implications of theological consensus, mutual recognition, convenanting together and eventual reconciliation, The United Methodist Church wishes to join with other churches in moving from affirmation to action.

The plenary of the Consultation on Church Union in November 1984 will focus on the new theological statement of consensus, the implications of a developing covenant toward unity (that is expected to be before the General Conference of 1988) and liturgical expressions of both. These emphases are related to the new World Council of Churches statement on *Baptism, Eucharist and Ministry* currently being reviewed and responded to by United Methodists.

We have a stake in the faithful discipleship of other communions. Other churches have a stake in the faithful discipleship of The United Methodist Church. For it is the Church of Jesus Christ that is called to share in mission and ministry for the world. God's covenant is with the whole People of God. A concurrent expression of United Methodist seriousness in the cause of Christian unity is needed. Clear visible evidence that we understand ourselves to be part of the Body of Christ is needed.

Be It Resolved, that participation with voice in United Methodist governing bodies and agencies and the joining in our liturgical celebrations by representatives from other communions are both symbols of the oneness of the Church of which we are a part and signs to others of our ecumenical seriousness.

To manifest our integrity as part of the Church of Jesus Christ, several items of legislation are proposed to the General Conference, including the permissive inclusion (outside of quota requirements) of representatives from other communions in General Conference, Annual Conferences, general and conference boards and other agencies. This resolution supplements that legislation with specific recommendations which relate to annual conferences and local churches, namely:

1. That United Methodist Annual Conferences be empowered, encouraged, and enabled to invite official representatives from other denominations, especially from member churches of the Consultation on Church Union, to their sessions and committees with voice and

that United Methodist judicatory leaders nominate representatives to the official church bodies of other denominations where invited to do so.

2. That representatives of other denominations be invited to participate in the laying on of hands in annual conference ordination ceremonies, symbolizing the catholicity of our ministry.

3. That Annual Conference Commissions on Christian Unity and Interreligious Concerns and Conference Councils on Ministry be alert to and consider carefully the development by the Consultation on Church Union of 1984 of: a) the principles and the text of an "Act of Covenanting"; b) development by them of enabling acts related to possible representation in "Councils of Oversight" that may be formed at middle judicatory levels of the COCU member churches; and c) encourage responsiveness to liturgical formulations developed by COCU which will be based on theological consensus and the covenanting processes.

4. That United Methodist local churches be encouraged to invite representatives from other denominations to participate in celebrations such as World Communion Sunday, baptism, and confirmation, and in special commemorative occasions in the congregation's life.

5. That local churches be urged to take initiatives in cooperation with congregations of other denominations in issues of racial and social justice, in mission and evangelism, and in occasions of special study and celebration (such as Advent, Lent, Easter, and Pentecost); and that special efforts be made to share persons with special skills, talents and imagination between denominations in order to strengthen the whole body of Christ in its nature and witness.

6. That local churches and Annual Conferences, aided by the General Commission on Christian Unity and Interreligious Concerns, study the COCU publication of a seven-chapter consensus on *In Quest of a Church of Christ Uniting* and respond to the GCCUIC.

ADOPTED 1984

See Social Principles, ¶ 72.B, "Toward an Ecumenical Future," "A Continuing Membership in the Consultation on Church Union."

National Convocation on the Ordained Ministry for Native Americans

Whereas, there is a shortage of Native American pastors within The United Methodist Church; and

WHEREAS, non-Native Americans are frequently appointed to serve Native American United Methodist Churches with little knowledge of the culture, values, and unique relationship Native Americans have with the federal government; and

WHEREAS, the responsibility of the Board of Ordained Ministry is to study ministerial needs and resources in The United Methodist Church and to cooperate with appropriate groups in the interpretation of ministry as a vocation, in an effort to enlist suitable persons for ministry; and

WHEREAS, the Board of Ordained Ministry is to provide for recruiting and preparation of persons for ministry among ethnic groups, including Black Americans, Hispanic Americans, Native Americans, Asian Americans, and those of other national and ethnic origin;

Therefore, be it resolved, that the General Board of Higher Education and ministry jointly with the National United Methodist Native American Center sponsor a National Convocation, "The Ordained Ministry" early in the 1996–1996 quadrennium.

ADOPTED 1992

See Social Principles, ¶ 72, "Native American Social Witness Program," "Native American Representation in The United Methodist Church," "Native American History and Contemporary Culture as Related to Effective Church Participation."

Native American History and Contemporary Culture as Related to Effective Church Participation

WHEREAS, current literature and research suggest a substantial "communication gap" between Native Americans and non-Indian United Methodist Church entities, specifically as it related to non-Indian entities comprehending the concept of Native American life, culture, language, spirit, values, etc.; and

WHEREAS, this vague communication has been a consistent problem over history with minimal effort from non-Indian entities to change their attitudes toward Native Americans until recent trends; and

WHEREAS, such attitude of society reflects a growing trend toward developing and implementing a system accommodating, to a high degree, cultural diversity; generally speaking, society is beginning to demonstrate comprehension of the term *multicultural education* as related to the year 2000 and making efforts to become even more informed; services which once perpetuated eurocentric society only, are now examining the values of the ever-growing ethnic populations and attempting to integrate these values in their service activities (education, government, health, business, etc.); and

WHEREAS, there are substantial numbers of ethnic professionals capable of providing effective instruction in cultural diversity as related to The United Methodist Church current and future thrusts; and

WHEREAS, there still is a critical need for The United Methodist Church to become concretely familiar with its Native American membership in order to assure their religious, denominational, spiritual, and emotional well-being; and

WHEREAS, there is an expressed concern from The United Methodist Church's Native American membership that racism and prejudice are significant contributors to the absence of Native American representation in the church's hierarchy; and

WHEREAS, the formal means of eliminating this condition is through the formal instruction in Native American history, culture, and contemporary affairs of non-Indian entities of The United Methodist Church;

Therefore, be it resolved, that General Conference advocate the development and implementation of a training policy whereby Native American history, culture, and contemporary affairs will be an integral part of ministry and administrative training for all aspects of The United Methodist Church;

Be it further resolved, that General Conference designate the National United Methodist Native American Center, Inc., as the center for the research, development, and training components of the requested curriculum;

Be it further resolved, that General Conference support a policy that the concept of "Indian preference" be utilized in the selection of instructors and speakers for the proposed training components.

ADOPTED 1992

See Social Principles, ¶ 72, "The United Methodist Church and America's Native People," "National Convocation on the Ordained Ministry for Native Americans," "Native American Social Witness Program," "Native American Representation in The United Methodist Church."

Native American Representation in the United Methodist Church

WHEREAS, the population of Native Americans has grown dramatically during the past two decades; and

WHEREAS, this trend of population growth is accompanied by a substantial positive interest in Native American culture and history in regard to The United Methodist Church participation among traditionally non-interested individuals; and

WHEREAS, leadership of The United Methodist Church has recently demonstrated a sincere desire to "include" Native Americans in the decision-making activity of the church; and

WHEREAS, there is a significant need to recruit Native Americans into "role model" positions within the church as a means to enhance church membership, ministry numbers, and an overall understanding of contemporary Native American life as related to racial communication; and

WHEREAS, current attitudes among Native Americans reflect a critical desire to present and communicate accurate Native American perspectives to, and for, decision-making bodies of The United Methodist Church; and

WHEREAS, there is currently a minute number of Native Americans serving on the national United Methodist Church policy-making boards, management committees, education boards, finance committees, information areas, etc.; and

WHEREAS, current trends suggest a decrease in church membership and attendance among Native American citizenry;

Therefore, be it resolved, that General Conference strongly support the following tasks as related to accurate Native American representation and participation on local, regional, and national policy-making, managerial, and implementation/evaluation boards/committees of The United Methodist Church:

- Establish a policy of defining Native American identity as "any individual who can provide verification of membership in a tribe of the United States.
- Develop a policy which will ensure that Native Americans will be identified, selected, and placed on pertinent boards and/or committees as previously stated.
- Urge national, regional, and annual conference activities to select Native American representation from Native American individuals who have a background of relevant Native American history, cultural sensitivity, and contemporary affairs.

Be it further resolved, that The United Methodist Church supports the integration of a policy on Native American definition within *The Book of Discipline*, specific to the current and future regard of Native American representation on such national, regional, and local efforts.

ADOPTED 1992

See Social Principles, ¶ 72.A, "Native American Young Adults in Mission," "Native American Social Witness Program," "Promote the Observance of Native American Awareness Sunday."

Native American Social Witness Program

WHEREAS, Native American churches have historically been seen as being on the receiving end of mission and ministry; and

WHEREAS, yet many social concerns are presently being addressed by Native American communities; and

WHEREAS, the potential and need for social justice ministries among Native Americans is tremendous, and Native American congregations have been put into the role of recipient rather than being empowered;

Therefore be it resolved, that the General Board of Church and Society make available, on request, to every Native American United Methodist church, ministry training and consultation on social witness during the 1992–1996 quadrennium. Such program will be designed and patterned after the gospel of Jesus Christ, which will empower congregations to engage in social witness to their respective Native American communities,.

ADOPTED 1992

See Social Principles, ¶ 72, "Native American Representation in The United Methodist Church," "The United Methodist Church and America's Native People."

Native American Young Adults in Mission

WHEREAS, by treaty obligation many Native American tribes are recognized as "nations" within the territorial boundaries of the United States; and

WHEREAS, the National and World Divisions and the Mission Personnel Resources Program Department of the General Board of Global Ministries of The United Methodist Church sponsor the Mission Intern Program, the World Division assigns young adults overseas to develop leadership skills, and the National Division assigns young adults within the boundaries of the United States to develop leadership skills; and

WHEREAS, opportunities for mission and evangelism exist within Native American nations and tribes within the territorial boundaries of the United States;

Therefore, be it resolved, that the Mission Personnel Resources Program Department, World and National Divisions be directed to assign Native American young adults in "Native American Nations and Tribes" within the boundaries of the United States and in overseas assignments.

ADOPTED 1992

See Social Principles, ¶ 72.A, "Native American Social Witness Program," "Native American Representation in The United Methodist Church."

New Developments in Genetic Science

I. Foreword

The 1988 General Conference approved a statement affirming the positive prospects and warning of the potential dangers of genetic technologies. The General Conference authorized the establishment of a representative task force to: review and assess scientific developments in genetics and their implications for all life; take initiatives with industrial, governmental, and educational institutions involved in genetic engineering to discuss further projections and possible impact; convey to industry and government the sense of urgency to protect the environment as well as animal and human life; support a moratorium on animal patenting until the task force has explored the ethical issues involved; cooperate with other churches, faith groups, and ecumenical bodies sharing similar concerns; explore the effects of the concentration of genetic engineering research tasks and applications in a few crops; and recommend to the 1992 General Conference such further responses and actions as may be deemed appropriate. The term "genetic science" was adopted to identify collectively the aforementioned issues and the task force was thus named the Genetic Science Task Force.

The task force was appointed in March, 1989. Task-force members include scientists, educators, health professionals, ethicists, theologians, a social worker, a lawyer, and a farmer. Informational hearings in the following areas provided basic data on the issues: Houston and

College Station, Tex.; Boston, Mass.; Washington, D.C.; San Leandro, Calif.: Ames, Ia.; Durham, N.C.; and Oak Ridge, Tenn.

Testimony was received from geneticists, physicians, theologians, ethicists, social workers, attorneys, officers of biotechnology companies, journalists, insurance executives, governmental regulatory agency representatives, educators, and persons with genetic disorders and the family members of such persons. The hearing process formed the basis of the recommendations contained in this resolution. A more complete discussion of issues can be found in the complete report of the task force to General Conference.

II. Our Theological Grounding

The United Methodist doctrinal/theological statement affirms, "new issues continually arise that summon us to fresh theological inquiry. Daily we are presented with an array of concerns that challenge our proclamation of God's reign over all of human existence" (1988 Book of Discipline, ¶ 69).

One of the concerns which merits critique in light of theological understandings is genetic science. The urgent task of interpreting the faith in light of the biotechnology revolution and evaluating the rapidly emerging genetic science and technology has only begun. The issues demand continuing dialogue at all levels of the church as persons from diverse perspectives seek to discern and live out God's vision for creation.

The following affirmations provide the theological/doctrinal foundation of the task force's work and recommendations. These historic affirmations represent criteria by which developments and potential developments in biotechnology are evaluated by the community of faith, the church. The task force urges the whole church to join in the urgent task of theological inquiry in what has been called the genetic age.

All Creation Belongs to God the Creator

Creation has its origin, existence, value, and destiny in God. Creation belongs to God, whose power and grace brings the cosmos out of nothingness, order out of chaos, and life out of death. Creation is a realm of divine activity as God continually seeks to bring healing, wholeness, and peace. All creation is accountable to God; therefore, all existence is contingent, finite, and limited. Creation has been declared "good" by the Creator and its goodness inheres in its fulfillment of the divine purpose. The goodness of our genetic diversity is grounded in our creation by God.

Human Beings Are Stewards of Creation

While human beings share with other species the limitations of finite creatures who owe their existence to God, their special creation "in the image of God" gives them the freedom and authority to exercise stewardship responsibly. This includes the knowledge of human life and behavior as it is being expanded by genetic science. The biblical imperative is that human beings are to nurture, cultivate, and serve God's creation so that it might be sustained. Humans are to participate in, manage, nurture, justly distribute, employ, develop, and enhance creation's resources in accordance with their finite discernment of God's purposes. Their divinely conferred dominion over nature does not sanction exploitation and waste; neither does responsible stewardship imply refusal to act creatively with intelligence, skill, and foresight.

The image of God, in which humanity is created, confers both power and responsibility to use power as God does: neither by coercion nor tyranny, but by love. Failure to accept limits by rejecting or ignoring accountability to God and interdependency with the whole of creation is the essence of sin. Therefore, the question is not, can we perform all prodigious work of research and technology? but, should we? The notion that the ability to do something is permission to do it ignores the fundamental biblical understanding of human beings as stewards accountable to the Creator and as contingent, interdependent creatures. Although the pursuit of knowledge is a divine gift, it must be used appropriately with the principle of accountability to God and to the human community and the sustainability of all creation.

Technology in Service to Humanity and God

God has given human beings the capacity for research and technological invention, but the worship of science is idolatry.

Genetic techniques have enormous potential for enhancing creation and human life when they are applied to environmental, agricultural, and medical problems. When wisely used, they often provide positive, though limited and imperfect, solutions to such perplexing social problems as insufficient food supply, spread of disease, ecological deterioration, overpopulation, and human suffering. When used recklessly, for greedy profit, or for calculated improvement of the human race (eugenics), genetic technology becomes corrupted by sin. Moreover, we recognize that even the careful use of genetic technologies for good ends may lead to unintended consequences. We confess that even our intended consequences may not be in the best interest of all.

From Creation to Redemption and Salvation

Redemption and salvation become realities by divine grace as we respond in faith to God's action in Jesus Christ to defeat the powers of sin which enslave the human spirit and thwart the realization of God's purposes for creation. Jesus Christ is the incarnation of God's eternal word and wisdom. His redemptive life, ministry, death, resurrection, and sending of the Spirit reveal God's vision for humanity. Having distorted God's good intention for us in creation, we now are called to be conformed to God's true image in Jesus Christ.

Through the affirmation of the goodness of creation and the saving work of Christ, God has claimed all persons as beloved sons and daughters with inherent worth and dignity. Therefore, we understand that our worth as children of God is irrespective of genetic qualities, personal attributes, or achievements. Barriers and prejudices based on biological characteristics fracture the human family and distort God's goal for humanity. The community of Christ bears witness to the truth that all persons have unity by virtue of having been redeemed by Christ. Such unity respects and embraces genetic diversity which accounts for many differences among people. Love and justice, which the scriptures uplift and which Jesus Christ supremely expresses, require that the worth and dignity of the defenseless be preserved and protected. As the community of Christ, the Church seeks to embody love and justice and to give of itself on behalf of the powerless and voiceless.

God's Reign is for All Creation

The coming of God's reign is the guiding hope for all creation. Hebrew Scripture and the life, teaching, death, and resurrection of Jesus Christ affirm that God's reign is characterized by liberation from all forms of oppression, justice in all relationships, peace and goodwill among all peoples, and the healing of all creation. It is both the vision of God's new heaven and new earth and the recognition of our limits which must inform and shape our role as stewards of earth and life in the emerging age of genetics. It is in the context of God's sovereignty over all existence, our hope for the coming of God's reign, our awareness of our own finitude, and our responsibility as stewards that we consider these issues and the following recommendations.

III. Issues in the Development of Genetic Research and Technology

A. Why the church is addressing these issues.

God's sovereignty over all creation, our status as stewards of creation's resources, and the Church's nature as a nurturing and prophetic community living toward God's reign over all existence propel us to consider the theological/ethical implications of genetic science. As genetic science probes the very structure of biological life and develops means to alter the nature of life itself, the potential for relief of suffering and the healing of creation is enormous. But the potential for added physical and emotional suffering and social and economic injustice also exists. Developments in genetic science compel our reevaluation of accepted theological/ethical issues, including determinism versus free will, the nature of sin, just distribution of resources, the status of human beings in relation to other forms of life, and the meaning of personhood.,

B. Genetic science affects every area of our lives.

The food we eat, the health care we receive, our biological traits, and the environment in which we live are all affected by research and developments in genetic science. As stewards of and participants in life and its resources, we seek to understand, to evaluate, and to utilize responsibly the emerging genetic technologies in accordance with our finite understanding of God's purposes for creation. The divine purpose includes justice, health, and peace for all persons and the integrity and ecological balance of creation. The uses of genetic science have the potential for promoting as well as thwarting these aspects of the divine purpose.

Genetic issues are much more pressing than is generally recognized. Every community contains individuals and families who daily face genetic concerns in the workplace or as result of their own genetic makeup. The rapid growth of genetic science has increased our awareness of these concerns, has created new concerns, and has accelerated the theological, ethical, and pastoral challenges that genetics poses to persons of faith.

C. *Scientific change now leads societal change.*

The rise in importance of science and technology has been one of the most significant developments in the last 400 years. Beginning with the industrial revolution, we have witnessed a succession of revolutions: the technological, the atomic, and biological. Each of these revolutions has presented society with a host of religious challenges and threats that have taken enormous and ongoing efforts to resolve constructively. The very nature of work, perceptions of the world, international relations, and family life have changed in part because of these revolutions.

A major dimension of the biological revolution is genetic science. Less than 50 years ago, the actual genetic substance of living cells, DNA, was firmly identified. Now, altering DNA in plants and animals, even humans, in order to correct disorders or to introduce more desirable characteristics is being done. Genetic developments in medicine and agriculture promise to alter the very nature of society, the natural environment, and even human nature. Christians must evaluate these developments in light of our basic understanding of God as creator and of humans as stewards of creation, including technology.

D. *Genetic science challenges society.*

Biotechnology based on genetic research is already upon us. Thousands of people and millions of dollars are devoted to genetic science. Gene therapy has already been introduced as an experimental medical treatment. Extensive research is being conducted in plant and animal genetics with significant implications for the food supply, farm policy, agricultural economics, and ecological balance. The efforts to identify the estimated one hundred thousand human genes (The Human Genome Project) are well underway with funding from both the National Institutes of Health and the U.S. Department of Energy.

In spite of the rapid growth in genetic research, many people tend to see genetics merely as an extension of the changes in medical, agricultural, and other technologies. In fact, genetic science crosses new frontiers as it explores the essence of life. The implications of genetic research and development are so far-reaching that society must consider the effect of these developments on persons, animal and plant life, the environment, agriculture, the food supply, patent policies, and medicine. Delays in commercializing some of the technologies may afford society and the church additional time to address the implications, but the time available for serious reflection on the consequences of these technologies prior to their implementation is brief.

IV. Questions about Biotechnology

New developments in technology always challenge society's imagination and understanding. Technology is often viewed either with awe or with fear. The popular view of the geneticist alternates between a saint who cures all disease and a mad scientist who creates monsters or perverts life. The extreme image must be avoided as society raises questions about the technologies themselves and questions how they should be properly developed and controlled. Although genetic technologies are similar to other technologies, genetic science and technology force us to examine, as never before, the meaning of life, our understanding of ourselves as humans, and our proper role in God's creation.

Several basic questions can provide a framework within which to evaluate the effect of genetics (or any other new technology) on any segment of society. The questions revolve around issues of appropriateness, availability, efficacy, and accessibility.

V. The Patenting of Life Forms

The patenting of life forms is a crucial issue in the debate over access to genetic technologies. Some claim that patenting of life will give complete control to the owner and so limit access. Others insist that the scientists and funding agencies or institutions must have some return on their investment. A compromise that many societies have worked out in order to provide economic returns for those who have developed a technology while providing access, eventually, to the entire society is the patent, or exclusive control of a technological invention for a period of years. But should exclusive ownership rights apply to the gene pool? In 1984, the General Conference of The United Methodist Church declared genes to be a part of the common heritage of all peoples. The position taken by the church in 1984 is consistent with our understanding of the sanctity of God's creation and God's ownership of life. Therefore, exclusive ownership rights of genes as a means of making genetic technologies accessible raises serious theological concerns. While patents on organisms themselves are opposed, process patents, wherein the method for engineering a new organism is patented, provide a means of economic return on investment while avoiding exclusive ownership of the organism and can be supported.

VI. Affirmations/Recommendations/Conclusions

A. General

1. We affirm that knowledge of genetics is a resource over which we are to exercise stewardship responsibly in accordance with God's reign over creation. The use of genetic knowledge in ways which destabilize and fragment creation is resisted as a violation of God's vision of justice, peace, and wholeness.

2. We caution that the prevalent principle in research that what can be done should be done is insufficient rationale for genetic science. This principle should be subject to legal and ethical oversight in research design and should not be the prevalent principle guiding the development of new technologies. Applications of research to technologies need moral and ethical guidance.

3. We urge adequate public funding of genetic research so that projects not likely to be funded by private grants will receive adequate support and so that there will be greater accountability to the public by those involved in setting the direction of genetic research.

4. We urge that genes and genetically modified organisms (human, plant, animal) be held as common resources and not be exclusively controlled, or patented. We support improvements in the procedures for granting patents on processes and techniques as a way to reward new developments in this area.

B. Medical Recommendations

1. Testing and Treatment

a. We support the right of all persons to health care and health-care resources regardless of their genetic or medical conditions.

b. We support equal access to medical resources including genetic testing and genetic counseling by appropriately educated and trained health-care professionals. We affirm that responsible stewardship of God's gift of human life implies access of all persons to genetic counseling throughout their reproductive life.

c. We support human gene therapies that produce changes that cannot be passed on to offspring (somatic), but believe that they should be limited to the alleviation of suffering caused by disease. We urge that guidelines and government regulations be developed for the use of all gene therapies. We oppose therapy that results in changes that can be passed to offspring (germ-line therapy) until its safety and the certainty of its effects can be demonstrated and until risks to human life can be demonstrated to be minimal.

d. We support the use of recombinant DNA for the purposes of genetic therapy and the prevention of genetic disorders. However, we oppose its use for eugenic purposes or genetic enhancements designed merely for cosmetic purposes or social advantage.

2. *Privacy and Confidentiality of Genetic Information*

a. We support the privacy of genetic information. Genetic data of individuals and their families shall be kept secret and held in strict confidence unless confidentiality is waived by the individual or his or her family, or unless the collection and use of genetic identification data are supported by an appropriate court order.
b. We support increased study of the social, moral, and ethical implications of the Human Genome Project. We support wide public access to genetic data that do not identify particular individuals.
c. We oppose the discriminatory or manipulative use of genetic information, such as the limitation, termination, or denial of insurance or employment.

C. *Agriculture*

1. We support public involvement in initiating, evaluating, regulating and funding of agricultural genetic research.

a. We believe the public has an important policy and financial role in ensuring the continuation of research which furthers the goal of a safe, nutritious, and affordable food supply.
b. We believe that the public should have input into whether a research effort, or its products, will serve an unmet need in food and fiber production and processing. We urge United Methodists to be active participants in achieving this accountability in all areas of the world.
c. We believe that the benefits of research applications should accrue to the broadest possible public, including farmers and consumers.
2. We support the sustainability of family farms, natural resource, and rural communities and urge that genetic research in agriculture and food products promote these goals.

D. *Environment*

1. As stewards of the planet Earth, we should strive to perpetuate all of God's living creations as long as possible. We should be

concerned not only with the well-being of humans, but also with the wholeness of the rest of creation. We should try to maintain ecological balance as God intended. Technologies such as genetic engineering can effect ecological balance. Genetic technologies must be used carefully to help sustain the planet.

2. We caution that genetically engineered organisms be released into the environment only after careful testing in a controlled setting that stimulates each environment in which the organisms are to be used.

3. We urge the development of criteria and methodologies to anticipate and assess possible adverse environmental responses to the release of genetically engineered organisms.

4. We urge that prior to the release of each organism, plans and procedures be developed to destroy genetically engineered organisms that may cause adverse environmental responses.

E. What the Church Can Do

1. Expand education and dialogue around ethical issues in the development of genetic science and technology.

    a. We request that The United Methodist Church and its appropriate boards and agencies educate laity and clergy on the issues of genetic science, theology, and ethics by conducting workshops and seminars, producing resource materials, and training pastors and lay persons to deal constructively with these issues. Sessions on the ethical implications of genetics technology should be included as part of seminary training, continuing education requirements for clergy, Christian educators' training events, adult and youth Sunday school curriculum, schools of mission and schools of church and society, and campus ministry programs.

    b. We request that clergy be trained to provide pastoral counseling for persons with genetic disorders and their families as well as those facing difficult choices as a result of genetic testing. These choices might include decisions such as those related to reproduction, employment, and living wills. Churches are encouraged to provide support groups for individuals and families affected by genetic disorders.

c. We call on the church to support persons who, because of the likelihood of severe genetic disorders, must make difficult decisions regarding reproduction. We reaffirm the 1988 General Conference (*1988 Book of Discipline* ¶71.G) position opposing the termination of pregnancy solely for the purpose of gender selection.

d. We urge theological seminaries to offer courses and continuing education events which equip clergy to address theological and ethnical issues raised by scientific research and technology.

e. We urge the church to establish and maintain dialogue with those persons working to develop or promote genetics-based technologies.

The complexity and multi-faceted implications of genetic science require continuing interaction among scientists, technologists, theologians, ethicists, industrial and corporate leaders, government officials, and the general public. The church can facilitate dialogue on the emerging issues. The Genetic Science Task Force hearings revealed a strong interest on the part of persons from various perspectives, experiences, and interests in exploring the ethical, theological, and societal implications of developments in genetics. Providing a forum for informed discussion will enable the church to inform the public, raise relevant theological/ethical concerns, expand and deepen theological exploration in light of contemporary developments, and more adequately support scientists and technologists who seek to live out their faith in their vocations.

The ethical concerns of the church need to be interjected into the laboratory, factory, and the halls of government in an ongoing manner. Local churches, districts, annual conferences, and appropriate general agencies should participate in dialogues with university, industry and government bodies.

2. Produce resources to educate on genetics issues. General agencies of the church should develop additional interpretive resources on genetics issues.

a. United Methodist Communications is urged to cooperate with the General Board of Church and Society to develop an episode of "Catch the Spirit" highlighting persons who testified to the Genetics Science Task Force.

b. The Board of Discipleship is urged to develop curriculum materials stressing the ethical dimensions of the widespread use of genetic technologies in health, agriculture, and other industries.

c. The Division of Health and Welfare Ministries of the General Board of Global Ministries is urged to develop materials in cooperation with United Methodist-affiliated hospitals on the ethical issues families may face regarding the use of new diagnostic tests and other procedures.

d. The General Board of Higher Education and Ministry is urged to survey seminaries and United Methodist-affiliated schools for academic courses related to genetic science and to make this listing available through its publications.

e. The General Council on Ministries Research Section is urged to survey United Methodist general agencies and annual conferences requesting the names of informed speakers in the following categories:

(1) Families affected by genetic disorders.

(2) Clergy with experience in the fields of genetics research, or genetics counseling.

(3) Genetic counselors, social workers, psychologists, and other counseling professionals who work with individuals and families with genetic disorders.

(4) Social and physical scientists researching the effect of genetics technologies on society.

(5) Environmental, agricultural, and biomedical scientists.

(6) Theologians and ethicists.

(7) Farmers and others concerned about agricultural and environmental effects of these technologies.

(8) Technologists and representatives of industry.

(9) Physicians knowledgeable in genetic issues, especially obstetrician-gynecologists and pediatricians.

(10) Educators.

3. Continue and increase The United Methodist Church's work in the area of genetics.

a. The General Council on Ministries is urged to convene a meeting of general agency staff in early 1993 to review the work each agency plans in the 1993–96 quadrennium relative to the ethics of genetic science technologies.

b. The General Board of Church and Society is urged to continue its work in these areas, to publish a summary of the hearings it conducted on genetic science, and monitor legislative and governmental actions related to genetic technologies.

c. All general agencies are urged to cooperate with ecumenical groups as they seek to coordinate actions regarding the use of knowledge gained from genetic science. Concern for justice for persons and the integrity of all life should form the basis of our ecumenical witness.

d. Local churches are urged to study the issues raised in this statement and to act on the recommendations.

ADOPTED 1992

See Social Principles, ¶ 72, "U.S. Agriculture and Rural Communities in Crisis."

Observance of Dr. Martin Luther King, Jr. Day

WHEREAS, the observance of Dr. Martin Luther King, Jr. Day is in keeping with the spirit of the Social Principles of The United Methodist Church and the inclusiveness of the denomination;

Be it therefore resolved, that each annual conference observe Martin Luther King, Jr. Day with appropriate services of commemoration in recognition of Dr. King; and

On that day we recommend that we close the bishop's office, all conference offices, all district offices, all local church offices, and, where feasible, business offices of church-related institutions; and

Support local activities surrounding the celebration of Dr. King's life and ministry; and

Encourage local school districts not to hold classes on Dr. Martin Luther King, Jr., Day; or

If local school districts hold classes, encourage them to use Dr. Martin Luther King, Jr., Day to celebrate Dr. King's work and address the need for the continuing struggle for justice.

ADOPTED 1992

See Social Principles, ¶ 72.A, "A Charter for Racial Justice Policies in an Interdependent Global Community."

The Oxford House Model for Treatment of Drug and Alcohol Abuse

WHEREAS, 12.1 million U.S. citizens have one or more symptoms of alcoholism[1]; and

---

[1]"National Institute on Alcohol Abuse and Alcoholism, a Working Paper: Projections of Alcohol Abusers," January, 1985.

WHEREAS, Oxford Houses are self-run, self-supporting, non-subsidized, shared-residence programs utilizing ordinary rental housing in order to provide effective peer support (rather than governmentally, or institutionally, or staff-dependent support) for persons in recovery; and

WHEREAS, a 1988 poll of some 1,200 persons who had lived in Oxford Houses for some period during the previous 12 years showed that some 80 percent had maintained sobriety (as contrasted to the 20 percent rate of the abuse-free maintenance that is customarily reported for those who have completed rehabilitation programs without subsequent residence in Oxford House); and

WHEREAS, a 1991 survey of 45 residents of six newly formed Oxford Houses by Dr. William Spillane of the Catholic University of America, Washington, D.C., indicated a relapse rate of only 9.3 percent;

Be it therefore resolved, that General Conference hereby encourages each of its member congregations to become knowledgeable about the Oxford House model so that these congregations might provide all feasible support and assistance in the creation and maintenance of such recovery houses in their respective local communities;

Be it further resolved, that the General Conference direct the Health and Welfare Department of the General Board of Global Ministries to provide appropriate informational assistance in this effort, within the constraints of the current budgetary allotments.

ADOPTED 1992

See Social Principles, ¶ 72, "Drug and Alcohol Concerns."

Pacific Islanders Included as Racial and Ethnic Minority Group

WHEREAS, the Pacific Islander population is continuing to grow in the United States and in The United Methodist Church; and

WHEREAS, the United Methodist Pacific Islander constituency has requested to be considered as a racial and ethnic minority group on its own; and

WHEREAS, the National Federation of Asian American United Methodists has recognized the Pacific Islanders as a different racial and ethnic minority group; and

WHEREAS, the General Commission on Religion and Race has also recognized the Pacific Islanders as an additional ethnic and racial minority group within the denomination;

Therefore, be it resolved, that General Conference of 1992 mandates the category of Pacific Islanders be included as a racial and ethnic minority group in the *Book of Discipline* wherever the other four racial and ethnic minority groups are mentioned (e.g., Asians, Blacks, Hispanics, Pacific Islanders, and Native Americans).

ADOPTED 1992

See Social Principles, ¶ 72.

Pan Methodist Unity

WHEREAS, the Constitution of The United Methodist Church calls for our church to "seek, and work for unity at all levels of church life . . . through plans of union with churches of Methodist and other denominational traditions" (*Constitution*, 5); and

WHEREAS, on March 22, 1991, the Fifth Consultation of Methodist Bishops, consisting of bishops of the African Methodist Episcopal, African Methodist Episcopal Zion, Christian Methodist Episcopal, and United Methodist Churches passed the following resolution:

> In the Fifth Consultation of Methodist Bishops at St. Simon's Island, as an outgrowth of presentation of papers dealing with the global and national witness of the Christian faith in our world of the present day and accepting the challenge for the church to begin to set its house in order as it relates to the absence of unity within the Body of Christ, this Consultation of Methodist Bishops responds by supporting the following:

WHEREAS, a consensus developed among those bishops attending the Consultation that the mission of the church compels us to reexamine the relationships and cooperative structures of the African Methodist Episcopal Church, the African Methodist Episcopal Zion Church, the Christian Methodist Episcopal Church, and The United Methodist Church; and

WHEREAS, these four denominations share a common history and heritage, with similar polity, episcopal form of leadership, itineracy, and Wesleyan priorities; and

WHEREAS, new forms of relationships, missional structures, and possible merger would make a powerful witness to Christ in a world torn by such evils as injustice and racism;

Therefore, be it resolved, that the bishops of each of our four churches petition their respective General Conferences to authorize a Study

Commission for the purpose of exploring possible merger. Each such petition should request that:

1. Each respective General Conference provide for five representatives to this commission reflecting the wholeness of the Church and provide needed financial support;

2. The commission be authorized to seek such staff support from existing denominational staff as it shall deem needful;

3. Progress reports be made regularly to each body of bishops and that a final report should be prepared for each General Conference no later than 1996;

4. The task of the commission shall include, but not be limited to, the following:

A. Keeping clear the missional reasons for this exploration and ensuring that such a mission focus be written into any proposal or plan;

B. Ensuring that all proposals provide recognition of each denomination's heritage and appropriate representation of persons in any future structures;

C. Developing a plan of merger that includes a proposed constitution, organizational plan, and continuation of the episcopacy and itineracy;

D. Recognizing the global nature, polity, and mission of our churches.

5. The chairperson of the commission shall rotate among the participating denominations in alphabetical order with each denomination choosing its chairperson from among its representatives;

6. We hold open the possibility of other Methodist denominations joining us in this quest for unity and wholeness.

7. This proposal does not discourage the continuation of any existing merger conversations.

Now therefore be it further resolved, that the General Conference of The United Methodist Church authorizes participation of The United Methodist Church in the Study Commission proposed in the Bishops Consultation resolution, with five members reflecting the wholeness of the Church to be appointed by the Council of Bishops. Funding will be provided by the General Council on Finance and Administration.

Be it further resolved, that the work of the commission proceed according to the guidelines of the Bishops Consultation resolution of

March 22, 1991, except that the report to the 1996 General Conference shall not necessarily be a final report.

ADOPTED 1992

See Social Principles, ¶ 72.A, "History of Blacks in the United Methodist Church."

Population

The creation of the world out of chaos into order is the initial biblical witness. In this witness is the affirmation of the freedom and responsibility of humankind. We affirm God to be the Creator, the one who grants us freedom, and the one to whom we are responsible.

God's ongoing creative and re-creative concern for the universe was expressed through Jesus Christ, who has called us to find the meaning of our lives in dual love of God and neighbor. In this context we live responsibly before God, writing history by the actions of our lives. The imperative upon the individual Christian and the Christian community is to seek patterns of life, shape the structures of society, and foster those values which will dignify human life for all.

In this quest we must not "quench the Spirit" but allow the spirit to lead us into God's new day for all people, a new day which calls for the compassionate and passionate desire to see a new birth out of justice.

We believe that history is not finished, but that we are engaged in a history. This is an age of possibility in which we are called under God to serve the future with hope and confidence. Christians have no alternative to involvement in seeking solutions for the great and complex set of problems which faces the world today. All these issues are closely interrelated: hunger, poverty, denial of human rights, economic exploitation and overconsumption by the rich, technologies that are inadequate or inappropriate, depletion of resources, and rapid population growth.

Hunger and poverty, injustice and violence in the world cannot simplistically be blamed on population growth, yet the rapidly swelling numbers of humankind are making it increasingly difficult to solve the other interconnected problems. There is much we do not yet know about the relationship between population size and the sustaining environment, but clearly we do know there can be too many people.

Programs aimed at reducing population growth should not be ends in themselves, not substitutes for other measures necessary to eliminate hunger and poverty. The Church supports population programs as needed to move toward its goal of a just and humane world order.

The population situation is different in different societies, and therefore nations must be free to develop policies in keeping with their own needs and cultures. These global and regional aspects affect all humankind and can only be solved by international cooperation.

At the individual level, our Church has long recognized the basic human right to have the education and means to plan one's family. For women, particularly, the ability to control fertility is a liberating force, making it possible to assume other roles and responsibilities in society. Men and women alike bear responsibility for family planning and contraceptives practices.

Today there are those who claim that some nations are beyond help because of their rapid population growth. The Christian church cannot accept these voices of despair. Even as just means for achieving stabilization are urgently sought, the Christian church must reaffirm the sacredness of each individual and stand fast against attitudes and practices which treat people as mere numbers or masses.

We welcome the growing understanding of what just and desirable means for lowering fertility rates may encompass, and we affirm that the use of such means must take into consideration the critical importance and interrelated nature of these aspects: better education, and the opportunity for people to participate in decisions that shape their lives; the provision of basic economic security, including old-age security; upgrading the status of women; improved maternal and child health care; and finally, a strong birth control program.

The Church should take the lead in actions which can help focus on the problems caused by rapid population growth and to support measures to deal with them. We therefore call on the people and agencies of the Church:

1. To recognize rapid population growth to be a matter of great religious and moral concern, to develop education and action programs on the issues raised, and to increase understanding of the interrelationships between population growth and other world problems. Education must include sensitivity toward the existence of varying sociological patterns and religious philosophies.

2. To develop programs to increase understanding of the meaning in today's world of responsible parenthood. Churches can encourage acceptance of the idea that not everyone needs to be a parent and that those who choose to have children should accept the small family norm as responsible practice in today's world.

3. To help the affluent realize the devastating impact on the world and its people of wasteful consumption patterns and exploitative economic systems, and to develop resources and curricula which encourage change in overmaterialistic lifestyles.

4. To urge that United Methodist medical and mission facilities and programs provide a full range of fertility-related and family-planning information and services. The Church should exert leadership in making possible the safe and legal availability of sterilization procedures for both men and women, and of abortion where appropriate.

The Church should offer informed counseling and support to both men and women on all options regarding childbearing. The Church bears a particular responsibility to stand guard against coercive use of birth control practices aimed at the poor and powerless.

5. To take the lead in measures to upgrade the status of women in societies and to include them in all development planning and processes, and give increased support to policies which will further the goal of equal rights for women, such as the Equal Rights Amendment in the United States.

6. To call on all governments to give priority to implementing the provisions of the World Population Plan of Action which the United Nations approved in 1974, and which called for population policies in a context of total social and economic development planning. We especially call on the United States government to develop a national population policy that would include the goal of stabilizing the United States population, and recommendations on population distribution and land and resource use.

7. To call on the United States Congress and legislative bodies of the affluent nations to recognize the crucial nature of population growth, and to give maximum feasible funding to programs of population, health, agriculture, and other technological assistance programs for the poor nations. International assistance programs should be based on mutual cooperation, should recognize the

diversities of culture, should encourage self development and not dependency, and should not attempt to require "effective population programs" as a prerequisite for other developmental assistance.

8. To call for government and private agencies to place a higher priority on research aimed at developing a range of safe, inexpensive contraceptives that can be used in a variety of societies and medical situations.

A high priority should also be given to research aimed at gaining greater understanding of attitudes, motivations, and social and economic factors affecting childbearing.

Even as we urge individuals and governments to intensify efforts immediately to achieve population stability as soon as possible, the churches need to keep before people the moral reasons why we need to be concerned with the population problem. Our goal in history is that everyone may have the conditions of existence necessary for the fulfillment of God's intentions for humanity. Our context in history is the preciousness of life and the love of God and all creation.

ADOPTED 1980, REVISED 1992

See Social Principles, ¶ 72.H, "A Call for Increased Commitment to End World Hunger and Poverty," "Justice, Peace and the Integrity of Creation."

Prejudice Against Muslims and Arabs in the U.S.A.

Today in the U.S.A. there are approximately 3 million persons who are adherents of Islam. Arab-Americans, both Christian and Muslim, constitute an ever larger number of persons in the American population. These persons are suffering the effects of a particularly virulent prejudice too often aided and abetted by statements and images in the media and by rhetoric from some of the highest political leadership.

As part of the fabric of racism in the U.S.A. in which both subtle and violent acts continue against ethnic minority groups and persons, so too have such acts been perpetuated against the Arab and Muslim communities in the U.S.A.

Arab-American organization offices, mosques and Islamic centers have been bombed and torched. Leaders of the community have been murdered. Questionable uses of law have been utilized to stifle the rights of association and freedom of expression. Though discriminatory acts against Arabs and Muslims do not stand in isolation from similar acts perpetuated against other racial/ethnic minority persons in the U.S.A., their existence and effects upon Arabs and Muslims has been little acknowledged in U.S. society, with concomitant deleterious effect on U.S. perceptions, internationally, as they touch upon relations with predominantly Arab and Muslim nations and organizations.

Therefore, The United Methodist Church, in the knowledge that Jesus calls us to the blessings of peacemaking and reminds us that the highest law is to love God and neighbor, calls its members:

1. To oppose demagoguery, manipulation and image-making which seek to label Arabs and Muslims in a negative way.
2. To counter stereotypical and bigoted statements made against Muslims and Islam, Arabs and Arabic culture.
3. To increase knowledge of neighbor by study and personal contact which yield a greater appreciation of the Muslim and Arabic contributions to society.
4. To act decisively to include Arabs and Muslims in interfaith and community organizations.
5. To pray for the perfection of community among us and to participate fully in the process of bringing it into being.

To aid United Methodists to respond to this call, all boards, agencies, and institutions of The United Methodist Church are requested to provide resources and program, and where appropriate, to act in advocacy.

ADOPTED 1988

See Social Principles, ¶ 72.B, "Eradication of Racism," "A Charter for Racial Justice Policies in an Interdependent Global Community," "Our Muslim Neighbors."

Program to Emphasize Inclusiveness in All Dimensions of the Church

Develop a program that places fresh emphasis upon "Inclusiveness": (multicultural, multiracial, multilingual gender) inclusiveness in the life and ministry of The United Methodist Church in all dimensions and at all levels. Such an emphasis will include the following provisions:

1. That each annual conference, led by the bishop and cabinet, develop a conferencewide program with clear goals and strategies; this program to be reviewed and evaluated by the General Commission on Religion and Race, in consultation with the other general program agencies; this annual conference plan to be ready by July 1, 1994.

2. That this program include a conferencewide enlistment and recruitment program that seeks clergy and laity who will give themselves to cross-cultural appointments, to begin new Sunday schools and congregations among poor people and people of color.

3. That the program include a determined effort to enlist and recruit some of the most competent, experienced pastors for such appointments rather than simply enlisting the newest clergy.

4. That the General Conference make it possible for the bishop to appoint clergy who work at other jobs and who will not obligate the conference in salary or pension to be appointed to start new congregations or strengthen other congregations.

5. That this "inclusive" emphasis include asking and actively encouraging all multi-staff congregations to deliberately make their staffs inclusive in gender and people of color.

6. That goals and strategies be established in each conference so that cross-racial and cross-cultural appointments become normative for the conference and one of the essential ways in which the conference engages in the mission of Christ.

7. That the program include measures to increase the conference lay and clergy leadership in knowledge and understanding of all the people and cultures who reside within the borders of the conference.

8. That this conference program include programs for children and youth, such as "multicultural camps," human relations conference/ seminars, and various kinds of work camps (for example, an evangelism work camp).

9. That the conference program include the enlisting and recruitment of young adults to become "people in mission" who work on a subsistence basis or pay their own way.

10. That this program will create new congregations—rural, suburban and urban—in town and country.

11. That this program will encourage diversity in styles and kinds of ministries, in worship styles, in language and thought forms in

order to enable the gospel and The United Methodist Church again to have impact on working-class people, the poor, people of color, and other target groups of people. The United Methodist Church must recover the passion for advancing scriptural holiness and reforming the nation.

12. That this program make appointments of "tentmaker" clergy to ministries of justice and peace, to ministries of prevention and rehabilitation in drug abuse and to children and young people caught in the spiraling crisis of drugs, violence, racism, and poverty.

13. That each conference program will include the assisting of local congregations and pastors in developing an "inclusive" model for the congregation, even though worship services occur in several languages, and in eliminating the "landlord" model.

14. That the program include a provision that we will no longer sell church buildings in the urban areas to churches of other denominations but will instead place "tentmaker" clergy and laity in those situations, assisting them in finding the way to create a new people in that place for mission to the people in that community.

15. That the conference program will include a major training and additional skills strategy, using pastors' schools, annual conference sessions, and United Methodist theological schools (where a United Methodist seminary is not within the bounds of the conference or area, the conference should enlist schools of other denominations) to create resources for the inclusive ministry and to empower conference clergy and laity.

16. That this conference program also include an effort to develop what Black Methodists for Church Renewal call "outrageous ministries," innovative ministries in urban, suburban, and rural areas so that an unfettered gospel can do the work of the crucified and Risen One.

17. That each annual conference report back to the General Conference in 1996 their program and progress. That these reports come through the report of the General Commission on Religion and Race.

18. That the General Conference of 1996 evaluate this entire effort and then encourage and strengthen it for the next quadrennium.

ADOPTED 1992

See Social Principles, ¶ 72, "Elimination of Racism in The United Methodist Church," "Strengthening the Black Church for the 21st Century."

Project Equality

In consideration of long established support, by The United Methodist Church, for fair employment practices;

In consideration of national policy for fair employment practices in the United States, which policy embraces legislation against unemployment discrimination;

In recognition of The United Methodist Church's responsibility to make ethical use of its own financial resources; through effective use of equal employment opportunity as one of its purchasing criteria;

In recognition that Project Equality provides a technical assistance resource to agencies and institutions of The United Methodist Church in the development of equal employment and affirmative action programs;

In the conviction that "Project Equality," a voluntary cooperative interdenominational enterprise of churches, synagogues, and related institutions, provides a responsible, consistent, ethical, practical, effective, and positive means whereby The United Methodist Church and other churches can support fair employment practices in the United States:

The United Methodist Church endorses "Project Equality," and recommends cooperation, both through participation and financial support, on the part of all United Methodist annual conferences, local churches, local or national institutions, agencies, and organizations.

ADOPTED 1968, REVISED 1988

See Social Principles, ¶ 72.A, "A Charter for Racial Justice Policies in an Interdependent Global Community," "Economic Justice."

Promote the Observance of Native American Awareness Sunday

WHEREAS, the Native American population continues to shift in larger numbers from the rural areas to the urban population centers; and

WHEREAS, the human conditions of numerous Native Americans in the rural and urban environments reflect a legacy of poverty and socioeconomic denial; and

WHEREAS, there is a serious shortage of Native American pastors and trained professionals to respond to the human conditions in the Native American communities; and

WHEREAS, there is a National United Methodist Native American Center which has been created to recruit, train, and deploy Native American leadership; and

WHEREAS, the financial support which is required to sustain the center is beyond the capability of the Native American communities; and

WHEREAS, the 1988 General Conference approved Native American Awareness Sunday as a means for providing opportunities for the denomination to support Native American ministries;

Therefore, be it resolved, that all annual conferences promote the observance of the Native American Awareness Sunday and encourage local churches to support the Sunday with programming and offerings.

Be it further resolved, that the agencies which develop and provide resources for this special day report to the General Commission on Religion and Race their plans, strategies, and timelines for addressing the goals and objectives related to Native American Awareness Sunday.

ADOPTED 1992

See Social Principles, ¶ 72, "The United Methodist Church and America's Native People," "Shared Financial Support for the Native American Center."

Protecting and Sustaining Children

"And they were bringing children to him that he might touch them . . . Let the children come to me, do not hinder them, for to such belongs the Kingdom of God. Truly, I say to you, whoever does not receive the Kingdom of God like a child shall not enter it. And he took them in his arms and blessed them, laying his hands upon them." (Mark 10:13-16)

"Fear not, O my servant Jacob, O Jeshurun, whom I chose, for I pour water on the thirsty land and streams on the dry ground, I pour my spirit on your children, my blessings on your offspring, till they spring up like grass among the waters, like willows by a watercourse" (Isaiah 44:3-4.)

"We are guilty of many errors and many faults, but our worst crime is abandoning the children, neglecting the foundation of life. Many of the things we need can wait. The child cannot. Right now is the time its bones are being formed, blood is being made and senses are being developed. To this child we cannot answer, 'Tomorrow.' This child's name is 'Today.' " (Gabriela Mistral, Nobel Prize-winning poet from Chile)

Introduction

Children are powerless. The future of the human race is in our children, but in decision-making they are voiceless and powerless. Children cannot speak for themselves. They depend on us to speak for them and to be their advocates. They suffer most when resources are misappropriated. They need us to bring their very special needs to the notice of societies and those in power.

Who will survive? And how has the world protected its children? By killing and maiming millions of them through war and an unjust global economic system. "The children of the world are already living in the rubble of World War III," Dr. Bernard Lowe, co-president of the International Physicians for the Prevention of Nuclear War stated in 1986, ". . . Every three days 120,000 children die unnecessarily—the very toll of casualties following the atomic bombing of Hiroshima." United Nations Children's Fund (UNICEF) 1987 "State of the World's Children" says that 14 million innocent children under five die each year from preventable undernutrition and infection, twenty-seven every minute of the day and night.

An escalating arms race and misdirected priorities doubly threaten children's survival: a single hour's global military expenditure could save 3.5 million children otherwise destined to die annually from preventable infectious diseases. Yet every minute of the day, 1.9 million dollars is spent by leaders of nations around the world—not only superpowers—on an arms race that assumes the existence of a political issue worth destroying all the children in the world.

Survival Often Means a Lifetime of Suffering and Neglect

Those children who do survive often grow up under a blanket of poverty and despair. In Asia, Africa and Latin America, many children go hungry, remain poor, suffer from preventable diseases, lack education, lack fuel and clean water.

Causes and Extent of Child Poverty and Neglect

Poverty is the cause of early deaths, ill health and poor physical and intellectual growth among many of the world's children. In the 1980's, progress against that poverty has been slowed, and in many nations thrown into reverse, by the effects of long-running world recession.

Governments, almost universally, have responded to the recession by decreasing the share of social expenditures as a proportion of total government spending, either by stopping the expansion of services or by dropping the quality of existing services.

There is a clear correlation between reductions in government spending and a deterioration in children's welfare. While the richer people manage to remain relatively isolated from the effects of the world economic recession, the children of the poor (and in some countries the children of the lower middle class) have borne the brunt of a significant and global cutback in services. This has resulted in a loss of the civil, political, social and economic rights of the world's children, and is manifested by:

- Frequent infection and widespread undernutrition kills over a quarter of a million children every week. These children do not die of exotic diseases requiring sophisticated cures. They die in the long drawn-out process of frequent illness and poor nutrition which gradually loosens their grip on life.
- Millions of children are forced into prostitution, pornography and other forms of abuse and exploitation. More than 100 million children are employed under hazardous and often fatal working conditions.
- The use and manipulation of children as soldiers, targets for assassination, torture and imprisonment without trial has increased as armed conflict and civil unrest rises. The situation in South Africa is a prime example of a deliberate policy by the government to terrorize and subjugate black children and youth, with thousands detained without trial.
- The manipulation and institutionalized control of children's minds and values by: the media, war toys, the education system, and sometimes, subconsciously, the family and church, which leads to false stereotypes and the perpetuation of systems of injustice and violence.

- Armed conflict, civil unrest and famine displace children and separate them from their families. Children make up more than 70 percent of the population in many refugee camps, while 80 million children are homeless worldwide.
- The availability of formal education has decreased. In 1970, if all the world's children who did not have access to school held hands, they would go around the world three times. In 1985, they would go around the world four times.
- Youth unemployment is now at epidemic proportions. Youth have been forced into a critical situation where they lack basic skills and training in societies with high unemployment and underemployment.
- Urban unemployment and underemployment, low wages, loss of rural profits, and decreases in services for the poor have been partly responsible for detrimental changes in child rearing and protection practices.

Children and Poverty in the United States

And it is not just in Bangladesh, Sri Lanka, or El Salvador that children are dying unnecessarily. In the United States in 1987, poverty killed 10,000 children, one every-fifty-three minutes. In fact, the United States has slipped from sixth to a tie for last place among twenty industrialized nations in keeping babies alive in the first year of life.

In the United States children are the largest single age group living in poverty. For the more than 13 million who are poor, childhood can be a time of privation and violence, loneliness and hunger—a time when they and their families must focus on a vision of basic survival. In the most affluent nation in the world, in 1987, one out of three children did not see a dentist; two out of three poor children had no regular health insurance; and 6.5 million children lived in families with annual incomes less than $5,000. But statistics alone cannot measure the prevailing sense of hopelessness and lack of life options faced by poor children in the United States.

The cultural and educational impact of poverty upon children is immeasurable. Eighty-seven percent of U.S. children from all income groups is educated in the public school system; yet the public schools are failing to educate many, especially those from economically disadvantaged backgrounds.

The failure of our educational system to provide all children with a solid base of academic skills hurts young people and society in the long run. When compared to those with above-average skills, youths reaching age 18 with the weakest reading and math skills are:
• eight times more likely to have children out of wedlock;
• eight times more likely to drop out of school before graduation;
• four times more likely to be both out of work and out of school;
• four times more likely to be forced to turn to public assistance for basic income support.

Racial Injustice and Children in the United States

Poverty disproportionately affects children of color; therefore, child poverty cannot be fully understood without addressing the issue of racism. According to the resolution "Children and Their Welfare and Health Care": "Racism does its most serious damage to children who already have much against them—poverty, broken homes, hunger, crowded living conditions." In order to diminish child poverty in the world, we must work toward societies in which each person's value is recognized, maintained, and strengthened. In more concrete terms, as stated in the Social Principles, "We assert the obligation of society, and groups within society, to implement compensatory programs that redress long-standing systematic social deprivation of racial and ethnic minorities."

Prevention of Child Poverty Is Cost Effective

Budget cuts that affect children, made as a result of recession and budget deficits, are inhuman and shortsighted. Nations must invest in their children, because children are the future of the world.

Research substantiates that children's programs providing services like prenatal care, immunizations and primary health care save more money than they cost. For example, in the U.S. it costs about $10 to provide a baby with a series of immunizations, compared with hundreds of thousands of dollars for a lifetime of care for a disabled child. Every dollar spent on comprehensive prenatal care saves more than $3 in health care in just the first year of an infant's life. UNICEF estimates that a $5 course of immunizations per child could save as many as 5 million children each year.

The federal budget deficit and world economic recession are the most frequently heard political excuses for neglecting children. Our response is five-fold: 1) children did not cause the deficit nor the world economic crisis, and hurting them more will not cure it; 2) children and their families have sacrificed proportionately more than any other group as nations cut back on their government programs; 3) investing in children now saves money later—to fail to prevent sickness, malnutrition, and illiteracy is to perpetuate the very dependence cycle and high remediation costs so many currently decry; 4) investing in children is feasible: we know how to do it and how to achieve positive results for relatively modest investment; 5) children are dying right now unnecessarily—one every fifty-three minutes in the United States, one every two seconds in the world. How can we dare not save them if we believe God exists?

Statement of Christian Conviction

It is not only sensible but right and just to protect our children, who are the least among us. "The death of one child, when that death could have been avoided," United Nations Secretary General Javier Perez de Cuellar said in 1986, "is a rebuke to all humanity." The death of millions of children from preventable poverty and disease at home and abroad is a rebuke to the God who saved Isaac and Ishmael, the sons of Abraham, and the God who sent Christ in the form of a child as the messenger to bring good news to the poor. Christ rebuked those who sought to push children aside, saying: "Whoever receives this child in my name receives me; and among you all, he is the greatest." (Matthew 18:3-4)

Children are our gift of hope for a future time when our broken and injured world is healed and our relationship with God becomes whole and just. Adults are called to protect and advocate for the world's children as a thankful response to the covenant God has made with us and which has been extended to us down through the ages. How do we protect and nurture our children? What gifts do we give them to enable them to survive in wholeness and justice? Do we pass on our brokenness, or do we find ways to strengthen and share in the light and freshness that they bring to the task of mending this world?

As we look at poverty through the eyes of children, we see the hope, faithfulness and courage that children bring to the world—and we observe the barriers and obstacles that are placed in the way of their special contributions. We remind ourselves that as Christians we are called to dissolve those obstacles and to pursue public policies at the local, national and international levels that nurture and celebrate the hope that rests in children.

Summary

There are many issues adversely affecting children in the United States and the world that cannot be covered in one resolution; however, most fall under the themes of child survival and preventive investment in children. Therefore, The United Methodist Church encourages all general boards, conferences, their related institutions and committees, and congregations to become involved in the following related topics of concern:
• teenage pregnancy
• abuse of children (physical and sexual)
• children of South Africa
• children who have never known peace
• children who are imprisoned
• disappeared children
• refugee children
• abandoned children
• pedophilia
• sex tourism
• torture
• children without education
• children and labor
• substance abuse

The Challenge

The overall message is that the methods of alleviating child death and poverty are now proven and tested, available and affordable. We know the way . . . we need the will.

A principle challenge of the next decade is the protection of the world's children from lifelong poverty and death. Between now and the year 2000, the nations of the world must mount a carefully conceived, comprehensive human investment effort to ensure that every child has basic health, nutrition, shelter and education and training. Surely the time has come to put the massive deaths and suffering of children alongside slavery, racism, and apartheid on the shelf reserved for those things which are simply no longer acceptable.

The long-term solution lies in implementing structural changes within nations—including land reform, the redistribution of income-earning opportunities, and economic policies designed to empower women and poor people. Similarly, structural changes between nations—including fairer and more stable commodity prices, more market access for the manufactured good of the developing world, a reform of the international monetary system, and an increase in both official aid and low interest loans—are also fundamental to the creation of the conditions in which the vast majority of the world's families can earn enough, through their own efforts, to improve the quality of life for themselves and their families.

Recommendations to The United Methodist Church

The Rights of Children

WHEREAS The Social Principles upholds the rights of children to growth and development, adequate nutrition, health services, housing, education, recreation, protection against all forms of racial discrimination, cruelty, neglect, and exploitation;

Therefore, be it resolved that The United Methodist Church shall uphold the rights of children, speak out when abuses occur, and advocate for the strengthening and strict enforcement of these rights.

Racial Justice

WHEREAS racism robs and deprives children of their basic rights and diminishes their opportunities; and

WHEREAS the "aim of The United Methodist Church is nothing less than an inclusive church in an inclusive society";

Therefore, be it resolved that The United Methodist Church calls upon all its people to perform those faithful deeds of love and justice in both the church and the community that will bring this aim into reality by actively implementing the Charter for Racial Justice Policies.

Outside our own Community

WHEREAS The United Methodist Church affirms that child advocacy begins at home,

Therefore, be it resolved that The United Methodist Church urges:

• Local congregations to give ample opportunity to children to share in the central worship life of the congregation as full participants.

• Local congregations and the United Methodist general agencies to enable adequate provision for Christian education for children within the life of the congregation. Children should also be included in the mission life of the congregation in age-appropriate ways.

• Conferences, their related institutions and committees, congregations, and the United Methodist Women, to give heightened attention and focus to public education, direct involvement and legislative advocacy on behalf of children.

The Child Survival Revolution

This program promotes breast-feeding, immunization, growth monitoring, and oral rehydration therapy (ORT). In several nations, including Bangladesh and Nicaragua, these low-cost child protection strategies have gone into action on a large scale.

WHEREAS, the same kind of public support and momentum which has been mobilized against famine and starvation is now needed for the global implementation of the Child Survival Revolution;

Therefore, be it resolved that The United Methodist Church calls upon all general boards, conferences, their related institutions and committees, and congregations to:

• Educate church members and society at large about the revolution in child health and survival.

• Encourage financial contributions to and volunteer participation in UNICEF's Child Survival Campaign.

• Support the United Methodist Committee on Relief (UMCOR) in its efforts to enhance child health and survival.

• Support the effort of Women's Division and World Division, General Board of Global Ministries to work with Methodist women's organizations around the world in strengthening ministry with and advocacy for women and children.

• Support the efforts of the General Board of Church and Society in advocating for federal policies that significantly increase United States support for United Nations Children's Fund (UNICEF) and funding for the U.S. Agency for International Development's "Child Survival Fund."

Preventive Investment in Children in the United States

WHEREAS one out of five children in the United States lives in poverty, and it is time to begin the hard but necessary task of readjusting our national priorities;

Therefore, be it resolved that The United Methodist Church calls upon all general boards, conferences, their related institutions and committees, and congregations to:

• Educate all church members and society at large about the needs of children in the United States and encourage preventive investment in children before they get sick, drop out of school, or get into trouble.

• Support United Methodist agencies, including the Institutional Ministries of the National Division of the General Board of Global Ministries, which work to alleviate child poverty and neglect in local communities and states.

• Advocate for federal and state policies which provide preventive programs for children, ensuring basic health, nutrition, and early childhood services. These include: prenatal and maternity care programs (including Medicaid), job training programs, child care and protective services.

• Support educational proposals to help children with special needs, including expanding successful federal programs as well as supporting promising new efforts. These include: Chapter I, Head Start, bilingual education, desegregation assistance, education for children with handicapping conditions, dropout prevention, and "community learning centers." In addition, encourage parental and guardian involvement in their children's education.

• Engage in denominational and ecumenical efforts to end child poverty.

• Be aware and supportive of the United Methodist Women's "Campaign for Children in the United States," the purpose of which is to focus on the critical needs of children in poverty in local communities.

• Continue to advocate for systemic changes affecting children and their families, such as welfare reform, increase in the minimum wage, national health insurance, and job creation.

ADOPTED 1988

See Social Principles, ¶ 72.C, "Ministry to Runaway Children," "Medical Rights for Children and Youth."

Racial Harassment

The first two chapters of the book of Genesis describe the creative genius of God. The writers tell us that God created heavens and earth and gave life to woman and man. Animals, vegetation, and the entire universe were the product of God's grace and work. The Psalmist of Psalm 24 reaffirms the relationship between all of God's creation and the divinity of God.

Yet, in spite of humanity's common legacy as God's descendants, we have consistently established differences among God's children because of their race. We have continuously engaged in verbal exchanges and behavioral demonstrations which have rejected the sacredness of all persons. The belief that one race is superior to others has permeated our lives, thus creating the perception of inferiority of some persons because of their skin color, features, language, and their racial/ethnic heritage.

When this prejudicial and/or racist attitude is expressed in a behavior that is focused specifically in the abuse, humiliation, and defamation of persons because of their race or ethnicity, it has become racial harassment.

Racial harassment is in reality an act of covert or overt racism. The United Methodist Church, committed to the elimination of racism, cannot tolerate this racist manifestation. Because of the many definitions of racial harassment currently found in society which are too general and even confusing, precise guidelines are needed from the denomination which will enable local churches, conferences, agencies, and church organizations to identify conditions or for situations of racial harassment.

Therefore, be it resolved, that the General Conference of 1992 defines the following conditions as racial harassment:

1. Abusive and/or derogatory language that in a subtle or overt manner belittles, humiliates, impugns, or defames a person or a group of persons based on racial and ethnic traits, heritage, and characteristics.

2. A behavior (individual, group, or institutional) which abuses, belittles, humiliates, defames, or demeans a person or a group of persons based on racial and ethnic traits, heritage, and characteristics.

3. Documentation, printed or visual, which abuses humiliates, defames, or demeans a person or group of persons based on racial and ethnic heritage and traits, heritage, and characteristics.

Be it further resolved, that The United Methodist Church and all its agencies:

1. Encourage law enforcement personnel to maintain accurate records on hate crimes and bring to justice the perpetrators of such violence and intimidation.

2. Support hearings on hate crimes, particularly in those states where statistics reveal an increase in the activity of the Ku Klux Klan and other hate groups.

3. Support congressional hearings when there are allegations of government involvement or negligence exacerbating such violence.

ADOPTED 1992

See Social Principles, ¶ 72.A, "A Charter for Racial Justice Policies in an Interdependent Global Community," "Eradication of Racism," "Global Racism."

Recruitment and Development Plan for Local Pastors

WHEREAS, the legacy of great black preachers like Harry Hoosier, Tallulah Williams, J. Jeanmette Cooper, Bishop Leontine Kelly, and Henry Evans is a celebration note for United Methodists in particular and all Christians in general; their preaching brought power, zeal, and spiritual awakening to all who heard them; and

WHEREAS, these giants and many others who have preached, witnessed, lived out the gospel, and built great congregations that have acted in witness and mission in the Black community and in the society at large for the past 200 years; and

WHEREAS, Blacks in The United Methodist Church as well as Blacks in the society have progressed over the past two centuries in spite of the opposition and second-class citizenship that have been imposed on them by the church and the society; and

WHEREAS, they have created and sustained ministries and vital, faithful congregations in communities of poverty with second-rate education and third-rate facilities; and

WHEREAS, many of the most effective pastoral leaders in sustaining vital, effective ministries and congregations, witnessing to the gospel, and participating as full partners in God's mission have been local pastors who understood and had a keen interest in the development of the community; and

WHEREAS, the growth trend among Black congregations in The United Methodist Church indicates that the diversity within the population group warrants more than one model of pastoral leadership; and

WHEREAS, a pastoral leadership model is needed that along with and in addition to the elder can reach to unleash the power and zeal of people mired in the tribulations of the growing underclass in this country; and

WHEREAS, self-determination is essential for the long-term development and growth of vital congregations in the Black community; and

WHEREAS, effective pastoral leadership in the Black community requires persons with natural spiritual nurturing ability and an intellect that reflects the hurts, pain, hopes, and aspirations of the community;

Therefore, be it resolved, that the Board of Higher Education, Division of Ordained Ministry, affirm local pastors as an effective and legitimate clergy-leadership appointment in the development, maintenance, and growth of Black congregations;

Be it further resolved, that the Board of Higher Education, Division of Ordained Ministry, in consultation with annual conference boards of ordained ministry and district boards of ordained ministry, develop a recruitment and career development plan specifically focused on lay persons in Black congregations who can serve as local pastors, and make a report on the implementation of that plan to the 1996 General Conference.

ADOPTED 1992

See Social Principles, ¶ 72, "Considering Community Contexts in the Appointment Process."

Relationship between The United Methodist Church and The New Affiliated Autonomous Methodist Church of Puerto Rico

This is to petition the General Conference to establish the foundations to govern the relationship between The United Methodist Church and The Methodist Church of Puerto Rico during the interim period before the formal signing of an Act of Covenanting in accordance with the *1988 Book of Discipline*, ¶ 648 and ¶ 650. The unique character of this process is acknowledged due to the close relationship between both churches, as well as the unique link between the United States and Puerto Rico.

1. The advent of the new Methodist Church in Puerto Rico is celebrated and supported as part of a growth process and self-determination. The United Methodist Church in its global vision of the church affirms that the new Methodist Church of Puerto Rico must be viewed as a powerful ally in meeting the needs of and challenges to Hispanics on the United States mainland. It will also be a link between the United States, the Caribbean, and Latin America.

2. As a means for the empowerment of the new Methodist Church in Puerto Rico throughout its formation period of two quadrennia (1992–2000), the following principles are established:

2.1 That The Methodist Church of Puerto Rico constitutes a unique case and shall be considered the most favorable manner by the general agencies of The United Methodist Church.

2.2 The general agencies will give equal access and consideration to petitions and requests for resources from The Methodist Church of Puerto Rico for the transition period, in the manner provided to any other United Methodist annual conference.

2.3 All of the agreements between the general agencies and the Puerto Rico Annual Conference entered into the records of the general agencies and the Puerto Rico Annual Conference for the transition period will be honored by the general agencies and The Methodist Church of Puerto Rico.

2.4 All decisions that affect The Methodist Church of Puerto Rico shall be made in consultation with The Methodist Church of Puerto Rico; no unilateral decisions are to be made that in any way will weaken the local mission as it has developed during the last 92 years.

2.5 In order that no action shall be taken that can be construed as having vestiges of racism or discrimination, the General Commission on Religion and Race will retain jurisdiction on this matter through the 1992–2000 time period.

2.6 The Methodist Church of Puerto Rico will continue providing significant pastoral leadership for Hispanic ministries in The United

Methodist Church. The Evangelical Seminary of Puerto Rico will continue as a center for the theological education of Hispanic ministers, both for the United States and for Puerto Rico.

2.7 The above-mentioned principles shall govern all agreements with the general agencies of The United Methodist Church.

3. To facilitate the coordination of mission efforts between The Methodist Church of Puerto Rico and The United Methodist Church, a provision is made in order that the bishop of The Methodist Church of Puerto Rico will sit with voice but no vote in The United Methodist Council of Bishops. Periodic episcopal visitation from The United Methodist Church will be welcomed by The Methodist Church of Puerto Rico (¶ 648.4).

4. The Methodist Church of Puerto Rico shall be entitled to continue to send two delegates, one clergy and one lay, to the General Conference of The United Methodist Church with all rights and privileges. The United Methodist Church shall be entitled to send two delegates, one clergy and one lay, to the General Conference of The Methodist Church of Puerto Rico with all rights and privileges (¶ 602.1B and ¶ 12.2 of the Constitution).

5. In order to provide adequate coordination and programmatic support during the 1992–2000 period, The Methodist Church of Puerto Rico will continue its membership in the Board of Directors of the following agencies: General Council on Ministries, General Board of Global Ministries, General Board of Church and Society, General Board of Discipleship, Board of Global Higher Education and Ministry, General Commission on the Status and Role of Women, and General Commission of Religion and Race (¶ 805.1, 2).

6. The Methodist Church of Puerto Rico is committed to contribute at least at the present level to the general benevolence fund of The United Methodist Church for the 1992–2000 period. The Methodist Church of Puerto Rico is also committed to continue purchasing and using printed and other resources produced by The United Methodist Church.

ADOPTED 1992

See Social Principles, ¶¶ 72 and 75, "Puerto Rico and Vieques."

Resourcing Black Churches in Urban Communities

WHEREAS, the struggle for social, economic, and political survival of Black people in the United States is manifested in their historical migration to urban centers; and

WHEREAS, the problems that have evolved through the decade now face this population of people, isolated from access to the material resources needed to unleash its power and creativity in a manner that will build rather than destroy communities; and

WHEREAS, the Black United Methodist churches in urban communities have historically been centers of spiritual nurture, social and political action that have cared for the youth and offered viable alternatives to the negative aspects of decaying urban centers; and

WHEREAS, there is a demonstrated need in all urban communities in this country for strong, vital Black congregations to reach into the hurts and pains of the community and provide the spiritual revival that is needed in order to reclaim individuals and communities and manifest the healing power of God to combat drugs, violence, and a growing sense of hopelessness; and

WHEREAS, the gospel mandates that we "seek the welfare of the city where I have sent you into exile, and pray to the Lord on its behalf, for in its welfare you will find your welfare" (Jer. 29:7); and

WHEREAS, Black United Methodist congregations in urban communities are called as are all churches to minister to the needs of persons in the communities where the church is located; and

WHEREAS, the conditions in urban communities for Black persons continue to worsen and the need for grounding in a faith and reliance on the power of God for the strength and vision to reclaim and rebuild strong, proud, faith-centered communities grows daily while the resources and persons in Black urban congregations decrease;

Therefore, be it resolved, that the General Conference directs the General Board of Discipleship to develop programs and strategies which will enable the development of Black leadership, and specific programs and strategies that will foster financial self-sufficiency, such as launching a stewardship education program.

Be it further resolved, that the General Board of Global Ministries, National Division, work with existing Black churches in urban communities to develop and maintain vital congregations providing practical ministries that address the spiritual, social, and economic decline in these communities.

Be it further resolved, that the National Division coordinate its work in strengthening Black urban congregations with the General Board of Discipleship, the annual conferences and urban ministry units of annual conferences, the General Board of Global Ministries, and the

General Board of Discipleship, and provide a comprehensive progress report—including activities, human resources, and funds that have been committed to this effort—to the General Council on Ministries by December 31, 1994.

ADOPTED 1992

See Social Principles, ¶ 72.A, "Black Church Growth," "Church and Community Workers."

Rights of Native People of the Americas

WHEREAS, many of the Native People living in the Americas are held captive by policies that violate their rights as human beings; and,

WHEREAS, these policies deny the worth and God-given right of every human being to live free of injustice, discrimination, and fear; and,

WHEREAS, the human rights of Native People of the Americas have been and continue to be grossly violated by various governments which suppress freedom; and,

WHEREAS, Native Peoples of the Americas are in countries experiencing civil war and their lives are continually threatened and endangered; and,

WHEREAS, our religious faith calls us to affirm the dignity and worth of every human being and to struggle with our oppressed brothers and sisters for justice. We are called to "proclaim release to the captives, to set at liberty those who are oppressed";

Therefore be it resolved, that we petition the 1988 General Conference to direct the General Board of Church and Society to design, coordinate, and facilitate, in consultation with the Native American International Caucus, the Oklahoma Indian Missionary Conference, and all other appropriate United Methodist Native American organizations, a strategy that will bring the power of moral and religious influence to bear upon the struggles of the oppressed Native People of the Americas.

ADOPTED 1988

See Social Principles, ¶ 72, "The United Methodist Church and America's Native People," "American Indian Religious Freedom Act," "Toward a New Beginning beyond 1992."

Rural Chaplaincy as a Ministry of Laity and Clergy

WHEREAS, continued decline of rural America constitutes an ongoing struggle which holds rural communities in long-term crisis; and

WHEREAS, the need for specialized and caring ministries in rural communities has become critical; and

WHEREAS, the Rural Chaplains Association is providing training for the certification of laity and clergy as rural chaplains; and

WHEREAS, rural chaplains are persons called by God whose gifts and graces are uniquely suited for mission and ministry with town and rural persons, families, communities, and churches; and

WHEREAS, rural chaplains respond to spiritual dimensions of life when rural peoples who relate to farming, mining, timbering, fishing, rural industries, and businesses, etc., experience harmful, social, technological, and economic changes; and

WHEREAS, rural chaplains advocate the provision of human services that respond to the needs of persons, families, and communities; and

WHEREAS, rural chaplains are interpreters of town and rural issues to denominational, local, and denominational forms of the church, and also to local communities and society at all levels; and

WHEREAS, rural chaplains provide encouragement to persons who choose to integrate their theological and ethical understandings of society and creation in a life-style that calls for a just, participatory, and sustainable economy, and also challenge secular perceptions of environmental and ecological issues; and

WHEREAS, rural chaplains have long-term commitments to serve in communities where they have been appointed or called by the church, and to use their skills for the purposes given above by participating in a network for fellowship, encouragement, and sharing; and

WHEREAS, 40 rural chaplains, including seven lay persons and nine women, from 22 annual conferences and five jurisdictions now have been certified;

Therefore be it resolved, that The United Methodist Church affirm rural chaplaincy as a viable and specialized ministry for town, country, and rural settings; and

Be it further resolved, that The United Methodist Church affirm rural chaplaincy as a ministry of both laity and clergy.

ADOPTED 1992

See Social Principles, ¶ 72, "An Affirmation of Basic Rural Worth," "Appointment of Clergy to Rural Ministry," "The Church's Response to Changing Rural Issues."

Sale and Use of Alcohol and Tobacco on Church Property

The United Methodist Church opposes the sale and discourages the consumption or use of alcoholic beverages and tobacco products within the confines of church buildings, including worship centers, halls, and educational areas.

ADOPTED 1976

See Social Principles, ¶¶ 72.I and J, "Drug and Alcohol Concerns."

School Busing

WHEREAS, The Supreme Court in 1954 ruled that segregated public schools are inherently unequal and that dejure segregation in such schools is unconstitutional; and

WHEREAS, Integrated schools provide the best means for reducing racial bias and may be useful in providing beneficial learning experiences; and

WHEREAS, The busing of pupils is often the only method available to achieve racial integration and quality education in the public schools;

Resolved, That we call upon The United Methodist Church to support the use of busing where appropriate for school integration and to oppose legislative action or constitutional amendments prohibiting such busing.

ADOPTED 1972

See Social Principles, ¶ 72.A, "Church/Government Relations," "Public Education in the United States," "The United Methodist Church and Church/Government Relations."

Shared Financial Support for the Native American Center

WHEREAS, the National United Methodist Native American Center, Inc. (NUMNAC), has functioned as one of four national centers focused on ethnic enlistment, training, and assistance in the deployment of ordained and diaconal ministry, and other professional leaders in their respective communities; and

WHEREAS, NUMNAC has operated admirably with a limited staff of the executive director, associate director, and an administrative assistant; and

WHEREAS, NUMNAC's previous funding was authorized by the General Conference with linkage responsibilities resting on the General Board of Higher Education and Ministry (GBHEM); and

WHEREAS, NUMNAC's service record over the past eight years has been extremely contributory to active Native American recruitment into the ordained ministry, higher education opportunities for United

Methodist Native American students, Native American youth involvement in The United Methodist Church, pastoral care and training for current ministry, spiritual reinforcement in Native American congregations, communication between Native American and non-Indian churches, research relating to the growing cultural diversity within the United Methodist Church; and

WHEREAS, there exists a continuous need for Native American understanding, sensitivity, input, and participation among, and within, the church administration and general community; and

WHEREAS, NUMNAC's past funding of approximately $160,000 per year from the General Board of Higher Education and Ministry has been insufficient for carrying out assigned goals, and the current level of proposed funding is less than one-half of last year's budget;

Therefore, be it resolved, that in 1992 the General Conference endorse the quadrennium funding, 1993-1996, of NUMNAC through a "shared focus" among the Board of Higher Education and Ministry (GBHEM), General Board of Global Ministries (GBGM), General Board of Discipleship (GBOD), and the General Board of Church and Society (GBCS) and that the General Council on Finance and Administration (GCFA) appropriate money for this purpose. NUMNAC board and staff will raise any additional funds needed to fulfill program goals and needs.

Be it further resolved, that the General Conference endorse NUMNAC's current functions and roles as related to its initial goals and objectives, its proposed activities for the next quadrennium, and that it be supported by related entities of the United Methodist Church as a center for Native American cultural, spiritual, and contemporary training for United Methodist lay people.

GCFA recommends that the General Council on Ministries, prior to the end of the 1989-92 quadrennium, convene representatives of the General Board of Higher Education and Ministry, the General Board of Global Ministries, and the center to recommend to GCFA the amount and source of additional funding for the center from their budgets or other sources. The center is also encouraged to seek approval for funding through general Advance Special gifts.

ADOPTED 1992

See Social Principles ¶ 72, "The United Methodist Church and America's Native People," "National Convocation on the Ordained Ministry for Native Americans," "Native American Representation in The United Methodist Church."

Spanish Language Hymnal

WHEREAS, The General Board of Discipleship and The United Methodist Publishing House have agreed to create a one-volume Spanish Language Hymnal for The United Methodist Church, which will consist primarily of hymns, including both traditional and contemporary texts and tunes, as well as additional worship resources needed by a congregation, such as services of Holy Communion and Holy Baptism, psalms, and some other acts of worship; and

WHEREAS, The General Board of Discipleship and The United Methodist Publishing House have agreed to fund jointly the work of the committee; and

WHEREAS, Bishop Woodie White, President of The General Board of Discipleship, appointed in the summer of 1991 a representative committee of Hispanics to create the resource, under provisions of the 1988 *Book of Discipline*, ¶ 1214.3; and

WHEREAS, the committee began its work in the fall of 1991 to create this new resource; and

WHEREAS, there is an urgent need to create and publish such a book for our Spanish-speaking congregations;

Therefore, be it resolved, that the 1992 General Conference of The United Methodist Church: (1) commend the General Board of Discipleship and The United Methodist Publishing House for their efforts, (2) endorse the creation and work of the Spanish Language United Methodist Hymnal Committee, (3) urge the publication of the resource as soon as possible, and (4) commend the completed and published book to the 1996 General Conference for inclusion as an approved official hymnal of the denomination in the *Book of Discipline*, ¶ 1214.3.

ADOPTED 1992

See Social Principles, ¶ 72.A, "Program to Emphasize Inclusiveness in All Dimensions of the Church," "Support to Strengthen the Ethnic Minority Local Church."

Special Emphasis on Reclaiming the Cities

WHEREAS, the Christian Church—and the Methodist Church in particular—originated in the city; and

WHEREAS, the fastest-growing populations in the United States are among the Asians, Hispanic, and African-American people; and

WHEREAS, The United Methodist Church has had its greatest growth among the poor and "underclass," and our inner cities have become the home of the masses; and

WHEREAS, the Bishops' Initiative has shown that a great deal of human deprivation and desolation are concentrated in our cities—and especially among African-American and Hispanic males;

Be it therefore resolved, that there be a United Methodist Church special emphasis on "Reclaiming the Cities" by:

1. evangelizing the poor and oppressed;

2. giving special leadership and more quality time to the cities;

3. putting more of our human, financial, and other material resources in the cities;

4. uniting our Methodist families—the African Methodist Episcopal, the African Methodist Episcopal Zion, the Christian Methodist Episcopal and the United Methodist Church—to make one powerful Methodist voice and presence in our cities; and

5. leading the way for an ecumenical thrust to save the cities of our nation.

Be it further resolved, that this special emphasis be implemented, as appropriate, by each program board and agency and coordinated by the GCOM.

ADOPTED 1992

See Social Principles, ¶ 72.N.

The Status of Women

I

Christianity was born in a world of male preference and dominance. Practices, traditions, and attitudes in almost all societies viewed women as inferior to men, as having few talents and contributions to make to the general well-being of society aside from their biological roles. This was true of the Judaic society of which Jesus was a part.

But the life of Jesus, the redeemer of human life, stood as a witness against such cultural patterns and prejudices. Consistently he related to women as persons of intelligence and capabilities. He charged women as well as men to use their talents significantly in the cause of God's kingdom. His acts of healing and ministry were extended without distinction to women and men.

The central theme of Jesus' teaching is love for God and neighbor. Jesus embodied this message in his life and, in the early Church, women held prominent positions of leadership. Christian love as exemplified in the New Testament requires that we relate to others as persons of worth. To regard another as an inferior is to break the covenant of love: denying equality demeans, perpetuates injustice, and falls short of the example of Jesus and the early Church.

II

The movement to improve the status of women is one of the most profoundly hopeful of our times. The United Methodist Church in various ways has sought to support that movement. Although change is taking place, in most societies women are still not accorded equal rights and responsibilities.

There is increasing awareness that we cannot solve world problems of hunger, population growth, poverty, and peace so long as the talents and potential of half the world's people are disregarded and even repressed. There are strong interrelationships between all these problems and the status of women.

The years from 1975 to 1985 have been designated the Decade for Women, a time for correcting these ancient injustices. For Christians, it is a time for repentance and for new dedication to Christ's ideal of equality. It is a time for examining specific areas which need to be addressed in societies:

Economics. Often the productive labor of women is ignored in economic statistics, reinforcing the impression that work done by women is peripheral, of secondary importance, even dispensable. For that reason, few studies have actually evaluated the importance of contributions by women. As one example, when women grow food to feed their families, they are "just" tending kitchen gardens, but when men grow cash crops like tobacco and coffee, they are engaged in agricultural and commercial enterprises. In more industrialized societies, the enormous amount of volunteer work done by women is not counted as adding to the nation's wealth.

In the United States, nearly half of all women are working outside the home in the paid labor force and there are well-publicized professional successes, yet actually the earning gap between men and women is greater than it was in the 1950's. Everywhere, women tend to be clustered in the lower-paying jobs and in certain stereotyped job fields.

Legal Rights. In 1945, only 31 countries allowed women to vote; today women have the right in more than 125 nations. Only eight countries exclude women entirely from political processes open to men. Still, many areas of legal discrimination remain. In some nations, women are still considered the chattels of their husbands, with few rights in family law, landholding, inheritance, and guardianship of children.

In the United States some of the more glaring inequities are being corrected step by step. Nonetheless, a 1978 report of the Civil Rights Commission noted continuing discrimination on the basis of sex in the Federal Statutes.[1]

Cultural Factors. The perception of women as inferior and dependent is perpetuated through many institutions in society—the media, school textbooks and curricula, political structures, and often religious organizations. Education is one of the principal ways of opening doors to wider participation in society. Thus, it is distressing that, while the percentage of literate women is at an all-time high, the absolute number of illiterate women is greater than at any time in the past. The fact that two-thirds of the world's illiterates are female is evidence of continuing disparity in importance given to the education of boys and girls.

Traditional perceptions of female qualities also are a factor in the widespread domestic violence against women, now coming to be recognized as a tragically widespread occurrence.

Human Rights in Fertility Decisions. Through the centuries, women have been little consulted or involved in the decisions regarding fertility-related laws or practices. For women particularly, the ability to make choices concerning fertility is a liberating force, helping to safeguard their health and that of their children, to plan for the future, to assume wider roles and responsibilities in society.

The United Nations has declared that education and access to means for determining the number and spacing of children is a human right, yet this is an ideal far from realization.

Coercion is still common, sometimes aimed at increasing births, sometimes at limiting them. Evidence now clearly shows that many

---

[1]Statement on Equal Rights Amendment, U.S. Commission on Civil Rights Clearinghouse Publication 56, December 1978, page 5.

poor, particularly ethnic, women have been sterilized without their understanding of what was being done to them and without their informed consent. In many places, safe and legal abortion is denied, in some cases even to save the life of the pregnant woman. In other cases, women are threatened that welfare payments or aid programs will be cut if the pregnancy continues. Such inconsistency reflects lack of value-centered decision-making, as well as in sensitivity to the personhood of the woman involved.

While societal needs more and more should be considered in fertility matters, this should never be at the price of demeaning the individual or applying restrictive measures only to the poor. Women should be fully informed and fully involved in the decision-making.

Development Programs. National and international development programs now often stress the need to "integrate" women into the development process. Full recognition is seldom given to the contributions women already make to economic and social progress. For example, women make up 60-80 percent of the agricultural workers of the world; in some parts of Africa women manage a third of the farms. Yet few programs of agricultural development seek to upgrade the skills of women, provide easier access to credit, assure them the right to land titles in their own names, etc. In some cases, modernization actually degrades the already low status of women.

III

Across the nations of the world, new movements are growing which address the serious handicaps and harsh realities of the lives of many women. In the context of this increasing momentum for a more just society, we call on local congregations and the agencies of the Church:

1. To exert leadership in working wherever possible for legal recognition of equal rights for women. In the United States, this means a strengthened determination to secure passage of the Equal Rights Amendment,[2] in line with the United Methodist General

[2]Proposed 27th Amendment:
Sec. 1. Equality of rights under the law shall not be denied or abridged by the United States or by any State on account of sex.
Sec. 2. The Congress shall have the power to enforce, by appropriate legislation, the provisions of this article.
Sec. 3. This amendment shall take effect two years after the date of ratification.

Conference affirmations of 1972 and 1976. We need to recognize that this measure has become a symbol of the drive for equality. It has meaning far beyond the borders of one nation in the search for equal rights in other societies.

2. To urge governments to ratify the Convention on the Elimination of Discrimination Against Women which was adopted by the United Nations, December, 1979.

3. To encourage support of studies by scientific and governmental bodies of the economic contributions made by women outside the formal economic sector, and to include this information in the Gross National Product of nations or compilations of national wealth.

4. To examine governmental policies and practices, including development assistance, as to their impact on women's lives; to work to ensure that policies upgrade the status of women, and that women are included in decision-making regarding development goals and programs. The key roles of women as workers and consumers and as transmitters of culture must be given adequate weight in national development activities.

5. To examine the impact of transnational corporations on women's lives, and to work to eradicate exploitative practices where identified. One such area is the promotion and selling of inappropriate products and technologies.

6. To encourage private charitable organizations, including churches, to initiate and support more programs of leadership education for women and other educational programs that upgrade the status of women.

7. To monitor printed and audio-visual media and other means of communication on their portrayals of the roles and nature of women and men, and to seek ways to eradicate narrow stereotypes which limit the possibilities of useful contributions by both sexes. The Church should encourage study of the impact of Western, particularly U.S., television, radio, and other media on cultural patterns and national development around the world, and should draw public attention to cases where such influence is destructive of other cultures.

8. To support programs providing knowledge of and access to services in the area of family-planning and contraception, and to involve women in planning and implementation of such services. This effort should include support for public funding for these

programs; for access to safe, legal, and non-coercive contraception, sterilization, and abortion services; and for improved educational efforts on responsible sexuality and parenthood for both men and women. Attention should particularly be paid to ensuring high standards for clinics performing abortions; to monitoring enforcement of regulations designed to ensure informed consent for sterilization procedures; to opposing profit-making referral agencies, which charge fees for providing information freely available elsewhere.

9. To examine the impact of judicial decisions at all levels upon the daily lives of women in such areas as child custody, employment, civil rights, racial and sexual discrimination, credit practices, estate settlements, reproduction and education, and socio-economic status.

IV

The words and acts of Jesus give the Christian a vision of what a just society should be. Discipleship to Jesus requires both men and women to measure their attitudes about themselves and all others by his values and to act in accord with those values. The full worth and dignity of each person is to be acknowledged and expressed. The Church may help the vision of Jesus to be realized by proclaiming that women are persons created in the image of God, here to serve with men in the breaking forth of the Kingdom.

ADOPTED 1980

See Social Principles, ¶ 72.F, "Equal Rights of Women," "Full Personhood," "Ecumenical Decade: Churches in Solidarity with Women."

Strengthening the Black Church for the 21st Century

Direct the General Council on Ministries (GCOM) to include within its regular evaluation processes with the general program agencies a review of each agency's effectiveness in strengthening the Black church from the period 1972-1993, including a review of the strengths and weaknesses of what has been accomplished and including attention to areas such as: new church development, leadership development, and ministerial recruitment. GCOM is asked to report the results of this evaluation in its report to the 1996 General Conference.

Direct GCOM to convene a panel of 10 persons, composed of five GCOM members representing the five jurisdictions and five persons outside the GCOM membership, to review the evaluations of the General Program agencies mentioned above, and make any recommendations deemed necessary to the 1996 General Conference relating to new plans and strategies to strengthen the Black church into the 21st Century.

ADOPTED 1992

See Social Principles, ¶ 72, "Black Church Growth," "Black Leadership," "Program to Emphasize Inclusiveness in All Dimensions of the Church," "Resourcing Black Churches in Urban Communities."

Suicide: A Challenge to Ministry

The apostle Paul, rooted in his experience of the resurrected Christ, affirms the power of divine love to overcome the divisive realities of human life, including suicide:

"For I am persuaded that neither death nor life, nor angels nor principalities, nor powers, nor things present nor things to come, nor height nor depth, nor any other creature shall be able to separate us from the love of God, which is in Christ Jesus" (Romans 8:38-39).

Paul's words are indeed sources of hope and renewal for persons who contemplate suicide, for those who grieve the death of friends and family members who have committed suicide. These words affirm that in those human moments when all seems lost, all may yet be found through full faith.

A Christian perspective on suicide thus begins with an affirmation of faith: suicide does not separate us from the love of God.

Unfortunately, the Church throughout much of its history has taught just the opposite, that suicide is an unforgivable sin. As a result, Christians, acting out of a sincere concern to prevent suicide, often have contradicted Christ's call to compassion.

For example, victims have been denounced and presumed to be in hell, and families have been stigmatized with guilt and inflicted with economic and social penalties.

This statement is intended to be a guide and a challenge for United Methodist ministry as it relates to suicide in light of such attitudes and actions by the Church. Its purpose is to encourage the sharing of

God's grace in circumstances involving suicide and to offer a word of faith and hope to all who are affected by the tragedy of suicide.

Demography of Suicide

Although suicide rates in the United States have remained steady over the past few decades, new phenomena have arisen. Suicide victims in the past were most typically older white males who had suffered loss of family or material security and who may have first turned to the use of alcohol or drugs as a means of escape. The picture is quite different in the 1980s. The rate of suicide among teens and young adults has increased dramatically. There is also a small but noticeable increase in suicide among women and ethnic minorities as well as a rapid increase among white male youth.

According to data from the National Center for Health Statistics, the annual suicide rate among 15-24 year-olds increased 129 percent from 1960 to 1983, from 5.2 to 11.9 suicides per 100,000 youth. During 1983, 28,295 Americans took their lives. That averages 14 suicides per day and of these, 5,050 were between the ages of 5 and 24 years old.

These official, well-researched reports document circumstances in which there is little doubt about the intent of the victim. The actual number of deaths due to suicide may be twice as high as the reported incidence.

Many coroners and medical examiners are reluctant to list suicide as the cause of death because of the stigma attached to it. Listing suicide as the cause of death is further complicated because: 1) there is no commonly recognized definition of suicide (one that specifies factors that identify a suicide-caused death—for example, the existence of a note); and, 2) families feel the need to mask the death as a traffic fatality, a mixing of lethal combinations of drugs (i.e. alcohol and barbiturates), or other "accidents."

Causes of Suicide

The Centers for Disease Control (CDC) of the U.S. Public Health Service have been able to identify causes of many suicides. Specific groups in society appear more *vulnerable* to suicide than others. People in such groups are at special risk of committing suicide, especially if they experience certain precipitants (events in their lives like disease, loss of family, friends, job, etc.) and have access to a method for ending their lives, that is, an *enabling environment*. These factors—

vulnerability, precipitating events, enabling environment—must be recognized and addressed if there is to be any reduction in the suicide rate.

The problem of suicide and suicide accempts is extremely serious in this country. One in five women fall into the vulnerable group and the female to male rate of suicide completion of suicide is about 3.5 to one. In the past, women have used passive methods to attempt suicide. However, now the enabling environment, in terms of both attitude and access to weaponry, has changed and the ratios are changing

Societal Attitudes

The prevailing attitudes of society, both secular and religious, have been to condemn the victim and ignore victim's family and friends, and survivors.

"There are always two parties to a death; the person who dies and the survivors who are bereaved . . . the sting of death is less sharp for the person who dies than it is for the bereaved survivor. This, as I see it, is the capital fact about the relation between the living and the dying. There are two parties to the suffering that death inflicts; and in the apportionment of the suffering the survivor takes the brunt." Arnold Toynbee, *Man's Concern with Death.*

Churches sometimes have denied funerals and memorial services to bereaved families. Victim's remains have been banned from cemeteries. Medical examiners have falsified records for families so they can receive economic aid. The U.S. Office of the Inspector General conducted a national survey on societal attitudes related to suicide, when the teen suicide crisis became evident. The finding of that study, quoted below, provide a picture of these observations and factors related to suicide:

—"Youth at risk of suicide come from various walks of life and personal experiences. They come from dysfunctional families, as well as loving, supportive families. However, health, educational and social service agencies describe increasing trends in (a) the number of very young (aged ten and under) attempters, (b) suicide ideation (ideas, concern with, sometimes obsession with suicide) among youth of all ages, (c) multiple forms of self-destructive behavior, and (d) a sense of futility among youth.

—"Suicide is the ultimate form of self-destructive behavior. It is a symptom and should not be dealt with in isolation from other self-destructive behaviors or from social, health and educational problems.

—"Community response to suicide ranges from fear, denial and resistance to widespread support for suicide prevention.

—"Many youth who eventually kill themselves never enter the health service system and those who do often drop out prior to completing treatment. This is due, in part, to a stigma associated with mental health problems and suicide.

—"Lack of financial resources or private insurance limits access to mental health treatment.

—"More than half the study respondents cited family problems as contributing factors to suicidal risk. Family support is key to (a) getting youth into treatment, (b) assuring they do not drop out of treatment, and (c) effecting a successful outcome.

—"The most significant gaps in the service system include (a) too few inpatient psychiatric adolescent beds, particularly for public pay patients who, if admitted, are discharged prematurely, (b) limited subacute (non-critical) and alternative living arrangements, including residential treatment, day treatment, group homes and foster care, (c) limited outpatient treatment in community mental health centers where demand is greater than supply, and (d) scarce crisis intervention programs and hotlines with a special focus for youth.

—"Suicide prevention must be community based. School programs are key and should be developed in coordination with existing community resources, including mental health and crisis intervention programs. Networking is crucial to keeping youth from falling through the cracks."

The Church's Response

Recognizing that the church's historical response to suicide includes punitive measures intended to prevent suicide, and that there is no clear biblical stance on suicide, the General Conference of The United Methodist Church strongly urges the employment of major initiatives to prevent suicide. Additionally, the General Conference recommends to the boards, agencies, institutions and local churches of The United Methodist Church that the ministry of suicide prevention should receive urgent attention. The families of victims should also receive priority concern in the overall ministry of the Church. Harsh and punitive measures (such as denial of funeral or memorial services, or ministerial visits) imposed upon families of suicide victims should be denounced and abandoned. The Church should participate in and urge others to participate in a full community-based effort to address the needs of potential suicide victims and their families. Each annual conference and local church should respond to issues of ministry related to suicide prevention and family support services.

It must be emphasized that suicide increases in an environment or society that does not demonstrate a caring attitude toward all persons. The Church has a special role in changing societal attitudes and the social environment of individuals and families. To promote this effort, the Church should do the following:

(1) The General Board of Discipleship shall develop curriculum for biblical and theological study of suicide and related mental and environmental health problems and promote the programs recommended by the American Association of Pastoral Counseling and the use of the scientific research of the Centers for Disease Control and the American Association of Suicidology.

(2) The General Board of Higher Education and Ministry shall develop materials for United Methodist related seminaries to train church professionals to recognize treatable mental illness associated with suicide (e.g., depression) and realize when and how to refer persons for treatment; it shall insure that all pastoral counseling programs include such training and strategies for ministry to families of suicide victims.

(3) The General Board of Church and Society shall support public policies that (a) promote access to mental health services for all persons regardless of age, (b) remove the stigma associated with mental illness and (c) encourage "help seeking behavior."

(4) Embrace all persons affected by suicide in loving community through support groups and responsive social institutions, call upon society through the media to reinforce the importance of human life and to advocate that public policies include all persons' welfare and work against policies that devalue human life (i.e. nuclear armaments, war, etc.).

(5) Affirm that we can destroy our physical bodies but not our being in God and affirm that a person stands in relationship to others. The loss of every person is a loss in community.

(6) Support the United Methodist child care institutions which provide treatment for emotionally disturbed children, youth and their families.

(7) Strengthen the youth ministries of the local church, helping the young people experience the saving grace of Jesus Christ and participate in the caring fellowship of the church.

Conclusion:

"The church is called to proclaim the gospel of grace and, in its own life, to embody that Gospel. It embodies that Gospel when it is particularly solicitous of those within its number who are most troubled, and when it reaches beyond its own membership to such people who stand alone." (Dr. Philip Wogaman, Professor of Christian Social Ethics, Wesley Theological seminary.)

ADOPTED 1988

See Social Principles, ¶ 72, "Understanding Living and Dying as a Faithful Christian."

Support the Consultation on Church Union Proposal

WHEREAS, the principles and procedures of the Church of Christ Uniting and the Consultation on Church Union (COCU) are a viable format for continuing discussion of the unity of the Church; and

WHEREAS, through the Covenanting Proposal, meaningful dialogue is maintained with eight Christian communities besides our own; and

WHEREAS, that meaningful dialogue is extended to include advisory consultants from four other Christian communities; and

WHEREAS, by this effort we are also witness to many other Christian communities; and

WHEREAS, this covenant parallels the ecumenical discussion of *Baptism, Eucharist and Ministry* (Faith and Order Paper Number 111 of the World Council of Churches); and

WHEREAS, there is currently a COCU staff person holding discussion meetings in urban areas at which non-COCU communities have not only willingly participated, but in some cases asked to be included; and

WHEREAS, there is a need to increase awareness of the Covenanting Proposal; and

WHEREAS, the unity of the Church was the prayer of our Lord;

Therefore, be it resolved, that the General Conference of The United Methodist Church reaffirm support for the Consultation on Church Union and its covenanting proposals;

Be it further resolved, that the General Commission on Christian Unity and Interreligious Concerns be directed, within the framework of existing budget, to promote interest in the Covenanting Proposal and to develop for use by the fall of 1993 a "user-friendly" curriculum to study the document.

Be it further resolved, that the Council of Bishops encourage and support, within the financial limitations of their existing budget, the Covenanting Proposal of the consultation both through our continued denomination representation and through directions to local churches.

ADOPTED 1992

See Social Principles, ¶ 72, "Continuing Membership in the Consultation on Church Union," "Toward an Ecumenical Future."

Support to Strengthen Ethnic Minority Local Church

WHEREAS, it was the specific and intentional recommendation of the Missional Priority Coordinating Committee for the 1985-88 quadrennium that the various general boards and agencies and each annual conference incorporate into their program for the 1989-92 quadrennium continued support for ethnic-minority local church concerns; and

WHEREAS, for the most part, there has been only minimal continued support for these concerns, particularly at the annual conference level; and

WHEREAS, some of our ethnic-minority congregations are the fastest-growing congregations in the church; and

WHEREAS, there is still a great need for assistance to these congregations to help them grow; and

WHEREAS, the assistance previously given to these congregations from general boards and agencies, annual conference, and districts has proven to be a worthwhile investment; and

WHEREAS, the General Council on Ministries is recommending to the General Conference the sum of $5.5 million for continued ministries to develop and strengthen ethnic-minority churches;

Be it resolved, that each general board and agency and annual conference design intentional and specific programs to continue their support to develop and strengthen ethnic-minority local churches during the 1992-96 quadrennium;

Be it resolved, that adequate human and financial resources be committed to implement these programs.

ADOPTED 1992

See Social Principles, ¶ , "Strengthening the Black Church for the 21st Century," "Native American Social Witness Program."

Tent-Building Ministries

WHEREAS, many small churches/congregations are facing increasingly difficult financial situations; and

WHEREAS, pastoral support is the largest single item in the budgets of these churches; and

WHEREAS, many other denominations function successfully with pastors with secular jobs as their primary income;

Therefore, be it resolved, that we support encouraging more tent-building ministries as a help to these small churches/congregations.

ADOPTED 1992

See Social Principles, ¶ 72.

To Love the Sojourner

WHEREAS, that period of legalization for undocumented persons in the United States provided by the new Immigration Reform and Control Act of 1986 will expire on May 4, 1988, leaving millions of undocumented people without the legal recourse to change their status;

WHEREAS, The United Methodist Church called by its tradition, principles, and mission is compelled to extend its healing, pastoral ministry and protection to the men, women, and children who as undocumented people will be left in our midst;

WHEREAS, The Council of Bishops has recommended this document for study;

Therefore be it resolved that, The United Methodist Church through and with the assistance of the general boards make available the document *To Love the Sojourner* to all local churches as a study guide for better understanding of the history, root causes of the migration of peoples to this country and the responses through public policy which the United States has given through the years. This document will also serve as a guide for the development of comprehensive ministry and action strategies in response to the struggle of the undocumented people in this country.

ADOPTED 1988

See Social Principles, ¶¶ 72.H and 75.A, "Immigration," "U.S. Mexico Border," "Our Muslim Neighbors."

Toward an Ecumenical Future

WHEREAS, the Constitution of The United Methodist Church affirms that Jesus Christ is calling Christians everywhere to strive toward unity at all levels of church life (Division One, Article V); and

WHEREAS, the Council of Bishops has consistently upheld the commitment of The United Methodist Church to ecumenism, especially in the Report of the Conciliar Review Committee of the Council of Bishops in 1984; and

WHEREAS, The United Methodist Church or its predecessors have been founding members of ecumenical organizations such as the World Council of Churches, the National Council of the Churches of Christ in the U.S.A., the Consultation on Church Union (COCU), and the World Methodist Council; and

WHEREAS, three general conferences have affirmed the Consultation on Church Union's "Mutual Recognition of Members" and the 1988 General Conference adopted *The COCU Consensus: In Quest of a Church of Christ Uniting* as a sufficient theological basis for covenanting among the member churches; and

WHEREAS, the full United Methodist Church delegation appointed by the Council of Bishops and other member delegations voted unanimously at the 1988 COCU plenaries to send *Covenanting* to the churches for appropriate action;

Be it resolved, that the General Conference:

Direct the Council of Bishops and the General Commission on Christian Unity and Interreligious Concerns to develop a comprehensive policy for United Methodism's ecumenical involvement into the 21st century, for action at the 1996 General Conference, utilizing:

• the COCU proposal, *Churches in Covenant Communion,* including the concrete steps and procedures to prepare for a recognition of churches and reconciliation of ministries which would lead toward unity in eucharistic celebration and engaging in common mission;

• the contributions which dialogue among communions can make toward increased understanding and ecumenical hospitality;

• national and international expressions and relationships of Christian unity wherever the United Methodist Church exists, including relationships with conciliar organizations and Christian world communions;

• the Preamble of our Constitution, which states that "the Church of Jesus Christ exists in and for the world, and its very dividedness is a hindrance to its mission in the world."

ADOPTED 1992

See Social Principles, ¶ 72.B, "Ecumenical Interpretations of Doctrinal Standards," "Guidelines for Interreligious Relationships 'Called to Be Neighbors and Witnesses,'" "Support the Consultation on Church Union Proposal."

Toward a New Beginning Beyond 1992

The 1988 General Conference, in adopting petition number 1295, "A New Beginning," called United Methodists to declare 1992 "The Year of a New Beginning" through appropriate resolutions and legislation. It urged the 1992 General Conference to "take the necessary measures so that The United Methodist Church will place itself at the vanguard of the efforts to undo and correct the injustices and the misunderstandings of the last 500 years in this hemisphere."

For a "new beginning" to take place, new learnings resulting from the 1992 activities must shape perspectives, programs, and advocacy initiatives across the denomination for many years after 1992. This resolution recommends ways for individual local churches and the general church to respond and incorporate these concerns into their life and ministry.

The 1992 "celebration" in the western hemisphere and Europe has brought renewed attention to the consequences of the European colonial ventures in the Americas. The very use of the term "discovery" revealed the blindness of the "discoverers," who did not even acknowledge the humanity of the native inhabitants. It also justified the shameful stealing of their land and other goods and the cruel destruction of their culture, arts, religion and the environment and other living things on which their lives depended.

Eventually, oppression, exploitation, brutality, and enslavement led to the partial—and in some places, complete—extermination of the land's original inhabitants. The tragedy was compounded when African and Caribbean people were forced into slavery as a way to alleviate the problem. This only added countless new innocent people to the toll of those who suffered injustices, dispossession, and uprootedness.

A fair retelling of history, which is one of the goals of the church regarding quincentennary events, does not require us to assume that the native peoples were perfect. Yet, although humanly flawed (but not more so than their oppressors), history clearly demonstrates that their friendliness and good nature, as well as their initial goodwill, made them extremely vulnerable to the more aggressive, armed with more deadly weapons.

While Spain was the greatest offender 500 years ago, it was not only Spaniards or Roman Catholics who oppressed and exploited their colonial subjects. Other European powers proved equally inhuman and unjust. The sanitized version of the encounter of Indians and colonizers celebrated in the United States as Thanksgiving is very far from the Indian experience of oppression, exploitation, massacres, mass exclusion from their own lands, and an endless string of broken treaties and promises.

Unfortunately, the role of the churches in these events was ambiguous at best. Evangelization provided the excuse for the domination of indigenous peoples and Africans and for the destruction of their culture and religion. Nevertheless, evangelization did take place, in spite of the manipulation of religion for their own purposes by the colonizers. The power of the gospel of Christ to transcend human sinfulness was able to raise prophetic voices who denounced injustice and worked to alleviate the conditions of the oppressed. Still, centuries later, Protestant denominations divided the tribes among themselves just as the colonial powers had earlier divided the land.

While it is difficult to judge past events in light of contemporary moral sensibilities, Christians have the responsibility to understand them and face up to their contemporary consequences. Oppression, exploitation of people and their land, and cultural depreciation of people of color, minorities, and others suffering under structures of domination are still widely practiced, even if old-style colonialism has been defeated almost everywhere. Intolerance, racism, and greed are still the dominant value systems in many public and private centers of power in the world.

As people of faith, we confess that God is the creator of all that exists and that all humans are created equal in dignity, rights, and responsibilities. Therefore, we must challenge all value systems and structures which in theory and/or practice devalue human beings and rob them of their dignity and their relationship to the rest of God's creation which sustains us all. The Scriptures teach us that the earth is indeed the Lord's, and therefore we must oppose individual and corporate greed that seeks to take land away from the poor and often use it in ways that disregard ecological consequences.

When we today seek the face of our crucified and risen Lord, we hear the words that he can be found when we seek and serve "the least of these." We are, therefore, compelled to go beyond intellectual awareness of suffering an take concrete steps to walk in love and solidarity with those who today suffer the consequences of our past sins. Indeed, the resurrection of Jesus Christ is the greatest "new beginning." It inspires and empowers us to overcome the paralysis of guilt and move on to new opportunities for seeking peace with justice in eery corner of the world.

The Social Principles call us to be "faithful stewards of all that has been committed to us by God the Creator" (1988 Book of Discipline, Preamble to ¶ 70), while denying to "any person or group of persons exclusive and arbitrary control of any other part of the created universe" (¶ 73.A). It also denounces as immoral "an ordering of life that perpetuates injustice" (¶ 75.D).

Because of our biblical faith and our Social Principles, United Methodists cannot ignore the fact that the events which started 500 years ago were not a "discovery" but a conquest, not so much an exchange of cultures as an invasion by an occupying force, not so much a bringing of civilization as an imposition by force of a foreign culture and values on peoples who already had their own civilizations, history, culture, languages, and values. Again, because of our faith and principles, we cannot ignore that the five centuries since Columbus's arrival have left a legacy of violence and unjust socio-political and economic/ecological systems in the western hemisphere which has oppressed especially women, children, indigenous peoples, and people of African descent. The United Methodist "Charter for Racial Justice Policies" states that "during the early history of this country, Europeans assumed that their civilization and religion were innately superior to those of both the original inhabitants of the United States and the Africans who were forcibly brought to these shores to be slaves. The myth of European superiority persisted and persists" (*1988 Book of Resolutions*, p. 167). A basic step toward a new beginning requires us to abandon this Euro-centric myth that continues to operate in both church and society in most parts of the world.

United Methodists stand ready to accept the call to a "new beginning." Accepting this call means turning away from past practices and habits based on exploitation, racism, and injustice. It means affirming, respecting, celebrating, and seeking reconciliation with cultures other than those which are dominant in our societies, with particular attention to indigenous groups. In order to make this possible and to effect significant personal and institutional growth in the life of the church, several recommendations are proposed for the church in general and then for each specific level.

1. General recommendations:

All levels of the church are urged to provide leadership and resources to support United Methodist efforts toward a "new beginning" beyond 1992. The Council of Bishops is specially requested to lead the church by education and example on the issues raised by this resolution.

A first step in these efforts is to heed the call from the Seventh Assembly of the World Council of Churches that all member churches move beyond words to action, in these areas:

1. to negotiate with indigenous people to ascertain how lands

taken unjustly by churches from indigenous people can be returned to them;

2. to recognize, acknowledge, and vigorously support self-determination and sovereignty of indigenous people, as defined by them, in church and society; and

3. to oppose the continuing and now increasing exploitation of indigenous peoples' land and mineral resources.

2. Local church recommendations:

In the spirit of a new beginning, each local church, starting with its pastor and lay leaders, is to seek changes in the following areas:

Nurture. In preaching and Christian education, churches will seek to study and reflect on how the exploitation and genocide of natives and other racial/ethnic-minority peoples started with the colonial conquerors 500 years ago, was continued by their successors, and persists to this day. Special attention is to be given to Bible study and to local resources. Important also is to observe worship opportunities such as Native American Awareness Sunday, Human Relations Day, and Peace with Justice Sunday, where the congregation may find ways to meet with local people from racial/ethnic-minority communities in their own setting to hear ways to work with them.

Outreach. Identify discriminated, oppressed, or dominated groups in their community. Seek a new beginning with them through church programs. Provide resources for programs that promote empowerment, self-determination, and care for creation.

Witness. Accept the challenge of a new beginning in the approach of witnessing to new groups. The new approach would involve knowing the life of the people from inside; living, learning, and sharing with the people; believing that God is already present with the people; and calling the people into service. Witnessing also includes analysis of public policy formation and advocacy actions which lead to peace with justice in the name of Jesus Christ.

3. Annual conference recommendations:

In order to support the work of local churches, annual conferences will:

Stimulate and support local churches in implementing new beginning-inspired programs by developing appropriate programs and resources. Whenever resources are prepared, they should be explicit on how the issue discussed will affect people of color.

Provide training and educational opportunities for clergy and lay leadership to be held within an ethnic community in order to begin to hear, understand, and respect their culture and tradition and the issues related to this resolution. Special attention should be given to training in the dynamics of institutional racism and ways to eliminate it.

Use the guidelines and resources developed by Project Equality and make them available to local churches and all conference bodies.

Use publications and all other types of media available to keep issues before the people. Make sure writers/producers include people of color in the annual conference. Strengthen racial/ethnic-minority ministries and support significant programs such as the Hispanic and Native American comprehensive plans.

Identify, celebrate, and include racial- and ethnic-minority cultures and traditions within the life of the conference.

Support and be an advocate for the struggle for self-determination and other rights of indigenous people.

4. *General agency recommendations:*

The General Board of Discipleship is to develop appropriate curriculum and worship resources to support local churches in these efforts, while making sure that all curriculum and worship materials include racial/ethnic culture and traditions.

The General Board of Higher Education and Ministry is to request that United Methodist theological seminaries incorporate these concerns into the basic theological education curriculum. This is to be done also for the course of study programs for local pastors.

The General Board of Global Ministries is to develop ways to implement in its programs of mission and evangelism the perspectives advanced by this resolution. This includes the reviewing of all existing policies and procedures to make sure that funding, mission personnel, and other resources are fully available to racial/ethnic communities. Future mission studies, both ecumenical and United Methodist, should provide opportunities for studying the issues raised in this resolution and their mission implications. In line with our denominational affirmation of "the contributions which United Methodists of varying ethnic, language, cultural, and national groups make to one another and to our Church as a whole" (*Book of Discipline,* ¶ 68 section 4), this board is asked to take the initiative to enable the exploration of indigenous theologies in the Americas, including ecumenical and interfaith perspectives.

The General Board of Church and Society is to support and be an advocate for self-determination and empowerment of indigenous people and the just observance of international treaties with indigenous nations.

ADOPTED 1992

See Social Principles, ¶ 72, "A Charter for Racial Justice Policies in an Interdependent Global Community," "Rights of Native American People of the Americas," "The United Methodist Church and America's Native People."

The Treatment of Women in the United States Under Social Security

The Old and New Testaments share prophetic-messianic traditions in which God stands with the oppressed against a dehumanizing and destructive social order. The emphasis on the protection of those in deepest need was a theme of the events of Exodus. And Jesus, drawing on intimate knowledge of the Hebrew Scriptures, inaugurated his ministry with a quotation from Isaiah: "The Spirit of the Lord . . . has annointed me to preach good news to the poor . . . to set at liberty those who are oppressed. . ." (Luke 4:18-19; cf, Isa. 61:1-2).

The early Christian Church in Jerusalem, following this tradition, established a community in which all things were held in common. Special attention was given to those who were the neediest: widows, the elderly, the disabled. Israel and the early Church exemplify the role that a community of faith is called upon to play: concern for the welfare of the poor and establishment of a just social system.

In the United States, millions of aged and disabled persons, especially women, depend on the Social Security System for the necessities of life. For most Americans, especially aged women, the Social Security System is often the one program that stands between them and poverty.

Inequities in the system, however, also make it a program that tends to keep many women in poverty. Because of the important role of Social Security, people of faith have a special interest in ensuring that it is operated fairly and securely. Its benefits must be designed to overcome disadvantages of age, race, sex, or disability. And it must be regularly reviewed to assure that it is flexible enough to adjust to the changing needs of our society.

The Social Security System in the United States has historically functioned as a basic insurance program to provide income and medical expenses for those persons who are retired or disabled. It has helped to hold families together by maintaining income in times of personal hardship. It has relieved younger people of the necessity of total care for aging parents while also allowing retired persons the independence and dignity of their own income by providing basic benefits. Since its enactment in the 1930s, the program has been a cornerstone of the social policy of the United States. However, U.S. society has radically changed in the intervening years and modifications in the Social Security System are now required to meet those social changes.

When the Social Security System was first established, only 17 percent of the paid work force was female. Today over half of all women in the United States work outside the home. However, the wage differential between women and men has been deteriorating during the last 25 years. It is now about 60 cents to $1. Changes in the labor force, participation of women and the inequality of pay, combined with an increased divorce and remarriage rate and extended life expectancy of women, have resulted in an oppressive situation for many women under Social Security.

In 1980, approximately 52 percent of all Social Security recipients were women, either as workers or dependents. Thirteen percent were children and the remaining 35 percent were men. The average monthly Social Security benefit in 1982 for adult women was $308 compared to $430 for men. Retired female workers averaged $335 compared to $438 for men. Spouses of retired or disabled husbands averaged $196 and widows $351. The median annual income for all women over 65 from all sources was only $4757 as compared to $8173 for men in 1981. The figures for minority persons are painfully lower.

Clearly, the system needs attention. Widowed, divorced and never-married women account for 72 percent of all aged people living in poverty. Changes in the Social Security System are desperately needed in order to achieve equal and adequate treatment for all persons. Benefits are clearly inadequate for divorced women, widowed women, ethnic minority women, women who have never married, and women who are not citizens. The current benefit structure penalizes women who work regularly but who spend time out of the labor force to bear and raise children. Further, couples with one wage earner receive larger benefits than do two-earner couples with the same total earnings. Structural unemployment results in increased numbers of unemployed American women and, therefore, less Social Security coverage. Also, the growing issue of undocumented workers who pay into the Social Security System but receive no benefits from their payments needs to be addressed.

The 1983 report of the National Commission on Social Security Reform did not deal with basic systemic change in the gender-based system. However, after the report was released, a majority of the commissioners declared in favor of "earnings sharing," a concept that affirms marriage as a partnership, dividing equally any earnings by either spouse for Social Security purposes. Following that report, the General Boards of Global Ministries and Church and Society affirmed "earnings sharing" as a way of bringing greater equality to the Social Security System.

The United Methodist Church, in its Social Principles, urges social policies and programs that ensure to the aging the respect and dignity that is their right as senior members of society; affirms the need to support those in distress; and calls for the equal treatment of men and women in every aspect of their common life.

Therefore, be it resolved:

1. That the 1984 General Conference supports the effort to address the many inequities suffered by women in the Social Security System and urges that the governmental body established to consider these inequities should consult with older women, ethnic minority women and representatives of organizations dealing with older women's issues. Such a body should give special attention to:

a) The concept of "earnings sharing" with a "hold harmless" provision which would prevent persons now receiving benefits from being cut.

b) Social Security credits for the homemaker.

c) An allowance for more "child care" years spent out of the work force.

2. That the Secretary of the General Conference shall communicate this support to the appropriate officials in the executive and legislative branches of the U.S. government.

3. That the General Boards of Church and Society and Global Ministries shall continue to document social security issues and shall inform their constituencies about the needs for reform.

4. That The United Methodist Church shall educate its constituencies so that churches and individual United Methodists can encourage their legislators to support needed reform.

ADOPTED 1984

See Social Principles, ¶ 72.F. "Equal Rights of Women," "The Status of Women."

Universal Access to Health Care in the United States and Related Territories

The health care system in the United States is in need of serious systemic change. We call for legislation that will provide universal access to quality health care with effective cost controls.

John Wesley was always deeply concerned about health care, providing medical services at no cost to the poor in London and emphasizing preventive care. The first Methodist Social Creed (adopted in 1908) urged working conditions to safeguard the health of workers and community.

Through its many hospitals and health-care facilities around the world, as well as public-policy advocacy for health, The United Methodist Church continues to declare its commitment to quality and affordable health care as a right of all people.

The concern of The United Methodist Church for health is rooted in our biblical understanding that salvation embraces wholeness of mind, body, and spirit. Jesus revealed the meaning of divine love in his acts of healing for all and the meaning of justice in his inclusion of all persons in the healing and saving power of God. The redemptive ministry of Christ which focused on healing and wholeness—spiritual, mental, physical, and emotional—is our model for health ministry.

Persons in the United States have been conditioned to expect quality health care. The United States has one of the lowest overall mortality rates compared with other countries. Its medical technology expertise is evident in the many success stories of curing severe illness and prolonging life. The quality of medical training in the United States has also been very high, benefiting those who have access to the services of doctors and other health professionals.

Unfortunately, the excesses of the present system are beginning to erode many of these achievements. Nearly 37 million Americans are denied appropriate health care simply because of their economic status and/or disability. Within this group are some of the most vulnerable members of society, particularly 11 to 13 million children. Even those adults who are working are not spared: two-thirds of those without insurance belong to families with steadily employed workers. Many working people also belong to another large group in danger—more than 60 million with underinsurance.

Not surprisingly, the poor, the aging, women, children, persons with disabilities, and persons of color are most at risk in this system. The infant mortality rate in the United States is the worst among the "developed" countries. Black women die from cervical cancer at three times the rate of white women. Black Americans have a significantly lower life-span than white Americans—an average of six years less, and Hispanics have least access to the health-care system of any group. Native Americans, besides suffering greatly from alcoholism, have a tuberculosis rate 600 times higher than average U.S. rates. Recent immigrants who experience health problems find the health-care system poorly equipped to meet their needs.

Even persons with middle income have difficulty finding affordable quality care. Families in which a member suffers from catastrophic illness find their health insurance premiums priced so high they can no longer afford them, or in some cases, insurance is canceled. Businesses are overwhelmed with the cost of health insurance; a problem The United Methodist Church is also facing. The dissatisfaction with the U.S. health system ranks highest among the middle class in many surveys.

Despite these inadequacies, the health-care system is extremely costly, consuming 12 percent of the gross national product in 1990, while Canadian health-care costs still hold at 8 percent.

Finally, the providers of health care and corporate America both are unhappy with the present system. Doctors object to excessive paperwork, malpractice suits, and inadequate government programs. Hospitals can no longer stay financially sound under existing policies.

Corporate America has called for radical change because our economic position in the world is being eroded by rising health costs. Unions as well are unhappy, and a large number of strikes in recent years have stemmed from disputes over health care.

We therefore seek legislation that incorporates the following principles:

Principle 1

We seek a national health-care plan that serves and is sensitive to the diversity of all people in the United States and its territories.

Principle 2

We seek a national health-care plan that will provide comprehensive benefits to everyone, including preventive services, health promotion, primary and acute care, mental-health care, and extended care.

Principle 3

We seek a national health-care plan with an equitable and efficient financing system drawn from the broadest possible resource base.

Principle 4

We see a national health-care plan that provides services based on equity, efficiency, and quality, with payments to providers that are equitable, cost-efficient, and easy to administer and understand.

Principle 5

We seek a national health-care plan that reduces the current rapid inflation in costs through cost-containment measures.

Principle 6

We seek a national health-care plan that is sensitive to the needs of persons working in the various components of the health-care system and gives special attention to not only providing for affirmative action in the recruitment, training, and employment of workers, but also for just compensation for all workers at all levels and for retraining and placement of those displaced by changes in the health-care system.

Principle 7

We seek a national health-care plan that promotes effective and safe innovation and research for women and men in medical techniques, the delivery of health services, and health practices.

Principle 8

We seek a national health-care plan that assesses the health impacts of environmental and occupational safety, environmental pollution, sanitation, physical fitness, and standard-of-living issues such as housing and nutrition.

We, in The United Methodist Church, are called to a ministry of healing. Therefore, we challenge our church to:

1. Support the Interreligious Healthcare Access Campaign and its public-policy advocacy to provide access to universal health care for all.

2. Educate and motivate persons to pursue a healthy life style, thus avoiding health problems by practicing preventive medicine.

3. Affirm the role of Christ-like care in institutions which provide direct health services by units of The United Methodist Church.

4. Develop a curriculum model on universal health-care advocacy suitable for United Methodist Church seminaries.

5. Assure that persons representative of the groups most directly affected by inaccessibility to quality health care participate in all levels of efforts by The United Methodist Church directed toward the implementation of a national health-care policy.

ADOPTED 1992

See Social Principles, ¶ 72, "Health for All by the Year 2000," "Health in Mind and Body," "Health and Wholeness," "Medical Rights for Children and Youth."

The Use of Alcohol and Drugs on Campuses

WHEREAS United Methodist colleges should provide an environment suitable for pursuing a higher education in a Christian atmosphere;

Therefore, be it resolved, that The United Methodist Church addresses this issue by (1) promoting an alternative life style that encourages "wellness" without drugs and alcohol, (2) seeking authentic advocates for this alternative life style, and (3) having these advocates promote this image on United Methodist campuses across the nation.

ADOPTED 1984

See Social Principles, ¶ 72.I, "Drug and Alcohol Concerns," "Confronting the Drug Crisis."

Use of Church Facilities by Community Groups

Encouragement shall be given for the use of local church facilities by community groups and agencies which serve social and service needs of the total community.

ADOPTED 1970

See Social Principles, ¶ 72, "Church and Community Workers 1988," "Church and Community Workers 1992."

Vision Interfaith Satellite Network

From its inception, the Wesleyan tradition has made creative and responsible use of the most effective and modern forms of communication available. Just as the early circuit riders successfully used the power of face-to-face communication and the printed word to spread the gospel, the church today is challenged to use all forms of communication—including the electronic media—for ministry and witness.

In recent years, the world has been engaged in a revolutionary shift from a primary dependence upon the printed word to a recognition that the electronic media also have extraordinary power to shape values and affect behavior. If the church is to remain a viable instrument of God's will, it must continually seek to use all appropriate methods of communication.

Vision Interfaith Satellite Network (VISN), a cable network dedicated to faith- and values-oriented programming, offers The United Methodist Church an outstanding and timely opportunity to present the gospel of Jesus Christ in a clear, compelling, and appealing way to a television-oriented public, especially in view of the growing strength of the cable industry.

VISN was launched in September, 1988, and by the spring of 1991 had membership representing 54 faith groups. It is the only religious cable network owned and operated by a consortium of faith groups rather than by one denomination, faith group, or individual. This cooperative effort toward a common goal is made real in VISN's programming standards, which are unique in the television industry:

VISN does not allow programming that attacks or maligns any religious faith.

VISN encourages faith groups to present clearly their beliefs and witness, but it does not allow proselytizing.

VISN does not allow any self-serving on-air fund raising. VISN is not an electronic congregation; rather, it invites viewers to join in the faith journey through participation in a local congregation.

We celebrate the strength of VISN and the opportunity it offers The United Methodist Church to witness and minister to our own members and the general public in a responsible and respected context.

We celebrate VISN's ability to distribute a wide variety of United Methodist programming to viewers and families across the nation.

We commend those in the cable television industry who are committed to serving the needs of local communities and the interests of viewers for their initiative and the significant financial support they have provided to enable the launching and operation of VISN.

We commend communications, leaders of The United Methodist Church at all levels for their foresight in understanding the potential of an interfaith cable network.

We commend United Methodists at conference, district, and local levels who have succeeded in bringing VISN to their communities.

Further, we urge pastors and laypersons to take the initiative in their communities to work with other faith-group leaders in making VISN available.

We urge pastors and laypersons to support the production and airing of local programs for VISN.

We urge pastors and laypersons to support VISN once it is placed in their communities, to encourage others to watch it, and to utilize it creatively as a resource of mission and witness in congregations and communities.

ADOPTED 1992

See Social Principles, ¶ 72.O, "The Church in a Mass Media Culture."

THE ECONOMIC COMMUNITY

Appalachian Challenge

Be it resolved, that United Methodists reaffirm their commitment to ministry and mission in Appalachia illustrated by projects throughout the region such as the Red Bird Missionary Conference (Kentucky), Hinton Rural Life Center (North Carolina), Upper Sand Mountain Cooperative Parish (Alabama), Jackson Area Ministries (Ohio), Heart and Hand House (West Virginia), Connellsville Cooperative Ministry (Pennsylvania) and in other areas;

Further be it resolved that The United Methodist Church continue its mission and ministry denominationally as directed by the General Conference of 1968, through the coordination of the United Methodist Appalachian Development Committee, and ecumenically through the Commission on Religion in Appalachia; and *further,* we call upon all levels of the Church to reevaluate current programs, to reorder priorities, and to work with other religious groups ecumenically, and in conjunction with government and community organizations, to respond to the hurts, needs and empowerment of Appalachian peoples and communities through a comprehensive program of spiritual renewal, social recovery, economic transformation and political responsibility and compassion.

ADOPTED 1988

See Social Principles, ¶ 73.E, "Appalachian Mission."

The Appalachian Mission

WHEREAS, The United Methodist Church has engaged in ministry and mission in the Appalachian region since the beginnings of the denomination; and

WHEREAS, conditions among people in this region are actually worsening, according to numerous social, economic, and religious indicators; and

WHEREAS, according to the latest census figures the Appalachian region (in the eastern mountainous section of the United States, northern Alabama to lower New York, 398 counties in 13 states) is home to 20.5 million people, of which 9 percent are United Methodists—more than double the proportion in the nation as a whole—although membership has declined over the past decades; and

WHEREAS, per capita income in Appalachia is 69.95 percent of the U. S. average, a decline of 5.35 percent during the past 10 years; 25 percent of the region's children live in poverty; unemployment is above 20 percent in many portions of the region; and opportunities continue to decline with the exodus of industry and the growing mechanization of coal mining and timbering; and

WHEREAS, in many counties only 20 percent of the land is owned and controlled by indigenous people, with large holdings of the federal government and multi-national corporations being operated for the benefit of outsiders, and vast areas of the region becoming a dumping ground for the entire Eastern seaboard; and

WHEREAS, reduction of federal assistance programs and inequitable taxation mean that the suffering of people here increases in terms of health care, education, housing, transportation, and economic opportunity; and

WHEREAS, for many years there have been numerous creative outreach programs by the 24 annual conferences serving here and by the general church program boards, supported in large measure by people from the entire church; and

WHEREAS, among the all-too-few signs of hope in the region are the ministries of the church, many of which are the result of ecumenical cooperation and joint action, and in partnership with broad-based community organizations controlled by Appalachian people

Be it resolved, that The United Methodist Church reaffirm its commitment to mission and ministry here denominationally through the coordination of the Appalachian Development Committee, and ecumenically through the Commission on Religion in Appalachia; and

Be it further resolved, that all levels of the church be called upon to consider the worsening conditions in Appalachia, to reexamine mission and ministry and the priorities set, and to work with other groups ecumenically and in conjunction with government and community organizations to respond to the hurts and needs of Appalachian people and communities through a comprehensive program of spiritual renewal, social recovery, empowerment, economic transformation, and political responsibility and compassion.

ADOPTED 1992

See Social Principles, ¶ 73, "Appalachian Challenge," "Employment," "A Call for Increased Committment to End World Hunger and Poverty."

Economic Justice

I. *Introduction*

The results of rapid consolidation of wealth and power by fewer individuals, corporations and banks, the shift in government priorities from social to military expenditures; and the growing inter-connections between national economies have led to increases in poverty, hunger and despair in the human family. Materialism and selfishness are undermining the values of community and mutual sharing. Within this situation, The United Methodist Church, following its traditional commitment, is called to analyze international economics and work for biblical justice.

II. *Biblical/Theological Background*

God has created us for wholeness (shalom) and interdependence. God's creation is such that our well-being is dependent upon the well-being of all creation. Created in the image of God (Gen. 1:27), we are accountable to God, the Creator, in caring for the earth in ways that will bring wholeness to all of creation.

Within the universal gift of God's creation we are called into the particular tradition and mission of being a covenant people. In response to God's gift of grace, centered in the biblical experiences of exodus and resurrection, we are to live in relationship to God as communities of witness in the midst of the world (Ex. 19:4-6). In covenant we are committed to the welfare of our neighbors, and this must include our economic and political relationships. Covenant people are committed to equitable distribution of resources to meet basic human needs and to social systems that provide ongoing access to those resources. Covenant people are equally committed to decision-making and the use of power in a social order that is characterized by justice. The biblical mandate is to uphold the right of all persons to fullness of life and to confront all people and systems which would deny this right to others.

Covenant relationship to God and neighbors were expressed in concrete social structures as seen in Israel's law codes. The Ten Commandments (Ex. 20:2-17) emphasize that loyalty to God alone is tied to responsible life in human relationships of respect and equity. Law codes in Exodus, Leviticus, and Deuteronomy show a special concern for the resources necessary to meet human needs and guarantee basic rights such as food (Lev. 19:9-10; Deut. 23:21-22, 24:19-22), clothing (Ex. 26-27), just business dealings (Deut. 25:13-16), and access to just juridical process (Ex. 23:6-8). Special concern is expressed for those who are marginal in society: the poor (Ex. 23:6, Deut. 15:7-11), the stranger (Ex. 21:21-24), the sojourner (Deut. 10:19), the widow and the orphan (Deut. 24:19-22). To periodically re-balance economic inequities, the covenant community was called to observe sabbatical years in which the land was not worked and its produce was available to the poor (Ex. 23:10-11) and slaves were set free (Ex. 21:2). In the fiftieth year the Jubilee is to be celebrated (Lev. 25:8-55) as the year of God's release when prisoners are set free, debts are cancelled and land is returned to families.

Israel again broke its covenant with God during the period of the kings when the people began to turn away from Yahweh to patterns of idolatry, greed, privilege, materialism and oppressive power. The economic system of the community was no longer based on equality and concern for those who were powerless in the community but on economic privilege to the benefit of the rich and powerful. The prophets warned again and again that an economic system based on greed, economic exploitation and indifference to the needs of the poor was contrary to God's will (Amos 8:4-6, Jer. 22:131-7).

Like the Hebrew prophets who took their stand with the poor, Jesus embodied the messianic promise to the poor and alienated. As indicated in Luke 4:18-19, Jesus began his public ministry with these words:

"The Spirit of the Lord is upon me, because God has anointed me to preach good news to the poor. God has sent me to proclaim release to the captives and recovery of sight to the blind, to set at liberty those who are oppressed, to proclaim the acceptable year of the Lord."

Jesus Christ is proclaimed as new creation and new covenant. In him dividing walls of hostility are broken down, the far-off are brought near, those divided are made one (Eph. 2). Those who follow Christ as the center of their faith must take notice of his concern for both physical and spiritual wholeness, and his care for the poor and the oppressed. Jesus' frequent teachings on economic matters reveal his concern that faith brings forth efforts for social, as well as spiritual, well-being. This was evident in the early church as it shared all that it had and especially cared for the widows and the orphans (Acts 2:44-45, II Cor. 8:13-15).

Today, we are called to patterns of community that take seriously our roots in biblical faith as well as a sensitivity to what God is doing in our own time. Acknowledging that we are part of God's creation, called into covenant community and empowered by the model of Jesus Christ, we must analyze economic systems and their impact on justice and peace. We approach this responsibility as the church, a community transcending narrow interests of nation, race or class in obedience to the call to be God's people. We seek to express a love of God that can only be pursued by taking seriously the concern for our neighbor's well-being as our own.

III. *Tradition of The United Methodist Church Witness for Economic Justice*

The United Methodist Church and its predecessor bodies have a long history of public witness on matters of economic justice. John Wesley set the example in his famous sermon on "The Use of Money," his public stand against slavery, and his witness among England's working class. The 1908 "Social Creed" committed the Methodist Episcopal Church to work for the protection and rights of people disadvantaged by society. And the Evangelical United Brethren Church made a comparable commitment to personal, social, and international justice in its Discipline statement, "Moral Standards of the Evangelical United Brethren Church" (Section IX).

As United Methodists we are guided by "The Social Principles" as adopted in the *1984 Book of Discipline* (¶ 70-76). The "Economic Community" section begins with these words: "We claim all economic systems to be under the judgment of God, no less than other facets of the created order." "The Social Principles" contains basic principles that are useful in an analysis of contemporary economics.

IV. *Structures of Injustice in the Global Economy*

A. *Concentration of wealth and power*

"We support measures that would reduce the concentration of wealth in the hands of a few" (¶ 73).

The world economy has changed markedly over the past decades. Transnational corporations and banks have extended their ownership and control of agriculture, industry, land, finances and communications. As this process has taken place, two consequences have emerged:

1. The separation between the rich and the poor has become greater; and
2. many corporations have become increasingly unaccountable to their employees, to the communities in which they operate, and to governments.

B. *Production and work*

"Every person has the right and responsibility to work for the benefit of himself or herself and the enhancement of human life and community to receive adequate remuneration. . . We support the rights of workers to refuse to work in situations that endanger health and/or life, without jeopardy to their jobs" (¶ 73.c).

Transnational corporations have transferred much of the manufacturing base of industrial countries to developing countries, seeking cheaper labor and less stringent regulation of environmental practices, consumer protection, and occupational safety and health. They have also taken advantage of favorable tax treatment for overseas investment. In many cases, this has resulted in a "global assembly line" made up of workers who receive low wages, have few rights, and are forbidden to join democratic labor unions. Many of the workers on the global assembly line are women, particularly young women, who toil under difficult and unsafe conditions.

In the United States, the decline in industrial jobs has coincided with a rise in high technology jobs; low-paying and part-time service jobs; information jobs; and in non-union jobs with minimal job security and benefits (e.g., fast food, retail, health care, maintenance, and computer). A growing number of the new jobs involve women, many of whom do sub-contract work in their homes, again under conditions of low pay and no benefits.

C. Export-led development

"We affirm the right and duty of the people of developing nations to determine their own destiny. We urge the major political powers to use their power to maximize the political, social, and economic self-determination of developing nations rather than to further their own special interests" (¶ 75.b).

The global economic system and external debts continue to force developing countries to allocate major resources to produce goods with heavy emphasis on production for export rather than for domestic use. Many developing nations are locked into exporting primary commodities at prices that fluctuate widely. Even those few developing nations that do export manufactured goods face uncertain markets due to growing protectionism. They commit their natural resources, environment and land to competition for world markets while they sacrifice their domestic economy, social welfare and human lives.

D. Debt crisis/financial crisis

"We applaud international efforts to develop a more just international economic order, in which the limited resources of the earth will be used to the maximum benefit of all nations and peoples. We urge Christians in every society, to encourage the governments under which they live, and the economic entities within their societies, to aid and to work for the development of more just economic orders" (¶ 75.b).

After more than a decade of heavy borrowing encouraged by

Western banks, many developing countries found that, by the early 1980s (when interest rates rose and raw material prices collapsed), they could no longer meet the service payments on their debts. The creditor banks and governments turned to the International Monetary Fund (IMF) which makes new loans contingent on strict austerity programs. IMF remedies have placed the burden of debt repayment squarely on the shoulders of poor and working people by devaluing currencies, freezing wages, curbing government price subsidies (on rice, cooking oil, beans and other essential items), and cutting subsidized credits in rural areas.

Simultaneously, the United States is having debt problems of its own. The federal budget is chronically in deficit; the foreign (trade) debt has become monumental; and consumers continue their heavy dependence on credit while foreclosures of farms and small businesses assume record proportions. The actual result of the pressing debt in both the Third World and the United States is that the poor, with and without employment, carry the burden.

E. *Military spending*

". . . human values must outweigh military claims as governments determine their priorities; . . . the militarization of society must be challenged and stopped; . . . the manufacture, sale and deployment of armaments must be reduced and controlled. . ." (¶ 75.c).

Many governments in shifting major resources to the military have hurt the most vulnerable people in their societies. Some economies, such as that of the United States, increasingly depend on the military for jobs, exports, and economic growth. Among developing countries, some produce weapons to pay their foreign debt while others import military equipment to control their own populations.

V. *The Effects of the Global Economic System*

Injustices are imposed on the people of the world by economies characterized by a concentration of wealth and power, an export-based development, heavy indebtedness, and reliance on a militarized national security system. The following are some reminders:

A. Poverty and hunger have increased, especially among women and children. In developing countries, this has been most marked in the growing shanty-towns that surround major cities as people leave rural areas. In the United States, it is estimated that as much as 20 percent of the population may be living in poverty. Blacks and Hispanics make up a disproportionate share of that group. Homelessness is rampant in cities, while rural communities are in rapid decline as farms go bankrupt in record numbers.

B. Unemployment and underemployment are unacceptably high; education and job training opportunities are inadequate; and increasingly meaningful work is difficult to secure. In some communities, the situation is so severe that employment is virtually non-existent.

C. The increasing ability of large corporations to shift their resources around the globe has contributed to an erosion of worker rights everywhere. Third World governments compete to offer the lowest labor costs to the transnational corporations while at the same time, in the United States, these same corporations win major concessions from workers and communities by threatening to move to lower wage areas. As wages and benefits decline, the number of full-time employees living in poverty increases.

D. The environment and fragile natural resource base of many countries are deteriorating. Developing countries desperate for employment and capital try to attract transnational corporations with weaker environmental regulations than those in much of the industrialized world. The effect is destruction of fragile topsoil and rain forests and a shift in agricultural production into chemically-dependent cash crops.

E. A strong belief that competition results in greater economic growth underlies much of the international economic order. In the production and consumption of goods, corporations are to compete with corporations; individuals with each other; and societies with other societies. The central value is "more." The corporate culture of materialism, of "more is better," has spread throughout the world by sophisticated advertising of Western images. It is a culture that has little use for those who lack the means to consume.

Churches and social service agencies have struggled to meet the spiritual and psychological needs these economic effects create in persons, families and communities. In communities under economic stress, there is a rising incidence of suicides, child and spouse abuse, family breakdown, drug and substance abuse, and other forms of anti-social behavior.

VI. *Actions for The United Methodist Church*

The United Methodist Church, as a covenant community committed to justice, must work toward a just global economy. Our "Social Principles" reminds us that:

"In spite of general affluence in the industrialized nations, the majority of persons in the world live in poverty. In order to provide basic needs such as food, clothing, shelter, education, health care and other necessities, ways must be found to share more equitably the resources of the world."

Faced with this task, we specifically call upon The United Methodist Church to:

A. Challenge each local congregation to study global economic justice issues, using this resolution as a basic resource. To assist this process:

1. The General Board of Discipleship, in co-operation with the General Boards of Church and Society and Global Ministries, shall prepare appropriate curricula, including Bible study, and study materials for all ages. These resources would help local congregations to understand the impact of global economics on individuals, communities, and nations and suggest appropriate tasks for Christian mission.

2. United Methodist Communications shall develop media resources on global economic justice issues to accompany this church-wide study.

3. The General Board of Higher Education and Ministry shall work with United Methodist theological seminaries to include Christian responsibility for economic justice as a necessary part of education for ministry.

B. Commit the General Board of Church and Society and the General Board of Global Ministries to engage in an on-going search for and study of alternative systems of economic order, for the purpose of addressing the needs of an increasingly interdependent global economy.

C. Urge the General Boards of Church and Society and Global Ministries to work with annual conferences to initiate and support legislative efforts at the local, state, and national levels that will address "The Structure of Injustice in the Global Economy" (Section IV). Priority attention should focus on the accountability of transnational corporations and banks; the need for land reform; and the increasing dependency of national economies on the military.

D. Challenge all bodies related to the church to be more energetic in using their investment portfolios to strengthen developing national economies and global economic justice.

E. Challenge annual conferences, local churches and individuals to a simpler, more modest life style, and bring church and community people together to identify specific economic issues that affect individuals, families, and communities, i.e., plant closing and relocation, deterioration of public education, homelessness, and lack of affordable housing; and to respond to these issues through the strategies of study, service, advocacy and community economic development.

Finally, as delegates to the 1988 General Conference, we resolve and covenant with others to do the following:

1. To lift up the concerns of people affected by global economic injustice in personal and corporate prayer;
2. And to initiate study and action programs for global economic justice in our local congregations and annual conferences.

ADOPTED 1988

See Social Principles, ¶ 73, "Pay Equity in the USA," "Extension of the Right to Organize and Bargain Collectively," "Global Debt Crisis," "Special Needs of Farm Workers," "Rights of Workers."

Extension of the Right to Organize and Bargain Collectively

Historically, The United Methodist Church has recognized and supported the right of workers to organize into unions of their own choosing and to bargain collectively over wages, hours, and conditions of employment. National policy since 1935 has codified procedures for the election of labor unions by industrial workers, for the recognition of those unions by management, and for collective bargaining with the result of lessened conflict in the private industrial sector of the economy.

However, a major category of employees was excluded from the coverage of the National Labor Relations Act. These are the employees working for the federal government and employees of any political subdivision such as a state or school district.

Unfortunately, social strife in the occupational markets of public employees has led to high social costs such as the interruption of vital community services and even the tragedy of death. In view of this continued unresolved strain and many attendant injustices, The United Methodist Church requests the Congress to amend the National Labor Relations Act to include under its coverage government employees, federal, state, and local and to institute methods, for example, various forms of arbitration, for resolving disputes that significantly affect the health and safety of the public.

ADOPTED 1976

See Social Principles, ¶ 73.B, "Economic Justice," "Rights of Workers."

Gambling

The Social Principles states that "Gambling is a menace to society, deadly to the best interests of moral, social, economic, and spiritual life, and destructive of good government. As an act of faith and love, Christians should abstain from gambling, and should strive to minister to those victimized by the practice. Community standards and personal lifestyles should be such as would make unnecessary and undesirable the resort to commercial gambling, including public lotteries, as a recreation, as an escape, or as a means of producing public revenue or funds for support of charities or government."

One of the essential commandments, according to Jesus, is "Love thy neighbor as thyself" (Matthew 22:39-40). This, together with loving God with all of one's being, summarizes all of the law.

Gambling, as a means of keeping material gain only by chance and at the neighbor's expense, is a menace to personal character and social morality. Gambling fosters greed and stimulates the fatalistic faith in chance. Organized and commercial gambling is a threat to business, breeds crime and poverty, and is destructive to the interests of good government.

We oppose the growing legalization and state promotion of gambling.

Dependence on gambling revenue has led many states to exploit the weakness of their own citizens, neglect the development of more equitable forms of taxation, and thereby further erode the citizens' confidence in government.

We oppose the legalization of pari-mutuel betting, for it has been the opening wedge in the legalization of other forms of gambling within the states, and has stimulated illegal bookmaking. We deplore the establishment of state lotteries and their use as a means of raising public revenues. The constant promotion and the wide advertising of lotteries have encouraged large numbers of persons to gamble for the first time.

We express an even more serious concern for the increasing development of the casino enterprise in the United States, for it has taken captive entire communities and has infiltrated many levels of government with its fiscal and political power.

Public apathy and a lack of awareness that petty gambling feeds organized crime have opened the door to the spread of numerous forms of legal and illegal gambling.

We support the strong enforcement of anti-gambling laws, the repeal of all laws that give gambling an acceptable and even advantageous place in our society, and the rehabilitation of compulsive gamblers.

The Church has a key role in fostering responsible government and in developing health and moral maturity which free persons from dependence on damaging social customs. It is expected that United Methodist churches abstain from the use of raffles, lotteries, Bingo, door prizes, other drawing schemes, and games of chance for the purpose of gambling or fund raising. We should refrain from all forms of gambling practices carried on in our communities and should work to influence community organizations to develop forms of funding which do not depend upon gambling.

ADOPTED 1980

See Social Principles, ¶ 73.G, "UMC Position on Gambling."

The United Methodist Church's Position on Gambling

WHEREAS, the Social Principles state in part: "Gambling is a menace to society, deadly to the best interests of moral, social, economic, and spiritual life, and destructive of good government. As an act of faith and love, Christians should abstain from gambling. . . . Community standards and personal life styles should be such as would make unnecessary and undesirable the resort to commercial gambling, including public lotteries, as a recreation, as an escape, or as a means of producing public revenue or funds for support of charities or government"; and

WHEREAS, the number of organizations and governments using lotteries, raffles, and bingo as a revenue resource has dramatically increased recently; and

WHEREAS, high-stakes gambling has led to tragedy and the disruption of community life; and

WHEREAS, raffles and other types of gambling methods are used in some United Methodist Churches; and

WHEREAS, many other Christian denominations rely heavily upon the proceeds from raffles, lotteries, and other gambling devices as means of fund raising;

Be it therefore resolved, that The United Methodist Church reaffirm its position on gambling; and

Be it further resolved, that the appropriate general agencies continue to provide material to the local churches for study and action to combat gambling and aid persons addicted to gambling.

ADOPTED 1992

See Social Principles, ¶ 73.G, "Gambling."

Global Debt Crisis

I. *Introduction*

The growth of the global debt has precipitated a crisis for business and industry, church and schools, and, above all, children, women and men. Countries in Africa, Asia, the Pacific, Latin America and the Caribbean now owe more than one trillion dollars to Western banks, governments and international financial institutions. The burden of repayment and current strategies for managing the crisis have contributed to a decline in living standards, employment, health and rising death rates. Farmers and workers in industrialized countries also have suffered losses as exports of the goods they produce to debt-ridden developing nations have fallen. It is urgent that United Methodists everywhere strengthen their advocacy for the poor, the farmers and the workers so severely affected by the debt crisis.

II. Causes of the Debt Crisis

The causes of the debt crisis are complex. One of the roots of the crisis lies in the legacy of colonialism, which enriched colonizing countries and exploited the land, resources, and people of the colonies. In the post-colonial era, the nations of Africa, Asia, the Pacific, Latin America, and the Caribbean struggled to gain full control of their land and resources. But the trading system gave former colonial powers an advantage in controlling international markets.

Although most of the former colonies gained their political independence from the late 1800's through the 1960's, economic independence still eludes most of them. Most developing countries continue to export (sell) raw materials and import (buy) manufactured goods. The international trading system continues to favor exporters of manufactured goods, as prices of raw material exports tend to rise less rapidly than manufactured imports. This inequality has grown even worse in the last decades. In 1986 alone, the United Nations estimated that the developing world lost $94 billion to the developed world due to these unfavorable price movements.

This debt crisis escalated in the late 1960's and 1970's as a result of trade imbalances. The oil producing nations deposited billions of dollars in Western commercial banks. In turn, many banks aggressively marketed their loans to developing countries who were short on cash, facing high oil costs, and eager to borrow. Banks' normal loan review procedures were often abandoned in the rush to lend large amounts of money quickly.

Some of the loans to developing countries went to productive uses, such as water purification and sewage systems, education and health programs and subsidies for basic food staples. Many, however, went for purposes that had little to do with the needs of the majority. For example, loans went toward large projects such as nuclear power plants and dams, many of which were never finished or had dramatic human and environmental costs. Other loans ended up with rich individuals who, with the assistance of the banks, quietly transferred the money out of their country. In case after case, the vast majority of the people knew nothing about nor benefitted from the borrowing.

The lending bonanza ended abruptly in the early 1980's when the Western countries decided to clamp down on inflation and contracted their economies. This led to a worldwide recession, lowering the demand for and prices of Third World exports. Meanwhile, interest rates skyrocketed, adding dramatically to debt service costs for debtors. In August, 1982, Mexico launched what is known as the debt crisis by announcing it could no longer service its debt. Debt services payments became so high that many developing nations found themselves borrowing money just to cover interest payments on their loans.

When debtor nations run into serious trouble paying either their debt or at least the interest on their debt, they have few options but to turn to the International Monetary Fund (IMF), the lender of last resort. In return for emergency loans, the IMF has required debtor governments to adopt certain policies often referred to as an "austerity package." In such packages, debtor governments are usually required to cut wages, increase exports and cut imports, cut subsidies for farmers, and eliminate low prices for vital foodstuffs and reduce government spending on items such as health and education. While such measures are designed to restore a country's credit worthiness in the future, the immediate impact is to disproportionately hurt the poor. The burden of repayment has forced debtor nations to gear their economies further toward exports since the debt has to be repaid in hard currencies, such as the dollar. This tends to divert resources from production to meet local needs, and benefits foreign and local elites who dominate export industries.

As developing country economies stagnate due to the austerity programs, most U.S. banks have turned to new growth areas: U.S. consumers, especially through credit card and home equity borrowing, and U.S. businesses which are taking over other companies in record numbers.

Recently, the U.S. government has become the world's largest debtor to foreign creditors. In October, 1987, the U.S. foreign debt was $450 billion and growing weekly as the interest rates climbed. As the U.S. has joined the ranks of the debtor world, it becomes increasingly vulnerable to shifts in the international economy.

III. *Consequences of the Global Debt Crisis*

The costs of the debt crisis have been staggering. For example, national development policies, poor people and United Methodist mission partners have felt the impact in the following ways:

Impact on National Development Policies:

• The World Bank estimates that the combination of debt repayments and the reduction of new lending has resulted in a negative transfer of nearly $30 billion from poor countries to the industrialized countries in 1986 alone, in addition to money loss due to unfavorable prices. This negative transfer deprives the developing countries of needed capital investment and economic growth.

• The export drive to earn foreign exchange in order to repay the banks has pushed several developing countries into the production and export of military equipment. Other governments, in response to the growing unrest of their impoverished populations, have imported more military hardware in order to control their own people.

• The combination of IMF austerity programs and the use of foreign exchange to service developing countries' debts have prevented developing countries from purchasing goods and services from industrialized countries and undercut prices of agricultural and manufactured goods. Over a million U.S. workers lost their jobs as U.S. exports to Brazil, Mexico and other debtor nations were cut.

Impact on People:

• Trends of migration from impoverished rural areas to even more impoverished urban areas have grown as have unemployment, poverty, social unrest, destruction of democratic institutions.

• Outside lending to developing countries for projects such as water, sewage, health facilities, housing, education, and nutrition has diminished, while at the same time these countries have had to divert local funds from these projects to service their foreign debts.

• Poor people in developing countries have been dramatically affected by the austerity programs because they have no cushion in their living standards. They have been among the first to lose their jobs or have their wages reduced. Because they do not receive benefits, such as unemployment insurance, they have been profoundly affected by the elimination of subsidies which once kept basic staples within reach. Food prices have doubled or tripled overnight in some countries when the local currency has been devalued.

• According to the United Nations Children's Fund or UNICEF, the wrenching economic adjustments taking place this decade, particularly in Africa and Latin America, have led not only to more people living in absolute poverty, but also increasing inequity among social groups. In its 1987 publication, "Adjustment With a Human Face", UNICEF points to the prospect of a lost generation of children due to deteriorating nutritional status, increasing infant morality rates in some countries, and declining access to and quality of health and educational services thus far in the 1980's. For example, UNICEF found that in Jamaica, public schools and health clinics were closed due to budget cuts. In Ghana diseases presumed to be eradicated, such as yaws and yellow fever, have reemerged, and in Peru and the Philippines, deaths from tuberculosis and the incidence of other communicable diseases were on the rise. In Chile cases of typhoid fever and hepatitis have increased following cuts in government spending on drinking water and sanitation. In many parts of the developing world, UNICEF concludes, "Permanent damage has already been done to the physical and mental capacity of much of the future labor force." According to the Children's Defense Fund, the incidence of infectious mortality rates have increased among infants in the first 28 days of life.

• Even in industrialized nations, many family farmers and industrial workers have lost their means of livelihood. Many have lost jobs; many others have experienced reduction in wages and benefits, including denial of unemployment insurance. Whole communities have been threatened economically. Individuals have suffered psychologically, spiritually and physically.

Impact on Mission Partners:

• In the early 1980's the economic crisis impacted the churches so that many had to cut back mission outreach programs, freeze or in some cases cut back the salaries of pastors and lay workers. Some churches had totally to put aside general maintenance and upkeep of church buildings and property.

• In 1983 inflation in Zaire resulted in a 480% devaluation of its currency. The government drastically reduced its subsidies to medical and educational institutions overnight, personnel for support services were fired. Within the past three years, the government has virtually assigned the support and operation of schools and hospitals to the Church in Zaire.

• Inflation in Bolivia at one point passed 2,000 percent. Salaries of pastors dwindled from $150.00 U.S. a month to $10.00 U.S. This is in a country where a family of five needs at least $125.00 a month for food alone.

• The General Board of Global Ministries has received requests from Mozambique, Kenya and several other African countries for emergency grants to keep hospitals open which would have shut their doors due to lack of salaries for medical personnel, medical supplies and upkeep and maintenance of equipment and buildings. Even though Asia is not frequently in the international news for external debt problems, many Asian countries are in serious economic trouble. The deteriorating economic conditions of these Asian countries are impacting the mission and ministry of our partner churches. The churches in India, Malaysia, Indonesia and the Philippines have sought assistance from the General Board of Global Ministries to cope with their financial hardship in underwriting their programs and workers' salaries. These stories are being replicated throughout the Third World.

IV. *Biblical/Theological Background*

As Christians, we believe that all creation is a gift from God, that all people are created in God's image. We believe that every human being has personal worth and basic rights, including the right to affirm his or her dignity. We believe that when one of God's creatures is diminished, we all are diminished and thus our covenant with God is broken. We find many biblical references to indebtedness, especially in the Old Testament. The wealthy landowners of Israel lent money to the peasants who needed it because of their misfortune through drought, fire, floods, and for taxes. Because of the high interest rates and because the drought continued, they could not pay the debt or the interest. The peasants' first step was to sell their house and belongings, later their animals and land and finally themselves and their families. They had to work as slaves. The landowners added this money to the capital already invested in other projects, and thus continued to purchase land and to lend money. This pattern of accumulation of land and wealth was seen in the early biblical times and eventually led to the centralization of economic power and eventually enslaved even the Israelites.

Later the prophets, such as Isaiah, admonished the Israelites' behavior as they became selfish, more greedy and forgot the poor:

"You are doomed! You buy more houses and fields to add to those you already have. Soon there will be no place for anyone else to live and you alone will live in the land" (Isaiah 5:8).

Jesus Christ is proclaimed a new creation and new covenant. In him dividing walls of hostility are broken down and those who are divided are made one (Eph. 2). Jesus taught about the covenant relationship when he told the parable of the servant whose debt is generously forgiven, but deals harshly with those who owe him debts (Matt. 18:23-35). Such behavior is a violation of the kingdom and fails to understand Jesus' message that God's love is always tied to the love of the neighbor (Mk. 12:29-32).

The early church was committed to a covenant community as they shared their resources so that no one would be in need. Their concern about the use of wealth was that it not be used selfishly but to build community (Acts 2:44-47).

The problem of the global debt crisis today, as in the biblical communities, is that the debtors not only pay with their lives, but also with the lives of future generations. Part of God's creation has been diminished, the covenant broken. The covenant relationship demands justice.

V. *Principles to Guide Debt Crisis Solutions*

As Christians, our love of God and neighbor must be reflected by our actions within the global family. Thus we affirm the following policies and principles as needed in a just resolution to the debt crisis:

• As disciples of Christ we need to examine patterns of greed which may cause us as individuals and nations to become debtors and lenders. We encourage the development of patterns of giving our material wealth and our knowledge so that others are benefitted.

• The poor should not bear the burden of adjustment. Living standards of those least responsible and most vulnerable should not be sacrificed in order to meet external obligations. Developing countries should have the right to choose their own development paths with no military or economic interference from outside.

• The burden should be shared equitably among creditor institutions and the debtor governments, corporations and elites that incurred the debt.

• Factors adding to and perpetuating the debt problem but beyond the control of debtor countries—such as U.S. budget deficits, high interest rates, unfair commodity prices, and trade barriers—should be alleviated.

• Developing nations should not be forced to surrender their right to political or economic self-determination in exchange for relief.

• Debt relief should be fashioned in a way that benefits the poor and helps move debtors beyond debt repayment to development.

• Long-term solutions should promote a more just international economic system in order to prevent such crisis from recurring.

• Strong efforts should be made to encourage the easing of East-West tensions in order that military spending may be channeled to debt relief and humanitarian purposes.

VI. *Recommended Actions For The United Methodist Church Through its General Agencies and Local Congregations*

The United Methodist Church, as a covenant community committed to Christian discipleship and advocacy for the poor, must work toward "measures that would reduce the concentration of wealth in the hands of a few." Thus we specifically call upon The United Methodist Church through its general agencies and local congregations to

A. Continue to undergird mission partner churches and agencies through understanding their reality and responding to their needs as expressed in the programs of the General Board of Global Ministries.

B. Urge the General Boards of Church and Society and Global Ministries to work with annual conferences to become advocates for equitable resolutions of the global debt crisis which will protect the poor through public policy and corporate responsibility.

C. Challenge each local congregation to study the global debt crisis, using this resolution as the basic resource. To assist this process:

1. The General Board of Global Ministries shall facilitate speaking tours of Persons in Mission and other international guests to talk about the human side of the debt crisis and should develop audio- visual resources to help interpret the crisis.

2. The General Board of Global Ministries shall encourage study tours aimed at in depth study of the effect of the debt crisis and solutions coming from those affected.

3. The General Board of Discipleship, in cooperation with the General Boards of Church and Society and Global Ministries shall prepare appropriate curricula and study materials for all ages on the causes and affects of the global debt crisis.

4. United Methodist theological seminaries shall include Christian responsibility for economic justice, including the debt crisis, as a necessary part of education for ministry.

D. Challenge the General Boards of Church and Society and Global Ministries to conduct a study, reflection, action process on the effects of international speculation on the growing debt crises.

E. Strengthen public policy advocacy for reform of the international banking, trade, and corporate systems to ensure their accountability to the community as well as to shareholders.

F. Strengthen ecumenical and coalition work already being done on the debt crisis and economics.

G. Request the Council of Bishops with the cooperation and participation of the General Board of Global Ministries and other general agencies of the Church, to conduct hearings and to create major study documentation on the current global debt crisis and the international economic system.

H. Develop tours, curricula, study materials, seminary courses, ecumenical and coalition work, hearings and major study documentation. These recommended actions shall represent extensive research and include the benefits of borrowing and lending on individual, corporate and national levels, as well as the disadvantages and risks. They shall include reports on the standards of living in developing countries before and after the inceptions of international trade. Where appropriate, western systems of international economic relationships shall be compared with Asian systems. The preparation process shall include extensive consultation with United Methodist laity involved in international trade, banking, economic education, and the poor.

ADOPTED 1988

See Social Principles, ¶ 73, "Economic Justice."

Guidelines for Initating or Joining an Economic Boycott

Preamble

An economic boycott is understood to be a combined effort to abstain from the purchase or use of products or services provided by a targeted firm, government, or other agency. The purpose of a boycott is to persuade the targeted body to cease from certain practices judged to be unjust, and/or to perform certain practices deemed to be just.

Acknowledging "the boycott" as a legitimate Christian response to an identified social or economic injustice, we recommend the following criteria as a process for guiding the church and its agencies in decisions regarding boycott. This process includes the following steps:

> preparation;
> decision-making;
> monitoring;
> suspension/termination.

The decision-making body shall designate those persons who will perform the tasks of each step.

The twelve criteria are the minimal concerns to be addressed as a decisionmaking body secures information and data upon which to determine its action.

The questions following the criteria statements are not part of the criteria, but are given to help a decision-making body address specific areas of concern and secure information that will assist in its decision.

The gathered information and data are to be written and distributed to the decision-making body.

Clarifying Who May Call

Any local church, district or annual conference, general Church board or agency shall be empowered to initiate, participate in, monitor, and terminate a boycott in its own name. Such decision shall be made consistent with criteria established by General Conference.

Any of the above may request the General Conference to join it in the boycott in the names of The United Methodist Church. Only the

General Conference shall be empowered to initiate a boycott in the name of The United Methodist Church. It shall designate responsibility for monitoring and suspending and/or terminating such a boycott.

Preparation

I. Identify in writing the biblical and theological imperatives which address the issues involved in this particular conflict. How are the issues involved related to the purposes and mission of the decisionmaking body?

II. Document the social justice issues in the dispute through on-site investigation, interviews, hearings and study of literature, including input from:

A. each of the major parties in the dispute;

B. United Methodist sources, including the presiding bishop(s), leadership of the annual conferences, superintendent(s), and local church leadership (laity and clergy) in the region where the dispute or alleged injustice is occurring;

C. objective third parties.

1. How do the social justice issues affect various segments of society and the communities in the area?

2. What sources of political, economic, or social power does each party in the dispute or alleged injustice have?

3. How will a boycott affect a potential resolution of the situation?

4. Are the leaders in the dispute or grievance supported by the persons for whom they speak, and are they committed to nonviolent action?

5. What denominational reviews have been made on this issue?

6. What groups, agencies, or governmental bodies have been seeking resolution in the conflict?

III. Evaluate the conflict described by the gathered information in relation to the theological, ethical, and social principles of Christian tradition and The United Methodist Church.

1. Is intervention needed and what magnitude of response is appropriate to the scope of the injustice?

2. Is the desired end clearly specified?

IV. Generate a list of potential public and private means of intervention in the situation and evaluate the probable results of each.

1. What methods of mediation, dialogue, and negotiations have been attempted and evaluated?

2. Have these means of intervention been publicized and shared with connectional leadership in the region of the conflict and other constituencies?

3. Is the injustice of sufficient scope to warrant the mobilization of a boycott?

4. Is a boycott a more constructive and effective means of achieving justice than more coercive means?

5. What are likely to be the positive and negative consequences of a boycott?

6. What will the effects likely be in the local community?

7. Are the issues adequately clarified so as to provide support for a boycott?

8. How can negative stereotyping of contending parties be avoided?

V. Clearly state in writing the objectives potential boycott is intended to achieve.

1. How will these objectives be shared with the disputing parties?

2. Is it clear as to how the objectives of the potential boycott relate to other strategies being used by this or other church bodies?

3. Are these objectives in harmony with the theological, ethical, and social principles? (see I and III)

VI. Develop a plan and identify resources for carrying out a potential boycott, including mechanisms for:

A. communicating to church constituencies the objectives of the boycott, the issues as seen by the various parties, and the biblical, theological, and ethical imperatives for involvement;

B. informing disputing parties of an intention to call or participate in a boycott;

C. coordinating efforts with other United Methodist bodies, interfaith coalitions, and groups dealing with the issues;

D. monitoring the progress of the boycott (see crititeria VIII);

E. suspending/terminating the of the boycott when objectives are met (see criteria IX, X, XI);

F. developing ministries of reconciliation between aggrieved parties, during and following the boycott action.

1. What resources and plans have been made to insure that the potential boycott will be carried out effectively and responsibly?

2. Have the presiding bishop(s), council director(s), superintendent(s), pastors and membership in the region been afforded opportunity for participation in the development of this plan?

Decision

VII. On the basis of the information obtained in I-II above, decide whether a boycott action is merited.

1. What opportunity has been or will be provided for thorough consideration and debate of the issues?

2. Why is this the best time for this decision-making body to enter the boycott?

3. Is the boycott likely to achieve the stated objectives and assist in resolution of the dispute?

Monitoring

VIII. Designate a group of persons, including church representatives from the local area affected, who will monitor the boycott. Monitoring shall include:

A. regular evaluation and reporting of progress toward stated objective;

B. regular written reporting of such progress to the local area affected and to the constituencies of the decision-making bodies through appropriate denominational channels;

C. reporting substantial changes in the conditions under which the boycott is being carried out;

D. a process for issuing public statements;

E. coordination with designated coalitions and interfaith groups.

Suspension/Termination

IX. In those cases where circumstances have changed, making it unclear whether the objectives of the boycott are being met, in consultation with the designated coalition and/or participating d   groups that are coordinating the boycott action, the decision-making body, or its designate, may call for suspension of the boycott while monitoring and evaluation continues.

X. When the clearly stated written objectives of the boycott have been met, in consultation with the designated coalition and/or participating groups that are coordinating boycott action, the decision-making body or its designate shall terminate boycott participation.

XI. Notification of suspension/termination shall be made in writing to all parties in the dispute and all constituencies of the decision-making body.

XII. Following this notification, monitoring of compliance with objectives and ministries of reconciliation shall be continued by the decision-making body for a responsible period of time.

ADOPTED 1988

See Social Principles, ¶ 73, "Infant Formula Abuse."

Investment Ethics

The United Methodist Church and its predecessor denominations have a long history of witness for justice in the economic order. John Wesley and early Methodists, for instance, were staunchly opposed to the slave trade, to smuggling, and to conspicuous consumption. In fact, John Wesley refused to drink tea because of its relationship to the slave trade. Social creeds adopted by our predecessor churches, beginning in 1908, stressed social justice in the economic world, with special attention to the exploitation of child labor and inhumanely long working hours.

Throughout this century our church has promoted decent working conditions and the right to organize and bargain collectively, and opposed discrimination in the workplace on the basis of race, ethnic background, gender, age, or handicapping conditions. Historically our tradition has opposed church investments in companies manufacturing liquor or tobacco products or promoting gambling.

Since the 1960s our denomination and its predecessors have built a solid record expressing our ethics in our investment decisions. United Methodist agencies and conferences fought against the manufacture of napalm and were involved in the social-justice issues raised by religious shareholders. In the mid 1970s the General Council on

Finance and Administration (GCFA) began issuing official social-responsibility guidelines for general church investments.

While the issue of economic sanctions against *apartheid* in South Africa has engaged us more than any other, United Methodist agencies, affiliated institutions, conferences, congregations, and individual members have brought the church's Christian witness to business in relation to numerous issues, including employment discrimination, environmental preservation, militarism, nuclear weapons production, and infant formula abuse.

We affirm that all financial resources of the church and its members are God-given resources, to be held in trust for use or investment in ways which promote the reign of God on earth.

Further, we recognize that every investment has ethical dimensions. Financial investments have consequences which are both fiscal and social. We believe social justice and social usefulness must be given consideration together with financial security and financial yield in the investment of funds by United Methodist Church agencies and affiliated institutions and congregations as well as individual United Methodists. Socially responsible investing by Christian institutions and individuals must take account of both sets of considerations.

Our church's witness through investments has taken three forms, each of which may be employed with the others. They are:

1. *Avoidance by Divestment.* This policy prohibits investment in enterprises that have policies or practices which are so morally reprehensible that investment in these companies is not tolerated by the church. Our denomination traditionally has avoided investments in liquor, tobacco, and gambling. Many church investors have refused to invest in major military contractors, companies with nuclear weapons contracts, or companies doing business in South Africa under *apartheid*. In some cases, they have divested of such companies, making public their action as a moral statement.

2. *Affirmative Choice.* This strategy is to choose intentionally enterprises for investment based on careful consideration of return, both in social values and in social justice as well as financial security and monetary profit. For United Methodist investors, the Social Principles and the *Book of Resolutions* delineate the social goals to which we expect all our investments to make a positive contribution. But with certain affirmative investments we may seek a very specific

social outcome, such as the construction of affordable housing, the renewal of a particular neighborhood, or the expansion of business ownership to those traditionally excluded.

3. *Shareholder Advocacy*. The practices of corporations in which the church invests may fall short of the moral standards expressed in the Social Principles and the *Book of Resolutions*. Responsible Christian investing includes seeking to change company policies for the better. Church investors have, as shareholders of corporations, engaged corporate management in a great variety of ways, from gentle persuasion to public pressure, from dialogue to voting proxies to filing shareholder resolutions. In many cases corporate policies have changed as a result.

Policy and Implementation of Policy

1. The policy goals of the General Conference of The United Methodist Church, its general agencies, and entities under its control shall be:

A. To invest as much as possible in entities that are making a positive contribution to the communities, societies, and world on which they have impact and to realization of the goals outlined in the Social Principles and the *Book of Resolutions* of our church.

B. To employ this combination of socially responsible approaches that contribute to economic justice and corporate responsibility:

1. Avoidance by non-purchase or divestment of holdings in companies which:

a. Produce tobacco products or alcoholic beverages, or manage or own gambling establishments, or have as their primary business the production, distribution, or sale of pornographic material;

b. Rank among the top 100 Department of Defense (DOD) contractors (those receiving the largest volume of prime contract awards) for the past three years; and have DOD contracts larger than 10 percent of sales for voting securities and 5 percent of sales for nonvoting securities; the GCFA shall publish the listing of the top 100 DOD contractors annually;

c. Make components for nuclear explosive devices; or

d. Manufacture chemical or biological warfare materials.

2. Affirmative investing in companies, banks, funds, or ventures which are seeing specific targeted social goals upon which the church places high value, such as those which:

a. Encourage recycling and use recycled products;

b. Work within legally imposed discharge limits for toxic chemicals, noise, and water temperature;

C. Do not sell chemicals that would be banned in the company's country of origin;

d. Invest in low-income housing;

e. Invest in companies which have positive records in hiring and promoting women and racial ethnic persons;

f. Are companies owned by women and racial ethnic persons.

3. Shareholder advocacy through which the agency exercises its rights as shareholder to persuade corporations to end irresponsible behavior or live up to high moral standards by using any combination of the following approaches:

• Letter of inquiry or expression of its position to management.
• Dialogue with management.
• Voting proxies.
• Soliciting votes for a particular reason.
• Soliciting or co-sponsoring resolutions for votes at stockholder meetings.
• Speaking at stockholder meetings.
• Legal action.
• Publicity.
• Working in coalitions with other concerned shareholders.
• Petitioning the SEC or Congress for changes in the proxy rules.

C. To maintain and promote economic pressure against South Africa by both divestment and shareholder advocacy until such time as *apartheid* is abolished and the vote is given to persons of all races, or those in the forefront of the struggle have concluded that the time has come to normalize relations with a new South Africa.

D. To seek opportunities to commend corporations publicly for socially responsible behavior and for excellence on social issues which are major concerns of The United Methodist Church.

E. To consider using investment portfolio managers and funds which specialize in corporate social responsibility screening.

2. The General Council on Finance and Administration is assigned responsibility by the *Book of Discipline* for preparing and distributing the Investment Guidelines that must be used by all general agencies receiving general church funds, including social responsibility guidelines. The council shall periodically review and update these

guidelines as needed, inviting the counsel of the agencies and other interested sectors of the church. The council encourages the active involvement of investing agencies in the overview of socially responsible investing described in this policy.

3. All general agencies receiving general church funds shall file a copy of their investment policy with the General Council of Finance and Administration. It shall be available upon request to any interested member of the church.

4. These policy goals are strongly recommended to all the institutions affiliated with The United Methodist Church and any of their entities, and to the annual conferences and local churches and any funds of foundations related to them. It is also recommended that a copy of their social responsibility investment guidelines be available upon request by any United Methodist Church member.

5. Where financial considerations preclude immediate divestment of securities held in violation of the above policy goals, boards, agencies, and institutions of The United Methodist Church shall develop a plan for meeting the criteria which will bring them into compliance no later than the 1996 General Conference.

6. These policy goals are also strongly recommended to all individual United Methodist investors and users of financial services.

ADOPTED 1992

See Social Principles, ¶ 73.

National Incomes Policy

Many Americans live today under economic conditions which do not permit them to meet their basic needs. This situation is deplorable because it is not necessary. The economic productivity of our society, instead of meeting the needs of all its people, serves the interest of special groups. The present programs for increasing employment are inadequate to meet the need. Likewise, various income transfer programs, such as public welfare, unemployment insurance, and even Social Security itself, have failed to make possible an adequate minimum standard of existence. While a national program of income maintenance is not a substitute for a full employment policy, neither is a full employment policy a substitute for an incomes policy. Both programs are needed, and if one or both are missing, we shall continue to block the development of the maximum productive skills of a tragically large number of citizens. Wage standards are needed which provide a living wage for all workers. It is also necessary to broaden and improve social welfare services.

Our present economic system functions imperfectly. It is the responsibility of society to develop new institutions which more adequately fulfill human rights—jobs, food, clothing, housing, education, and health care. As Christians we have the obligation to work with others to develop the moral foundation for public policies which will provide every family with the minimum income needed to participate as responsible and productive members of society.

We, as Christians, also recognize our obligation to work with others to develop in each person an attitude of responsible stewardship of time, talent, and resources that will enable the maximum number of families to be self-reliant and economically independent to the greatest possible extent.

Some basic objectives of a strategy for economic justice are:

1. A return to a full employment policy with the federal, state, and local government as the employers of the last resort.

2. A guaranteed minimum annual income sufficient for every family living in the United States based on the Bureau of Labor Statistics' lower budget.

3. Supportive social services in the fields of education, health, housing, job training, and particularly adequate, comprehensive child development and day-care services for all children, especially those of the poor and low-income groups.

4. Improvement and expansion of the food stamp program, school breakfast and lunch programs, and the creation of new means to ensure that no person be hungry in this society of abundance.

We call upon our churches and the general boards and agencies:

1. To study the various methods for providing every individual and family an income capable of supporting human life in dignity and decency.

2. To participate in the development and implementation of a national income policy which best fulfills the following criteria:

a) Designed to provide a means to an income adequate for living and available to all as a matter of right.

b) Adequate to maintain health and human well-being and adjusted to changes in the cost of living.

c) Administered so as to extend coverage to all persons in need.

d) Developed in a manner which will respect the freedom of persons to manage their own lives, increase their power to choose their own careers, and enable them to participate in meeting personal and community needs.

e) Designed to reward rather than penalize productive activity.

f) Designed in such a way that existing socially desirable programs and values are conserved and enhanced.

g) Federally standardized, taking into consideration local and regional differences in cost of living.

ADOPTED 1976

See Social Principles, ¶ 73, "Economic Justice," "Pay Equity in the U.S.A.," "Special Needs of Farm Workers."

Nuclear Weapons Production at the General Electric Company

The General Electric Company (G.E.) is an industry leader in the production of nuclear weapons and delivery systems, as well as a powerful force in the aggressive promotion of nuclear-weapons development through the activities of its 150-person lobbying office in Washington, D.C., and other company activities.

Public concern about the crucial role of G.E. in nuclear production has generated a growing grass-roots movement, calling upon G.E. to cease development of weapons of mass destruction. This movement is coordinated by INFACT and involves an increasing number of religious and health-care institutions.

A powerful demonstration of United Methodist concern has been the decision of the United Methodist General Board of Pensions in July, 1991, to divest its General Electric stock, valued at more than $23 million, by December 31, 1992, because of G.E.'s continued leadership and involvement in the manufacture of nuclear and conventional weaponry. Therefore, The United Methodist Church:

a) encourages all its related institutions, church bodies, and members to engage in dialogue with G.E. managers in their local areas regarding our Social Principles statement on war and peace, as well as related statements in the *Book of Resolutions,* and to urge General Electric to cease nuclear-weapons production and promotion and to convert to peace-oriented manufacturing;

b) asks all United Methodist-related institutions to establish purchasing policies that take into account the church's Social Principles and resolutions on disarmament, nuclear weapons, and peace and, specifically, to consider G.E.'s role in nuclear-weapons production and promotion as a factor in the decision whenever a purchase might include a G.E. product;

c) encourages all local churches, annual conferences, and other agencies to follow the good example of the Board of Pensions in divesting its G.E. stock and notifying G.E. of the reasons for its action;

d) instructs the United Methodist Association of Health and Welfare Ministries and Board of Higher Education and Ministry to communicate, interpret, and advocate for this concern with their affiliated institutions; and

e) directs the General Board of Church and Society to communicate this resolution to General Electric, serve as continuing advocate of the United Methodist position within The United Methodist Church and with General Electric, and monitor the implementation of this resolution for report at the next General Conference.

ADOPTED 1992

See Social Principles, ¶¶ 73 and 75, "Nuclear Disarmament: The Zero Option," "The United Methodist Church and Peace."

Pay Equity in the U.S.A.

I. Introduction

Pay equity or comparable worth (the terms are used interchangeably) is a remedy for wage discrimination. Its goal is to eliminate sex and race discrimination from the wage setting process. Pay equity ensures that compensation is based on relevant factors, such as skill, responsibility and working conditions. Simply stated, the concept means that if the same amount of effort, skill, responsibility, experience, and education is required to do two different jobs, then the persons doing those jobs should be paid the same.

II. Biblical & Theological Background

Our biblical faith affirms the inherent value and equal worth in God's sight of every person; it requires the faithful to be advocates for those who have suffered oppression and discrimination. In his ministry, Jesus continually lifted up women, poor people and social outcasts as deserving not only of special loving care but also of having the wrongs done them redressed by the community. When asked to read a passage from the prophet Isaiah in the synagogue, Jesus chose one which called the faithful to release prisoners, to restore sight to the blind, to set the oppressed at liberty and "to proclaim the acceptable year of the Lord" (Luke 4:16-19). This "acceptable year" or "year of the Lord's favor" is believed by scholars to refer to the year of Jubilee, a time when slaves were set free, debts were repaid and land and wealth were equitably redistributed (Lev. 25:10-17). It is significant that Jesus chose this passage to announce his ministry. An additional passage which speaks to the issue of workers' rights to fair compensation is I Timothy 5:18: "Those who work deserve their pay."

United Methodists have tried to be faithful to this mandate to protect the powerless and to restore the oppressed to their rightful place of dignity and equality. We have understood this responsibility to extend into the economic life of the community. In our Social Principles, we "assert the right of members of racial and ethnic minorities to equal opportunity in employment and promotion" (III. C.) and we "affirm the right of women to equal treatment in employment, responsibility, promotion and compensation" (III. F.). A 1984 General Conference resolution on the "Equal Rights of Women" committed United Methodists to "monitor public policies and practices which affect unemployment, pay inequity, inequality of opportunity . . . " It also calls us to "research policies that discriminate on the basis of gender and to advocate changes that enable equality of rights and opportunities." Taking these commitments and responsibilities seriously leads us to embrace the concept of pay equity.

III. The Context

Most women and most persons of color in the United States are still concentrated in low paying jobs with limited opportunities for advancement. These jobs have historically been underpaid and undervalued precisely because they have been held primarily by women and persons of color.

Women's earnings are an indispensible share of the incomes of more and more families. Families headed by women are the fastest growing segment of the poverty population and now represent 75 percent of all individuals in poverty. Many mothers must support their families on their incomes alone; a significant portion of these mothers are women of color. Thus, the elimination of wage-based sex and race discrimination in the labor force is an important element in ending the "feminization of poverty." Because men of color as well as women are at the lower end of the wage earning scale, pay equity is not only a "women's issue" but a quality of life family issue as well.

Women's involvement in the work force has increased dramatically during the last decade.

In 1985, women accounted for nearly half of all full-time workers.

It is projected that 67% of all new work force entrants between 1987 and 2000 will be female. The average full-time woman worker earned 64 cents for every dollar earned by a man in 1985. The wage gap was even greater for black and Hispanic women, who earned, respectively, 59 cents and 55 cents for every dollar earned by men. If the trend of low pay for jobs held primarily by women continues; it is estimated that by the year 2000 virtually all of the poverty population will be women and their children. While part of this gap can be attributed to differences in education, experience and job tenure, most of these wage gaps are due exclusively to occupational segregation and sex discrimination in the labor force. The value of a job to society has little or no current correlation to remuneration; sanitation workers continue to earn far more than child care workers.

Despite the fact that "equal pay for equal work" is the law (Equal Pay Act of 1963, Title VIII of the Civil Rights Act), the wage gap persists. This is due in large measure to the fact there are few white men in women dominated jobs; women and men must work in the same job in order to determine if there is a violation of the Equal Pay Act. It is at this point that there is a breakdown in the argument that legal remedies for wage discrimination already exist.

Two other frequently cited arguments against the concept of pay equity are that it will interfere with the free market law of supply and demand, and that its cost will be prohibitive. In fact, most current wage discrepancies can hardly be attributed to impartial market forces. Two current examples are: 1) a large city which pays its police dispatchers (mostly black women) several thousand dollars less than it pays its predominately white male fire dispatchers and 2) the fact that secretaries, who are in short supply, are paid less than truck drivers, who are in considerable surplus. On the cost question, public and private employers who have voluntarily implemented pay equity policies consistently report that it has not been as expensive as predicted and that, in fact, they have avoided prolonged litigation and costly settlements. It is well to remember that similar predictions of economic chaos preceded the adoption of minimum wage and child labor laws.

Pay equity is a growing national movement; support for it is steadily increasing across the country through collective bargaining, legislation, voluntary initiatives and litigation. Pay equity initiatives are moving at a rapid pace at state levels and significant gains have been made in the private sector as well. Well over 100 governmental units, both state and local, have taken actions on pay equity. Over 47 states are doing or have already completed studies to find if there is sex and race discrimination in how they pay their employees, and 20 states have begun to implement pay adjustment. The national conferences of both governors and mayors have adopted resolutions supporting pay equity. Some employers in the private sector have already voluntarily taken actions to remove wage discrimination from their work place, thus avoiding the time, expense and conflict resulting from lack of action. A 1984 survey by Marttila and Kiley of Boston revealed that a majority of U.S. workers think pay equity is necessary to remove sex and race bias in wages. There is a trend among private employers to support the elimination of wage discrimination between different jobs as "good business" and not inconsistent with remaining competitive in the marketplace.

Therefore be it resolved that we as United Methodists endorse the principle of pay equity, whereby wage structures in the church and in the public and private sectors are based on unbiased evaluation of the jobs' requirements and value to the employer

1. We call upon the General Council on Finance and Administration to evaluate internal wage structures and practices of general agencies in light of the principle of pay equity and to include this assessment in its regular monitoring of equal employment opportunity compliance (The Book of Discipline, Para. 907.7b.).
2. We call upon The United Methodist Church at all levels to:

a. Evaluate all internal church wage structures in light of the principle of pay equity and move with dispatch to correct any inequities;

b. Provide educational resources which will assist the church in understanding the issue of pay equity;

c. Monitor relevant federal, state and municipal legislation and advocate policies which lead to adoption of pay equity as a national standard;

d. Exercise shareholder rights by voting shares in favor of voluntary implementation of pay equity programs in companies which do not currently have them;

e. Encourage individual United Methodists to work for voluntary implementation of pay equity in their places of business;

f. Monitor and advocate for the strengthening of affirmative action and antidiscrimination efforts at national, state and local levels.

ADOPTED 1988

See Social Principles, ¶ 73, "Economic Justice," "Rights of Workers."

Rights of Workers

I. Concern of the Church

The concern of The United Methodist Church for the dignity of workers and the rights of employees to act collectively has been stated in its Social Principles (1984). Both employer and union are called to "bargain in good faith within the framework of the public interest" (73 B). However, given the new international economic setting, it is necessary to reaffirm once again the church's position.

Genesis teaches that human beings, as the image of God, have an innate dignity (1:27). It also declares that people are to work the land and replenish the world (1:28, 2:25). Work is one of the ways through which human beings exercise the self-creativity given by their creator.

Based on the dignity of both work and the worker, the church teaches that society should provide employment under safe and decent conditions so that the dignity of the workers can be elevated and their creativity exercised. (*Book of Resolutions, 1984*, pp. 237, 431).

In Scripture the emphasis on human dignity is complemented by a demand for justice. Justice, as taught by the Jubilee theme of Leviticus

(Chapter 25) and Deuteronomy (Chapter 15) and in the cries of the prophets, cautions against concentrated economic power, and demands that the poor be reinstated into the body of society as brother and sister. Jesus, in his parables of the rich man and Lazarus (Luke 16), the final judgment (Matthew 25), and the rich fool (Luke 12), affirms a similar message.

Scriptural teaching mandates that society and its institutions are to be structured so that the weaker and poorer groups can participate in the shaping of society and their own futures.

II. Characteristics of the International Economy

The economies of nations are becoming increasingly internationalized. Within that process, however, there are currents that pose serious threat to both the rights and the dignity of workers. Those currents include the following:

A. International Corporate Competition

The emerging world economy is dominated by transnational corporations and banks whose activities are often coordinated with their "home" governments. At times these corporations compete vigorously around the globe. At other times they conspire together to maintain shares of the market. Since they control a considerable portion of the world's resources, technologies, and investment capital, they are able to locate their facilities where an advantage of profit or market power can be gained. Other considerations, including the rights of labor and community, are made subservient to the corporation's drive for a more competitive profit.

B. Transformation of Industries and Jobs

New technologies are transforming the structures and the nature of businesses everywhere. Production technologies redefine jobs into widely disparate classes: some workers are upgraded to higher skills and professions while, at the same time, many are downgraded to levels of minimum skill, or their jobs eliminated altogether.

C. Increasing Centralization of Decision-making.

The speed and accuracy by which information is transmitted around the globe have made data processing and information services the largest and fastest growing sector of some economies.

These technologies make it possible for corporate headquarters in one location to control an industrial-financial empire that extends across the nations of the world. The capacity of executives to swiftly transfer business out of one place and into another may de-industralize Pittsburg, Pennsylvania, for example, while at the same time industrializing a remote village like Pohang, Korea.

In both situations, the basic decisions are made by corporations and/or governments with little or no input from the workers or citizens in either place.

III. Effects on Labor

The combined effect of these characteristics on labor has been immense:

A. In economic systems, labor is considered primarily as a cost of production. Its human aspects are often ignored. Modern technologies make it feasible for industries constantly to relocate in search of cheaper labor, thus pitting workers of various countries against each other and depressing wages and benefits in richer and poorer nations. Together corporate competition and skill-reducing technology tend to downgrade the humanity of labor.

B. The centralization of decision-making power under the control of a few corporate board members and executives usurps the rights of employees and communities to have a say in what determines their lives. In some countries, worker organizations are intentionally weakened and/or repressed altogether.

Some labor leaders have themselves adopted the thought patterns and values of big business, thus impeding the workers' ability to respond to the challenges of the corporation. Union support from the rank and file is weakened and solidarity is eroded. Worker loyalty is transferred to the company, or themselves, rather than to fellow workers.

C. A third effect of the internationalizing economy is the fracturing of many jobs into temporary, part-time, subcontracted and cottage-industry jobs which are claiming larger numbers of employees. The impacts are many:

1. wages of regular, full-time jobs are pressured downward, or the jobs are eliminated altogether;
2. benefits are reduced or eliminated;
3. low-paying jobs keep people and families in poverty;
4. women and children are increasingly employed in these jobs, thus perpetuating a poverty class with sex and race characteristics.

D. As the internationalizing process has taken place, labor unions have at times failed to uphold solidarity among the world's workers. Some unions have adopted thought patterns and values that impede their ability to adjust to today's transformation in jobs and industrial organization. Consequently, established unionism is often irrelevant to workers in many new sectors of the world's economy, and even in traditionally organized sectors rank and file members are at times alienated from their leadership.

E. In less industrialized countries, foreign businesses are induced to come by promises that there will be no labor union problems, workers being kept docile by threats of dismissal and/or police suppression.

IV. Policy Directions for the Church

Given the circumstances of an international economy, and the principles taught by Scripture and the Social Principles, The United Methodist Church should advocate for the following:

A. Support for internationally recognized worker rights based on ILO Conventions. (Places of employment should guarantee to the workers a safe work environment, fair compensations, just supervision and the right to representation by a worker's organization of their own choosing.)

B. Recognition of these rights of workers by international banks and corporations, and the obligation to practice them in their places of employment.

C. Acceptance of union responsibility to look beyond their own organizational benefit and be more active in organizing women, temporary employees, people of color, and others disadvantaged in the labor market.

D. Full participation of rank and file members in union decision making. Unions should defend the rights of the organized and unorganized and develop global solidarity across nations and industries.

E. Government passage and enforcement of legislation that protects workers' rights and guarantees collective bargaining.

V. *Actions by the Church*

Given the above policies, The United Methodist Church should take the following actions:

A. All churches and church agencies shall respect their employees' rights to good working conditions, fair compensation and collective action.

B. The General Board of Church and Society and the General Board of Global Ministries, in cooperation with Methodist churches in other countries, shall communicate to domestic and international banks and corporations the church's:

1) concern over low wages and inadequate benefits;
2) distress at unsafe and health-threatening working conditions.
3) expectation that employees have the freedom to organize unions of their own choosing without employer interference;
4) call for collective bargaining to be carried our promptly and in good faith.

C. The General Board of Church and Society and the General Board of Global Ministries, in conjunction with Annual Conference and local church leaders, shall sponsor religion and labor programs that: a) study the theological significance of work and employment; and, b) initiate cooperation with workers and labor unions about how best to protect and enhance the rights of all workers, especially those of women, children, and people of color.

D. The General Board of Church and Society and the General Board of Global Ministries, in conjunction with Annual Conference and local church leaders, shall support legislation that:

1) protects the health and safety of employees at their work place;
2) guarantees workers the right to freely organize unions of their own choosing;

3) facilitates the negotiating process for the signing of collective contracts between management and union;

4) controls and monitors plant relocations and closings.

ADOPTED, 1988

See Social Principles, ¶ 73, "Economic Justice," "Extension of the Right to Organize and Bargain Collectively."

Safety and Health in Workplace and Community

Just as biblical religion affirms that God is involved in the healing of individuals (Genesis 20:17; Matthew 8), so also does God's covenant with his people include the mandate to protect the community from dangers that threaten the health of the people (Leviticus 14:33–15:14). At the beginning of Methodism, John Wesley provided medicine and medical treatment at no cost to the poor in London and Bristol. In addition to pioneering free dispensaries in England, Wesley emphasized prevention of illness. In his book "Primitive Physic" he dealt with nutrition and hygiene, as well as treatment of the sick.

The first Social Creed, adopted by the 1908 General Conference of The Methodist Episcopal Church (North), declared that workers must be protected "from dangerous machinery, occupational diseases, injuries, and mortality," and that working conditions must be regulated to safeguard the physical and moral health of the community. Today as well, the Church is called to declare that the health of every individual is part of community health, including safe and healthy conditions in places where people work. The Church has a responsibility to pronounce clearly the implications of God's law of love for human health. Where human life and health are at stake, economic gain must not take precedence.

A. *Public Health Hazards*

Public health hazards originate from a variety of sources, including organisms (e.g., bacteria, fungi, and viruses), physical conditions (e.g., hazardous machinery and excessive noise), toxic chemicals, and radiation. Some public health hazards, such as veneral disease and lead poisoning, were known to our biblical forebearers and to other ancient civilizations. Other hazards such as toxic chemical wastes are products of the past century's rapid technological development. Such

443

hazards can produce infectious diseases, disabling injuries, incapacitating illnesses, and death. Toxic substances and related hazards such as ionizing radiation threaten the exposed individual to additional hazards such as cancer and sterility, and also threaten future generations with birth defects and gene mutations.

A single toxic substance may have wide-range usage from the home to the workplace to the environment. It may persist for years in the form of dangerous wastes and residues. The human consequences of such public health hazards are vast. In 1977, work-related injuries claimed 5.3 million victims, 4,760 of whom died.[1] In 1976, compensation payments of $7.5 billion were made for work-related deaths, disease, and disability.[2] Environmental and occupational cancer are estimated to represent 20-38 percent of all cancer.[3] One substance alone, asbestos, is expected to claim the lives of 1.6 million of the 4 million individuals heavily exposed since World War II, including a substantial number of shipyard workers.[4] These deaths, diseases, and disabilities have an additional impact on the affected individuals and their families in terms of medical costs, lost earning capacity, pain, suffering, and grief. When long-term diseases such as cancer, birth defects, and gene mutations are involved, the human consequences extend far beyond the immediately perceived hazards of infection or injury.

B. *Declaration*

Public health is dependent on effective prevention and active protection before illness or injury have occurred. To fulfill God's commandment to love our neighbor as ourselves, we should support action to protect each individual's health and to preserve the health of the community. To this end we declare:

---

[1] Statistical Abstract of the U.S., 1978, U.S. Department of Commerce, 99th edition. Paperback, 1057 pp. P. 78, No. 112, 5,203 deaths from industrial type accidents shown for 1976.
[2] Ibid. P. 354, Table No. 558, "Workmen's Compensation Payments . . ."
[3] "Estimates of the Fraction of Cancer in the United States Related to Occupational Factors," prepared by National Cancer Institute, National Institute of Environmental Health Sciences, National Institute for Occupational Safety and Health, Mimeographed Report, September 14, 1978, p. 24.
[4] "Estimates of the Fraction of Cancer in the United States Related to Occupational Factors," prepared by National Cancer Institute, National Institute of Environmental Health Sciences, National Institute for Occupational Safety and Health, Mimeographed Report, September 15, 1978, p. 9.

1. Every individual, including those with handicapping conditions and disabilities, has a right to a safe and healthful environment unendangered by a polluted natural world, a hazardous workplace, an unsanitary community, dangerous household products, unsafe drugs, and contaminated food. This human right must take precedence over property rights. Moreover, the necessary preservation of human life and health must not be sacrificed or diminished for economic gain. It is unconscionable that anyone should profit from conditions which lead to the disease, disability, or death of another. Furthermore, the essential protection of the physical and moral quality of human life must not be compromised by competing considerations of capital investment and return, or diminished by society's insistence on affluence, luxury, and convenience.

2. Public health hazards must be *prevented* in order to avoid the serious individual and community consequences of injury, illness, and untimely death, including disability, physical pain, mental anguish, lost human potential, family stress, and the diversion of scarce medical resources.

3. Public health hazards to future generations such as toxic substances and wastes which produce birth defects and gene mutations must be prevented in order to avoid a legacy of disease, disability, and untimely death. No generation has the right to assume risks that potentially endanger the viability of future life.

4. The public health risks of technological development must be fully and openly assessed before new technologies are introduced into the home, the work-place, the community, or the environment. Medical research should be required to give high priority to the identification of hazardous substances and processes.

5. The preservation and protection of human life from public health hazards is a fundamental responsibility of government which must be maintained by active public support and adequate public funds. Efficient administration and effective enforcement of public health laws including those governing the use and disposal of toxic substances should be supported at all levels of government.

6. Preventive health care should be taught in educational institutions to persons in every age group at every level of society. Health professionals in all branches of medicine and public health, and those in related fields, should be educated in practicing preventive medicine, implementing community preventive health

strategies, and assisting patients in the adoption of healthy lifestyles. Programs should be implemented that educate and inform consumers and workers about physical, chemical, biological, and radiological hazards of products, services, working conditions, and environment contaminants.

ADOPTED 1980

See Social Principles, ¶¶ 72 and 73, "Economic Justice," "Universal Access to Health Care in the U.S. and Related Territories."

Self-Help Efforts of Poor People

We note with satisfaction the recent upsurge of community-based, cooperative, self-help efforts on the part of groups of low-income rural people in all parts of the United States. However, we recognize that such efforts do not offer a total solution to the problem of rural poverty or obviate the necessity for massive efforts on the part of government and private sector to combat rural poverty in other ways.

The church of Jesus Christ is concerned for the fulfillment of whole persons in community. Economic development which produces human and community development is to be preferred over other forms of economic activity. In the cooperative and other community-based enterprise of poor people we find a combination of economic gain, personal fulfillment, and community development.

We applaud and we will support these indigenous and cooperative self-help efforts because we see in them social and spiritual as well as economic values of great consequence.

We call upon our general boards, jurisdictions, area offices, annual conferences, districts, local churches and members to seek ways to become acquainted with the self-help efforts of poor people in rural areas and to help them with grants, credit, technical assistance, and training facilities.

We call upon federal and state governments, private industry, banks, colleges and universities, foundations, and all other public and private agencies to provide massive resources, both financial and technical, to assist the valiant efforts of low-income rural people to solve their own problems through self-help.

ADOPTED 1976

See Social Principles, ¶ 73, "Rights of Workers," "Economic Justice."

Sexual Harassment in Church and Society in the U.S.A.

All human beings, both male and female, are created in the image of God, and thus have been made equal in Christ. From the beginning God intended us to live out our equality in relation with one another. Yet, in our human brokenness we have given greater value and power to men than to women. Jesus was sent into this world that we might experience whole relationships with each other and God. "There is neither Jew nor Greek, there is neither slave nor free, there is neither male nor female; for you are all one in Christ Jesus" (Galatians 3:28, RSV). Still both the church and the society condone and ignore personal and institutional abuse of women.

Sexual harassment is any unwanted sexual advance or demand, either verbal or physical, which is perceived by the recipient as demeaning, intimidating or coercive. Sexual harassment must be understood as an exploitation of a power relationship rather than as an exclusively sexual issue. Sexual harassment also includes the creation of a hostile or abusive working environment resulting from discrimination on the basis of gender. The successful 1986 Supreme Court case of *Meritor Savings Bank et al v. Vinson* substantially broadened the legal definition of sexual harassment, holding that it is a violation of federal anti-discrimination laws and saying that companies may be liable for the misbehavior of one employee. This decision upheld the 1981 guidelines of the Equal Employment Opportunity Commission (EEOC), which holds employers liable for all forms of sexual harassment, including co-worker harassment and harassment from clients and customers. From the EEOC guidelines it is clear that the employer bears an affirmative responsibility to maintain a work-place free from sexual harassment, to investigate quickly and impartially any charge of sexual harassment and to take action against all offenders.

At the work-place, at one extreme, sexual harassment is the demand for sexual compliance coupled with the threat of firing if the person refuses.

On the other, it is being forced to work in an environment in which, through various means, the person is subjected to stress or made to feel humiliated because of one's gender. Sexual harassment is behavior which becomes coercive because it occurs in the employment context, thus threatening both a person's job satisfaction and security. This critical problem affects all persons regardless of job category or description, age, race, economic or educational background.

It affects women who are church professionals as well as those who work in secular occupations. Sexual harassment has been documented in United Methodist churches, agencies and institutions, including seminaries. It is becoming clear as statistics emerge that whatever their occupation, women share a common problem—the possibility of sexual harassment. Men can also be the victims of sexual harassment.

National surveys done by the Working Women's Institute, *Redbook Magazine* and an independent study in Illinois from 1975 through 1980 found that from 59% to 88% of all women surveyed responded that they had been made to feel humiliated or threatened by sexual harassment in their present place of employment. A 1981 survey of crises experienced by United Methodist women revealed that even without being provided a definition of sexual harassment, one out of every eight respondents reported that she had been harassed on her job.

It is clear from currently available data that the Church suffers from the sin of sexual harassment in ways which mirror the society. However, more current research is needed. The Christian community has a responsibility to deal resolutely with the issue of sexual harassment. It demeans and destroys the dignity of the victim. Rather than affirming women as whole persons as Jesus did, it reinforces the idea of women as sexual objects. It challenges women's humanity, undermining their self-esteem, job satisfaction and self-confidence; and, it keeps women at lower status in the work force.

Therefore be it resolved that The United Methodist Church stands in opposition to the sin of sexual harassment in the Church and the society at large, and calls upon the Church at all levels to:

1. Provide educational resources to assist United Methodists in understanding the issue of sexual harassment;
2. Develop clear policies and procedures related to sexual harassment establishing grievance procedures for victims and penalties for offenders;
3. Monitor federal, state and local legislation, advocating for just laws which will help to eradicate sexual harassment;
4. Model in its own life an environment of hospitality where there is

not only an absence of harassment but the presence of welcome, respect, and equality.

And be it further resolved that a United States survey be conducted by the General Council on Ministries to determine the extent of sexual harassment and the policies and procedures to deal with it inside our own Church structures, including all related agencies and institutions. The findings and recommendations of this survey will be reported to agencies, annual conferences and local churches by December 1990.

ADOPTED 1988

See Social Principles, ¶¶ 72.F and 73.C, "Sexual Harassment and The United Methodist Church."

Sexual Harassment and The United Methodist Church

According to the 1988 resolution: "Sexual harassment is any unwanted sexual advance or demand, either verbal or physical, which is perceived by the recipient as demeaning, intimidating or coercive. Sexual harassment must be understood as an exploitation of a power relationship rather than as an exclusively sexual issue. Sexual harassment also includes the creation of a hostile or abusive working environment resulting from discrimination on the basis of gender" (see previous resolution).

In this context, the 1988 General Conference directed the General Council on Ministries (GCOM) to conduct a survey of United Methodist clergy, laity, college and seminary students, and non-clergy church employees. The General Council on Ministries reported its finding in 1990 to agencies, annual conferences, and local churches. The GCOM survey concluded that:

"The presence of sexual harassment in environments associated with The United Methodist Church interferes with the moral mission of the Church and disrupts the religious activity, career development, and academic progress of its participants. This study shows that unwanted sexual behavior takes place in a variety of circumstances in the church and has a range of negative consequences for its victims.

"Sexual harassment creates improper, cocercive, and abusive conditions wherever it occurs in society, and it undermines the social goal of equal opportunity and the climate of mutual respect between men and women. Unwanted sexual attention is wrong, discriminatory, and illegal. Its victims have formal recourse through public agencies and the courts, but they have hesitated to deal with their circumstances publicly. According to the results of this study, people in the Church who are subjected to unwanted sexual attention want most of all for it to cease through ignoring it and avoiding the person. Women especially have been socialized to be 'pleasant,' to avoid challenging men, and to adopt a wary attitude about the risks of resistance. Harassers then misuse their personal and organizational power by treating those in more vulnerable statuses as 'fair game.'

"The experience of sexual harassment can be devastating to its victims. Coerced relationships set up a climate of intimidation and humiliation. Unwanted behavior damages the moral environment where people worship, work, and learn. This study documented the large costs in the form of lowered self-esteem borne by respondents, especially students. Victims often suffer profound personal distress and cope alone with intolerable conditions. Also, sexist behavior wherever it occurs causes emotional and psychological pain not only to individuals but also to those they are responsible for: spouses and children. Family relationships undergo strain when victims are debilitated by anxiety and misplaced self-blame because of unwanted sexual advances and a hostile, offensive, and degrading social environment." (See "Sexual Harassment in The United Methodist Church," p. 11.)

The survey provided continuing documentation that sexual harassment is a significant problem in The United Methodist Church, and that it detracts from the ministry and mission of Jesus Christ. Specific survey findings are available from the General Council on Ministries or the General Commission on the Status and Role of Women.

Therefore, The United Methodist Church shall undertake the following plan to begin to eliminate sexual harassment in the denomination and its institutions in the following three areas:

Education

(1) The General Commission on the Status and Role of Women will work cooperatively with other church bodies to explore ways to develop educational resources (workshops, print, and audio-visual

materials, etc.) to assist United Methodists throughout the church in understanding the issues of sexual harassment.

(2) The General Commission on the Status and Role of Women will explore ways to develop relevant education resources on sexual harassment specific to those: in the ordained and diaconal ministry; students, faculty, and administrators of United Methodist-related educational institutions; laity, paid and volunteer, throughout The United Methodist Church.

(3) The General Commission on the Status and Role of Women will ensure that United Methodist Church-developed materials are made available to annual conference boards of ordained and diaconal ministry, United Methodist-related educational institutions, and other agencies, groups, and individuals throughout The United Methodist Church.

Policies and Procedures

(1) Each annual conference, general agency, and United Methodist-related educational institution will have a sexual harassment policy in place, including grievance procedures for victims and penalties for offenders. A copy of these policies is to be forwarded to the General Commission on the Status and Role of Women by January 1, 1995, to be summarized and reported to the 1996 General Conference. The General Commission on the Status and Role of Women will be available to provide resources and counsel on the components of effective policies.

(2) The General Board of Church and Society will continue to monitor federal legislation and compliance with EEOC regulations. The General Board of Church and Society will also continue to be an advocate for just laws which will help to eradicate sexual harassment. This information will be available upon request.

Continuing Self-Assessment

(1) The General Commission on the Status and Role of Women will explore with the General Council on Ministries and other appropriate church bodies ways to assess the effectiveness of the church's efforts to eradicate sexual harassment.

See Social Principles, ¶¶ 72.F and 73.C, "Sexual Harassment in Church and Society in the U.S.A."

Special Needs of Farm Workers

Calling for special attention is the situation of farm workers in the United States. Traditionally they have been among the most poorly paid, housed, educated, and poorly served by health, welfare, and other social agencies. They have been systematically excluded from all, or nearly all, the benefits of social legislation.

Specifically, they have been and are excluded from unemployment insurance and workmen's compensation. Their coverage by social security, minimum wage, and child labor laws has come belatedly and is still inferior to that of most workers in industry. We support legislation designed to correct these injustices and to handle the strain within the labor market of the agricultural sector so that public interest is protected.

For over fifty years the churches have sought to improve the lot of seasonal farm workers through the Migrant Ministry, an ecumenical program to which The United Methodist Church has given significant support. The Migrant Ministry sincerely sought to meet some of the most acute needs of these oppressed people.

In recent days, the churches have come to recognize that the most fundamental of all the needs of farm workers is the need for dignity, for self-determination and for self-organization. Benefits won by any other route are at best second-rate.

At last the ten-year struggle of the farm workers in California has led to a major legislative breakthrough that is designed to ensure seasonal and year-round farm workers an opportunity to vote in secret-ballot elections for the unions of their choice. The California Agricultural Labor Relation Act of 1975 provides a better framework for the working out of justice in the fields, but does not guarantee that justice will finally prevail. Farm workers in other states are struggling also to bargain as equals with their employers. We call upon the Congress to enact legislation which enables farm workers to organize into unions of their own choosing.

We commit The United Methodist Church to support state legislation similar to the California law in other states when farm workers are pressing for such legislation.

The United Methodist Church will continue to press for better educational opportunity, housing, and welfare services, more adequate minimum wages, and full coverage by all social legislation designed for the protection of workers.

We also call upon the federal government to allocate more attention and resources to the task of retraining and adjustment for those farm workers who are being progressively displaced by mechanization of agricultural operations.

We urge all United Methodists to monitor situations where farm workers have won elections but have not been able to negotiate effective agreements and, to use their personal and institutional resources to encourage bargaining in good faith.

We urge the California legislature, without further delay, to appropriate the funds which would allow the provisions of the Farm Labor Act to be carried out.

We urge the support of Farm Workers Week with special bulletin inserts and the invitation by local churches and/or districts to workers to inform the people of the week and the aspirations of these persons.

The United Methodist Church affirms in principle the position of the recently formed National Farm Worker Ministry (a continuation of the Migrant Ministry) that the Church's most significant role must be as advocate and supporter of the efforts of farm workers toward their own responsible self-organization and self-determination.

ADOPTED 1976

See Social Principles, ¶¶ 72.M and 73, "Economic Justice," "An Affirmation of Basic Rural Worth."

Unemployment

I. *Historic Commitments*

"Historically, The United Methodist Church has been concerned with the moral issues involved with the social problem of unemployment" (opening sentence, 1976 General Conference statement on "Unemployment").

Three key statements from the Social Principles provide the basis for the church's approach to this critical social concern:
• "Every person has the right and responsibility to work for the benefit of himself or herself and the enhancement of human life and community and to receive adequate remuneration" (¶ 73 c) "Work and Leisure").

• "We recognize the responsibility of governments to develop and implement sound fiscal and monetary policies that provide for the economic life of individuals and corporate entities, and that ensure full employment and adequate incomes with a minimum of inflation" (¶ 73, introductory paragraph, "The Economic Community").

• "We believe private and public economic enterprises are responsible for the social costs of doing business, such as unemployment . . . , and that they should be held accountable for these costs" (¶ 73, "The Economic Community").

The 1976 General Conference adopted the most recent statement on "Unemployment" (as part of a comprehensive resolution on "Human Relations") that built on the historic concern for translating these basic principles into " . . . governmental policies . . . that would ensure full employment in order that workers may fully participate in society with dignity, so that families may be economically secure, and so that the nation may achieve coherent high priority goals" (from introductory paragraph, 1976 General Conference statement on "Unemployment").

This 1984 resolution reaffirms and updates these historic commitments of our denomination.

II. *Present Situation*

In the intervening years since 1976, however, little has been done to resolve the issue of unemployment. In 1984 unemployment rates still remain at about 7.8 percent; underemployment results in large numbers of families living under the poverty level; and increasing numbers of people have become discouraged and have dropped out of the labor force altogether.

Furthermore, the levels of unemployment among Blacks, Native Americans, Hispanics and some other minorities have become a national disaster.

III. *Call to Action*

Once more it is necessary for the church to remind itself and the nation of this unhappy and unjust situation and to recommend, as it did in 1976, certain specific policy actions that will help move society towards full-employment.

A. The General Conference of The United Methodist Church calls upon the local, state, and federal governments in the United States to:

1. Develop policies and programs that will help achieve full-employment.

2. Cooperate with private business and labor to institute comprehensive job training programs. (These programs must be devised to meet the special needs of minorities and women who bear a disproportionate share of unemployment and underemployment.)

3. Cooperate with private business and labor to create the jobs needed to secure employment for all who wish to work. (It is to be remembered that government has the right responsibility to invest in the public service sectors of transportation, health, education, and environment, all of which create many jobs. Some funds presently going to production of military weapons converted to these public service purposes could supply the needed investment funds.)

4. Cooperate with private business and labor to provide the unemployed workers with an income adequate to meet their families' needs.

B. The General Conference also calls upon the churches to:

1. Prepare the moral climate/understanding that would enable the nation to discover the resolving unemployment, by (a) educating its own constituencies and the general public about the causes, effects, and victims of unemployment and underemployment in the current and emerging American and global economy; (b) undergirding this educational effort with the biblical-theological basis of Christian responsibility for helping to resolve these issues; (c) incorporating in this education an emphasis on a biblical and social ethical analysis of the interrelationships between unemployment and racism, sexism, classism, militarism, and other forms of social violence.

2. Provide *direct services* to address unmet needs for employment, food, clothing, shelter, health care, and emergency financial assistance; and for counseling and support groups to meet the personal and family, economic and spiritual needs of the victims of unemployment.

3. Support *community-based economic development ventures* that provide local job opportunities and the recycling of money within local communities.

4. Encourage and support *local, state, regional, and national coalitions* that constructively address private and public sector policies that relate to the issues of unemployment and underemployment, plant closings and economic dislocation, and other ancillary concerns.

ADOPTED 1984

See Social Principles, ¶ 73, "Economic Justice," "Self-help Efforts of Poor People," "National Incomes Policy."

THE POLITICAL COMMUNITY

A Call for Increased Commitment to End World Hunger and Poverty

I. Introduction

At the Last Judgment, the question is asked, "When did we see thee hungry and feed thee?" (Matt. 25:37). The answer follows, "As You did it to one of the least of these my brethren, you did it to me" (Matt. 25:40). St. Paul, interpreting the new ethic of the kingdom, instructed the early church to satisfy the hunger and thirst of enemies (Rom. 12:20).

From the earliest times, the Christian community, in response to these teachings, has expressed compassion and care for those in need. In recent years this has been expressed in the giving of millions of dollars for direct food distribution. More systemically, the church has deployed agricultural missionaries, supported demonstration farming and development programs, challenged unjust social and economic systems which condemn people to poverty, and witnessed for just public food policies at state and federal levels.

Scant progress has been made in meeting the food needs of the hungry on a continuing basis. Too often, the attention span of church leaders and those who follow is curtailed by institutional interests and program fads. Our involvement as the owners of lands and buildings, our identification with social, economic, and political establishments, and our approval of those values which limit productive and distributive justice work together to limit our ministries "to the least of these."

II. Analysis of Current Situation

Despite marked increases in food production throughout the world, poverty and subsequent hunger is increasing. Most of the world's underfed teenagers and most of the underfed mothers and fathers of hungry children help to grow and harvest the world's food supply. For example, men and women on the farms of Asia, Africa, and Latin America produce more than half of the world's supply of "coarse grains" such as maize, sorghum, and millet. Yet, in the countries of Africa and Asia 80-90 percent and in Latin America 60 percent of the populations, representing a total of at least half a billion people, are at constant risk of hunger. The food missing from the daily lives of these people amounts to a very small part of the world's annual harvest. Nevertheless, they face hunger day after day, year after year. Unfortunately, many of the circumstances contributing to their hunger and the hunger of people worldwide are beyond their control and will remain so until the systems underlying those circumstances change.

Hunger is growing even in the United States. Since the early 1970s, the income gaps between rich and poor families have widened significantly. In 1988, the richest fifth of all families in the United States received 44 percent of the national family income, while the poorest fifth of families received 4.6 percent. Among those most likely to be poor in the United States are racial/ethnic-minority families headed by single women, children, the elderly, and groups within geographic areas such as Appalachia and the Southwest border.[1] Economic changes in agriculture in the United States, particularly in continuing loss of family farm and the related rural crisis, have had a devastating effect. The rural U.S. poverty rate has increased even faster than that of urban centers.[2]

III. Causes of the World Food Crisis

Since 1980, the portion of the earth's population that is chronically malnourished (70 percent fewer calories than necessary for health) has grown from one-ninth to one-sixth. This has both precipitating causes and much deeper systemic causes.

A. *Precipitating Causes.* Among the many precipitating causes, these stand out: the weather, political decisions, war, economic problems, and wasteful consumerism. Hunger cannot be dissociated

---

[1] Center on Budget and Policy Priorities, Washington, D.C., April, 1990.
[2] For a longer discussion see General Conference resolution on "U.S. Agriculture and Rural Communities in Crisis."

from systems that keep people in poverty, therefore powerless. Politics draws the line between poverty and power. Poverty controls lives because it entails housing, water, heat, and other necessities of life. Working to alleviate the causes of hunger requires working against poverty. It also entails organizing the poor and building economic justice coalitions that can change or transform the power arrangements.

B. *Systemic Causes.* Beyond the immediate causes of malnourishment lie more fundamental structural constraints of which hunger and poverty are but symptoms.

1. *Unjust economic systems,* a legacy of colonialism. Almost without exception, the poor countries were at one time colonies of imperial powers. Colonialism developed them primarily for the export of raw materials, mainly mining products and agricultural crops (coffee, tea, sugar, rubber, cocoa, etc.). To achieve this, the colonial powers restructured traditional social and legal customs, land distribution and tenure, food production, political power, regional and international economic relations, and the economy. The colonial system depended upon depressed wages and local elites.

2. *Maldistribution of wealth.* Corrupt practices of entrenched politicians and neo-colonial governments favor monopolistic policies of privileged families and corporations.

3. *Policies of lending institutions.* The stiff policies and conditions imposed on undeveloped and underdeveloped nations by lending institutions, such as the World Bank (IBRD) and the International Monetary Fund (IMF), have resulted, in many cases, as in the Philippines, in unjustly favoring the interest of the privileged few, and further aggravating and perpetuating the sad state and the ill effects of poverty and dehumanization of peoples in weak and defenseless nations.

These lending practices are also widespread in disadvantaged communities in developed nations.

4. *Insufficient food production* in developing nations. A principal result from colonial policies has been the insufficient development of food production in many lower-income countries. This distortion occurs through market forces and tax policies which encourage the cultivation of a single crop for export rather than the balanced production of food for domestic use.

5. *Population growth.* Rapid population growth and inadequate food

supply have a common origin and a joint explanation. They both are symptoms of structural poverty—those economic and political frameworks in which poor people exist. The experience is worldwide. Wherever poverty gives way to a rising standard of living, the birth rate declines. Wherever the security of the family increases, the birth rate declines. Such family security depends on social and economic development, which is based on the values of justice and shared power.

6. *Maldevelopment in the rich nations.* While inadequate and unbalanced development exists in the low-income countries, acute maldevelopment exists in the rich nations. This maldevelopment is characterized by militarism, waste of resources by the production of unnecessary goods and services, degradation of the environment, increasing structural, unemployment, institutionalized consumerism, persistence of poverty, rising nationalism, and a crisis in values especially felt in the lives of the young.

In 1980, the rich nations with 24 percent of the earth's population consumed 79 percent of the world's goods and services, leaving 21 percent for the developing nations with 76 percent of the population. In public health expenditures, the rich nations consumed 92 percent of the goods and services; the developing nations received 8 percent. Without significant change, the structural distortions will continue their toll on the human family.

IV. Theological Bases for Hope

As Christians, the central question we must ask ourselves in this situation is: What does God require and enable us individually and corporately to do? Some of our central affirmations of faith provide at least a partial answer.

God is Creator of all, and loves and cares for all creation. Because every person is a creature loved of God, every person has a basic human right to food, a necessity for survival. Because all persons are creatures of God, equally subject to God's grace and claim, all are bound together in inseparable ties of solidarity. It is the task of God's people to show solidarity in support of adequate provision for basic human needs such as food.

In the incarnation, life, death, and resurrection of Jesus Christ, the promise and first fruits of redemption have been brought to our sinful and selfish humanity. Jesus' own concern for human need in his ministry is a model for the Church's concern. His opposition to those who would ignore the needs of the neighbor make clear that we grossly misunderstand and fail to grasp God's grace if we imagine that God overlooks, condones, or easily tolerates our indifference to the plight of our neighbors, our greed and selfishness, or our systems of injustice and oppression.

As Holy Spirit, God is at work in history today, refashioning lives, tearing down unjust structures, restoring community, engendering faith, hope, and love. It is the work of the Holy Spirit which impels us to take action even when perfect solutions are not apparent. Thus, we engage in the struggle for bread and justice for all in the confidence that God goes before us and that God's cause will prevail.

V. Goals for Action by Christians

In faithfulness to our understanding of God's good intentions for all peoples, we can set for ourselves no lesser goals than repentance for the existence of human hunger and an increased commitment to end world hunger and poverty. Movement toward that ultimate goal of the abolition of hunger from the earth requires commitment to such immediate and instrumental goals as the following:

A. The transformation of persons and institutions such as the World Bank and the International Monetary Fund, which create and perpetuate strongholds of power and privilege for some at the expense of many, into new personal, social, economic, and political environments which are committed to ending hunger and poverty, and which are more conductive to justice, liberation, self-development, a stabilized population, and a sustainable environment.

B. The simplification of urgently needed "interim" measures and long-term distributive systems which, recognizing the unique status of food as a commodity essential for survival, assure to every human being access to food as a matter of right and recognizing that the self-reliant agriculture must be a part of ending hunger and poverty.

VI. Conclusion

1. We call upon all nations, but particularly the developed nations, to examine those values, attitudes, and institutions which are the

basic causes of poverty and underdevelopment, the primary sources of world and domestic hunger.

2. We call for The United Methodist Church to engage in an educational effort that would provide information about the scale of world and domestic hunger and its causes, and engage in study and effort to integrate the church's missional programs into a coherent policy with respect to a just, sustainable, and participatory development.

3. We specifically call upon each local church, cooperative parish, district, and conference to increase sharing resources through support of church and community agencies dedicated to eliminating hunger and poverty at home and abroad.

4. We call for the United Methodist Church through its appropriate agencies to develop effective public-policy strategies that would enable church members to participate in efforts to:

a. Decrease mother/child mortality;

b. Promote environmental justice and sustainable practices for using and restoring natural resources;

c. Provide safe drinking water and sustainable water-management systems;

d. Support community organizing to effect change in systems that keep people poor and powerless;

e. Organize and work to retain programs such as Women, Infants and Children (WIC), food stamps, and food co-ops;

f. Develop and implement agricultural policies that increase food production on family farms, provide just wages and working conditions for farm workers, and which provide incentives for farmers to produce corps using appropriate technology with equitable access to land by all;

g. Become advocates for reduction of military spending and reallocation of resources to programs that provide human services, convert military facilities to provide for civilian needs, and protect and restore the environment. (See *1988 Book of Resolutions*, "Economic Justice," Item E, p. 336.);

h. Become advocates of trade policies which alleviate economic disparities between rich and poor countries while protecting labor and human rights, environmental, health, and safety standards, and respecting the need for agricultural and food security;

i. Protect crafts people and artisans from exploitative trade practices;

j. Support community-based economic development that provides jobs, recycles money within communities, provides low-cost, high-quality services to meet basic human needs, and combats unemployment and underemployment.

ADOPTED 1992

See Social Principles, ¶ 74, "Bishops' Call for Peace and Self-Development of Peoples."

Assistance and Sanctuary for Central American Refugees

WHEREAS, at various times in history the Christian Church has been called upon to give concrete evidence of its commitment to love and justice even when it seems contrary to public opinion; and

WHEREAS, according to the terms of the Refugee Act of 1980 the United States accords refugee or asylum status to persons who cannot return to their countries of origin because of persecution or fear of persecution, for reasons of race, religion, nationality, membership in a particular social group or political opinion; and

WHEREAS, refugees from Central America and other areas of Latin America and the Caribbean are fleeing to the United States to escape the persecution, torture, and murder of their civil-war-torn homelands; and

WHEREAS, many of these refugees have been tortured and murdered when forced to return to their homelands; and

WHEREAS, Scripture says not to mistreat foreigners who live in your land (Lev. 19:33) because sojourners and strangers have a special place in the heart of God.

Therefore, Be It Resolved, that The United Methodist Church strongly:

1. Urges the President of the United States, the Department of State, and Department of Justice, and the Congress, to grant "extended voluntary departure" legal status to refugees from El Salvador and Guatemala, and other areas of the Caribbean and Latin America.

2. Requests that annual conferences and local churches assist in ministries to Central American, Caribbean, and other Latin American refugees by providing them with legal assistance, bail bond funds, food, housing, and medical care.

3. Encourages congregations who take seriously the mandate to do justice and to resist the policy of the Immigration and Naturalization

Service by declaring their churches to be "sanctuaries" for refugees from El Salvador, Guatemala, and other areas of the Caribbean and Latin America.

4. Urges the United States to follow the United Nations definition of refugees.

ADOPTED 1984

See Social Principles, ¶¶ 74.A and B, 75.A, "Central America: Peace and Justice with Freedom," "Concern for El Salvador."

Bilingual Education

The United States is a country based on the contributions of different races, ethnic groups, languages, and traditions. The fabric of the U.S. society thus is a mosaic of diversity which has enriched its history and its common life as a nation.

Education has played a very important role in the development of this nation. To have access to it and to receive a sound education are considered inalienable rights of all children. Bilingual education has been and is a critical tool to ensure these rights for non-English-speaking children living now in this country. It has been an instrument of education for children to make the transition from their native tongues to English while at the same time staying at the level correspondent to their age.

WHEREAS, we believe that these values are part of the trust of this nation; and

WHEREAS, most educators have confirmed that non-English-speaking children will make the transition from their native tongues to English more easily within the context of a good bilingual program; and

WHEREAS, the growth of the non-English-speaking population continues to increase through immigration, and it is estimated to be even larger in the next few decades; and

WHEREAS, the percentage of Hispanic dropouts from school is one of the largest in the country, thus challenging the nation to provide resources for this segment of the population more effectively in both elementary and high schools; and

WHEREAS, projections of the future envision a larger demand in the fields of mathematics and sciences, precisely where women,

Hispanics, Blacks, and Native Americans are currently almost non-present; and

WHEREAS, more intentional efforts must be made to bring children and youth from these groups to the same level of the rest of the student population;

Be it resolved, that 1992 General Conference proclaim bilingual education to be an educational program needed for this country which must be not only perpetuated but strengthened; and

Be it resolved, that the General Conference affirm in writing to the President of the United States, the United States Congress, and the Department of Education that bilingual education is a right for all children and that by strengthening such a program the nation will be in reality laying the foundations for a better future in this land; and

Be it resolved, to forward this resolution to members of Congress, governors, and the legislatures of the 50 states and territories; and

Be it resolved, to commend this resolution to all annual conferences for promotion and interpretation, and to ask the General Board of Church and Society to make this resolution an important item in its program and work agenda.

ADOPTED 1992

See Social Principles, ¶ 74, "Public Education in the United States," "Protecting and Sustaining Children."

Capital Punishment

In spite of a common assumption to the contrary, "an eye for an eye and a tooth for a tooth," does not give justification for the imposing of the penalty of death. Jesus explicitly repudiated the *lex tallionis* (Matthew 5:38-39), and the Talmud denies its literal meaning and holds that it refers to financial indemnities.

When a woman was brought before Jesus, having committed a crime for which the death penalty was commonly imposed, our Lord so persisted in questioning the moral authority of those who were ready to conduct the execution, that they finally dismissed the charges (John 8:31f).

The Social Principles of The United Methodist Church condemns ". . . torture of persons by governments for any purpose," and asserts that it violates Christian teachings. The church through its

Social Principles further declares, "we oppose capital punishment and urge its elimination from all criminal codes."

After a moratorium of a full decade, the use of the death penalty in the United States has resumed. Other Western nations have largely abolished it during the 20th century. But a rapidly rising rate of crime and an even greater increase in the fear of crime has generated support within the American society for the institution of death as the punishment for certain forms of homicide. It is now being asserted, as it was often in the past, that capital punishment would deter criminals and would protect law-abiding citizens.

The United States Supreme Court, in *Gregg V. Georgia*, in permitting use of the death penalty, conceded the lack of evidence that it reduced violent crime, but permitted its use for purpose of sheer retribution.

The United Methodist Church cannot accept retribution or social vengeance as a reason for taking human life. It violates our deepest belief in God as the creator and the redeemer of humankind. In this respect, there can be no assertion that human life can be taken humanely by the state. Indeed, in the long run, the use of the death penalty by the state will increase the acceptance of revenge in our society and will give official sanction to a climate of violence.

The United Methodist Church is deeply concerned about the present high rate of crime in the United States, and about the value of a life taken in murder or homicide. When another life is taken through capital punishment, the life of the victim is further devalued. Moreover, the Church is convinced that the use of the death penalty would result in neither a net reduction of crime in general nor in a lessening of the particular kinds of crime against which it was directed. Homicide—the crime for which the death penalty has been used almost exclusively in recent decades—increased far less than other major crimes during the period of the moratorium. Progressively rigorous scientific studies, conducted over more than forty years, overwhelmingly failed to support the thesis that capital punishment deters homicide more effectively than does imprisonment. The most careful comparisons of homicide rates in similar states with and without use of the death penalty, and also of homicide rates in the same state in periods with and without it, have found as many or slightly more criminal homicides in states with use of the death penalty.

The death penalty also falls unfairly and unequally upon an outcast minority. Recent methods for selecting the few persons sentenced to die from among the larger number who are convicted of comparable offenses have not cured the arbitrariness and discrimination that have historically marked the administration of capital punishment in this country.

The United Methodist Church is convinced that the nation's leaders should give attention to the improvement of the total criminal justice system and to the elimination of social conditions which breed crime and cause disorder, rather than foster a false confidence in the effectiveness of the death penalty.

The United Methodist Church declares its opposition to the retention and use of capital punishment in any for or carried out by any means; the Church urges the abolition of capital punishment.

ADOPTED IN 1980

See Social Principles, ¶ 74.F, "Criminal Justice."

Certification of Conscientious Objectors

The United Methodist Church today nurtures a substantial number of conscientious objectors among its members. Since 1936, The United Methodist Church or one of its predecessors has provided to those of its members who claim to be conscientious objectors the opportunity to register. Certified copies of such registration are supplied for use with the draft authorities.

We support this procedure and propose that The United Methodist Church further develop a churchwide process that certifies the decision of its members who seek to be identified as conscientious objectors. That process should be created by the General Board of Church and Society in cooperation with the General Board of Discipleship.

The process may begin in the local church, where the pastor, in cooperation with the Pastor-Parish Relations Committee and the Council on Ministries, could select a person or committee to implement the process developed by the general agencies.

The United Methodist theological statements, Social Principles, and historic statements on war, peace, and conscription should be primary points of reference. It is the responsibility of the Church at all levels to inform its members of the fact that conscientious objection, as well as conscientious participation, is a valid option for Christians and is recognized in many countries as a legal alternative for persons liable to military conscription.

The local committee's action does not express agreement or disagreement with the convictions of the applicant member. Rather, the committee's task is to record which of the church's members are opposed to participation in military service on grounds of conscience and to assist them in securing proper counsel. When a member has registered and his/her registration has been certified to the proper authorities, that action should be recorded with the conference and General Board of Church and Society.

ADOPTED 1980

See Social Principles, ¶ 74.G, "Concerning the Draft in the United States," "The United Methodist Church and Peace," "Support of Conscientious Objectors to Registration."

Church/Government Relations

Introduction

In response to a question about paying taxes, Jesus said: "Render to Caesar the things that are Caesar's, and to God the things that are God's" (Luke 20:25). Although this statement refers specifically to taxation, its apparent implications are that there are separate obligations and responsibilities to government and to religion.

The Social Principles of The United Methodist Church asserts: "We believe that the state should not attempt to control the church, nor should the church seek to dominate the state. 'Separation of church and state' means no organic union of the two, but does permit interaction. The church should continually exert a strong ethical influence upon the state, supporting policies and programs deemed to be just and compassionate and opposing policies and programs which are not."

As we consider the religious protections of the First Amendment— the free exercise and non-establishment of religion—we are pro- foundly grateful for the major statement made by the 1968 General Conference on "Church/Government Relations." In recognizing that debt, we reaffirm much of the substance of that declaration prepared by two distinguished committees under the authority of the General Conference and operating over two quadrenniums of the life of the Church.

A Statement Concerning Church-Government Relations and Education

1

The fundamental purpose of universal public education at the elementary and secondary levels is to provide equal and adequate educational opportunities for all children and young people, and thereby insure the nation an enlightened citizenry.

We believe in the principle of universal public education, and we reaffirm our support of public educational institutions. At the same time, we recognize and pledge our continued allegiance to the U.S. constitutional principle that citizens have a right to establish and maintain private schools from private resources so long as such schools meet public standards of quality. Such schools have made a genuine contribution to society. We do not support the expansion or the strengthening of private schools with public funds. Furthermore, we oppose the establishment or strengthening of private schools that jeopardize the public school system or thwart valid public policy.

We specifically oppose tuition tax credits or any other mechanism which directly or indirectly allows government funds to support religious schools at the primary and secondary level. Persons of one particular faith should be free to use their own funds to strengthen the belief system of their particular religious group. But they should not expect all taxpayers, including those who adhere to other religious belief systems, to provide funds to teach religious views with which they do not agree.

To fulfill the government's responsibility in education, sometimes it and non-public educational institutions need to enter a cooperative relationship. But public funds should be used only in the best interests of the whole society. Extreme caution must be exercised to assure that religious institutions do not receive any aid directly or indirectly for the maintenance of their religious expression or the expansion of their institutional resources. Such funds must be used for the express purpose of fulfilling a strictly public responsibility, subject to public accountability.

Public schools have often been an important unifying force in modern pluralistic society by providing a setting for contact at an early age between children of vastly different backgrounds. We recognize in particular that persons of all religious backgrounds may have insight into the nature of ultimate reality which will help to enrich the common life. It is therefore essential that the public schools take seriously the religious integrity of each child entrusted to their care. Public schools may not properly establish any preferred form of religion for common exercises of worship, religious observance, or study. At the same time, however, education should provide an opportunity for the examination of the various religious traditions of humankind.

2

We believe that every person has a right to an education, including higher education, commensurate with his or her ability. It is society's responsibility to enable every person to enjoy this right. Public and private institutions should cooperate to provide for these educational opportunities.

3

Freedom of inquiry poses a risk for established ideas, beliefs, programs, and institutions. We accept that risk in the faith that all truth is of God. Colleges and universities can best perform their vital tasks of adding to knowledge and to the perception of truth in an atmosphere of genuine academic freedom.

We affirm the principle that freedom to inquire, to discuss, and to teach should be regulated by the self-discipline of scholarship and the critical examination of ideas in the context of free public dialogue, rather than by supervision, censorship, or any control imposed by churches, governments, or other organizations. In the educational process, individuals have the right to appropriate freely for themselves what they believe is real, important, useful, and satisfying.

4

Experience has demonstrated that freedom to inquire, to discuss, and to teach is best preserved when colleges and universities are not dependent upon a single base or a few sources of support. When an educational institution relies upon multiple sources of financial support, and where those sources tend to balance each other, the institution is in a position to resist undue pressures toward control exerted from any one source of support. In the case of church-related colleges and universities, we believe that tuitions, scholarships, investment returns, bequests, payments for services rendered, loans, government grants, and gifts from individuals, business corporations, foundations, and churches should be sought and accepted in as great a variety as possible. Care must be exercised to insure that all support from any of these sources is free from conditions which hinder the college or university in the maintenance of freedom of inquiry and expression for its faculty and students.

We are very much aware of the dangers of church-sponsored colleges and universities being overly dependent upon government funding. However, we are also aware that, given the independent thought of most college students today, there is little danger of using government funds to indoctrinate students with religious beliefs. Therefore, institutions of higher leaning should feel free to receive government funds (except for religious teaching and structures for worship). At the same time they should be eternally cognizant of the dangers of accompanying government oversight that might threaten the religious atmosphere or special independent character of church-sponsored educational institutions.

No church-sponsored higher education institution should become so dependent upon government grants, research projects, or support programs, that its academic freedom is jeopardized, its responsibility for social criticism (including criticism of governments) inhibited, or its spiritual values denied.

We recognize that the freedom necessary to the existence of a college or university in the classical sense may be threatened by forces other than those involved in the nature and source of the institution's financial support. Institutional freedom may be adversely affected by governmental requirements of loyalty oaths from teachers and students, by public interference with the free flow of information, or by accreditation and certification procedures and requirements aimed at dictating the content of college and university curricula.

With respect to church-related institutions of higher education, we deplore any ecclesiastical attempts to manipulate inquiry or the dissemination of knowledge, to use the academic community for the promotion of any particular point of view, to require ecclesiastical "loyalty oaths" designed to protect cherished truth claims, or to inhibit the social action activities of members of the academic community. We call upon all members of The United Methodist Church, in whatever capacity they may serve, to be especially sensitive to the need to protect individual and institutional freedom and responsibility in the context of the academic community.

5

We are persuaded that there may be circumstances or conditions in which the traditional forms of tax immunities granted to colleges and universities may be a necessary requirement for their freedom. Therefore, we urge a continuation of the public policy of granting reasonable and non-discriminatory tax immunities to all private colleges and universities, including those which are related to churches.

We believe that colleges and universities should consider the benefits, services, and protections which they receive from the community and its governmental agencies, and should examine their obligations to the community in the light of this support. We believe it is imperative that all church-related institutions of higher education determine on their own initiative what benefits, services, and opportunities they ought to provide for the community as a whole as distinct from their usual campus constituencies.

*A Statement Concerning Church-Government Relations
and Governmental Chaplaincies*

1

We recognize that military and public institutional chaplaincies represent efforts to provide for the religious needs of people for whom both churches and governments are responsible. We recognize that in such a broad and complex undertaking there are bound to exist real and serious tensions which produce genuine uneasiness on the part of government officials as well as church leaders. Great patience and skill are required to effect necessary accommodations with understanding and without compromising religious liberty.

2

We believe that there are both ethical and constitutional standards which must be observed by governments in the establishment and operation of public chaplaincies. At a minimum, those standards are as follows:

First, the only obligation which governments have is to assure the provision of opportunities for military personnel, patients of hospitals, and inmates of correctional institutions to engage in religious worship or have access to religious nurture.

Second, participation in religious activities must be on a purely voluntary basis; there must be neither penalties for non-participation nor any rewards for participation.

Third, no preferential treatment should be given any particular church, denomination, or religious group in the establishment and administration of governmental chaplaincies.

Fourth, considerable care should be exercised in the role assignments of chaplains so they are not identified as the enforcers of morals. Precaution should also be taken to avoid chaplains being given duties not clearly related to their primary tasks.

Standards should be maintained to protect the integrity of both churches and governments. The practice of staffing governmental chaplaincies with clergy personnel who have ecclesiastical endorsement should be continued. The practice of terminating the services of such personnel in any instance where it becomes necessary for ecclesiastical endorsement to be withdrawn should also be continued. Supervision of clergy personnel in the performance of their religious services in governmental chaplaincies should be clearly effected through ecclesiastical channels with the cooperation of the public agencies and institutions involved. In the performance of these administrative functions, churches and agencies of government have an obligation to be fair and responsible, and to insure that due process is observed in all proceedings.

3

The role of a governmental chaplain should be primarily pastoral but with important priestly, prophetic, and teaching roles. The chaplain has an obligation to perform these ministries in as broad an ecumenical context as possible. A chaplain is responsible for the spiritual welfare and religious life of all the personnel of the military unit or the public institution to which he/she is assigned.

There are many persons, and some groups, whose personal religious practices or whose church's rules make it impossible for them to accept the direct ministry of a particular chaplain. In such instances, the chaplain, to the full extent of his/her powers, has an obligation to make provision for worship by these persons or groups. A chaplain is expected to answer specific questions by members of faith groups other than his/her own. Chaplains must know the basic tenets of their denominations in order to protect such members in the expression and development of their faith. The absence of parochialism on the part of a chaplain is more than an attitude; it necessitates specific, detailed, and accurate knowledge regarding many religions.

4

The churches should strive to make public chaplaincies integral expressions of their ministry and to face the implications of this for supervision and budget. The chaplain represents the church by affirming the dignity of all persons in military service through the chaplain's function in upholding their freedom of religion and conscience. Every person exists within a broader set of values than those of the military, and within a broader spectrum of responsibilities than those created by military orders. The chaplain is a bearer of the gospel to affirm the freedom of the individual and represents The United Methodist Church at that point of tension. Whether the freedom of the gospel is compromised or limited may be a result of either external pressures or internal submission, or both. Failure to sustain the freedom of the gospel lies within any human system or any individual. It is the task of the church to confront prophetically institutions or chaplains who compromise the gospel. The United Methodist Church provides presence, oversight, and support to chaplains who risk ministry in such a setting.

There are degrees of tension in present arrangements whereby a chaplain is a commissioned officer of the armed forces or an employee of a public institution. As such, he/she is a member of the staff of the military commander or of the director of the public institution involved. Government regulations and manuals describe him/her as "the advisor on religion, morals, morale, and welfare." Therefore, we believe it is the chaplain's duty in faithfulness to his/her religious commitments to act in accordance with his/her conscience and make such viewpoints known in organizational matters affecting the total welfare of the people for whom the chaplain has any responsibility. The chaplain has the obligation and should have the opportunity to express his/her dissent within the structures in which the chaplain works, in instances where he/she feels this is necessary. With respect to such matters it is the obligation of religious bodies to give the chaplain full support.

Churches must encourage chaplains who serve in the armed forces to resist the exaltation of power and its exercise for its own sake. They must also encourage chaplains who serve in public institutions to maintain sensitivity to human anguish. Churches and chaplains have an obligation to speak out conscientiously against the unforgiving and intransigent spirit in people and nations wherever and whenever it appears.

A Statement Concerning Church-Government Relations and Tax Exemption

1

We believe that governments recognize that unique category of religious institutions. To be in this unique category is not a privilege held by these institutions for their own benefit or self-glorification but is an acknowledgement of their special identity designed to protect their independence and to enable them to serve humankind in a way not expected of other types of institutions.

2

We urge churches to consider at least the following factors in determining their response to the granting of immunity from property taxes:
1. Responsibility to make appropriate contributions for essential services provided by government;
2. The danger that churches become so dependent upon government that they compromise their integrity or fail to exert their critical influence upon public policy.

3

We support the abolition of all special privileges accorded to members of the clergy in U.S. tax laws and regulations and call upon the churches to deal with the consequent financial implications for their ministers. Conversely, we believe that all forms of discrimination against members of the clergy in U.S. tax legislation and administrative regulations should be discontinued. We believe that the status of an individual under ecclesiastical law or practice ought not to be the basis of governmental action either granting or withholding a special tax benefit.

A Statement Concerning Church Participation in Public Affairs

1

We recognize that churches exist within the body politic along with numerous other forms of human association. Like other social groups their existence affects, and is affected by, governments. We believe that churches have the right and the duty to speak and act corporately on those matters of public policy which involve basic moral or ethical issues and questions. Any concept of, or action regarding, church-government relations which denies churches this role in the body politic strikes at the very core of religious liberty.

The attempt to influence the formation and execution of public policy at all levels of government is often the most effective means available to churches to keep before humanity the ideal of a society in which power and order are made to serve the ends of justice and freedom for all people. Through such social action churches generate new ideas, challenge certain goals and methods, and help rearrange the emphasis on particular values in ways that facilitate the adoption and implementation of specific policies and programs which promote the goals of a responsible society.

We believe that any action that would deny the church the right to act corporately on public policy matters threatens religious liberty. We therefore oppose inclusion of churches in any lobby disclosure legislation.

This does not mean that, in any way, we wish to hide actions taken by the church on public issues. On the contrary, we are usually proud of such actions. It does recognize, however, that the church is already responding to members who request information with respect to church action on public policy questions. In effect, in accordance with legislation enacted by the 1976 General Conference, The United Methodist Church already has its own lobby disclosure provisions in place.

It is quite another matter, however, for the government to insist that it must know everything about what a church is saying in its private communications with its own members.

When the U.S. Supreme Court acted in the 1971 landmark case of Lemon v. Kurtzman (403 U.S. 602 at pp. 612, 613) the Court applied a test to determine the constitutionality of legislation on First Amendment grounds as it deals with religion. Among its three criteria were these two: (1) its principle or primary effect must neither advance nor inhibit religion; (2) the statute must not foster an excessive government entanglement with religion.

Lobby disclosure legislation before the U.S. Congress over the last several years has required (1) extremely burdensome recordkeeping and reporting of all legislative activity; (2) reporting of contributions of churches giving $3,000 or more annually to a national body if a part of this is used for legislative action; (3) criminal penalties with up to two years in jail for violations; (4) unwarranted subpoena powers to investigate church records.

Legislation which passed the House in 1978 would have required detailed records of expenditures of 22 items. As such, it would have been burdensome and would "inhibit religion" in that The United Methodist Church would have been severely handicapped in implementing its Social Principles due to being neutralized by minutia.

Furthermore, if the government insists on knowing everything the church is doing on public policy questions over a five-year period (as was required) and imposes a criminal sentence for violations, this could "inhibit religion" to the extent that the church might be tempted to limit severely its activity to avoid non-compliance.

If the government is going to require that religious groups keep burdensome records and make voluminous reports, and there is some question as to whether the churches are complying, federal authorities would be authorized to step in and check church records and files. Such action would undoubtedly represent an unconstitutional "excessive government entanglement with religion."

The United Methodist Church would have great difficulty in complying with the provision that all organizational contributions of $3,000 annually be reported if some of these funds are used for lobbying. Since local churches contribute generously to the World Service Dollar, and a small portion of those funds are used for legislative action, this brings our Church under coverage of this provision. Such a requirement could mean that reports of contributions of some 30,000 United Methodist churches would have to be made to the government shortly after the close of each year. This could not be done and we would be in violation having "knowingly" omitted material facts "required to be disclosed." As a result, Church officials would be subject to criminal penalties of up to two years in prison.

For these reasons, we oppose lobby disclosure measures for the churches. In its most stringent form this legislation would inhibit our free exercise of religion. It would be impossible for the Church to comply with certain provisions, thus subjecting our Church leaders to criminal penalties.

3

We believe that churches must behave responsibly in the arena of public affairs. Responsible behavior requires adherence to ethically sound substantive and procedural norms.

We live in a pluralistic society. In such a society, churches should not seek to use the authority of government to make the whole community conform to their particular moral codes. Rather, churches should seek to enlarge and clarify the ethical grounds of public discourse and to identify and define the foreseeable consequences of available choices of public policy.

In participating in the arena of public affairs, churches are not inherently superior to other participants; hence the stands which they take on particular issues of public policy are not above question or criticism.

Responsible behavior in the arena of public affairs requires churches to accept the fact that, in dealing with complex issues of public policy, good intentions and high ideals need to be combined with as much practical and technical knowledge of politics and economics as possible.

Another norm of responsible behavior derives from the fact that no particular public policy which may be endorsed by churches at a given point in time should be regarded as an ultimate expression of Christian ethics in society. Churches should not assume that any particular social pattern, political order, or economic ideology represents a complete embodiment of the Christian ethic.

When churches speak to government they also bear the responsibility to speak to their own memberships. Cultivation of ethically informed public opinion is particularly crucial in local congregations. It is essential to responsible behavior that procedures be established and maintained to insure full, frank, and informed discussion by members and constituents of churches of the decisions and actions of religious groups within the arena of public affairs. In the present period of human history, attention should be given to the dignity of every person and appeal should be made to the consciences of all persons of good will. Churches must acknowledge and respect the role of the laity as well as the clergy in determining their behavior in the arena of public affairs.

Because of their commitment to unity and in the interest of an effective strategy, churches should, to the maximum extent feasible, coordinate their own efforts and, where appropriate, cooperate with other organizations when they seek to influence properly the formation and execution of public policy at all levels of government.

Finally, churches should not seek to utilize the processes of public affairs to further their own institutional interests or to obtain special privileges for themselves.

4

United Methodism is a part of the universal Church. In the formulation and expression of the United Methodist voice in public affairs, we must listen to the concerns and insights of church members and churches in all nations. It is imperative that our expressions and actions be informed by participation in the universal Church.

5

With particular reference to The United Methodist Church and public affairs, we express the following convictions: Connectional units of the denomination (such as General Conference, Jurisdictional Conference, Annual Conference, local congregation, or general board or agency) should continue to exercise the right to advocate government policies which involve basic moral or ethical issues or questions. In exercising this right, each such connectional unit, or any other official group within The United Methodist Church, should always make explicit for whom or in whose name it speaks or acts in the arena of public affairs. Only the General Conference is competent to speak or act in the name of The United Methodist Church.

ADOPTED in 1980

See Social Principles, ¶ 74, "The United Methodist Church and Church/Government Relations," "Public Education in the United States," "Religious Liberty."

Church/Government Relations, The United Methodist Church and

A Statement Concerning Church-Government Relations and Social Welfare

1

The United Methodist Church is concerned about the health and well-being of all persons because it recognizes that physical health and social well-being are necessary pre-conditions to the complete fulfillment of man's personal and social possibilities in this world. Our Master himself cared for the sick and fed the multitudes in recognition that man's physical well-being cannot be divorced from his spiritual health.

Service to persons in need, along with social education and action to eliminate forces and structures that create or perpetuate conditions of need, is integral to the life and witness of Christians, both as individuals and as churches. However, there are no fixed institutional patterns for the rendering of such service. It may be rendered effectively as a Christian vocation or avocation, and through the channels of either a governmental or a private agency.

We recognize that churches are not the only institutions exercising a critical and prophetic role in the community and in society. They share that responsibility with many other institutions and agencies in such fields as law, education, social work, medicine, and the sciences. Yet churches cannot escape their special obligation to nurture and encourage a critical and prophetic quality in their own institutional life. That quality should be expressed also through their members—as they act as citizens, trustees of agencies and persons with professional skills. It should be understood that the performance of such roles by church members will often involve them in revaluing the norms avowed by churches as well as using such norms as a basis for judgment.

2

We recognize that governments at all levels in the United States have increasingly assumed responsibility for the performance of social welfare functions. There is reason to believe that this trend will continue and, perhaps, be accelerated. We assume that governments will continue to use private nonprofit agencies as instrumentalities for the implementation of publicly formulated social welfare policies. This means that private agencies will continue to face unprecedented demand for their services and have unprecedented access to government resources.

It is now evident that a variety of contributions is required to achieve a comprehensive social welfare policy for the nation, for the states, and for each community. Such a policy includes identification of the range of human needs, transformation of needs into effective demands, and development of programs to meet those demands. We believe that all the organizations and resources of the private sector, as well as those of governments, should be taken into account in the formulation and execution of social welfare policies.

We recognize that appropriate government bodies have the right to prescribe minimum standards for all private social welfare agencies. We believe that no private agency, because of its religious affiliations, ought to be exempted from any of the requirements of such standards.

3

Governmental provision of material support for church-related agencies inevitably raises important questions of religious establishment. In recognition, however, that some health, education, and welfare agencies have been founded by churches without regard to religious proselytizing, we consider that such agencies may, under certain circumstances, be proper channels for public programs in these fields. When government provides support for programs administered by private agencies, it has the most serious obligation to establish and enforce standards guaranteeing the equitable administration of such programs and the accountability of such agencies to the public authority. In particular, we believe that no government resources should be provided to any church-related agency for such purposes unless:

1. The services to be provided by the agency shall meet a genuine community need.

2. The services of the agency shall be designed and administered in such a way as to avoid serving a sectarian purpose or interest.

3. The services to be provided by the agency shall be available to all persons without regard to race, color, national origin, creed, or political persuasion.

4. The services to be rendered by the agency shall be performed in accordance with accepted professional and administrative standards.

5. Skill, competence, and integrity in the performance of duties shall be the principal considerations in the employment of personnel and shall not be superseded by any requirement of religious affiliation.

6. The right to collective bargaining shall be recognized by the agency.

4

We recognize that all of the values involved in the sponsorship of a social welfare agency by a church may not be fully expressed if that agency has to rely permanently on access to government resources for its existence. We are also aware that under certain circumstances sponsorship of a social welfare agency by a church may inhibit the development of comprehensive welfare services in the community. Therefore, the church and the agency should choose which pattern of service to offer: (1) channeling standardized and conventional services supplied or supported by government, or (2) attempting experimental or unconventional ministries and criticizing government programs when they prove inadequate. We believe that these two patterns are difficult, if not impossible, to combine in the same agency, and that the choice between them should be made before dependence upon government resources makes commitment to the first pattern irreversible.

5

We believe that persons in both public and private institutions of social welfare should have adequate opportunities for religious services and ministries of their own choosing. Such services and ministries should be available to all, but they should not be compulsory. Under certain circumstances, failure to provide such services and ministries may have a serious adverse effect on the free exercise of religion. Where, for medical or legal reasons, the free movement of individuals is curtailed, the institutions of social welfare involved ought to provide opportunities for religious worship.

6

There is a new awareness of the need for welfare services to be complemented by action for social change. We believe that agencies of social welfare to churches have an obligation to provide data and insights concerning the causes of specific social problems. It should be recognized that both remedial and preventive programs may require legislation, changes in political structures, and cooperation in direct action and community organization.

In their efforts to meet human needs, churches should never allow their preoccupation with remedial programs under their own direction to divert them or the larger community from a common search for basic solutions. In dealing with conditions of poverty, churches should have no stake in programs which continue dependency or which embody attitudes and practices which may be described as "welfare colonialism."

We believe that churches have a moral obligation to challenge violations of the civil rights of the poor. They ought to direct their efforts toward helping the poor overcome the powerlessness which makes such violations of civil rights possible. Specifically, churches ought to protest such policies and practices by welfare personnel as unwarranted invasions of privacy and requirement of attendance at church activities in order to qualify for social welfare services.

ADOPTED 1968

See Social Principles, ¶ 74.A, "Church Government Relations," "Public Education in the United States."

The Church in a Mass Media Culture

The world is moving from an agricultural and industrial dominance into the information and communication age. In the United States, more persons are employed in information-related industries than in all other types of work combined. Public governments and private industries control the technology and flow of information, wielding great power over the lives of billions of people.

All people are affected by the information revolution. Persons in developing countries may receive most of their news from First World news services while their crop development and natural resources may be surveyed by foreign satellite. Some Third World nations are leapfrogging past the wired nation into the satellite era.

In First World countries such as the United States, persons are spending more and more time in communication activities: viewing more television programming as cable and direct signals from satellites increase, using the home computer and playing video games.

This new development in world history is driven by quantum leaps in basic information management technology and can be described as a revolution because of its pervasive effects at several levels:

• The centralization of control and ownership of information in First World countries.

• The socializing acculturating effects of world media bringing the same messages and information to diverse audiences.

• The increasing amounts of time persons are interacting with media rather than with other persons and the passive nature of much media viewing.

• The incentive for a mass audience leads to dominant content of the entertainment and information media categorized by escapism, consumerism, violence and exclusion of minorities.

• The increasing involvement of the work force and capital investment in information technology-related endeavors in the developed and developing world.

As United Methodists, we have "emphasized God's endowment of each person with dignity and moral responsibility" (¶ 69, page 76, 1980 *Book of Discipline*). We recognize that "faith and good works belong together" (¶ 69, p. 77). We have a long history of concern for social justice, so it is within both a biblical and historical context that we as United Methodists speak to the communication and information revolution.

The goals of The United Methodist Church, based on our understanding of the gospel, are clear.

• Persons everywhere must be free in their efforts to live meaningful lives.

• Channels of communication must operate in open, authentic and humanizing ways.

• Christians should be involved seriously and continuously in the communication systems of their societies.

In the implementation of these goals, we must be aware of the power of the mass media. All media are educational. The mass media—especially radio, television, cable TV, motion pictures, newspapers, books and magazines—are pervasive and influential forces in our culture. The new media of video games, direct broadcast satellite, video recordings for home use and computers are increasing. Whether they deal with information, opinion, entertainment, escape, explicit behavioral models or subtle suggestion, the mass media always are involved, directly or indirectly, in values. Furthermore, all media messages speak from some theological assumptions. Therefore, we as Christians must ask such major questions as:

• Who controls the media in a country? Who determines the structures of and the public's access to the mass media? Will deregulation of radio, television and cable in the United States result in greater diversity, freedom and justice, or less? Who controls international technologies of communication?

• Who determines message content and within what guidelines of responsibility?

• Who uses the media and for what purposes?

• What rights do users have in determining media structure and content? What is the user's responsibility in bringing critical appraisal and judgment to the messages received?

• What is the appropriate response to the growing demands of developing countries that there be new and more just world information systems which meet their needs?

As Christians, we affirm the principle of freedom of expression as both an individual and corporate right. We oppose any laws or structures which attempt to abridge freedom of expression and we state our concern about the numerous incidents of repression of freedom of expression occurring in the United States and around the world. We believe:

• Freedom of expression—whether by spoken or printed word, or any visual or artistic medium—should be exercised within a framework of social responsibility. The church is opposed to censorship.

• The principle of freedom of the press must be maintained and must receive full support from the church and its constituents, even when the cost is high.

• The electronic spectrum is a limited natural resource. The airwaves should be held in trust for the public by radio and television broadcasters and regulated in behalf of the public by government. While the broadcaster has great discretion for the program content this does not abridge the public's "right to know," to be fairly represented and to have access to the media.

• Public broadcasting as it continues to develop should be supported by both public and private sectors of the society to help further the diversity of programming and information sources.

• All persons of every nation should have equal access to channels of communication so they can participate fully in the life of the world. We encourage United Methodist members and agencies to participate in the study and continuing dialogue across national boundaries concerning the development of fair and just communication and information systems within nations and between nations.

• No medium can be truly neutral. Each brings its own values, limitations, criteria, authoritarian or democratic structures and selection processes with it.

• Appropriate agencies of The United Methodist Church should keep abreast of new communication technologies and structures, helping the church to stay informed so it may respond to developments which affect the human condition.

While we acknowledge the practicality of the necessity of media professionals to determine the societal and moral content of mass media, we must continue to oppose the practices of those persons and systems which use media for purposes of exploitation. Exploitation comes in many forms:

• Emphasizing violence.
• Showing pornography.
• Appealing to self-indulgence.

- Presenting consumerism as a way of life.
- Offering easy solutions to complex problems.
- Favoring the mass audience to the exclusion of individual and minority needs.
- Withholding significant information.
- Treating news as entertainment.
- Presenting events in isolation from the larger social context.
- Stereotyping characters in terms of sex roles, ethnic or racial background, occupation, age, religion and economic status.
- Failing to deal with significant political and social issues objectively and in depth.
- Exhibiting an overriding concern for maximizing profit.
- Discriminating in employment practices.
- Presenting misleading or dangerous product information or omitting essential information.
- Failing to educate adequately and inform the public about the nature and processes of these media themselves.

We call upon the mass media industries and their leaders to recognize their power and to use this power responsibly in enabling persons to achieve their fullest potential as members of the family of God. We urge Christians and church members involved in the media industries to utilize their faith in their decision-making and in their work place, to find others with moral and ethical commitment, and to discuss ways of enabling their industries to exercise their power for the good of humankind.

We urge the church to devise ways of responding to the mass media, including the following:

- Participating in research on the effects of media and information technologies.
- Developing criteria and resources by which church members can evaluate and interpret what is being communicated to them through the mass media.
- Recognizing that all information and entertainment programs can be used for learning, thereby making use of mass media programming in the church's ministry.
- Recognizing that communication professions offer opportunities for ministry and service.
- Working with the mass media at local and national levels, linking the life of the church with the life of the community.

• Participating in the development of the regulatory requirements of media.

We urge our churches to communicate, minister, and serve their communities through the public media. This will require them to:

• Discover the needs of persons in the community and determine how the church can minister to those needs through the media.

• Work with other churches in an ecumenical spirit of service and ministry.

• Commit time, budget, and talent to ministry through the media.

• Recognize the variety of purposes the church can fulfill in communicating through mass media, such as education, witness, evangelism, information, social service, and ministry.

• Be advocates for those shut out of the media; the poor, less powerful, and those on the margins of society.

In our own communication structures and processes within the church, we need to establish models of communication which are freeing, which respect the dignity of the recipient, and which are participating and non-manipulative. We need to democratize our own media to allow access and open dialogue. As a major institution within our society, we can demonstrate to other institutions the power of a connectional church which structures its communication patterns not by concentrating media power but by emphasizing the values of the gospel which recognize the sanctity of every individual.

ADOPTED 1984

See Social Principles, ¶ 72.O, "Sexual Violence and Pornography," "Free Flow of Information Among All Peoples of the Earth."

Community Life

At the heart of the Christian faith is an abiding concern for persons. This concern is evidenced by the Christian's sensitivity to all factors which affect a person's life. In our society the community has become known as a gathering of people who nurture one another and create for all an atmosphere for general enhancement. The community should be characterized by good schools, adequate housing, spirit-filled churches, and creative community organizations.

The Church has always been interested in communities as arenas where people engage in the common experiences of life. It is in community that men, women, and youth discover and enhance their identity. And it is in community that all persons learn to appreciate social, religious, and ethical values.

Communities are undergoing serious changes. Perhaps the most serious of these changes are destructive of the forces which have built communities in the past. Integrated housing patterns are beginning to prevail in many sections all across America. The previous pattern was accentuated by massive flight of white residents to the suburbs and an entrenchment of blacks in the inner city. This polarization along racial lines serves to destroy the idea of a democratic community and has brought into being hostile entities along political, social, and educational lines.

The development of federal and state housing authorities with a democratic pattern for housing development has restored the faith of many that the possibilities of a new community are there. We affirm the 1972 Statement on Housing.

The Local Church and the Local Public Schools

In innumerable and concrete ways, the local church serves as interpreter of and witness to the gospel in the life of its community. Therefore, it is the primary channel through which the demands of the gospel are made known in society. By virtue of the nature of the church, there is nothing in the community outside its concern or beyond its ability to affect.

The local public schools historically represent one of the fundamental focal points in American communities. This is as it should be because the democratic approach to education is the bedrock of democratic, political, and economic systems. The local public schools also represent one of the largest financial outlays in any given community. In these days many public school systems have been caught in the whirling social and educational changes of the times and have fallen victim to influences and powers which have not kept the fundamental purposes of the public schools as highest priorities.

Some of the many challenging issues confronting the schools are: financial inadequacies, historic racial attitudes, busing, curriculum, growing professionalism of teachers and administrators, and the lack of well informed and sensitive school board members. Many times these issues are combined, making the problems that much more acute.

The issues confronting public schools may be different in the respective communities, as the church is different in its respective communities. Yet, by the virtue of its calling, the church must lead the communities in exploring the issues, and in identifying and seeking solutions to their particular problems.

In each community, the local United Methodist Church is responsible for being a catalyst in helping the entire community become sensitive to the issues of public education.

We encourage each local church to recognize the importance of the culture, history and important contributions of ethnic minorities to the educational process and the resulting loss when these are omitted from the curriculum. Local churches should take the initiative to be certain that local school boards in their area or communities at every level of education include in the total curricula all contributions of all peoples to the growth and development of the United States.

The lack of opportunities to learn and understand the history and cultures of all races is reflected in our present problems in human relations.

Our Judeo-Christian tradition reveals clearly our personal accountability to Almighty God in relation to our personal responsibility to and for our fellow human beings.

Where problems exist, it is especially important that the local United Methodist Church support and work with existing community groups and organizations in bringing solutions. It is also recommended that each local United Methodist church develop a committee or an informal group of members to keep the congregation and community aware of public school issues and their obligation to assist in finding meaningful solutions.

ADOPTED 1976

See Social Principles, ¶ 74, "The United Methodist Church and Church/Government Relations," "Public Education in the United States."

Concerning the Draft in the United States

The General Conference of 1980 in session in Indianapolis is to transmit by special messengers an urgent message to the President of the United States. Messengers for this mission shall be named by the Council of Bishops and include, in addition to the president of the Council, six persons: one laywoman, one clergywoman, one layman, one clergyman, and two youth members (one male and one female). At least two of the six members shall be of racial or ethnic minorities.

Such a plan for communicating with the President of the United States today, in a new kind of world and for a different purpose, is in keeping with a tradition of the early history of Methodism. Deputations of distinguished persons were sent from time to time to convey messages of support or commendation to the President from the General Conference. Among these communications, history records the visit to President George Washington in 1789, expressing gratitude to him "for the preservation of civil and religious liberties and for the glorious revolution." Again in 1864, when General Conference convened in Philadelphia, the first order of business after the flag raising was to name a delegation to call on President Lincoln to assure him of the unfaltering support of Methodists in the war against slavery. Lincoln's response expressed gratitude that "The Methodist Church sends more soldiers to the field, more nurses to the hospitals, and more prayers to heaven than any" (Charles Ferguson, *Organizing to Beat the Devil*).

The basic content and guidelines of the message to the President today shall be as follows:

The 1980 General Conference of The United Methodist Church, which includes 912 duly elected delegates from 73 annual conferences across the United States of America, respectfully calls upon the President of the United States to rescind his announced policy calling for registration of youths in this land. We believe this will lead to the possible renewal of the draft into military service. We also believe that such a presidential plan has already increased the war hysteria in our own nation and generated greater tension among the Middle East nations and their neighbors.

We acknowledge that the issues are complex in today's military-industrial economy, but we believe that a peace-minded nation, such as we claim to be, needs your leadership as a President committed to peace. Your State of the Union message and your call for a great and continuing increase in defense weaponry, renewed registration of youths for a potential draft, and greatly strengthened military power seem to rule out all means for peaceful negotiation and the resolution of the conflict through United Nations and/or in cooperation with other concerned nations.

In the words of the 1976 action of this governing body of The United Methodist Church, "One hard fact must be bluntly stated: The arms race goes on. The momentum never slackens, and the danger of a holocaust is imminent. Meanwhile, millions starve, development stagnates, and international cooperation is threatened." We, the policy-making body of this world-wide Church, pray that you will reverse your policy of dangerous military threats and fulfill your commitment to peace. We do not believe that one life, man's or woman's, should be sacrificed in a war in this period of history when the global community provides untapped means for negotiation and the reconciliation of differences.

Therefore it is with the deepest concern and the greatest urgency that we call upon you, as President of the United States, to end the threat in this nation of registration of the youths of this land. We believe that such an act is clearly a basic step toward reinstating the draft. The question before us at this time is not whether both men and women should be registered and drafted for military service. The issue, in this enlightened beginning of our third century as a nation, is leadership in a world where war seems imminent and where the peoples of the world cry out to be saved from nuclear holocaust. We pray that God will give you wisdom and courage to take the necessary action for peace on earth—now!

ADOPTED IN 1980

See Social Principles, ¶ 74.G, "Certification of Conscientious Objectors," "The United Methodist Church and Peace."

Criminal Justice

Justice is the basic principle upon which God's creation has been established. It is the necessary ingredient required for the achievement of humanity's ultimate purpose.

Justice is an integral and uncompromising part in God's redemptive process which assures wholeness. It is a quality relationship based on God's love and the human response motivated by love.

Justice is the theme which permeates the history of God's people as participants in the ongoing human drama of their daily existence.

The gospel, through the example of Jesus Christ, conveys the message for Christians to be healers, peacemakers, and reconcilers when faced with brokenness, violence, and vengeance. Through love, caring, and forgiveness, Jesus Christ was able to transform lives and restore the dignity and purpose in those who were willing to abide by his principles.

Jesus Christ was opposed to vengeance as the way to administer justice (Matt. 5:38-44).

As Christians we recognize that each person is unique and has great value before God. Human worth does not diminish when a person violates laws made by human beings, for human worth has been guaranteed even when God's law has been violated.

The Christian Church as an institution is charged with the responsibility to ensure that a system of justice safeguards the inherent right that human beings possess as God's creatures and objects of the love and care which derive from that relationship.

The primary purpose of the criminal justice system and its administration is to protect individuals and society from any violation of their legal and constitutional rights.

The criminal justice system in this country has been adversely affected by economic and social conditions which have resulted in discrimination against the poor, minorities, and women.

Too often prisons are places where dehumanizing conditions reinforce negative social behavior. This contributes to the high incidence of recidivism and perpetuates the cycle of violence, crime, and incarceration.

The administration of the criminal justice system has reached a level of saturation which leads to expediency rather than the even-handed application of justice and punishment.

As United Methodist Christians we are called to sensitize those institutions which operate within the criminal justice system to be responsible, more humane and just, to ensure the full participation in society by those who have deviated from laws established as normative guidelines for behavior. Therefore, we will:

1. Minister to prisoners, offenders, exoffenders, victims, and to the families involved. (This includes working toward the goal of restoration and reconciliation of victims and offenders.)

2. Develop and offer competent ministries of mediation and conflict resolution, within the criminal justice system.

3. Nurture members of The United Methodist Church and the general public in the insights of the faith as they provide guidance in

expressing redemption and reconciliation for those persons embroiled in the criminal justice system.

4. Develop attitudes of acceptance in the community and opportunities for employment for those persons who are released from imprisonment or who are participating in programs that assist them to re-enter community life.

5. Monitor governmental policies and programs in the field of criminal justice and respond to them from our faith perspective.

Law Enforcement and Courts

Because we believe in reconciliation and redemption, we will work for a criminal justice system that is just and humane and has as its goals restoration rather than vengeance. Toward this end we will support the following:

1. Provision of safeguards to ensure that the poor, minorities, and the inexperienced have available the legal assistance and other advantages available to the rich, powerful, and the experienced.

2. Elimination of influences and practices of discrimination based on race, ethnic, or cultural background, political identification, age, class, or sex.

3. Staffing of the criminal justice system at every level by persons who represent a diversity of backgrounds in our society and who meet high standards of training and experience, including cultural understanding and care about the persons who come under their jurisdiction.

4. Separation of juvenile offenders from adult offenders with correction given to them outside the traditional courts and correctional system.

With specific regard to law enforcement officials and the courts, we as United Methodists:

1. Support efforts to develop alternative methods to the use of deadly force by law enforcement officials.

2. Insist that accused persons should have competent legal assistance and be ensured a speedy trial.

3. Recognize that organized crime has corrupting power over the racial, political, and economic life of our nations and support efforts to oppose it through effective legislation, strong law enforcement, and the development of public awareness.

Sentences

The primary purpose of a sentence for a crime is to protect society from future crimes by the offender, the deterrence of offenders from committing a crime, restitution of the victim, and assistance to the offender to become a law-abiding citizen.

Believing in the love of Christ who came to save those who are lost and vulnerable, we urge the creation of a genuinely new system and programs for rehabilitation that will restore, preserve, and nurture the total humanity of the imprisoned. We believe that sentences should hold within them the possibilities of reconciliation and restoration. Therefore we assert that:

1. In the sentencing by the courts and in the implementation of the sentences, the criminal justice system should use all resources and knowledge available to ensure that sentencing embodies the possibility of rehabilitation and reconciliation.

2. Imprisonment should be imposed only when the continued freedom of the offender poses a direct threat to society and when no acceptable alternative exists.

3. Capital punishment should be eliminated since it violates the concept of sacredness of human life and is contrary to our belief that sentences should hold within them the possibilities of reconciliation and restoration.

4. Sentences to restitution, community service, and other non-imprisonment alternatives provide economical, rational and humane systems of justice for non-dangerous offenders and provide justice for the victim.

5. Community involvement and concern is needed to monitor the policies and practices of the criminal justice system.

6. The criminal justice system must be accessible to all persons.

7. Accused persons must not be prejudged for detention before trial on the basis of their character, race, culture, gender, or class.

8. Percentage-of-sentence limitations on "good behavior" paroles violate the Christian mandates for redemption and reconciliation.

ADOPTED 1984

See Social Principles, ¶ 74.F., "Equal Justice," "Grand Jury Abuse," "Juvenile Justice," "Local Church and the Local Jail," "Penal Reform," "Police Firearms Policies," "Victims of Crime."

Domestic Surveillance

Openness is a redemptive gift of God, calling for trust and honesty between various segments of the community. Justice is the cornerstone of that trust we have come to expect in our elective and appointive representatives of the community. Communal wholeness is attained through the concerted use of these elements.

Domestic surveillance is an issue which, without adequate safeguards of civil rights, threatens the moral and legal fiber of our society.

Domestic surveillance is the gathering of information pertaining to the intent, capabilities, and activities of individuals and/or groups involved in criminal activities for a foreign agent or power. The intent is to root out elements that threaten or harm the national security of a country. Yet, congressional hearings, over time, have revealed that intelligence agencies often misuse and abuse surveillance activities: "Domestic intelligence has threatened and undermined the constitutional rights of Americans to free speech, associations, and privacy. It has done so primarily because the constitutional system for checking abuse of power has not been applied" (1976, Senator Church's Committee Report on Intelligence).

Examples of abuse include:

1. The use of grand jury investigations to harrass American citizens and groups exercising their freedom of speech under the First Amendment. Those under subpoena to grand juries have been incarcerated after exercising their rights under the Fifth Amendment.

2. The surveillance, disruption, infiltration and harassment of, and thefts from peace groups during the Vietnam era, and later, anti-nuclear, anti-war groups.

3. The active surveillance and infiltration of church and missional programs, environmental groups, civil and constitutional rights groups, etc.

Governmental directives and policies have been formulated that provide the intelligence agencies with a wider latitude in initiating domestic investigations. Recent directives expand the role these agencies play in conducting surveillance, and use techniques that heretofore had been considered violent and extreme. These directives legitimize abuses by giving the intelligence agencies the power to:

1. Conduct warrantless searches and seizures, in direct violation of

the Fourth Amendment of the Bill of Rights, including electronic surveillance, unconsented physical surveillance, and mail surveillance.

2. Direct intelligence techniques toward anyone who comes in contact with a foreign person or organization, i.e., "foreign" friends, members of the United Nations, church and related support agencies.

3. Infiltrate and influence the activities of law-abiding organizations in the United States, without valid reason to suspect or allege illegal activities.

4. Use journalists, missionaries, students, business-persons, and teachers as undercover agents, oftentimes without their expressed knowledge.

5. Conduct secret campus research, if authorized by undefined "appropriate officials."

As United Methodists, the issue of domestice surveillance and its misuse and abuse deserves a renewed focus. As stated in the Social Principles:

> We also strongly reject domestic surveillance and intimidation of political opponents by governments in power, and all other misuse of elective and appointive offices. Citizens of all countries should have access to all essential information regarding their government and its policies. Illegal and unconscionable activities directed against persons or groups by their government or governments must not be justified or kept secret even under the guise of national security.

We therefore call upon The United Methodist Church at all levels to:

1. Affirm the rights of individuals and groups to address governmental policies that reject the freedom to associate and the freedom of speech, especially to the beliefs that enhance the political, social, economic, and spiritual quality of life.

2. Recommend revocation of directives and policies that reduce public review of executive, judicial, and legislative procedures.

3. Support the continuing need for the present Freedom of Information Act. Actions to weaken FOIA and to restrict public access to local, state, and federal documents violate the principles of trust and openness, elements that enhance human development.

4. Affirm the responsibility of governments to ensure the national security of its people. We reject the use of "national security" as a guise for illegal and unconstitutional actions of governments. Invocation of the term "national security" for unjust reasons

undermines the credibility of governments and threatens the safety of its citizenry at home and abroad.

5. Support local, state, and federal actions and policies that respond adequately to the needs of the citizenry and ensure their fundamental moral and legal rights. Local, state and federal agencies should work together with community representatives in formulating policies that account for these needs.

ADOPTED 1984

See Social Principles, ¶¶ 74.A and C, "Repression and the Right to Privacy."

Enabling Financial Support for Domestic Programs

The United Methodist Church has declared war to be "incompatible with the teachings of Jesus Christ"; and

Dr. Martin Luther King, Jr., wrote that "racism and its perennial ally" economic exploitation "provide the key to understanding most of the international complications of this generation"; and

General Colin Powell offered testimony to the Congressional Black Caucus that the military presently provided the only means whereby thousands of Black youth and young adults could obtain a decent standard of living and an education, going on to say that such opportunities should also be made available by the private and the rest of the public sectors; and

While there is unemployment among other minority groups, tens of thousands of African-American male and female young adults have never been employed and are, therefore, not counted in current unemployment statistics; and

The majority of public school districts (especially those which serve the masses of urban black, Hispanic, and poor people) find themselves facing severe financial shortfalls, staff cuts, the elimination of vital programs, and school closings; and

Those same communities are experiencing social trauma due to plant closings and the relocation of industry to countries where the wages are from $.50 to $1.00 an hour; and

The Free Trade Agreement, proposed by President George Bush, will facilitate further plant closings and create further hardships for Black, Hispanic, and other poor communities.

We petition the President and Congress of the United States to reduce the U.S. military presence by recognizing principles of sovereignty in every region of the world.

We petition the President and Congress of the United States to reapportion dollars, saved by reduced military spending and base closings, for domestic programs that will enable the financial support for an increase in quality educational offerings in the public school systems of the country, adequate health care, the creation of sufficient employment opportunities, and a new comprehensive employment training act, which will appropriate federal dollars into elements of the private sector that are currently in compliance with affirmative action guidelines, for the purpose of encouraging their participation in the retraining of U.S. workers, and redevelopment of plants within the continental United States.

ADOPTED 1992

See Social Principles, ¶ 74, "The United Methodist Church and Peace," "U.S.-Mexico Border," "Unemployment."

Equal Justice

It must be remembered that the advice, "Let every person be subject to the governing authorities" (Romans 13:1), is preceded by: "Live in harmony with another, do not be haughty, but associate with the lowly, never be conceited. Repay no one evil for evil, but take thought for what is noble in the sight of all" (Romans 12:16ff).

The admonition is directed to the authorities who govern as well as those who may be subject.

The Social Principles of The United Methodist Church states that, "The Church should continually exert a strong ethical influence upon the state, supporting policies and programs deemed to be just and compassionate and opposing policies and programs which are not." "We support governmental measures designed to reduce and eliminate crime, consistent with respect for the basic freedom of persons. We reject all misuse of these necessary mechanisms, including their use for the purpose of persecuting or intimidating those whose race, appearance, lifestyle, economic conditions, or beliefs differ from those in authority, and we reject all careless, callous, or discriminatory enforcement of law."

The Police

In our democratic society, the police fill a position of extraordinary trust and power. Usually the decision of whether a citizen is to be taken into custody rests solely with the police. For these reasons, law enforcement officers must be persons who possess good judgment, sound discretion, proper temperament, and are physically and mentally alert.

Unusual care must be exercised in the selection of those persons to serve as police officers. We recommend pyschological testing prior to employment of police officers and periodically thereafter. During the period of training and continually thereafter, police must be instilled with the knowledge that the rights of many will never be secured if the government through its police powers is permitted to prefer some of its citizens over others. The practice of citizen preference in the enforcement of our criminal laws must not be tolerated. Our laws must be fairly enforced and impartially administered. No one is immune from the requirements of the law because of power, position, or economic station in life. Further, the power of the police must never be used to harass and provoke the young, the poor, the unpopular, and the members of racial and cultural minorities.

Where there is heavy pressure upon police officers by police departments to make regularly a large number of arrests as a demonstration of their initiative and professional performance, we urge that such practice be discontinued.

In a democratic society, however, a large majority of police work encompasses peacekeeping and social services rather than crime control functions. Police routinely use more than 85 percent of their duty time in giving assistance to citizens and making referrals to other governmental agencies. It is important for police to be recognized and promoted for their effectiveness in such roles as diverting youths from disorderly activities, peacefully intervening in domestic quarrels, anticipating disturbances through the channeling of grievances, and the building of good community relationships.

The United Methodist Church recommends that police departments publicly establish standards of police conduct and policies for promotion. To this end congregations should encourage the police to conduct public hearings among all classes of citizens, giving adequate weight to peacekeeping, life-protecting, and other service roles, as well as the bringing of criminal offenders to justice. The standards must include strict limits on the police use of guns.

We further recommend that police officers live within the jurisdiction in which they are employed.

We make these recommendations not only in concern about the frequent abuses of people by the police, but also because we are concerned for more effective control of crime. We observe that only about one half the victims of serious crime and a far smaller proportion of witnesses report to the police. If offenders are to be apprehended and convicted, police and law-abiding citizens must work closely together. Such cooperation can occur only when the police are fair and humane and when they are publicly known to be sensitive and considerate.

The United Methodist Church urges that communities establish adequate salary scales for police officers and develop high standards for recruiting both men and women, and members of all ethnic groups. Recruitment must be followed by adequate training in social relations and dispute settlement as well as in law and the skills of crime detection investigation, and the apprehension of offenders. As police officers continue to meet those improved qualifications, we will recognize law enforcement as a profession with status and respect.

Criminal Laws and the Courts

Where the law recognizes and permits plea bargaining, and in those instances where the ends of justice dictate that a negotiated plea be considered, we recommend it should be permitted and approved only after full disclosure in open court of the terms and conditions of such plea bargaining agreement. Equal justice requires that all trials and the sentencing of those convicted under our criminal laws must be conducted in the public court room.

Since at present 90 percent of all criminal convictions are by guilty pleas—an unknown but large proportion of those by plea bargaining—this recommendation would mean a large increase in the work of the criminal courts. However, that work should be correspondingly eased by changes in the law such as the moving of most traffic offenses out of criminal court to administrative procedures, and by relieving the court of great numbers of civil cases through the adoption of genuine no-fault motor vehicle insurance laws. The courts must also organize their work efficiently, employing modern management procedures. Many improvements could be made by the use of administrative volunteers, including retirees who can furnish professional services at minimal costs to the court.

Other changes needed to obtain equal justice in the courts include:

1. The repeal of some criminal laws against certain personal conditions or individual misconduct. Examples are criminal prohibitions of vagrancy, personal gambling, public drunkenness, and prostitution. Together, these items alone account for more than half of all arrests in some jurisdictions. They result in little social good but great evil in class discrimination, alienation, and waste of resources needed for other purposes. Some related laws such as those against drunken driving and those limiting and controlling the operation of gambling establishments need to be tightened.

2. The adoption of systematic new penal codes prescribing penalties proportionate to the predictable damage done by the various kinds of crime, without regard to the class of the offender.

3. The training of judges of juvenile and criminal courts in the use of nonincarcerating community sanctions wherever the offense does not involve persistent violence.

4. The adoption of systematic new penal codes prescribing a range of penalties without regard to the class of the offender, but utilizing non-incarceration community sanctions wherever possible. The provision for court-fixed sentences, rather than mandatory ones, in order to draw upon the skill and the training of qualified judges.

5. Statement by the sentencing judge of the reason or reasons why he or she is selecting from the range permitted by the law the particular sentence being pronounced.

6. The development of appropriate jury selection procedures which would insure most inclusive representation including representatives of the socio-economic class and ethnic group of the defendants.

7. The adoption by all courts of: (a) speedy trial provisions which the constitution guarantees, and (b) that degree of personal recognizance and supervision which each defendant's situation warrants, in place of the present inherently discriminatory bail bond pre-trial release process that exists in some courts.

8. When fines are assessed, they should be scaled to the magnitude of the crime and the ability of the offender to pay. In suitable cases, fines should be made payable in installments.

9. Governmental regulated programs of compensation for reimbursement of financial loss incurred by innocent victims of crime should be encouraged.

We recommend that local churches consider setting up court monitoring panels to observe the court operations and proceedings. Such panels may well adopt a role of "friends of the court" or of advocacy on behalf of accused persons. They may adopt other appropriate procedures in the interest of criminal justice, including close scrutiny of plea bargaining and/or evidence of unequal imposition of sentences.

ADOPTED 1980

See Social Principles, ¶ 74.F, "Criminal Justice," "Grand Jury Abuse," "Juvenile Justice," "Victims of Crime."

Grand Jury Abuse

Jesus' words, "Judge not that you may not be judged . . ." (Matthew 7:1) surely imply that all judgments are judged in the light of God's truth. The Social Principles of The United Methodist Church state boldly that ". . . governments, no less than individuals, are subject to the judgment of God."

Such a social principle causes us appropriately to view with concern the government's use of the Grand Jury to control dissent and harass those who act under the constraint of conscience.

The Grand Jury is envisioned in American law as a protector of citizens from unwarranted prosecutions. It is for this reason that its proceedings are secret and it has the power to subpoena witnesses.

Evidence indicates that in recent years the extraordinary powers of the Grand Jury often have been used—not for the protection of citizens—but in subjecting them to harassment and intimidation. Historically, political dissidents, anti-war activists, and leaders of minority groups and religious organizations have been particularly vulnerable to these abuses.

A government prosecutor can control the Grand Jury, thus distorting the Grand Jury's power to monitor and moderate the actions of the prosecution.

The prosecutor can use the subpoena powers of the Grand Jury to conduct investigations which are the responsibility of law enforcement agencies. As an example, Congress has never given the Federal Bureau of Investigation subpoena powers, yet agents routinely threaten uncooperative persons with subpoenas from a Grand Jury. In fact, subpoenas are often served at the request of the Federal Bureau of Investigation.

The use of the powers of the Grand Jury to harass and pursue political dissidents is a departure from its proper constitutional function, and is a threat to public order, lawful government, and true domestic security.

Witnesses called before a Grand Jury may be given little or no warning of their subpoenas, may be forced to travel to courts at distances from their homes, may not know whether they are targets of prosecution, may have little understanding of their rights, and cannot have legal counsel in the chambers.

Comprehensive Grand Jury reform legislation is needed to restore the constitutional guarantees of protection for citizens. The Fifth Amendment right against self-incrimination and false accusation must be re-established and reinforced.

The United Methodist Church, therefore, supports legislation designed to enhance the rights to due process of law, freedom of association, effective legal counsel, the presumption of innocence, and the privilege against self-incrimination of persons subpoenaed to testify before Grand Juries.

ADOPTED 1980

See Social Principles, ¶ 74.F, "Equal Justice," "Criminal Justice."

Gun Control

With the mounting proliferation of firearms in American society, the safety of our citizens cannot be guaranteed. Crime in city streets climbs, accidents abound, and suicides soar.

Christians concerned about reverence for life care about what is happening to many victims of gun murders and assaults. In the name of Christ, who came that persons might know abundant life, we call upon the Church to affirm its faith through vigorous efforts to curb gun violence.

In 1974, the last year for which complete figures are available, there were some 32,000 firearms deaths in the United States. Of these approximately 15,000 were murders, 14,000 suicides and about 3,000 accidents. The handgun was used in the largest proportion of these deaths. We know, for example, that 54 percent of the murders occurring in 1974 were by handguns.

Behind the statistics often lies great tragedy: children and teachers are being shot in school; depressed persons are taking their lives with guns left around the house; householders purchasing guns to protect their homes often end up using them to kill a loved one; police officers are being gunned down in increasing numbers in the course of duty.

As Christians who are deeply concerned about human life, we intend to do something about the unregulated access to guns in this shooting gallery called America.

We do not believe there is any constitutional personal right to bear arms. As the United Sates Supreme Court has ruled a number of times, the Second Amendment has to do with the militia, currently comparable to the National Guard.

The United States might well learn from the experience of other societies where stringent gun control laws are enforced. The gun murder rate per 100,000 population in the United States is 100 times greater than in England and Wales, where strict gun laws prevail; it is 200 times greater than in Japan, where it is impossible for the public to secure handguns legally. We believe that the time has come when the United States should move toward a less violent and more civilized society.

Therefore, The United Methodist Church declares its support for the licensing of all gun owners and the registration of all firearms. Licensing provisions should require adequate identification of gun owners and provide basic standards with respect to age, absence of mental illness, and lack of a serious criminal record. These and other objective standards should be applied in determining the granting or denial of any license.

In addition, special controls should be applied to the handgun, for it is the most deadly and least utilitarian weapon in American society. Because the handgun is concealable, it is the weapon of crime; because the handgun is available, it is the instrument used in suicides and crimes of passion.

Therefore, we call upon the United States government to establish a national ban on the importation, manufacture, sale, and possession of handguns and handgun ammunition with reasonable limited exceptions. Such exceptions should be restricted to: the police, the military, licensed security guards, antique dealers who maintain guns in unfireable condition, and licensed pistol clubs where firearms are kept on the premises under secure conditions.

In fairness to handgun owners, we propose that those who comply with the law and turn in their guns be compensated at fair value through a cash payment or tax credit.

ADOPTED 1976

See Social Principles, ¶ 74.F, "Police Firearms Policies," "U.S. Gun Violence."

Human Rights

Mindful of the tradition in which we stand, we see the struggle for human rights for all people of God to be a continuous unfolding of the gospel. It is an unfinished task. Our participation in this struggle means that we must identify those principalities and powers that militate against the worth of persons and groups, that seek to devalue life by denying basic rights, or that claim an ultimacy for themselves rather than for the persons they are designed to serve.

We affirm that all persons and groups are of equal worth in the sight of God. We therefore work toward societies in which each person's or group's worth is recognized, maintained, and strengthened. We deplore all political and economic ideologies that lead to repression or totalitarianism, that pit persons against each other, that deny hope, that seek to enhance privilege and power of the few at the expense of the well-being of the many. We condemn violations of human rights in all political and economic structures. The Church, while proclaiming the gospel message of a God of love and justice, must be wary lest it compromise its own witness and unwittingly become an uncritical ally of repressive power and privilege in society around it.

As United Methodists throughout the world give more attention to human rights, we must constantly examine or change our own practices in every locale where the basic rights of persons or groups may have been denied. The church in each community should be the means for removing the blindness from our eyes so that we perceive rights denied and redress imperfections.

Often the relationship of one country to another has been dictated by military and economic interests which tend to shape foreign policy and override moral imperatives to defend human rights. The Church should not sanction nor should foreign governments support those governments or regimes that deny people the right of speech, assembly, dissent, education, health, worship, or other rights.

Therefore we urge:

1. That The United Methodist Church on all levels continually examine the biblical and theological bases which call us to our own commitment to human rights.

2. That The United Methodist Church urge governments to cease all financial, military, open, or covert support of those governments or regimes that systematically violate the rights of their citizens.

3. That The United Methodist Church urge governments—nationally, regionally, and locally—to accord basic human rights to all persons residing within their boundaries regardless of citizenship. These rights include the right to an education, adequate health care, due process and redress of law, and protection against social and economic exploitation.

4. That United Methodist agencies join in efforts—ecumenical, denominational, or international—on behalf of human rights, informing our people of developments in the struggles and offering them means of constructive responses.

5. That The United Methodist Church designate human rights as a continuing study emphasis to be carried on in every local church, utilizing in part the Social Principles and materials published in 1979 by the National Council of Churches and the Board of Global Ministries for the study theme, "Human Rights and the International Order."

ADOPTED 1980

See Social Principles, ¶ 74.A, "Domestic Surveillance," "Repression and the Right to Privacy," "Ratification of Human Rights Covenants and Conventions," "New Issues in Human Rights."

Immigration

I. *Biblical/Theological Reflection*

The Old Testament is the story of a people on the move, often as immigrants and refugees, frequently as seekers of a better homeland. It is the story of suffering and repression and God's liberating action in the midst of that history. The sojourn of Ruth and the fleeing of Jacob and his sons to avoid famine are just two of the many stories related by the witness of the Old Testament. The Hebrew people, pilgrims themselves, were also reminded by their leaders and prophets: "Do not mistreat or oppress a foreigner; you know how it feels to be a foreigner because you were foreigners in Egypt" (Exod. 23:9), and "You are strangers and sojourners with me" (Lev. 25:23).

The New Testament story begins by reaffirming this heritage of uprootedness as the infant Jesus and his family fled to Egypt to avoid political persecution. Jesus' life from that beginning was marked by uprootedness: "Foxes have holes, wild birds have nests, but the Son of man has nowhere to lay his head" (Matt. 8:20). His friends and disciples were neither the "pillars of society" nor the holders of power, but those who were themselves homeless and often poor, powerless, despised, and rejected. His encounters were often with people who were direct challenges to the political and social sterotypes of his own nation-state.

Into a world of ethnic diversity, racial fears and nationalistic insecurities, Jesus brought a grace and power to overcome those fears. His new way was: "Love one another. As I have loved you, so must you love one another" (John 12:34-35). Love is fulfilled in the love of the stranger and sojourner. As stated in Heb. 13:1-2: "Let . . . love continue. Do not neglect to show hospitality to strangers for thereby some have entertained angels unawares."

II. *Historical Background*

Nearly all the citizens of the United States have come from other parts of the world. Since the 17th century, millions of immigrants came to the colonies and the United States, often to seek greater freedom and broader opportunities in a new land. No other nation has welcomed so many immigrants from so many parts of the world for so many centuries. Nevertheless, the history of immigration policy in the United States has been heavily influenced by public views on economics and racism. Since 1798 with the passage of the Alien Act until the present, the U.S. immigration policy has at times encouraged the presence of immigrants who could provide the cheap hard labor to build canals and railroads, help with the harvesting of crops, and supply industry with needed workers. At other times U.S. immigration has sytematically excluded immigrants because of racial, ethnic, religious, or other prejudicial reasons. Examples are the Chinese Exclusion Act of 1882, Immigration Act of 1924, designed to deport Mexican laborers, the Quota Law of 1921, and the Refugee Act of 1980, which denied Haitian, Ethiopian, and Latin Americans the classifications of refugees. While changes in immigration law and policy are necessary, we as the church need to be mindful of our tradition as stated in our Social Principles: "The church must regard nations as accountable for unjust treatment of their citizens and others living within their borders."

Therefore, we call the leaders of the United States of America:

1. To continue to strive to make the United States a model of social justice in its domestic immigration policies as well as in its foreign policy and diplomatic relations with other nations.

2. To interpret broadly the immigration laws of the United States a) by providing sanctuary for those fleeing because of well-founded fear of persecution due to their political affiliation, religious orientation and/or racial origin; and b) by adopting reasonable standards of proof of eligibility as refugees for those seeking asylum.

3. To withhold support to governments with a documented recent history of abuses and disregard for human rights.

4. To eliminate within the Immigration and Naturalization Service (INS) all abuses of civil and human rights including such practices as the violation of due process, denial of bail, or hasty deportation of the undocumented and overstayed.

5. To strengthen the service arm of the INS by increasing availability of personnel at the administrative levels in order to process applications and diminish the backlog of immigration applications.

6. To monitor all attempted reforms on immigration policy to ensure fair and adequate process in regards to judicial review, quota systems, and family reunification.

7. To reject the use of an identification card as a measure to control immigrants.

We urge the leaders of all nations:

1. To alleviate conditions and change internal politics that create a momentum for the migration of people over the world. (This means working for agrarian reform, social justice, and an adequate measure of economic security of all peoples.)

2. To create international economic policies that use capital, technology, labor, and land in a manner that gives priority to employment and production of basic human necessities. (At the same time such policies should not give inordinate power to transnational corporations and should avoid displacing people from their land.)

3. To recognize and respond to the causes and consequences of internally displaced people.

4. To seek an end to hostilities and terrorism through the just resolution of the socio-political conflicts which spawn such activities and give rise to large numbers of refugees.

5. To ensure protection of the basic human rights of immigrants (such as the right to an education, adequate health care, due process and redress of law, protection against social and economic exploitation, the right to a cultural and social indentity, and access to the social and economic life of nations) for both documented and undocumented, permanent or transient refugees or immigrants.

6. To welcome generous numbers of persons and families dislocated by natural disasters, war, political turmoil, repression, persecution, discrimination, or economic hardship.

7. To stop all military and financial aid and certification of governments which disregard human rights.

We speak to the whole church, and specifically call upon United Methodist churches and agencies to devote special attention and resources to the care of the legal, social, and other needs of over-stayed and of undocumented persons. We instruct the General Board of Church and Society and the General Board of Global Ministries to:

1. Continue explorations of solutions to the problems of the overstayed and of undocumented persons.

2. Serve as advocate on behalf of The United Methodist Church in support of the immigration principles of family unity and documentation for other cases of a hardship nature.

3. Monitor cases of possible human rights violations in the area of immigration and give guidance to United Methodists in responding to such cases.

4. Provide technical and financial assistance to local churches in active ministry to overstayed and undocumented persons.

5. Continue the task of educating United Methodists on the subject of immigration.

ADOPTED 1984

See Social Principles, ¶ ¶ 74.A and B, 75. A and B, "Assistance and Sanctuary for Central American Refugees," "U.S. Mexico Border."

Juvenile Justice

Our Lord particularly identified with children and illustrated the loving care which they need to grow and mature (Mark 9:36-37, Mark 9:42).

The Social Principles of The United Methodist Church calls for special attention to the rights of children and youth. From these perspectives we are concerned that in many states children are arrested and incarcerated for truancy, incorrigibility, stubborn altercations with parents, and other conduct which would not be criminal if performed by an adult. Such status offenses should not be considered as grounds for involving a juvenile in processes of criminal procedure or even of delinquency procedures. Rather, a child in trouble should be helped by agencies for domestic assistance.

There is considerable evidence that the methods of dealing with the child have a major part in developing criminal tendencies. Most violent adults persistently repeating crimes began their conflict with law and order as children ten to fourteen years old. If treatment by the state or local agencies leads the child to think of himself or herself as a tough young criminal, he or she is likely to act out that role.

The United Methodist Church urges that all status offenses be eliminated from the juvenile codes and from the processes for determining juvenile delinquency. We urge further that all offenses by children and youth be handled with extreme reluctance to incarcerate the offender. We especially oppose solitary confinement of children and youths in official detention. Institutions where juveniles classified as delinquent often are segregated from the general population often become schools of crime. As an alternative, we encourage greater use of supportive services for parents and children in their home settings; foster child care; neighborhood group homes, Parents Anonymous, and other alternatives.

There are communities within the states in which children are routinely locked up in jails because of a lack of temporary shelter care or an unwillingness to use home detention. We urge the prohibition of placing dependent and neglected children in jails or facilities for juvenile delinquents.

ADOPTED 1980

See Social Principles, ¶¶ 72.C, and 74.F, "Ministry to Runaway Children," "Criminal Justice," "Prevention and Reduction of Juvenile Delinquency."

Literacy, The Right to Learn: A Basic Human Right

I. Introduction

The United Methodist Church respects the inestimable worth of each person and his or her potential contribution to the transformation of the world. We, therefore, recognize and support the right of basic education for all so that individuals may determine their own lives and participate fully in social and political decisions. The Protestant Reformation was fueled by the ability of persons to read and interpret the Bible for themselves. Historically The United Methodist Church and its predecessor denominations have placed high priority on equipping persons to read and interpret the Bible. Through these efforts we have experienced the power of the Word to liberate and transform both persons and societies.

Literacy skills of reading, writing, and numeracy as well as the skills needed to function in a complex economic and technical world are tools needed in the advancement of society. We have come to understand that literacy is a process by which women and men can learn to organize themselves and to help to change the lives and conditions which hinder their quality of life.

II. Literacy as a social force for change

Although our world is still defined by borders, peoples of all nations are profoundly influenced by each other through global communication and travel. All peoples and nations are needed in the work of social transformation. Unfortunately, large segments of the world's population lack access to education. Some 960 million adults—15 years and older—cannot read, compute, or express themselves in writing. Industrialized countries, including the United States, report that from 10 to 15 percent of the adult population lacks the skills and knowledge required to function in a complex society. There are more than 100 million children throughout the world who have no access to primary schooling. Women and girls suffer a woeful lack of opportunity for basic education worldwide, but especially in countries with large rural populations.

Women, according to UNESCO estimates, make up nearly two-thirds of all persons who are not literate. Girls constitute 60 percent of the 116 million children unable to attend primary school in 1985. This discrimination stems, at times, from cultural bias favoring men and boys. Also, women and girls carry heavier responsibility for reproduction and expected economic production roles, without the education and training needed for their work or for building their self-esteem.

III. Biblical and theological references

The United Methodist Church clearly affirms that all human beings are created in the image of God. We are called to live according to Christ's words, "I have come in order that you might have life—life in all its fullness" (John 10:10b). We understand that if one of us is denied participation in the fullness of life, we are all diminished by it and that enabling others to achieve fullness of life allows the image of God to shine through all of us. We recognize our potential as a faith community to participate in peoples' self-development. We understand the influence we can have on governments' education policies and on the use and the distribution of national resources that support life.

Through our Social Creed, we commit ourselves to the rights of women, men, and children and to the improvement of the quality of life for all. Local and national governments must provide basic literacy programs needed for the development and free expression of peoples. The right to literacy extends beyond national boundaries and calls for the commitment and support of the international community.

There is need for a distribution system which acknowledge the worth of each person. The movement toward literacy for all is a step forward for a more just international economic order. Oppression of certain segments of population, including the abuse of the right to literacy, violates the principle of fullness of life for all. The world's people can only come near to their potential if the gifts and creativity of women, men, and children everywhere are set free through acceptance, respect, education, and the opportunity for full participation. The commitment to the fullness of life for all challenges us to recognize the importance of basic education, including literary, so that it influences the program policy and the allocation of resources of The United Methodist Church.

IV. *Illiteracy inhibits the development of a more just society*

Access to literacy skills and basic education expands personal choice, increases control over one's environment and allows for collective action not otherwise possible. Access to literacy and basic education not only empowers women, but, in many countries, is the key to the intellectual and physical well-being of children. In some cases, children's very survival depends solely upon their mother's level of literacy. In almost all cases, raising this level is the most direct way to raise the literacy level of the family as a whole, because it is the mother who educates the children. In brief, literacy is one tool for creating a just society and for helping people to act upon forces blocking other life goals.

The problem of poverty is closely linked to the lack of access to basic literacy and functional literacy skills. It follows that human and community development can be greatly enhanced when children, women, and men are literate. Literacy education enables the increase of productivity, enhances social and cultural awareness, and promotes international understanding. When literacy training is appropriate and well applied, it enables people to work for a fair, equitable distribution of resources and the necessary structural changes in society. Therefore, when The United Methodist Church commits itself to the fullness of life for all persons through its concerns that equitable literacy training be made available to all, it is at the same time a commitment to political, social, and economic equality and justice.

V. *Conclusion*

The United Methodist Church supports the basic belief in people's ability to empower themselves. Literacy is a basic human right. It is defined not only as the ability to function in a modern society but also to understand the context of one's life. Therefore, The United Methodist Church challenges national governments to provide and maintain public literacy education which recognizes the learner's dignity, fosters cooperative rather than competitive learning skills, and enables the learner to be prepared for democratic participation. It also encourages other nongovernmental agencies to renew their commitment to the right to literacy by allocating resources equal to its importance. All boards, agencies, and members are called to give strong and special support to the right to literacy through allocation of human and financial resources, advocacy, and collaborative action with ecumenical and nongovernmental agencies.

VI. *Recommendations for action*

To implement its commitment to the right of all persons to learn, The United Methodist Church strongly:

1. Commends to every level of the denomination the Right to Learn Declaration. "The Right to Learn is a fundamental human right whose legitimacy is universal: the right to learn cannot be confined to one section of humanity; it must not be the exclusive privilege of men, or of the industrialized countries, or the wealthy classes, or those young people fortunate enough to receive schooling."

2. Urges all leaders of nations—industrialized and nonindustrialized—to make and implement policies in which human values outweigh military claims as their governments determine priorities.

3. Requests that annual conferences, local churches, and individual members advocate, on the local and national level, public education for all children and for continuing literacy education for all adults who lack literacy skills or who do not have the skills required to participate fully in a complex society.

4. Recommends that boards and agencies make adequate funds available to support the efforts of partner churches and agencies to provide basic literacy for children and adults.

5. Recommends that United Methodist agencies consider "The Right to Learn" resolution a priority and design communication resources—print, audio-visual, and electronic—for its interpretation and promotion.

6. Encourages its congregations and members to:

a. participate in literacy projects existing in local communities as part of the church's mission and ministry;

b. become informed and supportive of legislative actions at the local and national level regarding literacy and the right to learn;

c. learn about the effects the lack of access to literacy has on the adult population, particularly on women, at the local, national, and international level;

d. continue support in local churches in the United States for partnership in literacy in cooperation with the Working Group on Literacy of the National Council of Churches and other ecumenical bodies;

e. promote the work of literacy in colleges, churches, and women's organizations in the worldwide struggle for self-determination and justice.

ADOPTED 1992

See Social Principles, ¶¶ 72 and 74.D, "Public Education in the United States."

The Local Church and the Local Jail

The writer of the Letter to the Hebrews, in suggesting conduct consistent with the new covenant brought through the mediation of Jesus, advises, "Remember those who are in prison as though in prison with them" (Hebrews 13:3).

The Social Principles of The United Methodist Church urges that the love of Christ be translated into "new systems of rehabilitation that will restore, preserve, and nurture the humanity of the imprisoned." This concern must be expressed in local communities by local congregations, for most of those imprisoned in the United States are in city and county jails.

Citizens pay millions of dollars for the support of jails in their local communities each year; yet, for the individuals who are detained in them, jail life is a particularly dehumanizing experience accompanied by the loss of freedom, the loss of contact with family and friends, and the loss of self-determination.

According to recent studies, most local jails provide inadequate food services, minimal medical care, no libraries or recreational facilities, no educational programs, and only a limited religious ministry. These conditions are physically injurious, mentally deteriorating, and spiritually destructive to those who are confined.

Most of the persons detained in local jails are being held for trial and actually are serving sentences prior to their conviction.

Since incarceration is by its very nature dehumanizing and destructive, The United Methodist Church states its belief that every responsible means should be used to reduce the present jail population and to use methods (such as release on recognizance, bail, probation, etc.) to keep persons out of jail.

All citizens have a fundamental right and obligation to know how the jails in their communities are being administered, how prisoners are being treated, and under what conditions they are being confined.

They should have further concern for the losses in human relationships and personal welfare which are suffered by those who are held in local jails.

The United Methodist Church urges its members to inform themselves about local jails through participation in citizen inspections; to establish programs of regular volunteer visitation with both individual staff members and confined residents of jails; to support chaplaincy programs within jails; and to seek diligently the alleviation of the present inhumane conditions while working for the eventual elimination of jails, except as necessary places of detention for dangerous criminals. Members of churches are further urged to support and fund organizations in their local communities which advocate the protection of the rights of all citizens. Where conditions are found to be substandard, United Methodist Church members are urged to request formal inquiry procedures.

ADOPTED 1980

See Social Principles, ¶ 74.F, "Penal Reform," "Equal Justice," "Criminal Justice."

New Issues in Human Rights

"God created human beings
in the image of God they were created;
male and female were created."
(Paraphrased from Genesis 1:26-27)

This biblical passage shows us that in our spiritual identity, we possess a God-given worth and dignity. The biblical tradition demands that we live in an interdependent relationship with God and our neighbor. That moves us to respond to human need at every community level.

"Now therefore, if you will obey my voice and keep my covenant, you shall be my own possession among all people for all the earth is mine, and you shall be to me a kingdom of priests and a holy nation." (Exodus 19:5-6, Revised Standard Version).

"You shall love the Lord your God with all your heart, with all your soul, with all your strength and with your mind and your neighbor as ourself." (Luke 10:27-28)

As covenant people of God who are a part to this covenant, we are called to responsibility rather than privilege.

God's vision for humanity as revealed in the life, death and resurrection of Jesus Christ demands the total fulfillment of human rights in an interdependent global community. It is a vision of life where needs of the community have priority over individual fears and where redemption and reconciliation are available to all. Human rights are holistic in nature and therefore indivisible in their social, civil, political, cultural and economic aspects. The omission of any of these aspects deny our God-given human dignity.

Further, we receive and carry, as Christians, a mandate to seek justice and liberation. That mandate calls us to safeguard the dignity of all persons, whether they are the oppressed or the oppressors by identifying and eliminating the root causes of human rights violations throughout our global community.

Therefore, The United Methodist Church reinforces its commitment to human rights and God's covenant by critically assessing and safeguarding the following principles in human rights:

1) All persons are of equal worth and dignity.
2) All persons have the right to the basic necessities of life, as defined in the United Nations Declaration of Human Rights.
3) All persons have the right to self-determination, cultural identify and minority distinction.
4) All persons have the right to religious expression and practice. As a people "committed to Christ" and "called to change", we are responsible for securing the integrity of our covenant in the midst of new imposing human rights developments.

In this spirit, we call upon citizens within the church and society to critically analyze trends and developments which may impinge upon human rights. These include:

1) The increase of capital intensive technology.
2) The intentional use of data banks to provide pervasive information.
3) The growing phenomenon of an "underclass" of persons domestically and internationally excluded from full participation in society due to educational, cultural, economic and political conditions.
4) The possible economic and political scape-goating of such an "underclass" for technological and social displacement. The

criterion of a "Fourth World" and its potential scapegoat for the social displacement resulting from technological advances.

5) Increasing extrajudicial executions, torture and disappearances of dissenters, their families and communities.

6) The growth of militarism and the imposition of military-like behavior on civilians.

7) The increase of terrorism and the growth of less publicized racist movements such as the paramilitary units of the Ku Klux Klan, the Posse Comitatus, etc. and so-called "National Fronts" in Britain and France.

8) The decreasing control in many countries of domestic and international units as well as increasing surveillance of their own citizenry perceived under the guise of a potential threat to national security.

9) The conflict of rising expectations of developing countries and the disproportionate sharing of global resources.

History teaches us that militarism and greed can overwhelm and undermine movements to secure human rights. Moreover, as humanity approaches the 21st Century the role of the church as advocate, healer, and servant of the poor and oppressed, including the indigenous people, is necessary. In the political, social and economic quest for justice and peace, the insatiable demand for material gain requires the church to be an advocate for the human rights of all.

Meanwhile, we commend those positive trends lending impetus to the human rights movement. Among them:

—The growing acceptance of universal standards for human rights.

—The increasing consensus against war as a viable solution to international conflicts.

—Recent moves to include "basic human needs" criteria in international aid packages and financial aid programming.

—The acknowledgement by the international community of a bona fide human role for the church.

—The establishment of human rights offices within governments of several nations.

—The growing emphasis on the technology appropriate to the cultural setting.

We hereby call upon all governments to renew their obligation to human rights by refraining from repressive, torture and violence against all persons. We further call upon all governments to fulfill their positive obligations to human rights to ratifying and implementing international conventions, covenants and protocols addressing human rights in the context of justice and peace.

We call the Church to be a place of refuge for the "heavy laden" and uprooted of the global community.

While recognition and protection of human rights is an essential part of our Christian obligations, we must remember that human rights alone do not assure individual redemption and wholeness. The Church must keep before the global community the claims of Christ upon humanity to seek lovingly to fulfill his mandate expressed in the Great Commission.

Therefore, we call upon all members of The United Methodist Church to do all within their power to further these objectives.

ADOPTED 1988

See Social Principles, ¶ 74.A, "Human Rights," "Repression and the Right to Privacy," "Domestic Surveillance."

Opposition to a Call for a Constitutional Convention

As United Methodists, we are grateful that for almost 200 years the Constitution of the United States has provided a basis for cherished religious and civil liberties. The document, drawn up by persons, including many descendants of those who fled to America because of persecution for their religious beliefs, has served as the cornerstone of our freedoms. The Social Principles statement of The United Methodist Church "acknowledge(s) the vital function of government as a principal vehicle for the ordering of society." With the rules for governing, a constitutional convention would become a vehicle of disorder rather than order.

We are therefore deeply concerned about state efforts to mandate that Congress call a convention which would re-open the Constitution and possibly jeopardize its provisions.

I. Background

Unknown to most citizens of the United States, state legislatures have petitioned Congress for a constitutional convention. Only seven more are needed to make up the three-fourths required by the

Constitution. This would be the first constitutional convention since 1787 which was called to amend the Articles of Confederation. There are two forces behind the movement. One desires to add an amendment declaring a fetus a human person at the moment of conception, thus prohibiting abortions for any reason. Another force seeks an amendment to require a balanced federal budget.

The Constitution provides two methods for proposing amendments. One is the familiar route used to adopt all of the twenty-six present amendments. Five others were approved by Congress but not ratified by the states. Two are still pending. Both methods are described in Article V of the Constitution:

The Congress, whenever two-thirds of both Houses shall deem it necessary, shall propose amendments to this Constitution, or on the application of the legislatures of two-thirds of the several states, shall call a convention for proposing amendments, which, in either case, shall be valid to all intents and purposes of this Constitution, when ratified by the legislatures of three-fourths of the several states, or by conventions in three-fourths thereof, as the one or the other mode of ratification may be proposed by the Congress.

Since 1787 there have been over 300 applications for a constitutional convention but no single proposal has ever been endorsed by two-thirds of the states at the same time. The closest approach occurred in the mid-1960's when thirty-three state legislatures petitioned Congress to call a convention to overrule the "one person, one vote" decision of the Supreme Court dealing with equitable apportionment of state legislatures.

II. Reasons for Opposition to a Constitutional Convention

We state the following concerns as our reasons for opposing a constitutional convention.

1. There are virtually no guidelines regarding the specific rules for calling a convention and, if it were called, for determining how it would be run.

Since the language of the Constitution is vague, serious questions have been raised which constitutional scholars and jurists are unable to answer. What constitutes a valid application to Congress by a state legislature for an amending convention? Do all state petitions have to have the same wording, the same provisions, and the same subject matter? If the two-thirds of the legislatures do adopt a resolution, is Congress obliged to call a convention? Must all applications for a convention on a given issue be submitted to the same Congress, or is an application adopted in 1975, for example, still valid? If an amending convention were called, could it be limited to a single issue or might it open the entire constitution for change? How would delegates be selected and how would votes in the convention be allocated? What would Congress' role be in this amending method? Would disputes over calling a convention and over its procedures be reviewable by the courts?

The complexity of the questions, and the fact that "experts" have no answers, illustrates the seriousness of attempting an uncharted route for changing the most fundamental document of our government.

2. This Constitutional convention process of amendment has been a less democratic procedure than the traditional means of amendment.

The fact that in almost 200 years there have been only twenty-six amendments to the Constitution attests to the fact that the traditional amendment route is constructed to assure wide national debate on each amendment and careful consideration by a three-fourths majority of the legislatures.

The process of calling for a constitutional convention has not been marked by careful consideration and democratic procedures. Of the twenty-seven states which have adopted the resolution, only six legislatures held hearings where the public was able to testify on the implications of the convention. In most instances there has been only cursory debate before adopting the resolution. In two states no committees considered the petitions before they were passed by the two bodies of the legislature. Committee reports were issued in only six states, explaining the proposed action. In one state, the senate committee discussed the petition for thirty minutes; the house committee discussed it six minutes.

Further, the people of the United States would have no direct vote on the results of the convention. State constitutional conventions, which are quite common, submit the proposed state constitutional changes to the voters. This has prevented the passage of changes pushed by small pressure groups, frequently over highly emotional issues. But the voters would have no ability to vote on a national constitutional revision, a matter affecting their most precious liberties.

3. Forces behind the call for a constitutional convention are dealing with highly emotional and highly complex issues which should be dealt with in the established manner for amending the Constitution.

"Right to Life" advocates, frustrated by their inability to succeed in their goals of eliminating all abortions through the normal legislative process are now trying the constitutional convention route. Yet such an amendment, declaring the fetus a person from the moment of conception, would be, in effect, to write one theological position into the Constitution. Various faith groups, including The United Methodist Church, do not share that theology. Such a position would be tantamount to declaring an abortion for any reason a murder. It would also inhibit the use of contraceptives such as the inter-uterine device (IUD). This would be contrary to the doctrine of separation of church and state embodied in the Constitution, and would impinge on freedom of religion, guaranteed in the First Amendment.

While the idea of a balanced federal budget has wide popular support, economists are highly uncertain of its effect on the economy. Many believe that it would not cut spending, as the public believes, but instead might require higher taxes and higher revenues. Both Republican and Democratic leaders oppose such an amendment because of its inflexibility. The budget and the economy are closely interrelated. When unemployment goes up only one percentage point, the deficit swells by some $20 billion due to lost tax revenues and increased social welfare costs such as unemployment compensation. A constitutional amendment would make it impossible to deal with such situations. Congressional leadership also points to the fact that the federal budget could be balanced fairly easily—by eliminating the current $82 billion in aid to state and local governments. But the same states calling for an amendment do not want the budget balanced at the cost of lost revenue to their states.

In summary, the present move towards a constitutional convention is ill-conceived and is being promoted by persons looking for easy solutions to complex problems. The Constitution should not have to suffer at the expense of frustrations that should be dealt with in the normal procedural manner which has served us well for two centuries.

Therefore, Be It Resolved, that the General Conference:

1. Oppose efforts of state legislatures to petition Congress to call a constitutional convention;

2. Inform local congregations regarding the factors involved in proposing a constitutional convention; and

3. Urge United Methodists to communicate their opposition to such a convention to their state legislatures and, in states that have adopted such a resolution, to urge its withdrawal.

ADOPTED 1980

See Social Principles, ¶ 74.B, "The United Methodist Church and Church-Governmental Relations."

Penal Reform

Our Lord began his ministry by declaring "release to the captives . . . " (Luke 4:18) and he distinguished those who would receive a blessing at the last judgment by saying, "I was in prison and you came to me." The Christian, therefore, naturally has concern for those who are captive, for those who are imprisoned, and for the human conditions under which persons are incarcerated.

The Social Principles of The United Methodist Church asserts the need for "new systems of rehabilitation that will restore, preserve, and nurture the humanity of the imprisoned."

There is not one, but many correctional systems in the United States which bear the responsibility for the confinement or supervision of persons convicted of crimes. For the most part the systems are capable neither of rehabilitating criminals nor of protecting society. They are, in fact, institutions where persons are further conditioned in criminal conduct and where advanced skills in crime are taught. More often than not correctional institutions have created crime rather than deterred criminals. They represent an indescribable failure and have been subjected to a gross neglect by the rest of society.

The Church has participated in the neglect of the correctional system by being blind to the inhumanities which the system perpetuates and being silent about the social ills that it intensifies. The Church has challenged neither society nor itself to accept responsibility for making those critically needed changes in the penal system which would permit it to motivate improvement and offer hope to those detained within it.

Major changes are needed in the nation's correctional systems in order for them to become positive factors in the restoration of persons and the stabilization of society. Support needs to be given to alternatives to incarceration to reduce mounting costs, by using additional rehabilitative resources.

The United Methodist Church calls upon its members to express a practical faith in redemptive love through the supporting of:

1. The greater use of alternatives to pretrial detention for persons accused of crimes such as: (a) release on recognizance; (b) the setting of reasonable and equitable bail; (c) the payment of a modest percentage in cash of the designated bail.

2. The use of alternatives to prosecution such as dispute settlement services and conflict resolution programs and the diverting of persons formally subject to criminal prosecution for drunkenness, vagrancy, and juvenile "status offenses" into those organized programs which furnish noncriminal justice services.

3. The use of alternatives to incarceration for those convicted of crimes such as: fines, payments of restitution to victims of offenders' crimes, social service sentences, and probation.

The United Methodist Church further urges its congregations and members to support those penal policies which:

1. Promote social rehabilitation of convicted persons in preference to punitive confinement.

2. Develop and support a range of community-based alternatives to institutional incarceration such as work release programs.

3. Establish and maintain prisons and jails which have healthful and humane surroundings and a climate conducive to human growth and development.

4. Guarantee and maintain the rights of offenders to legal and medical services. Guarantee the freedom of expression, association and religion, protect the lives and persons of offenders from abuse from staff and other inmates, and furnish effective procedures for the redress of grievances.

5. Establish uniform disciplinary procedures within correctional institutions.

6. Provide cooperation with community agencies.

7. Allow an optimal maintenance of relationships with the outside world, especially to preserve wholesome marriage and family ties; arrange for conjugal visits of husbands and wives following medical examinations and interviews for the purpose of insuring that mutual

desire exists. Arrange visits of families with as much privacy as security will permit. Encourage friends and friendly counselors to make visits as well.

ADOPTED 1980

See Social Principles, ¶ 74.F, "Criminal Justice," "Equal Justice," "The Local Church and the Local Jail."

Police Firearms Policies

We deplore the killing and injuring of police officers by citizens and the unnecessary and unwarranted killing of persons by police. We, therefore, not only call for the tightening of legal control over citizens' ownership of firearms or of guns, but we also call for the formulation of more clearly defined written firearms policies by every agency of law enforcement in the country.

ADOPTED 1976

See Social Principles, ¶ 74.F, "U.S. Gun Violence."

Prevention and Reduction of Juvenile Delinquency

WHEREAS, the abhorrent ills of our society (child abuse and neglect, teenage pregnancy, suicide, veneral diseases, drug and alcohol abuse) that relentlessly assail children have a profound effect on the quality of their lives, and without proper intervention, are often manifested in destructive behavior within the school setting;

WHEREAS, these debilitating effects often become cyclical, appearing in generations after generations, and result in the loss to society of fully functioning and competent adults;

WHEREAS, our school systems emphasize remediation at the secondary level to prevent delinquency;

Be It Resolved, that all United Methodists work through the appropriate structures and channels to provide guidance counseling at the elementary level of all schools in prevention of delinquency.

Be It Further Resolved, that United Methodist pastors are encouraged to develop cooperative relationships with persons doing such counseling.

ADOPTED 1984

See Social Principles, ¶¶ 72.C and 74.F, "Juvenile Justice."

Public Education in the United States

I. Introduction

In the 1980s several studies highly critical of public education in the United States have been published. Issues of the new technologies have coupled with the older problems of discipline, quality of instruction, finances, and race relations to challenge the established public education system.

II. Affirmation of the Church

The church teaches that all are created in the image of God and blessed by the Creator with the gifts of creativity, morality, and reason. In a pluralistic and democratic society, such as the United States, a quality public education system is the best means whereby these gifts can be nurtured and a community of equality transcending differences of race, ethnic origins, and gender can be built.

III. Concerns of the Church

Given the church's affirmation in support of universal public education, it becomes necessary to address some of the issues now confronting the public school system.

A. Society must again recommit itself to public education and be willing to pay taxes sufficient to develop quality education and attract and retain quality teachers. We support the continuing education and training of teachers to better prepare them to deal with the cultural diversity of students. Priority should be placed on recruitment of ethnic minorities in a national training plan, for these teachers serve as positive role models and instill cultural pride in minority students. Within the global society, it is important that children in the U.S.A. be bilingual and that this is facilitated in the public school system.

B. The United Methodist Church supports freedom of intellectual inquiry in the public schools. Children need to be taught to reason, to analyse and evaluate. Censorship of textbooks and other educational material is not acceptable, nor are attempts to limit enquiry in some prescribed direction. We particularly deplore recent tendencies toward ignoring religious heritages.

527

C. Though state and local governments have a primary responsibility for public education, the federal government's responsibility is also to be affirmed. In such areas as racial integration and education for the disadvantaged, the involvement of the federal government is crucial.

D. As the nation seeks to increase excellence in education, it must continue to provide quality education for all. New immigrants, persons with handicapping conditions, poor persons, racial minorities, and women must have equal access to quality education.

E. A democratic and pluralistic society, such as the United States, is built on the foundation of certain commonly shared values. Schools have the right and obligation to transmit personal values such as honesty, truthfulness, fairness, and responsibility. They also have the task of teaching the social values of equality amid diversity, civic participation, and justice for all.

The continuation of a democratic and free society in the United States requires a public education system that produces quality education for every student so that all might contribute to the building of community.

F. We encourage states' governments to budget adequately for quality education rather than to tie this important function to risk funding such as lotteries.

ADOPTED 1988

See Social Principles, ¶ 74.D, "The United Methodist Church and Church-Government Relations," "Church/Government Relations," "Community Life."

Ratification for District of Columbia Representation

The Scriptures tell us clearly that "God shows no partiality" (Acts 10:34). The Social Principles of The United Methodist Church cites "the full and willing participation of its citizens" as a key factor in the strength of our political system.

In keeping with the idea of impartiality and the call for citizen participation, we are concerned about the lagging issue of ratification of the Constitutional Amendment providing for full representation of the District of Columbia in the Congress. We are well aware that the population of the District of Columbia is powerless with respect to our national legislative body.

In October of 1971 a statement of the Board of Christian Social Concerns of The United Methodist Church asked the United States

Congress to "provide the District of Columbia with two voting U.S. Senators plus the number of voting U.S. Representatives it would be entitled to if it were a State." This position was reaffirmed by the Board of Church and Society in October of 1978.

In 1978 The U.S. Congress passed a Constitutional Amendment providing for full voting representation of the District of Columbia in both the House and the Senate.

This amendment is now before the various state legislatures and, to become law, must be ratified by 38 states by 1985. A number of states have already ratified the amendment.

The District of Columbia contains about 750,000 residents. This represents a population equal to or greater than seven states—each of which has full voting representation in the Congress. Each year District residents pay more than $1 billion into the Federal treasury, yet they are not permitted to have voting representation in the Congress. Such a practice appears to violate our American heritage of "no taxation without representation."

In terms of simple justice we believe it is appropriate that District of Columbia citizens should have the right to elect national legislators who make the laws under which they, too, must live. Therefore, we urge all uncommitted state legislatures to ratify the Constitutional Amendment providing the District of Columbia with full voting representation in the Congress. We further encourage all United Methodists to support their state legislators in this endeavor.

ADOPTED 1980

See Social Principles, ¶ 74.B.

Religious Liberty

The United Methodist Church, as a world-wide denomination, declares religious liberty, the freedom of belief, to be a basic human right that has its roots in the Bible. Paul admonished Christians with these words: "Who are you to pass judgment on the servant of another." (Romans 14:4) This understanding is fundamental to our religious heritage which requires that we honor God, not by placing our demands on all persons, but by making true account of our own selves.

The preamble to the Universal Declaration of Human Rights states that, "the advent of a world in which human beings shall enjoy freedom of speech and belief . . . has been proclaimed as the highest aspiration of the common people."

Minimal standards of the right of belief are amplified by the international community in the Declaration on the Elimination of All Forms of Intolerance and of Discrimination Based on Religion or Belief, adopted by the General Assembly of the United Nations on November 25, 1981. It declares that the right to freedom of thought, conscience, religion or belief is basic to the following freedoms:

1. To assemble and to worship;
2. To establish and to maintain places for those purposes;
3. To establish and to maintain charitable, humanitarian, and social outreach institutions;
4. To produce and to possess articles necessary to the rites and customs of a religion or belief;
5. To write, to issue, and to disseminate relevant publications;
6. To teach religious beliefs;
7. To solicit and to receive voluntary financial and other contributions from individuals and institutions;
8. To train, to appoint, to elect, or to designate by succession necessary leaders;
9. To observe days of rest and to celebrate holidays and ceremonies in accordance with the precepts of one's religion or belief;
10. To establish and to maintain communications with individuals and religious communities in matters of religion and belief at the national and international levels.

The declaration further establishes the rights of parents to provide religious training for their children.

Our test of religious liberty is not limited by these standards. We also believe that religious liberty includes the freedom to doubt or to deny the existence of God, and to refrain from observing religious practices. Further, we believe that persons of faith have the right to propagate their faith through evangelistic outreach. Persons must be allowed to live within the constraints and the demands of their convictions. We believe it is the right of a person to be allowed to follow the call of conscience when it becomes impossible to live by both the dictates of the state and the decisions of faith.

Threats to Religious Liberty

Religious liberty involves much more than the right to worship within the walls of a house of worship. Religious individuals, institutions, and their members have the right—indeed, the obligation—to be engaged in faith-based witness on issues of state and society. Broad latitude must be allowed in defining this religious function.

Theocracies or other governments and societies that give special privileges to adherents of one religion or ideology have a particular responsibility to insure and guarantee not only the religious rights, but also the political, economic, social and cultural rights of those who are not members of the favored group.

A grave threat to religious liberty exists in nation states where all forms of voluntary association—even for purposes of private religious worship—are limited or prohibited. In such situations special accommodation, which uses the United Nations Declaration as a minimum standard, must be made for the observance of religious functions.

Religious liberty is menaced in other ways. Governments or political movements have used religious institutions or organizations for their own purposes by compromising their personnel through offering power, or by manipulation, infiltration, or control. Governments also subvert religious organizations by means of surveillance of their legitimate activities through use of informers, covert searches of religious property and politically motivated threats to the safety of religious leaders or the financial operation of religious institutions. We pledge our continual efforts to protect against these activities.

We recognize that situations exist where religious observances seem to threaten the health or safety of a society. However, the importance of religious liberty dictates that restrictions of religious observances which are alleged to be contrary to government policy on the presumption that health or safety is threatened must be carefully examined. They must only be imposed in the midst of clear and serious danger to society beyond that of the observant adult.

Denominational Action to Expand Religious Liberty

The United Methodist Church places a high priority on the struggle to maintain freedom of religious belief and practice in the world.

Religiously observant persons in some societies are denied the rights on which there have been international agreements. Our members have an obligation to speak out on behalf of those for whom such freedoms are abridged.

In carrying out their responsibilities, United Methodists, United Methodist agencies and institutions, shall:

1. Affirm and support these concerns for religious liberty in the ecumenical groups in which we participate.
2. Pursue application of these minimal standards of the human right of religious liberty in all societies, and to work toward conditions where governmental units neither inhibit nor encourage religion.
3. Advocate, through education and political action, to gain religious liberty in all places where it is lacking.
4. Extend the compassionate ministry of the church to persons who suffer because either religious or governmental authorities seek to deny these rights to them, assuming a special responsibility to work on behalf of "unregistered," in addition to governmentally sanctioned, religious institutions.
5. Educate ourselves so that we will be able to identify and respond to violations of religious liberty both in our own and in other societies.
6. Offer support to the Office of the United Nations Special Rapporteur on Religious Intolerance.

ADOPTED 1988

See Social Principles, ¶¶ 74.B and 75.A, "The United Methodist Church and Church-Government Relations."

Repression and the Right to Privacy

The Social Principles of The United Methodist Church affirms that "national security must not be extended to justify or keep secret maladministration or illegal and unconscionable activities directed against persons or groups by their own governments. We also strongly reject the domestic surveillance and intimidation of political opponents by governments in power, and all other misuses of elective or appointive offices."

The prophets of Israel denounced the repression of the poor, widows, orphans, and others of their society, and our Lord's ministry began with the announced purpose to set at liberty the poor and disadvantaged. In our biblical tradition we raise the following issues:

Repression

We have lived in a time when the accumulated hopes of racial and cultural minorities combined with a growing dissent in the United States were met by mounting fears and rising anxieties of the dominant group within the population. Seized with apprehension, many became obsessed with establishing a climate of security—even by sacrificing of creating and maintaining justice and protecting the rights and liberties of individuals.

The institutions of this society began to reflect the fears of the majority of the population and established policies and procedures that, in the short range, provided expedient control. These policies, however, were seen as repressive measures by those who sought legitimate rights and new opportunities.

In the immediate past, we sounded a call to concern because we recognized that society can become repressive in nature with hardly a trace of consciousness by the mass of the people, particularly if that people is feverishly fearful and has developed the readiness to accept any measure that seems to offer a new form of protection.

It is deplorable that in a society which is democratic in theory and structure there are signs of increasing repression: dragnet arrests; police and the intelligence community's harassment of minority leaders; charges of conspiracy; summary acquittals of police accused of brutality; the rising militance of rank and file police; support for the use of preventative detention; the utilization of wire taps; censorship of journalism in educational institutions; heavy punitive action against dissidents; the confinement of those who protested within the military forces; the use of police to control dissent within the churches; utilizing grand juries for the purposes of harassment rather than indictment; and the use of church members, clergy, and missionaries for secret intelligence purposes by local police departments, the Federal Bureau of Investigation, and the Central Intelligence Agency.

We affirm the many civil, school, and church authorities who are working toward the elimination of these abuses through their work and example; and we note that many of the most flagrant of these acts of repression no longer occur. Congress, the press, and the American people have begun watching agency activities more closely and with a greater demand for public accountability.

This vigilance must not be relaxed, for if it is there may be renewed acts of repression and fresh attempts to curtail the rights of citizens whenever redress is sought for economic and social grievances.

Therefore, we urge that all Church members and leaders continue to be sensitive to this situation in their local community and in the nation by:

1. Seeking to understand and undergird responsible institutions and agencies of the community and being supportive of measurements that will improve them and upgrade their personnel.
2. Establishing programs in the community sponsored by local churches to: (a) educate church members and their wider community about the potential for repression in the institutions of society; (b) study and affirm the biblical and constitutional basis for justice under law; (c) work in state and federal legislatures to bring about just and responsible criminal code revisions which do not reinforce repressive elements in our nation's life; oppose forms of legislation which would legalize repression; support legislation which would prohibit intelligence agencies from conducting surveillance or disruption of lawful political activities or otherwise violating constitutional rights; (d) develop an awareness of the rights and protection citizens should expect; (e) work for institutional change in situations where rights are not respected and protection is not furnished.

The Right to Privacy

The Christian faith stresses the dignity of and respect for human personality. Invasion of the privacy of an ordinary citizen of society negates this dignity and respect. Further, the Christian faith is supportive of a society which elicits hope and trust, not a society that foments fear and threatens with oppression.

The revelation that intelligence agencies, local police, and the United States Army have over a number of years developed a domestic espionage apparatus involving the gathering of information about the lawful political activities of millions of citizens is a cause for concern.

The Constituional Rights Subcommittee and the Privacy Commission Report provided substantial information which demonstrated that privacy lies in jeopardy as a result of the use of long, personal government questionnaires. Much government data is collected under the threat of jail or fine. As useful as such information may be to the government and to private agencies, the misuse of data banks is an imminent and serious threat to constitutional liberties.

We are concerned about the increased amount of government wiretapping and electronic surveillance which has taken place in recent years.

Although it is now illegal for any governmental unit to engage in any kind of wiretapping without a warrant of a court, we urge restraint in the use of wiretapping and electronic surveillance, for its prevalency creates an air of suspicion throughout the whole society and contributes to the insecurity of law-abiding American citizens.

Therefore, we respectfully request the Congress of the United States to:

1. Enact comprehensive charter legislation for all of the intelligence agencies which would prohibit them from engaging in surveillance, or disruption of lawful political activity. We oppose any charter provision which permits intelligence agencies to recruit and use as agents clergy or missionaries.
2. Place statutory limitations upon the demand by governmental bureaus and agencies for personal information about any citizen or family for statistical purposes. When such requests by agencies are for information not required by law, the respondent should be informed that compliance is voluntary. Restrictions should be placed by law on private agencies in gathering, storing, and disseminating personal information.
3. Retain the Freedom of Information Act as it is, in support of the right of all citizens to know the actions of their government.

ADOPTED 1980

See Social Principles, ¶¶ 74.A and 75.A, "Human Rights."

Support of Conscientious Objectors to Registration

The United Methodist Church supports all persons who make decisions of conscience in regard to military service. The ministry of the church is not limited to those who conscientiously serve in the armed forces of their nation. It is also extended to those who, as a matter of conscience, refuse to serve in the armed forces, to cooperate with systems of military conscription, or to accept alternate service. (Social Principles V.G. UMC and Peace V.2)

535

In order to demonstrate this ministry, institutions of higher education affiliated with the various entitles of The United Methodist Church are expected to affirm that participation in systems of military conscription, including draft registration, will not be considered a prerequisite to eligibility either for enrollment, or for institutionally controlled student aid funds.

Therefore, be it resolved that the General Conference of The United Methodist Church encourage all United Methodist institutions of higher education to respect those students who conscientiously refuse to cooperate with the draft registration and provide them equal access to institutional financial aid resources to which they may be entitled.

ADOPTED 1988

See Social Principles, ¶ 74.G, "Concerning the Draft in the United States," "Certification of Conscientious Objectors."

Support Legislation Prohibiting Malicious Harassments

The United Methodist Church encourages and supports the introduction, passage, and funding of legislation which prohibits malicious and intimidating actions that are reasonably related to, associated with, or directed toward a person's race, color, religion, ancestry, national origin, sexual orientation, age, gender, or handicap.

ADOPTED 1992

See Social Principles, ¶¶ 72 and 74, "Racial Harassment," "Sexual Harassment and The United Methodist Church," "Sexual Harassment in Church and Society in the U.S.A.," "The Church and Persons with Mentally, Physically and/or Psychologically Handicapping Conditions."

U.S. Gun Violence

Gun violence around the world is a growing menace. In the United States today, deaths and assaults by guns of all kinds have reached devastating proportions. Each year, there are more than thirty thousand (30,000) women, men, young people, and children for whom guns are instruments of death, whether by suicide, homicide, or accident. Approximately 250,000 persons suffer injuries from misuse of guns, resulting in a financial toll of over $14.4 billion for the duration of the survivors' lives. Gun violence is a matter of deepening concern to the religious community as well as the entire society.

Most of these gun-related deaths and injuries are by handguns originally acquired for personal protection, target shooting, gun collection, and even hunting. Some are by shotguns and rifles, most often acquired for legitimate sporting or collecting; an increasing number of deaths and maimings are by semi-automatic or automatic guns often referred to as assault weapons. These result in the most dramatic and visible tragedies, especially when used in mass shootings such as in Stockton, California, and Louisville, Kentucky, during 1989. Whatever the purpose for which guns are acquired, deaths and injuries resulting from their use contribute to the atmosphere of violence, fear, and alienation that is a daily part of life in the United States today. There are an estimated 65 million handguns and 200 million firearms of all types in this country.

While not the sole cause of the nation's crisis of violence, the ready availability of guns for purchase, accessibility to children, and their convenience to those contemplating criminal activity or suicide make gun violence a major social problem. Even many of the sports and hunting magazines geared toward children advertise gun sales to children.

It is estimated by the Coalition to Stop Gun Violence that at least 8,000 handgun deaths in any one year could be avoided if regulatory legislation were in place.

The mobility of the United States citizens and the proximity of jurisdictions with a patchwork of laws make localized gun control only a partial solution. Federal gun control laws or uniform state legislation, as well as extensive public education on gun safety, violence, and issues, are needed. Public opinion polls indicate that two-thirds of U.S. citizens favor gun control laws that are more strict and more comprehensive than those few currently enacted.

As people of faith, we recognize the inherent goodness in all creation. This is a point of departure toward our understanding of God as the giver and sustainer of all life. We also recognize that the ultimate purpose of creation is to reveal God's reign of justice and peace.

The biblical admonition to choose life instead of death sets the tone for all human activity. "I call heaven and earth to witness against you this day, that I have set before you life and death, blessing and curse; therefore, choose life, that you and your descendants may live" (Deut. 30:19). Through these words, we are called to order our communities in such a way that all human relationships reflect God's justice and the promise of *shalom*. As God has established just laws that call forth redemptive power and creation, so we as a part of that creation are called to be life givers, to transform chaos into order.

The U.S. Constitution is invoked in support of unlimited and unregulated gun ownership. Although there is vagarious debate over the meaning of the Second Amendment to the Constitution, which speaks to the right to keep and bear arms, the United States Supreme Court and lower federal courts have held that the private ownership of guns is not protected by the Second Amendment. The United Methodist Church is among those religious communions calling for social policies and personal life-styles to contain gun violence.

The church as an instrument of reconciliation needs to bring an end to the senseless violence, suffering, and human loss caused by the unrestricted availability of handguns and assault weapons used by ordinary people to act out their aggression and conflicts or disputes with friends, families, and others.

Gun violence is a deep concern to the community of faith whose members are called to a vision of the peaceable kingdom, a society in which God's justice reigns, where reconciliation replaces alienation, where an open hand and a turned cheek replace retaliation, where love of enemies is as important as love of neighbor. The religious community must also take seriously the risk of idolatry which could result from an unwarranted fascination with guns, and which overlooks or ignores the social consequences of ther misuse.

Once again, the church dare not to be silent. Because our society is experiencing increasing gun violence, The United Methodist Church regards effective gun control and regulation to be a matter of spiritual concren and public responsibility.

Therefore, as United Methodists, we recommend the following:

1. That the United Methodists work toward discouraging the graphic depiction and glorification of violence by the entertainment industry, which greatly influences our society. Further, that these issues be addressed through education and consciousness raising, and we urge that this be done at all levels.

2. That all United Methodists and others who are members of gun clubs and associations continue to expand their educational programs on gun safety.

3. That all governing bodies, congregations, and members join in dialogue with gun clubs and similar associations in the effort to establish responsible gun regulations, to build a safer and less violent society, and to ask sports people to agree to incur some small inconveniences such as waiting periods before purchases in order to reduce the senseless deaths of many people.

4. That all congregations and members study the subject of gun violence and its implications for the church and the community.

5. That all congregations and members become involved in coalitions with other religious, professional, educational, and community-based organizations that support gun control legislation, consistent with the resolutions and recommendations stated by General Conference.

6. That the Secretary of General Conference and the Council of Bishops be directed to communicate this resolution and background information on gun violence to the Congress and to the President of the United States as well as appropriate members of the cabinet and state legislatures.

7. That the General Board of Church and Society give emphasis to this issue, and work with other organizations to develop model legislation and guidelines for implementations.

Furthermore, we call upon the United States government to:

1. Establish meaningful and effective federal legislation to regulate the importation, manufacture, sale, and possession of guns and ammunition by the general public. Such legislation should include provisions for the registration and licensing of gun purchasers and owners, appropriate background investigation and waiting periods prior to gun purchase, and regulation of subsequent sale.

2. Address more urgently the societal situations, including the clmate of fear, violence—including family and child violence—vengeance, and despair, in which persons turn to guns.

3. Provide significant assistance to victims of gun violence and their families.

4. Outlaw the sales and manufacture of all automatic-weapon conversion kits since their only purpose is to produce illegal firearms.

5. Outlaw the manfacture and sale of guns that cannot be detected with standard detectors.

ADOPTED 1992

See Social Principles, ¶ 74, and "Gun Control," "Police Firearms Policies."

Use of Church Facilities for Operating Private Schools

The General Conference is urged to adopt appropriate legislation designed to make unlawful the formation and operation within the physical facilities of the local United Methodist Churches of private elementary and secondary schools where a major purpose of the formation and organization of such private schools is to preserve racially segregated education.

ADOPTED 1970

See Social Principles, ¶ 74.D.

Victims of Crime

Jesus answered the question of "Who is my neighbor? by telling the parable of the Good Samaritan (Luke 10:25-37). The priest and Levite failed to respond. The Samaritan did respond, and we are to do likewise. The neighbor was the victim of crime, he had fallen among robbers, who not only stole his money, but stripped him, beat him, and left him half dead. The Samaritan had compassion, stopped, bandaged his wounds, cared for him, took him to an inn, and took responsibility for the cost of his stay.

Many people are victims or relatives of victims of crime. They suffer shock and a sense of helplessness. In addition to financial loss there is a spiritual and emotional trauma and often a lack of support and direction. There is no doubt that many feel frustrated because often there seems to be no provision for them to be heard, or their injuries redressed and they are not notified of the court procedures.

This is an area where the church has an opportunity to minister.

Therefore, we call upon the members of The United Methodist Church to minister to the victims of crime and to be advocates for them, and we call upon the General Conference:

1) To direct the General Board of Church and Society to work for the recognition of the needs of victims of crimes and survivors to certain rights.

2) To support laws at both the federal and state levels with respect of compensation to victims of crime and work for the adoption of such laws in those jurisdictions where there are now no such provisions.

3) Recognize that the constitutional rights of the accused must be provided. Victims of crime or their lawful representatives, including

the next of kin of homicide victims, are entitled to be kept informed during criminal proceedings, to be present at the trial, and to be heard at the sentencing hearing as well as an impact statement of the time of the parole consideration.

4) To encourage seminaries to develop continuing education programs on this subject.

5) To direct the General Board of Discipleship to develop guidelines, programs, and study materials for pastors and others in providing spiritual support and understanding for victims and families.

6) To urge all members of The United Methodist Church to initiate presence, prayers, and support for victims and survivors as well as strategies to bring about necessary changes in the criminal justice system.

ADOPTED 1988

See Social Principles ¶ 74.F "Equal Justice," "Criminal Justice."

THE WORLD COMMUNITY

The Arab-Israeli Conflict

The Middle East continues to be the location of some of the most serious international conflicts facing the world today. Though the area includes the birthplaces of three historically linked religions—Judaism, Christianity, and Islam—its problems are not primarily religious but ones of conflicting national and class interests.

Iran and Iraq are at war; the Kurdish people's aspirations to national self-determination remain unfulfilled; Lebanon, already torn by years of civil strife and the presence of Syrian and Palestine Liberation Organization (PLO) forces now suffers from the effects of invasion by Israel. It is still occupied and its territorial and national integrity remain threatened. Any timely or effective proposal for peace must take seriously the complexity of the entire Middle East.

For two quadrennia the General Conference of The United Methodist Church has given attention to the serious problems of the Middle East. Two aspects demand the continued concern of the church: The Arab-Israeli conflict, and the homelessness of the Palestinian people.

The Historical Context

The long history of oppression suffered by Jews—especially in the Western world—prompted nineteenth century European Jewish leaders to seek a Jewish homeland. Some urged return to the land which held so much historic national and religious significance. The oppression culminated in the Nazi holocaust and the extermination of millions of persons. Spurred by the holocaust and the unwillingness of nations to open their borders to Jewish refugees, the State of Israel

542

was born. From its creation in 1948 as a result of the United Nations Partition Resolution to the present, Israel has lived in a state of war with Arab nations hostile to its existence. Continuing and resurgent anti-Semitism, together with fears of a second holocaust, have given "The Land" new theological, political and pragmatic meaning to many Jews around the world.

The Arabs of Palestine and the surrounding region, emerging from centuries of Ottoman colonial rule, aspired to independence which was thwarted by the establishment of British and French authority over the area in the wake of World War I. The 1947 U.N. Partition Resolution had also promised an Arab state in Palestine, but was rejected as inadequate by Arab leadership. The resulting conflict between the armies of Israel and the Arab states displaced and dispossessed large numbers of Palestinian Arabs. In the wake of the fighting, Israel occupied territory beyond that allotted to it by the partition plan, and Egypt and Jordan occupied what remained of the territory.

From 1948 to the present, the Palestinian Arab people, among whom are Christian brothers and sisters, have suffered in many ways. Those who were dispossessed and are in exile suffer from deprivation in refugee camps, violence and repression. In the Occupied Territories, the effects of military rule and the continuing establishment of Israeli settlements on expropriated Arab land have led to increased tensions between Palestinian Arabs and Israeli Jews. Palestinians remain in the state of Israel as citizens, but suffer political and economic discrimination, especially with regard to ownership of land and homes. These conditions have rendered reconciliation between the two peoples more difficult.

The signing of a peace treaty between Egypt and Israel in 1979 was welcomed by many as a sign of, and a first step toward overall peace. Others warned that this separate agreement would make comprehensive peace more difficult to realize. Similar hopes and fears exist as a consequence of the 1983 peace accord between Lebanon and Israel. However well-intentioned, peace initiatives so far have either ignored the Palestinians' aspirations to statehood, or have not had the opportunity to bear fruit. All such initiatives have been flawed by the refusal to allow Palestinians to speak on their own behalf. Thus, they have failed to achieve their objectives—security for Israel, self-determination for the Palestinians, and peace for the region. Consequently, both the Israeli Jews and the Palestinian Arabs still live under conditions of instability and insecurity.

The Search for Peace

Integral to the solution of the Middle East conflict is the recognition of the right to self-determination of both the Israeli Jews and the Palestinian Arabs. This recognition demands affirmation of the right of the State of Israel to exist, and support for the rights of the Palestinian people to self-determination within historic Palestine, including the option of a sovereign state apart from the Hashemite Kingdom of Jordan. Both entities would be expected to pursue non-discriminatory policies towards domestic minorities.

We call for peace initiatives which are comprehensive. We affirm the continuing efforts of the United Nations to maintain peace and resolve the conflict. We affirm the courage of leaders who are willing to take the risk for peace. We condemn persistent conditions which perpetuate injustice and armed conflict and recognize that true peace must meet the needs of both the Israeli and Palestinian peoples. We affirm those forces and voices in Israel, the Arab world, and the United States—Jews, Christians, and Muslims—who have been in the forefront of the struggle for a peaceful resolution of the conflict.

We call upon the Arab nations to commit themselves, singly and together, to a course of peace with Israel. And we call upon the PLO leadership to offer its own bold and creative initiatives toward peace through some combination of the following: cessation of hostilities against Israel, a public statement of its commitment to a peaceful solution, and an explicit recognition of the right of Israel to exist. We also call upon the government of Israel to commit itself to a course that will lead to a just and peaceful resolution of Palestinian aspirations, through some combination of the following: cessation of policies of annexation, land expropriation, expulsions, collective punishment, and a freeze on settlements in the Occupied Territories, especially in the West Bank; a willingness to be in discussion with the PLO as a representative voice for the Palestinians; and a public openness to a democratic process by which the Palestinian people can move toward national self-determination.

With an urgency for the sovereignty of Lebanon, both its territory and its government, we affirm Israel's stated intention to withdraw from Lebanon and call for a similar disengagement of Syria and the disarming of remaining PLO forces. A similar ugency about the integrity of the Lebanese-Israeli border demands that we call upon Israel to respect it and to refrain from the use and support of seccessionist forces within Lebanon. We urge the government of Lebanon to ensure that southern Lebanon no longer be used as a base for attacks upon Israel. We call for the exchange or release of prisoners seized during and since the 1982 invasion of Lebanon, particularly the thousands held by Israel, the Lebanese army and various private militias.

As territorial compromise is a necessary factor in any peaceful settlement, we affirm Israel's return of the Sinai to Egypt as part of the Egyptian-Israeli peace process, we urge the demilitarization of the Golan Heights, and we consider the realization of Palestinian self-determination on the West Bank and Gaza Strip vital to a comprehensive peace.

The United States and the Arab-Israeli Conflict

The United States, the U.S.S.R., and other nations have become increasingly involved in the Middle East politically, economically and militarily, and it is incumbent upon the churches and their members to examine critically the reasons for and implications of such involvement. The Middle East, as a whole, remains an arena of a furious arms race. The supply of weaponry provided to Israel and its Arab neighbors continues to escalate and makes true and lasting peace more difficult to achieve. There is a danger that the arms race in general will have an adverse effect on the possibility of achieving an overall solution. The use and re-export of U.S. weapons in violation of treaty regulations that specify that these arms are not for offensive use and not for re-export raise concern about the continued U.S. supply of weapons.

Therefore, we urge the President of the United States through his reports to Congress and his executive powers to ensure that the U.S. laws governing the sale or grant of weapons be effectively and immediately applied in light of the extensive use of U.S. supplied arms throughout the region. We further urge the President to initiate a U.S. embargo on arms to the entire Middle East, and to seek similar action from the U.S.S.R., the United Kingdom, France, and other suppliers.

We urge U.S. citizens and the U.S. government instead to support increased levels of funding for programs in the Middle East designed to meet basic human needs.

We call on the U.S. government and others, in line with the precedent established by the U.N. Security Council in 1976 and the general tone of the Soviet-American statement on the Middle East in 1977, to engage in discussions with the PLO with the aim of furthering the peace process.

We reaffirm the need for governmental officials to seek an overall solution within a multilateral context, rather than pursuing narrow self-interest which may set states against one another and increase the isolation of the insecure and dispossessed.

The United Methodist Church

We urge that United Methodist members, local churches, and agencies take the following specific actions:

1. Pray for peace in the Middle East—in personal and corporate worship.

2 Request that the governments outside the region not fund the militarization of any state in the Middle East, but rather improve levels of funding to meet basic human needs, and organize action programs at all levels to oppose the continuing flow of arms from all sources to the Middle East.

3. Affirm and continue the support of United Methodist members, local churches, and Annual Conferences of church-related programs of relief to refugees, reconstruction and development through U.M.C.O.R., World Division, and the programs of the National Council of Churches, the World Council of Churches, and the Middle East Council of Churches.

4. Resist simplistic theologies, both in the Middle East and the U.S., which would either support uncritically Israeli policies on the grounds of exclusive claims to "The Land" or seek to deny the living covenantal relationship of God with Jews through its supposed supersedence by a new covenant.

5. Reject stereotypes of both Jews and Arabs as racist and instead seek opportunities to heighten sensitivity and increase awareness, out of which can grow a greater appreciation for the beliefs and values of Jews, Muslims, and Christians of Middle Eastern churches.

6. Participate in and promote educational programs aimed at helping United Methodists understand the intricacies of the Arab-Israeli conflict. Specific action should include:

a) Initiation of programs involving contact with and among Christians, Muslims, and Jews from the Middle East.

b) Encouragement of all leaders of and participants in "Holy Land tours" to contact indigenous Christian leaders in the Middle East, and to hear the concerns of both the Israelis and Palestinians who live there, as well as visit the biblical and historical sites.

c) Evaluation of the treatment of the conflict in United Methodist curricula and media.

d) Collaboration of appropriate boards and agencies to develop a packet of educational program materials.

e) Development of denominational participation in ecumenical and interreligious networks to raise consciousness, provide information about the Middle East, and to stimulate action to promote peace in the Middle East.

ADOPTED 1984

See Social Principles, ¶ 75, "Current Arab-Israeli Crisis."

Bishops' Call for Peace and the Self-Development of Peoples

The "basic beliefs" of the former Evangelical United Brethren Church stated forthrightly "that war and bloodshed . . . are not compatible with the gospel and spirit of Christ." The Methodist Social Creed said, "We must actively and constantly create the conditions of peace." World peace, a requisite for human survival, is a fundamental objective of Christians everywhere.

In a recent survey, United Methodists expressed their profound concern about the cheapness with which human life is treated and the possibility of the total extinction of the race; they revealed an overriding concern about world peace and the morality of war.[1] In response to this concern, in the light of traditional denominational teachings and on the basis of a biblical faith, the Council of Bishops of The United Methodist Church issues this call for peace and the self-development of people.

---

[1]Virgil Wesley Sexton, Listening to the Church (Abingdon Press, 1971), pp. 55, 62-68.

The Nature of Peace

Peace is not simply the absence of war—a nuclear stalemate or combination of uneasy cease-fires. It is that emerging dynamic reality envisioned by prophets where spears and swords give way to implements of peace (Isa. 2:1-4); where historic antagonists dwell together in trust (Isa. 11:4-11); and where righteousness and justice prevail. There will be no peace with justice until unselfish and informed love are structured into political processes and international arrangements.

The enemies of peace are many. War results from a complex of personal, social, economic, and political forces. If war is to be overcome, its root causes must be isolated and dealt with.

The Enemies of Peace

1. Blind self-interest is an enemy of peace. The history of war is a history of unbridled greed, ambition, and self-centeredness. Nations have been willing to gain their own security and advantage at the expense of other weaker nations. Persons obsessed with their "rightness" and power have sought to impose their wills on their surroundings. Self-aggrandizement has too often prevailed over human rights and international justice. Vain self-assertion has been the "nature" of persons, and in no small measure, it has shaped their "destiny."

The self-interest that gives birth to war is both personal and social. Policy-makers are individuals. Their decisions are moral decisions. Whether they live in a tribal culture, a representative democracy, or a totalitarian police state, they are individually responsible. By their greed and cowardice, silence and truculence, arrogance and apathy, they contribute to the dismemberment of true community.

But self-interest is also institutionalized. Nation-states, economic systems, political and military forces, and the structures of our corporate life, serving their own interests, become self-seeking antagonists destroying the unity of humankind.

2. Economic exploitation is an enemy of peace. No economic system is divinely inspired and every economic system should be judged by the ethical imperatives of the gospel of Jesus Christ. Personal fulfillment and international stability are impossible in a world where

two out of three people go to bed hungry every night and where the chasm between "haves" and "have nots" grows wider day by day.

One cannot understand current events without taking into account the colonial policies of an earlier era. World powers carved up continents and divided the spoils. Third World nations and underdeveloped peoples are now reacting with bitterness and suspicion toward those forces that systematically exploited their personal and natural resources.

The Third World is understandably concerned about American domination of the world market, is wary of strings-attached aid programs, and is determined to assert its independent selfhood. The "superpowers" are the new imperialists. With networks of economic and military interests intruding into almost every land, they frustrate authentic self-determination, manipulate power relationships, and disturb the essential ingredients of international community.

3. Racism is an enemy of peace. Whether its attitudes and institutions disturb domestic tranquility, contravene justice, or erupt in bloody skirmishes, racism stands opposed to every humanizing process. Racist presuppositions are implicit in Western attitudes and policies toward Asia, Africa, the Middle East, and Latin America, as well as toward black, brown, yellow, and red persons in subcultures controlled by white majorities.

4. Population explosion is an enemy of peace. Nations often justify expansionist policies on the basis of overcrowded homelands.

Human congestion, linked with poverty, hunger, and filth, gives rise to frustration, despair, and violence.

In affluent societies, an increasing population intensifies the ecological crisis as wealth multiplies industrial waste, pollutes air and water, and jeopardizes the delicate balance of nature.

Both poverty and wealth, when complicated by over-population, aggravate hostilities and negate human values.

5. Nation worship is an enemy of peace. Insulated, self-serving nationalism must yield to genuine international cooperation if people are to survive. The unilateral intervention of superpowers in the affairs of smaller nations (Hungary, Vietnam, Laos, Cambodia, Czechoslovakia, the Dominican Republic, and Guatemala) must be ended. International anarchy is the most dangerous form of lawlessness confronting the human family today.

6. Continued reliance upon military violence is an enemy of peace.

There have been more war casualties in the twentieth century than in all previous centuries of recorded history combined. Nuclear and biochemical weaponry and new technological war-making equipment have thrust the human race into an indefensible posture. It is alleged that 90 percent of the war casualties in Indochina have been civilian. Old "just war" theories need to be carefully rethought in the light of present reality. Wars fought in the national interest will doubtless continue, but violence begets violence, and in today's world extinction could result from irrational accident or momentary madness.

7. The arms race is an enemy of peace. Arms races have always resulted in the utilization of their products. In spite of Strategic Arms Limitation Talks, the superpowers have continued with the development of ABM and anti-ABM hardware, and MIRV has been deployed. The current overkill capacities of the Soviet Union and the United States, coupled with the fact that there are now five nuclear powers, make future prospects for world harmony bleak indeed.

Dehumanization, a special threat in a materialistic, technocratic society, is implicit in almost all the "enemies of peace" we have outlined. The gospel of Jesus Christ proclaims the inestimable worth of each individual. It is "personal" in the most radical sense of the word. It seeks to humanize, and would make common cause with those values and forces that are working for the fulfillment of the human potential in today's world.

The Sources of Peace

Peace is the gift of God, a gift that comes when persons meet the conditions of God.

The God who gives us peace is the Father of all peoples and the Judge of all nations. He has revealed his perfect will through Jesus Christ, the Lord of history and the Prince of Peace. God's Holy Spirit, the cleansing and unifying presence in our midst, is able to work through current conflict and disruption that the divine will might be done on earth.

And what are God's "conditions" for peace? There are many. They are personal and cultural; theological and practical; attitudinal and systemic.

God calls us to penitence and new life. In the light of present crisis we are called upon to be "heartily sorry for these our misdoings." We have been vain and self-serving, indifferent to poverty and hunger, insensitive in the face of exploitation and suffering; we have enthroned the values of a materialistic society; we have reflected racist attitudes and participated in racist systems; we have worshipped our native land, had undue faith in military violence, and permitted concepts of "national honor" to take precedence over the well-being of brutalized persons in distant places. Each of us, in the light of misguided loyalties and present apathy, is called upon to pray earnestly the familiar prayer, "O God, be merciful to me a sinner."

Genuine repentance can lead to new life. One of the central injunctions of a biblical faith is, "Repent, and believe . . ." (Mark 1:15). "When anyone is united to Christ, there is a new world; the old order has gone, and a new order has already begun" (II Cor. 5:17). New life based upon an honest awareness of past failures and sins is a requisite for peace within and world peace. Old values and allegiances are replaced by a new ethic in "the new being."

If God's "conditions" for peace include penitence and new life, they can also be summarized with one word: love. Mature love is neither sensuality nor sentimentality. It is not a refuge for the naïve. It is an unswerving and uncompromising way of life. It goes a second mile, turns the other cheek, and accepts and offers itself for friend and enemy alike. It feeds the hungry, clothes the naked, seeks out the rejected, and liberates the oppressed. Freedom is love's expression. Justice is love's demand. Believing that those who live by the sword will perish by the sword, and that those who find their security in nuclear stockpiles may well be destroyed by that weaponry, love seeks to overcome evil with good. "God was in Christ reconciling the world to himself . . . and . . . he has entrusted us with the message of reconciliation" (II Cor. 5:19).

Even as God is the source of our peace, he has called us to be his servants; custodians of his message; "peacemakers."

We have mentioned "the enemies of peace." Each of these enemies needs to be dealt with specifically.

If war results from greed, ambition, and sinful self-interest, peace requires the literal conversion of person, of attitudes and values. It also requires a radical redefinition of institutional goals and priorities. Self-interest must be seen in relationship to love for God and our brothers and sisters (Luke 10:25-28).

If extremes of poverty and hunger are to be overcome, development programs must be based upon principles of global need and accountability. They should not be designed to reinforce particular economic systems or protect the markets of privileged nations. Development, however, involves more than economic improvement. It refers to self-reliance and self-determination. The self-development of people requires equality of opportunity, full participation in decision-making processes, and a diffusion of political power from the few to the many.

There will be no peace with justice unless liberation is gained by those who have been manipulated and victimized by interests that have been willing to profit from the continued deprivation of the weak and the powerless. But the oppressor needs to be liberated as truly as the oppressed. Liberation affects the whole person. It is salvation; it is humanization. It is social, economic, political, and spiritual. It calls for the structural implementation of those values announced by our Lord when he said he had come that the "broken victims" of life might "go free" (Luke 4:18).

Racism must give way to justice if peace is to become a reality. This justice, based upon new attitudes, understandings, and relationships, will be reflected in the laws, policies, structures, and practices of both church and state.

If dignity and self-determination are human rights, then respect for and the preservation of particular ethnic, cultural, and racial traditions and values should be encouraged and assured. It is not the function of Christian witness to "westernize," "easternize," "Americanize," or in other ways acculturate human attitudes and responses. It is the function of the Christian to bring the full dimensions of a gospel of love and justice to bear upon the human situation.

Concerned and adequate population control programs must be developed if the planet is not to be crowded beyond its capacity to support human life.

If peace is to come, nation worship must be supplanted by the loyalty implicit in the declaration, "God so loved the world. . . ." Persons are normally patriots. They love the soil of their native land and the heritage that has shaped their days. Grateful for home and heritage they are now called to a higher patriotism. Once people were forced to organize as tribes for self-protection, then tribes as city-states and city-states as nation-states. Today we are called to look beyond the limited and competing boundaries of nation-states to the larger and more inclusive community of persons.

This movement from narrow nationalism to global loyalties requires both international law and international organization. The development of international law has included landmark treaties resulting from conferences at The Hague, Dumbarton Oaks, and the Geneva Conventions. Structures of international order have been anticipated by the ill-fated League of Nations and the United Nations. If peace with justice is to come, nation-states should utilize the United Nations and the International Court of Justice, as well as international trade, relief and scientific institutions, while seeking to perfect the instruments of international organization.

If peace is to come, our present reliance upon military institutions and domination by a military-industrial complex must be replaced by civilian control of the military. An ordered society must be policed by forces responsible to that same society. Self-serving national military forces must eventually give way to duly constituted international peacekeeping units.

The tradition of nonviolent love is a fundamental dimension of the Christian faith. Christians are challenged to consider and embrace this personal stance, thus providing a redemptive witness in society.

There must be eventual disarmament. We cannot be certain of the causes of a particular war. "Causes" may be simply pretexts. In the final analysis, it is the presence of military institutions in the nations of the world that makes wars possible and arms races probable. The tide must be turned. Recognizing the strategic dangers of unilateral disarmament, nations can begin processes of military disengagement and move toward bilateral and multilateral disarmament agreements within the framework of the United Nations. Our suicidal confidence in arms and military systems must give way to a radical reordering of priorities and an awareness of overriding human values.

The ingredients of peace are indivisible. Its realization cannot be achieved apart from theological, ethical, and practical sources. Individuals must assume their full responsibility for peacemaking. The Church must be far more faithful to its Lord, the Prince of Peace, than it has been willing to be in the past. And nations must become more deeply involved in the continuing processes of the self-development of people and the creation of a just and peaceful world order. Unless the most powerful and responsible members of the human family are willing to deal with the root causes of war, running the essential risks and making the necessary sacrifices, the human family will destroy itself.

"[Christ Jesus] is himself our peace . . . and in his own body of flesh and blood has broken down the enmity which stood like a dividing wall. . . . For he [came] to create . . . a single new humanity in himself, thereby making peace."—Ephesians 2:13-16

ADOPTED 1972

See Social Principles, ¶ 75, "The United Methodist Church and Peace," "Peace with Justice as a Special Program," "Christian Faith and Disarmament," "Comprehensive Test Ban Treaty," "Justice, Peace and the Integrity of Creation."

The Black Hills Alliance

The Black Hills, historically the sacred, ancestral lands of the Lakota people, is designated a "national sacrifice area" in a federal plan known as Project Independence. Large scale plans are underway for the mining of uranium, coal, and taconite iron deposits, using open pits, strip mines, and solution mines. It is estimated that within 35 years the water tables will be exhausted. Radioactive by-products will pollute the air. Unrestricted strip mining will devastate the land.

We therefore affirm: 1) the right of native people to keep sacred their ancestral burial grounds and their right to determine the responsible use of natural resources; 2) the necessity to consider the long-range consequences of depleting the water supply, as opposed to the short-range benefits of obtaining additional coal and other mineral resources; and 3) the position of the Black Hills Alliance, an organization of persons who live in the Black Hills region who are dedicated to a safe and healthy future for their children, and who maintain research, education, and action projects in support of their cause.

ADOPTED 1980

See Social Principles, ¶¶ 75.A and 72.A, "American Indian Religious Freedom Act," "The Fort Laramie Treaty," "Toward a New Beginning Beyond 1992."

Boycott of Royal Dutch/Shell

Introduction

Apartheid is sin and . . . the moral and theological justification of it is a travesty of the gospel and, in its persistent disobedience to the Word of God, a theological heresy.

—General Council
of the World Alliance
of Reformed Churches, 1982.

South Africa is a nation without its own supply of oil. Only with the support of international oil corporations can the apartheid regime survive. South African law considers oil supplies "munitions of war."

Shell USA is a wholly owned subsidiary of the Shell Group (Royal Dutch Petroleum of the Netherlands and the Shell Transport and Trading Company p.l.c. of the United Kingdom). Shell USA accounts for over 20% of the product sales of the parent company. Shell South Africa is included in the Group.

Royal Dutch/Shell co-owns or operates oil refinery facilities in South Africa. It is a primary petroleum interest in South Africa. The oil refined by Shell in South Africa supplies government agencies, including the police and military, which are used to maintain *apartheid*.

For years, British, Dutch and US churches have been in dialogue with Shell.

The 1984 General Conference of the United Methodist Church, in the resolution "Southern Africa," specifically urged:

—Divestment from corporations doing business in South Africa.

—An end to any collaboration with South Africa by opposing expanded participation of corporations in the South African economy.

—Support of United Nations' sanctions against South Africa.

The South African Council of Churches states:

The South African Council of Churches joins the majority of the people of South Africa in calling for immediate, comprehensive and mandatory sanctions that are aimed at sapping the energy of the *apartheid* state. We believe that the imposition of such sanctions is the only way to effect change in South Africa with minimum violence. (October, 1987)

The Methodist Church of Southern Africa States:

The responsibility for any hardship that may arise from sanctions lies with the South Africa government and not with the people struggling to free themselves from the snare that is *apartheid*.

Conditions in South Africa continue to worsen. Organizations devoted to peaceful protest against *apartheid* have been banned.

Denominations and faith groups boycotting Shell include:

The American Baptist Churches, General Board.

The Executive Council of the United Church of Christ.

Various orders of The Roman Catholic Church.

The Unitarian Universalist Association.

The General Boards of Church and Society
and Global Ministries
of the United Methodist Church.

Recommendations and Actions

The United Methodist Church joins the boycott of Royal Dutch/Shell and asks that its units and members refrain from purchasing Shell products so long as the boycott continues. Participation in the boycott will end when Royal Dutch/Shell withdraws from South Africa and terminates all license and franchise agreements with South African entities or when the *apartheid* system ceases.

Implementation

1. The boycott of Royal Dutch/Shell and its subsidiaries is effective immediately.
2. The General Board of Church and Society is asked to monitor the boycott pursuant to agency and denominational boycott guidelines and to present a report at each regular meeting of the board.

3. The General Board of Church and Society shall be responsible for preparation and distribution of educational materials about the boycott throughout the church.

4. Communication regarding the boycott decision will be sent to the South African Council of Churches and to the Methodist Church of Southern Africa.

ADOPTED 1988

Passed by General Conference but enjoined from carrying it out pending a review by the Judicial Council.

See Social Principles, ¶¶ 72.A, 73, and 75.A, "Southern Africa," "Web of *Apartheid*, South Africa and the Destabilization of Its Neighbors," "Guidelines for Initiating of Joining an Economic Boycott."

Central America: Peace and Justice with Freedom

Grace upon Grace, the mission statement of The United Methodist Church, written by a study commission established by the 1984 General Conference, received by the 1988 General Conference and recommended to the churches for study, states:

Jesus Christ is the Lord who is servant and the servant who is Lord. As Lord, Jesus inaugurates and promises the kingdom of God. God's sovereign rule has been asserted in our world. As servant, Jesus identifies with the human condition and expresses his glory through suffering. We acknowledge Jesus as Lord by participating in his kingdom and in his servant ministry. He who was greatest became the least and invites us to identify with him through sacrificial love. We who receive grace are to share grace, for grace is the heart of the gospel.

Jesus sets the ground for and the course of mission. In the gospels we see Christ Jesus:

preaching good news, healing the sick, calling the righteous to new commitments to the kingdom, feeding the hungry, raising the dead, overturning the tables of corruption, teaching the signs of the kingdom, liberating the captives, giving sight to the blind, dying on the cross, rising from the dead, living among his people. (*Grace upon Grace,* p. 19.

Today the experience of Central America exemplifies unrest and the denial of a just life. The decade of the 1980s has brought misery and increased suffering. In this decade we, the Church, have witnessed the unending persecutions, kidnapping, rapes, and assassinations of the people, particularly of people who attempted to respond to the calling of servanthood in the name of Christ. Similarly, natural disasters, diseases, and grinding poverty have been aggravated by the presence of war and military interventions.

We, the Church, have witnessed the plight of Indian communities in Central America and in many instances genocidal practices against them.

Women and children have been particularly impacted by the economic and political struggles, and the desire of the powerful to resolve these conflicts through military resolutions rather than political negotiations.

Socio-economic studies of the decade indicate that all the countries of the region had negative per capita economic growth. Latin American economist Xabier Gorostiago, citing the United Nations Economic Commission for Latin America, reports that the number of poor in Latin America has surpassed the 1980 figure of 110 million, and that number is 180 million for 1990.

The cry of our brothers and sisters in the continent has gone unheard. In 1983 the Executive Committee of the Latin American Council of Churches issued a plea that:

In the name of millions of indigenous farmers of Central America who have been thrown off their lands, whose right to life and personal safety has been taken away; in the name of the malnourished and sick children who die each day with no hope in their countries; in the name of political, student, union, and religious leaders who have been killed, or disappeared, or put in jail; in the name of innumerable refugees going through a dark night of exile and desolation, [and] in the name of thousands of Christian martyrs, who pleaded to heaven and earth for justice, for full and genuine liberation and peace for these nations.

This plea has, in fact, been responded to with an invasion of Panama and the low-intensity conflict that forced nations to choose peace but not justice in their electoral process.

Given the gravity of the Central American situation, leaders of the

Central American nations continue to work toward peaceful resolution of their conflicts as established in the Esquipulas II agreements, signed by all of the Central American presidents on August 7, 1987, that calls for:
• the formations of national committees for reconciliation;
• decrease of military presence in the region;
• the right of each nation to its own economic and socio-political self-determination.

Religious leaders, labor union leaders, peasants, students, merchants, women's associations, etc., in Central America are calling for a concerted effort to change the course of the political and economic processes towards an alternative that may lead to lasting peace with justice in the region.

Because of our conviction that injustice and war do not lead to peace;

Because the government of the United States has actively participated in low-intensity conflict, which includes "clandestine and covert operations, support for counterinsurgency and counterrevolutionary campaigns, terrorist strikes and other low level missions, makes sparing use of U.S. soldiers" and continues to support economically military forces and maintains several military bases across the region, particularly in Honduras and Panama;

Because of the call embodied in the mission statement of The United Methodist Church, *Grace upon Grace*, and the example of the ministry of Christ as presented in Luke (4:16-21);

We call upon the government of the United States to:

1. Support aid to a reconstruction fund which can be used to rebuild the Salvadoran nation;

2. Actively support accords made by the Central American nations in search for alternative solutions other than military;

3. Withdraw all U.S. military presence in Panama and honor the Torrijos-Carter treaty agreements, and fulfill its responsibilities for damages to human life, property, housing, and the economic system caused by the 1989 invasion;

4. Refrain from any activity—military, economic or of any other nature, covert or overt—directed against any sovereign state in Central America;

5. Apply human rights certification based upon U.S. law (Section 502b of the Foreign Assistance Act of 1960 as amended) and data from

Amnesty International and the United Nations Human Rights Commission as criteria for economic assistance to governments in the region;

6. Urge the U.S. government to abide by the decision of the International Court of Justice (The Hague) and pay reparations to Nicaragua;

7. Respect and recognize each nation's sovereignty and rights to self-determination and cease imposing its own political, military, and economic system on the countries of Central America;

8. Seek "temporary protected status" for persons fleeing repression and war in Central America.

We call upon the United Nations to:

1. Continue active support in finding political solutions that insure the participation of all segments of the population;

2. Continue to oversee and report any violations of human rights according to its Human Rights Declaration;

3. Support nongovernmental and civic organizations of the region in their efforts to work towards a unified solution so that peace and justice may prevail in the region;

4. Work in support of efforts to demilitarize the region and support alternatives for economic development;

5. Support the efforts of organizations in their work to alleviate the plight of Central American refugees.

We call upon United Methodists to continue to:

1. Learn about and better understand the hopes and aspirations of the people of Central America;

2. Strengthen our ties of solidarity with the people of Central America by deepening our understanding of the history and cultures of the region;

3. Encourage the use of curriculum materials, study guides, and other resources prepared by the general boards and agencies;

4. Encourage annual conferences and Central American churches to continue to support each other through prayer, exchange, and dialogue of persons, and the physical accompaniment of persons where appropriate;

5. Encourage the understanding that there are different expressions of the presence, witness, and theological views of Christians in the region;

6. Increase efforts to assist and participate in the reconstruction of the war-torn nations through sharing of resources;

7. Advocate and support policies and programs by The United Methodist Church directed to the rehabilitation of youth and young adults; victims of war; protection, defense, and promotion of the indigenous communities; and the promotion and support of programs for children and women;

8. Pray that peace, justice, and political solutions leading to development for life prevail in Central America.

ADOPTED 1992

See Social Principles, ¶ 75, "Concern for El Salvador."

Christian Faith and Disarmament

The prophecy of Isaiah to Ahaz, King of Judah, declared that security cannot be gained in foreign alliances, intensified hatreds, or strengthened defenses. Isaiah's action program was for the king to "Take heed, be quiet, do not fear, and do not let your heart be faint. . ." (Isa. 7:4).

Isaiah had named his son, "A remnant shall return," which offered God's hope for those who remained faithful, a foretelling of the failure of those who rely on force of arms to survive (Isa. 7; II Kings 17; II Chron. 28).

We affirm Isaiah's words as a standard for today. They are consistent with our denominational history and our contemporary stance. We remember the words of the bishops of the Evangelical Association who said in 1816, "War and the shedding of blood are incompatible with the teachings and example of Christ." Thus we place ourselves with those who reject planning for war as a path to peace.

We also affirm Isaiah's words of hope. We are not called to despair. The landmark study "The Christian Faith and War in the Nuclear Age," directed by the 1960 General Conference of The Methodist Church and given to the church in 1963, said: "The Christian Church and the individual must accept responsibility for the creation of a climate of opinion in which creative changes can occur." It called work for these creative alternatives, "Our mission field as we live as disciples of the Prince of Peace".

We recognize the current situation which is described as a "nuclear dilemma," presents the possibility that, referring to Isaiah's prophecy of a faithful remnant, there may not be a remnant left.

But we also recognize our own responsibility to act, on the basis of our faith, to establish alternatives to war as outlined in the Social Principles and "The United Methodist Church and Peace."

In that mission, we recognize certain events and rejoice in the work that is being done:

—We stand with and affirm our bishops as they lead us through their ministry for peace, especially as it was represented by their Pastoral Letter of April, 1982. We rejoice in their challenge to all United Methodists to join together in seeking an end to the arms race and dedicate ourselves to accept their challenge to be peacemakers. We especially affirm and support the statements of the Council of Bishops in their 1986 pastoral letter, "In Defense of Creation", and the accompanying foundation document. We urge our bishops to keep this concern before the Church. We request that the General Board of Discipleship produce new and updated educational materials for children, youth and adults to study the issues of peace and justice and the effects of the nuclear weapons crisis.

—We praise the American Conference of Catholic Bishops for their Pastoral Letter, "The Challenge of Peace: God's Promise and Our Response." We are strengthened in our understanding and actions through their studied biblical/theological analysis as well as by their analysis of our global situation.

—We rejoice that a challenge to the escalating nuclear arms race has been developed by the National Movement for a Nuclear Freeze in the United States, and has been affirmed internationally in the United Nations. We commend and encourage our congregations and members who are leaders in that movement at all levels. We support a mutually verifiable freeze of nuclear weapons as a politically viable first step toward achieving our goal of the elimination of the production, possession, or use of nuclear weapons.

—We also rejoice that many United Methodists throughout the world participate in various other movements designed to seek alternatives to armaments. In these actions, they are joining together corporately to fulfill the request of the 1963 study which says the Christian must act and must "not sit on the sidelines while momentous decisions are being made."

In order to fulfill our obligations to witness to God's hope for the future we pledge ourselves to these actions:

—We, as United Methodist Christians, must build the conditions for peace through development of confidence and trust between peoples and governments. We stand unalterably opposed to those who would instill hate for one people and nation in the people of another nation. As a worldwide church, we recognize in Christ the unity of all humanity. There must be no hatred between sisters and brothers. We must seek out and struggle against any attempt to instill hatred of any, whether a country, people, or national symbol.

—United Methodist and other Christians must recognize that conflict can be alleviated by accepting the validity of political and economic systems in other counties, and by pledging to work to eliminate attempts to impose systems developed in countries other than their own. That recognition is a necessary first step toward stopping the threat to one system by the government of the other.

—Our goal of world disarmament must be achieved through intermediate steps of arms reduction. We reject deterrence as a permanent basis for the securing and maintenance of peace. It can only be tolerated as a temporary expedient and while real measures of disarmament are set in motion. We affirm measures, particularly between the U.S.S.R. and the United States which develop trust in negotiating postures, and deplore words and actions of one or the other of the major nuclear powers designed to threaten the other.

—We seek to include "no first-strike" pledges in disarmament agreements. We oppose development of weapons systems which lead to automated, hair-trigger responses or pre-emptive strikes. Such systems radically shorten time available for rational response to presumed nuclear attack.

—We continue to urge ratification by all nations of international treaties designed to curb the spread of all types of weapons, both on earth and in outer space. We pledge ourselves to aid in the development of situations where no-nuclear countries do not feel compelled to seek nuclear weapons. We ask governments to structure appropriate political and economic relations with such countries that will encourage them in their non-nuclear path.

—We encourage our local churches and members also to engage in other actions that lead to a disarmed world, including prayer services, vigils, petition drives, and contacts with public officials. To these ends we support those Christians who feel called upon by God to participate in acts of non-violent civil disobedience.

—Disarmament and peace depend upon all nations discovering a prophetic vision of justice and tranquility, as well as the intentions of the Preamble of the U.S. Constitution. We, therefore, call upon The United Methodist Church to establish justice ministries committed to spreading scriptural holiness and reforming the land. Justice requires the end of racism, poverty and violence, and the emergence everywhere of reconciliation. For that reason we reaffirm the program emphasis of Peace With Justice.

ADOPTED 1988

See Social Principles, ¶ 75.C, "Comprehensive Test Ban Treaty," "The United Methodist Church and Peace," "Nuclear Disarmament: the Zero Option," "Nuclear-Free Pacific."

The Church and the Global HIV/AIDS Epidemic

The United Methodist Church will work cooperatively with colleague churches in every region in response to the global HIV/AIDS epidemic which is affecting the health and well-being of individuals and communities worldwide. The Old Testament is replete with calls to the nations and religious leaders to address the needs of the people who are in distress, who are suffering and ill. The New Testament presents a Jesus who reached out and healed those who came to him, including those who were despised and rejected because of their illnesses and afflictions. Jesus' identification with those who suffer was made clear in his admonition to his disciples, that "whatsoever you do to the least of these you do also unto me" (Matt. 25:40). His great commission to his followers to go and do as he has done is a mandate to the church for full involvement and compassionate response.

The Geneva-based World Health Organization estimates that by the year 2000, the number of people infected with the Human Immunodeficiency Virus (HIV), which cause HIV-related illnesses including AIDS (Acquired Immune Deficiency Syndrome), will reach

40 million. The suffering being borne by individuals, families, and entire communities, and the strain being placed on health facilities and national economies, call for intensified cooperative efforts by every sector of society to slow and prevent the spread of infection, to provide appropriate care for those already infected and ill, to speed the development of effective affordable treatment and vaccines to be available in all countries, and to provide support to care providers, communities, health-care workers, health facilities, and programs. The presence of HIV infection has been found in all five geographical regions and HIV illnesses have been reported to the World Health Organization by nearly 200 countries.

Worldwide, HIV infection has been transmitted primarily through heterosexual intercourse with infected persons, as well as in some regions through homosexual/bisexual sexual contact with infected persons, through blood-to-blood contact, including the transfusion of infected blood and blood products, through infected transplanted organs and donated semen, through the use of infected instruments as well as skin-piercing objects associated with ceremonial or traditional healing practices, through sharing of infected needles and equipment by injection drug users, from an infected woman to her fetus-infant before or during childbirth, and, in some instances, after delivery through infected breast milk,.

The impact of HIV infection and related illnesses on economic, social, demographic, political, and health systems is being felt in innumerable ways. Worldwide, women and children increasingly are being affected by the spread of HIV infection. As larger numbers of women of child-bearing age are infected and give birth, larger numbers of infants are born with HIV infection. As larger numbers of parents are infected and die, larger numbers of children are orphaned and extended families are called upon to provide care for greater numbers of family members.

Population growth rates, age structures, labor supply, and agricultural productivity will suffer negative effects as younger-age-group members and women are infected and become ill. The ramification of HIV infection and illness will be particularly grave for families and societies where the extended family is the main or only system of social security and care for family members who are aged or ill and for the nurture of orphaned children.

Gross national products may decrease in areas with high rates of

HIV infection, morbidity, and mortality. Crimes of hate and instances of neglect and rejection may increase against gay and bixsexual men, injection drug users, prostitutes, and others who are assumed to be carriers of HIV. Available health dollars and resources will be affected in the process of caring for larger numbers of persons with HIV illnesses, owning to the costs of securing, distributing, administering, and monitoring the effects of new treatments and drug therapies as they become more readily available. The advances of the "Child Survival Revolution" may be offset as the health of greater numbers of children are affected. It is not known how health systems in any region will be able to manage the additional case loads in a world in which as many as 40 million people may be infected with HIV by the year 2000. The potential to reject and refuse care to persons with HIV is likely to increase until such time as low-cost effective vaccines and therapeutic agents are produced and readily available to all.

In its 1988 Resolution, "AIDS and the Healing Ministry of the Church," General Conference affirmed that "the global AIDS pandemic provides an unparalleled opportunity for witness to the gospel and service to human need among persons." Across the world, United Methodist-related public health specialists, health workers, social workers, teachers, missionaries, clergy, and laity are living and working in cities, towns, and villages where HIV infection and illness are endemic. In all regions churches, congregations, health facilities, schools, men's, women's, and youth groups exist that can provide support, nurture, and education in the midst of the HIV epidemic.

The United Methodist Church urges:

A. Local congregations worldwide to:

• 1. Be places of openness where persons whose lives have been touched by HIV infection and illness can name their pain and reach out for compassion, understanding, and acceptance in the presence of persons who bear Christ's name;

• 2. Provide care and support to individuals and families whose lives have been touched by HIV infection and illness;

• 3. Be centers of education and provide group support and encouragement to help men, women, and youth refrain from activities and behaviors associated with transmission of HIV infection.

B. General program agencies to:

• 1. Assist related health institutions to obtain supplies and equipment to screen donated blood and provide voluntary HIV testing;
• 2. Support efforts by projects and mission personnel within regions to promote disease prevention and to respond to the needs of family care providers and extended families;
• 3. Facilitate partnership relationships between institutions and personnel from region to region, as appropriate, to share models and effective approaches regarding prevention, education, care, and support for individuals and families with HIV infection and illness;
• 4. Assist health workers to obtain regional specific timely updates on the diagnosis, treatment, and prevention of HIV infection and illness;
• 5. Facilitate the sharing of pastoral-care resources and materials dedicated to the care of persons and families whose lives have been touched by HIV;
• 6. Respond to request from the regions to develop training seminars and workshops for church-related personnel in cooperation with ecumenical efforts, private voluntary organizations, and programs already existing in the regions;
• 7. Advocate national, regional, and international cooperation in the development, availability, and transport of appropriate/relevant equipment and supplies for infection control, disease prevention, and treatment.

C. Annual conferences to:
• 1. Explore HIV prevention and care needs within their areas and to develop conferencewide plans for appropriate effective responses;
• 2. Promote pastoral responses to persons with HIV infection and related illnesses that affirm the presence of God's love, grace, and healing mercies;
• 3. Encourage every local church to reach out through proclamation and education to help prevent the spread of HIV infection and to utilize and strengthen the efforts and leadership potential of men's, women's, and youth groups.

D. Episcopal leadership in every region to:
• 1. Issue pastoral letters to the churches calling for compassionate ministries and the development of educational programs that recognize the HIV/AIDS epidemic as a public health threat of major global and regional significance;

• 2. Provide a level of leadership equal to the suffering and desperation being experienced by individuals, families, and the communities in which they live.

The unconditional love of God, witnessed to and manifested through Christ's healing ministry, provides an ever-present sign and call to the church and all persons of faith to be involved in efforts to prevent the spread of HIV infection, to provide care and treatment to those who are already infected and ill, to uphold the preciousness of God's creation through proclamation and affirmation and to be a harbinger of hope, mercy, goodness, forgiveness, and reconciliation within the world.

The United Methodist Church unequivocally condemns the rejection and neglect of persons with HIV infection and illness and all crimes of hate aimed at persons with HIV infection or who are presumed to be carriers of the virus. The United Methodist Church advocates the full involvement of the church at all levels to be in ministry with and to respond fully to the needs of persons, families, and communities whose lives have been affected by HIV infection and illness. In keeping with our faith in the risen Christ we confess our belief that God has received those who have died, that the wounds of living loved ones will be healed, and that Christ, through the Holy Spirit, is present among us as we strive to exemplify what it means to be bearers of Christ's name in the midst of the global HIV/AIDS epidemic.

ADOPTED 1992

See Social Principles, ¶ 71.H, "AIDS and the Healing Ministry of the Church," "Resources for AIDS Education," "Care Giving Teams for Persons with AIDS."

Comprehensive Test Ban Treaty

WHEREAS, The United Methodist Council of Bishops, in their 1986 Pastoral Letter, "In Defense of Creation" (p. 75), told us, "We support the completion at long last of a treaty banning all nuclear weapons testing. This action would redeem the solemn pledge of the 1963 Limited Test Ban Treaty and consummate two decades of nearly successful negotiations suspended in 1982. Such a treaty, perhaps more than any other step, would vindicate and strengthen the Non-Proliferation Treaty and thus help curb the spread of nuclear weapons. It would do much to halt the development of new nuclear weapons";

WHEREAS, the Non-Proliferation Treaty (NPT) is now in jeopardy because the United States has failed to stop nuclear weapons testing [The Fourth Review Conference of the Non-Proliferation Treaty in Geneva ended on September 15, 1990, without agreement. The non–nuclear weapons states, led by Mexico, refused to sign the Final Declaration and threatened to scrap the Non-Proliferation Treaty when it comes up for renewal in 1995. They argued that the United States had failed to abide by the fundamental agreement in Article VI of the Treaty, i.e., if the non-nuclear states refrained from acquiring nuclear weapons (horizontal proliferation) the United States and other nuclear states would agree to refrain from building more new weapons (vertical proliferation). Continued underground nuclear weapons testing is evidence that the United States has not stopped developing new nuclear weapons];

WHEREAS, the Non-Proliferation Treaty is not limited to nuclear weapons: Ronald Lehman, director of the United States Arms Control and Disarmament Agency, argued at the Review Conference that "Article VI is not limited to nuclear weapons. [It aims toward general and complete disarmament, which to achieve, would necessarily require a series of arms control steps in non-nuclear as well as nuclear areas . . .''];

WHEREAS, the United States scuttled the 1991 Amendment Conference to the Limited Test Ban Treaty [This Amendment Conference was designed to convert the Treaty into a CTBT by prohibiting underground tests. On January 18, 1991, the participating states, over the objections of the United States and the United Kingdom, agreed to work toward the end of the underground testing and to reconvene "at an appropriate time"];

Therefore, be it resolved, that the General Conference of The United Methodist Church ask the local churches under the guidance of their Church and Society committees to develop a climate of support (through dialogue, study, and prayer) for appropriate legislation which would complete a treaty banning all nuclear weapons testing;

Therefore, be it further resolved, that the Peace with Justice Committee provide the resources for study in the local church; and

Be it further resolved, that the General Conference of The United

Methodist Church instruct its secretary to communicate to President Bush, the United States Arms Control and Disarmament Agency, and the Secretary General of the United Nations, to support the Non-Proliferation Treaty and vigorously work to stop the proliferation of nuclear, chemical, and weapons of mass destruction.

ADOPTED 1992

See Social Principles, ¶ 75, "Christian Faith and Disarmament," "Nuclear Disarmament: the Zero Option," "Nuclear Weapons Production at the General Electric Company," and "The United Methodist Church and Peace."

Concern for El Salvador

General Conference adopts the following resolution for implementation through the General Board of Church on Society:

Be it resolved, that the 1992 General Conference:

1. Deplores the continuation of human-rights violations in El Salvador.

2. Encourages all other countries to halt all war-related aid to all parties in El Salvador.

3. Supports efforts in peacemaking and the current non-violent process of reconciliation supported by the United Nations.

4. Requests that Congress require that priority be given to the distribution of U.S. economic aid through church and humanitarian channels.

5. Supports the voluntary repatriation of Salvadoran refugees returning to places of their choice in their homeland, El Salvador.

ADOPTED 1992

See Social Principles, ¶ 75.

Consequences of Conflict

WHEREAS, contemporary warfare frequently involves a level of conflict short of formal and massive force engagement of two or more armies;

WHEREAS, such lower intensity forms of conflict are frequently undeclared or even covert, and often take the form of tragic civil war in which outside parties may or may not participate;

WHEREAS, such types of conflict are less amenable to international rules of warfare, particularly regarding the status of a non-combatants and prisoners of war;

Therefore, be it resolved:

1. That The United Methodist Church calls upon all who choose to take up arms, or who order others to do so, to evaluate their actions in accordance with historic Church teaching limiting resort to war, including questions of proportionality, legal authority, discrimination between combatants and non-combatants, just cause, and probability of success.

2. That The United Methodist Church urges the governments of the nations in which the church exists to support negotiations for peace and support the United Nations and other multinational, regional peacekeeping forces.

3. That the General Conference instruct its secretary to send a letter containing the admonition and support outlined above to the chief executive of the above nations and to the Secretary General of the United Nations.

ADOPTED 1992

See Social Principles, ¶¶ 74.G and 75.C, "The United Methodist Church and Peace."

The Current Arab-Israeli Crisis

In light of current events in the Middle East, The United Methodist Church reaffirms the 1984 resolution, "The Arab-Israeli Conflict." The continuing violent confrontation between the Israeli Army and Palestinian civilians living under military occupation in the West Bank and Gaza district and citizens within Israel itself is deeply disturbing to the whole human community. We believe that Israel's current iron-fist policy, which results in violence against Palestinian civilians, is totally unacceptable as civilized behavior. This violent behavior brutalizes human beings, both oppressed and oppressors, and leads to a deepening cycle of hatred and violence. We deplore violence and retaliation on either side in this conflict.

Therefore, we call upon the government of Israel to stop beatings, to end the killings, to cease destroying Palestinian homes, to stop deporting Palestinians, to enter into negotiations with Palestinian civilians and the Palestine Liberation Organization over their legitimate demands, including the fair and just distribution of disputed lands.

We call upon Palestinians, including the Palestinian Liberation Organization to recognize the State of Israel with secure and recognized borders, and to offer to enter negotiations leading toward self-determination of all persons in the territories under military occupation, and to cease the support or initiation of all terrorist activities.

We call upon the United States government to resist efforts to move the United States Embassy from Tel Aviv to Jerusalem, and to support efforts to keep Jerusalem an open city with access to all religious groups.

We also call upon the United States government to support international efforts for Palestinian self-determination, and enter into negotiations with the Palestine Liberation Organization regarding peaceful solutions for the region's problems.

We call upon the United States government to oppose new settlements in the occupied territory, and to stop military and security assistance to Israel until Israel ceases the repression of Palestinians in the occupied territories.

We further recommend, as stated in the 1984 resolution, "Arab-Israeli Conflict," the "Development of denominational participation in ecumenical and interreligious networks to raise consciousness, provide information about the Middle East, and to stimulate action to promote peace in the Middle East."

Therefore, we commend the new organization "U.S. Interreligious Committee for Peace in the Middle East" whose Call for Peace in the Middle East we affirm:

"Peace in the Middle East is essential for the future of Israel, for the Palestinians and Arab states, and for the whole world. But the promise of peace remains unfilfilled. There is daily suffering and danger of greater violence and another war if there is no peace.

"*We Jews, Christians and Muslims Say—In the Name of God, Who Is Compassionate and Just—It Is Time For Peace.* We are motivated by our deepest religious convictions. Working for peace is not optional: it is fundamental to our faith.

"It is time to end the Arab-Israeli-Palestinian conflict. It is time for all parties to stop terror and violence. Peace cannot be achieved by force. It can only be achieved by negotiations. *It Is Time For Peace.*

"*We Call Upon Our Own United States Government to Make Peace a Priority* and use diplomacy to promote negotiations for a just peace based on the following:

"*Israel's Right to Secure Borders and Peace With Her Neighbors,* as an expression of the Jewish people's right of self determination. The principles embodied in UN Security Council Resolutions 242 and 338 provide an agreed upon formula to achieve security and peace for all states in the area in exchange for withdrawal from territories occupied in the 1967 war.

"The Palestinian People's Right of Self-Determination, including the right to choose their own independent leadership, is equally essential to peace. Evidence that Palestinians are willing to exercise their right of self-determination in the West Bank and Gaza alongside Israel, encourages prospects for peace.

"The Need For an International Conference For Peace. The complexity of the conflict and important interests of many countries in the Middle East require an international conference, involving all parties in the conflict as well as the five permanent members of the UN Security Council.

*"Jerusalem is of vital significance to Israelis and Palestinians, to Jews and Christians and Muslims. We believe negotiations, rather than unilateral action, can help assure that Jerusalem will be a city of peace."

Finally, we call upon the governments of all other countries, and especially those in which United Methodists are at work, to join in this effort to achieve a just peace with recognition of the rights of all parties.

ADOPTED 1988

See Social Principles, ¶ 75, "The Arab-Israeli Conflict."

End U.S. Military Presence in Bolivia

Since 1986, the United States has stationed military advisers in Bolivia, originally to fight communist subversion, and currently to fight a "war on drugs."

Because the production of coca is part of the history, culture, and religion of the Bolivian people; and

Because we believe that the war on drugs should be waged in the United States where money now spent on military efforts in Latin America could better be used for education, drug prevention, and rehabilitation; and

Because efforts in Bolivia could be better used in confronting the corruption caused by the narco-traffickers, the growing consumption of cocaine (1.5% of the population is currently affected), and the negative economic impact on the international community; and

Because we believe that the continuing buildup of U. S. military presence in Bolivia is part of a wider strategy of military/political control over governments, popular organizations, and resources, which violates the people's right to self-determination, perpetuates dependence, destroys the social fabric, and becomes an obstacle to a free and independent foreign policy; and

Because the people of Bolivia, who only recently have freed themselves of the power of military dictatorships, strongly object to the presence of U. S. military in their country;

We, as concerned members of The United Methodist Church, join with our brothers and sisters in Bolivia in calling for an end to the U. S. military presence in Bolivia that could lead to further militarization of the country and the continent.

ADOPTED 1992

See Social Principles, ¶ 75, "The United Methodist Church and Peace."

The Fort Laramie Treaty

WHEREAS the 1868 Ft. Laramie Treaty was entered into by the United States of America, the Lakota Nation and other Indian nations, and was ratified by the Senate of the United States and proclaimed by its president in 1869;

WHEREAS this Treaty affirms the sovereignty of the people of all the nations involved;

WHEREAS treaties entered into by the United States government are considered to be the supreme law of the land equal to its Constitution;

WHEREAS treaties cannot be unilaterally abrogated, according to international law;

WHEREAS the 1868 Ft. Laramie Treaty has never been legally abrogated;

WHEREAS the 1868 Ft. Laramie Treaty has been repeatedly violated and ignored by the United States government;

WHEREAS these treaty violations have undermined both the moral integrity of the United States government and the respect for its laws by U.S. citizens;

WHEREAS these treaty violations have resulted in the loss of land and loss of self-government which have contributed to poverty, ill-health, unresponsive educational institutions, loss of self-determination, and loss of life for the Lakota people;

Be It Resolved that we, the members of The United Methodist Church, recognize and reaffirm the sovereignty and independence of the Lakota people.

Be It Further Resolved that we, the members of the General

Conference of The United Methodist Church call on our United States government to recognize the sovereignty and independence of the Lakota Nation through the 1868 Ft. Laramie Treaty. We call upon the President of the United States to form a Presidential Treaty Commission to meet with representatives selected by the Lakota people to redress the grievances caused by the U.S. violations of the 1868 Ft. Laramie Treaty to the mutual satisfaction of both nations, and to devise and implement specific steps to bring the United States into compliance with its treaty obligations with the Lakota Nation.

ADOPTED 1980

See Social Principles, ¶¶ 75.A and 72.A, "Rights of Native American People of the Americas."

Free Flow of Information Among All Peoples of the Earth

In the international arena there is widespread discussion of what is known as the "new world information and communication order." The discussion involves the worldwide flow of information in the light of such factors as governmental restraints, multinational commercial communication enterprises, and the modern technology of communication. The church has a witness to bear upon these issues.

1. The Scriptural Base

Scripture is replete with demands for freedom, truth, justice, and fair treatment of others.

The Old Testament records how, in the early history of the Hebrew people, God's law demanded truth, honesty, and equity. In the great nineteenth chapter of Leviticus God calls for equal treatment of the powerless (v. 15), for love and fair dealing toward the sojourner or stranger (v. 33-4), and for truth and honesty in all dealings (v. 35-6). The Ten Commandments forbid false witness (Deut. 5:20).

The prophets called for justice and righteousness. Amos gave God's word: "Let justice roll down like waters" (5:24). Micah declared that the Lord required of humans "to do justly and to love mercy" (6:8).

In the New Testament Jesus both demands and promises truth and freedom. In John's Gospel he says, "If you continue in my word, you are truly my disciples, and you will know the truth and the truth will make you free" (8:31-2). In the synoptic gospels he commands respect for others, especially those who are weak. Each person's responsibility toward the "little ones" (Matt. 18:5-6; Mark 9:42; Luke 17:2) may be seen also as a responsibility toward the powerless. By example he was an advocate for persons on the margins of society.

Paul, as he wrote the Galatians about freedom in Christ, called his readers to enjoy and use their freedom, but to use it as an opportunity to serve others (5:13-15).

As Christians of today we seek to apply these biblical concepts to the opportunities and problems of the modern media.

2. Our Historic Witness

The United Methodist Church and its predecessor denominations have a long history of defending freedom of religion, freedom of expression, and the rights of persons who are powerless because of political or economic conditions. This concern found expression in the original (1908) Social Creed and successor documents down to the present Social Principles, including today a specific call for freedom of information and protection of the people's right for access to the communication media (Section V). The concern is raised in actions of the 1980 General Conference as recorded in *The Book of Resolutions*. The resolution on Church-Government Relations urges Christians to participate meaningfully in public affairs. The resolution on the Church in a Mass Media Culture declares that channels of communication "must operate in open, humanizing ways." In the resolution on Open Meetings the church demands of itself the high standard of openness that it commends to others. *The Book of Discipline* instructs one of the church agencies to "work toward promotion and protection of the historic freedoms of religion and the press" (¶ 1106.5).

3. Problems in the Flow of Information

Nowhere in the world do people have full and free access to information about people and events elsewhere. Even in the United States, with a tradition of press freedom and constitutional guarantees, our view of the world is circumscribed by what is selected for us by newspaper and news magazine editors and radio/television news producers. A study of datelines in newspaper stories quickly reveals that most of the news pertains to our own country or Europe, and that news from countries elsewhere is likely to be filtered through Western conduits.

Persons in many countries, especially in developing nations, feel that they seldom have the opportunity to express themselves, or even describe themselves, in their own words and on their own terms. They feel that they are seen mainly through the eyes of foreigners—usually reporters for the commercial news services of Europe and North America.

Many persons live in countries where newspapers and broadcast news are controlled by governments. In many countries there is outright censorship. Some governments use the mass media for political purposes.

Modern technology, especially computer-based communications and transmission by satellite, makes global communications possible on a scale and with an immediacy never possible before. But the cost is beyond the reach of all but the most affluent countries or corporations. Those who control communication technology have the power to determine what is known about others. The same technology makes it possible to treat information as a commodity to be bought and sold, to be shared or withheld for payment or consideration.

In the United States the broadcast and print media increasingly have turned viewers and readers into a product to be delivered to the sponsors. As a result, the media's goal becomes to reach and hold the largest possible audience, regardless of other journalistic objectives.

These, and other related concerns, demand serious thought in all countries, especially those countries that have the power to create and control the media of communication. The light of the Christian gospel must be applied to these questions.

4. *Statement of Principles*

In view of inequities in the flow of information among the peoples of the world, and in the light of our own understanding of the gospel, we state these principles:

• All peoples of earth have a right to free flow of information.

• Peoples have a right to originate information and make statements about themselves in terms of their own culture and self-view.

• Journalists must be given access to information within their own countries and across international frontiers.

• Journalists have a responsibility for accuracy and fairness in all that they write, photograph, edit, publish or broadcast. Part of this responsibility includes cross-cultural sensitivity and awareness as well as freedom from language bias.

• The licensing of publications or of journalists violates freedom.

• Information is a human right and not only a commodity to be bought and sold. (However, those who gather, edit and transmit information are entitled to fair rewards for their efforts.)

• Every citizen has a right to be informed in order to participate in politics intelligently.

• Censorship by governments or by those who control news media is abhorrent and should not be permitted; neither should there be legal restrictions to the free flow of information. The withholding of information for security reasons must be limited by publicly-stated guidelines.

• Readers and viewers in every land have a right to a broad view of the world, drawing upon multiple sources of information.

• The churches should be primary advocates for a free flow of information and diversity of sources. The churches should oppose the practice of those persons and systems which use media for purposes of human exploitation, political control, or excessive private profit.

5. Recommended Actions

This resolution is commended to the churches and to individual United Methodists for study and action, such as monitoring local and national media and legislation and instituting appropriate follow-up. Dialog with journalists, publishers and broadcasters is recommended.

The United Methodist Church must ensure that, in its own communications, persons of other countries and cultures speak for themselves.

Individuals, local churches, and local church groups are urged to join with other Christians in their communities in study and action on the issues and principles stated in this resolution.

The results of local study may indicate suggestions to local media. Recommendations may be made to representatives in local, state or national government. Viewpoints may be registered also with governmental agencies, such as the Federal Communications Commission, and with intergovernmental or international agencies.

General agencies of the church, particularly United Methodist Communications, the General Board of Church and Society and the General Board of Global Ministries, are directed to provide coordinated resources and guides for study and action.

ADOPTED 1984

See Social Principles, ¶¶ 74.C and 75, "Justice, Peace and the Integrity of Creation," "The United Methodist Church and Peace."

The Global Nature of The United Methodist Church

WHEREAS, there must be developed a truly global church which has an integrity which affords dignity to all parts of the United Methodist Church; our church must be an expression of the global nature of our church membership: "A member of a local United Methodist Church is a member of the total United Methodist connection" (¶ 210); and

WHEREAS, there must be equity (parity) between what are now called central conferences and jurisdictional conferences; and

WHEREAS, we must provide for connectional unity with the flexibility and freedom for meeting regional needs; and

WHEREAS, we must redefine some General Conference responsibilties as regional ones; much of the current General Conference agenda is focused exclusively on United States issues and needs; at least some of this agenda could be handled in a North American Regional Conference, just as similar regional agenda could be addressed in other regional conference; and

WHEREAS, we must be sensitive to how God seeks to manifest the gospel in each unique culture and nation; we must also maintain a vital global connection in order to prevent both narrow parochialism and detrimental regionalism; and

WHEREAS, our global vision for The United Methodist Church includes, but is not limited to, the following:

1. Provision of a means by which the United Methodist family can live and serve together in a common dignity and respect as together we respond to the mission of Jesus Christ;

2. A serious responsiveness to the unique needs and expressions of faith in each of the regions of the world and provision for freedom for creative response to unique characteristics;

3. Connection of our global United Methodist membership at essential points and through common global mission;

4. Responsiveness to the radically changed and changing world culture in which we are called to do ministry in Christ's name;

Therefore, be it resolved, that the General Conference authorize the Council of Bishops, in cooperation with the General Council on Ministries, the General Council on Finance and Administration, the General Board of Global Ministries, the General Commission on Christian Unity and Interreligious Concerns, and the Commission on Central Conference Affairs (selecting at least three non-episcopal members) to continue to develop this proposal on the Global Nature of The United Methodist Church and to report to the General Conference 1996; and

Be it further resolved, that the Council of Bishops submit the attached report as a progress report to the General Conference.

ADOPTED 1992

See Social Principles, ¶ 75, "Understanding the United Methodist Church as a Global Church," "New House of Europe."

Holy Land Tours

Concern has been raised across the church about special opportunities that are often being missed by United Methodists traveling to Israel/Palestine, often called the Holy Land.

Christians indigenous to the area have also sharpened the question by wondering why they are so often ignored by Christian pilgrims to the region. Why, they ask, do travelers tend to honor the inanimate stones which testify to Jesus' life and ministry while ignoring the "living stone," the indigenous Christians who represent an unbroken line of discipleship to Jesus in the land which he called home?

Travelers to this land have the opportunity to be ambassadors of unity and concern to the churches and Christians in a troubled land. They also have an opportunity to learn from the spiritual traditions of the churches indigenous to the Middle East. Further, they have a special opportunity to discover firsthand the realities of a region of deep meaning and vital importance to Christians, as well as to Jews and Muslims.

Therefore, The United Methodist Church:

A) Strongly affirms the resolution of the 1984 General Conference, offering: "Encouragement of all leaders of and participants in 'Holy Land tours' to contact indigenous Christian leaders in the Middle East, and to hear the concerns of both the Israelis and Palestinians who live there, as well as visit the biblical and historical sites" ("The Arab-Israeli Conflict," 6.b);

B) Asks the bishops, clergy, members, agencies, and congregations of The United Methodist Church, as they plan visits to the Holy Land, to devote at least 20 percent of the program time to contact with indigenous Christian leaders and to hearing the concerns of Palestinians and Israelis on the current crisis of Palestinian self-determination;

C) Recommends that United Methodists planning individual or group tours to Israel/Palestine consult with the United Methodist liaison in Jerusalem and the Middle East Council of Churches Ecumenical Travel Office to seek opportunities to worship with indigenous Christian congregations and to visit United Methodist-supported mission sites;

D) Asks the General Board of Global Ministries and General Board of Church and Society to prepare specific recommendations for United Methodists traveling in the Middle East and other sensitive regions of the world;

E) Recommends that United Methodist-sponsored tours use the denomination's joint seminar program in pre-departure seminars for the travelers; and

F) Urges that travelers use, as advance study materials, positions adopted by General Conference and by general church agencies relating to the Middle East.

ADOPTED 1992

See Social Principles, ¶ 75, "The Arab-Israeli Conflict," "Current Arab-Israeli Conflict."

In Support of Self-Determination and Non-Intervention

Interventions of nations into the affairs of other nations, frustrating justice and self-determination, are a reality of our time. The United Methodist Church stands unequivocally against such interventions.

The Hebrew prophets call us to a world in which all peoples are secure in their own land and on their own mountains. God breaks the bars of the yoke of oppression and feeds the people in justice (Ezekiel 34). Our Savior, Jesus Christ, calls us to be peacemakers, to live in justice and in peace with one another (Matthew 5).

The Social Principles of our church offers guidance:

—The first moral duty of all nations is to resolve by peaceful means every dispute that arises between or among them.

—We affirm the right and duty of the people of all nations to determine their own destiny.

—Upon the powerful (nations) rests a special responsibility to exercise their wealth and influence with restraint.

The United Nations Charter provides mandates. All member states shall:

—Settle international disputes by peaceful means.

—Respect the principle of equal rights and self-determination of peoples.

—Refrain from the threat or use of force against the territorial integrity or political independence of any other State.

—Undertake to comply with the decision of the International Court of Justice in any case to which it is a party.

The Charter of the Organization of American States offers an additional directive:

—No State or group of States has the right to intervene in any way, directly or indirectly, for any reason whatever, in the internal or external affairs of any other State.

In spite of the mandates of international law and the cries of the people for a world of peace with justice, we are faced with continuing interventions of all kinds. These actions undermine international law, breed injustice, frustrate the self-determination of peoples, and are responsible for untold human suffering.

"Intervention," as used in this resolution, is defined as the knowing and willful intrusion by one nation into the affairs of another country with the purpose of changing its policies or its culture. It includes any activity, military, economic, political, social, cultural; covert or overt; designed to stabilize or destabilize an existing government.

We are guided in our activities for self-determination and non-intervention by our biblical faith, the Social Principles and the principles of international law. Specifically, we adopt the following guidelines:

1. The United Methodist Church categorically opposes interventions by more powerful nations against weaker ones. Such actions violate our Social Principles and are contrary to the United Nations Charter and international law and treaties.

2. We oppose clandestine operations, such as political assassinations; political and military coups; sabotage; guerilla activities; atrocities, particularly those directed at children; paramilitary

efforts; military training; weapons support and supply; mining of navigable waters; economic pressures; political or economic blackmail; and propaganda aimed at de-stabilizing other governments. We oppose activities where national or international intelligence agencies engage in political or military operations beyond the gathering of information.

3. We support multilateral diplomatic efforts, for example the Contadora peace process and the Afrias Initiative (Esquipulas II) which have been used in Central America, as a means of settling disputes among nations. We support regional and international negotiations arranged in cooperation with the United Nations and held without resort to political rhetoric and public posturing.

4. To deepen understanding among nations and to affirm the diversities among peoples, their politics and culture, we support increased contacts between peoples—between East and West, North and South, between the peoples of the Soviet Union and the United States, between the peoples of Nicaragua and the United States, and between the peoples of Afghanistan and the Soviet Union. These contacts could include cultural exchanges, tourism, educational and scientific seminars, church visitations. We applaud and encourage the development of covenant relationships between United Methodist congregations in countries with differing social or economic systems.

5. We support affirmative United Nations policies and actions to assist peoples of the world, particularly of developing nations, in achieving self-determination. We support the development and implementation of United Nations sanctions against those nations that intervene unilaterally in the affairs of other nations in violation of international law.

6. We support United Nations and regional policies and actions designed to isolate and quarantine any nation which consistently denies fundamental human rights, as enumerated in the Universal Declaration of Human Rights, to any segment of its people. Through collective action, wars fought to achieve justice might be averted or diminished. Such measures include: "complete or partial interruption of economic relations and of rail, sea, air, postal, telegraphic, radio, and other means of communication, and the severance of diplomatic relations." (Article 41, United Nations Charter)

Therefore, we call upon all United Methodists, United Methodist agencies and institutions, to:

1. Study the issue of intervention and to hold their own governments accountable to the United Nations Charter and other international laws and treaties.
2. Deliver this resolution to their governmental leaders and to discuss its contents with them, urging its support and implementation.
3. Monitor their own governments and to support appropriate actions to hold their governments accountable to the United Nations Charter and international laws and treaties.

ADOPTED 1988

See Social Principles, ¶¶ 75.B and D, "End U.S. Military Presence in Bolivia," "Oppose Food and Medicine Blockades or Embargoes," "The United Methodist Church and Peace."

Infant Formula Abuse

Breastfeeding is the healthiest, most nutritious method of feeding newborn infants and is virtually universally recommended as the preferential means of feeding infants. Conversely the misuse of infant formula and bottlefeeding causes health problems, illness, and even death for hundreds of thousands of babies each year. We support full compliance with the WHO/UNICEF Code of Marketing of Breast Milk Substitutes as one vital means of promoting breastfeeding and protecting the health and lives of millions of infants.

During the past decade and a half The United Methodist Church has developed considerable knowledge in this arena and worked as an active global advocate for maternal and infant nutrition. In pursuing our goal of proper nutrition for infants we have supported the elements of the International Code of Marketing of Breast Milk Substitutes, supported UNICEF and their Baby Friendly Hospital Initiative, and challenged infant formula companies to comply with the code and end all practices, in the U.S. and around the world, that undermine breastfeeding. At times our voice has been heard in tones of quiet persuasion in meeting rooms while at other times it has been a forceful public challenge in arenas like company stockholder meetings. The Infant Formula Task Force of The United Methodist Church has also engaged in comprehensive monitoring in Third World countries of government and corporate adherence to the code.

"Then he took a child and set her in front of them, and put his arm around her. 'Whoever receives one of these children in my name,' he said, 'receives me; and whoever receives me, receives not me, but the One who sent me': (Mark 9:36-37).

Jesus, in these words, confirmed what the scriptures taught from ancient days, that how one treats the weakest and most helpless—the widow, the orphan, the alien, the child—was an expression of one's respect for God. God through Christ comes to us in the inversion of our images of power and omnipotence, in the persona of one in need of care. Those who cheat, steal, or profit from the weak and helpless are urged to change and if they remain impervious to correction, are driven out of the community of faithful.

In the present world of impersonal technology and high-pressure global sales strategies, those who deprive the children of their rightful heritage of health may never see the faces of those who suffer by their corporate decisions. But we are called, nevertheless, to hold up before them the children whose lives are stunted by their policies, and hold them accountable for the wasted lives, the stolen promises, the unnecessary premature deaths. God sets every child in our midst, reminding us that we are accountable to the Most Holy One for how our actions affect the weakest and most helpless of our brothers and sisters.

On the other hand, we are called to love those who cannot take care of themselves, such as infants, for they are powerless, vulnerable, have no claims on us, and cannot reward or repay us.

Children are a gift of God, a precious resource and our planet's future. Every year hundreds of thousands of newborn infants suffer needless sickness and even death when breastfeeding is not chosen and infant formula is misused. At the United Nations World Summit for Children in 1989, nations agreed to the "empowerment of all women to breastfeed their children exclusively for four to six months and to continue breastfeeding until complimentary food well into the second year." Breastfeeding passes on essential immunities to the infant from the first day of life, reducing infectious diseases and mortality; it also builds a special bond between mother and child.

In a 1991 communication to all heads of state in the world, UNICEF Executive Director James Grant and WHO Director-General Dr. Hiroshi Nakajima stated: "More than a million children would not have died last year if all mothers had been able to effectively breast-feed." Breastfeeding also significantly reduces the prospect of breast cancer.

Conversely, the misuse of infant formula feeding by the use of contaminated water or overdilution of the formula results in the very sickness and death that the WHO/UNICEF letter refers to. Health authorities, supported by our denomination, have vigorously opposed any actions, whether by a government or infant formula company, that discourage breastfeeding or inadequately warn mother and fathers about the dangers of bottlefeeding.

To express their deep conviction on this issue, the nations of the world voted in 1981 for the Code of Marketing of Breast Milk Substitutes. The code expressly opposes policies such as public advertising, lack of warnings on labels, sample packs to mothers leaving the hospital, public advertising, promotion of bottlefeeding over breastfeeding in literature, and free supplies of infant formula to hospitals. This code provides a basis of understanding for government health professionals and industry alike.

Recently WHO and UNICEF launched a Baby Friendly Hospital Initiative to encourage successful breastfeeding.

While infant formula companies have made many changes over the last decade, such as revising labels, ending sample packs to mothers, and public advertising in developing countries, they stubbornly refuse to affirm the universal nature of the code and to put its provisions fully into effect. For example, infant formula companies still provide free supplies of infant formula to hospitals, a vitally important marketing strategy since families usually continue to use the formula they start with in the hospital. WHO and UNICEF both believe these free supplies act to discourage breastfeeding and have recently set the end of 1992 as a deadline for ending free supplies. Industry has pledged its support for this deadline but refuse to end such supplies voluntarily, instead waiting for government agencies to legislate their end. We believe this code violation should be ended speedily; further, we urge companies to unilaterally end free supplies as well as supporting government action to do so.

In addition, there have been new public advertising and marketing campaigns in the United States that violate the code and discourage breastfeeding. Nestle/Carnation, Bristol-Myers Squibb, and Gerber have all begun mass-media advertising of new infant formula products. Claiming their formula is a "complete food" or "if it isn't from you, shouldn't it be from Gerber?", tens of millions of advertising dollars have been spent to attract consumers to these new formula products.

Such campaigns undermine breastfeeding in the pursuit of profit. These deceptive campaigns are vigorously opposed by health professionals, including the American Academy of Pediatrics.

The church is called to give leadership on this vital issue. After 15 years of involvement our expertise and effective public leadership is acknowledged as a vital moral voice. James Grant of UNICEF has commended the religious community's "moral imperative" on infant formula and urged us to continue this urgent work.

Many companies turn to the churches as a moral compass and public litmus test on this issue.

The United Methodist Church affirms the need for urgent action to support breastfeeding on a global basis and to end policies or practices by governments, corporations, or health authorities which promote bottlefeeding over breastfeeding. While we believe women and families should have information allowing a choice in how they feed their babies, information campaigns and education programs should support the primacy of breastfeeding.

In particular:

1. We recommend the continuation of an Infant Formula Monitoring and Action Committee with representation from a variety of United Methodist agencies to give leadership to the church in this new quadrennium. The committee is to be convened by the General Board of Church and Society (GBCS) and shall include one person from the 1984-88 Infant Formula Task Force, one person from the 1988-92 Infant Formula Task Force, two persons chosen at-large for their expertise on Infant Formula issues, and two members of GBCS.

2. We recommend that The United Methodist Church support WHO and UNICEF in their active initiatives for comprehensive global implementation of the code and the Baby Friendly Hospital Initiative.

3. We recommend that The United Methodist Church urge infant formula companies to implement fully and universally all provisions of the code and in particular cooperate with the WHO and UNICEF goal of ending free supplies of infant formula to hospitals by the end of 1992. These supplies can be ended using a variety of approaches, including government action and unilateral corporate withdrawal of free supplies to insure the end of the code abuse. We believe the 1992 deadline should not be negotiable.

4. We urge Nestle/Carnation, Bristol-Myers Squibb, and Gerber to end all public advertising of infant formula in the United States. This

advertising violates the code and the stated position of the American Academy of Pediatrics and numerous national health organizations opposing such widespread media advertising and promotes new brands of infant formula, undercutting breastfeeding.

5. We urge all United Methodist institutional and individual stockholders in infant formula companies to use their sharedholder leverage to encourage code compliance by these corporations, including dialogue and shareholder resolutions with selected companies. Further, we urge our partner churches around the world to raise these concerns with infant formula companies in their nations.

6. We urge all United Methodist-related hospitals to embrace the UNICEF Baby Friendly Initiative, a multi-pronged program for infant health and breastfeeding.

7. We urge United Methodist agencies to work ecumenically through the Interfaith Center on Corporate Responsibility and in partnership with leadership groups such as UNICEF, WHO, the American Academy of Pediatrics in support of these goals.

8. We support a campaign of education and advocacy for breastfeeding to help create a culture in the workplace, the church, the hospital, and the home supportive of breastfeeding, and commend to the churches the work of World Alliance for Breastfeeding Action (WABA), Penang, Malaysia, in this regard.

9. We urge individual United Methodists and appropriate agencies of the church to voice strong concern to the United States government about the pricing policies of the $2 billion federally funded WIC program (for women, infants and children) in light of a 1991 study which revealed a sharp decline in breastfeeding among WIC recipients.

10. We acknowledge the effectiveness of boycott action as a last resort to press corporations to act responsibly and request the General Board of Church and Society to initiate a study to see if the new massive advertising campaigns in the U.S. media warrants such boycott actions.

11. We urge governments and health authorities to take concrete steps to support breastfeeding and to end marketing and promotion tactics leading to bottlefeeding abuses.

ADOPTED 1992

See Social Principles, ¶ 75.

Justice for Reverend Alex Awad

The Rev. Alex Awad is a Palestianian-American who was commissioned a missionary in 1989 by the United Methodist General Board of Global Ministries to serve as pastor of the East Jerusalem Baptism Church. Since that time, however, the Israeli government has repeatedly refused to grant him a visa for entry into Jerusalem.

Although the reason given for the refusal relates to visa problems with Rev. Awad some years past, it is more likely that he is being prevented from pastoring this church because he is the brother of Mubarak Awad, founder of the Palestinian Center for the Study of Nonviolence, who was deported by the Israeli government in 1988. Rev. Awad has no history of political activity and wishes to assume his role as pastor of the East Jerusalem Baptist Church for religious, and not political, reasons. He and his wife Brenda have also been asked to teach at the Bethlehem Bible College.

Rev. Awad has been formally issued a call by the East Jerusalem Baptist Church to serve as its pastor. His congregation has suffered patiently without a pastor throughout these years as he has petitioned the Israeli government for a visa.

Support for indigenous Christian congregations is especially important during this time of great stress, which has led to increased Christian emigration from East Jerusalem, the West Bank, and Gaza in response to the sufferings of Palestinians under Israeli occupation.

The Social Principles clearly state the moral obligation for all governments to provide freedom of religion: "We hold governments responsible for the protection of the rights of the people to free and fair elections and to the freedoms of speech, religion, assembly, and communications media" (74A). The resolution "Religious Liberty," in the *Book of Resolutions* restates and expands the church's commitment to religious freedom.

Despite numerous pleas from United Methodist Church officials (including a November, 1991, meeting of bishops and top mission staff with Israeli embassy officials), U.S. congresspersons, concerned citizens, peace and rabbinical organizations in Israel, and church officials from other denominations in Europe and the United States, the government of Israel has persisted in denial of a visa to Rev. Awad and his family.

Israel's refusal to grant a visa to Rev. Awad represents:

1) a denial of the freedom of religion which Israel espouses for Jerusalem;

2) an affront to The United Methodist Church, whose mission board has found him suitable in every way to serve under its auspices and has formally commissioned him and his family to serve in Jerusalem;

3) a spiritual burden upon the congregation in Jerusalem, which has been without a pastor this long period;

4) a source of grave concern as to whether this is part of a policy to intimidate and reduce the Palestinian population of Jerusalem; and

5) a travail for the Awad family and their young children, who have been forced to move at least yearly throughout this time of waiting.

Therefore, The United Methodist Church:

1) expresses its gratitude for all of those religious groups, government officials, concerned individuals, and organizations who have joined with United Methodist members and officials in calling for an end to this denial of religious freedom and for the granting of a visa to Rev. Alex Awad and his family;

2) extends our church's continuing prayerful concern and support for Rev. Awad and his family during this difficult time, and expresses our deep appreciation for his ongoing ministry of mission interpretation within our church during this interim period;

3) protests in the strongest terms the refusal of the Israeli government to grant a visa to Rev. Awad, a commissioned missionary and a United States citizen;

4) requests that church agencies, annual conferences, and congregations monitor the case of Rev. Awad and voice their concern about religious freedom to the Israeli Embassy;

5) requests that the General Board of Global Ministries, the General Board of Church and Society, and the Council of Bishops to intensify their advocacy for the free practice of religion in Jerusalem, the rights of the Palestinian people, and the granting of a visa to Rev. Awad;

6) urges all United Methodists who travel to Israel/Palestine to:

a) share with Israeli authorities their deep concern about this denial of religious freedom, and

b) use the special opportunity afforded by their travel to learn about and share with the Palestinian Christian community;

7) encourages United Methodist congregations to learn about the

life and challenges facing Palestinian Christians and other Christians in the Middle East.

ADOPTED 1992

See Social Principles, ¶ 75, "The Arab-Israeli Conflict," "Current Arab-Israeli Crisis."

Justice, Peace, and the Integrity of Creation

"Justice, Peace and the Integrity of Creation" was the theme of a process initiated by the World Council of Churches, Sixth Assembly, in Vancouver, Canada, in 1983. In Canberra, Australia, in 1991 the World Council of Churches adopted this emphasis as a priority area for the council's programmes. To join the issues of peace, justice, and the well-being of creation is to create a common understanding of their interconnectedness.

A World Convocation was held in Seoul, Republic of Korea, in March, 1990, "to engage member churches in a conciliar process of mutual commitment to justice, peace and the integrity of creation." A set of 10 affirmations was approved by the convocation for a process of covenanting:

1. We affirm that all forms of human power and authority are subject to God and accountable to people. This means the right of people to full participation. In Christ, God decisively revealed the meaning of power as compassionate love that prevails over the forces of death.

2. We affirm God's preferential option for the poor and state that as Christians our duty is to embrace God's action in the struggles of the poor in the liberation of us all.

3. We affirm that people of every race, caste, and ethnic group are of equal value. In the very diversity of their cultures and traditions, they reflect the rich plurality of God's creation.

4. We affirm the creative power given to women to stand for life wherever there is death. In Jesus' community women find acceptance and dignity and with them he shared the imperative to carry the good news.

5. We affirm that access to truth and education, information, and means of communication are basic human rights. All people have the right to be educated, to tell their own stories, to speak their own convictions and beliefs, to be heard by others, and to have the power to distinguish truth from falsehood.

6. We affirm the full meaning of God's peace. We are called to seek

every possible means of establishing justice, achieving peace, and solving conflicts by active nonviolence.

7. We affirm that the world, as God's handiwork, has its own inherent integrity; that land, waters, air, forests, mountains, and all creatures, including humanity, are "good" in God's sight. The integrity of Creation has a social aspect which we recognize as peace with justice, and an ecological aspect which we recognize in the self-renewing, sustainable character of natural ecosystems.

8. We affirm that the land belongs to God. Human use of land and waters should release the earth to replenish regularly its life-giving power, protecting its integrity and providing spaces for its creatures.

9. We affirm the dignity of children which derives from their particular vulnerability and need for nurturing love; the creative and sacrificial role that the young people are playing in building a new society, recognizing their right to have a prophetic voice in the structures that affect their life and their community; the rights and needs of the younger generation as basic for establishing educational and developmental priorities.

10. We affirm that human rights are God-given and that their promotion and protection are essential for freedom, justice, and peace. To protect and defend human rights, an independent judicial system is necessary.

The Social Principles of The United Methodist Church clearly reflects our commitment to justice, peace, and the integrity of creation. In addition, The United Methodist Church has demonstrated its support for justice, peace, and the integrity of creation through its complementary Peace with Justice Program.

In affirming its participation in the justice, peace, and the integrity of creation process of the World Council of Churches, The United Methodist Church specifically pledges to:

1. encourage local churches and individuals to study the documents of "Justice, Peace and the Integrity of Creation" in order to develop greater understand and support for those movements of people who struggle for human dignity, liberation, and for just and participatory forms of government and economic structures;

2. join the worldwide ecumenical movement to articulate its vision for all people living on earth and caring for creation;

3. urge the General Board of Global Ministries and the General Board of Church and Society to give priority to integrated programs

supportive of the four covenants affirmed by the convocation in Seoul, Korea, which advocate:

• a just economic order and liberation from the bondage of foreign debt;
• true security of all nations and people;
• the building of a culture that can live in harmony with creation's integrity; and
• the eradication of racism and discrimination on national and international levels for all people;

4. urge all United Methodists to implement the Social Principles and General Conference resolutions which address these issues, especially "Economic Justice," "The United Methodist Church and Peace," "Environmental Stewardship," "Global Racism," and "An Ecumenical Decade: Churches in Solidarity with Women";

5. urge all United Methodists to join in covenant with Christians around the world to work to fulfill the goals of justice, peace, and the integrity of creation.

ADOPTED 1992

See Social Principles, ¶¶ 70, 73, and 75; "The United Methodist Church and Peace," "Peace with Justice as a Special Program," "Environmental Justice for a Sustainable Future."

Mission and Aging of Global Population

The church is being asked to respond to a rapidly expanding number of older persons throughout the world, many of whom live in precarious circumstances in societies hard pressed to find the economic resources to cope with them. The situation holds possibilities for an invigorated ministry by, for, and with these older persons, however, and the challenge is to change some of our perceptions of older persons and their abilities and also of our complacence about so-called advanced societies.

A primary reason for the church to be concerned about the aging of the global population is rooted in the Bible. The creation stories in Genesis were not merely about youth and middle age; they also dealt with the promise of a blessed future. These promises took on more material form in the patriarchal stories where individuals lived hundreds of years—an expression of the belief that life itself was good and therefore extended life was very good. The birth of children to Sarah and other women of advanced age fulfilled God's intent that older persons were of worth all their years. The ninetieth Psalm's "three-score and ten / or even by reason of strength fourscore" was expressed in the context of transient life but at the same time life lived confidently in God's care. When Jesus spoke of the commandments, he included honor for father and mother (Mark 10:19, with parallels in Matthew and Luke), and it can be assumed that when Paul spoke of giving "honor to whom honor is due" (Rom. 13:7), he meant to include respect for older persons. The term "elder" used in the New Testament gravitated to a title for certain roles in the church, but it could only have been used in a community in which "older" called for honor and reverence.

Through the centuries the church has held varying attitudes toward older persons, but the strongest traditions were those that accorded dignity to persons in old age. These traditions contributed to our United Methodist Social Principles statement on rights of the aging, in which social policies and programs are called for "that ensure to the aging the respect and dignity that is their right as senior members of the human community."

The facts are clear: demographic data reveal that every month the world population of older persons, ages 55 and over, increases by more than one million persons. Eight percent of the increase occurs in so-called developing countries. Today these countries contain about 370 million older persons, but projections are that by the year 2020 they will contain more than one billion. The rate of growth of older persons is faster in these countries than others.

Advances in public health and education, as well as control of infectious diseases, have contributed to these changes. Nevertheless, the biblical hope for a blessed old age never becomes reality for many older persons because of extreme conditions of poverty, war, and hunger. Eldercide is becoming more frequent. Social security coverage applies only to a small minority of citizens in some countries.

Many of these older persons live in situations that make them very vulnerable. They live in rural areas, working the land; are predominantly female; and are illiterate. Rural areas have much older populations, since younger people tend to migrate to cities. Older persons are heavily concentrated in agriculture, with manufacturing jobs ranking a distant second. Women outlive men in virtually all countries. Most women past age 65 are widows, a trend that is likely to continue. Less than 10 percent of older women in many poor societies are literate. Older persons belong to families, but traditional

594

social support based on family structures is eroding, leaving many in isolation and without persons to care for them in their last years.

Many of these poor societies are more advanced than our own in one respect, however: older persons are held in love and respect precisely because of their experience and their symbolic place as the wise leaders and survivors of families and communities. Contrast this love and respect with some of the attitudes in the United States and other Western countries, where old age is depreciated because it is less "productive," and because physical energy and young ideals of style and beauty are held to be more valuable than spiritual energy and the beauty of the inner soul. For this reason, the United States and other societies are "developing" and can learn much from other societies.

Those in the United States can celebrate the improved health and social security provided to older persons in recent decades, as well as the important role that very large nonprofit associations of older persons play in policy development and legislation. Those in The United Methodist Church also celebrate the inclusion of older persons in structures throughout the church and the increasing quality of care provided for these persons in retirement and older adult facilities. Gratitude for these advances does not, however, blind us to efforts to depict older persons as benefiting from the plight of the very young, to the low quality of care in many nursing homes, and to outright abuses in families, institutions, and organizations that employ older persons.

The United Methodist Church calls upon:

A. Local churches to:

1. Involve older adults intergenerationally and in ways that empower and encourage them to be resources for skills, knowledge, experience, and spiritual insight;

2. Use resources from general agencies of The United Methodist Church that suggest actions and models for learning from other cultures and countries in their understanding and appreciation of older persons.

B. Annual conferences to:

1. Involve older adults in the full range of programs of the conference, including volunteer-in-mission (VIM) projects; health ministries in which able older adults care for the frail elderly; and use of resources and action suggestions from the Advisory/Coordinating Committee of Older Adult Ministries and its successor in The United Methodist Church.

2. Ask itinerating missionaries to speak to constructive ways churches in the United States can (a) learn from the customs, values, and practices of churches in other countries and cultures, and (b) support older persons in these other countries and cultures through Advance Specials, VIM projects, and mission support.

C. All general program agencies of The United Methodist Church to:

1. Identify specific actions in their ongoing programs and ministries by which families on a global basis can be assisted in caring for their frail elderly; and

2. Include older persons in training for care giving in relation to mission and ministry globally.

D. The General Board of Church and Society and the General Board of Global Ministries to:

1. Advocate support for older persons in governmental and nongovernmental organizations, including the United Nations, the U.S. government, and ecumenical and other nongovernmental, international organizations; and

2. Study and share with the whole church pertinent issues related to the well-being of older persons, such as allocation of governmental resources for support and care, end-of-life issues, and avoidance of age-ism in employment and community life.

E. The General Board of Global Ministries to include in mission education:

1. Positive images of older persons in all countries and cultures along with images depicting realistically the difficulties many of these persons have under conditions of poverty and isolation;

2. Information about the "double bind" in which many poor societies find themselves by virtue of the demands of a growing young population and the demands of a growing older population; and

3. Resources for annual conferences and local churches that provide models for appropriate mission and ministry on the local level and specific action and program suggestions.

F. All general agencies and all episcopal leadership to:

1. Include older persons as full participants in programs and ministries from planning through decision making and evaluation;

2. Seek opportunities by which The United Methodist Church can affirm its aging membership while finding ways by which this membership can collaborate with younger persons in evangelism and

renewal of the whole church, to the end that persons of all ages are called to the discipleship of Jesus Christ; and

3. Lift the prophetic voice of Christian faith in a critique of the limits and values of self-help efforts, such as asking older persons to take responsibility for their own health and well-being, and to proclaim a vision of human community in which older persons are accorded respect and dignity as those made in the image of God and part of the human family.

ADOPTED 1992

See Social Principles, ¶ 72.E, "Aging in the United States of America."

"New House" of Europe

United Methodism in a New Europe

The United Methodist Church recognizes, with deep gratitude, the positive developments which have taken place in Europe. President Gorbachev accelerated the process toward change with new polices of openness (glasnost) and reconstruction (perestroika). This process has provided room for development of the liberation movements which have been growing in eastern Europe. The fall of the Berlin wall was a symbol of a new order. From these changes a "New House" of Europe is emerging which is reshaping the political, social, and economic fabric of the continent.

We affirm that many people, among them numerous Christians including United Methodists, stood and suffered against oppressing political powers which used coercion to extinguish any spark of opposition.

At the same time, the violence which too often accompanies change causes us grief. There is civil war going on in many parts of Europe. We encourage development and application of peaceful means while change continues in these regions. We point to the liberation movements in central Europe as models for change.

We commend the reconciliation that occurred among the western European nations during the last four decades. However, some countries still struggle for identity and recognition, e.g., the Republic of Macedonia. We are concerned, therefore, that a special effort should be made by governments so that consensus and harmony can now be extended to the whole of Europe. The United Methodist Church needs to raise its members' awareness of the issues, thus involving them in the efforts to build a "new house" in which all people will feel at home. Consensus and harmony can now be extended to the whole of Europe.

The process for change has been strengthened by confidence-building measures promoted within the Helsinki process (the Conference on Security and Cooperation in Europe or CSCE). Churches in Europe and North America have participated together in that process through The Churches' Human Rights Program on the Helsinki Final Act, a joint program of the Conference of European Churches, the National Council of Churches of Christ-USA, and the Canadian Council of Churches.

We are aware of the dangers which continue to threaten the process toward a new Europe: self-serving nationalism, serious economic problems, and social upheaval. The necessary transformation which nations make into market economies will not provide easy answers to their circumstances. We encourage all the peoples in the "New House" of Europe to show concern and support for their neighbors in the struggle for economic, social, and political equality. The current priorities of the church's human rights program are:
• national minorities and groups in minority-like situations such as foreigners and indigenous populations;
• protection of refugees, migrants, asylum seekers, and displaced people;
• development of the common rule of law in a manner that favors people's well-being;
• religious freedom;
• social policy questions such as capital punishment, conscientious objection, and social rights for all, including justice for women and children;
• environmental and energy policies for a sustainable way of life.

A strong and united Europe can offer positive support to the developing nations elsewhere in the world. On the other hand, many developing nations see a strong Europe as a potential threat to their interests. We urge the European nations to refrain from economic and other practices which work against the peoples of developing countries.

As United Methodists, we support efforts for the creation of a new world of interdependent regional communities of nations, especially CSCE. This new set of conditions also demands new thinking and behavior on our part, including the acceptance of our responsibilities as The United Methodist Church.

We live in a time in which there is a great need for the gospel of reconciliation, a time when we can share the joys and sorrows of Christians living in faith together, yet having been physically separated, for so many years. Now it is possible to recount to each other our past failures and successes as we attempted to be faithful servants of Christ in a divided world.

In the old Europe, there were Christians, both east and west, who were faithful witnesses to the Good News of Jesus Christ. Those from the east must be encouraged to maintain that faithfulness and not become beggars dependent upon the largesse of the west. Those from the west must be encouraged to maintain their faithfulness and allow and encourage the independent witness of those in the east.

Contacts between Christians and between churches which were developed at a time of closed political borders are still important. Contacts were established in order to strengthen relationships across those borders. Christians must not now assume that open borders and new political structures have eliminated the need for the continuation of these contacts. Such relationships can also be of exceptional value between churches in Europe and throughout the world.

New relationships among churches must be carefully prepared and implemented through a process of mutual discovery and sharing. They must be based upon the connectional nature of The United Methodist Church.

Valuable and limited church resources (e.g., money, time, travel costs, food) are best used in local ministries rather than in demonstrations of hospitality for visitors.

Relationships often result in partnerships—a mutual sharing between specific congregations. These partnerships must minimize the formation of privileged and non-privileged churches. Such arrangements are not only unfair but are destructive of the Christian family. Partnerships must not exist solely on the basis of money. Personal contacts, exchange of information, and correspondence are as important as material support.

The most important relationship to be developed is the essential understanding that we are all one in Christ. This basic premise of the gospel be kept without violation. Oneness in Christ is equality.

Ministry in community is the purpose of the church. Therefore, in all cases the following principles are recommended:
• The offices of the bishops involved, and the appropriate general

agencies working together, will arrange and coordinate all partnerships, and will provide information on special projects and answers to questions. This procedure will prevent inappropriate concentration of attention on one congregation or pastor.

• All financial contributions will be made through authorized denominational channels.

• Visits between Christians are still needed. However, bishops should be informed of denominational visits.

Enormous challenges lie ahead for European peoples before the goal of a "New House" of Europe is reached, a Europe at peace and with justice. The United Methodist Church is called upon to advance that goal.

ADOPTED 1992

See Social Principles, ¶ 75, "Understanding the United Methodist Church as a Global Church."

Nuclear Disarmament: The Zero Option

Saying "No" to Nuclear Deterrence

In 1986, The United Methodist Council of Bishops, after nearly two years of prayerful and penitent study, adopted a pastoral letter and foundation document entitled *In Defense of Creation: The Nuclear Crisis and a Just Peace.*[1] The bishop's statement was deeply rooted in biblical faith. They wrote:

At the heart of the Old Testament is the testimony to *shalom*, that marvelous Hebrew word that means peace. But the peace that is *shalom* is not negative or one-dimensional. It is much more than the absence of war. *Shalom* is positive peace: Harmony, wholeness, health, and well-being in all human relationships. It is the natural state of humanity as birthed by God. It is harmony between humanity and all of God's good creation. All of creation is interrelated. Every creature, every element, every force of nature participates in the whole of creation. If any person is denied *shalom*, all are thereby diminished. . . .

New Testament faith presupposes a radical break between the follies, or much so-called conventional wisdom about power and security, on the one hand, and the transcendent wisdom of *shalom*, on the other. Ultimately, New Testament faith is a message of hope about

---

[1]United Methodist Council of Bishops, In Defense of Creation: The Nuclear Crisis and a Just Peace. Nashville: Graded Press, 1986, p. 24.

God's plan and purpose for human destiny. It is a redemptive vision that refuses to wallow in doom. (pp. 24, 28)

Based upon this faith the bishops in their pastoral letter stated unequivocally that "we say a clear and unconditional *No* to nuclear war and to any use of nuclear weapons. We conclude that nuclear deterrence is a position that cannot receive the church's blessing" (p. 92).

The implication is clear. If nuclear weapons cannot be legitimately used for either deterrence or war fighting, no nation should possess them. Accordingly, in the foundation document the bishops indicated:

We support the earliest possible negotiation of phased but rapid reduction of nuclear arsenals, while calling upon all other nuclear-weapon states to agree to parallel arms reductions, to the eventual goal of a mutual and verifiable dismantling of all nuclear armaments. (p. 76)

The World Today

Since 1986, remarkable events have occurred. The Cold War between the United States and the Soviet Union has ended. The Berlin Wall has fallen. Eastern Europe is free from Soviet control. The Warsaw Pact has gone out of existence. The Soviet Union itself has dissolved. Most of the independent republics of the former U.S.S.R. are committed to democracy and a free-market economy. Together they form a weak confederation, the Commonwealth of Independent States (C.I.S.). This transition holds great promise but also has many uncertainties and potential instability.

The Cold War was the primary reason that the global nuclear arsenal grew to enormous size. The United States and the Soviet Union developed their fleets of strategic bombers, intercontinental ballistic missile (ICBMs), and submarine-launched ballistic missiles (SLBMs) to hold each other hostage under a doctrine of mutual assured destruction. The first nuclear weapons were deployed in Europe because of Cold War confrontation between the two blocs. Great Britain, France, and China became nuclear nations as a by-product of the Cold War.

With the Cold War ended, now is the time to exercise the zero option: to eliminate all nuclear weapons throughout the globe. That means reducing to zero the supply of all types of nuclear weapons held by all possessors. It means a halt to all testing and weapons production. It means preventing all non-possessor nations from acquiring nuclear weapons.

A promising start on the journey has occurred through the initiative taken by U.S. President George Bush on September 21, 1991, to commence the withdrawal of nuclear weapons and the response of Soviet President Mikhail Gorbachev on October 5. Since them, President Bush and Russian President Boris Yeltsin have offered further proposals to reduce the nuclear arsenal. We welcome these initiatives. They constitute a good beginning. But much more should be done promptly. Therefore, we call for further steps of nuclear arms reduction.

Strategic Nuclear Weapons: Zero

Approximately one-half of the global nuclear arsenal is composed of strategic weapons designed to attack the adversary's homeland from afar. They can be launched from land, sea, and air. In spite of entering a new era of cooperation, the United States and the Commonwealth of Independent States continue to target one another with these highly lethal weapons. From the perspective of both nations these strategic weapons are the only danger of foreign attack. Accordingly:

• We recommend that the United States and the Commonwealth of Independent States immediately and concurrently deactivate their entire land- and sea-based strategic arsenal. They should:

—bring all strategic submarines into port, remove their missiles, and take off the warheads;

—open all ICBM silos, take out the missiles, place them on the ground, and remove the warheads.

• We hope that Great Britain, France, and China will understand the necessity to deactivate immediately their strategic arsenal: land-, air-, and sea-based.

• After deactivation is accomplished, the United States and the Commonwealth of Independent States should work out a schedule for dismantling all strategic nuclear weapons and delivery vehicles and destroying their warheads. Great Britain, France, and China should join this schedule. The process should be implemented in an agreed and verified sequence that is balanced so that at no stage could any nation gain an advantage.

Tactical Nuclear Weapons: Zero

The other half of the global nuclear arsenal is composed of tactical nuclear weapons with relatively short range and intended for combat use on land, at sea, and in the air.

• We praise President Bush's decision to eliminate the United States' entire worldwide inventory of nuclear artillery shells and short-range ballistic missile warheads. Based in Europe and South Korea, and perhaps elsewhere, they have no military utility because their use would have devastating effects on the countries they are intended to defend. With the Soviet army leaving central and eastern Europe there is no adversary possessing theater nuclear weapons. Likewise in Korea the U.S. tactical nuclear force was arrayed against an adversary not possessing this type of weapon.

• We support the withdrawal of all U.S. tactical nuclear weapons from surface ships and attack submarines and from land-based naval aircraft. We urge that all of the warheads be dismantled and destroyed, not leaving any in storage for future use.

• We also call for elimination of all U.S. nuclear bombs and missiles carried on tactical aircraft, a significant omission from President Bush's proposal. In Europe, U.S. tactical aircraft have no adversaries to target with nuclear weapons because of the dissolution of the Warsaw Pact, the freeing of Eastern Europe, and the achievement of independence by the republics of the former Soviet Union and their commitment to democracy and a free-market economy. Moreover, there are no other legitimate targets for U.S. tactical nuclear bombs and air-launched missiles anywhere else on earth.

• We praise the commitment made by former Soviet President Gorbachev to eliminate the entire Soviet inventory of nuclear artillery, nuclear warheads for short-range ballistic missiles, and nuclear land mines. They have no military utility in international warfare, and their elimination will prevent their use in any future conflict within and between the republics of the Commonwealth of Independent States.

• We support the withdrawal of all Soviet tactical nuclear weapons from surface ships and multi-purpose submarines and the removal of all nuclear warheads from anti-aircraft missiles. We urge that all of these missiles and warheads be dismantled and destroyed, not leaving any in storage for future use.

• All nations possessing tactical nuclear weapons should eliminate them in an agreed and verified sequence that is balanced so that at no stage could any nation gain an advantage.

Testing and Production: Zero

With a commitment to move to global nuclear disarmament—the zero option—there is no further need to develop, test, and produce new nuclear warheads and delivery vehicles. Therefore:
• We call upon all nuclear weapons states immediately to:
— cease production of nuclear weapons material.
— halt all testing of nuclear warheads.
— stop assemblage of new warheads.
• We also call upon all nuclear weapon states to discontinue the manufacture of new missiles, bombers, and strategic submarines.
• We recommend the closure of all nuclear weapons production facilities, except as they might be used to disassemble nuclear warheads and convert nuclear material to non-weapon use.
• We recommend a program to assist workers, companies, and communities engaged in producing nuclear weapon and delivery vehicles to convert to nonmilitary activities.

Nonproliferation: Universal

It is essential that no other nation acquire nuclear weapons and delivery capacity while the current possessors are eliminating their nuclear arsenal. Accordingly:
• We call upon all nations to become signatories of the Treaty on the Non-Proliferation of Nuclear Weapons (NPT) and to abide by its provisions.
• We call for strengthening provisions of the Non-Proliferation Treaty and for vigorous enforcement.
• We call for an international system to prevent the development, production, and deployment of ballistic missiles that can be used to attack an adversary's homeland and for the destruction of all such missiles now in existence.

Strategic Defense: Unnecessary

By moving promptly and resolutely to complete strategic disarmament and by achieving a diligent nonproliferation regime to block the spread of nuclear weapons and ballistic missiles, no system of strategic defense will be required. The zero option provides necessary homeland security. Therefore:

• We call for the United States and the Commonwealth of Independent States to disband all efforts to develop and deploy a strategic defense system.

• We call upon the Commonwealth of Independent States to dismantle its existing ground-based strategic defense.

• We believe that the danger of any new nation developing nuclear weapons and ICBM delivery capacity can be handled through an effective international nonproliferation regime. A strategic defense network is not needed for that purpose.

Conclusion

We fervently believe that these recommendations will greatly enhance global security by eliminating the possibility of nuclear war. Furthermore, the resources of human talent, production capacity, and money released can become available to deal with urgent human problems around the globe. The zero option provides great hope for global peace and prosperity.

ADOPTED 1992

See Social Principles, ¶ 75, "Christian Faith and Disarmament," "Comprehensive Test Ban Treaty," "The United Methodist Church and Peace."

Nuclear-Free Pacific

The United Methodist Church affirms its commitment to a Nuclear-Free Pacific. As Christian people committed to stewardship, justice and peacemaking, we oppose and condemn the use of the Pacific for tests, storage, and transportation of nuclear weapons and weapons delivery systems and the disposal of radioactive wastes. We further affirm the right of all indigenous people to control their health and well-being.

ADOPTED 1984

See Social Principles, ¶¶ 70.A and 75.C, "Nuclear Disarmament: the Zero Option," "Comprehensive Test Ban Treaty."

Oppose Food and Medicine Blockade or Embargoes

Whereas, as Christians we have a moral obligation to support life and stand against any force or action that causes suffering and death; and

605

WHEREAS, the gospel mandates that we feed the hungry, stand in solidarity with the poor and the oppressed, and promote health and human well-being; and

WHEREAS, some governments and/or groups of nations and/or factions within a country have stopped the flow and free marketing of food and medicines, seeking political gains; and

WHEREAS, such practices cause pain and suffering, malnutrition, or starvation with all its detrimental consequences to the innocent civilian population, especially the children; and

WHEREAS, the blockade of food and medicines is done many times to force riots in the general population, putting them in greater danger; and

WHEREAS, the media have brought to us the terrible images of children and women suffering, sick, and starving due to the blockade of food and medicines in recent conflicts;

Therefore, as United Methodists, we request the United Nations to declare the practice of impeding the flow or free commerce of food and medicines to be a crime against humanity; and, as such, not to be permitted in or by the Security Council;

And be it further resolved, that as United Methodists we request the United States President and the United States Congress to abstain from using embargoes or blockades of food and medicines, with no exceptions, as an instrument of foreign policy;

And we, as Christians, call upon world leaders to affirm life, to affirm and guarantee the right of all human beings to have access to food and adequate health care, regardless of their political or ideological views.

ADOPTED 1992

See Social Principles, ¶ 75, "The United Methodist Church and Peace," "Recognition of Cuba."

Our Muslim Neighbors

Christians are called to initiate and promote better relationships between Christians and Muslims on the basis of informed understanding, critical appreciation, and balanced perspective of each other's basic beliefs.

The Historical Context

United Methodists, seeking to be faithful neighbors and witnesses to other members of the human family, recognize with respect peoples of the religion of Islam, who number about one-fifth of the human race.

Christians and Muslims acknowledge common roots, along with Jews, in the faith of Abraham, Sarah, and Hagar. As members of one of the monotheistic world religions, Muslims worship and serve the one God with disciplined devotion. Both Christians and Muslims believe that God is ever inclined toward humankind in justice and mercy. The two faiths sometimes understand differently the particular ways in which God deals with human beings, but they agree that the proper human response to the Almighty is a life of humble obedience, including repentance, faith, and good works. Muslims believe that in their scriptures, the Qur'an, they find set forth for believers the principles for righteous conduct and a harmonious life in society. The following verses from the Qur'an show that these principles are similar to the ones found in the Christian scriptures:

O believers, be steadfast witnesses for God with justice. Do not let the hatred of a people make you act unjustly. Be just, for justice is next to piety. (5:8)

Worship only God; be good to parents and kindred, to orphans and the poor; speak kindly to others. 92:83)

Do not mix truth with falsehood, nor knowingly conceal the truth. (2:42)

O believers, fulfill your obligations. (5:1)

Hold to forgiveness and enjoin good; turn aside from the foolish. (7:199)

It may be that God will bring about friendship between you and those whom you hold to be your enemies. (60:7)

The Need for Understanding

United Methodists live together with Muslims in many countries of the world and in a variety of social environments. Indeed, in the United States of America, Muslims comprise one of the most rapidly growing religious communities. In places around the world, Muslims may constitute the majority of the population, and in other places, Christians may be the majority. As believers of the two religions build their lives in the same general area, they are often affected by patterns of religious antagonism inherited from the past history of disputes and misunderstanding between the two.

Also, Muslims and Christians experience varying degrees of political and social discrimination, depending on the particular circumstances of each country. In certain areas of tension—for example, Indonesia, Malaysia, Palestine, Sudan, West Africa, the Philippines, Europe, and the United States of America—believers in the two faiths are caught up in struggles for economic, political, and human rights.

We believe that sustained and ever-renewed initiatives of open discussion and sharing of concerns in interfaith settings contribute to the achievement of social justice.

By this statement we express solidarity with those of either religion who suffer oppression or discrimination.

By this statement, we make a step toward more hospitable and cooperative relationships and encourage dialogical relations.

Basic United Methodist Documents

A. *Called to be Neighbors*

A clear biblical basis for discussion in interfaith settings is set forth in *Guidelines for Interreligious Relationships*:

In conversation with a lawyer (Luke 10:25), Jesus reminded him that his neighbor, the one to whom he should show love and compassion, included a stranger, a Samaritan. Today, Christ's call to neighborliness (Luke 10:27) includes the "stranger" of other faiths. It is not just that historical events have forced us together. The Christian faith itself impels us to love our neighbors of other faiths and to seek to live in contact and mutually beneficial relationship, in community with them.

B. *The Social Community*

In our United Methodist Social Principles we affirm all persons as equally valuable in the sight of God and determine to work towards societies in which each person's value is recognized, maintained, and strengthened.

Religious persecution has been common in the history of civilization. We urge policies and practices that ensure the right of every religious group to exercise its faith free from legal, political, or economic restrictions. In particular, we condemn anti-Semite, anti-Muslim, and anti-Christian attitudes and practices in both their overt and covert forms, being especially sensitive to their expression in media stereotyping.

C. Our Theological Task

In our United Methodist Doctrinal Standards, our relationship with adherents of other living faiths of the world is set in the context of our ecumenical commitment. We are encouraged to enter into serious interfaith encounters and explorations between Christians and adherents of other living faiths of the world. Scripture calls us to be both neighbors and witnesses to all people. Such encounters require us to reflect anew on our faith and seek guidance for our witness among neighbors of other faiths.

When Christians enter into such dialogue, they come to it consciously as they seek to live as one people, under the living God who is "the Creator of all humankind, the One who is above all and through all and in all" (Eph. 4:6).

This theological understanding compels us to a particular kind of dialogue, one in which we reflect critically upon our Christian tradition, gain accurate appreciation of the traditions of others, and engage with love and generosity of spirit as we seek "to raise all such relationships to the highest possible level of human fellowship and understanding."

Christian-Muslim Discussions

The long-standing commitment of The United Methodist Church to social justice, to theological inquiry, and to just and open relationships places a particular responsibility on its members to develop discussions between Christians and Muslims.

Although the movement is still small, there is increasing evidence that groups of Christians and Muslims are coming together to witness to their faith and acknowledge the power of God in their lives, to identify problems that challenge all on the deepest theological and moral level, and to try to understand better the complex factors that determine the crucial decisions being made by governments around the world.

Through such interactions, Christians and Muslims are finding that working for better exchange of information and for ways to cooperate in solving mutual problems and concerns often leads to discovery and growth, adding to the depth and understanding of each tradition.

If we observe the unfolding of events in today's world and assess Islamic movements as only reactionary and threatening, we will hinder the advancement of justice and peace and neither gain from nor contribute to mutual understanding.

If we develop friendships with Muslims as members of the human community from whom and with whom we have much to learn, we will increase our respect for Islam as a way of life that calls its millions of followers to the highest moral ideals and satisfies their deepest spiritual aspirations.

Action Statement

Local congregations and United Methodist agencies at all levels are encouraged to develop ongoing relationships with Muslims and their respective organizations. They are urged to initiate conversations, programs, and dialogues leading to the understanding of both Islam and Christianity, appreciation of their particular gifts, discovering of commonalites and differences, and to seek areas of mutual cooperation. They are also urged to exchange information and discuss ways to cooperate when they deal with common problems and concerns.

Recommendations

We request the Council of Bishops to support, participate in, and assist United Methodists in implementing this resolution.

We call upon the General Board of Global Ministries, and particularly its Women's Division, to promote a program of ongoing relationships with Muslim women, seeking areas of mutual concern about how to live ethically, morally, and responsibly in today's world and to join in common struggles for peace and justice.

We urge the General Board of Church and Society to work with Muslims in activities designed to achieve common political, social, economic, and ecological goals.

We urge that the General Board of Global Ministries and the General Board of Church and Society develop advocacy programs on behalf of religious freedom and minority rights particularly regarding nations which are experiencing crisis in Christian-Muslim conflicts in which religious minorities are harassed or persecuted. These advocacy programs should be directed toward, among others, the U.S. Department of State and the United Nations Human Rights Commission.

We recommend that the General Commission on Christian Unity and Interreligious Concerns as it initiates and engages in dialogue with representatives of Islam remain mindful of the evangelism imperatives of the gospel and the gospel mandate to seek justice for those who are oppressed.

We recommend that the United Methodist Communications, through its Division of Public Media and News Service, monitor and call attention to discrimination against Muslims in both the religious and secular media.

We urge United Methodist members, local churches, and agencies to take the following specific actions:

1. Study Islam, using resources such as: *Guidelines on Dialogue with People of Living Faiths and Ideologies*, World Council of Churches, Geneva, 1990; *God Is One: The Way of Islam*, R. Marston Speight, Friendship Press, New York, 1989; resources available from the Office of Christian-Muslim Concerns, The National Council of the Churches of Christ in the U.S.A., 77 Sherman Street, Hartford, CT 06105; *Striving Together: A Way Forward in Christian-Muslim Relations*, Charles Kimball, Orbis Books, New York, 1991; *The Holy Qur'an*, trans. 'Abdullah Yusuf' Alli, New Revised Edition, Amana Corp., Brentwood, Md., 1989; periodicals such as *The Muslim World, Islamic Studies*.

2. Initiate dialogue with Muslims, utilizing as our guide the resolution of the 1980 General Conference, *Called to be Neighbors and Witnesses, Guidelines for Interreligious Relationships*, and models of dialogue developed by the General Commission on Christian Unity and Interreligious Concerns.

3. Develop awareness of the concerns of particular Muslim

populations through implementation of other applicable General Conference Resolutions in *the 1992 Book of Resolutions*, such as:

The Arab-Israeli Conflict; The Current Arab-Israeli Crisis; Prejudice Against Muslims and Arabs in the U.S.A.

4. Promote understanding between Christians and Muslims in local communities through:

• arranging visits to local mosques;

• developing and participating in cultural exchanges with Muslims;

• inviting Muslims to social occasions;

• seeking Muslim participation in local interfaith councils and interfaith worship;

• sending messages of greeting and goodwill to Muslims upon the occasion of their religious festivals;

• encouraging authorities of schools, hospitals, prisons, factories, and places of business and government to respect particular features of Muslim life;

• upholding the dignity of individuals, families, and communities and;

• seeking to remedy situations in which Muslims encounter misunderstanding, prejudice, stereotyping, or even hostility from the neighborhood or population when they desire to express their faith in everyday life.

ADOPTED 1992

See Social Principles, ¶ 72.B, "Prejudice Against Muslims and Arabs in the U.S.A.," "The Current Arab-Israeli Crisis," "Guidelines for Interreligious Relationships 'Called to Be Neighbors and Witnesses.'"

Peace Colleges

Be it resolved that all United Methodist institutions of higher education be encouraged to be sensitive to the following issues:

1) Interpersonal communication and techniques.

2) Cultural differences including languages (i.e. national and tribal).

3) Be inclusive in regard to the politics, the economics, and the cultures of the world.

4) Consider offering education events for pastors and laity in the areas of interpersonal communications, cultural differences, economics, and political dynamics, and peacemaking, so that we may further

witness to the world our seriousness about world peace and our willingness to be instruments of God's peace.

ADOPTED 1988

See Social Principles, ¶ 75, "The United Methodist Church and Peace," "Peace with Justice as a Special Program."

Peace, Justice, and the Reunification of Korea

Christians in Korea, rooted in a biblical passion for justice, have spoken prophetically and at great risk about the urgency of the reunification of their nation. Celebrating 100 years of Korean Methodism in 1985, the Korean Methodist Church in its Centennial Statement said:

"Faced as we are with the forty years' tragic division of the Korean peninsula, we express our longing for unification of the nation in any form possible through peaceful means in the earliest possible time. This must be done through establishing a democratic political structure based upon freedom and human rights, and must be fulfilled by working toward the establishment of a just society built for the sake of the people. Therefore, we reject any form whatever of dictatorship. Deploring the long history of our nation in which the reality has been the sacrifice of our country's political life, and now with a definite sense of national self-determination which rejects any domination by the superpowers, we disavow any form of war or the taking of life, and commit the whole strength of the Korean Methodist Church to the peaceful reunification of our country."

Now is a time for repentance, a time for reconciliation, a time for justice, a time for peace. For the nation of Korea, divided for more than forty years, justice, peace and reconciliation are tragically overdue. In 1945 just before the end of World War II, the United States proposed and the Soviet Union agreed to the division of Korea. The division was to have been temporary to facilitate the surrender of Japanese troops in Korea. More than four decades later the country is still divided into the Republic of Korea (ROK) and the Democratic Peoples Republic of Korea (DPRK). The enmity between the superpowers has been played out in the Korean tragedy of war and death, dictatorship and militarization, separation of one people into two hostile camps and divided families with no contact at all. All members of the Body of Christ, but especially Christians in the United States, have a special responsibility to support the Korean people in their attempts to build democracy, reduce tension, create trust on the Korean peninsula, heal the divisions and reunite their country. God's reconciling activity in Jesus Christ calls us as Christians to the ministry of reconciliation.

Now is the time of urgency. The hunger for democracy and respect for human rights grows strong and promises political change." In the Democratic People's Republic of Korea (DPRK), people's struggle for human rights and political freedom is completely repressed and there is no sign of improvement at this time. In the Republic of Korea (ROK), the political situation has been much improved with the constitutional change and the direct presidential election. However, there still exist elements of political repression. The threat to peace remains critical with the world's fifth and sixth largest armies facing each other across the Demilitarized Zone. Nuclear weapons back up 40,000 U.S. troops in the south, and the U.S.S.R. and the U.S. have nuclear weapons in the region targeted on Korea. The 1953 Armistice has not yet led to a peace treaty. These political and military divisions inevitably have led to a separation in the Body of Christ, so that Korean Christians, who once worshipped and served our Lord together, now live in isolation from one another. Ten million Korean people separated from their families, divided since the 1950's with no contact, are growing older and dying. The divisions deepen with distorted rhetoric.

In many ways the Korean people, north and south, have expressed their strong desire for reunification. Since 1984 there have been official contacts and conversations on economic and humanitarian issues between ROK and DPRK. Emergency assistance, following devastating floods in the south, was offered by the DPRK and accepted by the ROK. The first government-sponsored exchange of visits between divided family members occurred in 1985. Christians from north and south met in 1986 in Glion, Switzerland, as part of an ecumenical process on peace and the reunification of Korea led by the World Council of Churches. In 1987 both sides offered proposals to lower military tensions on the peninsula.

In 1986, as a result of consultations in Korea, north and south, with Christians and government representatives, the National Council of Churches of Christ in the U.S.A. (NCCCUSA) adopted an important policy statement on "Peace and the Reunification of Korea." United Methodist representatives participated fully in the development of this statement, in consultations on peace and reunification, and in an official ecumenical delegation to North and South Korea in the summer of 1987.

In support of the Korean people and in cooperation with partner Christian groups, it is recommended that The United Methodist Church, its members, local churches, annual conferences, and agencies, undertake the following actions through intercession, education, public advocacy, and support of programs furthering justice, peace, and reconciliation:

1. Engage in prayer of penitence and petition with the Korean people and with Christians in the north and south, scarred and pained by the division of their nation and yearning for reunion, and support the efforts of the Korean Methodist Church and the National Council of Churches of Korea to seek peace and reconciliation.

2. Commend the policy statement on "Peace and the Reunification of Korea" of the National Council of the Churches of Christ in the USA (NCCCUSA), November, 1986, to annual conferences and local churches for study and action. The policy statement affirms the desire of the Korean people for restoration of national unity and reunion of separate families, traces the history of division and hopeful steps toward change, and outlines recommendations for Advocacy and Action in the areas of "Healing and Reconciliation," "Peace With Justice," and "New Directions for US policy." Recommendations 3, 4, and 5 which follow are in line with the policy statement.

3. Participate in the ecumenical effort of the World Council of Churches (WCC) and NCCCUSA to facilitate the reunion of separated Korean families, including Korean residents in the US and their family members in the DPRK.

4. Urge all governments which have relations with the ROK or the DPRK or both to exercise their influence to further mediation, interchange, peace, and reunification.

5. Urge all governments involved to forthright commitment to the following policy directions in support of Korean efforts for peace and reunification:

    a) The peaceful reunification of Korea should be a formal U.S. policy goal.

    b) A Peace Treaty should be signed among the nations involved to eliminate the threat of war, establish an enduring peace, and minimize tension in the Korean peninsula. The Peace Treaty, replacing the existing Armistice Treaty, should be based on the conditions of a Non-aggression Pact between the Republic of Korea and the Democratic People's Republic of Korea, with the full participation of the United States and the People's Republic of China as well as other related countries.

c) ROK and DPRK contacts should be encouraged.

d) Bilateral diplomatic and human contacts between the Republic of Korea and the People's Republic of China and between the Republic of Korea and the USSR and bilaterally between the United States and the DPRK should be enhanced.

e) Upon the ratification of a peace settlement in the Korean peninsula based on the spirit of the Peace Treaty and the Non-agression Pact and the restoration of mutual trust between the Republic of Korea and the Democratic People's Republic of Korea, U.S. troops in Korea should be withdrawn and, accordingly, the U.N. command should be dissolved. At the same time, all nuclear weapons in Korea and all U.S. and U.S.S.R. nuclear weapons targeted on Korea which threaten the survival of the Korean people and those of the world should be removed. Any type of military exercises in Korea that affect the peace of the Korean peninsula should be mutually suspended:

f) The U.S. should negotiate to end the war and to seek a comprehensive peace settlement in Korea.

6. Call on governments, churches and other groups to support the struggle of the people of Korea for human rights and democracy by:

a) Making efforts to lessen the international climate of polarization, hostility and fear of war that leads to political repression, imprisonment, torture, the militarization of society, and international acts of political violence in air, sea, and land.

b) Encouraging dialogue and reconciliation among parties, regions, and classes to resolve long held grievances and prejudices for the sake of a just, inclusive society;

c) Emphasizing the importance of open social institutions, including freedom for press, political, academic, religious, and cultural activities, in order to build a strong, unified Korea;

d) Supporting international economic relations with Korea that enhance economic justice for workers, farmers, and small businesses and that protect the environment.

7. Encourage United Methodists to use the occasion of the 1988 Olympics and other opportunities for visitation and interchange

to come to a deeper understanding of the Korean situation, the witness of the church, and the achievements, aspirations and contributions of Korean people in Korea and in various parts of the world, including the U.S.

ADOPTED 1988

See Social Principles, ¶ 75.

Peace, The United Methodist Church and

"Peace is not simply the absence of war, a nuclear stalemate or combination of uneasy cease-fires. It is that emerging dynamic reality envisioned by prophets where spears and swords give way to implements of peace (Isa. 2:1-4); where historic antagonists dwell together in trust (Isa. 11:4-11); and where righteousness and justice prevail. There will be no peace with justice until unselfish and informed life is structured into political processes and international arrangements" (Bishops' Call for Peace and the Self-Development of Peoples).

The mission of Jesus Christ and his Church is to serve all peoples regardless of their government, ideology, place of residence, or status. Surely the welfare of humanity is more important in God's sight than the power or even the continued existence of any state. Therefore, the Church is called to look beyond human boundaries of nation, race, class, sex, political ideology, or economic theory, and to proclaim the demands of social righteousness essential to peace.

The following are interrelated areas which must be dealt with concurrently in a quest for lasting peace in a world community.

I. *Disarmament*

One hard fact must be stated bluntly: the arms race goes on, the momentum of the race never slackens, and the danger of a holocaust is imminent. Meanwhile, millions starve, development stagnates, and international cooperation is threatened. Increasingly sophisticated weapons systems accelerate arms spending and heighten anxieties without adding to the security of the nations. Again and again, regional tensions grow, conflicts erupt, and great powers intervene to advance or protect their interests without regard to international law or human rights.

True priorities in national budgeting are distorted by present expenditures on weapons. Because of fear of unemployment, desire for profits, and contributions to the national balance of payments, the arms industry engenders great political power. Arms-producing nations seek to create markets, then vie with one another to become champion among the arms merchants of the world. Food, health, social services, jobs, and education are vital to the welfare of nations. Yet the availability of all of these is constantly threatened because of the overriding priority given by governments to what is called "defense."

If humanity is to move out of this period of futility and constant peril, the search for new weapons systems must be halted through comprehensive international agreements. Moreover, disarmament negotiations should include all nations with substantial armaments systems. The vast stockpiles of nuclear bombs and conventional weapons must be dismantled under international supervision, and the resources being used for arms must be diverted to programs designed to affirm life rather than destroy it. Serious consideration should be given by nations to unilateral initiatives which might stimulate the reaching of international agreement.

World public opinion justly condemns the use of chemical or biological weapons. Governments must renounce use of these particularly inhumane weapons as part of their national policy.

Where nations in a specific region band together to bar nuclear weapons from the area as encouraged by the international community, we commend such constructive agreements and urge other countries, particularly the great powers, to respect them.

We affirm peoples' movements directed to abolition of the tools of war. Governments must not impede public debate on this issue of universal concern.

The goal of world disarmament, demanding a radical reordering of priorities and coupled with an effective system of international peacemaking, must be kept constantly before peoples and governments by the church.

II. *Democracy and Freedom*

Millions of people still live under oppressive rule and various forms of exploitation. Millions more live under deplorable conditions of racial, sexual, and class discrimination. In many countries many persons, including Christians, are suffering repression, imprisonment, and torture, as a result of their efforts to speak truth to those in power.

Action by governments to encourage liberation and economic justice is essential but must be supported by parallel action on the part of private citizens and institutions, including the churches, if peaceful measures are to succeed. Unless the prevailing oppression and denial of basic human rights are ended, violence on an increasing scale will erupt in many nations, and may spread throughout the world. The human toll in such a conflict could be enormous and could result in new oppression and further dehumanization.

We are concerned for areas where oppression and discrimination take place, and specifically for Namibia and South Africa, where White minorities continue to oppress and discriminate against Black majorities through legal systems.

This concern extends to all situations where external commercial, industrial, and military interests are related to national oligarchies which resist justice and liberation for the masses of people. It is essential that governments which support or condone these activities alter their policies to permit and enable people to achieve genuine self-determination.

III. *The United Nations*

International justice requires the participation and determination of all peoples. We are called to look beyond the "limited and competing boundaries of nation-states to the larger and more inclusive community of humanity" (Bishops' Call for Peace and the Self-Development of Peoples).

There has been unprecedented international cooperation through the United Nations and its specialized agencies as they have worked to solve international problems of health, education, and the welfare of people. The United Nations Children's Fund (UNICEF) is one of the agencies that has been successful in this area.

These achievements are to be commended. However, in other areas political considerations have diminished the support needed for the United Nations to achieve its goals. Many nations, including the most powerful, participate in some programs only when those actions do not interfere with national advantage.

We believe the United Nations and its agencies must be supported, strengthened, and improved. We recommend that Christians work for the following actions in their respective nations:

1. The Universal Declaration of Human Rights is a standard of achievement for all peoples and nations. International covenants and conventions which seek to implement the Declaration should be universally ratified.

2. Peace and world order require the development of an effective and enforceable framework of international law which provides protection for human rights and guarantees of justice for all people.

3. Greater use should be made of the International Court of Justice. Nations should remove any restrictions they have adopted which impair the court's effective functioning.

4. Development agencies should not be dominated by the industrialized world. Efforts to make controlling bodies of these agencies more representative should be supported.

5. International agencies designed to help nations or peoples escape from domination by other nations or transnational enterprises must continue to be created and strengthened.

6. Issues of food, energy, raw materials, and other commodities are greatly affected by economic and political considerations. Efforts in the United Nations to achieve new levels of justice in the world economic order should be considered, reviewed, and supported.

7. Collective action against threats to peace must be supported. Wars fought in the search for justice might well be averted or diminished if the nations of the world would work vigorously and in concert in seeking changes in oppressive political and economic systems.

IV. *World Trade and Economic Development*

The gap between rich and poor countries continues to widen. Human rights are denied when the surpluses of some arise in part as a result of continued deprivation of others. This growing inequity exists in our own communities and in all our nations. Our past efforts to alleviate these conditions have failed. Too often these efforts have been limited by our own unwillingness to act or have been frustrated by private interests and governments striving to protect the wealthy and the powerful.

In order to eliminate inequities in the control and distribution of the common goods of humanity, we are called to join the search for more just and equitable international economic structures and relationships. We seek a society that will assure all persons and nations the opportunity to achieve their maximum potential.

In working toward that purpose, we believe these steps are needed:

• Economic systems structured to cope with the needs of the world's peoples must be conceived and developed.

• Measures which will free peoples and nations from reliance on financial arrangements which place them in economic bondage must be implemented.

• Policies and practices for the exchange of commodities and raw materials which establish just prices and avoid damaging fluctuations in price must be developed.

• Control of international monetary facilities should be more equitably shared by all the nations, including the needy and less powerful.

• Agreements which affirm the common heritage principle (that resources of the seabed, subsoil, outer space and those outside national jurisdiction are the heritage of humanity) should be accepted by all nations.

• Multilateral, rather than bilateral, assistance programs should be encouraged for secular as well as religious bodies. They must be designed to respond to the growing desire of the "developing world" to become self-reliant.

• Nations which possess less military and economic power than others must be protected, through international agreements, from loss of control of their own resources and means of production to either transnational enterprises or other governments.

These international policies will not narrow the rich-poor gap within nations unless the powerless poor are enabled to take control of their own political and economic destinies. We support people's organizations designed to enable the discovery of local areas of exploitation and development of methods to alleviate these problems.

Economic and political turmoil within many developing nations has been promoted and used by other powers as an excuse to intervene through subversive activities or military force in furtherance of their own national interests. We condemn this version of imperialism which often parades as international responsibility.

We support the United Nations' efforts to develop international law to govern the sea and to ensure that the world's common resources will be used cooperatively and equitably for the welfare of humankind.

We urge the appropriate boards and agencies of The United Methodist Church to continue and expand efforts to bring about justice in cooperative action between peoples of all countries.

V. *Military Conscription, Training, and Service*

1. *Conscription.* We affirm our historic opposition to compulsory military training and service. We urge that military conscription laws be repealed; we also warn that elements of compulsion in any national service program will jeopardize seriously the service motive and introduce new forms of coercion into national life. We advocate and will continue to work for the inclusion of the abolition of military conscription in disarmament agreements.

2. *Conscientious objection.* Each person must face conscientiously the dilemmas of conscription, military training, and service and decide his or her own responsible course of action. We affirm the historic statement: "What the Christian citizen may not do is to obey persons rather than God, or overlook the degree of compromise in even our best actis, or gloss over the sinfulness of war. The church must hold within its fellowship persons who sincerely differ at this point of critical decision, call all to repentance, mediate to all God's mercy, minister to all in Christ's name" (The United Methodist Church and Peace, 1968 General Conference).

Christian teaching supports conscientious objection to all war as an ethically valid position. It also asserts that ethical decisions on political matters must be made in the context of the competing claims of biblical revelation, church doctrine, civil law, and one's own understanding of what God calls him or her to do.

We, therefore, support all those who conscientiously object: to preparation for or participation in any specific war or all wars; to cooperation with military conscription; or to the payment of taxes for military purposes; and we ask that they be granted legal recognition.

3. *Amnesty and reconciliation.* We urge understanding of and full amnesty or pardon for persons in all countries whose refusal to participate in war has placed them in legal jeopardy.

VI. *Peace Research, Education, and Action*

We call upon The United Methodist Church in the light of its historical teachings and its commitment to peace and self-development of peoples to:

1. Seek the establishment of educational institutions devoted to the study of peace (such as the National Academy of Peace and Conflict Resolution).

2. Develop alternatives to vocations that work against peace and support individuals in their quest.

3. Explore and apply ways of resolving domestic and international differences which affirm human fulfillment rather than exploitation and violence.

4. Affirm and employ methods that build confidence and trust between peoples and countries, rejecting all promotion of hatred and mistrust.

5. Continue to develop and implement the search for peace through educational experiences, including church school classes, schools of Christian mission and other settings throughout the church.

6. Encourage local churches and members to take actions that make for peace, and to act in concert with other peoples and groups of good will toward the achievement of a peaceful world.

ADOPTED 1984

See Social Principles, ¶ 75.C, "Bishops' Call for Peace and the Self Development of Peoples," "Peace with Justice as a Special Program," "Christian Faith and Disarmament," "Nuclear Disarmament: the Zero Option," "Justice, Peace and the Integrity of Creation."

Peace with Justice as a Special Program

Background: From Despair to Hope

Since 1980 we have seen a worsening of living conditions for poor people in the United States and elsewhere in the world. Affordable housing for persons of modest income is becoming scarce. Homelessness is increasing. Unemployment rates for minority youth and persons lacking skills are astonishingly high. Hard-working industrial workers are losing their jobs as a result of global economic change. Hard-working farmers are being displaced from productive land. Family stability is threatened by economic insecurity. The number of single-parent households is on the rise. Immigrants who have come to the United States to escape persecution and to seek economic opportunity face obstacles in law and community acceptance. Many Native Americans, Blacks, Hispanics, and Asians still suffer from discrimination and other manifestations of inequality. So do women. Many millions of persons, particularly elderly persons and low-income women and children, receive inadequate or no health care. Persons have been discharged from mental hospitals with little or no provision of the community-based services they need. Victims of the spreading AIDS epidemic confront prejudice and insufficient care facilities.

Historically, and presently, issues of injustice are disproportionately experienced by racial/ethnic people. A disproportionate number of racial ethnic persons are victimized by poverty, poor or no health care, violence, limited educational opportunities, and higher frequencies of environmental pollution. Racial/ethnic persons are most severely affected by the militarization of our economy.

Daily we experience the disintegration of creation. We consume earth's resources without regard to the processes of regeneration of the earth. Regional environmental issues—water scarcity, loss of precious topsoil, pollution of natural resources, the over-harvesting of timber, the encroachment of development in wildlife habitats, and the use of arable land to grow cities and parking lots rather than farms—plague our nation. In other sectors of our world, we see the processes of desertification, acid rain, and loss of tropical rain forest, destroying our natural world. The implications and far-reaching effects of global warming put our whole world at risk.

Many of the economic problems and the decline in community services can be traced to the militarization of the U.S. and world economies. The United States has gorged itself with military expenditure but refused to pay the full bill through taxes. As a result, the federal deficit has almost tripled, thus mortgaging the future for coming generations. Similar distortion occurred in the Soviet Union, contributing to its dissolution. It has also happened in a number of Third World countries, which can ill afford such waste. For parts of the Third World, the situation is made worse by civil and regional wars, low intensity conflicts, and military intervention by the United States and other nations.

While these harmful trends have been occurring, many people in the United States and elsewhere have raised their voices in protest. They have urged an end to nuclear madness, to undue reliance on military force as the primary instrument of foreign policy, to neglect of urgent human needs. The 1984 General Conference of The United Methodist Church spoke out on a number of these issues of peace and justice. The United Methodist Council of Bishops offered a prophetic vision in the pastoral letter and foundation document, *In Defense of*

Creation. Roman Catholic bishops in the United States have spoken eloquently on the need for a reversal of U.S. nuclear policy and for introduction of greater justice into the U.S. economy. Other religious denominations have added their voices. An increasing number of political leaders are insisting that there must be better ways of conducting the world's business.

Changes taking place in our global community give us hope for potential future reductions in military expenditures. This will free up resources of money and talent to be used for meeting urgent social needs.

This is happening at the same time that an increasing number of persons and institutions are expressing a strong determination and commitment to address the social and economic crisis that confronts the poor, those displaced by economic change, and those who never achieved full equality of opportunity. This, then has set the stage for a social transformation, for the quest to open the doors of opportunity for all, to distribute resources more equitably, to provide better care for persons in need.

Biblical Basis for Response

The United Methodist Church, with its historic commitment to peace and justice, can and should provide leadership to this social transformation. This heritage is expressed in the Social Principles and the Social Creed. It gained eloquent articulation by the United Methodist Council of Bishops in the foundation document, *In Defense of Creation: The Nuclear Crisis and a Just Peace*, which offers a well-grounded biblical analysis for peace with justice. The bishops wrote:

At the heart of the Old Testament is the testimony to *shalom*, that marvelous Hebrew word that means peace. But the peace that is *shalom* is not negative or one-dimensional. It is much more than the absence of war. *Shalom* is positive peace: harmony, wholeness, health, and well-being in all human relationships. It is the natural state of humanity as birthed by God. It is harmony between humanity and all of God's good creation. All of creation is interrelated. Every creature, every element, every force of nature participates in the whole of creation. If any person is denied *shalom*, all are thereby diminished. . . .

The Old Testament speaks of God's sovereignty in terms of *covenant*, more particularly the "covenant of peace" with Israel, which binds that people to God's *shalom* (Isaiah 54:10; Ezekiel 37:26). In the covenant of *shalom*, there is no contradiction between justice and peace or between peace and security or between love and justice (Jeremiah 29:7). In Isaiah's prophecy, when "the Spirit is poured upon us from on high," we will know that these laws of God are one and indivisible:

Then justice will dwell in the wilderness,
and righteousness abide in the fruitful field.
And the effect of righteousness will be peace,
and the result of righteousness, quietness and trust forever.
My people will abide in a peaceful habitation,
in secure dwellings, and in quiet resting places. (Isaiah 32:16-18)

Shalom, then, is the sum total of moral and spiritual qualities in a community whose life is in harmony with God's good creation. . . . (pp. 24, 25-26)

In their analysis, the United Methodist bishops pointed out that when the elders of Israel forsook their moral covenant for warrior-kings, the nation descended into generations of exploitation, repression, and aggression—then into chaos, captivity, and exile in Babylon. Yet We must look to the great prophets of that bitter period of Exile for the renewed vision of *shalom*. If Exodus is liberation, Exile is renewal. Ezekiel and Isaiah (40–66) reaffirm God's creation and redemption as universal in scope. Narrow nationalism is repudiated. Servanthood is exalted as the hopeful path to *shalom*. (p. 27)

And the prophets' images—swords into plowshares, peaceable kingdoms, new covenants written on the heart—"forecast the coming of One who will be the Prince of Peace."

And so he comes. He comes heralded by angels who sing: "Glory to God in the highest, and on earth peace!" He invokes the most special blessings upon peacemakers. He exalts the humanity of aliens. He commands us to love our enemies; for he knows, even if we do not, that if we hate our enemies, we blind and destroy ourselves. *Shalom,* after all, is the heart of God and the law of creation. It cannot be broken with impunity. . . .

New Testament faith presupposes a radical break between the follies, or much so-called conventional wisdom about power and security, on the one hand, the transcendent wisdom of *shalom,* on the other. Ultimately, New Testament faith is a message of hope about God's plan and purpose for human destiny. It is a redemptive vision that refuses to wallow in doom. . . .

Paul's letters announce that Jesus Christ is "our peace." It is Christ who has "broken down the dividing wall of hostility," creating one humanity, overcoming enmity, so making peace (Ephesians 2:14-19). It is Christ who ordains a ministry of reconciliation. Repentance prepares us for reconciliation. Then we shall open ourselves to the transforming power of God's grace in Christ. Then we shall know what it means to be "in Christ." Then we are to become ambassadors of a new creation, a new Kingdom, a new order of love and justice (2 Corinthians 5:17-20). . . .

The promise of peace envisioned by Israel's prophets of the Exile at the climax of the Old Testament is celebrated once more at the climax of the New Testament. The Revelation of John, in the darkest night of despair, sings of a new earth, radiant with infinite love and compassion, in which all nations and peoples come together peaceably before the Lord God and in which hunger and hurt and sorrow are no more (Revelation 7). (pp. 27-30)

This is the foundation of faith that enables us in The United Methodist Church to offer hope to those who despair and to bring forth joy to replace sadness. As Saint Francis of Assisi prayed to act in the spirit of Christ, so we too can sow love where there is hatred; where injury, pardon; where darkness, light. As instruments of peace and justice, we can seek to replace discord with harmony and to repair the brokenness that shatters the wholeness of *shalom.*

Program Activities

The General Board of Church and Society will carry out the following "Peace with Justice" activities:

(1) Implement "Policies for a Just Peace" as specified in the Council of Bishops' Foundation Document;

(2) Implement the process of "Justice, Peace and the Integrity of Creation" as adopted by the 1990 World Convocation for Justice, Peace and the Integrity of Creation in Seoul, Republic of Korea;

(3) Work for social-justice policies and programs that seek the wholeness of shalom, including provision of greater economic opportunity, affordable housing, adequate food, and proper health care for poor people, displaced industrial workers, displaced farmers, and other persons faced with economic insecurity;

(4) Work to eradicate attitudinal and systemic behavior patterns that perpetuate the sin of racism as it is lived out in the areas of peace, justice, and the integrity of creation.

To achieve these objectives, the General Board of Church and Society may:

(a) Assist annual conferences, districts, and local churches to organize and carry out peace with justice activities, and to promote the Peace with Justice Special Sunday Offering;

(b) Provide a regular flow of information on public issues to local churches, districts, and annual conferences;

(c) Strengthen its staff capability to act as a public-policy advocate or measures that improve U.S. global relations and move toward nuclear disarmament and measures that provide jobs, housing, food, health care, and income support for lower-income families and individuals;

(d) Assist annual conferences and/or local churches to assess and respond to the disproportionate effect of injustices on racial/ethnic persons.

For the purpose of financing activities (a) to achieve the "Policies for a Just Peace" contained in the Council of Bishops' Foundation Document In Defense of Creation and (b) to pursue other justice and peace objectives contained within the vision of shalom in this same document, revenue shall come from the Peace with Justice offering and other possible sources in accordance with ¶ 275.5 and World Service special gifts:

Assignment

The Peace with Justice Special Program shall be assigned to the General Board of Church and Society.

ADOPTED 1992

See Social Principles, ¶ 75, "Justice, Peace, and the Integrity of Creation," "The United Methodist Church and Peace."

Persons Missing in Action

We affirm and rejoice in the negotiations which have resulted in the return to their families of the remains of combatants from southeast Asia, and encourage the continuation and expansion of these efforts. We urge further negotiations in order to fulfill the Paris Accords by all parties, including the United States and Vietnam, which will result in open borders and other conditions so as to allow:

1) the return of other human remains to their families; and
2) verification regarding the residential desire of each former foreign combatant.

We also ask the U.S. Congress and the Administration to move toward full recognition of Vietnam, and to engage in the diplomatic relations that will more quickly bring the MIA issue to the most satisfactory closure.

ADOPTED 1988

See Social Principles, ¶ 75.

The Philippines

"Then justice will dwell in the wilderness, and righteousness abide in the fruitful field. And the effect of righteousness will be peace." (Isaiah 32:16-17.)

The Republic of the Philippines claimed the attention and respect of the world with the heartening changes which took place there in 1986. United Methodists and other Christian people were filled with thanksgiving as Filipino hopes soared. The witness of Christians in the Philippines and the support of the churches for justice, peace, and reconciliation were inspiring. Even in prison and in the midst of uncertainty, conflict and persecution, the Christian message of love through crucifixion and resurrection rang out.

The End of a Dictatorship: People's Power

Ferdinand Marcos was removed from power in February, 1986, in a remarkable display of people's participation. Hopes were raised by the election of Corazon Aquino, the release of political prisoners, the reopening of newspapers, the resumption of lively public debate, the cease fire and peace talks, a new constitution with a mandate for

President Aquino, new local and provincial elections, and modest progress made in recovering stolen wealth and confronting an age-old system of favor and corruption. Hopes were raised that an opportunity for fundamental but non-violent change might be grasped through broad participation and patient negotiation. Especially encouraging was the leadership of President Corazon C. Aquino and many others who gave of their talents and energies, seeking true democratic change.

Disturbing Trends

But disturbing trends persist. Deep poverty remains in most parts of the nation. Rural people have sought without success a land reform program to end hunger, malnutrition and exploitation. Workers continue to be at the mercy of Filipino and multinational businesses making high profits but paying less than subsistence wages. The national debt oppresses the entire nation.

The military continues to exert a dominant influence in government. A succession of coup attempts seems designed to push the civilian government closer to the military and the wealthy minority and away from the concerns of the majority of the people. The arming and condoning of civilian death squads, operating outside the law, have brought increased terror and murder to the countryside, resulting in the dramatic rise of human rights violations. Negotiations between the government and insurgent forces, including the New Peoples Army, have given way to hardened hostility and a return to war in many parts of the country.

United States' Interests

The United States has played a major role in Philippine history since the 1898 Spanish-American War and the destruction of the Philippine struggle for independence at the turn of the century. For more than four decades, the U.S. exercised colonial oversight, ending with Philippine political independence in 1946. Since then, the U.S. has continued to be a controlling presence through economic investment and military bases.

With the fall of Marcos, the support of the United States and other countries for the principle of democratic civilian government in the

Philippines has been very important. But parallel with this support have been forms of U.S. involvement which continue to strengthen forces contrary to democracy and the welfare of the Filipino people. Such forms include military aid and pressure solely for military solutions to counter the threat of popular protest and communist insurgency. In addition, there are signs that the doctrine of "Low Intensity Conflict" is being applied in the Philippines. This strategy pits Filipinos against each other by supplying arms to opposing groups within the country, as it calls for provision of maximum military aid short of commitment of U.S. troops.

The presence of the largest U.S. military bases outside the United States also contributes to many social problems such as the involvement of tens of thousands of women and children driven by poverty into prostitution with the accompanying spread of sexually transmitted diseases.

Other outside groups have been divisive as well. The presence of the Unification Church's political arm CAUSA and other international militantly anti-communist organizations, many with ties to the U.S., appear to be contributing to the destabilization of democraic processes. Fanatical religious and para-religious groups also polarize and spread enmity among the Filipino people. Many electronic church programs, originating in the U.S., seem to be set over against the pastoral and prophetic ministries of Filipino Protestants and Catholics.

As United Methodists, we are deeply concerned about the people of the Philippines and the future of their country. We are dismayed at forces which are destroying the lives of Filipinos and the fabric of their society. While confessing complicity in sin, we also confess that Jesus is Lord and that God's purpose is redemption and fullness of life for all people.

In this spirit, it is recommended that The United Methodist Church, its members, local churches, annual conferences, central conferences and agencies:

1. Support the witness of Christians in the Philippines, including The United Methodist Church, the United Church of Christ in the Philippines, and the National Council of Churches in the Philippines, in prayers and programs which move toward peace, justice and reconciliation among the Filipino people;

2. Support the rights of the Filipino people to self-determination and national sovereignty, including decisions regarding the future of foreign military bases, full and equitable control of their land and other forms of national wealth, and freedom from outside intervention;

3. Support defense of the basic human rights of the Filipino people, giving special attention to the rights of the poorest, including freedom from terror, murder, and poverty;

4. Urge our governments, especially the government of the United States, to:

   a. Continue to be supportive of democratic civilian government;

   b. End military aid, and increase economic aid through channels which seek effectively to improve the plight of the poor, reduce the burden of external debt and end economic and political dependency;

   c. Call for investigative hearings into covert activities and the use of the strategy of low intensity conflict by U.S. government-related and private organizations;

   d. Respect the will of the Filipino people with regard to their desire to eliminate nuclear weapons from their territory as stated in their new constitution;

5. Study and challenge the impact of U.S. and other religious groups and electronic church programs whose effect is either directly or indirectly to divide churches and destabilize the society, both in the philippines and in other parts of the world;

6. Participate fully in the 1989-90 Mission Study on the Philippines, using the opportunity to understand better the history and hopes of the Filipino people, the witness of the churches, and the role of the United States.

ADOPTED 1988

See Social Principles, ¶ 75.A.B, "In Support of Self Determination and Non-intervention."

Puerto Rico and Vieques

The theme of human liberation is found again and again in the Bible, from Moses' leadership of the Hebrew people out of Egypt to Jesus in the synagogue proclaiming the acceptable year of the Lord.

The United Methodist Church has long stood for an end to colonialism and for the self-determination of all peoples. At the same time, the people of Puerto Rico have lived under the sovereignty of the United States in what can be described as a form of colonialism. Though plebiscites have been held and a degree of local autonomy granted, all of the island's political parties in recent years have expressed their dissatisfaction with Puerto Rico's political status. The situation has been aggravated by the U.S. Navy's bombing practice and related activities on and around two off-shore islands, at first Culebra and now Vieques.

The General Conference of The United Methodist Church:

1. Asks that the people of Puerto Rico be accorded full opportunity for self-determination of their future political status under conditions that assure a genuinely free choice with generous provisions for adjustment to any new status chosen;

2. Expresses its solidarity with the people of Vieques in their most ardent desire that the United States Navy cease its military activity that adversely affects the citizens of Vieques, and that the United States Navy repair whatever damages it has caused to the people of Vieques.

To these ends the General Conference directs the attention of United Methodists and the general agencies of the denomination to the need for information and action.

ADOPTED 1980

See Social Principles, ¶ 75.B.

Ratification of Human Rights Covenants and Conventions

The United Methodist Church commends the Senate of the United States for action which completed ratification of the International Convention on the Prevention and Punishment of Genocide during the Ninety-Ninth Congress and of the Convention against Torture and Other Cruel, Inhuman, or Degrading Treatment or Punishment, ratified during the One Hundred First Congress, and the International Covenant on Civil and Political Rights ratified during the One Hundred Second Congress.

However, the Senate has not pursued those steps which will complete ratification of the International Covenant on Economic,

Social and Cultural Rights, and the International Convention on the Elimination of all Forms of Racial Discrimination, which were signed and transmitted to the Senate of the Ninety-Fifth Congress by President Jimmy Carter, and the Convention on the Elimination of all Forms of Discrimination Against Women, which was signed on behalf of the President of the United States in Copenhagen on July 17, 1980, and transmitted to the United States Senate in October, 1980. It is imperative that the United States Senate act promptly to give its "advice and consent" to the ratification of these instruemnts.

The Convention on the Rights of the Child was approved by the United Nations General Assembly on November 20, 1989. However, the President of the United States has neither signed this treaty nor submitted it to the Senate. We urge the President of the United States to sign the Convention on the Rights of the Child and submit it to the Senate that ratification may be completed, with any reservations that may be necessary to protect the rights and safety of children and the proper responsibilities of parents.

ADOPTED 1992

See Social Principles, ¶ 75, "The United Methodist Church and Peace," "Human Rights."

Recognition of Cuba

The United Methodist Church is linked in Christ with the Methodist Church of Cuba. We share a common heritage and mission. We are mutually responsible for the proclamation of God's love and the nurturing of neighbor-love.

"God's world is one world." The Social Principles requires us to make the community of God a reality as we "pledge ourselves to seek the meaning of the gospel in all issues that divide people and threaten the growth of world community." Such a world cannot exist when nations refuse to give diplomatic recognition to one another.

For over 20 years the government of the United States has not maintained diplomatic relations with the government of Cuba and has instead pursued an economic embargo prohibiting any kinds of trade with Cuba. This policy has resulted in the loss of an important commerical market and trade partner for the United States, and in the heightening of tensions in the Caribbean. The objectives sought by the proponents of this policy were to force a change in Cuban foreign policy and to halt the growth and development of Soviet influence in that country.

It is now clear that the embargo policy has not succeeded with those objectives. If anything, its most evident result has been to force Cuba to an even closer political and military reliance on the Soviet Union.

WHEREAS, the Methodist Church in 1964 made an historical statement entitled the "Re-examination of Policy Toward Mainline China, Cuba and other Countries," which said: "The Christian gospel involves reconciliation by encounter and by communication regardless of political considerations. Therefore, we cannot accept the expression of hostility by any country, its policies, or its ideologies as excuses for the failure of Christians to press persistently, realistically, and creatively toward a growing understanding among the peoples of all countries";

WHEREAS, the government of the United States is the only major Western country pursuing a policy of non-relations with Cuba, while Canada, France, Great Britain, West Germany, Japan, Mexico, Argentina, Bolivia and almost all other countries of the western alliance maintain normal diplomatic and/or economic relations with Cuba; and

WHEREAS, the government of the United States has in recent years strengthened its commercial and diplomatic relations with other Communist countries such as the Soviet Union itself, China, Hungary, Poland, and Romania, independently of their foreign policy which differs and often collides with that of the United States; and

WHEREAS, the Reagan administration declared that the United States will not use food as a foreign policy instrument when it lifted the grain embargo imposed against the Soviet Union by the Carter administration in order to protest the Soviet intervention in the conflict in Afghanistan; and

WHEREAS, the lifting of the economic embargo against Cuba would help relieve tensions in the Caribbean while creating a new and important market for American industry and agriculture, especially at a time of high unemployment in this country; and

WHEREAS, the Ecumenical Council of Cuba of which the Methodist Church of Cuba is a member, the Cuban Conference of Roman Catholic Bishops, and several other international as well as U.S. religious bodies such as the United Church of Christ, the Presbyterian

Church (USA), and the American Baptist Churches have passed resolutions in favor of lifting the embargo;

Therefore Be It Resolved, that The United Methodist Church, from its Christian and humanitarian perspective, hereby petitions the government of the United States to lift its economic embargo against Cuba and to seek negotiations with the Cuban government for the purpose of resuming normal diplomatic relations.

ADOPTED 1984

See Social Principles, ¶ 75.

Southern Africa

God, sovereign over all nations, has made of one blood all the peoples of the earth. The belief in racial superiority is totally incompatible with the gospel. We, therefore, unite with all who have condemned racism as sin, and *apartheid* as heresy.

United Methodists affirm the witness of all churches inside and outside Southern Africa in the struggle to dismantle *apartheid*. Participation in this struggle is one sign of bearing the Cross of Christ today. Many languish in prison, are condemned to torture, brainwashing and death. We join the lament of their families "How long Oh Lord, How long?"

United Methodists stand together both judged and reconciled with our sisters and brothers in South Africa and Namibia who bear so much suffering. Their pain judges us. Their anguish shames us. Their courage inspires our hope that justice will one day roll down like the waters and reconciliation will bring healing to our nations.

We rely on the grace of the Holy Spirit who alone is able to gather our brokenness and recreate us into a new community of truth, of justice and of peace. This is the true basis of our hope, the assurance given us that God is at work in our world. With anticipation, we pray, Thy Kingdom come, Thy will be done in South Africa, in Namibia, and everywhere on earth.

We know that goodness, justice, and love will triumph; that tyranny and oppression even in South Africa and Namibia will not last forever. We know that the tears of the "Rachels" weeping for the children in the "Sowetos" will be wiped away. Our task is to support our sisters and brothers in Southern Africa in their struggle.

United Methodists reaffirm our denomination's Charter on Racial Justice Policies in an Interdependent Global Community (1980) and the Southern Africa resolutions (1980 and 1984). Furthermore, we acknowledge our denomination's resolutions prior to 1980. These resolutions oppose apartheid and have laid the groundwork for our continuing efforts.

The Situation in Southern Africa:

United Methodists view with grave concern the escalating violence by the government of South Africa. These governmental policies are supported by powerful allies. Black townships are militarized and occupied by soldiers and police. Severe media censorships is in effect. Thousands of black children under the age of 18 have been imprisoned or detained without charge or trial and denied parental access. Children have been tortured and shot. Black children are denied access to quality education, decent housing and basic health care in contrast to the high quality services received by white children. Pneumonia, diarrhea, and premature births are still the common causes of infant deaths. Increasing violence, especially since the state of emergency declared on June 12, 1986, has created further worldwide concern.

The situation in Namibia is also characterized by mounting repression. Cruel and inhuman treatment of the population is the rule of the day. Infant mortality for black children in Namibia is eight times that of white children. South Africa, the occupying power, refuses to implement Resolution 435, the 1978 United Nations Security Council Resolution calling for the early independence of Namibia through free and fair elections under the supervision and control of the United Nations.

South Africa's aggression in the neighboring countries of Angola, Botswana, Lesotho, Mozambique, Swaziland, Zambia, and Zimbabwe goes unabated. It is a threat to peace against the entire continent of Africa. South Africa, alone, or with the assistance of surrogate forces, targets the infrastructure of these countries for destruction through diplomatic coercion, destabilization of the economies, military intervention and occupation.

Call To Action:

Conscious of the intensity of suffering in Southern Africa, the fifteenth World Methodist Conference meeting in Nairobi, Kenya, in July 1986, expressed deep concern for the critical situation. The conference called for steps to be taken to bring about positive change, to establish a just and free society in South Africa and Namibia, and to encourage and invest in those institutions and agencies that are struggling for change against restrictive systems within Southern Africa.

In the same spirit, we call upon United Methodists to:

1. Educate themselves about the current situation in Southern Africa through mission studies, church school curricula and community opportunities.
2. Participate in Southern Africa ecumenical observances, especially the June 16th "Soweto Uprising" commemorating the courageous witness of children and youth against *apartheid*. Resources to be coordinated and developed by the General Boards of Church and Society and Global Ministries.
3. Explore participation in boycotts of corporations doing business in South Africa and Namibia.
4. Support city, state, and national legislation which establishes selective purchasing guidelines limiting purchases from companies doing business in South Africa or Namibia.
5. Support General Board of Global Ministries efforts to minister to persons who are displaced, exiled, unemployed, and in critical need.

We call upon The United Methodist Church (its agencies, boards, local churches, colleges and related institutions) to use its moral and corporate resources to promote the dismantling of *apartheid*. We acknowledge disagreement among informed Christians regarding the most effective means of achieving this end. Our efforts may include, but shall not be limited to, efforts to promote complete disengagement of companies and banks as long as *apartheid* continues by doing the following:

1. Urging corporations to withdraw all business ties from South Africa and Namibia, including contracts, franchises, licensing or management agreements, as well as direct investments.

2. Refraining from doing business with banks with operations in or loans to South Africa or Namibia.
3. Pressuring, as shareholders or clients, such banks and other financial institutions to cease making loans to the private sector, in South Africa and Namibia.
4. Consulting with United Methodist agencies and ecumenical coalitions to either:
   a. Fully divest of stocks and bonds in all companies operating in South Africa and Namibia, or
   b. Selectively divest of stocks and bonds in specific corporations operating in South Africa (to be chosen according to the strategic nature of their product and size of their operations in South Africa and Namibia) coupled with a vigorous use of shareholder resolutions advocating corporate disengagement from South Africa and Namibia.

Furthermore, we urge corporations and banks withdrawing from South Africa and Namibia to relocate and invest in other countries of Southern Africa.

We also urge all governments to:

1. Implement a policy of comprehensive economic sanctions against South Africa and Namibia through multilateral efforts and the United Nations Security Council.
2. Support the implementation of United Nations Security Council Resolution 435 calling for the independence of Namibia.
3. Work to end support by their own or other governments or oragnizations which destabilize the governmetns of Angola and Mozambique (such as RENAMO/-MNR—Resistencia Nacional de Mocambicana and UNITA—Union for the Total Independence of Angola).
4. Provide strong economic and political support to the efforts of the "frontline countries"[1] in Southern Africa to end their dependence on the Republic of South Africa. In particular, we call for financial and other support for the Southern Africa Development Coordination Conference (SADCC) which coordinates the efforts of the nations of Southern Africa to liberate their economies from their dependence on South Africa.

We specifically urge the United States government to extend full

---

[1]Angola, Botswana, Mozambique, Zambia, Zimbabwe, United Republic of Tanzania.

and immediate recognition to the government of Angola (Israel, South Africa and the United States are the only remaining nations that do not recognize the government of Angola).

Further, we urge the government of South Africa to:

1. Lift the state of emergency in South Africa.
2. Provide children, regardless of their race or color, with access to integrated education, to decent housing, and basic health care.
3. Release the political prisoners and detainees.
4. Negotiate the political and economic future of South Africa with all the representative leaders of the people.
5. Allow South Africans living in exile to return home.
6. End the violence and resulting loss of life in South Africa, Namibia, and the neighboring countries.
7. Withdraw the South African Territorial Force from Namibia and grant Namibia's independence.

Conclusion:

We believe that the people of Southern Africa will continue to look primarily to themselves to determine their destiny without the intervention of outside foreign powers. Our concern and support must continue to be demonstrated by our commitment to the principle of self-determination and by our belief that we are all made in God's image.

We pray for the end to unjust rule in South Africa and Namibia, and affirm our belief in God's power over the forces of sin and evil, and the capacity of God's grace to restore human life to physical and spiritual wholeness.

ADOPTED 1988

See Social Principles, ¶ 75A.B., "Boycott of Royal Dutch/Shell," "Web of *Apartheid*, South Africa and the Destabilization of Its Neighbors," "Support and Concern to Mozambique."

Support Amnesty International

WHEREAS, Amnesty International has documented and verified political imprisonments, tortures, and killings over the last few years, involving government linked forces by governments of widely differing ideologies in more than 20 countries on four continents;

AND WHEREAS, Amnesty International has mounted a campaign to publicize such crimes against humanity which involve thousands of victims, and in this way to bring pressure upon the governments involved;

Be It Resolved, that The United Methodist Church adds its endorsement and support to Amnesty International, along with that already given by the Central Committee of the World Council of Churches, the National Council of the Churches of Christ in the U.S.A., and the American Baptist Churches, USA.

And Be It Further Resolved, that notice of this support be sent to Amnesty International, USA, to the Secretary General of the United Nations, and to the media.

ADOPTED 1984

See Social Principles, ¶ 75, "In Support of Self-determination and Non-intervention," "Human Rights."

Support and Concern to Mozambique

The burdens of the people of Mozambique weigh heavily upon us. They suffer extreme hunger and poverty. Hungry and homeless people gather in camps for food and shelter. The major reason for the famine is the war being waged against the government by RENAMO (the MNR), a guerrilla movement.

The MNR burn whole villages, plunder farms, and burn the crops. They steal the clothes from people's backs, leaving families walking naked down the road, seeking some safe haven. Women are raped. Men, women, and children are maliciously crippled, maimed, deformed, or scarred for life. Trucks and farm vehicles are stopped, food supplies destroyed, and drivers kidnapped or killed. These killers enter villages, clinics, and hospitals, indiscriminately shooting everyone in sight.

Teachers, health workers, and church leaders have become primary targets of terror by the MNR. Whole missions have been invaded. The Cambine United Methodist Mission suffered an attack which caused extraordinary destruction and loss of life.

Having suffered perhaps more than any other African nation under colonial rule, the people of Mozambique yearn for true independence, free from exploitation from east or west.

Significantly, the Assemblia of Mozambique, recently adopted a new constitution allowing multiparty elections, economic development, and strengthening the commitment to self-determination.

The United States has continued to seek ways to increase friendship with Mozambique. However, there continues to be a movement within Congress, led by Senator Jesse Helms, to abandon Mozambique, recognize the MNR, and join South Africa in providing aid and support to the campaign of destruction and destabilization.

The Christian Council of Mozambique has called upon the churches of the world to aid Mozambique, help feed the people, redevelop the nation, and condemn the action of South Africa and the MNR.

In the midst of these most difficult times, The United Methodist Church of Mozambique is growing, full of faith and hope. Re-opening the Chicuque Hospital, continued growth of Ricatla United Seminary, building new congregations, demonstrating self-sufficiency farming, providing new opportunities for mission, and bringing new converts to Christ and his Church, the church of Mozambique is an inspiration to us all.

The government of the Republic of Mozambique has initiated conversations with RENAMO in order to advance peace, and these conversations are now at an advanced state. The Bishop of the United Methodist Church of Mozambique, Joas Somane Machado, is involved in these conversations on behalf of the Christian Council of Mozambique. We have a strong hope that peace will come soon to Mozambique, even though we are unable to say when.

Therefore, The United Methodist Church:

a) Offers a special message of support and concern to the churches and people of Mozambique, encouraging them in their struggle for self-determination and freedom;

b) Pledges to make this support tangible through its continuing support for the Africa Church Growth and Development Fund and UMCOR's program in Mozambique, and urges the agencies and congregations of The United Methodist Church to participate in these endeavors, including the Advance Specials for Mozambique;

c) Sends a message to the delegations of the Mozambican government and RENAMO, meeting in Rome, encouraging them to work with all possible speed to find ways to overcome obstacles so as to declare a cease-fire and end the suffering of the people of Mozambique;

d) Opposes any efforts by any government, individuals, or nongovernmental organizations to support RENAMO (MNR);

e) Urges our governments, especially the United States of America, to pressure the government of South Africa to cease funding RENAMO and to desist from all other efforts to destabilize the government of Mozambique; and

f) Supports and encourages the people of Mozambique in their struggle for self-determination and freedom.

ADOPTED 1992

See Social Principles, ¶ 75, "Web of *Apartheid,* South Africa and the Destabilization of its Neighbors," "Southern Africa."

Terrorism

WHEREAS, the increase in terrorism from 1970 to 1990 has caused a fear among international people that creates a sense of hopelessness and instability and reveals the weakness in the present world system of international peace and security; and

WHEREAS, there is no significant difference between "state terrorism," as the "overkill" response of a state, and group terrorism, inasmuch as the innocent suffer;

Therefore, as United Methodist Christians, we:

1. Will examine critically the causes of terrorism and nations' involvement with it.

2. Firmly support the United Nations as an agency for conflict resolution and as a viable alternative to the resort to war and/or terrorism.

3. Urge the President of the United States to repudiate violence and to adhere to the statement that retaliation could be a terrorist act in itself and the killing and victimizing of innocent people.

4. Oppose the use of indiscriminate military force to combat terrorism except as a final resort, especially where the use of such force results in casualties among noncombatant citizens who are not themselves perpetrators of terrorist acts, and urge support of United Nations' Resolution 40-61, which addresses international cooperation regarding terrorist acts.

5. Condemn the use of extremist tactics which resort to violence within our own domestic society as an expression of ideological differences, racism, and anti-Semitism.

6. Direct the General Board of Church and Society to formulate a study to show how to deal with acts of terrorism that we face as a society and give direction as to how the church and annual conferences leaders and members can and should respond.

ADOPTED 1992

See Social Principles, ¶ 75.

United States-Mexico Border

The United States-Mexico border is a 2,000-mile-long area where the socio economic dynamics of two interacting cultures have a negative impact on the quality of life of adjoining populations. This adverse situation has been exacerbated by domestic and international policies espoused by the U.S. and Mexican governments.

The border region is characterized by:
• political domination by a minority of rich and powerful families;
• drastic economic disparity between segments of the population;
• constant deterioration of the health conditions, particularly affecting the poor;
• high incidence of crime and drug trafficking; and
• high rates of unemployment and underemployment, and (in the United States) the lowest per-capita income.

These detrimental conditions also effect the constant influx of thousands of refugees and undocumented persons coming to the United States seeking safe haven or better economic conditions. This situation of pain and suffering affects millions of women, children, and men residing on both sides of the border. The impact of these dynamics reaches well into the interiors of both countries.

Confronted by this human suffering along the United States-Mexico border region, we recognize that the vision of the "new heaven and new earth" (Rev. 21) will be only an illusion as long as "one of the least" (Matt. 25) continues to suffer.

As Christians and United Methodists, we express our sorrow and indignation and accept the responsibility to use our resources toward the elimination of the root causes creating this tragic human problem. We are particularly concerned about the following conditions:

1. Environmental

a. The constant indiscriminate use of pesticides in the growing and harvesting of agricultural products, a problem on both sides of the border. Pesticides banned or restricted in one nation are being exported for use in the other.

b. The water contamination caused by corporations dumping industrial toxic waste and the flushing of poisonous compounds into the Rio Grande, the Colorado, and other rivers.

c. Air pollution, a growing problem on both sides of the border.

2. Health

a. The use of toxic materials in production without informing workers of their hazards or providing education or proper equipment, leading to a high incidence of birth defects and other health problems.

b. The high incidence of dysentery, tuberculosis, and hepatitis caused by lack of adequate water waste facilities, lack of healthy drinking water, hunger and malnutrition, particularly among the "Colonias"—rural unincorporated areas—and, more specifically, as they affect children.

c. The lack of minimum adequate and affordable housing for workers in the Maquiladoras, leading to informal shanty towns without sanitation or other social facilities, and the use of unsafe and crowded barracks for workers.

d. The strained and inaccessible public services, such as health, education, and welfare, that seem to perpetuate the cycle of poverty and dehumanization.

3. Economic

a. Wages kept low by repression of workers' bargaining rights, keeping the border region below the average of Mexican industrial wage levels, despite the fact that the Maquiladoras are the second largest producers of export income for the country (after oil), and the largest source of income for the Mexican border region.

b. The lack of long-range economic and industrial development strategies, making the economies of both sides of the border more dependent on "quick economic fixes" such as "maquiladoras," "quick cash crops," tourism, and services that can help temporarily and superficially, but ignoring the economic needs of most of the present and future generations.

c. The trade agreements (such as the proposed North American Free Trade Agreement), which may worsen the existing economic dependencies and foster the exploitation of human and natural resources.

d. The low educational attainment level, high incidence of illiteracy, the high drop-out rate, and the ready availability and constant influx of drugs, which heighten the vulnerability of the low-income population along the border.

4. Political

a. The prevalent existence of political styles that benefit only those who want to perpetuate models of feudalistic governments that leave control in the hands of the powerful few, a situation creating the political climate that disempowers the poor.

5. Civil and Human Rights

a. The constant influx of people from south of the borders, heightening the anxieties of those who perceive immigrants as unwelcomed foreigners who pose a threat to the U.S. social, political, and economic security.

b. Strategies devised by governmental agencies and groups to harass, intimidate, and repress legal and illegal foreign entrants into the U.S. territory.

c. The poor administration of justice; the cultural insensitivity of Border Patrol agents; the high incidence of illegal use of force; and the constant violation of the civil and human rights of those detained or deported, creating an atmosphere of tension and distrust that exacerbates the social dynamics, contributing to the polarization between white and non-white residents and transients.

As people of faith, we are urged by God through Christ to love our neighbor and to do what we must to bring healing in the midst of pain, and to restore to wholeness those whose lives are shattered by injustice and oppression. "I have come in order that you might have life—life in all its fullness" (John 10:10).

Therefore, we recommend and urge the Mexican and U.S. governments to:
• develop national and international policies that bring more economic parity between the two countries, as the integral part of any trade agreement;
• appropriate sufficient resources to develop new industrial and economic development programs that are long-range, mutually beneficial, and more sensitive to the well-being of all women, children, and men of that area;
• develop bi-national and multilateral agreements that improve the quality of life, safeguard the water rights, and prevent the contamination of air, water, and land of the area;
• develop binding and enforceable mechanisms with respect to labor and human rights; agriculture, including farm workers; environmental standards; and health and safety standards for both nations and in any agreements to which they are a party;
• develop national and international policies that facilitate the migration and immigration of peoples across the border without the violation of their rights and aspirations; and
• find alternative and creative ways to reduce the foreign debt of Mexico.

Furthermore, we urge The United Methodist Church to continue its support of the U.S.-Mexico Border Bilateral Advisory Committee within the General Board of Global Ministries to provide coordination and facilitate a holistic approach to addressing the structural causes of the problems in this region.

We further recommend that the General Board of Church and Society, with churches in Mexico, the United States, and Canada, seek ways to network on fair trade, labor and human rights, agricultural and environmental concerns.

ADOPTED 1992

See Social Principles, ¶ 75, "Immigration," "Human Rights."

Understanding The United Methodist Church as a Global Church

WHEREAS, modern developments in transportation, communications, and technology have brought peoples and nations closer together; and

WHEREAS, globality tends to be understood in The United Methodist

Church basically in terms of the United Methodist presence beyond the boundaries of the United States and almost exclusively in relation to those sections of the church which are structurally within it; and

WHEREAS, there are a number of churches in the Methodist family which out of a sense of calling by the Holy Spirit, a desire to affirm their own identity, and their need for self-determination have elected be become autonomous;

Therefore, be it resolved, that The United Methodist Church:

1. Celebrate the God-given diversity of race, culture, and people at every level of church life in our worship and other activities;

2. Celebrate the global dimension brought to The United Methodist Church by sisters and brothers from all over the globe and the Native American nations, who are a part of U.S. society and The United Methodist Church;

3. Celebrate the autonomous affiliated Methodist churches and the Central Conference of The United Methodist Church as important expressions of the diversity of cultures and peoples called by God to be the Church Universal;

4. Work for a future where The United Methodist Church and the autonomous Methodist churches throughout the world, expressing their faith through their unique, God-given culture, will share resources, personnel, and perspectives as equals in their common task of evangelizing all the world;

5. Continue and strengthen its ecumenical commitment;

6. Embody this vision as possible in all United Methodist programs.

ADOPTED 1992

See Social Principles, ¶ 75, "The Global Nature of The United Methodist Church," "United Methodism in a New Europe."

In Support of the United Nations

This General Conference affirms its historic support for the United Nations. Today we rejoice that since 1945 the United Nations has been a functioning organization working for international peace and justice. In that time it has:

• Provided mechanisms for the peaceful settlement of disputes.
• Provided an arena for promotion of a just and equitable world economic system.

• Provided assistance through United Nations Educational, Scientific and Cultural Organization, United Nations Development Program, United Nations Children's Fund (UNICEF), World Health Organization, and its other agencies to persons who are usually neglected.
• Established peace-keeping forces in troubled areas.
• Defused big power confrontations.
• Provided a forum for discussion of difficult issues, such as decolonization.

International relations are entering a new era. Governments turn to the United Nations as they recognize that they must address their problems multilaterally. The use of consultation and compromise as solutions intensifies. Nations acting together can, for the first time in history, enforce observance of international law. We are encouraged that nations show a new willingness to work together for peace.

However, we are not convinced that the move toward cooperation among governments is inevitable. Nations might still return to unilateral acts of violence. Conflicts persist. The arms buildup has not ceased. Regional wars will continue to break out. The Security Council does not have the mechanism to implement fully the intent of the charter for collective action. Those aspects of the charter must be implemented which will protect the organization from undue reliance on the military of one or a few powerful states.

We encourage the governments of the world to discard old systems of nationalistic self-will and to let the ideals and visions of the Charter of the United Nations serve as their guide to a new spirit of international cooperation.

The pursuit of peace is thwarted when misunderstandings about the purpose and possibilities of the United Nations are widely promoted and believed. Therefore, we commend to the churches a wider study of the United Nations in order that Christians might be enabled to work in unity for peace and justice in the world.

To that end:

1. We reaffirm decisions of the General Conference beginning in 1944 to establish "an international office of education and publicity for peace." These decisions resulted in establishment of the Methodist Office for the United Nations and, in 1963, in construction of the Church Center for the United Nations.

2. We particularly commend the program "United Methodist Seminars on National and International Affairs" to local church,

district, and annual conference groups as a way to experience firsthand the work of the United Nations as it grapples with the work for peace.

3. We also reaffirm the importance of celebrating the signing of the Charter of the United Nations on October 24, 1945, with an emphasis in local churches on World Order Sunday, observed on that date or the Sunday preceding it.

ADOPTED 1992

See Social Principles, ¶ 75, "On the United Nations," "The United Methodist Church and Peace."

On the United Nations

Recognizing the fact that for the past 46 years the United Nations has been a unifying force that encourages international cooperation and dialogue in a world often divided by vast ideological and cultural differences;

And that the United Nations was awarded the 1988 Nobel Peace Prize for negotiating the Soviet withdrawal from Afghanistan, for mediating a cease-fire between Iran and Iraq, and for peace-keeping efforts in other parts of the world;

And that the United Nations forged the international treaty that will halt the production and consumption of chemicals that damage the earth's ozone layer;

And that the United Nations World Health Organization brought nations together to coordinate the battle against AIDS, which now afflicts people in 137 countries;

And that the United Nations provided assistance through U.N. Educational Scientific and Cultural Organization, U.N. Development Program, U.N. Children's Fund, World Health Organization, and its other agencies to persons who are usually neglected;

Therefore, we urge the United States government to provide its full share of financial support for the United Nations, related international organizations, and U.N. peace-keeping forces.

Furthermore, we call upon United Methodists to celebrate each year the founding of the United Nations on October 24, and affirm their commitment to the principles and goals of the United Nations charter; and we urge them to participate in the Ecumenical Study of the

National Council of Churches prepared to celebrate the fiftieth (50) anniversary of the United Nations, looking toward the new century.

Furthermore, we call upon The United Methodist Church through its conferences, districts, and local congregations to integrate information on the United Nations and its services, functions, and goals into discussion of issues and problems.

Finally, we call upon United Methodists to encourage their governments to strengthen the United Nations so that it may more effectively relieve the suffering of millions, protect our planet's environment, promote human rights, and bring about genuine and lasting peace in the world.

ADOPTED 1992

See Social Principles, ¶ 75, "The United Methodist Church and Peace," "In Support of the United Nations."

United States–China Political Relations

Our Political Understandings

In late 1978 the governments of the United States and the People's Republic of China (P.R.C.) reached agreement establishing full diplomatic relations. The United States ended official relations—diplomatic and military—with the authorities on Taiwan. (In March 1979 the U.S. Congress passed the Taiwan Relations Act putting U.S. relations with Taiwan on an unofficial basis). The United States recognized the People' Republic of China as the "sole legal government of China," but reserved the right over P.R.C. objections to sell "defensive" weapons to Taiwan. At the time of normalization the P.R.C. refused to rule out the possibility of reunifying with the island of Taiwan by force, but offered to allow Taiwan to maintain the political, economic, and military status quo if Taiwan were to recognize P.R.C. sovereignty.

This normalization agreement ended a 30-year period in which formal American commitments to the authorities on Taiwan blocked closer relations with the People's Republic of China. It laid the foundations for framework of cooperation and exchanges which continue to develop. Highlights include:

• Government-to-government agreements covering consular relations and embassies, civil aviation, scientific and technical cooperation, educational exchange, trade and credit, fisheries and a wide range of other fields.

• Substantial expansion of tourism and specialized visits.

• Educational programs facilitating nearly 10,500 scholars and teachers (10,000 Chinese; 500 Americans) to be resident in the other country.

• Numerous governmental and private institutional exchange agreements in education, the fine and performing arts, cinema, publishing, etc.

• Sister state-province and city-to-city agreements calling for various kinds of cooperation.

• Increased two-way trade.

• Discussions at the highest governmental levels about strategic and military concerns and cooperation.

The rapid growth and elaboration of these bilateral relations have been unusual and, to many, unexpected. While the direction is generally positive and the initial results heartening, the relationship is still in its early stages. Because the P.R.C. and U.S. systems are so different, translating worthwhile goals into concrete practice has often been difficult.

Fundamentally, the two countries have yet to determine what kind of long-term relationship they want. Misperceptions and misunderstandings are all too commonplace on both sides, even on basic principles.

As a case in point, the two sides had sharp disagreements during 1981 and 1982 over the issue of continuing U.S. arms sales to Taiwan. By August 1982, Washington and Beijing had clarified their understanding on this question: the P.R.C. stated that its "fundamental policy" was to "strive for peaceful reunification" with Taiwan. In that context, the U.S. government pledged not to increase and in fact to reduce its sale of arms to Taiwan. But this agreement only holds in abeyance a resolution of the Taiwan issue.

Recommendations on U.S.–China Political Relations

The United Methodist Church:
1. Affirms the establishment of full diplomatic relations between the United States and the People's Republic of China as an important

step toward mutual cooperation and understanding and toward world peace.

2. Advocates that the U.S. government, in accordance with the Joint Communique of December 1978, should continue to deal with the people of Taiwan on an unofficial basis.

3. Recognizes the necessity for China to continue its economic and social development and urges U.S. cooperation to that end within the context of Chinese independence and selfhood.

4. Feels the long-term basis of U.S.-China relations should emphasize people-to-people, educational, social, and economic cooperation based on mutual understanding and benefit, not short-term or expedient military or strategic interests; expresses deep concern about the anti-Soviet rationale used to explain U.S.-P.R.C. relations; opposes the sale of U.S. military equipment to the P.R.C.

5. Endorses a peaceful approach to ending the long-standing conflict between the governments in the People's Republic of China and in Taiwan while recognizing that the resolution of the status of Taiwan is a matter for the Chinese people themselves, and in that context supports the continued reduction and early cessation of U.S. arms sales to Taiwan.

6. Declares our continuing concern regarding the human rights of all people on both sides of the Taiwan Straits.

7. Recognizes that U.S.-P.R.C. relations have an important influence on the peace and stability of the Asian region, particularly in Southeast Asia; and urges both the United States, and the People's Republic of China to seek peaceful means to contribute to the peace and stability of the region.

ADOPTED 1984

See Social Principles, ¶ 75.B, "United States Church-China Church Relations."

United States Church–China Church Relations

Our faith affirmations and historical understandings of a relationship with the church in the People's Republic of China. Throughout the history of the Christian church, changes in the social, political, economic and cultural environment have elicited new, different, sometimes creative, sometimes destructive, responses in the ministry and witness of the church.

The church which re-emerged in the People's Republic of China (P.R.C.) in 1979, having been officially closed during the Cultural Revolution in 1966-1976, is striving to shape a new church, a new ministry, a new witness in China. A fundamental task for United Methodists is to develop the perceptiveness and spiritual depth that will enable us to enter into new relationships with the P.R.C. and with this new church. Entering this new relationship requires an honest examination of past patterns of work and relationships, a rethinking of our understanding of the task of the church, and an openness to new ways of being, relating and doing under the guidance of the Holy Spirit.

God's Church is called to mission. Individually and together, both the church in the People's Republic of China and the church in the United States are called to find their place in God's mission. This understanding, which forms the basic approach of the United Methodist China Program, is founded on certain affirmations drawn from biblical faith and shaped by our contemporary social and historical context.

I. Our faith is in God, who is one, the only transcending reality, who is creator of heaven and earth, who has made humankind one, and who continues to work in human history. God's love is expressed in great cosmic and human events; it is also very personal and individual. Created by God, each individual is loved of God, made for God, and drawn to God.

Faith in God as Creator affirms a common humanity with the Chinese people, a recognition that God relates to and has always been at work in Chinese history and culture and in individual persons. Persons in other cultures have much to learn from the Chinese people and from their experiences. Western values and assumptions cannot be projected as universal for all peoples.

II. God has called into being, through Jesus Christ, a particular people, the Church, and has made them one and has sent them into the world in mission and service to all humankind. Christians are linked to Christians in every nation and place through Jesus Christ. Living their daily lives in separate nations and cultures, Christians seek relationships which draw them into fuller expressions of unity while allowing for diversity and independence.

Churches within each nation have a primary link with one another and are the Body of Christ, the church in that place. They are also linked with churches, the Church, in every other nation, and together are the one Body of Christ in the world. Their unity is a sign to the world of God's intention to reconcile and unite humankind. As God continues working in human history, creating, judging, reconciling and redeeming, so the Church, and the churches are called to share in this mission to the world.

Fundamental to the mission are acts of thanksgiving:

We give thanks for all those persons, both indigenous and expatriate, through whose lives and ministries the Church has come into being throughout the world.

We rejoice that God stands with all people, especially the poor and the oppressed of the earth.

Christians give thanks wherever the poor of the earth are receiving new life, and affirm this as part of God's work.

Fundamental to mission also are acts of repentance. We are aware of historic links between the missionary movement and Western influence. Christianity must not be used as a tool of Western penetration. While all are sinners and offered God's grace and forgiveness, the Church is called to stand especially with those who are "sinned against." As the Church renews its covenant of witness, ministry, and mission, it does so with deep repentance and humility, accepting God's forgiveness and seeking the forgiveness of those it has wronged. Trusting God's grace and guidance, the Church moves forward with courage to seek new relationships in mission and service.

III. Through the Holy Spirit the Christian community, within and outside the People's Republic of China, is being challenged to respond in new ways to a new China. Together, the Chinese government and people have brought about many improvements in basic physical needs. The attitudes of the people are also changing. Liberation from foreign domination has brought a renewed sense of pride and dignity in being Chinese. Growing self-reliance in overcoming seemingly insurmountable problems has underscored this feeling of self-respect and self-esteem.

In 1949 many Chinese viewed the church in China as a foreign institution, largely supported by foreign funds and personnel, and closely allied with those who opposed the Revolution. While the Chinese Communist Party and Chinese church differ on their views of religious belief, the Constitution now provides for both the policy and practice of religious freedom.

Chinese Christians now reaffirm their responsibility to bear witness to the gospel in the People's Republic of China through Christian communities that are self-governing, self-supporting, and self-propagating. Responsibility for Christian mission in the People's Republic of China is with the Christians in the P.R.C. Their leaders want no assistance from outside organizations or individuals without mutual consultation and decision. The Chinese Protestant Three-Self Patriotic Movement and the China Christian Council are institutional expressions of these affirmations.

The life of the church in China, as in other countries, is a precious gift offering a powerful witness to the world. Part of the task of the churches outside China is to receive that witness and to allow time and space for it to grow.

In its centuries-old struggle for survival, China is an inspiration and a challenge to United Methodists. Where is God in the struggle and pathos of the Chinese people? How does the Church of Jesus Christ share in this history? Our historical involvement as United Methodists with the people of China offers a rare opportunity for us to look at the ambiguous relationships between the Chinese people and ourselves. It forces us toward a new understanding of faith in the gospel which seeks to unite all things in Jesus Christ. A new understanding is primary in all that we do in cooperation with the people of China, and the church in China. Christians in China have requested our new understanding and underlined this need by asking us to pray for them and for ourselves.

Recommendations on U.S. Church–China Church Relations

1. That The United Methodist Church provide information, guidance, and encouragement to help its constituency understand the struggles of the people of China, and to pray fervently with informed sensitivity for the people and the church in China.

The church in the People's Republic of China has declared itself to be self-governing, self-supporting, and self-propagating. The primary responsibility for Christian mission in the People's Republic of China belongs to the church there. We must not act as if the church in the People's Republic of China does not exist, or as if only we are called in mission. We thank God that the church lives in China, and that it is a Chinese church.

2. That The United Methodist Church affirm the selfhood of, respect the autonomy of, and reaffirm our readiness to hear and interact with, the church in the People's Republic of China as together we shape future relationships based on mutuality.

Christians in the Peoples's Republic of China have declared themselves to be in a "post-denominational era." There are now no denominations in the People's Republic of China. There is no Chinese body of Christian believers having an agreed upon polity, creed, rites, etc. What future form of organization, doctrine, ritual the church will take is yet to be determined. Chinese Christians are now concerned that they be allowed to determine these issues within their understanding of the Holy Spirit's leading and without foreign interference. The de-emphasis on denominations in the church in the People's Republic of China is a reminder to United Methodists that the whole Church of Jesus Christ must manifest unity as a sign and sacrament of the unity of humankind.

3. That The United Methodist Church reaffirm its continuing commitment to work ecumenically with other Christian bodies in relating to the church in the People's Republic of China and with the Chinese people.

Christians in the People's Republic of China have made us sensitively aware of the imbalances of relationships between China and ourselves. They have also pointed out the growing disparities between the rich and the poor nations. They have challenged us to examine our involvement with the poor and oppressed in our own society.

4. That The United Methodist Church recommit itself a) to a sustained program for awareness of the disparities between the rich and the poor; and b) to work with faithfulness and integrity to create new attitudes and institutional structures which more perfectly manifest the gospel of Christ that all humankind be united. Such efforts include:

• Being sensitive to areas of our national life which exploit peoples of other societies as well as our own.

• Standing with the poor and the oppressed in the United States as well as in other countries.

• Examining and learning from the accomplishments and the mistakes in past and present missionary efforts in China and other parts of the world.

• Being available for mutual ministry with Christians in China, in the United States, and in other countries.

5. That The United Methodist Church also commit itself to a strengthened program of communication and dialogue within The United Methodist Church about the People's Republic of China and the church there.

ADOPTED 1984

See Social Principles, ¶ 75A.B, "United States-China Political Relations."

Web of *Apartheid,* South Africa and the Destabilization of Its Neighbors

We rejoice with the people of Southern Africa who appear to be on the threshold of change. At the same time, we stand by the assertion that *apartheid,* in its legal form or in its de facto expression through racism, is a sin and must be condemned unequivocally—within South Africa and neighboring countries and throughout the world, including our own communities in the United States.

In discerning change in the region, we as Christians, and particularly as United Methodists, affirm our faith in a God who stands with the most vulnerable in society. Their well-being must serve as a guidepost for justice in the region. We therefore remain ever vigilant in the face of reforms and negotiations, listening more attentively than ever to the churches and movements in the region.

We express our concern about the continued violence in South Africa, recognizing that structural violence, evident in a political system which denies people of color the ability to participate in the governing of their land, intensifies, polarizes and creates political and ethnic divisions. Government-instigated violence has clearly been evident and must be denounced. Reported violence in the townships must be investigated and analyzed, recognizing the causes and conditions which create that dynamic.

The destabilization acts of South Africa continue to maim neighboring countries as well. As these countries achieve independence, South Africa seeks to exert economic pressure, arm insurgency movements, and take direct military actions to undermine the newly formed governments. This contrived conflict has produced a generation of citizens in the region who have never known peace.

Since their independence in 1975, Mozambicans have been plagued by the Mozambique National Resistance (MNR or RENAMO), a destabilization force, financed by agents of South Africa and private individuals and groups in the United States, whose primary targets are transportation and health services. Although starvation and infant mortality are catastrophically high, attempts to relieve suffering through development projects are quickly undermined by RENAMO.

In Angola, South Africa and the United States until recently waged an undeclared war against the Popular Movement for the Liberation of Angola (MPLA) Government through their support of the National Union for the Total Independence of Angola (UNITA). The lengthy war has come to an end with the recently signed Peace Accord between the government and UNITA. The bombings and South African incursions into this country have left the population with the largest number of amputees in the world and tremendous devastation.

Plagued by violence at home, refugees and displaced persons exist in catastrophic numbers in the region. Within Mozambique, 2 million persons are internally displaced. Of the 1.4 million Mozambicans living as refugees outside of the country, 909,000 have settled in the tiny country of Malawi, producing a severe strain on that country's social services. According to the World Bank, one in three Malawian children die before the age of five. One-quarter million Mozambicans in South Africa illegally neither have status as refugees nor receive any assistance from the United Nations High Commission for Refugees (UNHCR).

The Republic of Namibia gained its independence on March 21, 1990, and held its first free and fair elections under the supervision of the United Nations. Independence was gained after a long protracted struggle by the people of Namibia. We rejoice with them in their victory and acknowledge the prophetic and pastoral role played by the churches in Namibia.

The struggle has not ended for Namibia. Not only has Namibia repatriated more than 41,000 former refugees, but an estimated 25,000 Angolans have entered Northern Namibia since independence, fleeing the violence in their own country. Namibia's task of nation-building is further threatened by the lingering arm of South African control. The former occupying force has continued its claim on Walvis Bay, Namibia's only deep-sea harbor. Once in the hands of Namibia, Walvis Bay could play a key role in the Southern Africa Development Coordination Conference (SADCC) which seeks to coordinate efforts of the nations of Southern Africa to liberate their economies from their dependence on South Africa.

Our acts of solidarity must not only focus on ending the historical process of destabilization of the region of Southern Africa, but also contribute toward a future of stabilization and development in that region. United Methodist Social Principles assert the government responsibility for "the protection of the rights of the people to free and fair elections . . . to adequate food, clothing, shelter, education, and health care."

Development and stabilization will require just relations between economic institution at home and in the region. Therefore, we call for the maintenance of economic pressures on South Africa until an interim government is installed that will transfer power from the hands of those who traditionally have supported *apartheid* and into a democratic structure that will create a new constitution. Once that has been accomplished, companies and banks should be encouraged to reinvest in South Africa under the conditions and priorities set by the organizations (such as the trade unions, churches, and liberation movements) which represent the majority of South Africans.

Restitution for past oppression will also be a requirement for development. As stated in the United Methodist Social Principles under "Rights of Racial and Ethnic Persons": "We assert the obligation of society, and groups within the society, to implement compensatory programs that redress long-standing systemic social deprivation of racial and ethnic minorities" (72.A.). Therefore, we affirm the Rustenburg Declaration's "support for acts of restitution in the areas of health care, psychological healing, education, housing, employment, economic infrastructure and land ownership."

Recognizing that true peace in Southern Africa can only be based on justice, and that all neighboring countries are affected by the destabilization efforts of South Africa, United Methodists call for an end to the heretical and immoral system of *apartheid* and support the creation of a united, nonracial and non-sexist democratic society in South Africa as well as sustainable and equitable development throughout the region.

We call upon United Methodists to:
• Recognize, acknowledge, and confront the racism that is a part of each of our lives.
• Continue to advocate and support sanctions against South Africa until the creation of an interim government.
• Enable The United Methodist Church to provide moral and financial support to the churches in the region of Southern Africa.
• Make use of available resources to become familiar with the region of Southern Africa and keep informed of recent developments.
• Include the people of the region in prayers and liturgies.

We call upon The United Methodist Church to:
• Continue providing information to United Methodists and policy makers regarding the status of current changes in South Africa and the need for appropriateness of continuing economic pressures.
• Encourage companies and banks to reinvest in South Africa, once an interim government is in place, according to the conditions and priorities articulated by organizations (such as trade unions, churches, democratic and liberation movements).
• Support independent research and development programs within Southern Africa—especially those related to law and education.
• Support independent organizations which monitor human rights, assisting with advocacy for identified victims.
• Assist in creating an atmosphere of just peace, where persons must not flee their homes in terror.
• Assist with the repatriation and resettlement of refugees.

We call upon all governments to:
• Maintain sanctions against South Africa until an interim government has been established.
• Support peaceful negotiations with all parties in South Africa.
• Respect human rights in the region and implement policies which insure the rights of refugees and displaced persons.
• Press for an end to private U.S. logistical and financial aid to RENAMO in Mozambique.

• Normalize relations with the neighboring countries of South Africa, providing the economic and political support needed to relieve these countries of their dependence on South Africa. Among such aid is support for the Southern Africa Development Coordination Conference (SADCC).

ADOPTED 1992

See Social Principles, ¶¶ 74.A, 72.A, and 75, "Support and Concern to Mozambique," "The United Methodist Church and Peace."

OTHER RESOLUTIONS

Biblical Language

The United Methodist Church affirms the right and custom of the use of biblical language and images in all its forms in worship and in our common life together. Phrases such as "Lord" and "King" and "Father" are an integral part of the rich heritage of the faith. A truly inclusive church will not restrict its people as to what is appropriate and what is inappropriate language and imagery about God. We, therefore, affirm the use of biblical language and images in all its forms as appropriate for use in hymns, liturgy, teaching and in all areas of our common life together.

ADOPTED 1988

Make Evangelism the Number One Priority for the Next Quadrennium

Evangelism shall become the number one priority of The United Methodist Church for the next quadrennium. Evangelism shall also become the number one priority of all our mission work around the world—and of all our commissions, boards, and agencies at all levels—for the purpose of persuading men, women, and children to come to Jesus Christ and so be reconciled to God. It is imperative for us to fulfill the Great Commission, left us by Jesus Christ, God's Son, to go into all the world in the power of the Holy Spirit, to influence the unsaved persons of our world to receive Jesus Christ as Savior and Lord.

ADOPTED 1992

Proper Use of Name: The United Methodist Church

WHEREAS, The Methodist Church and The Evangelical United Brethren Church were united under the name The United Methodist

663

Church in the year 1968 and that the uniting name has great historical significance for both bodies;

Be it resolved that insofar as possible all materials used in correspondence, advertisements, and signs of the said churches and other denominational organizations use the complete proper name "The United Methodist Church," capitalizing the word "The," when referring to the denomination as a whole.

ADOPTED 1980

Spiritual Directors' Program

WHEREAS, the importance of a person of faith listening to, sharing with, and guiding another is clearly told in the scripture (as examples, Elijah guiding Elisha, the spiritual friendship of Naomi and Ruth, Jesus leading the Samaritan woman to truth, Philip guiding the eunuch, Paul nurturing Timothy); and

WHEREAS, the Church through the ages has benefitted from the spiritual guidance given by such prayerful persons as Ignatius of Loyola, Teresa of Avia, Thomas Merton, and Douglas Steer; and

WHEREAS, our own history as United Methodists is informed by John Wesley's probing question, "How is it with your soul?"; by the spiritual nurturing he shared with Peter Boehler; and the spiritual guidance of the class meeting; and

WHEREAS, many in our dizzying culture are seeking to discern the subtle threads and blessings woven by the mysterious movement of the Spirit;

WHEREAS, the interest in and training of spiritual directors is beginning to occur in may Protestant circles; and

WHEREAS, a great service could be passed on to the church through encouragement, networking, information-sharing, and training of spiritual guides;

Therefore, be it resolved, that General Conference recommends that *The Upper Room* explore ways of supplying resources to and networking with United Methodists and others involved in and interested in spiritual direction work; and

Be it further resolved, That General Conference further recommends that *The Upper Room* in consultation with other boards and agencies (such as the Board of Higher Education and Ministry) plan a consultation/workshop in the next quadrennium that would enhance the gifts and skills of spiritual directors and those interested and serve as a way to link with others for support; and

Be it further resolved, that the costs for these actions be assumed within the normal funding of *The Upper Room* and those boards and agencies consulted.

ADOPTED 1992

A Tithing Church

Scripture

WHEREAS: In Numbers and Deuteronomy, Moses stated all the laws of God has commanded him to pass on to Israel. After describing the three different kinds of tithes God requires of us, Moses said, "The purpose of tithing is to teach us to always put God first in our lives," so that "Jehovah, our God, will bless us and our work." (Num. 18:21/24, Deut. 14:23c and 14:29d TLB), and

WHEREAS: In the Sermon on the Mount, Jesus proclaimed, "You cannot serve two masters, God and money, for you will hate one and love the other, or the other way around." (Matt. 6:24), and

Tradition

WHEREAS: Tithing has been the Christian minimum standard of giving for many years, and

Reason

WHEREAS: In the 1987 Journal of Stewardship published by the National Council of Churches, the giving level per number of the United Methodist Church ranks 28th out of the 30 United States denominations reporting, and

Experience

WHEREAS: There is always the need to be continually reminded that God is to be first in our lives,

THEREFORE, BE IT RESOLVED that the General Conference of the United Methodist Church determine that we will be a tithing church and that the practice of tithing be lifted up to each congregation from the pulpit and through other channels of communication, and that workshops on the spiritual blessings of tithing will be held in each Annual Conference a minimum of once a year as a part of Christian Stewardship.

ADOPTED 1988

A New Beginning

WHEREAS, Indigenous People welcomed the arrival of Europeans of 1492, sharing their gifts with the newcomers; and

WHEREAS, we recognize that conquerors and colonizers took the land, lives, and cultures of Indigenous People; and

WHEREAS, we recall that imperialism and colonialism brought Africans to the Americas in dehumanizing slavery; and

WHEREAS, we realize that the United States and other countries are planning to celebrate the five hundredth anniversary of the so-called "discovery" of the continents of North and South America; and

WHEREAS, reaffirming that the Indigenous People have a voice and vision to offer to The United Methodist Church;

Therefore be it resolved, that the Native American International Caucus call upon United Methodists to reflect and analyze, beginning in the year 1992, the differing effects that colonialism has brought to our various people; to analyze and assess the effects that colonialism has had on both the colonizer and the colonized; and to act faithfully and prophetically on their analysis, assessment, and reflection.

ADOPTED 1992

TOPIC AND CATEGORY INDEX

Accessibility/Equal Access
Accessibility of Meeting Places Beyond the Local Church.................................151
Affirmative Action...159
Affirmative Action Plans and People with Disabilities...161
Annual Accessibility Audit..184
Barrier-free Construction for the Handicapped..189
Bilingual Education..464
Church and Persons with Mentally, Physically, and/or Psychologically
   Handicapping Conditions, The...200
Communications Access for Persons Who Have Hearing
   and Sight Impairments...207
Compliance with the Americans with Disabilities Act for Employers..................208
Equal Justice..499
Inclusiveness of the Physically Challenged at all Conferences............................304
Pay Equity in the U. S. A...434
Project Equality..349

Administrative Guidelines
Biblical Language...663
Ethnic Membership on Boards and Agencies...254
Evangelism the #1 Priority for the Next Quadrennium, Make............................663
Guidelines for Initiating or Joining an Economic Boycott...................................423
Observance of Dr. Martin Luther King Jr. Day..338
Program to Emphasize Inclusiveness in All Dimensions of the Church..............346
Proper Use of Name: The United Methodist Church..663
Recruitment and Development Plan for Local Pastors...361

African American
Affirmation of Zoar United Methodist Church of Philadelphia...........................158
African-American Family Life..164
Black Church Growth...190
Black Leadership..191
Black-owned Farm Land..53
Declare Zoar United Methodist Church a Primary Historical Emphasis.............219
History of Blacks in The United Methodist Church..285
Resourcing Black Churches in Urban Communities...364
Strengthening the Black Church for the 21st Century..376

Age Level Ministries
Aging in the United States of America..165
Dependent Care...219
Enlist and Involve the Youth in the Life of the Church.......................................249

Infant Formula Abuse...584
In Support of Women, Infants, and Children's Supplemental
    Food and Nutrition Education Program (WIC Program)..............................302
Juvenile Justice..511
Medical Rights for Children and Youth..308
Ministry to Runaway Children...317
Mission and Aging of Global Population...593
Native American Young Adults in Mission..324
Prevention and Reduction of Juvenile Delinquency.....................................526
Protecting and Sustaining Children...350

Children
Dependent Care...219
In Support of Women, Infants, and Children's Supplemental
    Food and Nutrition Education Program (WIC Program)..............................302
Medical Rights for Children and Youth..308
Ministry to Runaway Children...317
Protecting and Sustaining Children...350

Communications
Church in a Mass Media Culture, The..484
Free Flow of Information Among All Peoples of the Earth...............................575
Vision Interfaith Satellite Network..399

Community
Church and Community Workers, 1988...199
Church and Community Workers, 1992...200
Church/Government Relations..468
Church/Government Relations, The United Methodist Church and..........................480
Community Life...488
Ministries in Social Conflict..312
Population...342

Country/region concerns
Arab-Israel Conflict, The..542
Boycott of Royal Dutch/Shell...555
Central America: Peace and Justice with Freedom......................................557
Concern for El Salvador..570
Current Arab-Israel Crisis, The..571
End U. S. Military Presence in Bolivia...573
Global Nature of The United Methodist Church, The....................................579
Holy Land Tours..580
In Support of Self-determination and Non-intervention................................581
Justice for the Reverend Alex Awad...589
"New House" of Europe..597
Nuclear-Free Pacific...604
Oppose Food and Medicine Blockades or Embargoes......................................605
Peace, Justice, and Reunification of Korea...613
Persons Missing in Action..629
Philippines, The...629
Puerto Rico and Vieques..632
Recognition of Cuba..634
Southern Africa..636
Support and Concern to Mozambique..641
Understanding The United Methodist Church as a Global Church..........................647
United States-China Political Relations..651

United States Church-China Church Relations...653
Web of Apartheid, South Africa and the Destabilization
  of its Neighbors... 658

Disarmament
Christian Faith and Disarmament.. 561
Comprehensive Test Ban Treaty... 568
Nuclear Disarmament: the Zero Option.. 600
Nuclear-Free Pacific... 604
Nuclear Weapons Production at the General Electric Company........................ 433
Peace, The United Methodist Church and.. 617

Drug and Alcohol
Ban on Alcohol Beverage Advertisements.. 189
Confronting the Drug Crisis... 211
Driving under the Influence...228
Drug and Alcohol Concerns...229
Education on Alcohol and Substance Abuse..246
Oxford House Model for Drug and Alcohol Abuse, The................................338
Sale and Use of Alcohol and Tobacco on Church Property............................ 367
Use of Alcohol and Drugs on Campus, The..398

Economics
A Call for Increased Commitment to End World Hunger and Poverty.................457
Appalachian Challenge...401
Church/Government Relations...468
Church/Government Relations, The United Methodist Church and................... 480
Economic Justice.. 403
Enabling Financial Support for Domestic Programs...................................... 498
Environmental Stewardship...70
Extension of the Right to Organize and Bargain Collectively........................... 411
Global Debt Crisis... 414
Infant Formula Abuse... 584
Investment Ethics...427
Justice, Peace and the Integrity of Creation...591
National Incomes Policy.. 431
Pay Equity in the U. S. A... 434
Rights of Workers... 438
Self-help Efforts of Poor People...446
Tithing Church, A... 665
Unemployment.. 453
Peace, The United Methodist Church and.. 617

Ecumenical/Interfaith/Cooperative Relations
Act of Covenanting Between Other Christian Churches and The
  United Methodist Church..153
Appalachian Challenge...401
COCU Consensus: in Quest of a Church of Christ Uniting............................205
Comity Agreements Affecting Development of Native American Ministry
  by The United Methodist Church... 206
Continuing Membership in the Consultation on Church Union........................ 217
Continuing Membership in the National Council of the Churches of
  Christ/U.S.A... 217
Continuing Membership in the World Council of Churches............................ 218
Ecumenical Decade: Churches in Solidarity with Women.............................242
Ecumenical Interpretations of Doctrinal Standards...................................... 245

TOPIC AND CATEGORY INDEX

Guidelines for Interreligious Relationships "Called to Be Neighbors and Witness"263
Mutual Recognition of Members..318
Our Muslim Neighbors.. 606
Pan Methodist Unity...340
Relationship Between The United Methodist Church and the New
  Affiliated Autonomous Methodist Church of Puerto Rico..............................362
Support the Consultation on Church Union Proposal.....................................382
Toward an Ecumenical Future...385
United States Church-China Church Relations..653
Use of Church Facilities by Community Groups...399

Education
A Call for Increased Commitment to End World Hunger and Poverty................457
Access of Hispanics to Higher Education..151
Bilingual Education..464
Celebrating 100 Years of Lay Education in the Tradition of
  Scarritt-Bennett Center.. 194
Church/Government Relations..468
Continuance of Funding to the Evangelical Seminary of Puerto Rico..................216
Enlist and Involve the Youth in the Life of the Church.................................249
Higher Education Training and Scholarships..284
Increased Support for Programs Impacting the Higher Education
  of Native Americans... 304
Literacy, the Right to Learn: A Basic Human Right.....................................512
Peace Colleges.. 612
Public Education in the United States... 527
School Busing... 368
Spiritual Directors' Program..664
Use of Church Facilities for Operating Private Schools................................ 540

Environment/Energy
Black Hills Alliance, The.. 554
Common Heritage..54
Energy Policy Statement..57
Environmental Justice for a Sustainable Future.. 62
Environmental Racism.. 67
Environmental Stewardship..70
Indoor Air Pollution..77
Law of the Sea, The..79
Nuclear Safety in the United States.. 80
Reduction of Water Usage by United Methodists.. 87
Use of Reclaimed Paper.. 112

Family
Adoption...113
African-American Family Life...164
"May" as Christian Home Month..122
Responsible Parenthood.. 125
Supportive Policies for Families with Children.. 135

Gambling
Gambling.. 412
Gambling, The United Methodist Church's Position on................................. 413

Health
AIDS and the Healing Ministry of the Church.. 115
Care-Giving Teams for Persons with Aids.. 120

TOPIC AND CATEGORY INDEX

Church and Persons with Mentally, Physically, and/or Psychologically Handicapping Conditions, The..............200
Church and the Global HIV/AIDS Epidemic, The............564
Circumcision..............121
Federal Funds for Indian Health Services............254
Health and Wholeness............273
Health for All by the Year 2000............278
Health in Mind and Body............280
Infant Formula Abuse............584
Medical Rights for Children and Youth............308
Ministries on Mental Illness............313
Organ and Tissue Donation............123
Pastoral Care and the AIDS Epidemic in Native American Communities............123
Resources for AIDS education............124
Safety and Health in Workplace and Community............443
Suicide: A Challenge to Ministry............377
Understanding Living and Dying as a Faithful Christian............140
Universal Access to Health Care in the U. S. and Related Territories............395

Hispanic
Access of Hispanics to Higher Education............151
Spanish Language Hymnal............370

Housing and Homelessness
Available and Affordable Housing............185
Homelessness in the U. S. A............286
Housing............293

Human Sexuality
Against Sterilization Abuse............113
Condemning Legal Prostitution............121
Domestic Violence and Sexual Abuse............223
Sexual Harassment and The United Methodist Church............449
Sexual Harassment in Church and Society in the U. S. A............447
Sexual Violence and Pornography............128

Human Rights
Equal Rights of Women............251
Human Rights............506
Literacy, the Right to Learn: A Basic Human Right............512
New Issues in Human Rights............517
Ratification of Human Rights Covenants and Conventions............633
Religious Liberty............529
Support Amnesty International............640

Immigration/Refugee
Assistance and Sanctuary for Central American Refugees............463
Immigration............507
To Love the Sojourner............384
U. S.-Mexico Border............644

Indigenous Peoples
America's Native People, The United Methodist Church and............178
Arab-Israel Conflict, The............542
Black Hills Alliance, The............554

TOPIC AND CATEGORY INDEX

Comity Agreements Affecting Development of Native American Ministry
by The United Methodist Church.. 206
Comprehensive Approach to Native American Ministries.. 209
Confession to Native Americans..210
Education Responsibilities Concerning Native American Cultural Traditions.........247
Federal Funds for Indian Health Services... 254
Fort Laramie Treaty, The...574
Increased Support for Programs Impacting the Higher Education of
Native Americans... 304
Indian Lands Used by The United Methodist Church... 76
American Indian Religious Freedom Act..176
National Convocation on the Ordained Ministry for Native Americans...............320
Native American History and Contemporary Culture as Related to
Effective Church Participation... 321
Native American Social Witness Program... 324
Native American Representation in The United Methodist Church....................322
Native American Young Adults in Mission...324
New Beginning, A...666
Nuclear-Free Pacific... 604
Pastoral Care and the AIDS Epidemic in Native American Communities............. 123
Promote the Observance of Native American Awareness Sunday.......................... 349
Protecting the Native American Land Base...86
Rights of Native People of the Americas.. 366
Shared Financial Support for the Native American Center..................................... 368
Toward a New Beginning Beyond 1992.. 386

International Law

Common Heritage...54
Human Rights.. 506
Law of the Sea, The...79
Ratification of Human Rights Covenants and Conventions...............................633
Terrorism.. 643

Intolerance/Tolerance

Affirming a Diversity of Language Usage in the United States and
Opposing a Constitutional Amendment Making English the Official Language.. 162
Ku Klux Klan and Other Hate Groups in the United States............................. 306
Membership in Clubs or Organizations that Practice Exclusivity....................... 311
Prejudice against Muslims and Arabs in the U. S. A...345
Racial Harassment... 360

Justice and Law

Capital Punishment... 465
Criminal Justice...492
Domestic Surveillance.. 496
Equal Justice... 499
Extension of the Right to Organize and Bargain Collectively....................... 411
Grand Jury Abuse... 503
Gun Control.. 504
Juvenile Justice... 511
Local Church and the Local Jail, The...516
Opposition to a Call for a Constitutional Convention.. 520
Penal Reform.. 524
Police Firearms Policy.. 526
Prevention and Reduction of Juvenile Delinquency... 526
Ratification for District of Columbia Representation.. 528

TOPIC AND CATEGORY INDEX

Repression and the Right to Privacy... 532
Support Legislation Prohibiting Malicious Harassments................................... 536
Terrorism.. 643
U. S. Gun Violence... 536
Victims of Crime.. 540

Militarism and the Draft
Certification of Conscientious Objectors.....................................467
Church/Government Relations..468
Concerning the Draft in the United States.................................... 490
Support of Conscientious Objectors to Registration........................ 535

Nuclear Issues
Nuclear-Free Pacific... 604
Nuclear Safety in the United States.. 80

Peace and War
Bishops' Call for Peace and the Self-development of Peoples........................... 547
Christian Faith and Disarmament... 561
Consequences of Conflict.. 570
Justice, Peace and the Integrity of Creation..................................... 591
Peace, The United Methodist Church and.................................... 617
Peace with Justice as a Special Program.. 623
United Nations, In Support of the.. 648
United Nations, On the.. 650

Race
Celebrate and Affirm the Work of the General Commission on Religion and Race 193
Charter for Racial Justice Policies in an Interdependent Global Community, A..... 196
Elimination of Racism in The United Methodist Church.................................. 248
Environmental Racism.. 67
Eradication of Racism..254
Global Racism..256
History of Racial/Ethnic United Methodists.................................... 285
Inclusive History.. 303
Membership in Clubs or Organizations which Practice Exclusivity................... 311
Pacific Islanders Included as Racial and Ethnic Minority Group........................339
Prejudice Against Muslims and Arabs in the U. S. A.....................................345
Project Equality...349
Racial Harassment.. 360
Support to Strengthen Ethnic Minority Local Church................................ 383

Rural/Urban Issues
Affirmation of Basic Rural Worth, An... 157
Appalachian Mission, The.. 401
Appointment of Clergy to Rural Ministry..................................... 185
Black-owned Farm Land.. 53
Call to the Bishops to undergird Cooperative Parish Ministry......................... 191
Church and Community Workers, 1988.....................................199
Church and Community Workers, 1992.......................................200
Church's Response to Changing Rural Issues, The................................ 204
Considering Community Contexts in the Appointment-Making Process..............215
Protecting the Native American Land Base..86
Resourcing Black Churches in Urban Communities.................................364
Rural Chaplaincy as a Ministry of Laity and Clergy....................................... 366
Special Emphasis on Reclaiming the Cities.....................................370

Special Needs of Farm Workers..452
Tent-Building Ministries.. 384
U. S. Agriculture and Rural Communities in Crisis....................................... 87

Science and Religion
New Developments in Genetic Science..325

Women
Anna Howard Shaw Day.. 182
Celebrate and Support the Ongoing Work of the General Commission on the
 Status and Role of Women... 192
Domestic Violence and Sexual Abuse.. 223
Ecumenical Decade: Churches in Solidarity with Women................................242
Equal Rights of Women... 251
Full Personhood... 255
Goals and Recommendations on Participation of Women..................................261
In Support of Women, Infants, and Children's Supplemental Food
 and Nutrition Education Program (WIC Program)..302
Status of Women, The... 371
Treatment of Women in the United States under Social Security, The................ 392

SUBJECT INDEX

A

Abortion 36, 126, 276, 374, 521
Abstinence 41, 232, 247
Academic Freedom 470, 527
Access Sunday 202
Access to Information 577
Accessibility 151, 172, 184, 189, 201, 207, 208, 395
Addiction 46
Adoption 37, 113
Advance Specials 369, 596
Advocacy 204, 223, 346, 429, 476, 611
Affirmative Action 40, 159, 203, 428
African American(s) 158, 164, 190, 191, 285, 303, 361, 364, 376, 396, 465, 498
  Colleges 54
  Farms 53, 93
African Methodist Episcopal Church 158, 340, 371
African Methodist Zion Church 340, 371
African National Congress (ANC) 260
Agency Review 376
Aging 39, 97, 165, 222, 276, 280, 299, 392, 593, 597
Agriculture 42, 87, 334, 462, 644
Aid to Families with Dependent Children (AFDC) 297
AIDS (See HIV)
Air (See Atmosphere)
Air Pollution 645
Alaskans 181
Alcohol 41, 189, 205, 211, 228, 229, 234, 246, 310, 367, 378, 398, 428
American Indian(s) 123, 176, 178, 206, 209, 210, 247, 254, 285, 289, 300, 303, 321, 323, 324, 349, 366, 387, 396, 465, 554
  Land 61, 76, 86, 93
  Religious Freedom Act 177, 211
Americans With Disabilities Act 207, 208
Amnesty 622
Amnesty International 640
Angola 640, 659

Animal Life 33
Anti-Semitism 306, 609, 643
Apartheid 243, 260, 357, 428, 555, 636, 658
Appalachia 401
Appalachian Development Committee (ADC) 401, 402
Appointments, Clergy 215, 347, 361
Arabs 345, 542, 571
Armaments 50, 276
Arms Embargo 545
  Race 550
Articles of Religion 245
Asian Americans 93, 285, 303
Asylum 509
Atmosphere 64, 74, 77
Autonomous Affiliated Methodist Churches (AAMC) 648
Awad, Alex 589

B

Baby Friendly Initiative 584
Baptism, Eucharist and Ministry 382
Barrier Free Construction (See Accessibility)
Basic Human Needs 404, 519
Bilingual Education 359
Bingo 413
Biotechnology 326, 331
Birth Control (See Contraception)
Bishops' Initiative on Drugs and Drug Violence 212
Blacks (See African Americans)
Black Colleges (See African American Colleges)
Black Hills Alliance 554
Black Methodists for Church Renewal (BMCR) 348
Blockade 605
Bolivia 573
Boycott (See Economic Boycott)
Breast Feeding 358, 584
  Milk Substitutes 584

Buddhists 267
Bussing, School 368

C

Campaign for Children in the United States 359
Canadian Council of Churches 598
Capital Punishment 465, 495
Caribbean 463, 634
Casino Gambling 413
Censorship 470, 528, 533, 576
Central America 463, 557
Chaplains 366, 472
Charter for Racial Justice Policies 258, 306, 357, 389, 637
Chemical/Biological Weapons 618
Chemicals/Agricultural 74
Child Abuse 526
  Abuse Prevention Month 228
  Advocacy 139, 358
  Care 394
  Survival Campaign (UNICEF) 358, 566
  Survival Fund (USAID) 359
Children 39, 125, 135, 220, 281, 294, 302, 308, 317, 350, 382, 511, 592, 634, 640
Children's Rights 357
China 651, 653
China Christian Council 655
Christian Council of Mozambique 642
Christian Faith and War in the Nuclear Age (1960) 561
Christian Home Month 122
Christian Methodist Episcopal Church 340, 371
Christian Nurture 34
Christian Unity 154
Christians 544, 580, 607, 613
Church and Community Workers 199, 200
Church Center for the United Nations 649
Church Facilities 399, 540
Church/State Relations 47, 468, 480, 523
Churches' Program on the Helsinki Final Act (CHRP) 598
Circumcision 121
Civil Disobedience 48
Civil Rights 496, 509, 633
Civil War 463
Class 518
Clergy Women 182
Coalitions 426
Cold War 601
Collective Bargaining 44, 411, 427, 442, 482
Colleges 398, 471, 497, 612
Colonialism 415, 459, 483, 630, 633, 641, 666
Columbus 386, 666

Comity Agreements 206
Commission on Religion in Appalachia (CORA) 401, 402
Commodities 90
Commonwealth of Independent States (CIS) 601
Common Heritage 54, 79, 621
Community 34, 49, 215, 443, 446, 488
Community Groups 399
Conference of European Churches (KEK) 598
Conference on Security and Cooperation in Europe (CSCE)
Confession 210, 258
Confidence Building Measures 563
Conflict Resolution 312, 424, 492, 643
Conscience 467, 474, 535, 622
Conscientious Objectors 49, 467, 535, 622
Conscription 49, 467, 468, 490, 535, 622
Conservation 32, 61, 99
Constitutional Convention 520
Consultation on Church Union (COCU) 205, 217, 319, 382, 385
Consumption 45
Contadora Peace Process 583
Contraception 125, 343, 374
Cooperative Housing Foundation 188
Cooperative Parish 191
Courts 494, 501
Covenanting 153, 217, 320, 382, 385, 591
Crack/Cocaine 238
Creation 32, 56, 62, 71, 75, 79, 169, 326, 405
Crime 48, 466, 492, 499
Criminal Code 534, 541
Crisis Intervention 312, 316
Cuba 634
Cults 269
Cultures 50, 391, 484, 490, 518, 533

D

Data Banks 518
Day Care 138
Day of Prayer and Action for Shelter 301
Deaconess 194
Death 37
  Penalty (See Capital Punishment)
  with Dignity 140
Debt 92, 407, 414
Democracy 528, 618
Dependent Care 219
Destabilization (See Intervention and Low Intensity Conflict)
Deterrence 563, 601
Dialogue 266
Disabilities (See Handicapping Conditions)

Disabled Persons (See Handicapping Conditions)
Disarmament 553, 561, 600, 617
Discrimination 170, 373, 376, 434, 493, 608, 623
District of Columbia 528
Divestment (See Investment)
Divorce 35
DNA 330
Doctrinal Standards 245, 262
Domestic Violence 205, 223, 228
  Awareness Month 228
Draft (See Conscription)
  Registration 490
Driving Under the Influence 228, 502
Drug(s) 41, 138, 189, 211, 228, 229, 246, 274, 281, 338, 348, 365, 378, 398, 410, 573
Drug Traffic 240
Dumbarton Oaks 553

E
Earnings Sharing 394
Ecology 62, 64, 98, 549, 592
Economic Boycott 45, 423, 555, 588, 638
  Development 620
  Embargo 605, 634
  Justice 619
  Sanctions 428, 584, 661
Economics 44, 372, 403, 453, 513, 548, 592
  Agricultural 91
Economy 427, 431, 439, 446, 620, 621, 624, 645
  Global 407
Ecumenical Decade for Women 242, 372
Ecumenical Relations 205, 206, 217, 218, 245, 319, 340, 382, 385, 401, 426, 479, 488, 507, 547, 596, 648
Education 47, 151, 194, 231, 258, 284, 304, 322, 358, 450, 464, 469, 470, 489, 498, 527, 664
Egypt 543
El Salvador 463, 559, 570
Eldercide 594
Electronic Church 632
Embargo (See Economic Embargo and Arms Embargo)
Employment 349, 353, 393, 432, 494
Enemy Image 627
Energy 33, 57, 65, 81, 85
English Only Movement 162, 464
Environment 60, 62, 67, 70, 274, 334, 407, 444, 460, 624, 644
Equal Access 299
Equal Employment 253
Equal Rights Amendment 253, 374

Ethics 427, 476
Ethnic 254, 259, 284, 285, 303, 321, 339, 383, 391, 623
  Local Church 248
Europe 597, 603
Evangelical Seminary of Puerto Rico 216
Evangelism 387, 611, 663
Exclusive Clubs 311
Exclusivity 311
Exploitation 548

F
Family 34, 127, 135, 164, 281, 293, 344, 436, 612, 615
  Farm 89, 462
  Planning 125, 375
Farm 42
  Crisis 89, 94
  Land 53
  Workers 452, 462
Farmworkers' Week 453
Firearms (See Guns)
Food 459
Fort Laramie Treaty 574
Forward Looking Strategies 242
Free Trade Agreement 498
Freedom 47, 530, 618
Freedom of Information 471, 486, 575
  Act 535
Front Line States 260, 637
Fuels 33

G
Gambling 46, 412, 413, 428, 502
General Electric (GE) 433
Genes 42
Genetic Science 42, 325
Genetics 100, 317
Geneva Conventions 553
Genocide 260, 633
Global Church 579, 647
Government 46
  Funding 471
"Grace Upon Grace" 557
Grand Jury 503, 533
Guatemala 463
Guns 504, 526, 536, 538

H
Habitat for Humanity 188, 301
Hague Peace Conference 553
Handguns (See Guns)
Handicapping Conditions 40, 151, 160, 161, 184, 189, 200, 207, 208, 222, 280, 298, 299, 304, 359, 392, 445, 528

Harassment 496, 503, 536
Hate Crimes 258, 361, 566
　Groups 258, 306, 519
Hawaiian 181
Health 137, 142, 167, 254, 273, 278, 280, 308,
　317, 333, 352, 395, 443, 480, 499, 567,
　595, 606, 645
　for All by the Year 2000 279
　Insurance 275, 360
　Maintenance 275
Helsinki Process (See CSCE)
Hindus 267
Hispanic Americans 151, 285, 303, 391, 464
History 285, 303, 321, 387
HIV (Human Immunodeficiency Virus) 115,
　120, 123, 124, 148, 289, 564, 624, 650
Holocaust 271, 542, 617
Holy Land Tours 547, 580
Holy Spirit 664
Homelessness 286
Homosexual Persons 36
Housing 137, 171, 185, 286, 293, 409
Human Genome Project 334
Human Relations Day, 390
Human Rights 36, 251, 506, 512, 517, 591,
　598, 614, 616, 632, 633, 653, 661
　Ratification of Covenants 199
Hunger 342, 351, 403, 457

I
Immigration 258, 384, 464, 507
Immunization 354
In Defense of Creation (1986) 562, 568, 600, 624
Incarceration 516
Inclusive 249, 254, 304, 346
Income 136, 171, 431, 453, 644
Indians (See American Indians)
Indigenous Peoples 178, 260, 366, 389, 402,
　605, 666
INFACT 433
Infant Formula 584
Infiltration 496
Inflation 418
Information, Freedom of 47
Institutional Racism (See Racism)
Integration 368, 489, 540
Interfaith Center on Corporate Responsibili-
　ty (ICCR) 588
Interfaith Relations 606
International Court of Justice 553
International Labor Organization (ILO) 441
International Monetary Fund (IMF) 417,
　459, 621
Interreligious Healthcare Access Campaign
　(IHAC) 398

Interreligious Relationships 263
Intervention 581, 637
Investment 428, 430, 438, 639, 661
Islam 271, 345, 606
Israel 271, 542, 571, 580, 589

J
Jails (See Prisons)
Jerusalem 589
Jews 267, 542, 580
Job Training 455
Jordan 544
Jury 502
"Just War" 550, 570
Justice 48, 50, 51, 59, 62, 88, 146, 274, 288,
　403, 424, 432, 461, 462, 492, 496, 499,
　503, 509, 511, 514, 519, 559, 591, 607,
　613, 631, 648
Justice, Peace and the Integrity of Creation
　(JPIC) 244, 591, 628
Juvenile Delinquency 526

K
King, Jr., Dr. Martin Luther, Day 338
Korea 613
Korean Methodist Church 613
Ku Klux Klan 258, 306, 361, 519
Kurds 542

L
Labor 44, 438
Lakota People 554, 574
Land 88
　Use 42, 75, 76, 86, 90
Language 164, 259, 346, 464
　Biblical 663
Latin America 463
Latin American Council of Churches 558
Law 48, 51, 494, 499, 503, 526, 621
　of the Sea 55, 79, 621
League of Nations 553
Lebanon 542
Leisure 45
Limited Test Ban Treaty 568
Literacy 304, 355, 373, 512
Lobby Disclosure 476
Lotteries 413, 528
Low Intensity Conflict 558, 631
LSD 240

M
Macedonia 597
Maquiladoras 645
Marijuana 235
Marriage 34

Media 43, 239, 352, 484, 576, 609
Violence 129
Mediation 425, 493, 499
Medical Ethics 148, 278, 336
Experimentation 41
Medicare 167
Men 40, 450
Mental Health 276, 280, 294, 313, 381
Methodist Church of South Africa 557
Methodist Youth Fellowship (MYF) 250
Mexico 644
Middle East 542, 571, 580
Migrants 46, 94, 287, 417, 453
Militarism 259, 352, 460, 490, 519, 624
Military 76, 408, 462, 467, 473, 498, 535, 549, 622, 630
Bases 630, 633
Service 49
Mining 98, 554
Minorities 38
Missing in Action 629
Mission Intern Program 324
Mission Partner Churches 418, 421
Missionaries 247, 497, 533, 589, 599
Moon 57
Mozambique 641
MPLA 659
Multicultural/Cross Cultural 259, 313, 321, 346
Multinational Corporations (See Transnational Corporations)
Murder 282, 466, 504, 536
Muslims 267, 345, 544, 580, 606

N
Name, Use of "The United Methodist Church" 663
Namibia 619, 636, 659
Narcotics 236
National Academy of Peace and Conflict Resolution 622
National Council of the Churches of Christ in the USA (NCCC/USA) 217, 385, 507, 516, 598, 614, 615, 651
National Health Care Plan 397
National Interfaith Conference on the Church and Homelessness 291
National Labor Relations Act 412
National United Methodist Native American Center (NUMNAC) 210, 248, 304, 322, 350, 368
National Youth Ministries Organization (NYMO) 250
Nationalism 549

Native American(s) (See American Indians)
Awareness Sunday 349, 390
International Caucus 366, 666
Land (See American Indian Land)
Natural Resources 56, 73
Neighbors 264
New Beginning 386, 666
New World Information and Communication Order (NWICO) 575
Nicaragua 560
No Fault Insurance 501
No First Strike 563
Non-Governmental Organizations (NGO) 245, 481, 560, 596
Non-Intervention 581
Non-Proliferation Treaty 568, 604
Non-violence 259, 592
Nuclear 80, 605
Energy 61
Freeze Movement 562
Waste 83
Weapons 433, 568, 600, 614

O
Obscenity (See Pornography)
Occupied Territories 543, 572
Olympics 616
"One Church—One Home" 291
Oppression 388, 435
Ordained Ministry, The/National Convocation on 321
Organ Donors 123, 145
Organization of American States (OAS) 582
Outrageous Ministries 348
Oxford House Model 338

P
Pacific 243, 605
Islanders 303, 339
Pain 147
Palestine Liberation Organization (PLO) 542, 571
Palestinians 542, 571, 580, 589
Pan Methodist 340, 371
Panama 558
Paper (Reclaimed) 112
Parenthood 125, 344
Parents Anonymous 511
Pari-Mutuel Betting 413
Paris Accords 629
Pastoral Care 143
Patents 332
Pathways to Promise 316
Pay Equity 434

SUBJECT INDEX

Peace 50, 467, 519, 547, 591, 612, 613, 617, 649, 650
Conditions for 550
Research 622
With Justice 548, 564, 592, 623
With Justice Sunday 390, 628
Pediatric Bill of Rights 309
Penal Reform 524
Pensions 39, 171, 174
Personhood, Full 255, 329
Persons In Mission 421
Pesticides 99, 645
Philippines 629
Police 499, 526
Political Prisoners 640
Pollution 77, 230, 445
Population 40, 114, 126, 342, 459, 549, 593
Pornography 128, 352, 429, 486
Poverty 45, 96, 185, 243, 252, 280, 288, 342, 353, 402, 403, 446, 457, 483, 514, 549, 552, 624, 645
Power 50
Power of Attorney, Binding 147
Prejudice 345, 360
Press Freedom (See Freedom of Information)
Prison Visitation 517
Prisons 31, 466, 493, 502, 516, 524
Privacy 334, 532
Private Schools 540
Project Equality 349, 391
Property 44
Property Tax 475
Prostitution 121, 352
Psychedelics 239
Public Broadcasting 486
Public Education (See Education)
Puerto Rico 216, 632
Methodist Church of 362
Punishment 492

R

Racial and Ethnic Persons 38, 490
Harassment 360
Racism 67, 163, 193, 196, 198, 245, 248, 254, 256, 280, 287, 296, 306, 345, 346, 354, 360, 363, 388, 455, 533, 549, 593, 634, 643m 661
Raffles 413
Rape 226
Reclaiming the Cities 370, 371
Reconciliation 599, 622
Redlining 299
Refugees 463, 542, 598, 661
Rehabilitation 41, 237, 495, 516, 524

Religious Liberty 176, 210, 472, 474, 476, 483, 520, 523, 529, 554, 576, 589, 598
RENAMO 639, 641, 659
Repentance 551
Repression 532
Reunification 613
Right to Life 523
Rights 47
Roman Catholic 246, 387
Bishops 562, 625
Royal Dutch/Shell 555
Runaway 317
Rural 42, 87, 157, 185, 199, 204, 243, 366, 446
Chaplains Association 367
Life Sunday 105

S

Sanctions (See Economic Sanctions)
Sanctuary 463, 509
Scarritt Bennett Center 194
School Prayer 48
Schools (See Education)
Science 33
Seabed (See Law of the Sea)
Sedatives 237
Self-Determination 50, 362, 390, 453, 516, 518, 544, 572, 573, 581, 633, 640, 642, 648
Development 461, 513, 547
Help 446
Interest 548
Seminar Program (United Methodist Seminars on National and International Affairs) 581, 649
Sentencing 495, 502
Settlements 572
Sexual Exploitation and Violence 39, 128, 192, 223
Harassment 447, 449
Sexuality 35, 126
Shalom vision 63, 71, 600, 625
Shaw, Anna Howard 182
Single Persons 35, 127, 135
Slavery 31, 47, 357
Small Churches 384
Social Creed, 1908 31, 405, 427
Our 51
Social Planning 43
Social Security 392, 595
Solitary Confinement 511
South Africa 260, 555, 619, 636, 642, 658
South African Council of Churches (SACC) 555
Southern Africa Development Coordination Conference (SADCC) 639, 660, 662
Soweto 638

Space 33
Spain 387
Spanish Language Hymnal 370
Special Emphasis 370, 371
Spiritual Director 664
Stereotyping 40, 257, 346, 425, 487, 609
Sterilization 113
Stewardship 58, 70, 87, 141, 158, 327, 665
Stimulants (See Drugs)
Substance Abuse (See Drugs)
Suicide 144, 282, 377, 536
Surveillance 47, 496, 534, 535
Sustainability 59, 64, 461
SWAPO 260
Syncretism 272
Syria 542

T
Taiwan 651
Tax Exemption 475
Immunities 472
Taxes 44
Technology 61, 76, 327
Tent Making Ministries 348, 384
Terrorism 510, 519, 643
"The Land" 546
Theocracy 531
Three Self Patriotic Movement (Chinese Protestant) 655
Tithing 665
"To Love the Sojourner" 385
Tobacco 41, 215, 234, 274, 367, 428
Torrijos-Carter Treaty 559
Torture 47, 465, 519, 633
Tourism 651
Townships 637, 658
Toxic Waste 32, 67, 73, 443, 605, 645
Trade 415, 462, 620
Unions 407, 411, 441
Transnational Corporations 258, 375, 406
Tuition Tax Credits 469

U
Undocumented Workers 385, 394, 510, 644
Unemployment 96, 402, 409, 431, 441, 453, 498, 644
Insurance 453
Unification Church 631
UNITA 639, 659
United Nations 51, 55, 79, 199, 227, 344, 373, 464, 491, 497, 532, 543, 558, 570, 571, 582, 596, 606, 619, 637, 643, 648, 650
Children's Fund (UNICEF) 351, 417, 584, 619, 650

Conference on Environment and Development 66
Convention/Racism 260
Religious Belief 530
Rights of the Child 227
Women 227, 375
Day 650
Decade for Women 242
High Commissioner for Refugees (UNHCR) 659
Human Rights Commission 559
Human Rights Covenants and Conventions 199, 619, 633
Security Council 546, 573, 639
Treaties 563, 568, 604
Universal Declaration of Human Rights 518, 530, 560, 584, 619
World Population Plan of Action 344
United States 545, 601, 614, 629, 644, 651
University Senate 153
Urban 42, 364, 370
US Interreligious Committee for Peace in the Middle East 572
USSR 545, 601, 614

V
Values 43, 59
Victims of Crime 49, 502, 540
Vieques 632
Vietnam 629
Violence 43, 128, 486, 536, 643
Vision Interfaith Satellite Network (VISN) 399
Volunteers-In-Mission (VIM) 188, 595
Voting Rights 529

W
War 50, 467, 498
Water 65, 75
Water Conservation 87
WCC Program to Combat Racism 260
Welfare 259, 480
White Flight 489
Wholeness 273
Witness 266, 390
Women 40, 192, 221, 242, 251, 255, 261, 302, 343, 371, 392, 435, 448, 450, 498, 634
Women, Infants, and Children's Supplemental Food and Nutrition Education Progr, 610 302, 462, 588
Women's Rights 373
Work 45, 136, 406, 443, 453
Workmen's Compensation 453
World Bank (IBRD) 417, 459, 621, 659

World Communion Sunday 320
World Council of Churches (WCC) 218, 242, 260, 382, 385, 389
World Health Organization (WHO) 279, 564, 584, 650
World Methodist Council 385, 638
World Order 620
World Order Sunday (See UN Day)

Y
Young Adults 39, 324
Youth 39, 249, 281, 308, 317, 379, 492, 502, 511
Youth Ministry 251

Z
Zero Option 602
Zoar UMC 158, 219